everyWORD

SCRIPTURE | OUTLINE | COMMENTARY

THE GOSPEL ACCORDING TO MARK

NEW TESTAMENT | ENGLISH STANDARD VERSION

LMW

LEADERSHIP MINISTRIES WORLDWIDE

CHATTANOOGA, TN

Please address all requests for information or permission to:
Leadership Ministries Worldwide
1928 Central Avenue
Chattanooga, TN 37408
Ph.# (423) 855-2181 FAX (423) 855-8616 E-Mail info@lmw.org
http://www.lmw.org

ISBN Softbound Edition: 978-1-57407-451-2
ISBN Casebound Edition: 978-1-57407-454-3

LEADERSHIP MINISTRIES WORLDWIDE
CHATTANOOGA, TN

Printed in the United States of America

DEDICATED

To all the men and women of the world who preach and teach the Gospel of our Lord Jesus Christ and to the Mercy and Grace of God

&

- Demonstrated to us in Christ Jesus our Lord.

  "In him we have redemption through his blood, the forgiveness of our trespasses, according to the riches of his grace." (Ep.1:7)

- Out of the mercy and grace of God, His Word has flowed. Let every person know that God will have mercy upon him, forgiving and using him to fulfill His glorious plan of salvation.

  "For God so loved the world, that he gave his only Son, that whoever believes in him should not perish but have eternal life. For God did not send his Son into the world to condemn the world, but in order that the world might be saved through him." (Jn.3:16–17)

  "This is good, and it is pleasing in the sight of God our Savior; who desires all men to be saved and to come unto the knowledge of the truth." (1 Ti.2:3–4)

everyWORD®

is written for God's servants to use in their study, teaching, and preaching of God's Holy Word . . .

- to share the Word of God with the world.
- to help believers, both ministers and laypersons, in their understanding, preaching, and teaching of God's Word.
- to do everything we possibly can to lead men, women, boys, and girls to give their hearts and lives to Jesus Christ and to secure the eternal life that He offers.
- to do all we can to minister to the needy of the world.
- to give Jesus Christ His proper place, the place the Word gives Him. Therefore, no work of Leadership Ministries Worldwide—no Outline Bible Resources—will ever be personalized.

CONTENTS

ACKNOWLEDGMENTS AND BIBLIOGRAPHY

Every child of God is precious to the Lord and deeply loved. And every child as a servant of the Lord touches the lives of those who come in contact with him or his ministry. The writing ministries of the following servants have touched this work, and we are grateful that God brought their writings our way. We hereby acknowledge their ministries to us, being fully aware that there are so many others down through the years whose writings have touched our lives and who deserve mention, but the weaknesses of our minds have caused them to fade from memory. May our wonderful Lord continue to bless the ministry of these dear servants, and the ministry of us all as we diligently labor to reach the world for Christ and to meet the desperate needs of those who suffer so much.

THE GREEK SOURCES

Balz, Horst and Schneider, Gerhard M. *Exegetical Dictionary of the New Testament*. Grand Rapids: Wm. B. Eerdmans Publishing Co., 2003. Via Wordsearch digital edition.

Black, David Alan. *Linguistics for Students of New Testament Greek*. Grand Rapids: Baker Publishing Group, 1988.

Burton, Ernest De Witt. *Syntax of the Moods and Tenses in New Testament Greek*. Grand Rapids: Kregel Publications, 1976. Via Wordsearch digital edition.

Cotterell, Peter and Turner, Max. *Linguistics and Biblical Interpretation*. Downers Grove, IL: InterVarsity Press, 1989.

Davis, William Hersey. *Beginner's Grammar of the Greek New Testament*. New York: Harper & Row, 1923.

Expositor's Greek Testament, Edited by W. Robertson Nicoll. Grand Rapids: Wm. B. Eerdmans Publishing Co., 1970.

Gilbrant, Thoralf and Harris, Ralph W. *The Complete Biblical Library Greek-English Dictionary*. Springfield, MO: World Library Press, Inc., 1989. Via Wordsearch digital edition.

Guthrie, George H. and Duval, J. Scott. *Biblical Greek Exegesis: A Graded Approach to Learning Intermediate and Advanced Greek*. Grand Rapids: Zondervan, 1998.

Harris, Murray J. *Exegetical Guide to the Greek New Testament: John*. Nashville: B & H Academic, 2015.

Kittel, Gerhard and Friedrich, Gerhard. *Theological Dictionary of the New Testament*. Grand Rapids: Wm. B. Eerdmans Publishing Co., 1977.

Kostenberger, Andreas J., Merkle, Benjamin L., and Plummer, Robert L. *Going Deeper with New Testament Greek: An Intermediate Study of the Grammar and Syntax of the New Testament*. Nashville: B & H Academic, 2016.

Kubo, Sakae. *A Reader's Greek-English Lexicon of the New Testament and a Beginner's Guide for the Translation of New Testament Greek*. Grand Rapids: Zondervan, 1975.

Moulton, Harold K., ed. *The Analytical Greek Lexicon Revised*. Grand Rapids: Zondervan, 1977.

Practical Word Studies in the New Testament. Chattanooga, TN: Leadership Ministries Worldwide, 1998. Via Wordsearch digital edition.

Robertson, A.T., *A Grammar of the Greek New Testament in the Light of Historical Research*. New York: George H. Doran Company, 1915.

_____. *A Short Grammar of the Greek New Testament*. New York: A.C. Armstrong & Son, 1909.

_____. *Word Pictures in the New Testament*. Nashville, TN: Broadman Press, 1930.

Staats, Gary. *Christological Greek Grammar*. Austin, TX: Wordsearch Bible Software, 2001.

Strong, James. *Strong's Greek and Hebrew Dictionary of the Bible*. Public Domain. Via Wordsearch digital edition.

Thayer, Joseph Henry. *Greek-English Lexicon of the New Testament*. New York: American Book Co, n.d.

Vincent, Marvin R. *Word Studies in the New Testament*. Grand Rapids: Wm. B. Eerdmans Publishing Co., 1969.

Vine, W.E. *Expository Dictionary of New Testament Words*. Old Tappan, NJ: Fleming H. Revell Co., n.d.

Wallace, Daniel B. *Greek Grammar Beyond the Basics: An Exegetical Syntax of New Testament with Scripture, Subject, and Greek Word Indexes*. Grand Rapids: Zondervan. 1997.

Wuest, Kenneth S. *Word Studies in the Greek New Testament*. Grand Rapids: Wm. B. Eerdmans Publishing Co., 1966.

Young, Richard A. *Intermediate New Testament Greek: A Linguistic and Exegetical Approach*. Nashville: Broadman & Holman, 1994.

Zodhiates, Spiros. *The Complete Word Study Dictionary: New Testament*. Chattanooga, TN: AMG Publishers, 1992. Via Wordsearch digital edition.

THE REFERENCE WORKS

Berkhof, Louis. *Principles of Biblical Interpretation*. Grand Rapids: Baker Book House, 1950.

Blomberg, Craig. *The Historical Reliability of the Gospels*. Downers Grove, IL: InterVarsity, 1987.

Bruce, F. F. *New Testament History*. New York: Doubleday, 1983. Via Wordsearch digital edition.

Bryant, T. Alton, ed. *The New Compact Bible Dictionary*. Grand Rapids: Zondervan Publishing House, 1967.

Butler, Trent C., ed. *Holman Bible Dictionary*. Nashville: Holman Bible Pub., 1991.

Carson, D. A. and Moo, Douglas. *An Introduction to the New Testament*. 2nd ed. Grand Rapids: Zondervan, 2005.

Cruden's Complete Concordance of the Old & New Testament. Philadelphia: The John C. Winston Co., 1930.

Easton, Matthew G. *Illustrated Bible Dictionary*. Public Domain. Via Wordsearch digital edition.

Edersheim, Alfred. *The Life and Times of Jesus the Messiah*. Peabody, MA: Hendrickson Publishers. 1993. Via Wordsearch digital edition.

Evans, Craig A. and Porter, Stanley E. *Dictionary of New Testament Background*. Downers Grove, IL: InterVarsity Press, 2000. Via Wordsearch digital edition.

Gromacki, Robert. *New Testament Survey*. Grand Rapids: Baker Book House, 1974.

Gundry, Robert. *Survey of the New Testament*. 4th ed. Grand Rapids: Zondervan, 2003.

Guthrie, Donald. *New Testament Introduction*. rev. ed. Downers Grove, IL: InterVarsity, 1981, 1064 pp.

Habermas, Gary R. *The Historical Jesus: Ancient Evidence for the Life of Christ*. Joplin, MO: College Press, 1996. Via Wordsearch digital edition.

Hiebert, D. Edmond. *An Introduction to the New Testament*. 3 vols. Chicago: Moody Press, 1975–77.

Jensen, Irving L. *Jensen's Survey of the New Testament*. Chicago: Moody Press, 1981.

Josephus' Complete Works. Grand Rapids: Kregel Publications, 1981.

Kaiser, Walter, Jr., and Silva, Moises. *An Introduction to Biblical Hermeneutics: The Search for Meaning*. Grand Rapids: Zondervan, 1994.

Klein, William W., Blomberg, Craig L., and Hubbard, Robert, Jr. *Introduction to Biblical Interpretation*. Nashville: W Publishing Group, 1993.

Larkin, Clarence. *Rightly Dividing the Word*. Philadelphia, PA: The Rev. Clarence Larkin Est., 1921.

Lockyer, Herbert. Series of books, including his books on *All the Men, Women, Miracles, and Parables of the Bible*. Grand Rapids: Zondervan Publishing House, 1958-1967.

Marshall, I. Howard. ed. *New Testament Interpretation*. Grand Rapids: Wm. B. Eerdmans Publishing Co., 1977, 406 pp.

Martin, Ralph. *New Testament Foundations*. 2 vols. Grand Rapids: Wm. B. Eerdmans Publishing Co., 1975–78.

McGarvey, John William. *Lands of the Bible: A Geographical and Topographical Description of Palestine*. Public Domain. Via Wordsearch digital edition.

Morris, Leon. *New Testament Theology*. Grand Rapids: Zondervan, 1996.

Nave's Topical Bible. Nashville, TN: The Southwestern Co., n.d.

Orr, James. *The International Standard Bible Encyclopedia*. Grand Rapids: Wm. B. Eerdmans Publishing Co., 1939. Via Wordsearch digital edition.

Ramm, Bernard. *Protestant Biblical Interpretation: A Textbook of Hermeneutics*. Grand Rapids: Baker Book House, 1970.

Ryrie, Charles. *Biblical Theology of the New Testament*. Chicago: Moody, 1959, 304 pp.

Scroggie, William G. *Guide to the Gospels*. London: Pickering and Inglis, 1948, rpt., 664 pp.

Tenney, Merrill C. *Genius of the Gospels*. Grand Rapids: Wm. B. Eerdmans Publishing Co., 1951, 124 pp.

_____. *New Testament Survey*. Grand Rapids: Wm. B. Eerdmans Publishing Co., 1961.

The Amplified New Testament. (Scripture Quotations are from the Amplified New Testament, Copyright 1954, 1958, 1987 by the Lockman Foundation. Used by permission.)

The Four Translation New Testament. (Including King James, New American Standard, Williams—New Testament in the Language of the People, Beck—New Testament in the Language of Today.) Minneapolis, MN: World Wide Publications.

The New Thompson Chain Reference Bible. Indianapolis: B.B. Kirkbride Bible Co., 1964,

Unger, Merrill F., Harrison R. K., (ed.). *The New Unger's Bible Dictionary*. Chicago: Moody Publishers, 2006. Via Wordsearch digital edition.

Water, Mark, *AMG's Encyclopedia of Jesus' Life & Time*. Chattanooga, TN: AMG Publishers, 2006. Via Wordsearch digital edition.

Willmington, Harold L. *Willmington's Bible Handbook*. Wheaton, IL: Tyndale House, 1997.

_____. *Willmington's Guide to the Bible*. Wheaton, IL: Tyndale House, 1981.

THE COMMENTARIES

Barclay, William. *Daily Study Bible Series*. Philadelphia, PA: Westminster Press, Began in 1953.

Barnes, Albert. *Barnes' Notes on the New Testament*. Grand Rapids: Kregel Classics, 1962. Via Wordsearch digital edition.

Barton, Bruce, ed. *Life Application Bible Commentary*. Carol Stream, IL: Tyndale House Publishers, Inc., various dates. Via Wordsearch digital edition.

Bock, Darrell L. *Cornerstone Biblical Commentary, The Gospel of Mark*. Wheaton, IL: Tyndale House, 2006

Burn, John Henry. *The Preacher's Complete Homiletic Commentary on the Gospel According to St. Mark*. Grand Rapids: Baker Books, 1996.

Calvin, John. *Calvin's Commentaries*. Public Domain. Via Wordsearch digital edition

Earle, Ralph. *Mark: The Gospel of Action*. Chicago: Moody Press, 1980.

Elwell, Walter A. *Baker Commentary on the Bible*. Grand Rapids: Baker Academic, 2001. Via Wordsearch digital edition.

Evans, Craig A. *The Holman Apologetics Commentary on the Bible, The Gospels and Acts*. Nashville: Broadman and Holman, 2013.

Exell, Joseph S. *The Biblical Illustrator, Mark*. Grand Rapids: Baker Book House, 1953.

France, R.T. *The New International Greek Testament Commentary, The Gospel of Mark*. Grand Rapids: Eerdmans, 2002.

Garland, David E. and Longman III, Tremper, ed. *The Expositor's Bible Commentary, Revised Edition, Volume 9: Matthew & Mark*: Grand Rapids: Zondervan, 2010.

Gilbrant, Thoralf and Harris, Ralph W. *The Complete Biblical Library New Testament Commentary*. Springfield, MO: World Library Press. 1992. Via Wordsearch digital edition.

Grogan, Geoffrey. *Focus on the Bible Commentary: Good News from Jerusalem*. Fearn, Ross-Shire, Scotland: Christian Focus Publications, 2003.

Gutzke, Manford George. *Plain Talk on Mark*. Grand Rapids: Zondervan, 1975.

Hendriksen, William. *Mark*. Grand Rapids: Baker Books, 1975.

Henry, Matthew. *Commentary on the Whole Bible*. Old Tappan, NJ: Fleming H. Revell Co.

Hiebert, D. Edmond. *The Gospel of Mark: An Expositional Commentary*. Greenville, SC: BJU Press, 1994.

Holman Bible editorial staff. *Holman New Testament Commentary*. Nashville: Holman Reference, 2001.

Hughes, R. Kent. *Mark: Jesus, Servant and Savior*. Wheaton, IL: Crossway Books, 2015.

Ironside, H.A. *Expository Notes on the Gospel of Mark*. New York: Loizeaux Brothers, 1948.

Jamieson, Robert; Fausset, A. R. and Brown, David. *Jamieson, Fausset & Brown's Commentary on the Whole Bible*. Public Domain. Via Wordsearch digital edition.

Lane, William L. *New International Commentary on the New Testament, The Gospel of Mark*. Grand Rapids: Eerdmans, 1974.

MacDonald, William. *Believer's Bible Commentary*. Nashville: Thomas Nelson, 1995.

MacLaren, Alexander. *Expositions of the Holy Scriptures* (17 volumes). Grand Rapids: Baker Publishing Group, 1988.

McGee, J. Vernon. *Through the Bible* (5 volumes). Nashville: Thomas Nelson, 1990. Via Wordsearch digital edition.

McKenna, David L. *The Preacher's Commentary Volume 25: Mark*. Nashville: Thomas Nelson, 2002.

Morris, Leon. *The Gospel According to John*. Grand Rapids: Wm. B. Eerdmans Publishing Co., 1971.

Pfeiffer, Charles F and Harrison, Everett F., eds. *The New Testament & Wycliffe Bible Commentary*. New York: The Iverson Associates, 1971. Produced for *Moody Monthly*. Chicago: Moody Press, 1962.

Phillips, John. *Phillips Commentary Series*. Grand Rapids: Kregel, 2006.

Poole, Matthew. *Matthew Poole's Commentary on the Holy Bible*. Peabody, MA: Hendrickson Publishers, 1985.

Stein, Robert H. *Baker Exegetical Commentary on the New Testament, Mark*. Grand Rapids: Baker Book House, 2008.

Swindoll, Charles R. *Mark: Swindoll's Living Insights Commentary*. Wheaton, IL: Tyndale House, 2016.

Tasker, RVG. *The Gospel According to St. John* (Tyndale New Testament Commentaries). Grand Rapids: Wm. B. Eerdmans Publishing Co., 1960.

The Pulpit Commentary, Edited by H.D.M. Spence & Joseph S. Exell. Grand Rapids: Wm. B. Eerdmans Publishing Co., 1950.

Tyndale New Testament Commentaries. Grand Rapids: Wm. B. Eerdmans Publishing Co., Began in 1958.

Various authors. *The IVP New Testament Commentary Series* (20 volumes). Downers Grove, IL: Inter-Varsity Press, 1991–2009. Via Wordsearch digital edition.

Various authors. *The New American Commentary* (43 volumes). Nashville: Broadman & Holman, various dates. Via Wordsearch digital edition.

Walker, Thomas. *Acts of the Apostles*. Chicago: Moody Press, 1965.

Walvoord, John. *The Thessalonian Epistles*. Grand Rapids: Zondervan Publishing House, 1973.

_____ and Roy B. Zuck, eds. *The Bible Knowledge Commentary New Testament: An Exposition of the Scriptures by Dallas Seminary Faculty*. Wheaton, IL: Victor Books. Via Wordsearch digital edition.

Wiersbe, Warren W. *The Bible Exposition Commentary*. Colorado Springs, CO: David C. Cook, 2004. Via Wordsearch digital edition.

ABBREVIATIONS

&	=	and	O.T.	=	Old Testament
bc.	=	because	p./pp.	=	page/pages
concl.	=	conclusion	pt.	=	point
cp.	=	compare	quest.	=	question
ct.	=	contrast	rel.	=	religion
e.g.	=	for example	rgt.	=	righteousness
f.	=	following	thru	=	through
illust.	=	illustration	v./vv.	=	verse/verses
N.T.	=	New Testament	vs.	=	versus

THE BOOKS OF THE OLD TESTAMENT

Book	Abbreviation	Chapters	Book	Abbreviation	Chapters
GENESIS	Gen. or Ge.	50	Ecclesiastes	Eccl. or Ec.	12
Exodus	Ex.	40	The Song of Solomon	S. of Sol. or Song	8
Leviticus	Lev. or Le.	27			
Numbers	Num. or Nu.	36	Isaiah	Is.	66
Deuteronomy	Dt. or De.	34	Jeremiah	Jer. or Je.	52
Joshua	Josh. or Jos.	24	Lamentations	Lam.	5
Judges	Judg. or Jud.	21	Ezekiel	Ezk. or Eze.	48
Ruth	Ruth or Ru.	4	Daniel	Dan. or Da.	12
1 Samuel	1 Sam. or 1 S.	31	Hosea	Hos. or Ho.	14
2 Samuel	2 Sam. or 2 S.	24	Joel	Joel	3
1 Kings	1 Ki. or 1 K.	22	Amos	Amos or Am.	9
2 Kings	2 Ki. or 2 K.	25	Obadiah	Obad. or Ob.	1
1 Chronicles	1 Chron. or 1 Chr.	29	Jonah	Jon. or Jona.	4
2 Chronicles	2 Chron. or 2 Chr.	36	Micah	Mic. or Mi.	7
Ezra	Ezra or Ezr.	10	Nahum	Nah. or Na.	3
Nehemiah	Neh. or Ne.	13	Habakkuk	Hab.	3
Esther	Est.	10	Zephaniah	Zeph. or Zep.	3
Job	Job or Jb.	42	Haggai	Hag.	2
Psalms	Ps.	150	Zechariah	Zech. or Zec.	14
Proverbs	Pr.	31	Malachi	Mal.	4

THE BOOKS OF THE NEW TESTAMENT

Book	Abbreviation	Chapters	Book	Abbreviation	Chapters
MATTHEW	Mt.	28	1 Timothy	1 Tim. or 1 Ti.	6
Mark	Mk.	16	2 Timothy	2 Tim. or 2 Ti.	4
Luke	Lk. or Lu.	24	Titus	Tit.	3
John	Jn.	21	Philemon	Phile. or Phm.	1
Acts	Acts or Ac.	28	Hebrews	Heb. or He.	13
Romans	Ro.	16	James	Jas. or Js.	5
1 Corinthians	1 Cor. or 1 Co.	16	1 Peter	1 Pt. or 1 Pe.	5
2 Corinthians	2 Cor. or 2 Co.	13	2 Peter	2 Pt. or 2 Pe.	3
Galatians	Gal. or Ga.	6	1 John	1 Jn.	5
Ephesians	Eph. or Ep.	6	2 John	2 Jn.	1
Philippians	Ph.	4	3 John	3 Jn.	1
Colossians	Col.	4	Jude	Jude	1
1 Thessalonians	1 Th.	5	Revelation	Rev. or Re.	22
2 Thessalonians	2 Th.	3			

HOW TO USE

everyWORD®

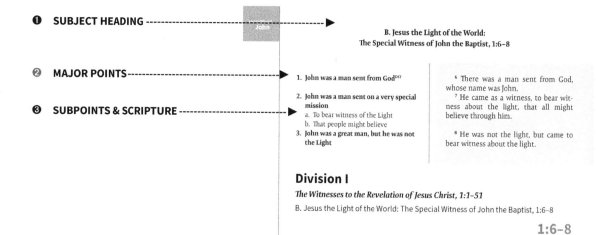

❶ **SUBJECT HEADING** ---------------------------------▶

❷ **MAJOR POINTS** ---------------------------------▶

❸ **SUBPOINTS & SCRIPTURE** ---------------------------------▶

B. Jesus the Light of the World:
The Special Witness of John the Baptist, 1:6–8

1. John was a man sent from God[DS1]

2. John was a man sent on a very special mission
   a. To bear witness of the Light
   b. That people might believe
3. John was a great man, but he was not the Light

⁶ There was a man sent from God, whose name was John.
⁷ He came as a witness, to bear witness about the light, that all might believe through him.

⁸ He was not the light, but came to bear witness about the light.

Division I

The Witnesses to the Revelation of Jesus Christ, 1:1–51

B. Jesus the Light of the World: The Special Witness of John the Baptist, 1:6–8

1:6–8
Introduction

❹ **COMMENTARY** ---------------------------------▶

Of all the people who bore witness of Jesus, one individual stands out as unique. John the Baptist was a very special witness of Christ. In fact, John's sole purpose on earth was to witness and to bear testimony of the Light of the world. His purpose stands as a dynamic example for us. As believers, our purpose is to bear the same witness as John: Jesus Christ is the Light of the world. This is, *Jesus the Light of the World: The Special Witness of John the Baptist, 1:6–8.*

1. John was a man sent from God (v.6).
2. John was a man sent on a very special mission (v.7).
3. John was a great man, but he was not the Light (v.8).

❶ Glance at the **Subject Heading.** Think about it for a moment.

❷ Glance at the **Subject Heading** again, and then the **Major Points** (1, 2, 3, etc.). Do this several times, reviewing them together while quickly grasping the overall subject.

❸ Glance at **both** the **Major Points** and **Subpoints** together while reading the **Scripture.** Do this slower than Step 2. Note how these points sit directly beside the related verse and simply restate what the Scripture is saying—in Outline form.

❹ Next read the **Commentary. Note** that the *Major Point Numbers* in the Outline match those in the Commentary. When applicable, a small raised number (**DS1, DS2, etc.**) at the end of a Subject Heading or Outline Point directs you to a related Deeper Study (shown on opposite page) in the Commentary.

❺ and ❻ Finally, read the **Thoughts** and **Support Scriptures** (shown on opposite page).

1:6

⁶ There was a man sent from God, whose name was John.

1 John was a man sent from God.
Scripture makes a strong contrast between what had been said about Christ and what is now being said about John. Christ "was in the beginning"; He was "with God," and He "was God" (vv.1–2). On the other hand, John was "a man" who had come into existence at birth, just like every other human who has ever lived. John had a biological mother and father, whereas Jesus Christ had no human father; He was the only begotten Son of God (v.14; Jn.3:16). John was not a divine being, not even an angel. He was a mere man.

This man, however, was *sent from God*; and he was sent on a very special mission. Two facts show this:

➤ The meaning of the word *sent* (see DEEPER STUDY # 1).
➤ The phrase *from God* (Gk. para Theou), which literally means "from beside God." John was not only sent by God, he was sent from the very side and heart of God. John was only a man, but a man of high calling and mission, of enormous responsibility and accountability. He was a man sent uniquely by God, not by some other person.

Luke recorded a fascinating fact about this unusual man: his name was not chosen by his parents, but by God Himself. The angel whom God sent to Zacharias, instructed him to name his son

8

The **every**WORD® series and study system contains everything you need for sermon preparation and Bible study:

1. The **Subject Heading** describes the overall theme of the passage and is located directly above the Outline and Scripture (keyed *alphabetically*).
2. **Major Points** are keyed with an outline *number* guiding you to related commentary.
3. **Subpoints** explain and clarify the Scripture as needed.
4. **Commentary** is fully researched and developed for every point.

John (Lk.1:13). The name *John* means *gracious.* John was a man sent forth with a name to match his message: *God's grace* is now to enter upon the scene of world history.

> John answered, "A person cannot receive even one thing unless it is given him from heaven." (Jn.3:27)

> What is man, that you make so much of him, and that you set your heart on him? (Jb.7:17)

> What is man that you are mindful of him, and the son of man that you care for him? (Ps.8:4)

> Do you not know? Do you not hear? Has it not been told you from the beginning? Have you not understood from the foundations of the earth? It is he [God] who sits above the circle of the earth, and its inhabitants are like grasshoppers; who stretches out the heavens like a curtain, and spreads them like a tent to dwell in. (Is.40:21–22)

THOUGHT 1. Like John, we too, as believers, are sent by God to bear witness of Jesus Christ. ◀----------------- ⑤ **THOUGHTS**
Note three significant points about the servants and messengers of God:

➤ First, the servants and messengers of God are not sent forth by another person, but by God. We are sent forth as the ambassadors of God.

➤ Second, God's messengers are sent forth *from* God, from the very side and heart of God.

➤ Third, as God's messengers, we have received the highest of all callings and missions, the calling of telling the world about Christ and the mission of bringing others into a saving relationship with Christ. This is an enormous responsibility, and we must never lose sight of the sobering fact that we are accountable to God Himself for our faithfulness to this holy task.

> "You did not choose me, but I chose you and appointed you that you should go and bear fruit and that your fruit should abide, so that whatever you ask the Father in my name, he may give it to you." (Jn.15:16)   ◀----------------- ⑥ **SUPPORT SCRIPTURE**

> Not that we are sufficient in ourselves to claim anything as coming from us, but our sufficiency is from God, who has made us sufficient to be ministers of a new covenant, not of the letter but of the Spirit. For the letter kills, but the Spirit gives life. (2 Co.3:5–6)

> All this is from God, who through Christ reconciled us to himself and gave us the ministry of reconciliation; that is, in Christ God was reconciling the world to himself, not counting their trespasses against them, and entrusting to us the message of reconciliation. Therefore, we are ambassadors for Christ, God making his appeal through us. We implore you on behalf of Christ, be reconciled to God. (2 Co.5:18–20)

> Of this gospel I was made a minister according to the gift of God's grace, which was given me by the working of his power. (Ep.3:7)

> I thank him who has given me strength, Christ Jesus our Lord, because he judged me faithful, appointing me to his service. (1 Ti.1:12)

DEEPER STUDY # 1   ◀----------------- ⑦ **DEEPER STUDY**

(1:6) **Sent—Apostle—Commission:** *Sent* (apestalmenos) means to send out; to commission as a representative, an ambassador, an envoy. Three things are true of the person sent from God.
1. He belongs to God, who has sent him out.
2. He is commissioned to be sent out.
3. He possesses all the authority and power of God, who has sent him out.

2 John was a man sent on a very special mission.

Two Old Testament prophets foretold John's special mission and purpose. Both Isaiah and Malachi prophesied that John would prepare the way of the Lord, who is the embodiment

1:7

⁷ He came as a witness, to bear witness about the light, that all might believe through him.   ◀----------- ⑧ **SCRIPTURE CALLOUTS**

9

5. **Thoughts** help apply the Scripture to daily life.
6. **Support Scripture** provides one or more Bible verses that correspond to the Major Points and Subpoints.
7. **Deeper Studies** provide in-depth discussions of key words or phrases.
8. **Scripture Callouts** repeat segments of Scripture used in the Scripture and Outline sections below the Subject Headings

"Woe to me, if I do not preach the gospel!"
(1 Co.9:16)

THE GOSPEL ACCORDING TO MARK

INTRODUCTION

AUTHOR: John Mark.

The early church fathers say that Mark was a companion of Peter. Some commentators claim that Peter furnished much of the material for the Gospel, whereas others say that Mark made notes of Peter's preaching and later used the notes to write the Gospel.

Papias says: "Mark, who was Peter's interpreter, wrote down carefully all that he remembered of what Christ had said or done, though not in order. For he had neither heard the Lord nor been His disciple; but afterwards, as I said, he had been Peter's disciple. Now Peter used to teach according to the needs, without giving an orderly summary of the Lord's sayings. So Mark was not wrong in writing down some things as he recalled them. For his one concern was this—not to omit nor to falsify anything that he had heard" (Papias, Frag.2:15. Quoted by William Barclay. *The Gospel of Mark*. "The Daily Study Bible." Philadelphia, PA: The Westminster Press, 1954, p. xvii).

Scripture gives a good deal of information about Mark (see notes—Ac.12:25; 13:13).

DATE: uncertain. Probably A.D. 67–70.

The fall of Jerusalem in A.D. 70 had not yet occurred (Mk.13). The church father, Irenaeus, says: "Matthew also issued a written Gospel among the Hebrews in their own dialect, while Peter and Paul were preaching at Rome and laying the foundations of the church. After their departure, Mark, the disciple and interpreter of Peter, did also hand down to us in writing what had been preached by Peter" (Irenaeus, *Against Heresies* III.I.1).

Note the word *departure*. It evidently means death. It is so used in referring to the Lord's death (Lu.9:31) and to Peter's impending death (2 Pe.1:15). The Anti-Marcionite Prologue says very clearly, "After the death of Peter himself, he [Mark] wrote down this same gospel. . . ." (Quoted from *The Gospel of Mark*. Introduction. "The New Testament and Wycliffe Bible Commentary," ed. by Charles F. Pfeiffer and Everett F. Harrison. Produced for Moody Monthly by the Iversen Associates, NY, 1971, p.113.)

The deaths of Peter and Paul are thought to have occurred around A.D. 65–70. (See Introductory Notes, Author, *1 Timothy* and *2 Timothy*.) Therefore, Mark's writing would have taken place somewhere around A.D. 67–70.

TO WHOM WRITTEN: to the Roman world, the world at large, the Gentile mind.

Mark's recipients are not familiar with Jewish terms and customs, for he constantly explains them. However, they are familiar with Christian history and terms. He never explains them (for example, John the Baptist, baptism, the Holy Spirit).

PLACE WRITTEN: most likely Rome.

PURPOSE: to show that Jesus is unquestionably the Son of God.

Mark states his purpose immediately upon beginning his Gospel: "The beginning of the gospel of Jesus Christ, the Son of God" (Mk.1:1). Jesus is declared to be the Son of God at His baptism and transfiguration by the thundering voice of God, "This is my beloved Son. . . ." (1:11; 9:7). Even demons cry out, "I know thee, who thou art, the Holy One of God" (1:24). The conclusion of the Centurion is, "Truly this was the Son of God" (15:39). Throughout His ministry Jesus Himself claims to be the Son of God time and again.

SPECIAL FEATURES:

1. *Mark* is *The Gospel of Realism*. Mark reports Jesus' life as it was with little interpretation. It is an *on-the-spot*, eyewitness account written in a straightforward manner. The account is unvarnished.

2. *Mark* is *The Gospel of Action*. The key word is *euthys* which means instantly, immediately, forthwith. It occurs well over thirty times. The Gospel paints a moving and vivid picture of the dramatic life of Christ. It rushes from event to event as if breathlessly moving toward one final ultimate climax.

3. *Mark* is *The Gospel of Humanity* or *The Gospel of Emotion*. Jesus' humanity is forcibly pictured. Jesus is the carpenter (6:3); He was moved with righteous anger (3:5; 8:33; 10:14); He became weary (4:38); He marveled at the people's unbelief (6:6); He became tired and needed rest (6:31); He was moved with compassion (6:34); He sighed (7:34; 8:12); He looked at the rich young ruler and loved him (10:21); He hungered (11:12).

4. *Mark* is *The Gospel of the Eyewitness*. Mark adds detail after detail to the events of Jesus' life, details that could come only from an eyewitness. During Jesus' temptation, He was with the wild beasts (1:13). Jesus named James and John "Boanerges" (3:17). "He was very displeased" with the disciples' rejection of little children (10:14). When Jesus foretold His death, the disciples "were amazed; and as they followed, they were afraid" (10:32). "The common people heard Him gladly" (12:37).

OUTLINE OF MARK

everyWORD® is *unique*. It differs from all other Study Bibles and Sermon Resource Materials in that every Passage and Subject are outlined right beside the Scripture. When you choose any *Subject* below and turn to the reference, you have not only the Scripture, but you also discover the Scripture and Subject *already outlined for you—verse by verse.*

For a quick example, choose one of the subjects below and turn over to the Scripture. There you will find this marvelous help for faster, easier, and more efficient use.

In addition, every point of the Scripture and Subject is *fully developed in a Commentary with Support Scripture* already written out for you. Again, this arrangement makes sermon or lesson preparation much simpler and quicker.

Note something else: The Subjects of *Mark* have titles that are both Biblical and *practical*. The practical titles usually appeal to more people. This benefit is clearly seen for use on billboards, bulletins, church newsletters, handouts, etc.

A suggestion: For the *quickest* overview of *Mark*, first read *all the Division titles* (I, II, III, etc.), then come back and read all the individual outline titles.

Outline of Mark

I. THE BEGINNING OF THE GOSPEL: JESUS CHRIST, THE SON OF GOD, 1:1–20
 A. Jesus Christ and John the Baptist: The Good News and the Messenger of God, 1:1–8
 B. Jesus Christ and His Baptism: A Decision for God, 1:9–11
 C. Jesus Christ and His Temptation: Dealing with Temptation, 1:12–13
 D. Jesus Christ and His Message: The Good News of God, 1:14–15
 E. Jesus Christ and His Disciples: The Kind of People Called, 1:16–20

II. THE SON OF GOD'S OPENING MINISTRY: JESUS' IMMEDIATE IMPACT, 1:21–3:35
 A. Jesus' Teaching and Its Impact: Launching a New Ministry, 1:21–22
 B. Jesus' Power over Evil Spirits and Its Impact: Delivering the Most Enslaved, 1:23–28
 C. Jesus' Power and Impact upon Each One: Caring for the Home and the Individual, 1:29–31
 D. Jesus' Power and Impact upon People in the Streets: Caring for the Whole World, 1:32–34
 E. Jesus' Source of Power and Its Impact: What Is the Source of Power, 1:35–39
 F. Jesus' Power over Leprosy and Its Impact: Cleansing the Most Unclean, 1:40–45
 G. Jesus' Power to Forgive Sin and Its Impact: Forgiveness of Sin, 2:1–12
 H. Jesus' Impact upon Matthew and His Friends: Reaching the Outcast and the Sinner, 2:13–17
 I. Jesus' Impact upon Young Disciples and Theologians: The Kind of Life Christ Brings, 2:18–22
 J. Jesus' Impact upon Religionists: Understanding the Sabbath, 2:23–28
 K. Jesus' Impact upon Authorities and Politicians: Understanding True Religion, 3:1–6
 L. Jesus' Impact upon Crowds and Evil Spirits: Seeking and Fearing Christ, 3:7–12
 M. Jesus' Impact upon the Twelve Disciples: Calling Choice People, 3:13–19
 N. Jesus' Impact upon Friends: Calling Jesus Mad and Insane, 3:20–21
 O. Jesus' Impact upon Religionists: Calling Jesus Demon-Possessed, 3:22–30
 P. Jesus' Impact upon His Own Family: Feeling Jesus Is an Embarrassment, 3:31–35

III. THE SON OF GOD'S CONTINUING MINISTRY: JESUS' PARABLES AND HIS AUTHORITY, 4:1–6:6
 A. The Parable of the Sower: How People Receive the Word of God, 4:1–20
 B. The Parables Dealing with Truth: Truth and Man's Duty, 4:21–25
 C. The Parable of the Growing Seed: The Growth of Believers, 4:26–29
 D. The Parable of the Mustard Seed: The Growth of God's Kingdom, 4:30–32
 E. The Use of Parables by Jesus: Why He Used Parables, 4:33–34
 F. The Authority of Jesus over Nature: Rest and Peace, 4:35–41
 G. The Authority of Jesus to Banish Demons: Hope for the Most Severely Affected, 5:1–20

CHAPTER 1

I. THE BEGINNING OF THE GOSPEL:
JESUS CHRIST, THE SON OF GOD, 1:1–20

A. Jesus Christ and John the Baptist:
The Good News and The Messenger of God, 1:1–8

(Mt.3:1–12; Lu.3:1–18; Jn.1:19–28)

The beginning of the gospel of Jesus Christ, the Son of God.

² As it is written in Isaiah the prophet, "Behold, I send my messenger before your face, who will prepare your way,"

³ "the voice of one crying in the wilderness: 'Prepare the way of the Lord, make his paths straight,'"
⁴ John appeared, baptizing in the wilderness and proclaiming a baptism of repentance for the forgiveness of sins.
⁵ And all the country of Judea and all Jerusalem were going out to him and were being baptized by him in the river Jordan, confessing their sins.
⁶ Now John was clothed with camel's hair and wore a leather belt around his waist and ate locusts and wild honey.
⁷ And he preached, saying, "After me comes he who is mightier than I, the strap of whose sandals I am not worthy to stoop down and untie.
⁸ I have baptized you with water, but he will baptize you with the Holy Spirit."

1. **The gospel of God**
   a. Concerns Jesus Christ,[DS1] the Son of God[DS2]
   b. Began long ago: The prophets foretold it
2. **The promise of God to send a messenger: To prepare for His Son**

3. **The mission of God's messenger**
   a. To be a voice: "Prepare"[DS3]

   b. To baptize
   c. To preach repentance and forgiveness of sins
4. **The impact of God's messenger: Many responded**
   a. They were baptized
   b. They confessed their sins
5. **The spirit of God's messenger: Self-denial**

6. **The message of God's messenger**
   a. The supremacy of Christ

   b. The power of Christ: To save and empower (baptize) you with His Spirit

Division I

The Beginning of the Gospel: Jesus Christ, the Son of God, 1:1–20

A. Jesus Christ and John the Baptist:
   The Good News and the Messenger of God, 1:1–8

(Mt.3:1–12; Lu.3:1–18; Jn.1:19–28)

1:1–8
Introduction

Mark begins his Gospel with the simple words "the beginning of." But the words that follow are not simple. They are profound and astounding: "the gospel [good news] of Jesus Christ, the Son of

God." Our hearts should leap with a grasping, vibrant joy at the sight of these words; for God truly exists, and God has sent a glorious message to us through His Son.

Mark wastes no time in sharing the good news about the coming of God's Son into human history. He jumps right to the subject of God's messenger whom God sent to prepare the way for His Son. This is, *Jesus Christ and John the Baptist: The Good News and the Messenger of God, 1:1-8.*

1. The gospel of God (v.1-2).
2. The promise of God to send a messenger: To prepare for His Son (vv.2-3).
3. The mission of God's messenger (vv.3-5).
4. The impact of God's messenger: Many responded (v.5).
5. The spirit of God's messenger: Self-denial (v.6).
6. The message of God's messenger (vv.7-8).

1:1-2

The beginning of the gospel of Jesus Christ, the Son of God.

² As it is written in Isaiah the prophet, "Behold, I send my messenger before your face, who will prepare your way,"

1 The gospel of God.

Mark opens his book by announcing his subject: the gospel of Jesus Christ. He says two things about the beginning of the gospel or *good news* (see note, *Gospel*—Ro.1:1-4 for more discussion).

a. Concerns Jesus Christ, the Son of God (v.1).

The gospel concerns "Jesus Christ, the Son of God." Note Mark's exact words: "the gospel of Jesus Christ." It is not the "gospel of Mark," but "the gospel of Jesus Christ." This statement conveys three critical truths:

- Jesus Christ is the Subject of the gospel (see DEEPER STUDIES 1, 2).
- Jesus Christ is the Author of the gospel. By Him and through Him the gospel is created and written. He brings the *good news* of God to the human race. He embodies, and He proclaims the *good news* about God to people (see DEEPER STUDIES 5, 6—Mt.1:21; DEEPER STUDY # 3—8:20).
- Jesus Christ is the Son of God (see notes—Jn.1:1-2; 1:34; 10:30-33; Ph.2:6; 2:7).

b. Began long ago: The prophets foretold it (v.2).

Although the Subject and the Author of the gospel is Jesus Christ, the gospel began long before the birth of Jesus and the ministry of John. The gospel began long ago in the *mind and plan* of God. God foretold the gospel through the prophets of old. Mark mentions specifically Isaiah's prophecy to point out that the message of Jesus Christ was not new. In essence, Mark says the same thing Paul would later say:

> To this day I have had the help that comes from God, and so I stand here testifying both to small and great, saying nothing but what the prophets and Moses said would come to pass. (Ac.26:22)

DEEPER STUDY # 1

(1:1) **Jesus** (Gk. Iesous; pronounced *ee-yay-soos*): Savior; He will save. The Hebrew form is *Joshua* (yasha), meaning Jehovah is salvation; He is the Savior (Mt.18:11; Lu.19:10; Ro.8:3; Ga.1:4; He.2:14-18; 7:25).

DEEPER STUDY # 2

(1:1) **Christ** (Christos): the words "Christ" and "Messiah" are the same name. Messiah is the Hebrew word, and Christ is the Greek word. Both words refer to the same person and mean the same thing: the *Anointed One*. The Messiah is the *Anointed One of God*. Matthew says Jesus "is called Christ" (Mt.1:16); that is, He is recognized as the *Anointed One of God*, the Messiah Himself.

In Jesus' day, people yearned for the coming of the long-promised Messiah. Most people's lives were harsh, hard, and impoverished. Under the Romans, the people felt that God could not wait much longer to fulfill His promise. Such longings for deliverance left the people gullible. Many arose who claimed to be the Messiah and led their trusting followers into rebellion against the Roman state. The insurrectionist Barabbas, who was set free in the place of Jesus at Jesus' trial, is an example (Mk.15:6f) (see notes—Mt.1:1; DEEPER STUDY # 3—3:11; notes—11:1-6; 11:2-3; DEEPER STUDY # 1—11:5; DEEPER STUDY # 2—11:6; note—Lu.7:21-23).

People assumed that the Messiah would be several things (see note, Davidic Prophecies—Lu.3:24-31):

1. Nationally, He would be the leader from David's line who would free the Jewish state to be an independent nation and lead it to be the greatest nation the world had ever known.

2. Militarily, He would be a great military leader who would lead Jewish armies victoriously over all the world.

3. Religiously, He would be a supernatural figure straight from God who would bring righteousness over all the earth.

4. Personally, He would be the One who would bring peace to the whole world.

Jesus Christ accepted the title of Messiah on three different occasions (Mt.16:17; Mk.14:61; Jn.4:26). The name "Jesus" shows Him to be man—a human being. The name "Christ" shows Him to be God's Anointed One, God's very own Son. *Christ* is Jesus' official title. It identifies Him officially as *Prophet* (De.18:15-19), *Priest* (Ps.110:4), and *King* (2 S.7:12-13). These three officials were always anointed with oil, a symbol of the Holy Spirit who was to perfectly anoint the Christ, the Messiah (Mt.3:16; Mk.1:10-11; Lu.3:21-22; Jn.1:32-33) (see note—Lu.3:32-38 for more discussion, verses and fulfillment).

2 The promise of God to send a messenger: To prepare for His Son.

1:2

God had promised to send a messenger, a forerunner to prepare the way for His Son. God made this promise through Malachi, the last of the Old Testament prophets:

² As it is written in Isaiah the prophet, "Behold, I send my messenger before your face, who will prepare your way,"

> Behold, I send my messenger, and he will prepare the way before me. And the Lord whom you seek will suddenly come to his temple; and the messenger of the covenant in whom you delight, behold, he is coming, says the LORD of hosts. (Mal.3:1; see Mt.11:10)

Isaiah, the most famous of the Old Testament prophets, predicted:

> A voice cries: "In the wilderness prepare the way of the LORD; make straight in the desert a highway for our God." (Is.40:3; see Mt.3:3)

THOUGHT 1. The Old Testament and the New Testament are one in purpose. They both point toward "the gospel" of Jesus Christ.

THOUGHT 2. A significant fact is seen here: God knows exactly what is needed to bring the gospel to humanity. He knew that a forerunner was needed; therefore, He planned and promised to send a forerunner. What was true of humanity as a whole is true with every one of us individually. God knows what is needed to bring the gospel to each of us. However, the responsibility to respond and to obey rests with us.

> The kingdom of heaven may be compared to a king who gave a wedding feast for his son, and sent his servants to call those who were invited to the wedding feast, but they would not come. (Mt.22:2-3)

> But he said to him, "A man once gave a great banquet and invited many. And at the time for the banquet he sent his servant to say to those who had been invited, 'Come, for everything is now ready.'" (Lu.14:16-17)

Therefore, we are ambassadors for Christ, God making his appeal through us. We implore you on behalf of Christ, be reconciled to God. (2 Co.5:20)

Behold, I stand at the door and knock. If anyone hears my voice and opens the door, I will come in to him and eat with him, and he with me. (Re.3:20)

I have sent to you all my servants the prophets, sending them persistently, saying, 'Turn now every one of you from his evil way, and amend your deeds, and do not go after other gods to serve them, and then you shall dwell in the land that I gave to you and your fathers.' But you did not incline your ear or listen to me. (Je.35:15)

1:3-5

³ "the voice of one crying in the wilderness: 'Prepare the way of the Lord, make his paths straight,'"

⁴ John appeared, baptizing in the wilderness and proclaiming a baptism of repentance for the forgiveness of sins.

⁵ And all the country of Judea and all Jerusalem were going out to him and were being baptized by him in the river Jordan, confessing their sins.

3 The mission of God's messenger.

God selected John the Baptist as the messenger who would pave the way for the Messiah. John was sent with a specific, threefold mission.

a. To be a voice: "prepare" (v.3).

John was to be a voice calling people to prepare the way of the Lord (see DEEPER STUDY # 3). Note that he was crying "in the wilderness." The wilderness is a picture of our lost, sin-cursed world. The world is a wilderness full of dangerous, rough, uneven, thorny, and rocky roads. It is easy to get lost in the wilderness of the world, to stumble and injure oneself (see notes—Mt.18:11; DEEPER STUDY # 1—Lu.15:4). It was in the wilderness of the world where the messenger of God had to cry, "Prepare—prepare the way of the Lord."

Therefore stay awake—for you do not know when the master of the house will come, in the evening, or at midnight, or when the rooster crows, or in the morning. (Mk.13:35)

Stay dressed for action and keep your lamps burning, and be like men who are waiting for their master to come home from the wedding feast, so that they may open the door to him at once when he comes and knocks. (Lu.12:35–36)

b. To baptize (v.4a).

John baptized all who genuinely repented and sought God's forgiveness for their sins. Their repentance was with a view to the coming Messiah; it prepared them to believe in and receive the Messiah when He arrived (see note—Mt.3:11).

c. To preach repentance and forgiveness of sins (v.4b).

John preached repentance and forgiveness of sins. He called the people to repent, to turn *from* their sins *to* God (see DEEPER STUDY # 1—Ac.17:29-30); then they were to be baptized in order to "fulfill all righteousness" (Mt.3:15). *Baptism was part of the act of repentance.* There was no true repentance without it. The people were called to acknowledge and feel genuine sorrow for their sin, turning from their sin to God. Part of their turning to God was being baptized. Those who were genuinely repenting would be willing to be baptized as an outward sign of their repentance. John's baptism was a baptism of repentance. Those who truly repented and received God's forgiveness were baptized (see DEEPER STUDY # 4—Mt.26:28).

No, I tell you; but unless you repent, you will all likewise perish. (Lu.13:3)

And Peter said to them, "Repent and be baptized every one of you in the name of Jesus Christ for the forgiveness of your sins, and you will receive the gift of the Holy Spirit." (Ac.2:38)

Repent therefore, and turn back, that your sins may be blotted out. (Ac.3:19)

If we confess our sins, he is faithful and just to forgive us our sins and to cleanse us from all unrighteousness. (1 Jn.1:9)

Whoever conceals his transgressions will not prosper, but he who confesses and forsakes them will obtain mercy. (Pr.28:13)

Let the wicked forsake his way, and the unrighteous man his thoughts; let him return to the LORD, that he may have compassion on him, and to our God, for he will abundantly pardon. (Is.55:7)

(1:3) **Roads—Prepare:** this is a graphic scene. In ancient days, most roads were hardly more than rough, dusty paths. When a king was about to visit a certain place, a runner would run some distance ahead of the king and shout, "Prepare! The king is coming." And the people would immediately begin to clean and level the road for the coming king. John was saying, "I am but a voice crying, 'Make ready! Prepare! The King is coming!'"

4 The impact of God's messenger: Many responded.

1:5

John's impact was enormous, both in Jerusalem and throughout the Judean region. Note the word "all." All were flocking out to him and being baptized. *Going out* or *went out* and *being baptized* or *baptized* are imperfect verbs in the Greek text, indicating continuous action. There was a "continual procession of people who kept going out to hear John's preaching and to be baptized by him."[1]

[5] And all the country of Judea and all Jerusalem were going out to him and were being baptized by him in the river Jordan, confessing their sins.

a. They were baptized.

The baptism of so many Jews was shocking, for Jews were never baptized. Baptism was only for Gentile converts to the Jewish faith (see note—Jn.1:24-26).

b. They confessed their sins.

Again, John's baptism was a baptism of repentance; therefore, the people confessed their sins. Confession is a part of repentance. It includes admitting or acknowledging our sins, but it is more than that. The Greek root word of *confessing* (homolegeō) means to agree with or say the same thing about. When we genuinely confess our sins, we not only admit to them, but we agree with God that we need to forsake them. This results in repentance, in turning from sin and to God.

THOUGHT 1. An enormous impact will be made for God if three things are true:
- if the messenger is truly called of God as John was called.
- if the messenger lives for God as John lived.
- if the messenger witnesses and preaches for God as John witnessed and preached.

5 The spirit of God's messenger: Self-denial.

1:6

John lived with a spirit of self-denial. His living quarters were in "the wilderness," that is, in the country (v.4). He deliberately chose to live away from the city with all its distractions and temptations, where he could be alone with God in meditation and prayer. Both his diet of locusts and wild honey (see Le.11:22-23) and his animal-hide clothing were simple.

[6] Now John was clothed with camel's hair and wore a leather belt around his waist and ate locusts and wild honey.

THOUGHT 1. John knew that life was more than food and clothing and housing. He knew that he must not allow anything to distract him or the people from God . . .
- not living in extravagant luxury.
- not being dressed in the latest and most expensive fashion.
- not eating the tastiest dainties.

---

1   John F. Walvoord, Roy B. Zuck, *The Bible Knowledge Commentary New Testament: An Exposition of the Scriptures by Dallas Seminary Faculty*, (Wheaton, IL: Victor Books, 1983), via Wordsearch digital edition.

Therefore, he denied himself; he actually practiced self-denial. What a lesson for all believers, preachers and laypeople alike! (Ro.14:17).

> **Then Jesus told his disciples, "If anyone would come after me, let him deny himself and take up his cross and follow me." (Mt.16:24)**
>
> **Whoever does not bear his own cross and come after me cannot be my disciple. (Lu.14:27)**
>
> **For if you live according to the flesh you will die, but if by the Spirit you put to death the deeds of the body, you will live. (Ro.8:13)**
>
> **And those who belong to Christ Jesus have crucified the flesh with its passions and desires. (Ga.5:24)**

1:7–8

⁷ And he preached, saying, "After me comes he who is mightier than I, the strap of whose sandals I am not worthy to stoop down and untie.
⁸ I have baptized you with water, but he will baptize you with the Holy Spirit."

6 The message of God's messenger.

John's message was clear and to the point. He did not try to draw a following for himself, but He called the people to look for Christ and to follow Him.

a. The supremacy of Christ (v.7).

John preached the preeminence of Christ and the *nothingness* of self. John said he himself was less than a slave. Slaves were the ones who removed the sandals of guests and washed their feet. John said the One coming was so mighty, John was not even worthy to untie His sandals, much less wash His feet.

b. The power of Christ: To save and empower (baptize) you with His Spirit (v.8).

John proclaimed the power of Christ, a power that far exceeded his. John said he could minister only physical substance: water baptism, a baptism that could only point toward God. But the One coming, the Messiah, would minister spiritual reality, the baptism of the Spirit of God Himself. John's baptism was but a symbol, an act that demonstrated repentance. But the baptism Christ would bring, the baptism of the Spirit, would empower people and change their lives.

THOUGHT 1. The message of the messenger is to point to Christ and to Him alone.

THOUGHT 2. The glorious message of the gospel is twofold.
1) The One "mightier than I" has come, the One who rises above all and holds the answer for all people.

> **He who comes from above is above all. He who is of the earth belongs to the earth and speaks in an earthly way. He who comes from heaven is above all. (Jn.3:31)**
>
> **Let all the house of Israel therefore know for certain that God has made him both Lord and Christ, this Jesus whom you crucified. (Ac.2:36)**
>
> **For to this end Christ died and lived again, that he might be Lord both of the dead and of the living. (Ro.14:9)**
>
> **Yet for us there is one God, the Father, from whom are all things and for whom we exist, and one Lord, Jesus Christ, through whom are all things and through whom we exist. (1 Co.8:6)**
>
> **And he is the head of the body, the church. He is the beginning, the firstborn from the dead, that in everything he might be preeminent. (Col.1:18)**

2) The One who can "baptize [immerse] us with the Holy Spirit" of God has come. The One who can fill us with "the divine nature" and save us from "the corruption that is in the world" has come (2 Pe.1:4).

> **And behold, I am sending the promise of my Father upon you. But stay in the city until you are clothed with power from on high. (Lu.24:49)**
>
> **Whoever believes in me, as the Scripture has said, 'Out of his heart will flow rivers of living water.' Now this he said about the Spirit, whom those who believed in him were to receive, for as yet the Spirit had not been given, because Jesus was not yet glorified. (Jn.7:38–39)**

And I will ask the Father, and he will give you another Helper, to be with you forever, even the Spirit of truth, whom the world cannot receive, because it neither sees him nor knows him. You know him, for he dwells with you and will be in you. "I will not leave you as orphans; I will come to you." (Jn.14:16–18)

Nevertheless, I tell you the truth: it is to your advantage that I go away, for if I do not go away, the Helper will not come to you. But if I go, I will send him to you. (Jn.16:7)

But you will receive power when the Holy Spirit has come upon you, and you will be my witnesses in Jerusalem and in all Judea and Samaria, and to the end of the earth. (Ac.1:8)

And Peter said to them, "Repent and be baptized every one of you in the name of Jesus Christ for the forgiveness of your sins, and you will receive the gift of the Holy Spirit." (Ac.2:38)

B. Jesus Christ and His Baptism: A Decision for God, 1:9–11

(Mt.3:13–17; Lu.3:21–22; Jn.1:29–34)

1. **His decision to be baptized and submission to God's will**
2. **His new beginning and the launching of His ministry**
3. **His commissioning and empowering by the Holy Spirit**

4. **His approval and encouragement by God**[DS1]

⁹ In those days Jesus came from Nazareth of Galilee and was baptized by John in the Jordan.

¹⁰ And when he came up out of the water, immediately he saw the heavens being torn open and the Spirit descending on him like a dove.

¹¹ And a voice came from heaven, "You are my beloved Son; with you I am well pleased."

Division I

The Beginning of the Gospel: Jesus Christ, the Son of God, 1:1–20

B. Jesus Christ and His Baptism: A Decision for God, 1:9–11

(Mt.3:13–17; Lu.3:21–22; Jn.1:29–34)

1:9–11
Introduction

At the very outset of Jesus' public ministry, He was baptized. Jesus' baptism serves as an example for us to follow, and it pictures what happens when a person makes a genuine decision for God. This is, *Jesus Christ and His Baptism: A Decision for God,* 1:9–11.

1. His decision to be baptized and submission to God's will (v.9).
2. His new beginning and the launching of His ministry (v.9).
3. His commissioning and empowering by the Holy Spirit (v.10).
4. His approval and encouragement by God (v.11).

1:9

⁹ In those days Jesus came from Nazareth of Galilee and was baptized by John in the Jordan.

1 His decision to be baptized and submission to God's will.

Jesus' baptism involved a momentous decision and a total surrender. Note the words "Jesus came from Nazareth . . . and was baptized in the Jordan." In Nazareth, Jesus had everything that most people dream about: a happy home, a close-knit family, a profitable occupation (carpenter), friends, and all the fond memories that accumulate through the years of childhood and youth. Yet, He left it all; He left Nazareth to be baptized by John in the Jordan River. Why? Within Jesus' mind was the call of God to launch the mission to save the world, a mission that demanded the sacrifice of everything:

- the sacrifice of all that He had in Nazareth.
- the sacrifice of a long earthly life. By choosing the mission of God, He was to be killed in only thirty-six months.

- the sacrifice of His godly righteousness. He was to become the sin-bearer for the world (see note, Justification—Ro.5:1; 1 Pe.2:21-24).
- the sacrifice of God's presence. In death, God was to forsake Him (see note—Mt.27:46-49).

It was a *momentous decision* for Jesus to leave Nazareth to be baptized. By being baptized, Jesus was *surrendering totally* to God's will and mission to save the world. He demonstrated what is involved in paying the ultimate price: the price of sacrificing oneself totally for the will of God. He showed the world what is involved in making a momentous decision and a total surrender to God.

THOUGHT 1. The decision to follow Jesus is a momentous decision. It involves the total surrender of all we are and have. If we genuinely decide to follow Jesus, we pay the price of sacrificing self completely. However, we must remember: a decision not to follow Christ will lead to discontent and drifting, a wasted and tragic life.

> And he said to all, "If anyone would come after me, let him deny himself and take up his cross daily and follow me." (Lu.9:23)

> So therefore, any one of you who does not renounce all that he has cannot be my disciple. (Lu.14:33)

> For if you live according to the flesh you will die, but if by the Spirit you put to death the deeds of the body, you will live. (Ro.8:13)

> And those who belong to Christ Jesus have crucified the flesh with its passions and desires. (Ga.5:24)

> Indeed, I count everything as loss because of the surpassing worth of knowing Christ Jesus my Lord. For his sake I have suffered the loss of all things and count them as rubbish, in order that I may gain Christ. (Ph.3:8)

2 His new beginning and the launching of His ministry.

1:9

Jesus' baptism involved a beginning and an identification. His baptism was a *beginning* in that it was the beginning of a new life, a new direction in His life. His baptism launched the mission of God to save the world. It was an *identification* in that He was identifying with John's ministry. John was proclaiming the coming of the Messiah, the Lamb of God. Through baptism Jesus was identifying Himself as the Messiah, the Lamb of God (see notes—Mt.3:13; 3:15).

⁹ In those days Jesus came from Nazareth of Galilee and was baptized by John in the Jordan.

THOUGHT 1. The decision to follow Jesus involves both baptism and the identifying of ourselves with Jesus the Messiah, the Lamb of God. If Jesus had not been baptized, He would not have identified Himself as the Messiah, nor would He have been known as the Messiah. Likewise, if we are not baptized, we do not identify ourselves with Jesus, nor are we known to be identified with Him. Baptism is the initial way the Lord has called us to identify publicly with Him.

> Whoever believes and is baptized will be saved, but whoever does not believe will be condemned. (Mk.16:16)

> And Peter said to them, "Repent and be baptized every one of you in the name of Jesus Christ for the forgiveness of your sins, and you will receive the gift of the Holy Spirit." (Ac.2:38)

> And he commanded them to be baptized in the name of Jesus Christ. Then they asked him to remain for some days. (Ac.10:48)

> And now why do you wait? Rise and be baptized and wash away your sins, calling on his name. (Ac.22:16)

3 His commissioning and empowering by the Holy Spirit.

Jesus' baptism involved a commissioning and an empowering. This is seen in the heavens' opening and the Spirit's descending upon Him.

1:10

¹⁰ And when he came up out of the water, immediately he saw the heavens being torn open and the Spirit descending on him like a dove.

Jesus' commissioning was a dramatic moment. The heavens were *torn open* (Gk. schizamenous)—rent asunder or torn apart. What does this mean? What exactly happened? It may have been a moment like rays of sunlight breaking through clouds ever so brilliantly after a thunderstorm. Or it may have been a moment when God miraculously tore apart the barrier between heaven and earth, allowing Jesus to see into the glory of heaven from where He had come.

Whatever happened, Jesus was being commissioned and set apart by heaven itself. God was giving His Son an experience that would make the commissioning unquestionable and unforgettable.

The empowering of Jesus was also a very dramatic moment. The Spirit of God descended on Jesus in the form of a dove. This event not only identified Jesus as the Messiah, it declared that the Spirit of God and His power were on Jesus. This man, Jesus of Nazareth, was being empowered by God's very own Spirit to do the work of God (see note—Jn.1:32-33).

The dove was a symbol of something else. The work which Jesus was to do would be the work of peace and purity (again, see note—Jn.1:32-33 for the symbolism of the dove). Luke points out that the Spirit came to Jesus while He was praying *after having been baptized* (Lu.3:21). The Spirit's descending *on* Him, as opposed to *in* Him, was definitely an empowering experience as well as an identifying experience.

THOUGHT 1. Every true believer is commissioned and empowered by God to do His work of. Some commissioning experiences are dramatic (the heavens are torn apart); other experiences are not so dramatic (the still small voice of God's Spirit tugs at the heart with an awareness that one is called). Nevertheless, every true believer is commissioned and empowered by God's Spirit.

The *awareness* of the commission and power, however, is a different matter. Too many are not aware of God's commission and of the Spirit's presence within. What makes the difference? The first two points: one's decision and submission, one's beginning and identification. Too many of us lack a consistent commitment in both steps. As a result, we wander through life unaware of God's commission and of the presence of the Spirit of God empowering us to do the task.

- Too many of us do not make a decision to follow Christ totally; we do not surrender all we are and have to Christ. Therefore, we are not aware of the great call and commission of Christ.
- Too many of us do not begin with Christ; we just never identify with Him. We may be baptized, but we never follow through with Christ. The world never knows that we are followers of Christ, not committed, genuine followers.

> You did not choose me, but I chose you and appointed you that you should go and bear fruit and that your fruit should abide, so that whatever you ask the Father in my name, he may give it to you. (Jn.15:16)

> But you will receive power when the Holy Spirit has come upon you, and you will be my witnesses in Jerusalem and in all Judea and Samaria, and to the end of the earth. (Ac.1:8)

> But rise and stand upon your feet, for I have appeared to you for this purpose, to appoint you as a servant and witness to the things in which you have seen me and to those in which I will appear to you. (Ac.26:16)

> Therefore, we are ambassadors for Christ, God making his appeal through us. We implore you on behalf of Christ, be reconciled to God. (2 Co.5:20)

> And I heard the voice of the Lord saying, "Whom shall I send, and who will go for us?" Then I said, "Here I am! Send me." (Is.6:8)

4 His approval and encouragement by God.

Jesus' baptism was gloriously blessed with a supernatural display of God's approval and encouragement. As Man—a human being—Jesus Christ needed the perfect assurance of God. So much was being required of Him, and He was to pay such an enormous price to serve God. He needed some clear confirmation, some special strength, some encouragement from God. What God did was profound: He spoke from heaven, declaring that Jesus was His beloved Son and that He was well pleased with Him (see Deeper Study # 1; note—Mt.3:16-17.)

11 And a voice came from heaven, "You are my beloved Son; with you I am well pleased."

THOUGHT 1. God meets the needs of His servants for assurance. He sees to it that we *know* His will and gives *assurance* that we are doing His will. He speaks to our hearts and gives signs of approval and *encouragement*.

> Go therefore and make disciples of all nations, baptizing them in the name of the Father and of the Son and of the Holy Spirit, teaching them to observe all that I have commanded you. And behold, I am with you always, to the end of the age. (Mt.28:19-20)

> And because of him you are in Christ Jesus, who became to us wisdom from God, righteousness and sanctification and redemption. (1 Co.1:30)

> The Lord is my strength and my shield; in him my heart trusts, and I am helped; my heart exults, and with my song I give thanks to him. (Ps.28:7)

> Fear not, for I am with you; be not dismayed, for I am your God; I will strengthen you, I will help you, I will uphold you with my righteous right hand. (Is.41:10)

> When you pass through the waters, I will be with you; and through the rivers, they shall not overwhelm you; when you walk through fire you shall not be burned, and the flame shall not consume you. (Is.43:2)

DEEPER STUDY # 1

(1:11) **Old Testament Reference:** see Ps.2:7; Is.42:1.

C. Jesus Christ and His Temptation: Dealing with Temptation, 1:12–13

(Mt.4:1–11; Lu.4:1–13)

1. Temptation follows decision
2. Temptation is used by God's Spirit
3. Temptation is a desert or wilderness experience
4. Temptation is of Satan
5. Temptation is overcome through God's help

¹² The Spirit immediately drove him out into the wilderness.

¹³ And he was in the wilderness forty days, being tempted by Satan. And he was with the wild animals, and the angels were ministering to him.

Division I

The Beginning of the Gospel: Jesus Christ, the Son of God, 1:1–20

C. Jesus Christ and His Temptation: Dealing with Temptation, 1:12–13

(Mt.4:1–11; Lu.4:1–13)

1:12–13
Introduction

The importance of understanding temptation cannot be overstressed. We face temptation every day of our lives. For this reason, we need to gain a thorough understanding of just what temptation is and how we can overcome it. At the outset of Christ's public ministry, He encountered a grueling time of severe temptation. Our Lord withstood Satan's fiercest attempts to bring Him down, leaving us a powerful example of how we too can overcome temptation. This is, *Jesus Christ and His Temptation: Dealing with Temptation,* 1:12–13 (see outlines and notes—Mt.4:1–11 for more discussion).

1. Temptation follows decision (v.12).
2. Temptation is used by God's Spirit (v.12).
3. Temptation is a desert or wilderness experience (v.13).
4. Temptation is of Satan (v.13).
5. Temptation is overcome through God's help (v.13).

1:12

¹² The Spirit immediately drove him out into the wilderness.

1 Temptation follows decision.

Jesus was tempted right after making the decision to be baptized. His baptism was a momentous decision, for Jesus was declaring His total commitment to God and to God's mission. The decision would lead to His death in less than thirty-six months. The point to see is that Satan immediately attacked Christ's decision. Jesus was tempted immediately after His clear-cut decision to follow God and to launch God's great mission of salvation (see DEEPER STUDIES 1, 2, 3—Mt.4:1–11 for more discussion).

THOUGHT 1. Wonderful things happen when you make a decision for God (see DEEPER STUDY # 1—Ro.1:16 for discussion). Satan, as the adversary of God and people, knows this; therefore, temptation always follows a decision for God. Satan always fights against you when you . . .

- are set free from selfishness and sin by God; when you are set at liberty to live a life of love and joy and peace (see note and DEEPER STUDY # 1—Ep.1:7).

> But the fruit of the Spirit is love, joy, peace, patience, kindness, goodness, faithfulness, gentleness, self-control; against such things there is no law. (Ga.5:22-23)

> In him we have redemption through his blood, the forgiveness of our trespasses, according to the riches of his grace, (Ep.1:7)

- are set free from death and the fear of death by God; when you are set at liberty to live a life of confidence and assurance—the confidence and assurance you have become a child of God.

> For you did not receive the spirit of slavery to fall back into fear, but you have received the Spirit of adoption as sons, by whom we cry, "Abba! Father!" (Ro.8:15)

> But when the fullness of time had come, God sent forth his Son, born of woman, born under the law, to redeem those who were under the law, so that we might receive adoption as sons. And because you are sons, God has sent the Spirit of his Son into our hearts, crying, "Abba! Father!" (Ga.4:4-6)

> Since therefore the children share in flesh and blood, he himself likewise partook of the same things, that through death he might destroy the one who has the power of death, that is, the devil, and deliver all those who through fear of death were subject to lifelong slavery. (He.2:14-15)

- are set free from condemnation and hell by God; when you are set at liberty to live life knowing that you will never be condemned by God; when you first know that you will live forever with God; when you begin living with the knowledge that nothing will ever separate you from the love of Christ.

> Truly, truly, I say to you, whoever hears my word and believes him who sent me has eternal life. He does not come into judgment, but has passed from death to life. (Jn.5:24)

> For I am sure that neither death nor life, nor angels nor rulers, nor things present nor things to come, nor powers, nor height nor depth, nor anything else in all creation, will be able to separate us from the love of God in Christ Jesus our Lord. (Ro.8:38-39)

Just imagine all that is involved in the above: the depth and the richness, the assurance and the confidence, the joy and the motivation, that fills a life that receives so much from the Lord. And not only does this happen when you truly make a decision for Christ, but all this shows itself through your life to others. Your family and friends see the depth and richness of your changed life. The result is heartwarming: usually some of them also come to know Christ as their personal Savior.

The adversary to God and humans is bound to tempt the new convert. Satan is definitely going to attack, attempting to overthrow the person's new decision for God. He attacks by causing the person to doubt, to question, to choose another way, to undertake another task, to seek something else. Satan knows that he cannot leave new converts alone lest they become strong in the Lord and in their witness for the Lord.

2 Temptation is used by God's Spirit.   1:12

The Holy Spirit uses temptation, overpowering Satan's attempts to destroy us by working out God's purpose in our lives. *Drove* or *impelled* (Gk. ekballei) means thrust, cast forth, driven forth, or forced. Jesus was compelled with great force to go into the wilderness. He was driven by the Spirit to be tried. Obviously, the Holy Spirit's purpose was *not to make Jesus fall*, but to make Him stronger and better prepared to do great things for God, His father (see note, pt.3—Mt.4:1).

> 12 The Spirit immediately drove him out into the wilderness.

THOUGHT 1. Trials and temptations are to be stepping stones, not stumbling blocks. They are opportunities for the Spirit of God to use in making us *stronger* and *more able* to do greater things for God.

> Not only that, but we rejoice in our sufferings, knowing that suffering produces endurance, and endurance produces character, and character produces hope. (Ro.5:3-4)

Count it all joy, my brothers, when you meet trials of various kinds, for you know that the testing of your faith produces steadfastness. And let steadfastness have its full effect, that you may be perfect and complete, lacking in nothing. If any of you lacks wisdom, let him ask God, who gives generously to all without reproach, and it will be given him. (Js.1:2-5)

So that the tested genuineness of your faith—more precious than gold that perishes though it is tested by fire—may be found to result in praise and glory and honor at the revelation of Jesus Christ. (1 Pe.1:7)

THOUGHT 2. After a significant decision or a mountaintop experience, it is very wise to get alone with God. You need to be spiritually strengthened and prepared to follow through with the new decision.

Let us draw near with a true heart in full assurance of faith, with our hearts sprinkled clean from an evil conscience and our bodies washed with pure water. (He.10:22)

The LORD is near to the brokenhearted and saves the crushed in spirit. (Ps.34:18)

But for me it is good to be near God; I have made the Lord GOD my refuge, that I may tell of all your works. (Ps.73:28)

The LORD is near to all who call on him, to all who call on him in truth. (Ps.145:18)

1:13

13 And he was in the wilderness forty days, being tempted by Satan. And he was with the wild animals, and the angels were ministering to him.

3 Temptation is a desert or wilderness experience.

Temptation is a wilderness experience. It is a discomforting, apprehensive, and threatening experience. Jesus faced all three experiences in His wilderness temptation (see notes—Mt.4:2-10 for a detailed discussion of Jesus' temptation).

- He was discomforted in that His peace and security in God were disturbed. He was made immediately aware of another choice, a choice that enticed His flesh to desire the forbidden thing: bread created from rocks (see note—Mt.4:2-4).
- He was apprehensive in that He was made immediately aware that a decision must be made, a decision that could be wrong and could result in bad consequences.
- He was threatened in that if He yielded to the temptation, the consequences of sin would result and God's purpose would not be fulfilled.

THOUGHT 1. Temptation is a wilderness experience, that is, a worldly experience. Consequently, temptation is not civilized, comforting, peaceful, secure, or safe. Note three things about the wilderness (world).

1) The life of the wilderness . . .
   - is covered with rocks and precipices (difficult, threatening situations) which can trip and injure.
   - is often a desert (dry, empty, purposeless times) in which a person can die from thirst and hunger.
   - is camouflaged with serpents (food and drink, worldly deceptions) which will strike and poison.
   - is filled with ravenous beasts (both people and things, whether friend or foe) which will consume.
2) The danger of the wilderness is that rocks, desert, serpents, or beasts will injure and consume us.
3) The call of the wilderness is adventuresome, stimulating, challenging, and exciting. It appeals to our *human nature*.

For what will it profit a man if he gains the whole world and forfeits his soul? Or what shall a man give in return for his soul? (Mt.16:26)

Do not be conformed to this world, but be transformed by the renewal of your mind, that by testing you may discern what is the will of God, what is good and acceptable and perfect. (Ro.12:2)

Among whom we all once lived in the passions of our flesh, carrying out the desires of the body and the mind, and were by nature children of wrath, like the rest of mankind. (Ep.2:3)

You adulterous people! Do you not know that friendship with the world is enmity with God? Therefore whoever wishes to be a friend of the world makes himself an enemy of God. (Js.4:4)

Do not love the world or the things in the world. If anyone loves the world, the love of the Father is not in him. For all that is in the world—the desires of the flesh and the desires of the eyes and pride of life—is not from the Father but is from the world. (1 Jn.2:15–16)

THOUGHT 2. God wills us to conquer the wild, to triumph over the wilderness experience, but His presence and power are needed to conquer and triumph. Note that God sent Jesus into the wilderness only after the Spirit had come upon Him.

No temptation has overtaken you that is not common to man. God is faithful, and he will not let you be tempted beyond your ability, but with the temptation he will also provide the way of escape, that you may be able to endure it. (1 Co.10:13)

For because he himself has suffered when tempted, he is able to help those who are being tempted. (He.2:18)

Then the Lord knows how to rescue the godly from trials, and to keep the unrighteous under punishment until the day of judgment. (2 Pe.2:9)

4 Temptation is of Satan.

1:13

Temptation is of Satan; it is not of God (see note—Mt.4:1 for discussion; also see DEEPER STUDY # 1—Lu.4:1-2; DEEPER STUDY # 1—Rev.12:9 for more discussion). Scripture clearly states that God never tempts anybody to sin:

¹³ And he was in the wilderness forty days, being tempted by Satan. And he was with the wild animals, and the angels were ministering to him.

Let no one say when he is tempted, "I am being tempted by God," for God cannot be tempted with evil, and he himself tempts no one. (Jas.1:13)

THOUGHT 1. So few people know and accept that temptation is of Satan. But the fact remains that temptation is a lie and a deception. It comes from the father of lies and deception. We must, therefore, reject temptation, for temptation has the potential to destroy us.

You are of your father the devil, and your will is to do your father's desires. He was a murderer from the beginning, and does not stand in the truth, because there is no truth in him. When he lies, he speaks out of his own character, for he is a liar and the father of lies. (Jn.8:44)

During supper, when the devil had already put it into the heart of Judas Iscariot, Simon's son, to betray him. (Jn.13:2)

In which you once walked, following the course of this world, following the prince of the power of the air, the spirit that is now at work in the sons of disobedience. (Ep.2:2)

Be sober-minded; be watchful. Your adversary the devil prowls around like a roaring lion, seeking someone to devour. (1 Pe.5:8)

5 Temptation is overcome through God's help.

We must never attempt to conquer temptation in our own strength. If we do, we will inevitably fall into its dangerous clutches. We can only overcome temptation with God's help. This truth is seen in three experiences of Jesus.

First, Jesus was with the wild beasts of the wilderness, yet they did not devour Him. The beasts of the wilderness would have included the leopard, lion, bear, wild boar, jackal, scorpion, and serpent. God protected Jesus from all these for forty days.

Second, Jesus was ministered to by angels. Jesus did not have to face the temptations alone. God saw to it that He had whatever provision was necessary.

> What then shall we say to these things? If God is for us, who can be against us? (Ro.8:31)

> For because he himself has suffered when tempted, he is able to help those who are being tempted. (He.2:18)

> Submit yourselves therefore to God. Resist the devil, and he will flee from you. (Js.4:7)

> Little children, you are from God and have overcome them, for he who is in you is greater than he who is in the world. (1 Jn.4:4)

Third, Jesus relied on God's Word to answer the temptations (see outline and Deeper Studies 1, 2, 3—Mt.4:1-11; Lu.4:1-13 for discussion). He fought temptation with "the sword of the Spirit, which is the word of God" (Ep.6:17).

THOUGHT 1. The armor of God is the glorious provision God provides for our victory over temptation (see outline and notes—Ep.6:10-20 for discussion). God promises that we can overcome Satan and his evil forces by clothing ourselves in this spiritual armor.

D. Jesus Christ and His Message:
The Good News of God, 1:14–15

(Mt.4:12–17; Lu.4:14, 19–20; Jn.4:1–4)

¹⁴ Now after John was arrested, Jesus came into Galilee, proclaiming the gospel of God,

¹⁵ and saying, "The time is fulfilled, and the kingdom of God is at hand; repent and believe in the gospel."

1. **Jesus preached the good news of God**[DS1]
   a. In Galilee
   b. After John was put in prison
2. **The time has come**
3. **The kingdom of God is near**
4. **The decision needed: Repent and believe**[DS2]

Division I

The Beginning of the Gospel: Jesus Christ, the Son of God, 1:1–20

D. Jesus Christ and His Message: The Good News of the Gospel, 1:14–15

(Mt.4:12–17; Lu.4:14, 19–20; Jn.4:1–4)

1:14–15
Introduction

This passage records an important transition, the transition from John the Baptist to Jesus as the primary messenger of God to the people. John had fulfilled his mission, and then God's Son took center stage to preach the gospel. This is, *Jesus Christ and His Message: The Good News of the Gospel,* 1:14–15.

1. Jesus preached the good news of God (v.14).
2. The time has come (v.15).
3. The kingdom of God is near (v.15).
4. The decision needed: Repent and believe (v.15).

1 Jesus preached the good news of God.

1:14

a. In Galilee

b. After John was put in prison

¹⁴ Now after John was arrested, Jesus came into Galilee, proclaiming the gospel of God,

Mark notes that Jesus began to preach the gospel—the good news of God—throughout Galilee when John was arrested and put in prison (see DEEPER STUDY # 1). This statement serves to establish the approximate time that Jesus began to minister in Galilee. One year had passed between verses 13 and 14 of Mark 1. Mark does not cover the events that took place between the temptation of Jesus and the imprisonment of John the Baptist. They are covered by John in his Gospel (Jn.1:19–4:54). Apparently, the order of events was as follows:

First, two of John's disciples, Andrew and Peter, became followers of Jesus right after Jesus' baptism (Jn.1:35–42).

Second, the very next day, Jesus, accompanied by Andrew and Peter, left Judea and went into Galilee. It was there that Philip and Nathaniel became followers of Jesus (Jn.1:43–51), and that the first miracle took place at Cana (Jn.2:1–11).

Third, Jesus then took His family and His followers and moved to Capernaum, which was to become His headquarters (see note—Mt.4:12–13). But He stayed there only a few days, probably just long enough to move His family's belongings.

Fourth, the Passover was at hand, so Jesus went to Jerusalem to celebrate it (Jn.2:13). It was while there that the first cleansing of the temple and the conversation with Nicodemus about the new birth took place (Jn.2:14–3:1f).

Fifth, Jesus then began to move about Judea and to openly preach and baptize (Jn.3:22). But His ministry posed a problem for John and incited the opposition of the religious leaders. Consequently, He left Judea and returned to Galilee (Jn.3:23–4:3).

It was at this point that Mark (and also Matthew) picked up the story of Jesus' ministry. The reasons why Jesus chose Galilee to be the center for most of His ministry should be closely examined (see notes—Mt.4:12–13).

DEEPER STUDY # 1

(1:14) **Gospel or Good News**: see DEEPER STUDY # 2—1 Co.15:1–11. See Ro.1:1–4.

1:15

[15] and saying, "The time is fulfilled, and the kingdom of God is at hand; repent and believe in the gospel."

2 The time has come.

The good news Jesus proclaimed was that the time had been fulfilled. The time had been fulfilled for what? For the coming of Christ, God's Messiah. It was time for the salvation of humanity to be fully revealed to the world. The strategic time had come for God's plan of redemption to be carried out (Ga.4:4–5).

World and religious events were ready for the coming of Christ (see DEEPER STUDY # 1—Ga.4:4 for discussion). The law had done its educational work. It had shown through the Jewish nation that all people are terrible transgressors. Despite all of God's favor and blessings, people still failed to worship God in love. The world now had a picture of humans' depraved hearts (see Ro.3:10–18 for a clear description of humanity's sinfulness).

The people of the world were spiritually starved. The worship of self, of pleasure, of false gods, and of philosophical ethics left many empty and barren. The human soul was now ready to have its hunger met.

The world was at peace under Roman rule. Strategically, the world was an open door for the spread of the gospel—without any restraint. An important factor in this was the establishment of Greek as a basic language for all the world. This common tongue made communication possible with many from all over the world. In addition, a system of roads for mass travel had been built, enabling Christian missionaries to reach the farthest parts of the earth. It also brought commercial travelers to metropolitan centers where Christian believers were concentrated.

> But when the fullness of time had come, God sent forth his Son, born of woman, born under the law, to redeem those who were under the law, so that we might receive adoption as sons. (Ga.4:4–5)

> For there is one God, and there is one mediator between God and men, the man Christ Jesus, who gave himself as a ransom for all, which is the testimony given at the proper time. (1 Ti.2:5–6)

> In hope of eternal life, which God, who never lies, promised before the ages began (Tit.1:2)

> For then he would have had to suffer repeatedly since the foundation of the world. But as it is, he has appeared once for all at the end of the ages to put away sin by the sacrifice of himself. (He.9:26)

Prophetic events associated with Christ's coming were being fulfilled. For example, God had foretold that Elijah must *first* come and prepare the way (Is.40:3; Mal.3:1). Elijah came in the person of John the Baptist (Mt.11:10). But now John was passing from the scene. His ministry of preparing the way for the Messiah was completed. It was now time for the Messiah to appear in full force, proclaiming the glorious gospel of God's kingdom.

Matthew and Peter, as well as Mark, stress that "the time was fulfilled" for the Messiah to appear. The fact that the time was stressed so much gives additional proof to His Messiahship.

> Now when he heard that John had been arrested, he withdrew into Galilee. . . . From that time Jesus began to preach, saying, "Repent, for the kingdom of heaven is at hand." (Mt.4:12, 17)

As for the word that he sent to Israel, preaching good news of peace through Jesus Christ (he is Lord of all), you yourselves know what happened throughout all Judea, beginning from Galilee after the baptism that John proclaimed. (Ac.10:36–37)

THOUGHT 1. Note two significant applications.

1) God prepared the way for His Son by moving world events. He controlled history and events, and He controls all events and circumstances for the sake of His people.

> And we know that for those who love God all things work together for good, for those who are called according to his purpose. (Ro.8:28)

2) God fulfilled His promise to prepare the way for His Son. He will fulfill His promises to believers. He prepares the way for every genuine believer, running ahead of us to take care of us.

> Fully convinced that God was able to do what he had promised. (Ro.4:21)

> For all the promises of God find their Yes in him. That is why it is through him that we utter our Amen to God for his glory. (2 Co.1:20)

> Even though I walk through the valley of the shadow of death, I will fear no evil, for you are with me; your rod and your staff, they comfort me. (Ps.23:4)

> When you pass through the waters, I will be with you; and through the rivers, they shall not overwhelm you; when you walk through fire you shall not be burned, and the flame shall not consume you. (Is.43:2)

3 The kingdom of God is near.

1:15

Jesus also preached the good news that the kingdom of God was at hand (see DEEPER STUDY # 3—Mt.19:23-24 for discussion). God's appointed and anointed king over His creation—the Messiah, God's Son—had arrived, meaning that His rule was near.

[15] and saying, "The time is fulfilled, and the kingdom of God is at hand; repent and believe in the gospel."

> And he lifted up his eyes on his disciples, and said: "Blessed are you who are poor, for yours is the kingdom of God." (Lu.6:20)

> The Law and the Prophets were until John; since then the good news of the kingdom of God is preached, and everyone forces his way into it. (Lu.16:16)

> Being asked by the Pharisees when the kingdom of God would come, he answered them, "The kingdom of God is not coming in ways that can be observed, nor will they say, 'Look, here it is!' or 'There!' for behold, the kingdom of God is in the midst of you.'" (Lu.17:20–21)

> Jesus answered him, "Truly, truly, I say to you, unless one is born again he cannot see the kingdom of God." . . . Jesus answered, "Truly, truly, I say to you, unless one is born of water and the Spirit, he cannot enter the kingdom of God." (Jn.3:3, 5)

> For the kingdom of God is not a matter of eating and drinking but of righteousness and peace and joy in the Holy Spirit. (Ro.14:17)

4 The decision needed: Repent and believe.

The gospel Jesus preached called people to repent and believe the gospel. Both repentance and belief (faith) are essential to salvation.

Repentance by itself does not satisfy the law which has been broken. People may repent and change from their former lives, but repentance is not enough. Payment and satisfaction must be made for the laws that have already been broken.

This is why a person must believe in the *good news* about Jesus Christ. Jesus kept the law perfectly. He lived a sinless life (see 2 Co.5:21; Heb.4:15; 7:26; 1 Pe.1:19; 2:22). He was perfectly righteous. As such, He satisfied God perfectly. He stood as the Perfect Man, the Ideal Man, the Pattern of what every human being should be. And as the *Ideal Man,* He could stand for every person and offer Himself to God as the *Ideal Payment,* the *Ideal Satisfaction* for all who had broken the law of God.

This is the glorious gospel, the *good news* preached by Jesus Christ throughout Galilee. The person who becomes acceptable to God is the person who repents and believes the gospel, who believes that Jesus is God's Son (Mk.1:1), that Jesus is the *Ideal Man* who has made the perfect payment, the perfect satisfaction for our sins. Jesus is the propitiation for sins (see notes—Ro.3:25; DEEPER STUDY # 1—1 Jn.2:2. Also see note, *Justification*—Ro.5:1.)

> For our sake he made him to be sin who knew no sin, so that in him we might become the righteousness of God. (2 Co.5:21)

> For we do not have a high priest who is unable to sympathize with our weaknesses, but one who in every respect has been tempted as we are, yet without sin. (He.4:15)

> Consequently, he is able to save to the uttermost those who draw near to God through him, since he always lives to make intercession for them. For it was indeed fitting that we should have such a high priest, holy, innocent, unstained, separated from sinners, and exalted above the heavens. (He.7:25–26)

> Knowing that you were ransomed from the futile ways inherited from your forefathers, not with perishable things such as silver or gold, but with the precious blood of Christ, like that of a lamb without blemish or spot. (1 Pe.1:18–19)

> He committed no sin, neither was deceit found in his mouth. When he was reviled, he did not revile in return; when he suffered, he did not threaten, but continued entrusting himself to him who judges justly. He himself bore our sins in his body on the tree, that we might die to sin and live to righteousness. By his wounds you have been healed. (1 Pe.2:22–24)

Moreover, faith by itself does not satisfy the law. Faith without repentance, without a true change of life, is insincere. It is merely a profession. It presumes upon God, thinking He will excuse a self-centered life just like a grandfather who unwisely indulges a spoiled grandchild. Faith in Christ, in His satisfaction for sin, and repentance are both essential to enter the Kingdom of God (see DEEPER STUDY # 1—Ac.17:29-30 for more discussion).

> "Repent, for the kingdom of heaven is at hand." (Mt.3:2)

> No, I tell you; but unless you repent, you will all likewise perish. (Lu.13:3)

> "For God so loved the world, that he gave his only Son, that whoever believes in him should not perish but have eternal life." (Jn.3:16)

> Repent therefore, and turn back, that your sins may be blotted out. (Ac.3:19)

> Because, if you confess with your mouth that Jesus is Lord and believe in your heart that God raised him from the dead, you will be saved. For with the heart one believes and is justified, and with the mouth one confesses and is saved. (Ro.10:9-10)

> Let the wicked forsake his way, and the unrighteous man his thoughts; let him return to the LORD, that he may have compassion on him, and to our God, for he will abundantly pardon. (Is.55:7)

DEEPER STUDY # 2

(1:15) **Believe:** see DEEPER STUDY # 2—Jn.2:24; DEEPER STUDY # 3—Ac.5:32; note—Ro.10:16-17; DEEPER STUDY # 1—He.10:38 for discussion.

E. Jesus Christ and His Disciples:
The Kind of People Called, 1:16–20

(Mt.4:18–22; Lu.5:1–11; Jn.1:35–51)

16 Passing alongside the Sea of Galilee, he saw Simon and Andrew the brother of Simon casting a net into the sea, for they were fishermen.

17 And Jesus said to them, "Follow me, and I will make you become fishers of men."

18 And immediately they left their nets and followed him.

19 And going on a little farther, he saw James the son of Zebedee and John his brother, who were in their boat mending the nets.

20 And immediately he called them, and they left their father Zebedee in the boat with the hired servants and followed him.

1. **They were industrious and hard-working**[DS1]

2. **They were visionaries: Looking for the Messiah and ready to follow Him**
   a. Their call
   b. Their response: Immediate and costly—gave up their business
3. **They were loyal and supportive**

4. **They were successful, but also sacrificial and considerate**

Division I

The Beginning of the Gospel: Jesus Christ, the Son of God, 1:1–20

E. Jesus Christ and His Disciples: The Kind of People Called, 1:16–20

(Mt.4:18–22; Lu.5:1–11; Jn.1:35–51)

1:16–20
Introduction

It has been said that the greatest ability required to serve the Lord is availability. This certainly proved true in Jesus' calling of His disciples. As Mark records in this passage, Jesus called simple men to follow Him most closely. They were *not . . .*

- religious leaders
- powerful men, not the political leaders of the nation's ruling body, the Sanhedrin (see note, Sanhedrin—Mt.26:59)
- of the priestly or ministerial profession
- students in the schools of higher learning

To the contrary, they were ordinary men, simple laypeople engaged in the affairs of life—just like all the laypeople of their day. Having said this, however, a question needs to be asked. If these men were just ordinary people, why did Jesus call them instead of calling the more gifted? The answer lies in some very special qualities that the disciples possessed—qualities that made them stand out from the average layperson. This passage reveals these qualities, painting a portrait of the kind of person Jesus calls (see outline and note—Mt.4:18–22 for additional thoughts on all these points). This is, *Jesus Christ and His Disciples: The Kind of People Called*, 1:16–20.

1. They were industrious and hard-working (v.16).
2. They were visionaries: Looking for the Messiah and ready to follow Him (vv.17–18).

3. They were loyal and supportive (v.19).

4. They were successful, but also sacrificial and considerate (v.20).

1:16

> [16] Passing alongside the Sea of Galilee, he saw Simon and Andrew the brother of Simon casting a net into the sea, for they were fishermen.

1 They were industrious and hard-working.

The disciples of Jesus were hard workers. When Jesus called them, they were working diligently in their businesses (also v.19). As the Lord strolled the shores of the Sea of Galilee, He noticed their industriousness (see DEEPER STUDY # 1). The Lord has no use for lazy, uncommitted workers. Jesus calls people who are industrious and hard-working. A study of God's call to various persons throughout Scripture makes this fact crystal clear:

- Compare the call of Amos.

> Then Amos answered and said to Amaziah, "I was no prophet, nor a prophet's son, but I was a herdsman and a dresser of sycamore figs. But the LORD took me from following the flock, and the LORD said to me, 'Go, prophesy to my people Israel.'" (Am.7:14–15)

- Compare the call of Elisha.

> So he departed from there and found Elisha the son of Shaphat, who was plowing with twelve yoke of oxen in front of him, and he was with the twelfth. Elijah passed by him and cast his cloak upon him. (1 K.19:19)

- Compare the call of Saul of Tarsus, a man who was anything but lazy (Ac.9:1).

> Therefore, my beloved brothers, be steadfast, immovable, always abounding in the work of the Lord, knowing that in the Lord your labor is not in vain. (1 Co.15:58)

THOUGHT 1. Throughout His teachings, Jesus emphasized that He expects His servants to be diligent and industrious:

> It is like a man going on a journey, when he leaves home and puts his servants in charge, each with his work, and commands the doorkeeper to stay awake. (Mk.13:34)

> He said therefore, "A nobleman went into a far country to receive for himself a kingdom and then return. Calling ten of his servants, he gave them ten minas, and said to them, 'Engage in business until I come.'" (Lu.19:12–13)

DEEPER STUDY # 1

(1:16) Sea of Galilee—Lake Gennesaret—Sea of Tiberias: a fresh water lake in northern Palestine. At its widest points, it was only about 13 miles north to south and 8 miles east to west. It would not be called a sea today because of its small size. There are several important facts to note about the lake.

1. The lake was known by several names: the Sea of Galilee (Mt.4:18; 15:29; Mk.1:16; 7:31), the Sea of Tiberias (Jn.6:1; 21:1), the Lake of Gennesaret (Lu.5:1), and simply the "Sea" (Jn.6:16–25) or the "Lake" (Lu.5:2; 8:22). In the Old Testament it was called the Sea of Chinnereth (meaning harp shaped, Nu.34:11; De.3:17; Jos.13:27) or Chinneroth (Jos.12:3; 1 K.15:20).

2. The lake was surrounded by some of the richest and most heavily populated areas of Palestine. Large towns flourished along its shores, towns which play a prominent role in Scripture: Capernaum (see outline and notes—Mt.4:12–13), Bethsaida (Mk.6:45), Chorazin (Lu.10:13), Magdala (Mt.15:39), and Gadara (Mk.5:1).

3. The lake is subject to violent storms. It sits 680 feet below sea level which gives it a warm climate, but it is in a pocket-like basin surrounded by steep, fast-rising hills (2,000 feet high) with funnel-like ravines. These deep gorges running down through the hills have resulted from many centuries of erosion. When cold fronts move in with their fierce winds, the cold whips through the gorges and mixes with the warm temperatures of the lake, often leading to unpredictable and terrifying storms (Mt.8:23–27; Mk.4:35–41; Lu.8:22–25).

2 They were visionaries: Looking for the Messiah and ready to follow Him.

The disciples of Jesus were visionaries; they were looking for the Messiah and were ready to follow Him no matter the cost. This was the quality that distinguished those Jesus called from many others. Some possessed the other qualities of the disciples (as they do in every generation), but this particular quality was found in few other people.

> [17] And Jesus said to them, "Follow me, and I will make you become fishers of men."
> [18] And immediately they left their nets and followed him.

a. Their call (v.17).

Jesus' call to these men was radical and uncompromising.

It was an "all or nothing" proposition. Jesus called them to leave their businesses and lifestyles behind and devote themselves fully to following Him.

But even more critical, Jesus' call was a call to a greater life, to something that was of greater significance. They would become fishers of *men*. Instead of meeting people's earthly, physical needs, as they had done through their businesses and professions, they would meet people's eternal, spiritual needs. The vision of having an eternal impact on souls compelled them to make a radical decision to devote their lives to such a worthy cause.

b. Their response: Immediate and costly—gave up their businesses (v.18).

Many were looking for the Messiah, but few were actually ready to follow Him. Few if any others would pay the cost of giving up their businesses and immediately follow Jesus. But these men were willing to follow Him, and they did follow Him! They were willing to sacrifice all in order to follow Christ.

THOUGHT 1. Few people have a strong vision—a vision so strong that they are willing to pay any price to follow Jesus. Giving up their professions or businesses, homes or environments, families or friends, is just too costly for most, because they lack the vision of what a life of utter devotion to Christ and His mission truly means.

> Whoever loves father or mother more than me is not worthy of me, and whoever loves son or daughter more than me is not worthy of me. And whoever does not take his cross and follow me is not worthy of me. Whoever finds his life will lose it, and whoever loses his life for my sake will find it. (Mt.10:37-39)

> So therefore, any one of you who does not renounce all that he has cannot be my disciple. (Lu.14:33)

> Indeed, I count everything as loss because of the surpassing worth of knowing Christ Jesus my Lord. For his sake I have suffered the loss of all things and count them as rubbish, in order that I may gain Christ. (Ph.3:8)

THOUGHT 2. Jesus calls people to a life of work, not to a life of ease and comfort. He calls people to invest their lives, not to waste them.

> And he said to all, "If anyone would come after me, let him deny himself and take up his cross daily and follow me. For whoever would save his life will lose it, but whoever loses his life for my sake will save it." (Lu.9:23-24)

> We must work the works of him who sent me while it is day; night is coming, when no one can work. (Jn.9:4)

> Moreover, it is required of stewards that they be found faithful. (1 Co.4:2)

> Whatever your hand finds to do, do it with your might, for there is no work or thought or knowledge or wisdom in Sheol, to which you are going. (Ec.9:10)

THOUGHT 3. Our primary call is to become "fishers of men," not to become teachers, preachers, counselors, administrators, builders, fundraisers or anything else. Yet, how easily we obscure and camouflage the evangelistic ministry of the church. While the Lord calls and gifts us for various areas of ministry, we need to be careful not to neglect His primary call to each of us.

Go therefore and make disciples of all nations, baptizing them in the name of the Father and of the Son and of the Holy Spirit, teaching them to observe all that I have commanded you. And behold, I am with you always, to the end of the age. (Mt.28:19–20; see Mt.20:28)

And he said to them, "Go into all the world and proclaim the gospel to the whole creation." (Mk.16:15)

For the Son of Man came to seek and to save the lost. (Lu.19:10)

Jesus said to them again, "Peace be with you. As the Father has sent me, even so I am sending you." (Jn.20:21)

But you will receive power when the Holy Spirit has come upon you, and you will be my witnesses in Jerusalem and in all Judea and Samaria, and to the end of the earth. (Ac.1:8)

1:19

¹⁹ And going on a little farther, he saw James the son of Zebedee and John his brother, who were in their boat mending the nets.

3 They were loyal and supportive.

Jesus' disciples were men who knew how to cooperate with others. Simon and Andrew were brothers, as were James, and John, and yet they were working together. The fact that they were working as a team speaks volumes of their family backgrounds. They had *good* parents who had taught them to love and care for one another. They came from closely knit families, families that worked together. They followed in the steps of their parents' teaching, maintaining a brotherly spirit throughout life, maintaining loyalty to each other while being supportive. They were just the kind of people Jesus needed as His closest associates, and they were the kind of people He needs in His churches today.

THOUGHT 1. The disciples' brotherly, cooperative spirit shows us three things.
1) The need for a brotherly spirit: the kind of spirit Christ desires of His followers. The kind of kingdom Christ is building is a kingdom of followers with a brotherly spirit.

> And a second is like it: You shall love your neighbor as yourself. (Mt.22:39)

> This is my commandment, that you love one another as I have loved you. (Jn.15:12; see Jn.13:35; 1 Pe.1:22)

> Love one another with brotherly affection. Outdo one another in showing honor. (Ro.12:10)

2) The need for reaching families: brothers and sisters reaching each other.

> He first found his own brother Simon and said to him, "We have found the Messiah" (which means Christ). He brought him to Jesus. Jesus looked at him and said, "You are Simon the son of John. You shall be called Cephas" (which means Peter). (Jn.1:41–42)

> The father knew that was the hour when Jesus had said to him, "Your son will live." And he himself believed, and all his household. (Jn.4:53)

> And after she was baptized, and her household as well, she urged us, saying, "If you have judged me to be faithful to the Lord, come to my house and stay." And she prevailed upon us. (Ac.16:15)

> Then he brought them out and said, "Sirs, what must I do to be saved?" And they said, "Believe in the Lord Jesus, and you will be saved, you and your household." (Ac.16:30–31)

3) The need for parents to train up their children in the way they should go (see outline and notes—Ep.6:1–4; Col.3:20–21; Pr.22:6).

> Fathers, do not provoke your children to anger, but bring them up in the discipline and instruction of the Lord. (Ep.6:4)

> You shall teach them diligently to your children, and shall talk of them when you sit in your house, and when you walk by the way, and when you lie down, and when you rise. (De.6:7)

> Train up a child in the way he should go; even when he is old he will not depart from it. (Pr.22:6)

4 They were successful, but also sacrificial and considerate.

Zebedee and his sons, James and John, were successful businessmen. Perhaps this is the reason John was able to enter the palace of the High Priest when Jesus was being tried for treason (Jn.18:15f). He probably provided fish for the palace (see notes—Mk.10:35–37; Jn.18:15–18). Mark includes a significant detail: the sons left their father with hired servants.

This detail speaks of the depth of James' and John's devotion to Christ and also of their character:

> 20 And immediately he called them, and they left their father Zebedee in the boat with the hired servants and followed him.

- James and John, despite their success as fellow laborers with their father, sacrificed their part of the family business. They were either present owners or would be future owners by inheritance. They gave it all up to follow Jesus. This, too, is a rare quality found in few people.
- James and John were considerate of their father. They did not leave him alone; they would have never done that! They cared for him, so they left him with adequate employees to carry on the business.

THOUGHT 1. How many would sacrifice their inheritance to follow Jesus?

> For where your treasure is, there your heart will be also. (Mt.6:21)

> And everyone who has left houses or brothers or sisters or father or mother or children or lands, for my name's sake, will receive a hundredfold and will inherit eternal life. (Mt.19:29)

> And Jesus, looking at him, loved him, and said to him, "You lack one thing: go, sell all that you have and give to the poor, and you will have treasure in heaven; and come, follow me." (Mk.10:21)

THOUGHT 2. How many adults care enough for their parents to see to it that they have plenty of help in tending to their affairs? The kind of person Jesus calls is a considerate person.

> For Moses said, "Honor your father and your mother"; and, "Whoever reviles father or mother must surely die." (Mk.7:10)

> But if a widow has children or grandchildren, let them first learn to show godliness to their own household and to make some return to their parents, for this is pleasing in the sight of God. . . . But if anyone does not provide for his relatives, and especially for members of his household, he has denied the faith and is worse than an unbeliever. (1 Ti.5:4, 8)

> You shall stand up before the gray head and honor the face of an old man, and you shall fear your God: I am the LORD. (Le.19:32)

II. THE SON OF GOD'S OPENING MINISTRY: JESUS' IMMEDIATE IMPACT, 1:21–3:35

A. Jesus' Teaching and Its Impact: Launching a New Ministry, 1:21–22

(Lu.4:31–32)

1. Jesus began with worship: Immediately—in the synagogue
2. Jesus seized the opportunity to teach
3. Jesus amazed the crowd
   a. His teaching, vv.14-15
   b. His authority

21 And they went into Capernaum, and immediately on the Sabbath he entered the synagogue and was teaching.

22 And they were astonished at his teaching, for he taught them as one who had authority, and not as the scribes.

Division II

The Son of God's Opening Ministry: Jesus' Immediate Impact, 1:21–3:35

A. Jesus' Teaching and Its Impact: Launching a New Ministry, 1:21–22

(Lu.4:31–32)

1:21–22
Introduction

Having chosen His first disciples, Jesus launched His ministry in full force. It might be said that this was the beginning, the opening of His ministry. What Jesus did at the outset of His ministry is important for us to see as we go forth serving our Lord. This is, *Jesus' Teaching and Its Impact: Launching a New Ministry*, 1:21–22.
1. Jesus began with worship: Immediately—in the synagogue (v.21).
2. Jesus seized the opportunity to teach (v.21).
3. Jesus amazed the crowd (v.22).

1:21

21 And they went into Capernaum, and immediately on the Sabbath he entered the synagogue and was teaching.

1 Jesus began with worship: Immediately—in the synagogue.

On the Sabbath, Jesus *immediately* went to the synagogue (see DEEPER STUDIES 1, 2; DEEPER STUDY # 2—Mt.4:23 for a discussion on the synagogue) and launched His ministry in worship. A new ministry should always begin in worship and be bathed in worship continually.

Jesus was faithful to *weekly worship* in the synagogue. The synagogue, with its leaders and its worshipers, was far from perfect; yet on the Sabbath day, Jesus entered and worshiped faithfully. Such an example leaves all without excuse.

THOUGHT 1. Like the synagogue of Jesus' day, churches today are far from perfect. Many people search for the perfect church, but they never find it. Why? Because it does not exist. Consequently, many hop from church to church, while others do not go to church at all.

We need to follow Jesus' example, worshiping and serving faithfully with other believers in God's house. Churches will never be perfect because they are made up of people! We must not let the shortcomings of churches keep us from worshiping and serving in them.

He went on from there and entered their synagogue. (Mt.12:9)

And they went into Capernaum, and immediately on the Sabbath he entered the synagogue and was teaching. (Mk.1:21)

And he came to Nazareth, where he had been brought up. And as was his custom, he went to the synagogue on the Sabbath day, and he stood up to read. (Lu.4:16)

But they went on from Perga and came to Antioch in Pisidia. And on the Sabbath day they went into the synagogue and sat down. (Ac.13:14)

Not neglecting to meet together, as is the habit of some, but encouraging one another, and all the more as you see the Day drawing near. (He.10:25)

DEEPER STUDY # 1

(1:21) **Synagogue** (Gk. synagoge): means a gathering, a community of people. It can also mean the building in which the gathering took place. Synagogues were often held in homes. In fact, if ten Jews lived in a community, they were bound by law to conduct a synagogue meeting someplace. If there were enough Jewish citizens in a place and the local laws allowed, they constructed a synagogue building. There is no sure mention of synagogues in the Old Testament, but they are mentioned over fifty times in the New Testament.

Synagogues began to rise either during or right after the Jews returned from the Babylonian captivity. The leaders became convinced that the nation could never survive unless its people really knew and practiced the law of God. Therefore, it was established that wherever ten or more Jews lived, they were to meet together on a regular basis in a synagogue meeting. They were to study and practice the law of God. The growth of synagogues was staggering. The number can be imagined by keeping in mind how the Jews had been deported and dispersed all over the world and by remembering that wherever ten Jews lived, they were to form a synagogue meeting (see Lu.4:16f; Ac.9:2).

The *synagogue ruler* was the administrator, handling the business affairs and overseeing the services. He arranged for speakers and readers and those who were to pray (see Mk.5:22; Lu.13:14; Ac.18:8). There was also the *chazzan* or sexton or minister. He was in charge of the sacred scrolls or Scripture, the teaching of the law in actual class sessions, and the care and maintenance of the synagogue building (see Lu.4:20).

The service of the synagogue meeting was very simple. There was prayer, the reading of the Scripture (scroll), and an exposition of the Scripture (see Lu.4:16f; Ac.13:14-52 for a picture of two services).

Bear in mind two important facts about the synagogue we learn from New Testament Scripture. (1) Its primary purpose was to teach the Word of God. All other functions were secondary. (2) There was no permanent preacher or teacher. It was the practice to call on both local and visiting teachers to give an exposition of the Scripture.

These two facts explain why Jesus, and later the apostles, were able to find an open pulpit in the synagogues as they carried out their mission throughout the world (see Ac.3:1; 10:2; 13:5; 13:14-52; 18:4; see also DEEPER STUDY # 2—Mt.4:23).

DEEPER STUDY # 2

(1:21) **Synagogue:** it is interesting to note that a Gentile centurion built this particular synagogue and gave it to the Jews as a special gift. Both Jewish and Gentile proselytes were present as Jesus ministered (see Lu.7:1-10, esp.5).

2 Jesus seized the opportunity to teach.

Mark's statement conveys that Jesus excitedly entered the synagogue and immediately began to teach. This was the very day He was to launch His ministry; this was the first chance He had to take the podium and teach. He immediately seized the opportunity.

1:21

²¹ And they went into Capernaum, and immediately on the Sabbath he entered the synagogue and was teaching.

THOUGHT 1. Opportunities must be seized when they present themselves. We must not let them pass. Several things can make us miss opportunities:
1) Not looking for opportunities.
2) Not grasping for the opportunities at the right time.
3) Not having the initiative to grab an opportunity when it arises.
4) Not handling the opportunity properly.

THOUGHT 2. Jesus utilized the moment. His time was short, so He seized the opportunity to teach. Our time is also short. We must use every minute to the fullest, for a day is coming when we can no longer work. We can make several mistakes with time:
1) We can lose time: just let it pass, never seize the opportunity.
2) We can ignore time: pay no attention to it, give it little if any thought.
3) We can neglect time: be unconcerned and non-caring, fail to realize its potential and exactly what could be achieved with its proper use.
4) We can abuse time: use time to do the opposite of what we should be doing; misuse time by using it half-heartedly, sloppily, inefficiently.

> We must work the works of him who sent me while it is day; night is coming, when no one can work. (Jn.9:4)

> Besides this you know the time, that the hour has come for you to wake from sleep. For salvation is nearer to us now than when we first believed. The night is far gone; the day is at hand. So then let us cast off the works of darkness and put on the armor of light. (Ro.13:11–12)

> This is what I mean, brothers: the appointed time has grown very short. From now on, let those who have wives live as though they had none, and those who mourn as though they were not mourning, and those who rejoice as though they were not rejoicing, and those who buy as though they had no goods, and those who deal with the world as though they had no dealings with it. For the present form of this world is passing away. . . . I say this for your own benefit, not to lay any restraint upon you, but to promote good order and to secure your undivided devotion to the Lord. (1 Co.7:29–31, 35)

> Look carefully then how you walk, not as unwise but as wise, making the best use of the time, because the days are evil. (Ep.5:15–16)

> So teach us to number our days that we may get a heart of wisdom. (Ps.90:12)

1:22

²² And they were astonished at his teaching, for he taught them as one who had authority, and not as the scribes.

3 Jesus amazed the crowd.

The crowd was astonished at Jesus' teaching. *Astonished* or *amazed* (ekplessonto) is a strong and expressive word. Its literal meaning is to be *struck in mind*, to be overwhelmed by an impact. The people were stricken, stirred, moved by the Lord's teaching.

a. **His teaching.**

Jesus astonished the crowd because His message was totally different from that of other Jewish teachers (see outline and notes—Mk.1:14–15). The people had never heard anything like the teaching of Jesus. They had never heard anybody speak the way Jesus spoke (Jn.7:46).

b. His authority.

Mark pointed out what made Jesus' teaching strikingly different from that of all the others: He taught with authority. Specifically, how was Jesus' teaching so superior, so much more authoritative, than that of the Jewish religious leaders?

First, other teachers relied on esteemed men, their traditions and teachings, and quoted them as their source of authority. But Jesus taught with a personal authority; He spoke independently of all others. He spoke with a certainty, a positiveness, a finality that no one else had ever possessed.

Second, other teachers stressed ritual, ceremony, and form. Jesus stressed the need and availability of power to overcome the trials and sufferings of life.

Third, the teaching by others revolved around humanistic laws, while Jesus' teaching was centered on spiritual truth. Other teachers reasoned and formulated law after law, teaching that these were the way to real life. Jesus spoke about matters of the heart and life, of the soul and spirit. The answers He gave were spiritual truths, not human thought and rationalism.

Fourth, other teachers preached their religion. Jesus, in contrast, preached life—a life to be lived abundantly and eternally.

Fifth, other teachers professed to follow God, but they twisted and interpreted the law of God to their own liking. What they followed was their own *man-made religion*. They were anything but followers of God. Jesus practiced and lived what He taught. His life was so different from other teachers that people sat up and took notice of what He had to say.

Heaven and earth will pass away, but my words will not pass away. (Mk.13:31)

It is the Spirit who gives life; the flesh is no help at all. The words that I have spoken to you are spirit and life. (Jn.6:63)

So Jesus answered them, "My teaching is not mine, but his who sent me." If anyone's will is to do God's will, he will know whether the teaching is from God or whether I am speaking on my own authority. The one who speaks on his own authority seeks his own glory; but the one who seeks the glory of him who sent him is true, and in him there is no falsehood. (Jn.7:16–18)

Do you not believe that I am in the Father and the Father is in me? The words that I say to you I do not speak on my own authority, but the Father who dwells in me does his works (Jn.14:10)

B. Jesus' Power over Evil Spirits and Its Impact:
Delivering the Most Enslaved, 1:23–28

(Lu.4:33–37)

1. The need of the possessed man
  a. He was in the synagogue

  b. He raged and cried out, sensed and recoiled from the purity, the holiness of Jesus
  c. He identified Jesus
2. The power of Jesus
  a. Jesus rebuked the evil spirit
  b. The evil spirit obeyed

3. The impact upon people
  a. The people were amazed
  b. The people questioned: What power, what new revelation (teaching) is this?
  c. The people spread Jesus' fame

²³ And immediately there was in their synagogue a man with an unclean spirit. And he cried out, ²⁴ "What have you to do with us, Jesus of Nazareth? Have you come to destroy us? I know who you are—the Holy One of God." ²⁵ But Jesus rebuked him, saying, "Be silent, and come out of him!" ²⁶ And the unclean spirit, convulsing him and crying out with a loud voice, came out of him. ²⁷ And they were all amazed, so that they questioned among themselves, saying, "What is this? A new teaching with authority! He commands even the unclean spirits, and they obey him." ²⁸ And at once his fame spread everywhere throughout all the surrounding region of Galilee.

Division II

The Son of God's Opening Ministry: Jesus' Immediate Impact, 1:21–3:35

B. Jesus' Power over Evil Spirits and Its Impact: Delivering the Most Enslaved, 1:23–28

(Lu.4:33–37)

1:23–28
Introduction

Jesus has the power to deliver us from whatever holds us in bondage (Ro.8:31; 1 Jn.4:4; see outline, notes and DEEPER STUDIES 1, 2—Mt.8:28–34; notes—17:14–21; Lu.8:26–39). People can even be delivered from unclean spirits that enslave them, no matter the grip of the enslavement. In this intense passage, Jesus demonstrates this supernatural power, confronting and conquering an unclean spirit. This is, *Jesus' Power over Evil Spirits and Its Impact: Delivering the Most Enslaved, 1:23–28*.

1. The need of the possessed man (vv.23–24).
2. The power of Jesus (vv.25–26).
3. The impact upon people (vv.27–28).

1 The need of the possessed man.

While in the synagogue, Jesus encountered a man with a desperate need: he was possessed by an unclean spirit—a demon. *With an unclean spirit* (Gk. en pneumati akatharto) can also be translated *in* (en) an unclean spirit. The man was in the grasp, in the possession of an unclean spirit. He was captured by this spirit and was subject to its will. Greek scholar Kenneth Wuest explains, "The unclean spirit was in the man in the sense that he, a [bodiless form] being entered the man's body, took up his residence in it, and controlled the person in whose body he dwelt. The man was in the demon in that he lived within the sphere of the demon's control."[1]

> 23 And immediately there was in their synagogue a man with an unclean spirit. And he cried out,
> 24 "What have you to do with us, Jesus of Nazareth? Have you come to destroy us? I know who you are—the Holy One of God."

To better understand the meaning, think of all the evil in the world, all the evil that occurs every hour and every day. John wrote that the world lies under the influence, power, bondage, will, and grip of the evil one (1 Jn.5:19). In the very same sense, this man was possessed by an unclean spirit (see DEEPER STUDY # 1—Mt.8:28-34 for a discussion of the Bible's teaching on evil spirits; Also see note—Lu.8:26-39).

a. He was in the synagogue (v.23).

The possessed man, surprisingly, was in the synagogue. What was he doing there? Was he a regular attendee or had he come just to hear Jesus? We are not told. But if he were a regular attendee, then the synagogue was spiritually dead. How do we know this? Because the man could attend services time after time and never be helped spiritually.

THOUGHT 1. How many worship services are *dead*, so *lifeless* that people with evil spirits can sit in the services and never be convicted or helped spiritually?

> Having the appearance of godliness, but denying its power. Avoid such people. (2 Ti.3:5)

> And the Lord said: "Because this people draw near with their mouth and honor me with their lips, while their hearts are far from me, and their fear of me is a commandment taught by men, therefore, behold, I will again do wonderful things with this people, with wonder upon wonder; and the wisdom of their wise men shall perish, and the discernment of their discerning men shall be hidden." (Is.29:13–15)

THOUGHT 2. How many sit in church and hear the Word of God week after week or live among believers and never make a decision to turn from their evil? They sit in service after service and brush shoulders with believers day by day, but they never decisively turn to God.

> You stiff-necked people, uncircumcised in heart and ears, you always resist the Holy Spirit. As your fathers did, so do you. (Ac.7:51)

> And Samuel said, "Has the LORD as great delight in burnt offerings and sacrifices, as in obeying the voice of the LORD? Behold, to obey is better than sacrifice, and to listen than the fat of rams." (1 S.15:22)

> For you will not delight in sacrifice, or I would give it; you will not be pleased with a burnt offering. (Ps.51:16)

> Guard your steps when you go to the house of God. To draw near to listen is better than to offer the sacrifice of fools, for they do not know that they are doing evil. (Ec.5:1)

> They have turned to me their back and not their face. And though I have taught them persistently, they have not listened to receive instruction. (Je.32:33)

> But they refused to pay attention and turned a stubborn shoulder and stopped their ears that they might not hear. (Zec.7:11)

---

1   Kenneth S. Wuest, *Wuest Word Studies from the Greek New Testament,* (Grand Rapids: MI, Wm. B. Eerdmans Publishing Co., 1980), via Wordsearch digital edition.

b. He raged and cried out, sensed and recoiled from the purity, the holiness of Jesus (v.24a).

The possessed man raged and cried out at the presence of Jesus. He sensed the Lord's purity and recoiled or jumped back when in His holy presence. Through the man, the unclean spirit cried out in recognition of the fact that it had nothing to do with Jesus. The unclean spirit was entirely different from Jesus, who is perfectly pure and sinless. The holiness of Christ is more than an external holiness, that is, a holiness of words and deeds. It is a holiness of spirit and desires; He is as spotless within as He is without. The unclean spirit could not tolerate Jesus' presence. It was diametrically opposed to our Savior's holiness.

THOUGHT 1. Sin, dirt, pollution, and uncleanness do not have a part or a place with Jesus. Jesus has no uncleanness in Him whatsoever.

The unclean spirit recognized that Jesus had come to destroy him (1 Jn.3:8). Down deep within, the unclean know they are to be judged and destroyed. They hate and despise, ignore and neglect, hide and rationalize, in order to continue their defiled ways. The paradox is that they know they will be judged, even while they are sinning and rebelling against God.

c. He identified Jesus (v.24b).

The possessed man identified Jesus. The unclean spirit confessed through the man that it knew who Jesus was. It told the truth about Jesus, that He is the Holy One of God (see DEEPER STUDY # 1, Evil Spirits—Mt.8:28-34; Son of God—Jn.1:34). As James says, even the demons believe in the one true God, and they tremble at the thought of Him (Js.2:19).

THOUGHT 1. What an indictment against so many! They deny the Lord, while devils confess Him.

> So everyone who acknowledges me before men, I also will acknowledge before my Father who is in heaven, but whoever denies me before men, I also will deny before my Father who is in heaven. (Mt.10:32–33)

> For whoever is ashamed of me and of my words in this adulterous and sinful generation, of him will the Son of Man also be ashamed when he comes in the glory of his Father with the holy angels. (Mk.8:38)

> Who is the liar but he who denies that Jesus is the Christ? This is the antichrist, he who denies the Father and the Son. No one who denies the Son has the Father. Whoever confesses the Son has the Father also. (1 Jn.2:22–23)

THOUGHT 2. Knowing that Jesus is the Holy One of God is not enough. A person has to believe in Christ and love Him and turn from sin to a clean and pure life.

> Since we have these promises, beloved, let us cleanse ourselves from every defilement of body and spirit, bringing holiness to completion in the fear of God. (2 Co.7:1)

> Therefore, if anyone cleanses himself from what is dishonorable, he will be a vessel for honorable use, set apart as holy, useful to the master of the house, ready for every good work. (2 Ti.2:21)

> Draw near to God, and he will draw near to you. Cleanse your hands, you sinners, and purify your hearts, you double-minded. (Js.4:8)

> Come now, let us reason together, says the LORD: though your sins are like scarlet, they shall be as white as snow; though they are red like crimson, they shall become like wool. (Is.1:18)

THOUGHT 3. One of Jesus' major purposes in confronting evil spirits was to prove His Messiahship (see DEEPER STUDY # 1—Mt.8:28-34). He is the Messiah!

> He said to them, "But who do you say that I am?" Simon Peter replied, "You are the Christ, the Son of the living God." And Jesus answered him, "Blessed are you, Simon Bar-Jonah! For flesh and blood has not revealed this to you, but my Father who is in heaven." (Mt.16:15–17)

> But Jesus remained silent. And the high priest said to him, "I adjure you by the living God, tell us if you are the Christ, the Son of God." Jesus said to him, "You have said so. But I tell

you, from now on you will see the Son of Man seated at the right hand of Power and coming on the clouds of heaven." (Mt.26:63–64)

The woman said to him, "I know that Messiah is coming (he who is called Christ). When he comes, he will tell us all things." Jesus said to her, "I who speak to you am he." (Jn.4:25–26)

So Jesus said to them, "When you have lifted up the Son of Man, then you will know that I am he, and that I do nothing on my own authority, but speak just as the Father taught me. And he who sent me is with me. He has not left me alone, for I always do the things that are pleasing to him." (Jn.8:28–29)

Jesus said to her, "I am the resurrection and the life. Whoever believes in me, though he die, yet shall he live, and everyone who lives and believes in me shall never die. Do you believe this?" She said to him, "Yes, Lord; I believe that you are the Christ, the Son of God, who is coming into the world." (Jn.11:25–27)

THOUGHT 4. Like the demon that possessed this man, the world cries out that it wants nothing to do with Christ. Why? Because He is the Son of God who demands belief and purity of life, self-denial and a life of sacrifice.

- Wealth cries, "Leave us alone. Let us secure ourselves, build up, and bank more and more."
- Power cries, "Leave us alone. Let us take over, exercise authority, rule and reign, dominate, maneuver and manipulate as we will."
- Ego cries, "Leave us alone. Let us seek recognition, attention, esteem, honor, and praise as we wish."
- Flesh cries, "Leave us alone. Let us excite, indulge, stimulate, relax, release, escape, party, revel, and carouse as we desire."

And he said to all, "If anyone would come after me, let him deny himself and take up his cross daily and follow me. For whoever would save his life will lose it, but whoever loses his life for my sake will save it." (Lu.9:23–24)

So therefore, any one of you who does not renounce all that he has cannot be my disciple. (Lu.14:33)

But watch yourselves lest your hearts be weighed down with dissipation and drunkenness and cares of this life, and that day come upon you suddenly like a trap. (Lu.21:34)

For if you live according to the flesh you will die, but if by the Spirit you put to death the deeds of the body, you will live. (Ro.8:13)

But put on the Lord Jesus Christ, and make no provision for the flesh, to gratify its desires. (Ro.13:14)

Beloved, I urge you as sojourners and exiles to abstain from the passions of the flesh, which wage war against your soul. (1 Pe.2:11)

2 The power of Jesus.

1:25–26

Demonic spirits are supernatural spirits. As such, they are more powerful than humans, for we possess only natural abilities. But their power cannot stand against the power of the Lord. When this unclean spirit was challenged by Jesus, it had to obey His almighty voice.

[25] But Jesus rebuked him, saying, "Be silent, and come out of him!"

[26] And the unclean spirit, convulsing him and crying out with a loud voice, came out of him.

a. Jesus rebuked the evil spirit (v.25).

Jesus' first word to the evil spirit was a word of rebuke: He ordered the demon to be quiet. Note a significant fact: Jesus did not accept demonic testimony to His Messiahship. Why? Such acknowledgment was involuntary, that is, of the mind only. It did not come from being born again. It came only from the demon's mental knowledge that Jesus is the Son of God. It was not of the demon's heart nor of its will to follow Jesus. The witness Jesus wants is the witness of a person who has made a deliberate decision to profess Him as Lord; the witness of a heart truly changed; the witness of a heart moved by the Spirit of God to confess that He is the Holy One of God (Mk.8:29; see Mk.1:34).

THOUGHT 1. We must make the true confession of Jesus, the confession of a believing and clean heart.

> I appeal to you therefore, brothers, by the mercies of God, to present your bodies as a living sacrifice, holy and acceptable to God, which is your spiritual worship. Do not be conformed to this world, but be transformed by the renewal of your mind, that by testing you may discern what is the will of God, what is good and acceptable and perfect. (Ro.12:1–2)

> But he who is joined to the Lord becomes one spirit with him. Flee from sexual immorality. Every other sin a person commits is outside the body, but the sexually immoral person sins against his own body. (1 Co.6:17–18)

b. The evil spirit obeyed (v.26).

When Jesus commanded the evil spirit to come out of the man, it obeyed. Note that the power of Jesus is in His Word. He cast the unclean spirit out by His Word, by simply saying, "Come out of him."

THOUGHT 1. Just meditate for a moment on the power of the Lord's Word. He simply spoke what He willed—for the unclean spirit to come out of the man—and what He willed happened. How we need to learn to depend on His Word as we confront the unclean spirits of this world and for every other need in our lives!

> For I am not ashamed of the gospel, for it is the power of God for salvation to everyone who believes, to the Jew first and also to the Greek. (Ro.1:16)

> For the word of God is living and active, sharper than any two-edged sword, piercing to the division of soul and of spirit, of joints and of marrow, and discerning the thoughts and intentions of the heart. (He.4:12)

> Is not my word like fire, declares the LORD, and like a hammer that breaks the rock in pieces? (Je.23:29)

Mark notes that the man was *convulsing* (sparaxan) as the demon came out of him. He shook violently and uncontrollably, as if he were having a seizure. In addition, the demon shrieked loudly as it yielded to the power of God's Son. The convulsion and cry indicate that the demon did not depart freely or peacefully from the man. It left the man, as we might say, kicking and screaming. The power of Christ forced the demon out of the man's body. The demon was furious and violent as it was conquered by Christ's power—involuntarily, against its will. The convulsion and cry testified of the power and Messiahship of Jesus. Jesus was actually conquering the force of evil within an individual, and only God has such power.

Evil and unclean spirits are powerful forces in the world, possessing enormous power to enslave and possess people. Their power is clearly seen in the way this demon caused the man to convulse and in the terrifying scene it created. People need to know that evil and unclean forces are true enemies of mankind—powerful forces who enslave people with their filthy, intoxicating, and immoral habits.

The convulsion and furious cry are also evidence of the unclean spirit's actually being in the man. The man was literally possessed by the demon.

THOUGHT 2. When the unclean spirit in this man was cast out, it was a convulsive experience. Similarly, *conversion* is a radical experience. When a person truly turns from sin and to Christ, really changes and is cleansed, he or she undergoes a radical change.

> Repent therefore, and turn back, that your sins may be blotted out. (Ac.3:19)

> Do you not know that if you present yourselves to anyone as obedient slaves, you are slaves of the one whom you obey, either of sin, which leads to death, or of obedience, which leads to righteousness? But thanks be to God, that you who were once slaves of sin have become obedient from the heart to the standard of teaching to which you were committed, and, having been set free from sin, have become slaves of righteousness. (Ro.6:16–18; see Ro.6:19–23)

> But I see in my members another law waging war against the law of my mind and making me captive to the law of sin that dwells in my members. Wretched man that I am! Who will deliver me from this body of death? Thanks be to God through Jesus Christ our Lord! So

then, I myself serve the law of God with my mind, but with my flesh I serve the law of sin. (Ro.7:23–25)

Therefore, if anyone is in Christ, he is a new creation. The old has passed away; behold, the new has come. (2 Co.5:17)

The law of the LORD is perfect, reviving the soul; the testimony of the LORD is sure, making wise the simple. (Ps.19:7)

3 The impact upon people.

The people were powerfully impacted by what they had witnessed. Consequently, they reacted in three ways.

[27] And they were all amazed, so that they questioned among themselves, saying, "What is this? A new teaching with authority! He commands even the unclean spirits, and they obey him."

[28] And at once his fame spread everywhere throughout all the surrounding region of Galilee.

a. The people were amazed (v.27a).

The people were *amazed* (ethambethesan), astonished. What the people had witnessed was unbelievable. Using no charms, no invocations, no exorcising devices, Jesus simply said, "Come out of him," and the unclean spirit was dramatically cast out of the man. The people were shocked and stunned.

b. The people questioned: What power, what new revelation (teaching) is this (v.27b)?

Those who witnessed the terrifying scene questioned and chattered among themselves, "What is this? What new power or revelation (teaching or doctrine) is this? What is God showing us? Is the revelation, the doctrine, the power we are witnessing truly from the Messiah?" They marveled at Jesus' authority over unclean spirits. The demon had to obey His command! The people were doing just what Jesus had wanted: they were asking if He were the Messiah.

c. The people spread Jesus' fame (v.28).

The amazed crowd spread the news about Jesus everywhere they went, all throughout Galilee. Imagine the conversation in the stores, businesses, homes, and streets as people travelled throughout the area and throughout the world.

THOUGHT 1. The impact on us should be the same as it was on those who witnessed Jesus' power. All three responses should characterize us as we witness the power of God in changing and healing lives. Yet, how *gospel-hardened* we can so easily become.

And what you have heard from me in the presence of many witnesses entrust to faithful men, who will be able to teach others also. (2 Ti.2:2)

But in your hearts honor Christ the Lord as holy, always being prepared to make a defense to anyone who asks you for a reason for the hope that is in you; yet do it with gentleness and respect. (1 Pe.3:15)

That which we have seen and heard we proclaim also to you, so that you too may have fellowship with us; and indeed our fellowship is with the Father and with his Son Jesus Christ. (1 Jn.1:3)

C. Jesus' Power and Impact upon Each One:
Caring for the Home and the Individual, 1:29–31

(Mt.8:14–15; Lu.4:38–39)

1. The disciples' worship of Jesus brought His presence into a house

2. The presence of Jesus brought hope to a house

3. The presence of Jesus brought healing and help to a house

4. The presence of Jesus brought devotion and service to a house

²⁹ And immediately he left the synagogue and entered the house of Simon and Andrew, with James and John.

³⁰ Now Simon's mother-in-law lay ill with a fever, and immediately they told him about her.

³¹ And he came and took her by the hand and lifted her up, and the fever left her, and she began to serve them.

Division II

The Son of God's Opening Ministry: Jesus' Immediate Impact, 1:21–3:35

C. Jesus' Power and Impact upon Each One: Caring for the Home and the Individual, 1:29–31

(Mt.8:14–15; Lu.4:38–39)

1:29–31
Introduction

The Lord Jesus cares for every individual and every family. In fact, the whole thrust of His heart and purpose in coming to earth was to seek and to save all who are lost (Lu.19:10). His care, presence, and power are available to anybody who will invite Him into their hearts and into their homes. This glorious truth is clearly demonstrated by what happened when Jesus came to Peter's house. This is, *Jesus' Power and Impact upon Each One: Caring for the Home and the Individual,* 1:29–31.

1. The disciples' worship of Jesus brought His presence into a house (v.29).
2. The presence of Jesus brought hope to a house (v.30).
3. The presence of Jesus brought healing and help to a house (v.31).
4. The presence of Jesus brought devotion and service to a house (v.31).

1:29

²⁹ And immediately he left the synagogue and entered the house of Simon and Andrew, with James and John.

1 The disciples' worship of Jesus brought His presence into a house.

It was the Sabbath, and Jesus and His disciples had gone to the synagogue to worship and teach (Mk.1:21–22). The service was now over, and Jesus had apparently entered Peter's home to have lunch. The main meal on the Sabbath came right after worship or twelve noon, which was the sixth hour (the Jewish day began at 6 a.m.).

A strong picture emerges here. Worship brought Jesus into Peter's home. Peter and the other three apostles had followed Jesus to worship. Upon leaving worship, Peter invited the Lord to be a guest in his home, and Jesus accepted the invitation to fellowship with him and his family.

THOUGHT 1. When we truly worship the Lord and invite Him into our homes, the Lord will enter and fellowship with us. He willingly becomes a guest of anyone who extends the invitation.

> Behold, I stand at the door and knock. If anyone hears my voice and opens the door, I will come in to him and eat with him, and he with me. (Re.3:20)

THOUGHT 2. When we truly worship the Lord, we can be assured of Christ's presence. Christ longs to live with us no matter how humble our home or dwelling is. If our dwelling is nothing more than a piece of ground under the open sky, the Lord will joyfully reside there with us.

> Teaching them to observe all that I have commanded you. And behold, I am with you always, to the end of the age. (Mt.28:20)

> While they were talking and discussing together, Jesus himself drew near and went with them. (Lu.24:15)

> Keep your life free from love of money, and be content with what you have, for he has said, "I will never leave you nor forsake you." (He.13:5)

THOUGHT 3. The person or family who worships is more likely to have the presence of the Lord in their home. Worship and faithfulness to God instill a sense of God's presence in the home more than any other thing.

> For where two or three are gathered in my name, there am I among them. (Mt.18:20)

> Whoever has my commandments and keeps them, he it is who loves me. And he who loves me will be loved by my Father, and I will love him and manifest myself to him. (Jn.14:21)

2 The presence of Jesus brought hope to a house.

Peter's mother-in-law was gravely sick with a fever. Luke adds that it was a *high fever,* an extreme fever which likely threatened the woman's life (Lu.4:38). The area was known for its swamps or marshes which were infested with disease-carrying insects, which may have caused the lady's illness.

> [30] Now Simon's mother-in-law lay ill with a fever, and immediately they told him about her.

The very moment that Jesus entered the home, the family was filled with hope. They *immediately* told Jesus about the dear lady's condition. There was a life-threatening sickness, a serious need in this home. One who had the power to help was a guest in the home. Naturally, hope was kindled.

The family believed that Jesus cared about their loved one and could help. Note that they had not known Jesus long. He was just beginning His ministry, yet they had already learned of His immense compassion and love, and His care and interest for people. Through this experience and many others yet to come, they were to learn to bring all their problems and sufferings to the Lord. Knowing of His care for people sparked the hope that He would help.

> Even as the Son of Man came not to be served but to serve, and to give his life as a ransom for many. (Mt.20:28)

> For we do not have a high priest who is unable to sympathize with our weaknesses, but one who in every respect has been tempted as we are, yet without sin. Let us then with confidence draw near to the throne of grace, that we may receive mercy and find grace to help in time of need. (He.4:15-16)

> Casting all your anxieties on him, because he cares for you. (1 Pe.5:7)

> In all their affliction he was afflicted, and the angel of his presence saved them; in his love and in his pity he redeemed them; he lifted them up and carried them all the days of old. (Is.63:9)

3 The presence of Jesus brought healing and help to a house.

Jesus responded to the family's request without delay. When they told Him of their loved one's sickness, He immediately went to her bedside. He did not ask questions or lay down conditions.

1:31

³¹ And he came and took her by the hand and lifted her up, and the fever left her, and she began to serve them.

He was a guest in Peter's home, and Peter had surrendered his life to the Lord—all he was and had, including His home. Jesus loved Peter for his surrender; therefore, when Peter had a need, the Lord *immediately came* to meet that need.

Brimming with love and compassion, Jesus approached the suffering lady and took her by the hand. He touched her. His touch was full of compassion and authority. (Nothing can compare to a touch given from a heart of love and care. Contrast the touch of the fist, claw, and executioner.) The fullness of God was in Jesus' body (Col.2:9), so when He lifted her up, the fever immediately left her. His authority was the authority of God, and His power was the power of God.

> And Jesus came and said to them, "All authority in heaven and on earth has been given to me." (Mt.28:18)

> How God anointed Jesus of Nazareth with the Holy Spirit and with power. He went about doing good and healing all who were oppressed by the devil, for God was with him. (Ac.10:38)

> Now to him who is able to do far more abundantly than all that we ask or think, according to the power at work within us. (Ep.3:20)

THOUGHT 1. Jesus possessed the power to meet Peter's need, that is, to heal Peter's mother-in-law. But note: He was able to help Peter because He was an invited guest in Peter's home. Think what Peter and his family would have experienced had they not invited Jesus into their home!

THOUGHT 2. The power of Jesus' touch is enormous.

- His touch has the power to cleanse from sin.

> And Jesus stretched out his hand and touched him, saying, "I will; be clean." And immediately his leprosy was cleansed. (Mt.8:3)

- His touch has the power to give sight to the blind.

> Then he touched their eyes, saying, "According to your faith be it done to you." And their eyes were opened. And Jesus sternly warned them, "See that no one knows about it." (Mt.9:29–30)

- His touch has the power to bless.

> And they were bringing children to him that he might touch them, and the disciples rebuked them. . . . And he took them in his arms and blessed them, laying his hands on them. (Mk.10:13, 16)

- His touch has the power to heal.

> And taking him aside from the crowd privately, he put his fingers into his ears, and after spitting touched his tongue. And his ears were opened, his tongue was released, and he spoke plainly. (Mk.7:33, 35)

1:31

³¹ And he came and took her by the hand and lifted her up, and the fever left her, and she began to serve them.

4 The presence of Jesus brought devotion and service to a house.

Upon being healed, Peter's mother-in-law immediately served the family and the guests. Jesus healed her so that she might serve. Though she was elderly, He did not heal her to sit and indulge her own whims and fancies and pass the time of her later years—doing nothing of real value. He healed her so that she might become devoted to Him and become a servant to all. And she fulfilled her purpose: she served them.

Jesus said to them, "My food is to do the will of him who sent me and to accomplish his work." (Jn.4:34)

We must work the works of him who sent me while it is day; night is coming, when no one can work. (Jn.9:4)

For this reason I remind you to fan into flame the gift of God, which is in you through the laying on of my hands. (2 Ti.1:6)

Older men are to be sober-minded, dignified, self-controlled, sound in faith, in love, and in steadfastness. Older women likewise are to be reverent in behavior, not slanderers or slaves to much wine. They are to teach what is good. (Tit.2:2–3)

D. Jesus' Power and Impact upon People in the Streets: Caring for the Whole World, 1:32–34

(Mt.8:16–17; Lu.4:40–41)

1. **Jesus can be approached at all hours**
2. **Jesus is acknowledged to be compassionate**
3. **Jesus has an open door for all**

4. **Jesus has compassion on all**
   a. He heals
   b. He restrains evil spirits

³² That evening at sundown they brought to him all who were sick or oppressed by demons. ³³ And the whole city was gathered together at the door. ³⁴ And he healed many who were sick with various diseases, and cast out many demons. And he would not permit the demons to speak, because they knew him.

Division II

The Son of God's Opening Ministry: Jesus' Immediate Impact, 1:21–3:35

D. Jesus' Power and Impact upon People in the Streets: Caring for the Whole World, 1:32–34

(Mt.8:16–17; Lu.4:40–41)

1:32–34
Introduction

The world is a paradox, a puzzling contradiction. It is filled with both good and evil, and the good and evil are clearly seen at every level. No matter how much people long for a perfect world, they discover that their world is desperately sick, a world . . .
- that is so beautiful, yet so corrupt
- that sees love, yet demonstrates hate
- that craves life, yet knows only death
- that desires more, yet deprives so many
- that desires peace, yet is at war
- that seeks health, yet is sick
- that has plenty, yet is starving

Two things are desperately needed in our sick world: hearing the good news that Jesus has the power to help, and coming to Jesus for help. Just imagine! The Son of God is available to help, to solve the world's problems. This is, *Jesus' Power and Impact upon People in the Streets: Caring for the Whole World*, 1:32–34.

1. Jesus can be approached at all hours (v.32).
2. Jesus is acknowledged to be compassionate (v.32).
3. Jesus has an open door for all (v.33).
4. Jesus has compassion on all (v.34).

1 Jesus can be approached at all hours.

Jesus was and can be approached at all hours. What happened in verse 32 is interesting. The people had heard about Jesus' teaching in the synagogue and the two miracles that had taken place. The news had spread like wildfire. It was also the Sabbath, and a Jew was not allowed to carry any kind of burden for any distance on the Sabbath. This included walking only a short distance; it even included carrying a sick person for medical help, unless it was a matter of life and death. Therefore, the people were forced by law to wait until the Sabbath was over to approach Jesus. The Jewish Sabbath began

> 32 That evening at sundown they brought to him all who were sick or oppressed by demons.

at 6 p.m. and ended at 6 p.m. As soon as night came, family and friends flocked to Jesus, bringing their sick to Him. Jesus received them without reservation. He did not mind that it was the end of the day. He welcomed people with needs at all hours of the day.

THOUGHT 1. It was not during the day—the active hours—that the people came to Jesus, but at night. It was an inopportune time, yet they came. The hour of the day was not going to keep them away. Their sense of desperation drove them to Jesus.

THOUGHT 2. Jesus was tired, very fatigued. The day had been long and full of stress, yet He made Himself available, even at an inconvenient hour. We can approach Jesus anyplace, anytime—at any hour of the day or night, and He will happily receive us.

> Come to me, all who labor and are heavy laden, and I will give you rest. Take my yoke upon you, and learn from me, for I am gentle and lowly in heart, and you will find rest for your souls. For my yoke is easy, and my burden is light. (Mt.11:28–30)

> The Spirit of the Lord is upon me, because he has anointed me to proclaim good news to the poor. He has sent me to proclaim liberty to the captives and recovering of sight to the blind, to set at liberty those who are oppressed (Lu.4:18)

2 Jesus is acknowledged to be compassionate.

The people knew of Jesus' compassion. Therefore, they did not hesitate to bring the needy to Him afterhours. They rushed to Him to ask if He would help. They simply accepted the fact that He would help, believing and trusting in *what they had heard*:

- They had heard that Jesus had the power to help.

> "But that you may know that the Son of Man has authority on earth to forgive sins"—he then said to the paralytic—"Rise, pick up your bed and go home." (Mt.9:6)

> And Jesus came and said to them, "All authority in heaven and on earth has been given to me." (Mt.28:18)

> How God anointed Jesus of Nazareth with the Holy Spirit and with power. He went about doing good and healing all who were oppressed by the devil, for God was with him. (Ac.10:38)

> Now to him who is able to do far more abundantly than all that we ask or think, according to the power at work within us. (Ep.3:20)

- They had heard that Jesus was compassionate, caring, and more than willing to help.

> Casting all your anxieties on him, because he cares for you. (1 Pe.5:7)

> As a father shows compassion to his children, so the LORD shows compassion to those who fear him. (Ps.103:13)

THOUGHT 1. What the people had heard is the crux of the gospel: Jesus has the power to help, and He cares about people and will help. All we need to do is believe and come to Him.

> Even as the Son of Man came not to be served but to serve, and to give his life as a ransom for many. (Mt.20:28)

> Therefore he had to be made like his brothers in every respect, so that he might become a merciful and faithful high priest in the service of God, to make propitiation for the sins of

the people. For because he himself has suffered when tempted, he is able to help those who are being tempted. (He.2:17–18)

For we do not have a high priest who is unable to sympathize with our weaknesses, but one who in every respect has been tempted as we are, yet without sin. Let us then with confidence draw near to the throne of grace, that we may receive mercy and find grace to help in time of need. (He.4:15–16)

1:33

³³ And the whole city was gathered together at the door.

3 Jesus has an open door for all.

The news of such power and compassion could not be overlooked and ignored. It had to be searched out and sought. It would be foolish to ignore the possibility of helping the needy of the community if help were available for the asking. Jesus was present and power was available. It was simply a matter of *gathering* at His door for help. The whole city came to Jesus, and He welcomed them all. Jesus' door was—and still is—open for everyone.

The crowd in the streets included three primary groups: the desperate who needed help, the family and friends who brought the desperate, and the observers. The observers were the curious people who had heard about Jesus and wanted to see what He was like. They too, gathered together with those who came to Jesus for help.

THOUGHT 1. How many hear and witness the power of Jesus in the lives of family and friends, yet they ignore and overlook Him?

THOUGHT 2. Our imagination makes us wonder how the observers or the curious responded to Jesus. Did they, too, begin to see needs which Jesus could meet, or did they detach themselves from the power of Him who had come with the message of God? Every church has its curiosity seekers who desperately need to see what Jesus can do for them. The great tragedy is that they are detached from Jesus. They have never experienced the power of God.

THOUGHT 3. Note that Jesus helps the person out in the street. He does not pick and choose whom He helps; He helps all. All can claim His power if they will but come to Him.

Come to me, all who labor and are heavy laden, and I will give you rest. (Mt.11:28)

Consequently, he is able to save to the uttermost those who draw near to God through him, since he always lives to make intercession for them. (He.7:25)

The Spirit and the Bride say, "Come." And let the one who hears say, "Come." And let the one who is thirsty come; let the one who desires take the water of life without price. (Re.22:17)

Come now, let us reason together, says the Lord: though your sins are like scarlet, they shall be as white as snow; though they are red like crimson, they shall become like wool. (Is.1:18)

Come, everyone who thirsts, come to the waters; and he who has no money, come, buy and eat! Come, buy wine and milk without money and without price. (Is.55:1)

1:34

³⁴ And he healed many who were sick with various diseases, and cast out many demons. And he would not permit the demons to speak, because they knew him.

4 Jesus has compassion on all.

Jesus had compassion on the people who so desperately need His touch. He demonstrated His Messiahship by manifesting His compassion and power for all.

a. He heals.

Many of the people brought to Jesus were sick with all sorts of diseases. These people suffered with troubled minds and painful bodies, and He healed many. *Healed many* does not mean nor suggest that Jesus did not heal all the people, that He chose not to heal some. It is "a Hebrew idiom meaning 'all who were brought.'"[1]

> He himself bore our sins in his body on the tree, that we might die to sin and live to righteousness. By his wounds you have been healed. (1 Pe.2:24)
>
> Who forgives all your iniquity, who heals all your diseases. (Ps.103:3)
>
> He heals the brokenhearted and binds up their wounds. (Ps.147:3)
>
> But he was pierced for our transgressions; he was crushed for our iniquities; upon him was the chastisement that brought us peace, and with his wounds we are healed. (Is.53:5)

b. He restrains evil spirits.

Many others were demon-possessed, and Jesus cast the evil spirits out of them. This time, Jesus did not allow the demons to speak as He had previously (see outline and notes—Mk.1:25–26 for discussion). He restrained them, and He still restrains evil spirits today.

THOUGHT 1. A myriad of selfish sins and demonic activity have resulted in our world being filled with disease and suffering. Is there a Savior with the power to heal and deliver, to save and set free? Yes! Jesus Christ, the Son of Man who came to seek and to save the lost (Lu.19:10).

> For God did not send his Son into the world to condemn the world, but in order that the world might be saved through him. (Jn.3:17)
>
> The thief comes only to steal and kill and destroy. I came that they may have life and have it abundantly. (Jn.10:10)
>
> If anyone hears my words and does not keep them, I do not judge him; for I did not come to judge the world but to save the world. (Jn.12:47)
>
> The saying is trustworthy and deserving of full acceptance, that Christ Jesus came into the world to save sinners, of whom I am the foremost. (1 Ti.1:15)

---

1   John Walvoord and Roy B. Zuck, eds., *The Bible Knowledge Commentary New Testament: An Exposition of the Scriptures by Dallas Seminary Faculty,* (Colorado Springs, CO: David C. Cook, 1983). Via Wordsearch digital edition.

**E. Jesus' Source of Power and Its Impact:
What Is the Source of Power? 1:35–39**

(Lu.4:42-44)

1. **Jesus' steadfast prayer life**
   a. When: Morning—very early, while it was still dark
   b. Where: Solitary place
2. **Jesus' mindfulness of His worldwide mission**
   a. The people sought to keep Jesus with them
   b. Jesus would not be deterred: He needed to spread the gospel
3. **Jesus' faithfulness**
   a. Preached everywhere
   b. Healed and cast out demons

35 And rising very early in the morning, while it was still dark, he departed and went out to a desolate place, and there he prayed.
36 And Simon and those who were with him searched for him,
37 and they found him and said to him, "Everyone is looking for you."
38 And he said to them, "Let us go on to the next towns, that I may preach there also, for that is why I came out."
39 And he went throughout all Galilee, preaching in their synagogues and casting out demons.

Division II

The Son of God's Opening Ministry: Jesus' Immediate Impact, 1:21–3:35

E. Jesus' Source of Power and Its Impact: What Is the Source of Power, 1:35–39

(Lu.4:42-44)

1:35–39
Introduction

We cannot be effective in the Lord's service without His power. But where and how does the servant of God receive power? From the very beginning of Jesus' earthly work, He ministered in the fullness of God's power. We can learn the secrets to being powerful in our service by studying the ministry of Jesus. This passage reveals in unmistakable terms where and how Jesus received His power. This is, *Jesus' Source of Power and Its Impact: What Is the Source of Power,* 1:35–39.

1. Jesus' steadfast prayer life (v.35).
2. Jesus' mindfulness of His worldwide mission (vv.36–38).
3. Jesus' faithfulness (v.39).

1:35

35 And rising very early in the morning, while it was still dark, he departed and went out to a desolate place, and there he prayed.

1 Jesus' steadfast prayer life.

Jesus' first source of power was His *steadfast prayer life.* Prayer was a priority for Jesus. He began the day by spending time alone with His Father in prayer. Note three facts about Jesus' prayer life in this passage.

On this particular morning, why did Jesus rise early to pray? First, Jesus was tired. The day before had drained and exhausted Him, probably to the point that every muscle in His body ached (vv.21-34). Teaching and ministering all day sapped the strength out of His body, both mentally and emotionally. In Jesus' case it actually drained virtue or energy out of Him (Mk.5:30). Mentally and emotionally, He was utterly exhausted. At such times the body does not want to move and the mind wanders more easily, making us more subject to temptation; therefore, we desperately need to pray.

Second, Jesus was launching His first missionary or evangelistic tour. Jesus sensed deeply that He had come to be an evangelist (v.38). Right before He was to launch His first tour, He felt a great need to pray. The people's needs were great, and their demands would be incessant. He would be bombarded by human needs and by the attacks of both Satan and institutional religion. The days would be long, taxing, and exhausting. He needed the strength of God and a special anointing as He went forth on this special mission.

Third, Jesus was confronted with the applause and praise of people (v.37). This presented the same temptation that He had faced earlier: to secure the loyalty of people by the spectacular (see note—Mt.4:5-7). After seeing the miracles, the crowds were ready to follow Jesus for what they could get out of Him. Jesus needed His purpose reinforced and a special infusion of God's strength to withstand the temptation of human applause and loyalty—applause and loyalty that arose from shallow and surface commitments.

a. When: Morning—very early, while it was still dark.

Jesus prayed early in the morning, long before sunrise. Remember, the day before had been the Sabbath, an extremely tiring day. He had expended enormous energy in teaching and ministering. He had been up late at night ministering to the whole city that had flocked to the house where He was staying (vv.21-34). Every muscle in His body must have ached, craving rest; yet, He rose before daybreak, went to a place where He could be alone with God, and prayed. He would not begin His day until He had spent time with His Father.

Early morning prayer must have been the habit of Jesus, for the fact that Jesus prayed in the pre-dawn hours made a lasting impression on the disciples. Remember, this scene is from the launch of Jesus' ministry, probably the first time the disciples had an opportunity to observe Jesus' prayer life. Mark gives a detailed description, the facts of which had probably come from Peter. Mark certainly felt that the fact was important enough to emphasize, for he not only shares what Jesus' ministry was like, he also shares what Jesus' prayer life was like.

b. Where: Solitary place.

Jesus went to a private place to pray. The specific place is not identified. It could have been some place out in the countryside, a quiet orchard, or an abandoned building. The fact of importance is that He had a place where He could be alone with God. He needed to be alone with God.

THOUGHT 1. If Jesus, the Son of Man, needed so much time alone with God in prayer, how much more do we? What an indictment against so many believers and their prayer life!

> Ask, and it will be given to you; seek, and you will find; knock, and it will be opened to you. (Mt.7:7)

> Until now you have asked nothing in my name. Ask, and you will receive, that your joy may be full. (Jn.16:24)

> Praying at all times in the Spirit, with all prayer and supplication. To that end, keep alert with all perseverance, making supplication for all the saints. (Ep.6:18)

> Pray without ceasing. (1 Th.5:17)

2 Jesus' mindfulness of His worldwide mission.

Jesus' second source of power was His *constant awareness of His mission*, a worldwide mission. Note what happened. When Peter and the others arose from sleeping, they discovered Jesus was missing. They searched for Him until they found Him (v.36). What they said to Jesus when they found Him reveals that they did not grasp the importance

36 And Simon and those who were with him searched for him,

37 and they found him and said to him, "Everyone is looking for you."

38 And he said to them, "Let us go on to the next towns, that I may preach there also, for that is why I came out."

of prayer. They told Jesus that all the people of the city were looking for Him, suggesting that the Lord should forgo praying in order to give them His attention (v.37). They were surely puzzled and possibly perturbed when Jesus replied that they were moving on to other towns (v.38).

a. The people sought to keep Jesus with them (v.37).

All the people were looking for Jesus. Luke adds that the people tried to keep Jesus from leaving Capernaum:

> **And when it was day, he departed and went into a desolate place. And the people sought him and came to him, and would have kept him from leaving them. (Lu.4:42)**

The word *keep* (Gk. kateichon, pronounced *ka-tech'-own*) is strong. It means to hold back, to hold fast. The imperfect verb indicates they persisted in their efforts; they would not take "no" for an answer. The people of Capernaum tried their best to detain Jesus. They were not going to let Him leave if they could prevent Him from doing so.

b. Jesus would not be deterred: He needed to spread the gospel (v.38).

The force of the urgings by the disciples and the people shows just how strongly convinced Jesus was of His mission. He had it made, so to speak, in Capernaum at this point in time. The people were stirred and motivated to follow God, and tremendous needs remained to be met in the city and surrounding area. A great ministry could be performed for God right in Capernaum. There was no need to go elsewhere, not in the people's minds. Jesus' response was forceful. He would not give in to the pressure to stay in Capernaum. He and His disciples would be moving on to other towns.

Jesus was thoroughly convinced: He must not be deterred nor sidetracked from His mission. Plenty of needs may still have existed, but two critical facts were being overlooked—facts which have been and are still being sadly overlooked by believers everywhere.

First, Capernaum and its people, at least many of its people, had already heard the gospel preached. If God's messenger (Jesus) had stayed in Capernaum, many throughout the world would never have heard the gospel.

Second, the people in Capernaum could now share the message themselves. God's messenger (Jesus) was not really needed to continue the ministry. The people were much more likely to assume the responsibility to carry on if Jesus left. But if Jesus had stayed, the people would have left most of the responsibility up to Him. The people would not become the witnesses they should.

THOUGHT 1. Jesus' response in Mark 1:38 is a powerful lesson that is clear and striking, and hopefully convicting. So much change is needed in institutional religion if the world is truly to be reached for Jesus. Courageous voices need to be raised for believers to begin doing what Jesus did . . .

- ministering
- making disciples
- preaching (witnessing, proclaiming the gospel)
- moving on to other needful and unevangelized villages and towns

> **Go therefore and make disciples of all nations, baptizing them in the name of the Father and of the Son and of the Holy Spirit, teaching them to observe all that I have commanded you. And behold, I am with you always, to the end of the age. (Mt.28:19–20)**

> **And he said to them, "Go into all the world and proclaim the gospel to the whole creation." (Mk.16:15)**

> **But you will receive power when the Holy Spirit has come upon you, and you will be my witnesses in Jerusalem and in all Judea and Samaria, and to the end of the earth. (Ac.1:8)**

THOUGHT 2. Jesus' exact words are of crucial importance. He stressed in no uncertain terms that His mission was primarily to *preach*. He set forth *preaching* as the *primary task* of the minister. Physical needs *were* present. They still existed in Capernaum, and they existed in all the towns where He would eventually go. He would meet as many of the needs as possible. But His primary task and mission was to proclaim the gospel of the Kingdom of Heaven (see DEEPER STUDY # 3—Mt.19:23–24).

> Jesus said to them again, "Peace be with you. As the Father has sent me, even so I am sending you." (Jn.20:21)

3 Jesus' faithfulness.

Jesus' third source of power was His *faithfulness* to His mission. He preached in the synagogues throughout all of Galilee. Galilee was densely populated. There were over two hundred cities in the district (see note—Mt.4:12-13). But Jesus went everywhere preaching, throughout the entire region. He left no place untouched. Note that He preached in the synagogues using the structure of established religion. He did this as long as He was allowed.

> 39 And he went throughout all Galilee, preaching in their synagogues and casting out demons.

Jesus continued to minister as well as preach. Preaching was His primary mission, but while He preached, He also ministered to the people's physical needs. People had physical, emotional, and mental needs as well as spiritual. Jesus validated and demonstrated both His mission and deity by healing and casting out demons.

THOUGHT 1. Faithfulness assures power. God will continue to give His power to the messenger who continues to be faithful. Likewise, He has to withdraw His power from the unfaithful messenger. He cannot give license to disobedience. A divided house cannot stand (see outline and notes—Mt.12:25–26 for more discussion).

> Moreover, it is required of stewards that they be found faithful. (1 Co.4:2)

> As each has received a gift, use it to serve one another, as good stewards of God's varied grace. (1 Pe.4:10)

> O Timothy, guard the deposit entrusted to you. Avoid the irreverent babble and contradictions of what is falsely called "knowledge." (1 Ti.6:20)

> By the Holy Spirit who dwells within us, guard the good deposit entrusted to you. (2 Ti.1:14)

F. Jesus' Power over Leprosy and Its Impact:
Cleansing the Most Unclean, 1:40–45

(Mt.8:2–4; Lu.5:12–15)

1. **Jesus is the great hope of the most unclean**[DS1]

2. **Jesus is moved with compassion for the most unclean**[DS2]
   a. Moved to touch
   b. Moved to speak
   c. Result: It was the power of His Word that cleansed and healed the most unclean
3. **Jesus sent the most unclean away with a stern warning**
   a. Warned to say nothing to others
   b. Warned to obey the law and give witness to His Messiahship

4. **Jesus made a great impact through the most unclean**
   a. The news spread
   b. Jesus could no longer minister in the cities: He had to stay out in the countryside

⁴⁰ And a leper came to him, imploring him, and kneeling said to him, "If you will, you can make me clean."
⁴¹ Moved with pity, he stretched out his hand and touched him and said to him, "I will; be clean."

⁴² And immediately the leprosy left him, and he was made clean.

⁴³ And Jesus sternly charged him and sent him away at once,
⁴⁴ and said to him, "See that you say nothing to anyone, but go, show yourself to the priest and offer for your cleansing what Moses commanded, for a proof to them."
⁴⁵ But he went out and began to talk freely about it, and to spread the news, so that Jesus could no longer openly enter a town, but was out in desolate places, and people were coming to him from every quarter.

Division II

The Son of God's Opening Ministry: Jesus' Immediate Impact, 1:21–3:35

F. Jesus' Power over Leprosy and Its Impact: Cleansing the Most Unclean, 1:40–45

(Mt.8:2–4; Lu.5:12–15)

1:40–45
Introduction

The most feared disease of the ancient world was leprosy. The leper was considered the most unclean, revolting, and hideous person imaginable. Leprosy itself was thought to be the result of terrible sin and actually became the most dramatic symbol of sin in people's minds. There was no known cure for leprosy; only God was considered powerful enough to cure the disease.

In this passage, Jesus healed a leper. In cleansing this helpless, hopeless man, Jesus was proving His Messiahship. He was demonstrating that He had the power to cleanse the most unclean, no matter how terrible their uncleanness (see Deeper Studies 1, 2, 3—Mt.8:1-4 for a more detailed discussion of leprosy and for more information on this event). This is, *Jesus' Power over Leprosy and Its Impact: Cleansing the Most Unclean*, 1:40-45.

1. Jesus is the great hope of the most unclean (v.40).
2. Jesus is moved with compassion for the most unclean (vv.41-42).

3. Jesus sent the most unclean away with a stern warning (vv.43–44).

4. Jesus made a great impact through the most unclean (v.45).

1 Jesus is the great hope of the most unclean.

The leper's experience was dramatic. He was full of leprosy (Lu.5:12); that is, he was completely covered by leprosy (see DEEPER STUDY # 1). His whole body was consumed with sores, perhaps some parts even eaten away by the cancerous disease. He was hopeless, for all were powerless to help him.

40 And a leper came to him, imploring him, and kneeling said to him, "If you will, you can make me clean."

But somewhere, somehow, he heard about Jesus and His miraculous power. Hope sprung up in his heart, and he began to search for Jesus. When he found out where Jesus was, he made his way to Him. Matthew tells us that he found Jesus on the mountain where Jesus was preaching the great *Sermon on the Mount* (Mt.8:1-4). He heard Jesus preach, and what Jesus said burned in his heart and turned his hope into enormous faith. As Jesus made His way down the mountain, the leper made his way to Him and fell at Jesus' feet.

The leper (the most unclean) was so desperate and so intent on seeking Jesus' help that he forgot everything else and everyone else. He forgot all about the law's requiring him to come no closer than six feet to any other person. He forgot all about the thronging crowd that surrounded Jesus. He saw no one and thought of no one except Jesus. It was his desperate need and the enormous hope sparked in him by Jesus that drove him to race through the crowd and fall on his face, begging for help.

Mark, Luke, and Matthew all highlight the *intensity* of the man's act, his falling down before the Lord in worship (Mt.8:2; Lu.5:12). The leper saw in Jesus the divine power of God Himself. This was evidenced by his worship of Jesus and the words he spoke to Jesus. Note he did not say, "You can ask God and God will make me clean." He said, "If _you_ will, if you are willing, you can make me clean." He was saying that Jesus possessed the power of God to cleanse him. Full of faith, he confessed that Jesus is the great hope of the most unclean.

THOUGHT 1. The leper is a picture of the sinner. Jesus will heal any individual who approaches Him as the leper did, even if he or she is the most unclean person—the wickedest sinner—on earth.

> And when Jesus heard it, he said to them, "Those who are well have no need of a physician, but those who are sick. I came not to call the righteous, but sinners." (Mk.2:17)

> And now why do you wait? Rise and be baptized and wash away your sins, calling on his name. (Ac.22:16)

> The saying is trustworthy and deserving of full acceptance, that Christ Jesus came into the world to save sinners, of whom I am the foremost. (1 Ti.1:15)

> Draw near to God, and he will draw near to you. Cleanse your hands, you sinners, and purify your hearts, you double-minded. (Js.4:8)

DEEPER STUDY # 1

(1:40) **Leprosy:** see DEEPER STUDY # 1—Mt.8:1-4.

2 Jesus was moved with compassion for the most unclean.

Looking down on the leper, Jesus knew the man through and through: his miserable condition, his heart, his hope, his

41 Moved with pity, he stretched out his hand and touched him and said to him, "I will; be clean."
42 And immediately the leprosy left him, and he was made clean.

faith. Our loving Lord was moved with compassion or pity for the suffering man, and He tenderly reached out to help him (see DEEPER STUDY # 2).

a. **Moved to touch (v.41a).**
Jesus was moved to reach out and touch the man; He did not ignore him. Jesus did not push him back or jump away from him for fear of catching his disease. He could have, for the man had no right to approach Jesus. But Jesus, knowing the man's heart, was moved with compassion; and He reached out and touched the leper (the most unclean).

> When he saw the crowds, he had compassion for them, because they were harassed and helpless, like sheep without a shepherd. (Mt.9:36)

> When he went ashore he saw a great crowd, and he had compassion on them and healed their sick. (Mt.14:14)

> As a father shows compassion to his children, so the LORD shows compassion to those who fear him. (Ps.103:13)

> In all their affliction he was afflicted, and the angel of his presence saved them; in his love and in his pity he redeemed them; he lifted them up and carried them all the days of old. (Is.63:9)

b. **Moved to speak (v.41b).**
Jesus was moved to speak the most wonderful words to the leprous man: He said that He was willing for the man to be healed, and He commanded that the man be cleansed. He spoke His Word of power.

c. **Result: It was the power of His Word that cleansed and healed the most unclean (v.42).**
The result was just as Jesus willed and spoke. His powerful Word cleansed and healed the man. In healing the man, Jesus demonstrated three things:

First, He cares and is moved with compassion by the plight of all people, even by the most unclean.

Second, He is most definitely the Son of God who possesses the very power of God to cleanse people of their sin and uncleanness. Leprosy was a symbol of sin, so in cleansing the man's leprosy, the man was being cleansed (healed) both physically and spiritually.

Third, He is superior to the law. He reached out and touched the man—which was against the law. Lepers were by law to remain at least six feet away from others, even from family members (see notes, *Jesus Christ, Fulfills Law*—Mt.5:17-18; DEEPER STUDY # 2—Ro.8:3 for more discussion).

THOUGHT 1. Remember, the leper is a picture of sinful humanity. We are all plagued with the deadly disease of sin. Jesus wills to make every sinful person clean. It is His will that every human being be made whole. But what is so desperately needed is for every sinner to approach Jesus just as this poor leper did.

> How God anointed Jesus of Nazareth with the Holy Spirit and with power. He went about doing good and healing all who were oppressed by the devil, for God was with him. (Ac.10:38)

> Consequently, he is able to save to the uttermost those who draw near to God through him, since he always lives to make intercession for them. (He.7:25)

> But he was pierced for our transgressions; he was crushed for our iniquities; upon him was the chastisement that brought us peace, and with his wounds we are healed. (Is.53:5)

> All these things my hand has made, and so all these things came to be, declares the LORD. But this is the one to whom I will look: he who is humble and contrite in spirit and trembles at my word. (Is.66:2)

DEEPER STUDY # 2

(1:41) **Compassion:** see note and DEEPER STUDY # 2—Mt.9:36.

3 Jesus sent the most unclean away with a stern warning.

Immediately after cleansing the leper, Jesus sent him away (v.43). As He was letting the man go, the Lord gave him strict instructions, sternly charging him to do two specific things.

a. Warned to say nothing to others (v.44a).

First, Jesus ordered the man to not tell others about His cleansing. Jesus had purposes for forbidding the man to speak of what Christ had done for Him. Perhaps one purpose was that He did not want the man to be filled with pride. Jesus was essentially saying, "Do not boast in your cleansing. Guard against pride, against feeling that God is partial to you and that you are a favorite of God and more special than *anyone* else." Apparently, there was something within this man that would tend toward pride (see note—Mt.8:4). His attention was not to be focused on what had happened to him (his cleansing and healing), but on Jesus, his compassionate and merciful Savior.

> [43] And Jesus sternly charged him and sent him away at once,
> [44] and said to him, "See that you say nothing to anyone, but go, show yourself to the priest and offer for your cleansing what Moses commanded, for a proof to them."

THOUGHT 1. Too often we look at the sinner and say, "*But for the grace of God, there go I.*" Such an attitude is boastful and prideful. It is true that the grace of God has saved us, but God did not save us because we are His favorites. We are not saved to compare ourselves with the sinner by going around saying (testifying) and thinking that we are above the sinner. We are saved to proclaim the grace of God to others. Our task is not to point to the one bound by sin and testify: "But for the grace of God, there go I." Our task is to reach out to those caught in sin's clutches and say, "The grace of God saves and cleanses from all sin. God has cleansed me, the sinner of sinners; His grace will cleanse you. There is cleansing and forgiveness for everyone."

b. Warned to obey the law and give witness to His Messiahship (v.44b).

Second, Jesus ordered the man to go to the priest and fulfill what the law required of cleansed lepers (Le.14:1-31). Jesus demanded this for three reasons:

- The man needed to obey the law, for he was not above the law. He was to live righteously just as the law demanded. Jesus did not annul or do away with the law. He fulfilled the law; therefore, He is greater than the law. The man was being taught to obey the law and more: he was being taught to obey Jesus *who includes the law and more* (see note—Mt.5:17-18 for discussion). Christ's righteous act was to be his primary witness, his first act of obedience.

THOUGHT 1. Obedience, that is, living righteously, is our primary witness for Christ. There is no real faith apart from obedience and works. This does not mean that we must do good works in order to be saved, but that if our faith is genuine, its fruit will be obedience and good works.

> **And being made perfect, he became the source of eternal salvation to all who obey him. (He.5:9)**

> **So also faith by itself, if it does not have works, is dead. (Js.2:17)**

- The man needed to be acknowledged by everyone as *cleansed*. People would not accept him until they knew he was cleansed. The priest had to *pronounce* him clean.

THOUGHT 2. Every cleansed (saved) person is to go to church, profess his cleansing, and become a part of God's society and family of believers.

> **So those who received his word were baptized, and there were added that day about three thousand souls. And they devoted themselves to the apostles' teaching and the fellowship, to the breaking of bread and the prayers. (Ac.2:41-42)**

> **Not neglecting to meet together, as is the habit of some, but encouraging one another, and all the more as you see the Day drawing near. (He.10:25)**

- The priest needed to testify to the divine power of Jesus. All the people knew that only God could cure leprosy. By declaring the man cleansed, the priest would be declaring Jesus to be the Son of God, the Messiah (see Lev.14:2–20).

THOUGHT 3. Every time a person is truly cleansed from sin, Jesus is proclaimed to be the Son of God, the Savior. A cleansed person becomes a living testimony and witness to the power of Jesus.

> **Therefore, if anyone is in Christ, he is a new creation. The old has passed away; behold, the new has come. All this is from God, who through Christ reconciled us to himself and gave us the ministry of reconciliation. That is, in Christ God was reconciling the world to himself, not counting their trespasses against them, and entrusting to us the message of reconciliation. Therefore, we are ambassadors for Christ, God making his appeal through us. We implore you on behalf of Christ, be reconciled to God. For our sake he made him to be sin who knew no sin, so that in him we might become the righteousness of God. (2 Co.5:17–21)**

> **I am writing to you, fathers, because you know him who is from the beginning. I am writing to you, young men, because you have overcome the evil one. I write to you, children, because you know the Father. I write to you, fathers, because you know him who is from the beginning. I write to you, young men, because you are strong, and the word of God abides in you, and you have overcome the evil one. Do not love the world or the things in the world. If anyone loves the world, the love of the Father is not in him. For all that is in the world—the desires of the flesh and the desires of the eyes and pride of life—is not from the Father but is from the world. (1 Jn.2:13–16)**

1:45

⁴⁵ But he went out and began to talk freely about it, and to spread the news, so that Jesus could no longer openly enter a town, but was out in desolate places, and people were coming to him from every quarter.

4 Jesus made a great impact through the most unclean.

Jesus' healing of the leper impacted the people of the city greatly. But the man's disobedience to Christ's orders resulted in Jesus having to make a change in His ministry.

a. The news spread.

In direct disobedience to the Lord's explicit command, the excited man spread the news of what Christ had done for Him. Again, Jesus had purposes for forbidding the man to speak of His miraculous healing. The man's disobedience defeated those purposes.

b. Jesus could no longer minister in the cities: He had to stay out in the countryside.

The text suggests that one of Jesus' purposes for commanding the man to keep silent about Jesus' healing of him was that Jesus wanted to continue ministering in the cities. The cities were where the most people were, and the synagogues were also in the cities. The man disobeyed Jesus (just as many of us so often do). Because of the man's disobedience, Jesus had to withdraw from the cities and to conduct His ministry in the open desert areas. However, when Jesus could not go to where the people were, the people came to Him. Mark notes that they made their way to Him from every direction.

THOUGHT 1. When we disobey Christ, Christ has to withdraw. His presence is no longer sensed by us or seen by our associates. It is as though He is forced into *a desert place*. It is interesting that nothing more is said about the disobedient leper. Imagine the people who were never helped because Jesus had to move His ministry out into a desert place!

We may not understand some of our Lord's commands, but we nevertheless need to obey them. The consequences of disobedience are too terrible, destroying lives through our lost witness.

> **If you love me, you will keep my commandments. (Jn.14:15)**

> **Wake up from your drunken stupor, as is right, and do not go on sinning. For some have no knowledge of God. I say this to your shame. (1 Co.15:34)**

I therefore, a prisoner for the Lord, urge you to walk in a manner worthy of the calling to which you have been called. (Ep.4:1)

And Samuel said, "Has the Lord as great delight in burnt offerings and sacrifices, as in obeying the voice of the Lord? Behold, to obey is better than sacrifice, and to listen than the fat of rams." (1 Sa.15:22)

CHAPTER 2

G. Jesus' Power to Forgive Sin and Its Impact:
Forgiveness of Sins, 2:1–12

(Mt.9:1-8; Lu.5:17-26)

1. **The setting: Jesus returned to Capernaum many months later**
   a. Jesus had returned home
   b. Crowds heard and flooded the house immediately
   c. Jesus preached the Word

2. **The prerequisites to being forgiven**
   a. Coming to Jesus
   b. Having a sincere and persevering faith in Jesus' power—a faith that will not quit[DS1]

3. **The reality of being forgiven[DS2]**
   a. Jesus saw their faith
   b. Jesus forgave the sick man's sins

4. **The question stirred by being forgiven**
   a. The religionists were silent
   b. The religionists thought to themselves: Who has the power to forgive?[DS3]

5. **The source of being forgiven**
   a. Jesus revealed that He knows people's hearts

   b. Jesus revealed His divine wisdom and fearlessness

   c. Jesus stated His purpose: To prove His Messiahship, that He is the Son of Man
   d. Jesus proved that He had the power to forgive sins

6. **The impact of being forgiven**
   a. The man walked before all—forgiven, healed
   b. The crowds marveled and praised God

And when he returned to Capernaum after some days, it was reported that he was at home.

² And many were gathered together, so that there was no more room, not even at the door. And he was preaching the word to them.

³ And they came, bringing to him a paralytic carried by four men.

⁴ And when they could not get near him because of the crowd, they removed the roof above him, and when they had made an opening, they let down the bed on which the paralytic lay.

⁵ And when Jesus saw their faith, he said to the paralytic, "Son, your sins are forgiven."

⁶ Now some of the scribes were sitting there, questioning in their hearts,

⁷ "Why does this man speak like that? He is blaspheming! Who can forgive sins but God alone?"

⁸ And immediately Jesus, perceiving in his spirit that they thus questioned within themselves, said to them, "Why do you question these things in your hearts?

⁹ Which is easier, to say to the paralytic, 'Your sins are forgiven,' or to say, 'Rise, take up your bed and walk'?

¹⁰ But that you may know that the Son of Man has authority on earth to forgive sins"—he said to the paralytic—

¹¹ "I say to you, rise, pick up your bed, and go home."

¹² And he rose and immediately picked up his bed and went out before them all, so that they were all amazed and glorified God, saying, "We never saw anything like this!"

Division II

The Son of God's Opening Ministry: Jesus' Immediate Impact, 1:21–3:35

G. Jesus' Power to Forgive Sin and Its Impact: Forgiveness of Sin, 2:1–12

(Mt.9:1–8; Lu.5:17–26)

2:1–12
Introduction

The greatest need of every person in the world is to be forgiven of our sins. God stands ready to forgive us, but we must first seek His forgiveness. Those who seek forgiveness of sins—truly seek with a desperation that will not quit—will be forgiven. This is the great lesson learned from this passage. This is, *Jesus' Power to Forgive Sin and Its Impact: Forgiveness of Sin, 2:1–12.*

1. The setting: Jesus returned to Capernaum many months later (vv.1-2).
2. The prerequisites to being forgiven (vv.3-4).
3. The reality of being forgiven (v.5).
4. The question stirred by being forgiven (vv.6-7).
5. The source of being forgiven (vv.8-11).
6. The impact of being forgiven (v.12).

1 The setting: Jesus returned to Capernaum many months later.

After many months of preaching throughout Galilee, Jesus returned to Capernaum (Mk.1:39). The preaching tour had lasted about twelve months.

> And when he returned to Capernaum after some days, it was reported that he was at home. ² And many were gathered together, so that there was no more room, not even at the door. And he was preaching the word to them.

a. Jesus had returned home (v.1).

Apparently, Jesus came back to Peter's house and lodged there. *At home* or *in the house* seems to refer to Peter's house, where the Lord had stayed previously (1:29). As always, the news spread quickly that Jesus was in town.

b. Crowds heard and flooded the house immediately (v.2a).

When the people of Capernaum heard that Jesus was back in town, a crowd quickly gathered at the house. They flooded the house, both inside and outside, to the point that nobody could even get near the door.

c. Jesus preached the Word (v.2b).

As the excited crowd swelled, Jesus focused on His *primary mission*: He preached the Word to them. No doubt many had come to have some need met or to be healed, and some had come merely out of curiosity. However, Jesus concentrated on the main work of God: He proclaimed the Word of God to people who were spiritually lost and facing an eternity separated from God.

2 The prerequisites to being forgiven.

Amidst the pushing and shoving of the eager throng, one sick man managed to get to Jesus. This man's actions demonstrate the prerequisites to being forgiven.

> ³ And they came, bringing to him a paralytic carried by four men. ⁴ And when they could not get near him because of the crowd, they removed the roof above him, and when they had made an opening, they let down the bed on which the paralytic lay.

a. Coming to Jesus (v.3).

The man came to Jesus. Actually, this man was brought to Jesus by four other men carrying him on a cot-like pallet.

The man was desperate for help and very hopeful, having heard about Jesus, but he was paralyzed; he could not get to Jesus on his own. Therefore, four of his friends carried him. Obviously, the paralyzed man was very dear to the four stretcher-bearers. This is indicated by the extreme action they took to reach Jesus.

The point is clear: the first prerequisite to forgiveness is coming to Jesus. A person must come to Jesus for forgiveness, even if he or she has to be brought. Compare the invitations of God to "come":

> Come to me, all who labor and are heavy laden, and I will give you rest. (Mt.11:28)

> The Spirit and the Bride say, "Come." And let the one who hears say, "Come." And let the one who is thirsty come; let the one who desires take the water of life without price. (Re.22:17)

> Come now, let us reason together, says the Lord: though your sins are like scarlet, they shall be as white as snow; though they are red like crimson, they shall become like wool. (Is.1:18)

> Come, everyone who thirsts, come to the waters; and he who has no money, come, buy and eat! Come, buy wine and milk without money and without price. (Is.55:1)

(See also Mt.22:4; Lu.14:17; Ge.7:1.)

b. **Having a sincere and persevering faith in Jesus' power—a faith that will not quit (v.4).**

The paralyzed man and his friends possessed a sincere, desperate faith in Jesus' power. Truly, their faith was a faith that would not quit. (See Deeper Study # 1; notes—Mt.9:23-27; 11:22-23 for discussion. Also see Js.2:26 where faith without works [action] is said to be dead, not really existing.) When the four men could not get to Jesus through the door, they found a way to get their needy friend to the Lord. They knew that Jesus could—and would—help him. They possessed solid and unwavering faith in Jesus, demonstrating the second prerequisite to being forgiven.

> And Jesus said to him, "'If you can'! All things are possible for one who believes." (Mk.9:23)

DEEPER STUDY # 1

(2:4) **Houses—Persevering Faith:** many houses of Jesus' day had an outside stairway that climbed up to a second floor. The roof was easily reached from this stairway. The roof was flat and made of tile-like rocks matted together with a straw and clay-like substance. The roofs were sturdy enough for people to sit on and carry on evening conversations and other activities (see Deeper Study # 2—Mt.24:17). These men dug and scooped out an opening through the roof. They were so sure of Jesus' power to help, and nothing was going to prevent them from getting to Jesus—a display of unwavering faith.

2:5

[5] And when Jesus saw their faith, he said to the paralytic, "Son, your sins are forgiven."

3 The reality of being forgiven.

When the afflicted man at last made it to Jesus, our gracious Lord met his greatest need, his most critical need. Jesus forgave his sins—saved his soul. For the first time in his life, this man knew the joyous reality of being forgiven.

a. **Jesus saw their faith.**

Jesus saw the faith of the man himself as well as the faith of the four men who brought him. The faith of the friends played a large part in the man's being healed and in his receiving forgiveness of sins (see notes—Mt.9:2; Mk.11:23).

> But a Samaritan, as he journeyed, came to where he was, and when he saw him, he had compassion. He went to him and bound up his wounds, pouring on oil and wine. Then he set him on his own animal and brought him to an inn and took care of him. (Lu.10:33–34)

> We who are strong have an obligation to bear with the failings of the weak, and not to please ourselves. (Ro.15:1)

Bear one another's burdens, and so fulfill the law of Christ . . . And let us not grow weary of doing good, for in due season we will reap, if we do not give up. (Ga.6:2, 9)

I was eyes to the blind and feet to the lame. I was a father to the needy, and I searched out the cause of him whom I did not know. (Jb.29:15–16)

She opens her hand to the poor and reaches out her hands to the needy. (Pr.31:20)

b. Jesus forgave the sick man's sins.

The very first thing Jesus did for the man was to forgive His sins. This brings us to a critical truth: forgiveness of sins is far more important than healing or anything else we may need from the Lord (Mk.2:10). A sound body assures life for only a few years at most; a sound soul assures life forever (see DEEPER STUDY # 2).

By first forgiving the paralyzed man's sins, Jesus taught that the most important thing we can do is seek forgiveness of our sins. Every person should always seek to be forgiven before anything else. Jesus wants us to live eternally, not just for a few short years here on earth. But before we can live eternally, we must willingly come to Jesus for forgiveness.

Jesus proclaimed forgiveness in tenderness and compassion. When we come to Jesus for forgiveness, Jesus does not . . .

- *accuse* us of past sins.
- *find fault* with us: what we have done—why we have come—from where we have come
- *begrudge* or *hesitate* in forgiving us

When we come to Jesus, He responds tenderly and compassionately. This is seen in the word "son." Son (Gk. teknon) means child. Looking at the paralyzed man lying at His feet, Jesus saw a child, and Jesus responded to the helpless man just as any of us would respond to a child lying helpless at our feet—tenderly and compassionately.

Jesus proclaimed forgiveness in His own authority. It is critical to see this. He did not say, "God, forgive this man," or "God, I wish You would forgive this man." Jesus said, "Child, your sins are forgiven." He forgave the man's sins Himself, in His own name, by His own power and authority.

The point is unmistakable. Jesus was claiming to be God, the very Son of God, and the people understood exactly what He was doing (vv.6–7).

THOUGHT 1. Jesus proclaims forgiveness, tenderly and compassionately, and He possesses the power to forgive sins because He is truly the Son of God. People are fools if they do not come to Jesus for forgiveness of sins.

God exalted him at his right hand as Leader and Savior, to give repentance to Israel and forgiveness of sins. (Ac.5:31)

Let it be known to you therefore, brothers, that through this man forgiveness of sins is proclaimed to you. (Ac.13:38)

In him we have redemption through his blood, the forgiveness of our trespasses, according to the riches of his grace. (Ep.1:7)

DEEPER STUDY # 2

(2:5) **Forgiveness**: see DEEPER STUDY # 4—Mt.26:28.

4 The question stirred by being forgiven.

Among those who had crowded the house were some religionists—strict adherents to a religion; in this case, Jewish religious leaders. When Jesus forgave the paralyzed man's sins, they were alarmed. Jesus' bold action stirred a skeptical, but reasonable, question in their hearts.

6 Now some of the scribes were sitting there, questioning in their hearts,
7 "Why does this man speak like that? He is blaspheming! Who can forgive sins but God alone?"

a. The religionists were silent (v.6).

Apparently, the ruling body in Jerusalem, the Sanhedrin, had heard about a prophet in Galilee who was carrying on an unusual ministry. Unbelievable miracles were being reported. The prophet, who called Himself Jesus of Nazareth, needed to be checked out to make sure He was not teaching error and misleading the people; not threatening insurrection against the Jewish religion and nation which was under Roman domination (see note—Mt.12:1-8; note and Deeper Study # 1—12:10; note—15:1-20; Deeper Study # 2—15:6-9). The Sanhedrin sent a delegation to Capernaum to investigate Jesus. The Scribes mentioned in these verses are that delegation.

Mark mentions a critical detail that must be noted: these men observed what was taking place *silently*. They did not say a word; they did not question Jesus aloud, only *in their hearts*.

b. The religionists thought to themselves: Who has the power to forgive? (v.7).

When the Scribes heard Jesus forgive the man's sins, they immediately saw the point Jesus was making. By doing what only God can do, He was declaring that He is God. They began to reason in their minds and hearts: "Why does this man blaspheme (see Deeper Study # 3)? Who can forgive sins but God only? Is He claiming to be God? The promised Messiah?" (see notes—Mk.3:1-2; outline and Deeper Study # 2—Mk.3:22).

THOUGHT 1. The Scribes' question was logical and reasonable.

1) Most people and religions in the world ask the very same question: "Who can forgive sins but God only?" They view Jesus only as a prophet or some great man. In their minds, He could never possess the right or power to forgive sins.

2) Some in the world simply ask, "Who can forgive sins?" And they rejoice when they find out that Jesus is the Son of God and that He does forgive sins.

> For God so loved the world, that he gave his only Son, that whoever believes in him should not perish but have eternal life. (Jn.3:16)

> Jesus heard that they had cast him out, and having found him he said, "Do you believe in the Son of Man?" He answered, "And who is he, sir, that I may believe in him?" Jesus said to him, "You have seen him, and it is he who is speaking to you." (Jn.9:35-37)

> Jesus said to her, "I am the resurrection and the life. Whoever believes in me, though he die, yet shall he live, and everyone who lives and believes in me shall never die. Do you believe this?" She said to him, "Yes, Lord; I believe that you are the Christ, the Son of God, who is coming into the world." (Jn.11:25-27)

THOUGHT 2. If Jesus were not the Son of God, then the Scribes were correct. Jesus was speaking blasphemy. However, since He is the Son of God, He truly forgave the man's sins. The conclusion is glorious: He can forgive our sins, too.

> And Peter said to them, "Repent and be baptized every one of you in the name of Jesus Christ for the forgiveness of your sins, and you will receive the gift of the Holy Spirit." (Ac.2:38)

> 'To open their eyes, so that they may turn from darkness to light and from the power of Satan to God, that they may receive forgiveness of sins and a place among those who are sanctified by faith in me.' (Ac.26:18)

> In whom we have redemption, the forgiveness of sins. (Col.1:14)

> If we confess our sins, he is faithful and just to forgive us our sins and to cleanse us from all unrighteousness. (1 Jn.1:9)

DEEPER STUDY # 3

(2:7) **Blasphemy:** see Deeper Study # 4—Mt.9:3.

5 The source of being forgiven.

Remarkably, Jesus addressed the Scribes' unspoken questions. By doing so, He demonstrated His omniscience, giving evidence that He was the Messiah—the Son of God and God the Son. In addition, Jesus revealed His power to forgive sins.

a. Jesus revealed that He knows people's hearts (v.8).

Jesus revealed that He knows the human heart: exactly what people think, our motives and reasonings (see note, pt.1—Mt.9:4-7 for discussion). Only God is omniscient—all-knowing; omniscience is one of God's exclusive attributes. By revealing what the Scribes were thinking, Jesus demonstrated His deity.

b. Jesus revealed His divine wisdom and fearlessness (v.9).

By confronting the Scribes' doubts, Jesus revealed His divine wisdom and fearlessness. He was not afraid of being challenged. He validated their skepticism, acknowledging that anybody could pronounce that sins were forgiven. Unlike healing or other physical miracles, forgiving sins produces no visible evidence. Jesus boldly suggested that He be tested with the impossible: healing the man of his paralysis (see note, pt.2—Mt.9:4-7 for discussion).

c. Jesus stated His purpose: To prove His Messiahship, that He is the Son of Man (v.10).

All of Jesus' miracles were for the purpose of proving that He was who He claimed to be. He clearly stated this was His purpose for the miracle He was about to perform—the healing of the paralyzed man. He wanted the Scribes and everyone else to know that He was the Messiah, the Son of God who became the Son of Man, the Savior, the only One who has the authority to forgive sins (see note, pt.3—Mt.9:4-7; DEEPER STUDY # 3—Mt.8:20 for discussion).

d. Jesus proved that He had the power to forgive sins (v.11).

Jesus proved His power to forgive sins. He must be able to forgive sins, for He healed the man and caused the man to arise and walk. His power is indisputable.

Note the proof of His power to forgive sins.

- Jesus *willed* the man to walk. He simply *spoke the Word*, and the man arose and walked. The power was in Jesus' *will and Word*. His will is His Word, and His Word is His will.
- It follows, then, that if Jesus *wills* to forgive sins, all He has to do is *speak the Word*, "Yours sins are forgiven," and the sins are forgiven (see Lu.24:47; Ac.5:31; 13:38; Ep.1:7; 1 Jn.1:9; 1 Jn.2:1-2).

> He himself bore our sins in his body on the tree, that we might die to sin and live to righteousness. By his wounds you have been healed. (1 Pe.2:24)

> Who forgives all your iniquity, who heals all your diseases. (Ps.103:3)

> But he was pierced for our transgressions; he was crushed for our iniquities; upon him was the chastisement that brought us peace, and with his wounds we are healed. (Is.53:5)

> Let the wicked forsake his way, and the unrighteous man his thoughts; let him return to the LORD, that he may have compassion on him, and to our God, for he will abundantly pardon. (Is.55:7)

8 And immediately Jesus, perceiving in his spirit that they thus questioned within themselves, said to them, "Why do you question these things in your hearts?
9 Which is easier, to say to the paralytic, 'Your sins are forgiven,' or to say, 'Rise, take up your bed and walk'?
10 But that you may know that the Son of Man has authority on earth to forgive sins"—he said to the paralytic—
11 "I say to you, rise, pick up your bed, and go home."

6 The impact of being forgiven.

Naturally, the miracle made a tremendous impact on all who witnessed it. But Jesus performed the miracle to impact the people with a greater truth: the man's sins had been forgiven, and their sins could be forgiven as well—if they believed in Him and came to Him for forgiveness, just as the man had.

12 And he rose and immediately picked up his bed and went out before them all, so that they were all amazed and glorified God, saying, "We never saw anything like this!"

a. **The man walked before all—forgiven, healed.**

Four men had carried their paralyzed friend to Jesus, but the man picked up his bed and walked away of his own power! This was a living testimony to the power of Jesus to forgive and heal a person's *whole being*.

b. **The crowds marveled and praised God.**

The people were amazed by what they had witnessed. They confessed that they had never seen anything like it. As a result, they praised God, giving Him the glory for what had taken place. But their response provokes a critical question: did they glorify God for the miracle they had *seen*, or for the miracle they *could not* see, the greater miracle; indeed, the greatest of all miracles—the forgiveness of sins.

THOUGHT 1. Jesus freely forgives the sin of any person, no matter how terrible the sin. When people's sins are forgiven, it should dramatically affect both them and those who know them. However, the great tragedy is that few pay attention to the claim that sins are forgiven. They ignore the fact and go on their merry way, continuing to walk in the selfishness of this world (see 1 Jn.2:15–16).

> And what you have heard from me in the presence of many witnesses entrust to faithful men, who will be able to teach others also. (2 Ti.2:2)

> But in your hearts honor Christ the Lord as holy, always being prepared to make a defense to anyone who asks you for a reason for the hope that is in you; yet do it with gentleness and respect. (1 Pe.3:15)

H. Jesus' Impact upon Matthew and His Friends: Reaching the Outcast and Sinner, 2:13–17

(Mt.9:9–13; Lu.5:27–32)

¹³ He went out again beside the sea, and all the crowd was coming to him, and he was teaching them.

¹⁴ And as he passed by, he saw Levi the son of Alphaeus sitting at the tax booth, and he said to him, "Follow me." And he rose and followed him.

¹⁵ And as he reclined at table in his house, many tax collectors and sinners were reclining with Jesus and his disciples, for there were many who followed him.

¹⁶ And the scribes of the Pharisees, when they saw that he was eating with sinners and tax collectors, said to his disciples, "Why does he eat with tax collectors and sinners?"

¹⁷ And when Jesus heard it, he said to them, "Those who are well have no need of a physician, but those who are sick. I came not to call the righteous, but sinners."

1. **Jesus went out to the lake**
   a. The crowds gathered
   b. Jesus taught them
2. **Jesus called the outcast and sinner**[DS1]
   a. He saw Levi, a tax collector
   b. He called Levi to abandon all
   c. The impact: Levi accepted the call; he left all
3. **Jesus associated with the outcast and sinner**
   a. Levi invited his associates and friends to a meal
   b. Jesus associated with them
   c. The impact: Many followed Him
4. **Jesus answered society's attitude toward the outcast and sinner**
   a. The religious leaders questioned Jesus' associations

   b. Jesus' reply: His very purpose was to call sinners to repentance

Division II

The Son of God's Opening Ministry: Jesus' Immediate Impact, 1:21–3:35

H. Jesus' Impact upon Matthew and His Friends: Reaching the Outcast and Sinner, 2:13–17

(Mt.9:9–13; Lu.5:27–32)

2:13–17
Introduction

Jesus loves and died for all people. He came to seek and to save the lost—all the lost. No matter how lost, how outcast, or how sinful a person is, Jesus came to save that person. Throughout the Lord's earthly ministry, He reached out to the lowest and most hated of society, setting an example for us to follow. In fact, Jesus expressly said that when we minister to such people, we are ministering to Him (Mt.25:35-40). This is, *Jesus' Impact upon Matthew and His Friends: Reaching the Outcast and Sinner, 2:13-17.*

1. Jesus went out to the lake (v.13).
2. Jesus called the outcast and sinner (v.14).
3. Jesus associated with the outcast and sinner (v.15).
4. Jesus answered society's attitude toward the outcast and sinner (vv.16-17).

1 Jesus went out to the lake.

2:13

Jesus went out by the shore of the Sea of Galilee. The mass of people now flocking to Him were so many that no building nor street was large enough to hold them. The religious leaders were also closing the synagogues to Him (see 2:6–7). However, Jesus was faithful in preaching and teaching despite the closed doors. His mission and call was to preach, and that is exactly what He did. He would not be stopped or silenced no matter what the challenges were.

¹³ He went out again beside the sea, and all the crowd was coming to him, and he was teaching them.

a. The crowds gathered.

The crowds gathered to hear Jesus preach. The text speaks of a huge crowd that followed and assembled around Him at the seashore.

THOUGHT 1. People should flock to the servant of God who truly teaches the Kingdom of God. Why? There is one simple reason: since Christ came, all things are now ready for the Kingdom of God. We should be eager and excited to hear the preaching and teaching of God's Word about His kingdom.

> And at the time for the banquet he sent his servant to say to those who had been invited, 'Come, for everything is now ready.' (Lu.14:17; see outline and notes—Lu.14:18–20 for a descriptive picture of the excuses given for not coming to Christ.)

b. Jesus taught them.

When people came to hear about the kingdom of God, Jesus taught them. He was the faithful servant of God, the obedient servant who seized every opportunity to teach (see outline and notes—Mk.1:14–15 for more discussion).

THOUGHT 1. God's servant should take advantage of every opportunity to teach and share Christ and His kingdom. Not a single opportunity should be missed. Faithfulness and obedience to one's call are the needs of the hour.

> We must work the works of him who sent me while it is day; night is coming, when no one can work. (Jn.9:4)

> Therefore, my beloved brothers, be steadfast, immovable, always abounding in the work of the Lord, knowing that in the Lord your labor is not in vain. (1 Co.15:58)

2:14

2 Jesus called the outcast and sinner.

At some point Jesus finished teaching the multitude and began walking along the seashore. He passed by the booth that had been set up to collect the taxes owed by incoming ships. Jesus called the tax collector, a despised outcast and wicked sinner in the people's eyes, to follow Him.

¹⁴ And as he passed by, he saw Levi the son of Alphaeus sitting at the tax booth, and he said to him, "Follow me." And he rose and followed him.

a. He saw Levi, a tax collector.

Jesus saw Levi, the tax collector in charge of the tax station or office. Levi is better known by the name, Matthew (see Deeper Study # 1). All tax collectors were ostracized and bitterly hated. In the minds of Jewish society, they were traitors, outcasts, and sinners, for they were looked upon as having sold their souls to the Roman authorities. The vast majority were thieves, cheats, and extortioners—always adding to the tax bill in order to fill their own pockets. Most tax collectors were wealthy, and the fact that Matthew had a house large enough to accommodate a large party points toward his being rich (see note—Mt.9:9).

b. He called Levi to abandon all.

Jesus called Levi to abandon his profession and to follow Him. The love of money and the lust for wealth was what made most Jewish tax collectors enter the tax-collecting service of the

Romans. This tells us that Matthew, as a young man, was consumed with greed and a craving for the so-called *good things* of life. He was so possessed by greed that he was willing to betray his country and people. His love of money and possessions made him willing to endure a lifetime of hatred by his own people.

However, in this passage, something else becomes evident about Matthew: the price he had paid for wealth was not worth it. His heart was cut by the piercing eyes, stinging words, isolation, and bitter hatred of the people. He ached for forgiveness and reconciliation, both with God and with his people. Jesus saw the hurt and the ache of Levi's wounded heart and appealed to him to abandon his sin of greed and to follow God.

THOUGHT 1. Jesus was always looking for the opportunity to reach individuals. He had just finished teaching the multitude, and He was probably tired. But as He was walking away from His meeting, He saw a soul needing His attention, so He stopped to witness to the man.

> Come to me, all who labor and are heavy laden, and I will give you rest. Take my yoke upon you, and learn from me, for I am gentle and lowly in heart, and you will find rest for your souls. For my yoke is easy, and my burden is light. (Mt.11:28-30)

> Come now, let us reason together, says the LORD: though your sins are like scarlet, they shall be as white as snow; though they are red like crimson, they shall become like wool. (Is.1:18)

> Come, everyone who thirsts, come to the waters; and he who has no money, come, buy and eat! Come, buy wine and milk without money and without price. (Is.55:1)

c. **The impact: Levi accepted the call; he left all.**

Jesus' call made an explosive impact on Matthew. He made an immediate, radical change in his life, leaving everything behind to accept Jesus' call to follow Him. Note two apparent facts:

- Matthew already knew of Jesus. Jesus had been teaching throughout Galilee for over a year. Like everyone else, Matthew had certainly heard of Jesus and had probably visited some of the Lord's meetings.
- Matthew gave up everything. In fact, the two major points to see in Matthew's call are: first, Jesus called a person who was a great *outcast* and a *sinner*; and, second, Matthew gave up everything to follow Jesus. Answering the Lord's call cost Matthew everything—his job and his enormous income. Most of the other disciples could return to their professions if things did not work out. But this was not so with Matthew. When he committed his life to Jesus, he literally committed everything. The call of Jesus disrupted his whole life (see note, *Self-Denial*—Lu.9:23 for development of this application).

> For whoever would save his life will lose it, but whoever loses his life for my sake and the gospel's will save it. For what does it profit a man to gain the whole world and forfeit his soul? (Mk.8:35-36)

> And he said to all, "If anyone would come after me, let him deny himself and take up his cross daily and follow me." (Lu.9:23)

> If anyone comes to me and does not hate his own father and mother and wife and children and brothers and sisters, yes, and even his own life, he cannot be my disciple. . . . So therefore, any one of you who does not renounce all that he has cannot be my disciple. (Lu.14:26, 33)

DEEPER STUDY # 1

(2:14) **Levi—Matthew:** this Levi is Matthew who wrote the first Gospel of the New Testament (see note—Mt.9:9). Apparently his given name was Levi, but Jesus changed his name to Matthew. It is significant that both Mark and Luke refer to him as Levi (Mk.2:14; Lu.5:27), but Matthew identified himself by the name Jesus gave him (Mt.9:9). The name Matthew or Matthias means the *gift of Jehovah*. When referring to himself, Matthew always stressed God's great mercy upon him. He wanted people to know that it was the glorious mercy of Jesus that had saved him, the outcast and sinner.

> But God, being rich in mercy, because of the great love with which he loved us, even when we were dead in our trespasses, made us alive together with Christ—by grace you have been saved. (Ep.2:4-5)

3 Jesus associated with the outcast and sinner.

After Matthew's decision to leave his corrupt business behind to follow Jesus, the Lord openly associated with this outcast and sinner. But Jesus not only befriended this man who was so bitterly despised by society, He chose to associate with Matthew's friends, people who were outcasts, just like him.

2:15

¹⁵ And as he reclined at table in his house, many tax collectors and sinners were reclining with Jesus and his disciples, for there were many who followed him.

a. Levi invited his associates and friends to a meal.

Immediately after his conversion, Levi or Matthew invited his associates and friends to a large feast (Lu.5:29). His friends were not the respectable people of society, but instead were greedy tax collectors (publicans) and sinners like him. They were foul-mouthed, angry, and rebellious. Together, they rejected both the restraints of society and God and represented the contemptible outcasts and non-religious of society.

But Matthew had discovered something wonderful: a glorious peace and joy of heart and mind. He had found it in Jesus. In fact, *in Jesus*, he had found what was actually a new life, and he desperately wanted his friends to discover the same peace and joy. So he planned a feast, and he invited all his friends to meet Jesus (see note—Mt.9:10–11).

THOUGHT 1. Matthew did not forget his sinful friends after his conversion. He wanted them to have the wonderful, life-changing experience with Jesus that he had come to know. So, he witnessed to them by arranging an encounter with Jesus, using the best method he knew. What a lesson for us!

THOUGHT 2. The command of Jesus is for us to go to our families and neighbors and friends first; to go to our own *Jerusalem* (Ac.1:8; see outline and DEEPER STUDY # 1—Mt.10:6; Lu.15:8–10; see also De.6:6–7; 1 Pe.3:15).

> But you will receive power when the Holy Spirit has come upon you, and you will be my witnesses in Jerusalem and in all Judea and Samaria, and to the end of the earth. (Ac.1:8)

> And what you have heard from me in the presence of many witnesses entrust to faithful men, who will be able to teach others also (2 Ti.2:2)

b. Jesus associated with them.

Jesus embraced the opportunity to meet with these outcasts and sinners. However, Jesus did *not* meet with the outcasts and sinners to condone their sin, but to turn them from their sin. They needed to experience the same change of life that Matthew had experienced.

Throughout Jesus' ministry, He reached out to outcasts and sinners. These reviled people had deep needs, and they were willing to confess them. They were responsive to having their needs met. The Gospels record the receptiveness of society's most loathed to Jesus' message:

• The despised tax collector and harlot.

> "Which of the two did the will of his father?" They said, "The first." Jesus said to them, "Truly, I say to you, the tax collectors and the prostitutes go into the kingdom of God before you." (Mt.21:31)

• The immoral person.

> Therefore I tell you, her sins, which are many, are forgiven—for she loved much. But he who is forgiven little, loves little. (Lu.7:47)

> She said, "No one, Lord." And Jesus said, "Neither do I condemn you; go, and from now on sin no more." (Jn.8:11)

• The sinner.

> And the Pharisees and the scribes grumbled, saying, "This man receives sinners and eats with them." (Lu.15:2)

• The thief.

> And he said to him, "Truly, I say to you, today you will be with me in paradise." (Lu.23:43)

- The rejected.

> Jesus heard that they had cast him out, and having found him he said, "Do you believe in the Son of Man?" (Jn.9:35)

THOUGHT 1. Christ cannot help people who are unwilling to confess their need. The self-righteous, self-sufficient, and self-dependent feel that they do not need help. Such feelings and beliefs, of course, are foolish; for disease, accident, and death confront everyone. When they do, all who refused to confess their need will stand alone at the threshold of eternity, facing vast darkness and eternal condemnation.

> So everyone who acknowledges me before men, I also will acknowledge before my Father who is in heaven, but whoever denies me before men, I also will deny before my Father who is in heaven. (Mt.10:32–33)

> Who is the liar but he who denies that Jesus is the Christ? This is the antichrist, he who denies the Father and the Son. No one who denies the Son has the Father. Whoever confesses the Son has the Father also. (1 Jn.2:22–23)

> Whoever confesses that Jesus is the Son of God, God abides in him, and he in God (1 Jn.4:15)

c. **The impact: Many followed Him.**

Jesus' impact on the outcasts and sinners was remarkable. Many of society's most-hated accepted Matthew's dinner invitation, and, upon feeling Jesus' love for them, followed Him.

THOUGHT 1. The outcast and sinner of Jesus' day ...

- saw His interest and acceptance, His care and compassion for any and all in need
- saw that any person with a need was not only welcomed by Jesus, but desired
- saw that Jesus did not act above or better, aloof or separate from sinners
- saw that, although Jesus never compromised His message of repentance, He loved and truly forgave and offered the greatest of challenges

> So that you may be sons of your Father who is in heaven. For he makes his sun rise on the evil and on the good, and sends rain on the just and on the unjust. (Mt.5:45)

> And they sent their disciples to him, along with the Herodians, saying, "Teacher, we know that you are true and teach the way of God truthfully, and you do not care about anyone's opinion, for you are not swayed by appearances." (Mt.22:16)

> For God shows no partiality. (Ro.2:11)

THOUGHT 2. Consider how uncomfortable the outcast and sinner (even the poorly dressed and unclean) often feel in church and among believers today. Tragically, this is true in part because of how uncomfortable the church feels when the outcast and sinner, the poorly dressed and unclean slip into services. Think of the enormous hesitation the poor have to overcome just to come into church! They slip in because they sense a need, yet they often end up sitting to the side by themselves.

> My brothers, show no partiality as you hold the faith in our Lord Jesus Christ, the Lord of glory. For if a man wearing a gold ring and fine clothing comes into your assembly, and a poor man in shabby clothing also comes in, and if you pay attention to the one who wears the fine clothing and say, "You sit here in a good place," while you say to the poor man, "You stand over there," or, "Sit down at my feet," have you not then made distinctions among yourselves and become judges with evil thoughts? (Jas.2:1–4)

> But the wisdom from above is first pure, then peaceable, gentle, open to reason, full of mercy and good fruits, impartial and sincere. (Jas.3:17)

4 Jesus answered society's attitude toward the outcast and sinner.

The Jewish religious leaders revealed their sinful attitude toward the tax collectors and sinners. Tragically, society's attitude has too often been the same as the Scribes' and Pharisees'

2:16–17

attitude—that of contempt and fear. Jesus answered their—and all judgmental people's—attitude toward society's outcasts and sinners.

¹⁶ And the scribes of the Pharisees, when they saw that he was eating with sinners and tax collectors, said to his disciples, "Why does he eat with tax collectors and sinners?"

¹⁷ And when Jesus heard it, he said to them, "Those who are well have no need of a physician, but those who are sick. I came not to call the righteous, but sinners."

a. The religious leaders questioned Jesus' associations (v.16).

The religious leaders voiced their objection to Jesus' associating with sinners. The religious and respectable of society hold open sinners in contempt because they live below their standards and discipline. Such elitists feel they are superior in beliefs and self-control. The blatantly sinful are thought to be either unprincipled or not disciplined enough to live by the rules.

The religious and respectable of society fear open sinners for two reasons. First, they fear being criticized and judged for associating with people of such low morals and behavior. They fear friends and neighbors' withdrawing from them because they associate with such people.

Second, they fear being contaminated and led astray themselves. They fear becoming dirty and defiled, dulled and weakened, in their own beliefs and principles.

THOUGHT 1. Some people are more principled and more disciplined than others. They had greater opportunity and more training as children because of parents, education, environment, and resources. This must always be remembered when dealing with others. So many traits and abilities, strengths and weaknesses, differ because of heritage and childhood opportunities.

THOUGHT 2. There is enormous hope for every individual, no matter how weak, unprincipled, or undisciplined. That hope is Jesus Christ. All can be *born again*—truly *born again*. Anybody can be *re-created* in Christ Jesus, made into a *new person*, a *new creation*.

> Therefore, if anyone is in Christ, he is a new creation. The old has passed away; behold, the new has come. (2 Co.5:17)

> And to be renewed in the spirit of your minds, and to put on the new self, created after the likeness of God in true righteousness and holiness. (Ep.4:23–24)

> And have put on the new self, which is being renewed in knowledge after the image of its creator. (Col.3:10)

> Who through him are believers in God, who raised him from the dead and gave him glory, so that your faith and hope are in God. (1 Pe.1:21)

b. Jesus' reply: His very purpose was to call sinners to repentance (v.17).

Jesus' reply to the religious leaders' objection was forceful. He stated clearly that He did not come to call the righteous, but sinners. Using an illustration of sick and well people, Jesus made two points.

The first point concerned the sick (sinner). The sick are the ones who need the physician (Him, the Savior). And note: the sick know they are sick and they ask for the physician.

The second point concerned Jesus Himself, His purpose as Messiah. He did not come to call the righteous (self-righteous), but sinners to repentance. Note three critical truths:

• The righteous (self-righteous) do not recognize their need of repentance.

> For, being ignorant of the righteousness of God, and seeking to establish their own, they did not submit to God's righteousness. (Ro.10:3)

> Not that we dare to classify or compare ourselves with some of those who are commending themselves. But when they measure themselves by one another and compare themselves with one another, they are without understanding. (2 Co.10:12)

> Many a man proclaims his own steadfast love, but a faithful man who can find? (Pr.20:6)

> There are those who are clean in their own eyes but are not washed of their filth. (Pr.30:12)

- The righteous (self-righteous) do not hear the call of Christ to repent. Sinners do hear the call.

> So Peter opened his mouth and said: "Truly I understand that God shows no partiality, but in every nation anyone who fears him and does what is right is acceptable to him." (Ac.10:34–35)

> For there is no distinction between Jew and Greek; for the same Lord is Lord of all, bestowing his riches on all who call on him. For "everyone who calls on the name of the Lord will be saved." (Ro.10:12–13)

> Behold, I stand at the door and knock. If anyone hears my voice and opens the door, I will come in to him and eat with him, and he with me. (Re.3:20)

> Who says to a king, 'Worthless one,' and to nobles, 'Wicked man,' who shows no partiality to princes, nor regards the rich more than the poor, for they are all the work of his hands? (Jb.34:18–19)

- Christ declared that He is the Great Physician. He is the One who calls people to repent. He is the Messiah, the Son of God Himself.

> And Peter said to them, "Repent and be baptized every one of you in the name of Jesus Christ for the forgiveness of your sins, and you will receive the gift of the Holy Spirit." (Ac.2:38)

> Repent therefore, and turn back, that your sins may be blotted out. (Ac.3:19)

> For there is no distinction between Jew and Greek; for the same Lord is Lord of all, bestowing his riches on all who call on him. For "everyone who calls on the name of the Lord will be saved." (Ro.10:12–13)

> Who desires all people to be saved and to come to the knowledge of the truth. For there is one God, and there is one mediator between God and men, the man Christ Jesus, who gave himself as a ransom for all, which is the testimony given at the proper time. (1 Ti.2:4–6)

I. Jesus' Impact upon Young Disciples and Theologians:
The Kind of Life Christ Brings, 2:18–22

(Mt.9:14–17; Lu.5:33–39)

1. **Christ provoked questions about fasting**[DS1]
   a. An unusual alliance: John's disciples and the Pharisees
   b. A justified question
2. **Christ brings a joyous life**[DS2,3]
   a. He is the bridegroom who stirs joy in His followers
   b. He stirs joy, not fasting, over a sad event
3. **Christ brings a seeking life**
   a. He will be taken away
   b. His followers will then fast
4. **Christ brings a new life**
   a. He is not attaching a new life to the old life of a person
   b. He is creating a totally new life, 2 Co.5:17
5. **Christ brings an adventurous life**
   a. He is not filling the old life with the new
   b. He is creating a totally new life, Jn.3:3; Ep.4:22–24

[18] Now John's disciples and the Pharisees were fasting. And people came and said to him, "Why do John's disciples and the disciples of the Pharisees fast, but your disciples do not fast?" [19] And Jesus said to them, "Can the wedding guests fast while the bridegroom is with them? As long as they have the bridegroom with them, they cannot fast." [20] "The days will come when the bridegroom is taken away from them, and then they will fast in that day." [21] "No one sews a piece of unshrunk cloth on an old garment. If he does, the patch tears away from it, the new from the old, and a worse tear is made."

[22] "And no one puts new wine into old wineskins. If he does, the wine will burst the skins—and the wine is destroyed, and so are the skins. But new wine is for fresh wineskins."

Division II

The Son of God's Opening Ministry: Jesus' Immediate Impact; 1:21–3:35

I. Jesus' Impact upon Young Disciples and Theologians: The Kind of Life Christ Brings, 2:18–22

(Mt.9:14–17; Lu.5:33–39)

2:18–22
Introduction

Jesus Christ knows the desperate need and cry among the people of the world for a changed life. He, and He alone, has the power to completely change lives, to make us new people, to give a new life. That new life is a radically different life, as explained by Jesus in this revealing passage. This is, *Jesus' Impact upon Young Disciples and Theologians: The Kind of Life Christ Brings, 2:18–22.*

1. Christ provoked questions about fasting (v.18).
2. Christ brings a joyous life (v.19).
3. Christ brings a seeking life (v.20).
4. Christ brings a new life (v.21).
5. Christ brings an adventurous life (v.22).

1 Christ provoked questions about fasting.

A discussion arose because John's disciples and the Pharisees were fasting, but Jesus' disciples were not (see DEEPER STUDY # 1). *Were fasting* (Gk. esan nesteuontes) means that the disciples of John and of the Pharisees were actually fasting when they asked Jesus this question. This provoked a sincere, justified question about fasting.

a. An unusual alliance: John's disciples and the Pharisees.

Certainly, it seems strange that John's disciples and the Pharisees seem to be in an alliance. What probably happened was this: religious Jews fasted twice every

18 Now John's disciples and the Pharisees were fasting. And people came and said to him, "Why do John's disciples and the disciples of the Pharisees fast, but your disciples do not fast?"

week—on Mondays and Thursdays (Lu.18:12). John was strict in his observance of the law, so he had taught his disciples to observe these two fasts. But now, John's disciples had a greater reason for fasting and for seeking God's presence. John, their teacher, was in prison and facing a death sentence. Therefore, they were fasting with increased fervency, beseeching God to deliver their revered prophet.

b. A justified question.

John's disciples were probably asking other Jewish believers to join them in their intercession and fast. Therefore, they could not understand Jesus' behavior. He was claiming unmistakably to be the Messiah to whom John had pointed. The one person who should be concerned over John's fate and over religious observances should be Jesus, the Messiah. Why did He not teach faithfulness to the religious ritual of fasting? And why was He not now having His followers fast and pray for John's release? They just did not understand.

- How could the *true* Messiah fail to teach faithfulness to religion?
- How could the *true* Messiah not fast and intercede for God's prophet, in particular when the prophet had meant so much to the Messiah's own ministry?

Their question about Jesus' not requiring His disciples to fast was a justified one. The matter of *Jesus' Messiahship* lay at the very root of the question. John's disciples knew that the Pharisees had also been asking how Jesus could break the rituals of their religion and be the true Messiah. So they joined with the Pharisees in asking Jesus the question. The two groups standing together before Jesus formed an unusual alliance. Remember, John had preached against the Pharisees and their hypocrisy, prophesying that they would suffer the most horrible fate if they did not repent (see Mt.3:7-10; see DEEPER STUDY # 3—Ac.23:8.)

THOUGHT 1. A believer should avoid judging other believers for not keeping religious rituals. Censuring and condemning others are uncalled for. Religious rituals are not the standard by which believers are to be judged. Neither are believers the judge of other believers. Christ alone is the Judge (Ro.14:4).

THOUGHT 2. Jesus does teach fasting, but there is a right and a wrong way to fast (see note—Mt.6:16-18 for more discussion).

DEEPER STUDY # 1

(2:18) **Fasting:** see note—Mt.6:16-18; Mk.2:20.

2 Christ brings a joyous life.

Jesus answered the question by pointing out that the kind of life He brings is a life of joy. This is the very reason Jesus did not teach His disciples to fast as a religious ritual. There is no need to fast incessantly when the presence and joy of Jesus fill a life. Jesus used a clear picture to teach what His mission was.

2:19

[19] And Jesus said to them, "Can the wedding guests fast while the bridegroom is with them? As long as they have the bridegroom with them, they cannot fast."

a. He is the bridegroom who stirs joy in His followers.

Jesus used the participants in a wedding to illustrate His ministry. Essentially, He said, "I am launching a new marriage of people to God. I am the Bridegroom (the Son of God Himself) who is to wed people to God, and My chosen disciples are the guests or friends of the Bridegroom" (see DEEPER STUDIES 2, 3).

b. He stirs joy, not fasting, over a sad event.

People usually fasted because of sad events—serious problems, tragedies, or challenges. A wedding is a joyful event; it is not a sad occasion that requires fasting. Jesus emphasized that His presence brings joy, not sadness, to those who follow Him. As long as He was with His people, they should rejoice, not mourn and fast (see note—Mt.9:15).

THOUGHT 1. The discovery of Christ and the day-by-day consciousness of His presence do bring joy to life. Christ is the secret to life and the joy in life. No matter how gloomy life may be or how far gone a person may feel, Christ can change the person's life and bring joy to the heart. Christ can convert a person from gloom and emptiness to joy and fulfillment.

The thief comes only to steal and kill and destroy. I came that they may have life and have it abundantly. (Jn.10:10)

These things I have spoken to you, that my joy may be in you, and that your joy may be full. (Jn.15:11)

Though you have not seen him, you love him. Though you do not now see him, you believe in him and rejoice with joy that is inexpressible and filled with glory. (1 Pe.1:8)

You make known to me the path of life; in your presence there is fullness of joy; at your right hand are pleasures forevermore. (Ps.16:11)

With joy you will draw water from the wells of salvation. (Is.12:3)

DEEPER STUDY # 2

(2:19) **Jesus Christ, Bridegroom:** see DEEPER STUDY # 2—Mt.25:1-13.

DEEPER STUDY # 3

(2:19) **Wedding, Jewish:** see DEEPER STUDY # 1—Mt.25:1-13.

2:20

[20] "The days will come when the bridegroom is taken away from them, and then they will fast in that day."

3 Christ brings a seeking life.

Jesus called attention to the fact that the kind of life He brings is a *seeking life*. It is a life that genuinely seeks Him, seeks His presence and power in a special way.

a. He will be taken away.

Jesus was blunt and honest. Despite the joy of His presence, He was going to be taken away from His followers. *Taken away* refers to the cross and Jesus' death. This is the first time in Mark's Gospel where Jesus says He is going to die a violent death.

> And said to them, "Thus it is written, that the Christ should suffer and on the third day rise from the dead." (Lu.24:46)

> But God shows his love for us in that while we were still sinners, Christ died for us. (Ro.5:8)

> He himself bore our sins in his body on the tree, that we might die to sin and live to righteousness. By his wounds you have been healed. (1 Pe.2:24)

b. His followers will then fast.

Once Jesus had died, the disciples would fast. They would seek Him—seek the joy and consciousness of His presence—through fasting.

Here Jesus states that there are two occasions when His followers should definitely want to fast. First, whenever His presence was removed. There are times when the presence of Christ is dimmed in the believer's life. Christ seems far away and absent; there is no sensing or no awareness of His presence. We need to fast and seek the Lord's presence during such times.

> Let us draw near with a true heart in full assurance of faith, with our hearts sprinkled clean from an evil conscience and our bodies washed with pure water. (He.10:22)

> Draw near to God, and he will draw near to you. Cleanse your hands, you sinners, and purify your hearts, you double-minded. (Js.4:8)

Second, believers should want to fast whenever His presence is especially needed. There are times when a special manifestation, a special empowering is needed. Fasting and intense prayer draw God close to the believer, to meet the believer who so greatly needs and desires closeness to God.

THOUGHT 1. All who will live godly in Christ Jesus will suffer in this world (2 Ti.3:12). Therefore, the godly need the very special presence of the Lord. We need to fast and pray often, ever seeking a deeper consciousness of His presence.

> And he told them a parable to the effect that they ought always to pray and not lose heart. (Lu.18:1)

> Is anyone among you suffering? Let him pray. Is anyone cheerful? Let him sing praise. (Js.5:13)

> Seek the Lord and his strength; seek his presence continually! (1 Chr.16:11)

> The Lord is near to the brokenhearted and saves the crushed in spirit. (Ps.34:18)

> Seek the Lord and his strength; seek his presence continually! (Ps.105:4)

> The Lord is near to all who call on him, to all who call on him in truth. (Ps.145:18)

4 Christ brings a new life.

Jesus proceeds to point out that He brings a new life. When a person repents and believes in Christ, he or she is a new creation (2 Co.5:17). This is why Jesus explains salvation as the new birth—being born again (Jn.3:3).

> 21 "No one sews a piece of unshrunk cloth on an old garment. If he does, the patch tears away from it, the new from the old, and a worse tear is made."

a. He is not attaching a new life to the old life of a person.

Jesus illustrates this truth by referring to the common practice of patching a worn-out or torn garment. Jesus is not a patch being sown to an old garment. He is not out to reform an old religion or an old life.

b. He is creating a totally new life (2 Co.5:17).

The life Jesus gives is a completely new life, and His day is a completely new day. It is not the day for patching up the old; it is time to create the new. His day is a day of regeneration, not of reformation (see outline and note—Mt.12:43-45 for more discussion).

> But to all who did receive him, who believed in his name, he gave the right to become children of God, who were born, not of blood nor of the will of the flesh nor of the will of man, but of God. (Jn.1:12-13)

> Jesus answered him, "Truly, truly, I say to you, unless one is born again he cannot see the kingdom of God." (Jn.3:3)

> He saved us, not because of works done by us in righteousness, but according to his own mercy, by the washing of regeneration and renewal of the Holy Spirit. (Tit.3:5)

> Since you have been born again, not of perishable seed but of imperishable, through the living and abiding word of God. (1 Pe.1:23)

> Everyone who believes that Jesus is the Christ has been born of God, and everyone who loves the Father loves whoever has been born of him. (1 Jn.5:1)

2:22

22 "And no one puts new wine into old wineskins. If he does, the wine will burst the skins—and the wine is destroyed, and so are the skins. But new wine is for fresh wineskins."

5 Christ brings an adventurous life.

The kind of life Christ brings is an adventurous life. It is bold, fresh, growing, and exciting. Once again, Jesus illustrates the truth by referring to a common practice: putting new wine into new wineskins.

a. He is not filling the old life with the new.

People did not put new wine into old wineskins. New wineskins were elastic and would expand as the gas of fermenting wine built up pressure. Old wineskins were hardened and would not expand, but rather would explode under pressure. The lesson: He was not merely filling the old life with the new. The old life—the old person, the fleshly nature—cannot contain the abundant spiritual life Jesus gives.

b. He is creating a totally new life (Jn.3:3; Ep.4:22-24).

Jesus says that He is bringing a new elasticity to life: a new expansion, a new adventure, a new excitement, a new life. Therefore, a new wineskin or life—a new person, a spiritual nature—is needed; a nature that can accommodate the abundant, ever-growing spiritual life Jesus gives is needed (Ep.4:22-24). For this reason, we must be born again (Jn.3:3).

THOUGHT 1. Life always presents opportunities for renewal, and history bears this out. The day for patching the old will not suffice. A new beginning and a new life must be launched or else we face uselessness, and death.

1) People will die in the *old garment of their flesh* unless they come to Christ for a new beginning.

> For God so loved the world, that he gave his only Son, that whoever believes in him should not perish but have eternal life. (Jn.3:16)

> Truly, truly, I say to you, whoever hears my word and believes him who sent me has eternal life. He does not come into judgment, but has passed from death to life. (Jn.5:24)

> Therefore, if anyone is in Christ, he is a new creation. The old has passed away; behold, the new has come. (2 Co.5:17)

> To put off your old self, which belongs to your former manner of life and is corrupt through deceitful desires, and to be renewed in the spirit of your minds, and to put on the new self, created after the likeness of God in true righteousness and holiness. (Ep.4:22-24)

> And have put on the new self, which is being renewed in knowledge after the image of its creator. (Col.3:10)

2) The programs, methods, organizations, and even religions of this world will die and become ineffective unless they are based upon Christ and His new beginning. The foundation of life is Christ and the *new garment of His righteousness* (2 Co.5:21).

For I tell you, unless your righteousness exceeds that of the scribes and Pharisees, you will never enter the kingdom of heaven. (Mt.5:20)

And because of him you are in Christ Jesus, who became to us wisdom from God, righteousness and sanctification and redemption. (1 Co.1:30)

For our sake he made him to be sin who knew no sin, so that in him we might become the righteousness of God. (2 Co.5:21)

And be found in him, not having a righteousness of my own that comes from the law, but that which comes through faith in Christ, the righteousness from God that depends on faith. (Ph.3:9)

THOUGHT 2. No greater adventure can be launched than the life that Christ gives to a person. No greater mission can be undertaken than His mission.

Even as the Son of Man came not to be served but to serve, and to give his life as a ransom for many. (Mt.20:28)

For the Son of Man came to seek and to save the lost. (Lu.19:10)

The thief comes only to steal and kill and destroy. I came that they may have life and have it abundantly. (Jn.10:10)

Jesus said to them again, "Peace be with you. As the Father has sent me, even so I am sending you." (Jn.20:21)

THOUGHT 3. We are to struggle against becoming set and fixed in our *own ways*. Instead, we are to be elastic, expanding, and adventurous in life (see He.11:1–40), constantly growing in holiness, and in service to Christ.

Rather, speaking the truth in love, we are to grow up in every way into him who is the head, into Christ. (Ep.4:15)

So as to walk in a manner worthy of the Lord, fully pleasing to him: bearing fruit in every good work and increasing in the knowledge of God (Col.1:10)

For this very reason, make every effort to supplement your faith with virtue, and virtue with knowledge, and knowledge with self-control, and self-control with steadfastness, and steadfastness with godliness. (2 Pe.1:5–6)

But grow in the grace and knowledge of our Lord and Savior Jesus Christ. To him be the glory both now and to the day of eternity. Amen. (2 Pe.3:18)

J. Jesus' Impact upon Religionists:
Understanding the Sabbath, 2:23–28

(Mt.12:1–8; Lu.6:1–5)

1. The Sabbath is not about rules and regulations
   a. Jesus passed through grain fields
   b. The disciples plucked and ate some grain
   c. The religionists questioned the picking of grain on the Sabbath

2. The Sabbath was given to help people[DS1]
   a. The illustration: David and his men were hungry
      1) He went into the house of God
      2) He ate the bread meant for priests alone
      3) He shared the bread with his men—an unlawful act

   b. The point: The Sabbath was given to meet the needs of people, not master and rule over them
3. The Sabbath is to be governed by the Son of Man

²³ One Sabbath he was going through the grainfields, and as they made their way, his disciples began to pluck heads of grain.

²⁴ And the Pharisees were saying to him, "Look, why are they doing what is not lawful on the Sabbath?"
²⁵ And he said to them, "Have you never read what David did, when he was in need and was hungry, he and those who were with him:
²⁶ how he entered the house of God, in the time of Abiathar the high priest, and ate the bread of the Presence, which it is not lawful for any but the priests to eat, and also gave it to those who were with him?"
²⁷ And he said to them, "The Sabbath was made for man, not man for the Sabbath."
²⁸ "So the Son of Man is lord even of the Sabbath."

Division II

The Son of God's Opening Ministry: Jesus' Immediate Impact, 1:21–3:35

J. Jesus' Impact upon Religionists: Understanding the Sabbath, 2:23–28

(Mt.12:1–8; Lu.6:1–5)

2:23–28
Introduction

The Sabbath is often abused. Under the law of Moses, the Sabbath was the seventh day of the week. The practice of the early church was to observe Sunday as the day for rest and worship, for our Lord rose from the grave on the first day of the week. Today, most believers follow the practice of the early church. Some, however, believe that Saturday should still be the day of the week for rest and worship. The principles Jesus' taught here apply to whichever day of the week believers choose to set aside for worship and rest. Throughout the commentary, the use of the word "Sabbath" is applied to God's commandment of a dedicated day for worship and not specifically to the seventh day of the week.

A person can abuse the Sabbath by being either too strict or too loose in observing the day. In Jesus' day, many were too strict. In the present generation, however, the problem is not in being too strict but in being too loose. Few ever give any thought to God's command to keep the Sabbath holy.

In this passage Jesus deals with the true meaning of Sabbath worship (or worship on Sunday for that matter): a critical issue for every generation (see outline and note—Mt.12:1-8 for more discussion). This is, *Jesus' Impact upon Religionists: Understanding the Sabbath,* 2:23-28.

1. The Sabbath is not about rules and regulations (vv.23-24).
2. The Sabbath was given to help people (vv.25-27).
3. The Sabbath is to be governed by the Son of Man (v.28).

1 The Sabbath is not about rules and regulations.

The point of this passage is vital: Sabbath worship is not about rules and regulations. The subpoints of the outline adequately convey what took place. Jesus and the disciples passed through a grain field on the way to worship. They had not eaten breakfast, so the disciples began to pluck a few head of grain and eat them. The extreme religionists, the Pharisees, saw them and accused them of breaking the

²³ One Sabbath he was going through the grainfields, and as they made their way, his disciples began to pluck heads of grain.

²⁴ And the Pharisees were saying to him, "Look, why are they doing what is not lawful on the Sabbath?"

Sabbath law; that is, they were charged with working on the Sabbath. Note two facts:

First, the disciples had broken the *ceremonial law*. The *ceremonial law* did not allow work on the Sabbath. The religionists were right in their accusation. The disciples had worked and broken the Sabbath law in two areas. They had plucked the heads of grain, and they had broken the kernels of grain off; or as Luke says, "[rubbed] them in their hands" (Lu.6:1) (see notes—Mt.12:1-8; 12:1-3 for a more detailed discussion).

Second, Jesus judged the disciples' work on the Sabbath as acceptable. He knew the law prohibited work on the Sabbath, and He knew the disciples were breaking the law—actually working on the Sabbath. Yet neither did He rebuke nor correct them. He allowed them to pluck and eat the grain despite the law. Why? There was one primary reason.

Resting and worshiping on the Sabbath is important and should be observed, but there is so much more to Sabbath worship than rules and regulations. Some things take precedence and are more needful than rules and regulations. Jesus simply knew that the disciples' need for food was greater than their need to keep a ceremonial rule. (In reality, Jesus is teaching that religion itself, in all its ritual and ceremony, is not about strict adherence to rules and regulations.)

THOUGHT 1. Rules and regulations, laws and commandments are made to help people, to govern our behavior and to show us the best way to live. Therefore, rules which guide us to dedicate a day to rest and worship each week are good and beneficial.

1) We should always recognize that guidelines emphasize the spirit of Sabbath observance. We need a day of rest and worship. We need to be physically refreshed and spiritually revived every week. God knew this, and this is precisely why He included this as one of His timeless commandments.

2) Sometimes a need arises that is greater than the need for rest and worship. Jesus recognized this. When a greater need arises, it should be met. But note: a temporary need does not do away with a permanent need. We are still to observe a day of rest and worship. In the event surrounding the disciples, Jesus judged the temporary need for food to be greater than the need for rest and worship on the Sabbath. However, addressing this temporary need was not to become the usual practice. Our permanent need is to worship and rest one day a week.

Of how much more value is a man than a sheep! So it is lawful to do good on the Sabbath. (Mt.12:12)

Not neglecting to meet together, as is the habit of some, but encouraging one another, and all the more as you see the Day drawing near. (He.10:25)

Remember the Sabbath day, to keep it holy. (Ex.20:8)

And if the peoples of the land bring in goods or any grain on the Sabbath day to sell, we will not buy from them on the Sabbath or on a holy day. And we will forego the crops of the seventh year and the exaction of every debt. (Ne.10:31; see Ne.13:15)

THOUGHT 2. When a person judges and censors another person's worship or devotion to God, he or she is committing a much more serious sin: the sin of forgetting mercy and forgiveness, love and ministry.

> **Judge not, that you be not judged. For with the judgment you pronounce you will be judged, and with the measure you use it will be measured to you. Why do you see the speck that is in your brother's eye, but do not notice the log that is in your own eye? Or how can you say to your brother, 'Let me take the speck out of your eye,' when there is the log in your own eye? You hypocrite, first take the log out of your own eye, and then you will see clearly to take the speck out of your brother's eye. (Mt.7:1–5)**

> **Therefore you have no excuse, O man, every one of you who judges. For in passing judgment on another you condemn yourself, because you, the judge, practice the very same things. (Ro.2:1)**

> **Who are you to pass judgment on the servant of another? It is before his own master that he stands or falls. And he will be upheld, for the Lord is able to make him stand. . . . Therefore let us not pass judgment on one another any longer, but rather decide never to put a stumbling block or hindrance in the way of a brother. (Ro.14:4, 13)**

> **Therefore do not pronounce judgment before the time, before the Lord comes, who will bring to light the things now hidden in darkness and will disclose the purposes of the heart. Then each one will receive his commendation from God. (1 Co.4:5)**

> **There is only one lawgiver and judge, he who is able to save and to destroy. But who are you to judge your neighbor? (Js.4:12)**

2:25–27

²⁵ And he said to them, "Have you never read what David did, when he was in need and was hungry, he and those who were with him:
²⁶ how he entered the house of God, in the time of Abiathar the high priest, and ate the bread of the Presence, which it is not lawful for any but the priests to eat, and also gave it to those who were with him?"
²⁷ And he said to them, "The Sabbath was made for man, not man for the Sabbath."

2 The Sabbath was given to help people.

God instituted the day of rest for our benefit, not His. He gave us this day to help us, to refresh us physically and renew us spiritually. Jesus got this truth across—as He so often did—by presenting an illustration.

a. The illustration: David and His men were hungry (vv.25–26).

Jesus told the story of what David had done in similar circumstances (1 S.21:1-6). David was fleeing from Saul, and he and his men were hungry, not having eaten for some time. In their flight they came upon the tabernacle in Nob. David went into the house of God and requested food from the priests, but there was no food. There was only the *bread of the Presence* (*showbread*—NKJV, KJV; *consecrated bread*—NASB, CSB, NIV) that was forbidden to be eaten by anyone other than the priests (see DEEPER STUDY # 1). Despite the law, David took five loaves and ate the bread meant for the priests alone. He shared the bread with his hungry men—a forbidden or unlawful act.

By using this illustration, Jesus was saying that a great man of God, a man after God's own heart, a man revered by the Jews, had broken the ceremonial law of God. Yet the man of God was justified because his need for bread was greater than his keeping a ceremonial law.

In addition, Jesus was showing that Scripture itself gives precedence for what His disciples were doing and reveals and justifies David's actions.

b. The point: The Sabbath was given to meet the needs of people, not master and rule over them (v.27).

Jesus states in this verse that the point of His illustration should be self-evident: the Sabbath (a day of rest and worship) is to serve people, not master people. Jesus simply says, "The Sabbath was made for man, not man for the sabbath." People and their needs take precedence over any ceremonial law—including ceremonial laws governing the Sabbath. Whatever serves us the most is exactly what is to be done on the holy day. The Sabbath was made for man, not man for the Sabbath.

But note a crucial fact. Two of the greatest needs of all people are for rest and worship, a day for physical refreshment and spiritual renewal every week. So the need has to be a desperate one, a need unable to be fulfilled any other way, for it to take precedence over the law. This is critical to understand, for we do not have license to break God's law at every whim and fancy. Breaking the law for selfish reasons—for fleshly desires and commercial pleasure—is not what Jesus is talking about. His point is that need, a true and real need, can take *temporary precedence* over the Sabbath.

The Sabbath or day of rest was made for us. It is to be used for our benefit, to gain rest and a revived sense of God's presence. But it is not our master. Our rest and worship may need to be temporarily interrupted in order to meet a greater need, a need that has suddenly come upon us (see outline, notes and DEEPER STUDY # 2—Mt.12:3-4).

THOUGHT 1. People are far more important than rules and regulations, far more important than ceremony, ritual, and religion. The first duty of all people is to worship God and to meet the needs of others. Nothing should ever take precedence over this first duty.

> Even as the Son of Man came not to be served but to serve, and to give his life as a ransom for many. (Mt.20:28)

> Jesus said to them again, "Peace be with you. As the Father has sent me, even so I am sending you." (Jn.20:21)

> In all things I have shown you that by working hard in this way we must help the weak and remember the words of the Lord Jesus, how he himself said, "It is more blessed to give than to receive." (Ac.20:35)

> We who are strong have an obligation to bear with the failings of the weak, and not to please ourselves. (Ro.15:1)

> Bear one another's burdens, and so fulfill the law of Christ. (Ga.6:2)

DEEPER STUDY # 1

(2:25-26) **Bread of the presence, showbread, or consecrated bread:** see DEEPER STUDY # 2—Mt.12:3-4.

3 The Sabbath is to be governed by the Son of Man.

2:28

Jesus, the Son of Man, is the Lord of the Sabbath. Therefore, the Sabbath is to be governed by Him. What He says supersedes all religious rules and regulations. By declaring Himself Lord of the Sabbath, Jesus is making two claims:

28 "So the Son of Man is lord even of the Sabbath."

- He is the true Messiah, the Son of Man (see DEEPER STUDY # 3—Mt.8:20).
- He is the One who gave the Sabbath. Therefore, He is the Lord who governs the Sabbath. People are to do exactly what Christ says to do on the Sabbath (see DEEPER STUDY # 1—Mt.12:1 for the scriptural teaching on the Sabbath.)

> And Jesus came and said to them, "All authority in heaven and on earth has been given to me." (Mt.28:18)

> Let all the house of Israel therefore know for certain that God has made him both Lord and Christ, this Jesus whom you crucified. (Ac.2:36)

> God exalted him at his right hand as Leader and Savior, to give repentance to Israel and forgiveness of sins. (Ac.5:31)

> Yet for us there is one God, the Father, from whom are all things and for whom we exist, and one Lord, Jesus Christ, through whom are all things and through whom we exist. (1 Co.8:6)

> And he put all things under his feet and gave him as head over all things to the church. (Ep.1:22)

> Who has gone into heaven and is at the right hand of God, with angels, authorities, and powers having been subjected to him. (1 Pe.3:22)

CHAPTER 3

K. Jesus' Impact upon Authorities and Politicians: Understanding True Religion, 3:1–6

(Mt.12:9–14; Lu.6:6–11)

1. **True religion is both worshiping and seeing those in need**
   a. Jesus entered the synagogue and encountered a man with a shriveled hand
   b. Jesus was closely watched by the religionists

2. **True religion is a willingness to stand up and obey Christ**
3. **True religion is doing good and saving lives**
   a. Not obeying rules, regulations
   b. Not refusing to face the truth
4. **True religion is righteous anger against error and evil**
   a. Feeling anger due to people's stubborn hearts[DS1]
   b. Feeling grief due to hardness
5. **True religion is restoring people to completeness and wholeness**
6. **True religion does not involve scheming or manipulation, nor is it destructive**

Again he entered the synagogue, and a man was there with a withered hand.

² And they watched Jesus, to see whether he would heal him on the Sabbath, so that they might accuse him. ³ And he said to the man with the withered hand, "Come here." ⁴ And he said to them, "Is it lawful on the Sabbath to do good or to do harm, to save life or to kill?" But they were silent.

⁵ And he looked around at them with anger, grieved at their hardness of heart, and said to the man, "Stretch out your hand." He stretched it out, and his hand was restored.

⁶ The Pharisees went out and immediately held counsel with the Herodians against him, how to destroy him.

Division II

The Son of God's Opening Ministry: Jesus' Immediate Impact, 1:21–3:35

K. Jesus' Impact upon Authorities and Politicians: Understanding True Religion, 3:1–6

(Mt.12:9–14; Lu.6:6–11)

3:1–6
Introduction

This passage presents a crucial event for Jesus—the climax of five conflicts with the religionists (Scribes and Pharisees). Time and again the religionists had attacked Jesus, accusing Him of teaching a false religion. In this climactic confrontation, Jesus used the man with a withered hand to demonstrate just what true religion is. The demonstration was so clear and forceful that the religionists were stunned. What is true religion? Jesus answered that question in this passage. This is, *Jesus' Impact upon Authorities and Politicians: Understanding True Religion, 3:1-6.*

1. True religion is both worshiping and seeing those in need (vv.1-2).
2. True religion is a willingness to stand up and obey Christ (v.3).
3. True religion is doing good and saving lives (v.4).
4. True religion is righteous anger against error and evil (v.5).
5. True religion is restoring people to completeness and wholeness (v.5).
6. True religion does not involve scheming or manipulation, nor is it destructive (v.6).

1 True religion is both worshiping and seeing those in need.

The synagogue was the stage for this showdown between Jesus and the religionists. To the Pharisees, religion revolved around a set of rules and regulations. To Jesus, religion revolved around worshiping God and helping those in need.

Again he entered the synagogue, and a man was there with a withered hand.
² And they watched Jesus, to see whether he would heal him on the Sabbath, so that they might accuse him.

a. Jesus entered the synagogue and encountered a man with a shriveled hand (v.1).

Upon entering the synagogue again, Jesus encountered an individual with a great need. *With* (or *who had*) *a withered hand* (Gk. exerammenen echon ten cheira; pronounced *ex-ay-ram'-en-ane ek'-own tane ka'-ra*) literally means "which had his hand withered" or "with a hand that had been withered." That is, his hand had been injured or had become diseased. He was not born this way. However, his plight had become desperate; for he was unable to work for a living due to his handicap. Tradition says he was a stone mason who asked Jesus to heal him so that he might not have to beg in shame (see note—Mt.12:9-13).

b. Jesus was closely watched by the religionists (v.2).

Jesus also encountered a group of Jewish religious leaders at the synagogue, probably the same delegation who had been sent earlier from the Sanhedrin to investigate His teaching (see note—Mk.2:6-7). It was their duty to protect the people from false teachers and to protect the nation from insurrectionists. They were not attending the synagogue to worship God. They were there to watch for Jesus to do something with which they disagreed in order that they might have a reason to accuse Him.

Jesus, however, was neither distracted nor intimidated by the Pharisees present. While they were watching Jesus, Jesus was focused on God and on those who needed a special touch from God. This—worshiping God and seeing those in need—is true religion.

THOUGHT 1. How many sit in church, watching and picking out wrong in others so that they might accuse them and gossip about them? Church is the place for worship and ministering to all with "withered hands"—hands that are unable to work and serve God, hands that are withered because of . . .

- dead spirits
- unlearned minds
- disturbed emotions
- misguided lives

Woe to you, scribes and Pharisees, hypocrites! For you tithe mint and dill and cumin, and have neglected the weightier matters of the law: justice and mercy and faithfulness. These you ought to have done, without neglecting the others. (Mt.23:23)

Bear one another's burdens, and so fulfill the law of Christ. (Ga.6:2)

If I delay, you may know how one ought to behave in the household of God, which is the church of the living God, a pillar and buttress of the truth. (1 Ti.3:15)

If anyone thinks he is religious and does not bridle his tongue but deceives his heart, this person's religion is worthless. (Js.1:26)

2 True religion is a willingness to stand up and obey Christ.

3:3

True religion is a *willingness to stand up and do what Christ has commanded us to do*. Jesus called the man with the withered man to come and stand before the congregation. *Come here* (egeirai eis to meson; pronounced *eh-gay'-reh ace tah meh'-sahn*) is most literally translated, "Rise up, stand up in the midst." Jesus was calling for the man's will—his willingness to do exactly what the Messiah was saying. The man had to want help enough to be willing to stand before the audience and before the scornful religionists. By such a stand, he would be *confessing his faith in Jesus and in His power to save and heal.*

³ And he said to the man with the withered hand, "Come here."

THOUGHT 1. Real religion is a willingness to stand in obedience to Christ. Christ calls all to *rise up, stand*, repent, and confess their faith in the Lord's power to save and heal them (see DEEPER STUDY # 1—Ac.17:29–30).

When he entered the house, the blind men came to him, and Jesus said to them, "Do you believe that I am able to do this?" They said to him, "Yes, Lord." (Mt.9:28)

So everyone who acknowledges me before men, I also will acknowledge before my Father who is in heaven, but whoever denies me before men, I also will deny before my Father who is in heaven. (Mt.10:32–33)

No one who denies the Son has the Father. Whoever confesses the Son has the Father also. (1 Jn.2:23)

How long will you lie there, O sluggard? When will you arise from your sleep? (Pr.6:9)

For there shall be a day when watchmen will call in the hill country of Ephraim: 'Arise, and let us go up to Zion, to the LORD our God.' (Je.31:6)

3:4

⁴ And he said to them, "Is it lawful on the Sabbath to do good or to do harm, to save life or to kill?" But they were silent.

3 True religion is doing good and saving lives.

After calling the handicapped man to come forward, Jesus confronted the Pharisees who were present. The religionists' problem with Jesus was His breaking of their ceremonial law. People by the thousands were flocking to Jesus for help, and every time He did not follow the law, He was teaching the people to discredit the ceremonial law. Therefore, they felt that Jesus was a serious threat to the Jewish religion and nation and to the leaders of the nation—both civil and religious (their security, position, and power; see notes—Mt.12:1–8; note and DEEPER STUDY # 1—12:10; note—15:1–20; DEEPER STUDY # 2—15:6–9 for a detailed discussion).

a. **Not obeying rules, regulations.**

Jesus taught and demonstrated that true religion is doing good and saving lives. True religion is not rules and regulations, not ceremony and ritual, no matter how good the rules and ceremony may be. If a person has a need, true religion meets that need. Jesus drove the point home by asking two questions.

First: "Is it lawful to do good on the Sabbath day, or to do harm (evil)?" Jesus had the power to do good by healing the man. Therefore, if He did not heal the man, He would be withholding good and doing evil. Yet the ceremonial law said that no work was to be done on the Sabbath.

Second: "Is it lawful to save life, or to kill?" Jesus had the power and wanted to save the man's life; the religionists had the civil authority and wanted to kill Jesus. The religionists were actually plotting His death, and He knew it. They knew what He was asking and saying. True religion does good and saves life, it does not live by rules and regulations, ceremonies and rituals; nor does it seek to isolate and cut off and kill people, even if they are judged to be threats.

b. Not refusing to face the truth.

The religionists said nothing in response to Jesus. They refused to face the truth; they closed their minds in obstinate unbelief (see DEEPER STUDY # 4—Mt.12:24; 12:31-32 for discussion). They preferred and chose a religion of ceremony and ritual to that of doing good and saving lives. True religion does not refuse to face the truth, especially when the truth is contrary to our opinions, preconceived ideas, or personal beliefs.

THOUGHT 1. True religion is doing good and saving lives, and it is accepting what God says as truth.

> And to love him with all the heart and with all the understanding and with all the strength, and to love one's neighbor as oneself, is much more than all whole burnt offerings and sacrifices. (Mk.12:33)

> Love does no wrong to a neighbor; therefore love is the fulfilling of the law. (Ro.13:10)

> Religion that is pure and undefiled before God the Father is this: to visit orphans and widows in their affliction, and to keep oneself unstained from the world. (Js.1:27)

> By this we know love, that he laid down his life for us, and we ought to lay down our lives for the brothers. But if anyone has the world's goods and sees his brother in need, yet closes his heart against him, how does God's love abide in him? Little children, let us not love in word or talk but in deed and in truth. By this we shall know that we are of the truth and reassure our heart before him; (1 Jn.3:16-19)

> For I desire steadfast love and not sacrifice, the knowledge of God rather than burnt offerings. (Ho.6:6)

> He has told you, O man, what is good; and what does the LORD require of you but to do justice, and to love kindness, and to walk humbly with your God? (Mi.6:8)

4 True religion is righteous anger against error and evil.

3:5a

When our religion is true, we cannot stand by unaffected by error and evil. When Jesus looked around at the religionists, when He saw their arrogant self-righteousness, their judgmentalism, and their total lack of compassion for the handicapped man, two strong emotions rose up within Him. His righteous feelings were kindled against the error and evil He observed.

> [5] And he looked around at them with anger, grieved at their hardness of heart, and said to the man, "Stretch out your hand." He stretched it out, and his hand was restored.

a. Feeling anger due to people's stubborn hearts.

Jesus was gripped by anger because of the hardness of the Pharisees' hearts. Many people wrongly assume that anger is a sin. The fact that Jesus became angry establishes that anger in and of itself is not a sin, for Jesus did not and could not sin. Scripture warns us that we must be careful not to sin when we become angry (Ep.4:26), but it is not a sin to become angry. If our religion is true, we cannot help but be angry when we see error and evil hurt those who need God most.

b. Feeling grief due to hardness.

Jesus was angry at the stiff-necked, unsympathetic Pharisees, but, at the same time, He was deeply concerned about them. He was grieved at the hardness of their hearts (see DEEPER STUDY # 1; DEEPER STUDY # 4—Mt.12:24; note—12:31-32).

THOUGHT 1. This is true religion: to hate the sin while simultaneously loving and caring about the sinner.

> Not everyone who says to me, "Lord, Lord," will enter the kingdom of heaven, but the one who does the will of my Father who is in heaven. (Mt.7:21)

> And he said to them, "Well did Isaiah prophesy of you hypocrites, as it is written, 'This people honors me with their lips, but their heart is far from me.'" (Mk.7:6)

Why do you call me "Lord, Lord," and not do what I tell you? (Lu.6:46)

They profess to know God, but they deny him by their works. They are detestable, disobedient, unfit for any good work. (Tit.1:16)

Little children, let us not love in word or talk but in deed and in truth. (1 Jn.3:18)

Deeper Study # 1

(3:5) **Grieved** (sullupoumenos): to sense grief, sorrow, empathy; to suffer with a person because they are injured. In this particular passage, Jesus' anger was combined with grief over people who harmed themselves. The anger of Jesus was a grieving anger over obstinate unbelief. The people who closed their minds—who remained obstinate in unbelief despite the evidence—incited a grieving anger within Him.

3:5b

⁵ And he looked around at them with anger, grieved at their hardness of heart, and said to the man, "Stretch out your hand." He stretched it out, and his hand was restored.

5 True religion is restoring people to completeness and wholeness.

Jesus demonstrated that true religion is *restoring people to wholeness*. True religion speaks and acts. Jesus spoke, "Stretch out your hand." The man did, and Jesus restored the man to wholeness. True religion does not hesitate to minister and restore people. It is love and service, not the keeping of rules and regulations, ceremonies and rituals. Rules and ceremonies are helpful; they are even necessary. But they are not true religion. The essence of religion is restoring people and making them whole in the name and power of Jesus.

THOUGHT 1. See outline and notes—Ro.12:1–21. A quick glance at the whole chapter will give an excellent description of what true religion is.

Even as the Son of Man came not to be served but to serve, and to give his life as a ransom for many. (Mt.20:28)

Jesus said to them again, "Peace be with you. As the Father has sent me, even so I am sending you." (Jn.20:21)

In all things I have shown you that by working hard in this way we must help the weak and remember the words of the Lord Jesus, how he himself said, "It is more blessed to give than to receive." (Ac.20:35)

We who are strong have an obligation to bear with the failings of the weak, and not to please ourselves. (Ro.15:1)

Bear one another's burdens, and so fulfill the law of Christ. (Ga.6:2)

3:6

⁶ The Pharisees went out and immediately held counsel with the Herodians against him, how to destroy him.

6 True religion does not involve scheming or manipulation, nor is it destructive.

Jesus had confronted the religionists with the truth. He taught them clearly and explicitly what true religion is. They were now faced with a dilemma: they had to either accept true religion, Jesus and His teaching, or else oppose Him. They chose to oppose Him, but they needed political help, so they went out and formed an alliance with the Herodians (see Deeper Study # 2—Mt.22:16). Note a significant fact: despite enormous philosophical differences, there was no difference in behavior between the religious and the political leaders (the Pharisees and the Herodians). Position, power, and security had corrupted their hearts and minds. They both plotted to destroy a person (Jesus) who opposed them (see note—Mt.12:1-8; note and Deeper Study # 1—12:10 for a detailed discussion of their opposition). The sinful actions of the Pharisees teach a critical truth: true religion does not involve scheming or manipulation, nor is it destructive.

THOUGHT 1. Every person is confronted with true religion in Jesus Christ. Every person is faced with the dilemma of choosing to follow true religion or to oppose Christ.

> Jesus said to him, "I am the way, and the truth, and the life. No one comes to the Father except through me." (Jn.14:6)

> For there is one God, and there is one mediator between God and men, the man Christ Jesus, who gave himself as a ransom for all, which is the testimony given at the proper time. (1 Ti.2:5–6)

> And this is the testimony, that God gave us eternal life, and this life is in his Son. Whoever has the Son has life; whoever does not have the Son of God does not have life. (1 Jn.5:11–12)

THOUGHT 2. How many within *religion* oppose Christ because of their position, power, and security? How many go along with questionable teachings, ideas, movements, and the religious fad of the day—all because they fear the reaction of the world and of their worldly-minded peers?

> And he said to all, "If anyone would come after me, let him deny himself and take up his cross daily and follow me." (Lu.9:23)

> Therefore go out from their midst, and be separate from them, says the Lord, and touch no unclean thing; then I will welcome you, and will be a father to you, and you shall be sons and daughters to me, says the Lord Almighty. (2 Co.6:17–18)

> Whoever says he abides in him ought to walk in the same way in which he walked. (1 Jn.2:6)

> And this is his commandment, that we believe in the name of his Son Jesus Christ and love one another, just as he has commanded us. (1 Jn.3:23)

L. Jesus' Impact upon Crowds and Evil Spirits:
Seeking and Fearing Christ, 3:7–12

(Mt.12:14–21)

1. **Jesus' withdrawal**[DS1]
2. **Jesus' impact upon people: A true seeking**
   a. Large crowds followed Him
      1) They came from near and far
      2) The reason: They heard what great things He did

   b. Large crowds crushed in upon Him
      1) Endangered His life

      2) Sought to touch Him

3. **Jesus' impact upon evil spirits: A terrible fear**
   a. They were subject to Him
   b. They acknowledged His Messiahship
   c. He rebuked the evil spirits' confession

⁷ Jesus withdrew with his disciples to the sea, and a great crowd followed, from Galilee and Judea

⁸ and Jerusalem and Idumea and from beyond the Jordan and from around Tyre and Sidon. When the great crowd heard all that he was doing, they came to him. ⁹ And he told his disciples to have a boat ready for him because of the crowd, lest they crush him, ¹⁰ for he had healed many, so that all who had diseases pressed around him to touch him. ¹¹ And whenever the unclean spirits saw him, they fell down before him and cried out, "You are the Son of God."

¹² And he strictly ordered them not to make him known.

Division II

The Son of God's Opening Ministry: Jesus' Immediate Impact, 1:21–3:35

L. Jesus' Impact upon Crowds and Evil Spirits: Seeking and Fearing Christ, 3:7–12

(Mt.12:14–21)

3:7–12
Introduction

Jesus' impact upon people was unbelievable; it was incomprehensible. In just a few months, the whole nation was seeking after the One called Jesus of Nazareth, the promised Messiah. A fact that is often unnoticed is the fact covered in this passage: a great crowd or multitude followed Him. The crowd is called "great" twice (vv.7, 8). The crowds were enormous (remember the feeding of five thousand men, not counting the women and children). The multitudes did what we so desperately need to do: they sincerely sought Jesus, even to the point of *crushing Him* (v.9) and *pressing in on Him* (v.10).

Jesus' impact upon evil spirits was just as dramatic. Demons were stricken to bow before Him and to acknowledge His Messiahship—two acts that desperately need to be done by all people. This is, *Jesus' Impact upon Crowds and Evil Spirits: Seeking and Fearing Christ, 3:7–12.*

1. Jesus' withdrawal (v.7).
2. Jesus' impact upon people: A true seeking (vv.7–10).
3. Jesus' impact upon evil spirits: A terrible fear (vv.11–12).

1 Jesus' withdrawal.

Because the leaders, both religious and political, were now plotting to kill Jesus (v.6; see note—Mt.12:14-16), the Savior was forced to withdraw to the Sea of Galilee (see DEEPER STUDY # 1). He still had much to teach before He could face the end of His earthly life and ministry. As He had said on several occasions, His hour had not yet come. He must not allow His death—not yet. Therefore, He had to move out of the synagogue into the open country.

7 Jesus withdrew with his disciples to the sea, and a great crowd followed, from Galilee and Judea

DEEPER STUDY # 1

(3:7) **Jesus Withdrew:** Mark also says Jesus withdrew in Mk.6:31, 46; 7:24, 31; 10:1; 14:34-35.

2 Jesus' impact upon people: A true seeking.

Jesus withdrew to the Sea of Galilee for a second reason: the crowds had become too large for the synagogues and the cities to handle. People by the multitudes were flocking to Him, even to the point of endangering His life by the crush of bodies (see vv.8-9).

Jesus' impact upon the crowds is often overlooked or minimized. It was nothing short of phenomenal. Both the sheer size of the crowds and their persistence demonstrate how eagerly we should seek after Jesus.

7 Jesus withdrew with his disciples to the sea, and a great crowd followed, from Galilee and Judea

8 and Jerusalem and Idumea and from beyond the Jordan and from around Tyre and Sidon. When the great crowd heard all that he was doing, they came to him.

9 And he told his disciples to have a boat ready for him because of the crowd, lest they crush him,

10 for he had healed many, so that all who had diseases pressed around him to touch him.

a. **Large crowds followed Him (vv.7b-8).**
Teeming multitudes flocked to Jesus and truly sought Him. They came from both near and far—from all over the nation, and some even came from foreign nations:

- Crowds came from all over Galilee (v.7b). Imagine a district so heavily populated that it embraced over two hundred cities with populations of fifteen thousand or more (see note—Mt.4:12-13). Teeming multitudes streamed to Jesus from all over this district.[1]
- Crowds came from Judea and Jerusalem (v.8a). This was a hundred-mile journey.
- Crowds came from Idumea which lay in the deep south, bordering Palestine and Arabia (v.8b). Idumea was the Greek and Roman name for Edom or the land of Esau (Ge.25:30; 36:1, 8). The significant point is that these people traveled a great distance to reach Jesus.
- Crowds came from beyond Jordan, which refers to the populations who lived on the east side of the Jordan River (v.8c).
- Crowds came from the north, from the foreign land of Phoenicia and from the nation's two major cities, Tyre and Sidon (v.8d).

Scripture clearly states the reasons the crowds flocked to Jesus (v.8e). The people had heard what great things He did. They had heard the testimony of those who had seen and heard Jesus themselves or else had been told by others about Jesus. The testimony that the Messiah had come—the prophet who could meet the needs of mankind—spread like wild-fire. And when the people heard, many arose, packed their bags, and came to Him.

---

1 William Barclay, *The Gospel of Matthew*, Vol.1. "The Daily Study Bible.," (Philadelphia, PA: The Westminster Press, 1956), p.66.

THOUGHT 1. The importance of witnessing and talking about the marvelous work of God's grace is strongly seen in Jesus' ministry. How many more would be flocking to Jesus and following Him if we were more faithful in sharing the glorious salvation found in Him.

> Go therefore and make disciples of all nations, baptizing them in the name of the Father and of the Son and of the Holy Spirit, teaching them to observe all that I have commanded you. And behold, I am with you always, to the end of the age. (Mt.28:19–20)

> As he was getting into the boat, the man who had been possessed with demons begged him that he might be with him. And he did not permit him but said to him, "Go home to your friends and tell them how much the Lord has done for you, and how he has had mercy on you." (Mk.5:18–19)

> But you will receive power when the Holy Spirit has come upon you, and you will be my witnesses in Jerusalem and in all Judea and Samaria, and to the end of the earth. (Ac.1:8)

> But in your hearts honor Christ the Lord as holy, always being prepared to make a defense to anyone who asks you for a reason for the hope that is in you; yet do it with gentleness and respect, (1 Pe.3:15)

> That which we have seen and heard we proclaim also to you, so that you too may have fellowship with us; and indeed our fellowship is with the Father and with his Son Jesus Christ. (1 Jn.1:3)

b. Large crowds crushed in upon Him (vv.9–10).

Multitudes thronged Jesus, endangering His life to the point of nearly crushing Him (v.9). They just wanted to touch Him, hoping that some *power* from Him might flow through their body and meet their need (v.10). The needy people were so forceful that Jesus had to order a small boat to sit just a short distance off shore to rescue Him in case the aggressive crowd became too much for Him to handle.

THOUGHT 1. How desperately people need the same kind of fervor to seek after Jesus today. We desperately need to touch Jesus. We need the *virtue, the saving strength, of Jesus.*

> Ask, and it will be given to you; seek, and you will find; knock, and it will be opened to you. (Mt.7:7)

> And behold, a woman who had suffered from a discharge of blood for twelve years came up behind him and touched the fringe of his garment, for she said to herself, "If I only touch his garment, I will be made well." (Mt.9:20–21)

> But from there you will seek the LORD your God and you will find him, if you search after him with all your heart and with all your soul. (De.4:29)

> Seek the LORD and his strength; seek his presence continually! (Ps.105:4)

> Seek the LORD while he may be found; call upon him while he is near. (Is.55:6)

> You will seek me and find me, when you seek me with all your heart. (Je.29:13)

3:11–12

[11] And whenever the unclean spirits saw him, they fell down before him and cried out, "You are the Son of God."
[12] And he strictly ordered them not to make him known.

3 Jesus' impact upon evil spirits: A terrible fear.

Jesus' impact upon evil spirits was dramatic. His very presence struck a terrible fear within them. Demons are powerful beings, far more powerful than we are. Our Lord's power over evil spirits is both comforting and assuring to us who believe in Him (see note—Lk.8:26–39).

a. They were subject to Him (v.11a).

The evil spirits were subject to Jesus. When they saw Jesus, they immediately fell down before Him. They knew Him, for He had been the greater power in the spiritual world or dimension of being. They could do nothing beyond His control.

b. **They acknowledged His Messiahship (v.11b).**

The evil spirits confessed that Jesus is the Son of God (see note—Mk.1:23-24 for more discussion). They acknowledged His Messiahship. The crowd had pressed in to touch Jesus, hoping and praying for help; but the evil spirits fell down before Him, being stricken to acknowledge His deity. But note: they did not fall down out of devotion—not because they were seeking Him—but they fell down because they . . .

- acknowledged Him to be who He claimed to be.
- feared Him, lest He cast them out, sending them to their destined hell before the end time.

THOUGHT 1. Every evil person needs to fall down before Christ—fearing, standing in awe, and confessing lest they be condemned to hell.

> So everyone who acknowledges me before men, I also will acknowledge before my Father who is in heaven, but whoever denies me before men, I also will deny before my Father who is in heaven. (Mt.10:32-33)

> And I tell you, everyone who acknowledges me before men, the Son of Man also will acknowledge before the angels of God, (Lu.12:8)

> Because, if you confess with your mouth that Jesus is Lord and believe in your heart that God raised him from the dead, you will be saved. For with the heart one believes and is justified, and with the mouth one confesses and is saved. (Ro.10:9-10)

> Whoever confesses that Jesus is the Son of God, God abides in him, and he in God. (1 Jn.4:15)

c. **He rebuked the evil spirits' confession (v.12).**

Jesus rebuked the confession of the evil spirits (see note—Mk.1:25-26). He sternly warned them that they were not to tell who He was. Christ issued this order for at least two critical reasons:

First, it is Christ's desire that the *people* whose lives have been changed by Him testify of who He is. Jesus refused to have demons testifying of Him.

Second, the demons would testify of Jesus in order to harm Him and hinder His ministry. The evil spirits may have fallen down before Jesus in His presence, but their mission was to destroy Him and those whose lives He would impact.

THOUGHT 1. The confession Christ wants is the confession of a broken and contrite heart, a changed and repentant life.

> The LORD is near to the brokenhearted and saves the crushed in spirit. (Ps.34:18)

> The sacrifices of God are a broken spirit; a broken and contrite heart, O God, you will not despise. (Ps.51:17)

> For thus says the One who is high and lifted up, who inhabits eternity, whose name is Holy: "I dwell in the high and holy place, and also with him who is of a contrite and lowly spirit, to revive the spirit of the lowly, and to revive the heart of the contrite." (Is.57:15)

> All these things my hand has made, and so all these things came to be, declares the LORD. But this is the one to whom I will look: he who is humble and contrite in spirit and trembles at my word. (Is.66:2)

M. Jesus' Impact upon the Twelve Disciples: Calling Choice Men, 3:13–19

(Mt.10:1–4; Lu.6:12–19; Ac.1:13–14)

1. **Men called by Jesus**

2. **Men appointed by Jesus**
   a. To be with Him
   b. To be sent out
   c. To preach[DS1, 2]
   d. To receive authority, power[DS3]

3. **Men changed by Jesus**[DS4–14]

[13] And he went up on the mountain and called to him those whom he desired, and they came to him. [14] And he appointed twelve (whom he also named apostles) so that they might be with him and he might send them out to preach [15] and have authority to cast out demons. [16] He appointed the twelve: Simon (to whom he gave the name Peter); [17] James the son of Zebedee and John the brother of James (to whom he gave the name Boanerges, that is, Sons of Thunder); [18] Andrew, and Philip, and Bartholomew, and Matthew, and Thomas, and James the son of Alphaeus, and Thaddaeus, and Simon the Zealot, [19] and Judas Iscariot, who betrayed him.

Division II

The Son of God's Opening Ministry: Jesus' Immediate Impact, 1:21–3:35

M. Jesus' Impact upon the Twelve Disciples: Calling Choice Men, 3:13–19

(Mt.10:1–4; Lu.6:12–19; Ac.1:13–14)

3:13–19
Introduction

Jesus calls choice people—individuals with hearts that can be melted and molded—to serve Him in a special way. He calls and appoints teachable, pliable people, and He changes them. This is what this passage is all about. This is, *Jesus' Impact upon the Twelve Disciples: Calling Choice People,* 3:13–19

1. Men called by Jesus (v.13).
2. Men appointed by Jesus (vv.14–15).
3. Men changed by Jesus (vv.16–19).

3:13

[13] And he went up on the mountain and called to him those whom he desired, and they came to him.

1 Men called by Jesus.

The twelve disciples were *men called by Jesus.* Jesus called, picked out, and chose them for His special purpose. Many people followed Him, but a few showed more interest and commitment. He noticed the ones . . .

- who listened with more attention
- who were more awake and alert
- who responded with a stirred heart
- who showed more attachment to Him after the crowds had gone
- who wanted to serve God with meaning and purpose

Jesus did not look at people's stature and physical qualities, not at their appearance and looks, not even at their ability and education. Jesus looked at people's hearts. When He saw a person listening, stirred, attached, and wanting to serve, He called that person.

Scripture expressly states that Jesus called whom He *desired* or *wanted*. His will was *the active power*. They did not choose Him, but He chose them. He did not call those whom the world thought more suitable and educated. He called those whose hearts were right and responsive. He knew the heart, and His call was based on the principle of *heart response* (see Jn.15:16).

When Jesus called these men, they came to Him. *Came* (Gk. apelthon) means went away, went off, or departed. The idea is that they left, forsook, and went away from their former work to undertake the new work assigned by Jesus.

THOUGHT 1. If we desire to be used by Jesus in a special way, we need to be listening for His call, and we need to respond as the disciples responded. We must be willing to follow the Lord in whatever way He chooses, to make ourselves available to go where He wants us to go and to do what He wants us to do.

Many are never used by the Lord to the extent that He wants to use them because they are not willing to *come to Him* as the disciples did. That is, they are not willing to depart, to go off. They are not willing to leave behind whatever must be left behind to follow Jesus, be it a job, a home or hometown, family and friends, a comfortable lifestyle, or anything else.

Jesus chooses those whose hearts are totally committed to Him, those who are available and willing to sacrifice anything and everything to *come to Him*.

Peter began to say to him, "See, we have left everything and followed you." (Mk.10:28)

And when they had brought their boats to land, they left everything and followed him. After this he went out and saw a tax collector named Levi, sitting at the tax booth. And he said to him, "Follow me." And leaving everything, he rose and followed him. (Lu.5:11, 27–28)

And he said to all, "If anyone would come after me, let him deny himself and take up his cross daily and follow me. For whoever would save his life will lose it, but whoever loses his life for my sake will save it." (Lu.9:23–24)

So therefore, any one of you who does not renounce all that he has cannot be my disciple. (Lu.14:33)

And he said to them, "Truly, I say to you, there is no one who has left house or wife or brothers or parents or children, for the sake of the kingdom of God, who will not receive many times more in this time, and in the age to come eternal life." (Lu.18:29–30)

2 Men appointed by Jesus.

Not only were the disciples men called by Jesus, they were men appointed by Jesus. Mark mentions four specific purposes for which they were appointed (see Deeper Study # 1).

¹⁴ And he appointed twelve (whom he also named apostles) so that they might be with him and he might send them out to preach
¹⁵ and have authority to cast out demons.

a. To be with Him (v.14a).

The disciples were appointed *to be with Jesus*. This was the first lesson Jesus wanted to teach us: that God wants our personal fellowship and devotion before all else. God wants people to *know* Him, *believe* Him and *understand* Him above all else (Is.43:10). The disciples were to live in Jesus' presence, ever learning of Him and drawing their spiritual nourishment and strength from Him.

God is faithful, by whom you were called into the fellowship of his Son, Jesus Christ our Lord. (1 Co.1:9)

Indeed, I count everything as loss because of the surpassing worth of knowing Christ Jesus my Lord. For his sake I have suffered the loss of all things and count them as rubbish, in order that I may gain Christ . . . that I may know him and the power of his resurrection, and may share his sufferings, becoming like him in his death. (Ph.3:8, 10)

Behold, I stand at the door and knock. If anyone hears my voice and opens the door, I will come in to him and eat with him, and he with me. (Re.3:20)

"You are my witnesses," declares the LORD, "and my servant whom I have chosen, that you may know and believe me and understand that I am he. Before me no god was formed, nor shall there be any after me." (Is.43:10)

b. To be sent out (v.14b).

The disciples were appointed to be *sent out*. They were to be Jesus' ambassadors, His representatives who moved out into the world. They were appointed for the purpose of representing Him among the people of the world (see DEEPER STUDY # 5—Mt.10:2 for discussion).

But rise and stand upon your feet, for I have appeared to you for this purpose, to appoint you as a servant and witness to the things in which you have seen me and to those in which I will appear to you. (Ac.26:16)

Therefore, we are ambassadors for Christ, God making his appeal through us. We implore you on behalf of Christ, be reconciled to God. (2 Co.5:20)

c. To preach (v.14c).

The disciples were appointed *to preach*. They were to be the heralds, the messengers of Jesus Christ. Jesus had a message for the world, and they were to proclaim His message to the world (see DEEPER STUDIES 1, 2; DEEPER STUDY # 1—Ro.1:1-7 for discussion).

And proclaim as you go, saying, 'The kingdom of heaven is at hand.' (Mt.10:7)

And he said to them, "Go into all the world and proclaim the gospel to the whole creation." (Mk.16:15)

And he sent them out to proclaim the kingdom of God and to heal. (Lu.9:2)

For if I preach the gospel, that gives me no ground for boasting. For necessity is laid upon me. Woe to me if I do not preach the gospel! (1 Co.9:16)

If I say, "I will not mention him, or speak any more in his name," there is in my heart as it were a burning fire shut up in my bones, and I am weary with holding it in, and I cannot. (Je.20:9)

The lion has roared; who will not fear? The Lord GOD has spoken; who can but prophesy? (Am.3:8)

d. To receive authority, power (v.15).

The disciples were appointed to *receive authority* or *power*. Jesus would give them the power to do works that no human authority can genuinely authorize or perform: to heal sicknesses and to cast out devils (see DEEPER STUDY # 3; note and DEEPER STUDIES 1, 2, 3—Mt.10:1 for discussion).

Behold, I have given you authority to tread on serpents and scorpions, and over all the power of the enemy, and nothing shall hurt you. Nevertheless, do not rejoice in this, that the spirits are subject to you, but rejoice that your names are written in heaven. (Lu.10:19-20)

But you will receive power when the Holy Spirit has come upon you, and you will be my witnesses in Jerusalem and in all Judea and Samaria, and to the end of the earth. (Ac.1:8)

And with great power the apostles were giving their testimony to the resurrection of the Lord Jesus, and great grace was upon them all. (Ac.4:33)

But they could not withstand the wisdom and the Spirit with which he was speaking. (Ac.6:10)

And what is the immeasurable greatness of his power toward us who believe, according to the working of his great might. (Ep.1:19)

Now to him who is able to do far more abundantly than all that we ask or think, according to the power at work within us. (Ep.3:20)

DEEPER STUDY # 1

(3:14) **Appointed—Ordained** (epoiesen; pronounced *ep-oi'-ay-sen*): *to be made* or *appointed*. The word is taken from the Greek word *poieo* which means *to do, to make, to appoint with credentials*. The word is often used to refer to a person being appointed to some high position or office. The picture is that of Jesus Christ, the Son of God, the King of the universe, taking twelve men and appointing them to the *office* of being His ministers and representatives on earth.

DEEPER STUDY # 2

(3:14) **Preach** (kerusso): to be a herald; to proclaim; to publish; to evangelize. The word carries with it the idea of intense feeling, gravity, and authority—so much so that it *must* be listened to and heeded. The person who preaches is the herald of Jesus Christ; that is, his message is to be the message of Christ, not of someone else. The herald does not share his own opinions and views; He *proclaims* the truth of Jesus Christ (see DEEPER STUDY # 5—Mt.10:2 for more discussion).

DEEPER STUDY # 3

(3:15) **Authority (Power)—Sicknesses—Demons:** the *Textus Receptus* Greek text includes the phrase *to heal sicknesses* (therepeuein tas nosous). Accordingly, the King James Version, New King James Version, Young's Literal Translation, and other English Bible translations from the *Textus Receptus* include this phrase. Throughout the Gospels, a distinction is commonly made between sickness and demon possession.

Note two significant facts about the word "authority" or "power":

1. The word for power here is not "*dunamis," the supernatural power of God*. It is "*exousia*," *a delegated power* or *authority*. The servant of God is not given the power of God to use as the servant wills, but the servant is given the authority to specifically minister by healing and casting out demons. The servant prays and speaks the word, and then God does the actual healing and casting out of the demon.

2. The emphasis of this delegated authority is casting out demons. The servant of Christ is given authority to cast out the evil spirits that rule people's lives. Note that the spiritual world or dimension of being is here acknowledged.

> **Whoever makes a practice of sinning is of the devil, for the devil has been sinning from the beginning. The reason the Son of God appeared was to destroy the works of the devil. (1 Jn.3:8)**

3 Men changed by Jesus.

The disciples were *men changed by Jesus*. But it is critical to keep in mind that each man had to be *willing* to be changed. One was not willing, Judas Iscariot. Jesus called them all, but only the ones willing to be changed were changed (see DEEPER STUDIES 4-14).

> **You did not choose me, but I chose you and appointed you that you should go and bear fruit and that your fruit should abide, so that whatever you ask the Father in my name, he may give it to you. (Jn.15:16)**

> **I appeal to you therefore, brothers, by the mercies of God, to present your bodies as a living sacrifice, holy and acceptable to God, which is your spiritual worship. Do not be conformed**

16 He appointed the twelve: Simon (to whom he gave the name Peter);

17 James the son of Zebedee and John the brother of James (to whom he gave the name Boanerges, that is, Sons of Thunder);

18 Andrew, and Philip, and Bartholomew, and Matthew, and Thomas, and James the son of Alphaeus, and Thaddaeus, and Simon the Zealot,

19 and Judas Iscariot, who betrayed him.

to this world, but be transformed by the renewal of your mind, that by testing you may discern what is the will of God, what is good and acceptable and perfect. (Ro.12:1–2)

Therefore, if anyone is in Christ, he is a new creation. The old has passed away; behold, the new has come. (2 Co.5:17)

DEEPER STUDY # 4

(3:16) **Simon—Peter (Greek, petros)—Cephas (Aramaic, kepha)**: Peter was a rough-hewn fisherman. He looked, acted, and spoke like any professional fisherman at the dock of a large lake or sea. Anyone who has been around a fisherman's dock or boat can picture Peter.

1. Peter had many commendable strengths.
   a. Peter was self-sacrificing, giving up all—even his home and business—to follow Jesus (see notes—Mk.1:16–18; Mt.8:14).
   b. Peter was spiritual-minded. He was the first to genuinely grasp who Jesus was (Mt.16:16–19).
   c. Peter was childlike and humble, often responding and leaping out to Jesus as a child does to his father (Mt.14:26–29; Mk.11:21; Jn.13:6–11).
   d. Peter was trusting, sometimes casting his whole being upon Jesus (Mt.14:26–29).
   e. Peter was tenderhearted and loving, caring deeply for his Lord (Mt.26:75; Jn.21:15–17).
   f. Peter was courageous, the only disciple who defended Jesus against arrest. He was also one of the two disciples who followed Jesus through His trials and crucifixion, although he followed *afar off* (Mt.26:51, 58).
   g. Peter would have been judged a hard-working, industrious man in any society.
2. Peter had some glaring weaknesses.
   a. Peter was prideful and presumptuous, a man who thought he knew best and who sometimes lorded it over others. He was always depending on human wisdom and strength, the arm of the flesh.
      - Peter thought he knew what was best for Jesus, insisting that Jesus did not have to die (Mt.16:22–23).
      - Peter tried to prevent Jesus' arrest by drawing his sword and wounding one of the arresting party (Mt.26:51; Mk.14:47; Lu.22:50).
      - Peter rebuked Jesus, overstepping the limits of his rights. When the crowd thronged Jesus, Jesus simply asked who had touched Him. Peter rebuked Jesus for asking such a question when there were so many people pressing in upon them (Lu.8:45).
      - Peter, in a self-abasing pride, refused to let Jesus wash his feet (Jn.13:6–11).
   b. Peter was slow to learn and to understand truth (Mt.15:15–16).
   c. Peter was self-seeking (Mt.19:27).
   d. Peter was disbelieving (Mt.14:30).
   e. Peter was overbearing, even to the point of instructing Jesus (Mt.16:22–23).
   f. Peter had a weak, cowardly trait, being the only disciple to vocally deny Jesus (Mt.26:69–74).
3. A chart showing some of the strengths and weaknesses of Peter can be pictured as follows:

• self-sacrificing (Mt.1:16–18; Mk.8:14)	• yet slow to learn spiritual truth (Mt.15:15–16)
• spiritual minded (Mt.16:16–19)	• yet presumptuous and prideful (Mt.16:22–23; 26:51; Lu.8:45)
• childlike and humble (Mk.11:21; Jn.13:6–11)	
• trusting (Mt.14:26–29)	• yet disbelieving (Mt.14:30)
• tenderhearted and loving (Mt.26:75; Jn.21:15–17)	• yet overbearing (Mt.16:22–23; 26:51)
• courageous (Mt.26:51; 26:58)	• yet cowardly (Mt.26:69–74)
• yet self-seeking (Mt.19:27)	

Peter was changed dramatically after Jesus' resurrection and after Pentecost. The presence of the living Lord in his life empowered him to great heights of sacrificial service to Christ. Peter was able to take charge of the frightened band of disciples and lead them to fearlessly proclaim the glorious news of the risen Savior (see note—Mt.8:14 and Master Subject Index for additional information on Peter).

DEEPER STUDY # 5

(3:17) **James and John:** these two men were brothers. They were the sons of Zebedee, likely a prosperous fisherman and a man of high social position. Apparently he was well acquainted with the High Priest and his household, probably providing fish for the palace. Their mother was Salome, who is thought by many to be the sister of Mary, the mother of Jesus. James and John were men of *stormy tempers*, so much so that Jesus called them the *sons of thunder*. Their tempers are seen when they ask Jesus to destroy a Samaritan village with fire for rejecting Him (Lu.9:54).

The two brothers were also gripped by *worldly ambition*. They wanted the highest offices in the coming kingdom of Jesus (Mt.20:20-21). However, Jesus dramatically changed the two men, transforming their stormy tempers into a burning zeal and ambition for God. They became two of the greatest witnesses for God ever known. James became the first of the twelve to be martyred, and John was the longest living disciple—becoming one of the greatest literary giants of all time (*The Gospel of John, The Three Epistles of John,* and *The Revelation*) (see notes—Mk.1:20; 10:35-45; DEEPER STUDY # 1—Lu.5:10. See Introduction—The Gospel of *John* and *Revelation*).

DEEPER STUDY # 6

(3:18) **Andrew:** Andrew was apparently the first disciple of our Lord. He had been a disciple of John the Baptist, longing for the Messianic hope. However, when John pointed out that Jesus was the Messiah, Andrew requested an interview with Jesus. From that point on, he was convinced that Jesus was the true Messiah, and Jesus granted him a very special friendship (Mk.13:3; Jn.1:35-37). Jesus met his craving for the Messianic hope and enlarged his gifts of love and caring (see Jn.1:41; 6:8-9; 12:21-22). Andrew was always helping people (Jn.6:8-9; 12:21-22).

Tradition says Andrew preached in Jerusalem and was crucified for preaching against idolatry. He was hung on a cross in the shape of an X.

DEEPER STUDY # 7

(3:18) **Philip:** Philip did not seek Jesus, but Jesus sought Philip (Jn.1:43f). This indicates that Philip was slow in responding and believing, and he almost missed the opportunity to become an apostle of Jesus. In fact, being slow to respond and fearing to act seem to be Philip's major weaknesses. He actually did miss the opportunity to demonstrate great faith when Jesus tested his faith in feeding the multitude. He was also slow in responding when some Greeks wanted to interview Jesus (Jn.12:21-22). Again, he was slow in understanding who Jesus was (Jn.14:8f). His faith and willingness to act were in constant need of being stirred and strengthened. Jesus changed him and made him a man of strong faith. This is seen in that he stood fast and fearless even in the face of martyrdom. Tradition tells us that he died as a martyr at Hierapolis.

DEEPER STUDY # 8

(3:18) **Bartholomew—Nathanael:** little is known about this disciple other than what is given by John (see outline, notes and DEEPER STUDIES 1, 2—Jn.1:46-49).

DEEPER STUDY # 9

(3:18) **Matthew—Levi:** Matthew was a tax collector, an outcast of society, a traitor to the Jewish people. He felt the alienation and rejection from his people ever so deeply. Yet Jesus took Matthew, changed His life, and met every need of his heart (see notes and DEEPER STUDY # 1—Mt.9:9-13; DEEPER STUDY # 1—Mk.2:14; see Introduction—The Gospel of Matthew).

DEEPER STUDY # 10

(3:18) **Thomas—Didymus** (meaning the *twin*): Thomas was a man of courage and loyalty. This is seen in his suggestion that the disciples follow Jesus even if it meant death (Jn.11:8, 16). But he was also a skeptic, a pessimist, a doubter. He was slow to understand Jesus' Messiahship (Jn.14:5-6), and he rejected the testimony of others that Jesus had actually risen from the dead (see outline and notes—Jn.20:24-29). However, the resurrection of Jesus changed Thomas—changed him completely. He has given to the world one of the strongest testimonies possible (Jn.20:28).

Tradition says that Thomas went to Parthia (India), carrying the gospel to that great continent. He is said to have died a martyr's death.

DEEPER STUDY # 11

(3:18) **James, the son of Alphaeus:** little is known about this James.
- His father was Alphaeus or Clopas (Jn.19:25).
- His mother was one of the women who stood by the cross and visited the tomb of Jesus (Jn.19:25).
- He had a brother, Joses, who was also a follower of Jesus (Mk.15:40; 16:1; Jn.19:25).

It is interesting to note that Matthew's father was also named Alphaeus. Thus, it is possible that James and Matthew were brothers. Tradition says that James was a tax collector just like Matthew. If true, this would give weight to their being brothers.

James was willing to be changed by Jesus, to become a true disciple of the Lord's. He did not forsake the disciples after the crucifixion but stayed right with them. Therefore, he was present when Jesus appeared to the disciples after His resurrection and began transforming the disciples into dynamic witnesses for Him.

DEEPER STUDY # 12

(3:18) **Thaddaeus—Lebbaeus—Judas (not Iscariot), Son or Brother (KJV) of James:** little is known about Thaddaeus. His name (Thaddaeus) means *breast* or *one that praises* or *man of heart.* The fact that Matthew and Mark call him by the name Thaddaeus, the man of heart, reveals that he was a man with a big heart, one who gave of himself to help and minister to others. The presence of the living Lord in his heart and life could only enlarge such a heart.

DEEPER STUDY # 13

(3:18) **Simon the Canaanite—Simon the Zealot:** Simon was a member of the fanatical Jewish party known as the Zealots. The party held that God alone was to be the Ruler and Lord of the Jewish nation. They hated and bitterly opposed all foreign (Roman) domination. They preached and led revolutionary uprisings against the government when they could be formed.

The power of Jesus to change a man's heart is seen in Simon the Zealot. Simon's fanatical devotion turned him into a zealot for Jesus. Note that he never changed the description of his fanatical nature. Even after his conversion and call, he still wanted his zeal to be known. He still wanted to be known as Simon the Zealot, one who was totally devoted to Jesus Christ, the true Messiah.

DEEPER STUDY # 14

(3:19) **Judas Iscariot:** Very simply, Judas was unwilling to have his heart and life changed by Jesus (see outlines and notes—Mt.26:14-16, 20-25; 27:3-5; Master Subject Index for discussion).

1. **The crowd: Was so zealous for Jesus that He was unable to eat**

2. **The friends or family: Acted in opposition to Jesus**
   a. Heard of His behavior
   b. Thought Him insane
   c. Sought custody

[20] Then he went home, and the crowd gathered again, so that they could not even eat.
[21] And when his family heard it, they went out to seize him, for they were saying, "He is out of his mind."

Division II

The Son of God's Opening Ministry: Jesus' Immediate Impact, 1:21–3:35

N. Jesus' Impact upon Friends: Calling Jesus Mad and Insane, 3:20–21

3:20–21
Introduction

Throughout history, no individual has been as misunderstood or misjudged as Jesus. As this passage records, even some close to Jesus did not understand Him. Thinking Him to be insane, they went out to forcefully take Him into their custody.

There is no noun in the Greek text to identify exactly who these people were who went out to seize Jesus. Consequently, Bible translations and commentators vary. The King James Version is probably correct in using "friends" here instead of family. Jesus' impact upon His family is discussed in Mark 3:31. This is, *Jesus' Impact upon Friends: Calling Jesus Mad and Insane, 3:20–21.*
1. The crowd: Was so zealous for Jesus that He was unable to eat (v.20).
2. The friends or family: Acted in opposition to Jesus (v.21).

3:20

[20] Then he went home, and the crowd gathered again, so that they could not even eat.

1 The crowd: Was so zealous for Jesus that He was unable to eat.

The zeal and enthusiasm of the crowd for Christ was great, so great that He was not able to take time to tend to His personal needs. He could not even find time to eat (see DEEPER STUDY # 1).

Jesus had not called for the crowd to come; they just came. They filled the house, overflowing into the street. Some had come more out of curiosity than need, but others had come to hear and learn. Still others had come to be helped and healed.

As stated, the crowd was so large and pressuring that Christ and the disciples were unable to take care of their physical needs. However, Christ did not turn the crowd away; neglecting His personal needs, He ministered to them.

THOUGHT 1. Zeal and enthusiasm for Christ are so desperately lacking. People should be flocking to Him by the multitudes, but they are not. Why?
- Do they love the world and the things of the world too much (1 Jn.2:15–16)?
- Do they love the flesh and its feelings too much?
- Do they love pride and fame and power too much?

- Do they just not know? Have they not heard (Ro.10:14–15)?
- Is the witness and life of believers too weak (Ep.4:17–24)?

THOUGHT 2. Christ ministered despite enormous inconvenience and disruption. A unique opportunity presented itself, and He grasped it. He denied Himself, His own needs, in order to help others. What a lesson for us!

> Come to me, all who labor and are heavy laden, and I will give you rest. (Mt.11:28)
>
> The Spirit and the Bride say, "Come." And let the one who hears say, "Come." And let the one who is thirsty come; let the one who desires take the water of life without price. (Re.22:17)
>
> Come, everyone who thirsts, come to the waters; and he who has no money, come, buy and eat! Come, buy wine and milk without money and without price. (Is.55:1)

DEEPER STUDY # 1

(3:20-21) **Response to Jesus Christ:** from this point to the end of the chapter Mark contrasts the feelings of the crowd and the feelings of others about Jesus. In verse 20 he first conveys the feelings and the support of the multitude. Then he contrasts the feelings of three groups who should have been the very ones to support Jesus. There are the contrasted feelings . . .

- of His friends—who charged Him with being mad and insane (Mk.3:21)
- of the religionists—who charged Him with being demon-possessed (Mk.3:22-30)
- of His very own family—who charged Him with being an embarrassment (Mk.3:31-35)

In Mark 3:20-21, the contrast between the feelings of the multitude and Jesus' friends is clearly seen. This contrast holds many lessons for us.

2 The friends or family: Acted in opposition to Jesus.

3:21

The way Jesus was treated by some friends (or family) differed enormously from the way the crowd treated Him. Whereas the crowd responded to Jesus, some friends heard of His behavior and concluded that He was insane, so they sought to take custody of Him. Apparently the friends were close to the family; therefore, they cared deeply for Jesus. They felt He was in danger and wanted to help the family and Him.

21 And when his family heard it, they went out to seize him, for they were saying, "He is out of his mind."

a. Heard of His behavior.

Some of Jesus' friends heard about what was going on. In the Greek *heard* (akousantes) is a participle, meaning "having heard." The idea is that the friends heard not only about the enormous crowds, but they heard *all about Jesus*: His amazing miracles, claims, and teachings; the prophetic esteem which the people heaped upon Him; the opposition which was now threatening His life.

b. Thought Him insane.

All this led the friends of the family to think Jesus was insane—mentally unfit or incapable of sound behavior. At least seven factors contributed to their conclusion of insanity.

First, they thought Jesus was insane because of the zeal and enthusiasm of the crowd. They assumed that the crowd's zeal had turned His head and caused Him to overly evaluate Himself. From their perspective, He was reveling in the crowd's attention and adulation. It was reported that Jesus was so caught up in the multitude's enthusiasm that He was neglecting the care of His body, even to the point of not eating meals.

Second, they thought Jesus was insane because of the response of the people and the esteem with which they held Him. They thought that such esteem had twisted His mind, causing Him to think too highly of Himself. There were reports that He was claiming to be the Messiah and even the Son of God Himself.

Third, they thought Jesus was mentally unfit because He was selecting an odd band of disciples: rough-hewn fishermen (Peter, James, and John); despised sinners and publicans (Matthew and probably James, the son of Alphaeus); a revolutionary zealot (Simon the Zealot); a seeker who was spiritually troubled (Nathaniel). A sane man set on religious purposes would never choose such men, not if he wished to succeed in society.

Fourth, they thought Jesus was insane because His life and behavior were so radically different from normal life and behavior. What He was doing and saying was diametrically opposed to the way anything had ever been done before. He differed so much from everyone else. His very life convicted any who confronted Him, and His words demanded either acceptance or rejection.

Fifth, they thought Jesus was insane because the authorities were opposing and threatening to kill Him, yet He refused to back down or flee. He even refused to move elsewhere. A normal person who had a mission to accomplish would at least flee elsewhere until he had time to regroup and plan some other way to achieve his purpose.

Sixth, they thought Jesus was insane because His healing ministry necessitated some explanation. There were so many healings, so many miraculous events, that a person was forced to come up with some theory to explain them. Jesus was either who He claimed to be, the Son of God; or He was filled with a supernatural spirit other than God's, a spirit that made Him crazy, the spirit of the devil. All kinds of theories were now running rampant. There were the theories that He was . . .

- John the Baptist raised from the dead (Mt.14:1–2)
- Elijah, Jeremiah, or some prophet sent back to life (Mt.16:14)
- Beelzebub (Mt.12:22–32; Mk.3:22–30).
- insane (Mk.3:21).

Seventh, they thought Jesus was mentally incompetent because His teaching and doctrine were so different from anyone else's. In fact, what He taught often radically differed from all that *had ever* been taught.

c. **Sought custody.**

Convinced that Jesus was insane, these people, whether friends or family, sought custody of Jesus. Their intention was to *seize* (kratesai; pronounced *kra-tay'-sigh*) Jesus—to take Him by force, against His will. While their conclusion was unquestionably wrong—Jesus was not insane—their hearts appear to be in the right place. Most likely, they thought they were protecting Jesus and acting in His best interests.

THOUGHT 1. Is Jesus truly the Son of God, as He claimed? Think of the alternatives:
1) He was devil-possessed; that is, His power came from an evil spirit.
2) He was insane, mad, mentally deceived, and deranged.
3) He was deliberately lying about being the Son of God, deliberately deceiving people in order to secure a following to boost His ego.

As many have said (most famously C. S. Lewis in *Mere Christianity*), Jesus must either be a liar or a lunatic or else Lord of lords. The call of the hour is: "Believe Jesus. Trust Him. He was not insane. He is truly the Son of the living God."

And those in the boat worshiped him, saying, "Truly you are the Son of God." (Mt.14:33)

The beginning of the gospel of Jesus Christ, the Son of God. (Mk.1:1)

And I have seen and have borne witness that this is the Son of God. (Jn.1:34)

For God so loved the world, that he gave his only Son, that whoever believes in him should not perish but have eternal life. For God did not send his Son into the world to condemn the world, but in order that the world might be saved through him. Whoever believes in him is

not condemned, but whoever does not believe is condemned already, because he has not believed in the name of the only Son of God. (Jn.3:16–18)

She said to him, "Yes, Lord; I believe that you are the Christ, the Son of God, who is coming into the world." (Jn.11:25–27)

Whoever confesses that Jesus is the Son of God, God abides in him, and he in God. (1 Jn.4:15)

THOUGHT 2. Friends can be wrong, no matter how much they esteem and love us. What they think and how they treat us can often be wrong. Even the friends of Jesus were wrong about Him.

THOUGHT 3. There are times when we must go against friends and family; we must vigorously surrender to God and do His will regardless of what our friends or family may think. If God calls us to serve Him, then serve Him we must. Friends and family can oppose God's will. They may have good intentions, but they cannot know God's will for another person's life. God deals, calls, and works with each of us individually and personally. We need to always be strong and stand firm in God's call and will—always.

After this many of his disciples turned back and no longer walked with him. So Jesus said to the twelve, "Do you want to go away as well?" Simon Peter answered him, "Lord, to whom shall we go? You have the words of eternal life." (Jn.6:66–68)

You did not choose me, but I chose you and appointed you that you should go and bear fruit and that your fruit should abide, so that whatever you ask the Father in my name, he may give it to you. (Jn.15:16)

But the Lord said to him, "Go, for he is a chosen instrument of mine to carry my name before the Gentiles and kings and the children of Israel." (Ac.9:15)

I appeal to you therefore, brothers, by the mercies of God, to present your bodies as a living sacrifice, holy and acceptable to God, which is your spiritual worship. Do not be conformed to this world, but be transformed by the renewal of your mind, that by testing you may discern what is the will of God, what is good and acceptable and perfect. (Ro.12:1–2)

Therefore, my beloved brothers, be steadfast, immovable, always abounding in the work of the Lord, knowing that in the Lord your labor is not in vain. (1 Co.15:58)

O. Jesus' Impact upon Religionists:
Calling Jesus Demon-Possessed, 3:22–30

(Mt.12:22–32; Lu.11:14–20)

1. **The setting: An investigative committee of Scribes gave their opinion about Jesus**
   a. The terrible charge: He is demon-possessed[DS1,2]
   b. The rebuttal by Jesus: A logical question

2. **Jesus' 1st rebuttal: Internal strife always divides and destroys**
   a. Internal strife destroys a kingdom
   b. Internal strife destroys a house

   c. Conclusion: Satan would be destroying his own kingdom

3. **Jesus' 2nd rebuttal: Satan's house (kingdom) has been broken into, and he has been made powerless, He.2:14–15**

4. **Jesus' 3rd rebuttal: God's love and forgiveness are universal**

5. **Jesus' 4th rebuttal: There is one danger, the unpardonable sin—blaspheming the Holy Spirit, continuing to reject God and ascribing His work to the devil**

22 And the scribes who came down from Jerusalem were saying, "He is possessed by Beelzebul," and "by the prince of demons he casts out the demons."

23 And he called them to him and said to them in parables, "How can Satan cast out Satan?"
24 "If a kingdom is divided against itself, that kingdom cannot stand.

25 And if a house is divided against itself, that house will not be able to stand.
26 And if Satan has risen up against himself and is divided, he cannot stand, but is coming to an end."
27 "But no one can enter a strong man's house and plunder his goods, unless he first binds the strong man. Then indeed he may plunder his house."
28 "Truly, I say to you, all sins will be forgiven the children of man, and whatever blasphemies they utter,"
29 "but whoever blasphemes against the Holy Spirit never has forgiveness, but is guilty of an eternal sin"—
30 for they were saying, "He has an unclean spirit."

Division II

The Son of God's Opening Ministry: Jesus' Immediate Impact, 1:21–3:35

O. Jesus' Impact upon Religionists: Calling Jesus Demon-Possessed, 3:22–30

(Mt.12:22–32; Lu.11:14–20)

3:22–30
Introduction

Who was Jesus Christ? Was He really of God, or was He of the devil? That is, was He evil, an imposter, a deceiver who set out to mislead the world into thinking that He was the Son of God? Is belief in Him really the only way to God? Are His teachings the *only way* to live and to experience deliverance now and eternally?

The religionists—Jewish religious leaders—of Jesus' day believed He was evil. In fact, they believed He was an embodiment of Satan himself. This passage discusses their charge and Jesus' answer. And it challenges people to believe the truth about Jesus. This is, *Jesus' Impact upon Religionists: Calling Jesus Demon-Possessed*, 3:22-30.

1. The setting: An investigative committee of Scribes gave their opinion about Jesus (vv.22-23).
2. Jesus' first rebuttal: Internal strife always divides and destroys (vv.24-26).
3. Jesus' second rebuttal: Satan's house (kingdom) has been broken into, and he has been made powerless, He.2:14-15 (v.27).
4. Jesus' third rebuttal: God's love and forgiveness are universal (v.28).
5. Jesus' fourth rebuttal: There is one danger, the unpardonable sin—blaspheming the Holy Spirit, continuing to reject God, and ascribing His work to the devil (vv.29-30).

1 The setting: An investigative committee of Scribes gave their opinion about Jesus.

A group of Scribes came down from Jerusalem to investigate Jesus. After observing Him and His ministry, they gave their judgment about Jesus (see notes—Mk.2:6-7; 3:1-2).

> 22 And the scribes who came down from Jerusalem were saying, "He is possessed by Beelzebul," and "by the prince of demons he casts out the demons."
>
> 23 And he called them to him and said to them in parables, "How can Satan cast out Satan?"

a. The terrible charge: He is demon-possessed (v.22).

The Scribes levied a terrible charge against the Messiah: He was possessed by Beelzebub (see DEEPER STUDY # 1). *Is possessed by* or *He has* (Gk. echei) means that He was *indwelt, controlled, under the supreme power* of Beelzebub, the supernatural power of evil. They were not saying that Jesus was in alliance with the devil. Their charge went much farther than an alliance. They were saying that Jesus was an incarnation of evil, of the devil himself.

The Gospels reveal that the religionists and people were vicious in their accusations against Jesus (see DEEPER STUDY # 2):

- They said He had a demon and was insane (Jn.10:20).
- They called Him a Samaritan (a racial epithet) and said He had a devil (Jn.8:48).
- They suggested He was born out of wedlock—a cause of great reproach and discrimination in the culture (Mt.1:18-19; Jn.8:41).
- They called Him a glutton, a drunkard, and a friend of [cohabiter with] sinners (Lu.7:34).

The religionists attacked Jesus so viciously because they could not deny His power: lives were being dramatically and radically changed; evil spirits were being cast out of people. This should not have prompted the religionists to accuse Jesus of being demon-possessed, for exorcism, the casting out of evil spirits, was neither a new nor unusual thing to the people of Jesus' day.

- Jesus referred to Jewish exorcists (Mt.12:27; Lu.11:19).
- The disciples referred to a man who professed to be a follower of Jesus and who was casting out demons in Jesus' name (Mk.9:38).
- There was a Jewish priest who had seven sons, and each of the sons claimed to be an exorcist (Ac.19:13-16).

The religionists were without excuse. They should have understood exorcism. The presence of evil spirits and men's attempting to cast them out were common enough occurrences for them to understand what Jesus was doing (see DEEPER STUDY # 4—Mt.12:24; 12:27-28).

The point is this: exorcism was not a *new* thing, but what Jesus was doing was new. Others were not always successful in casting out evil spirits. They failed, lacked permanent and perfect power to overcome the world of evil—but not Jesus. His power was universal and perfect, always effective. By just speaking a simple word, He produced the most powerful results imaginable. Evil spirits within people—spirits which corrupted their lives—were cast out, and the people were dramatically and forcefully changed.

The religionists could not deny this fact. They had to deal with the matter of Jesus' power. Some explanation, some theory had to be given. Their conclusion was that He was possessed by Beelzebub himself, the ruler of the demons, and He cast out demons by Beelzebub's power.

The religionists were deliberately trying to disprove Jesus' claim to be the Messiah, the Son of God. If they could prove He was an imposter, a fraud, a deceiver, an evil man misleading others, a man linked to evil and to the devil, then His claims would be refuted, and the people would stop following Him (see notes—Mt.12:1-8; 12:9-13; note and Deeper Study # 1—12:10).

b. The rebuttal by Jesus: A logical question (v.23).

Jesus had to answer the Scribes' outrageous charge. His rebuttal was a forceful argument. He asked *the logical and irrefutable* question: "How can Satan cast out Satan?" The answer was unavoidable: Satan would never cast out evil. If he did, he would be working against himself, and that is not his purpose. He is out to establish and expand evil, not to destroy it. To say otherwise is illogical; it does not make sense. Jesus proceeded to offer four rebuttals to prove His point (see outline and notes of this passage).

DEEPER STUDY # 1

(3:22) **Beelzebub:** an idol god of the ancient Philistines. The name means *the god of flies*. But the Jews called the idol *the god of filth* or *the god of dung* (Beelzebub). The name was eventually ascribed to Satan as the prince of unclean spirits (see Deeper Study # 1—Rev.12:9).

DEEPER STUDY # 2

(3:22) **Religionists—Jesus Christ, Opposed:** the religionists were bitter, stinging, rough, and cutting in their accusations against Jesus.

Why did the religionists (strict adherents to a religion; in relation to Jesus, Pharisees, Sadducees, and Scribes) oppose Jesus so vehemently? There were several reasons.

1. Religion gives a sense of security. It makes people secure and comfortable with themselves. Therefore, a truly professional and committed religionist opposes anything that threatens the security he or she has found.

2. Religionists oppose change. All true religionists believe *their* way is the way, the truth, and the life. There is no reason to change so long as one's needs are being met.

3. Religion can lead to position, pride, and a sense of importance. One of the most difficult things in the world is for people to give up their position and admit they are wrong. To do so is to deny their importance. Think about it—for this is exactly what Christ demands of every person (Lu.9:23). This is the reason so many of the gifted and the powerful of the world reject Christ and become hostile to Him (see outline—1 Co.1:26-31).

3:24-26

24 "If a kingdom is divided against itself, that kingdom cannot stand.
25 And if a house is divided against itself, that house will not be able to stand.
26 And if Satan has risen up against himself and is divided, he cannot stand, but is coming to an end."

2 Jesus' first rebuttal: Internal strife always divides and destroys.

Jesus' first rebuttal to the Scribe's slanderous accusation was that internal strife always divides and destroys. He gave two examples to reinforce His point (see note—Mt.12:25-26 for a more detailed explanation of this point).

a. Internal strife destroys a kingdom (v.24).

A kingdom divided against itself cannot stand. Civil war, internal strife, and divisiveness will cause a kingdom or nation to fall. It cannot last, not if its subjects fight among themselves.

b. Internal strife destroys a house (v.25).

A house divided against itself cannot stand. Constant bickering and arguing will cause the home to crumble. A family cannot last, not if its members strive, quarrel, and fight all the time. The house will break up.

c. Conclusion: Satan would be destroying his own kingdom (v.26).

If Satan were empowering Jesus to cast out demons, he would be rising up against himself. He would be casting out his own evil spirits and destroying his own kingdom of evil subjects. He would be breaking his rule and reign over lives.

There is no conceivable way Jesus is from anywhere other than from God. He had nothing whatsoever to do with evil or evil spirits, except to cast them out of people's lives. He came to free people in bondage to evil so that they might live righteously and godly in this present world. He is *God's* representative among humanity, not Satan's. He is exactly who He claims to be, the Son of God Himself. *To argue any other position is illogical.* (Again, see note—Mt.12:25-26 for a detailed discussion and application of this point. Also see note, Thought 1—Mk.3:21 for Jesus' claim to be the Son of God. See note—Jn.1:34 for many of the verses referring to Jesus as the Son of God.)

> **Whoever believes in him is not condemned, but whoever does not believe is condemned already, because he has not believed in the name of the only Son of God. (Jn.3:18)**

> **"Do you say of him whom the Father consecrated and sent into the world, 'You are blaspheming,' because I said, 'I am the Son of God'? If I am not doing the works of my Father, then do not believe me; but if I do them, even though you do not believe me, believe the works, that you may know and understand that the Father is in me and I am in the Father." (Jn.10:36-38)**

> **How much worse punishment, do you think, will be deserved by the one who has trampled underfoot the Son of God, and has profaned the blood of the covenant by which he was sanctified, and has outraged the Spirit of grace? (He.10:29)**

3 Jesus' second rebuttal: Satan's house (kingdom) has been broken into, and he has been made powerless (He.2:14-15).

3:27

The second rebuttal by Jesus is that Satan's kingdom had been breached. God had broken into Satan's house and kingdom by using the power of Christ to free those enslaved by Satan. Just as an invader enters a strong man's house, ties him up, and then steals his possessions, so Jesus has now invaded Satan's kingdom of evil. Christ is now setting people free, free from evil spirits. Satan is now being conquered. The power of Christ is now delivering people from the world and the enslavement of evil. They can now be set free from evil—even from the evil of death itself (see 1 Co.15:20-58; Col.2:15; Heb.2:14-15; see note—Mt.12:29 for a detailed discussion of this point).

27 "But no one can enter a strong man's house and plunder his goods, unless he first binds the strong man. Then indeed he may plunder his house."

> **Jesus answered, "This voice has come for your sake, not mine. Now is the judgment of this world; now will the ruler of this world be cast out." (Jn.12:30-31)**

> **But in fact Christ has been raised from the dead, the firstfruits of those who have fallen asleep. For as by a man came death, by a man has come also the resurrection of the dead. For as in Adam all die, so also in Christ shall all be made alive. But each in his own order: Christ the firstfruits, then at his coming those who belong to Christ. (1 Co.15:20-23)**

> **He disarmed the rulers and authorities and put them to open shame, by triumphing over them in him. (Col.2:15)**

> **Since therefore the children share in flesh and blood, he himself likewise partook of the same things, that through death he might destroy the one who has the power of death, that is, the devil, and deliver all those who through fear of death were subject to lifelong slavery. (He.2:14-15)**

> **Whoever makes a practice of sinning is of the devil, for the devil has been sinning from the beginning. The reason the Son of God appeared was to destroy the works of the devil. (1 Jn.3:8)**

4 Jesus' third rebuttal: God's love and forgiveness are universal.

Jesus' third rebuttal was that God's love is universal—available to all. God will forgive all sin—even blasphemy that insults, curses, and reviles God (see DEEPER STUDY # 4—Mt.9:3). All people need to know this glorious truth. There is no sin that God will not forgive. A person can be forgiven anything, no matter how terrible or vile. But they can only be forgiven if they will turn to Christ, confess their sin, and repent (see DEEPER STUDY # 4—Mt.26:28 for discussion).

3:28

28 "Truly, I say to you, all sins will be forgiven the children of man, and whatever blasphemies they utter,"

Jesus' behavior on the cross shows just how universal God's love really is. The savage treatment and the vulgar insults inflicted upon Jesus were horrible. Such treatment shows the vile, sinful nature of all human beings; yet Jesus prayed, "Father, forgive them" (Lu.23:34).

THOUGHT 1. God's love and forgiveness are available to all. God loves every individual and will forgive any person no matter how much that person has sinned and blasphemed God.

> Let it be known to you therefore, brothers, that through this man forgiveness of sins is proclaimed to you. (Ac.13:38)

> In him we have redemption through his blood, the forgiveness of our trespasses, according to the riches of his grace. (Ep.1:7)

> This is good, and it is pleasing in the sight of God our Savior, who desires all people to be saved and to come to the knowledge of the truth. For there is one God, and there is one mediator between God and men, the man Christ Jesus, who gave himself as a ransom for all, which is the testimony given at the proper time. (1 Ti.2:3-6)

> I, I am he who blots out your transgressions for my own sake, and I will not remember your sins. (Is.43:25)

> I have blotted out your transgressions like a cloud and your sins like mist; return to me, for I have redeemed you. (Is.44:22)

> Let the wicked forsake his way, and the unrighteous man his thoughts; let him return to the LORD, that he may have compassion on him, and to our God, for he will abundantly pardon. (Is.55:7)

3:29-30

29 "but whoever blasphemes against the Holy Spirit never has forgiveness, but is guilty of an eternal sin"—
30 for they were saying, "He has an unclean spirit."

5 Jesus' fourth rebuttal: There is one danger, the unpardonable sin—blaspheming the Holy Spirit, continuing to reject God and ascribing His work to the devil.

Jesus' fourth rebuttal serves a fearful warning to every human being: there is one danger—the danger of committing the unforgivable sin. The unforgivable sin is ascribing God's work to the devil (see note—Mt.12:31-32 for a detailed discussion and application of the Unpardonable Sin).

The unforgivable sin is committed by those who continue and continue . . .

- to reject the *promptings* of the Holy Spirit
- to blind themselves to the illumination of the Holy Spirit
- to willfully sin despite conviction by the Holy Spirit
- to insist on their own way
- to oppose the work of the Holy Spirit
- to justify themselves in their sinful behavior
- to say that the work of the Holy Spirit is actually the work of Satan.

> Whoever believes in the Son has eternal life; whoever does not obey the Son shall not see life, but the wrath of God remains on him. (Jn.3:36)

> I told you that you would die in your sins, for unless you believe that I am he you will die in your sins. (Jn.8:24)

> Take care, brothers, lest there be in any of you an evil, unbelieving heart, leading you to fall away from the living God. (He.3:12)

P. Jesus' Impact upon His Own Family: Feeling Jesus Is an Embarrassment, 3:31-35

(Mt.12:46-50; Lu.8:19-21)

31 And his mother and his brothers came, and standing outside they sent to him and called him.

32 And a crowd was sitting around him, and they said to him, "Your mother and your brothers are outside, seeking you."

33 And he answered them, "Who are my mother and my brothers?"

34 And looking about at those who sat around him, he said, "Here are my mother and my brothers!

35 For whoever does the will of God, he is my brother and sister and mother."

1. **Jesus' biological family**
   a. They were standing outside
   b. They sent someone in to get Him
   c. He was informed of the family's presence and embarrassment

2. **True kinship is more than being related by blood**
3. **True kinship is having a common relationship with God**
   a. It is being a disciple of Christ

   b. It is seeking to do God's will

Division II

The Son of God's Opening Ministry: Jesus' Immediate Impact, 1:21–3:35

P. Jesus' Impact upon His Own Family: Feeling Jesus Is an Embarrassment, 3:31–35

(Mt.12:46–50; Lu.8:19–21)

3:31–35
Introduction

Tongues were buzzing and rumors were flying about Jesus (see outline and DEEPER STUDY # 1—Mk.3:20–21; note—3:22-30). The rumors reached Mary and her other children back in Nazareth. They became extremely concerned over Jesus' welfare and were somewhat embarrassed by Jesus. So they decided to confront Him and force Him to come home with them before something terrible happened. When they arrived and Jesus was informed of their presence, He made a shocking claim: there is a greater family existing than the human family—a family that has supremacy over blood relationships. It is the family of God, the family of all those who do the will of God (see outline and notes—Mt.12:46-50; Lu.8:19-21 for more discussion). This is, *Jesus' Impact upon His Own Family: Feeling Jesus Is an Embarrassment, 3:31-35.*

1. Jesus' biological family (vv.31-32).
2. True kinship is more than being related by blood (v.33).
3. True kinship is having a common relationship with God (vv.34-35).

1 Jesus' biological family.

Jesus' family had not been with Him at this time in His ministry. They had probably remained in Nazareth. They came to the place where Jesus was ministering to bring Him home.

3:31-32

³¹ And his mother and his brothers came, and standing outside they sent to him and called him.
³² And a crowd was sitting around him, and they said to him, "Your mother and your brothers are outside, seeking you."

a. They were standing outside (v.31a).

Jesus' brother and mother were standing outside, apparently embarrassed. They probably did not want to approach Jesus in front of the crowd lest a scene be created.

b. They sent someone in to get Him (v.31b).

Apparently, Jesus' family sent someone else to let Him know they were there. This individual called to Jesus in order that His family could take Him home.

c. He was informed of the family's presence and embarrassment (v.32).

The crowd informed Jesus of the family's presence outside, saying that His family members were looking for Him. The crowd was apparently aware of the family's embarrassment and thoughts that He was mentally unstable and needed to be taken home.

Something significant had happened that brought Jesus' family to confront Him and take Him home. What happened that caused Mary and His brothers to come for Him? What was so serious that they would send someone else inside to get Him instead of going in themselves or at least waiting until the meeting was over? What would cause them to seek to interrupt and stop Jesus' preaching (see outline and notes—Mt.12:46-50)? What would cause Jesus to proclaim such shocking words at this time (vv.34-35)? There seem to be three reasons for their abrupt intervention.

First, the public, even some friends of Jesus and the family, were saying that Jesus was mad, insane, mentally unstable (Mk.3:20-21). They had observed that He was working very hard, in fact so hard that He did not even stop to eat (v.20). He was swamped by people to the extent that He was forced to skip meals and do without rest. His refusing to leave the frenzied atmosphere in order to eat and rest—such behavior going on day after day and month after month—led some to wonder if He were insane, abnormal in craving the attention and adulation and frenzy of the crowds.

Furthermore, Jesus was proclaiming Himself to be the Son of God. He made many claims that were so unusual that He was thought insane. (See outlines and notes—Jn.5:1-7:53; a quick glance at this passage will show just how phenomenal Jesus' claims were and why so many, even His own family, opposed Him.)

Second, the rulers, both political and religious, were increasingly opposing Jesus. The family was alarmed and feared for His life (see outline and notes—Mt.12:1-50; Mk.3:22-30).

Third, the news of Jesus' *claim* to be the Son of God reached the family, and the neighbors were saying that such a claim was preposterous, utter insanity. In addition, the neighbors and friends were whispering about His insanity and about His conflict with the leaders of the nation. These reports affected Mary and the family the way such news would affect any family: it caused concern and stirred a mother's deep love and responsibility for her Son. Mary left immediately to go for Jesus, to bring Him home in order to save Him from harm and to save the family from further embarrassment (Mt.12:14; Jn.7:1f).

THOUGHT 1. Some penetrating questions need to be asked and answered by all of us.

- Am I embarrassed by Jesus?
- Am I ashamed to stand up for Jesus and His claims?
- Do I fear what my neighbors and friends will say if I take a stand for Jesus?
- Do I want to keep Jesus private so His claims will not embarrass me or bother anyone?

> For whoever is ashamed of me and of my words in this adulterous and sinful generation, of him will the Son of Man also be ashamed when he comes in the glory of his Father with the holy angels. (Mk.8:38)

> For I am not ashamed of the gospel, for it is the power of God for salvation to everyone who believes, to the Jew first and also to the Greek. (Ro.1:16)

> As it is written, "Behold, I am laying in Zion a stone of stumbling, and a rock of offense; and whoever believes in him will not be put to shame." (Ro.9:33)

> As it is my eager expectation and hope that I will not be at all ashamed, but that with full courage now as always Christ will be honored in my body, whether by life or by death. (Ph.1:20)

At this point, a legitimate question needs to be asked: How could Mary not believe Jesus' claims after her experience with God concerning the birth of Jesus? The answer is given in an honest and open-hearted study of Scripture.

Mary was a wonderful woman, the woman chosen for a very special mission: to be the person through whom God would send His only begotten Son into the world (Jn.3:16). But we need to always remember that Mary was *only human*. She was a very special woman, yes; nevertheless, she was still only human. She was special only in that she was *highly favored* by God (Lu.1:28). Her being special was not because of any virtue or merit of her own. It was because of God, because of His mercy and His grace alone.

Mary's deep experience with God had happened some thirty years before. Thirty or more years is a long time for humans to maintain the reality and meaning of a religious experience. Human emotions rise and fall almost daily.

As a mother, as flesh and blood, Mary had a difficult time (as anyone in her situation would) understanding the mission and Messiahship of her Son, Jesus.

- Mary had believed God's messenger (Lu.1:45), but she had not fully understood. She apparently kept all these things to herself—wisely, we might add—and *pondered* them in her heart (Lu.2:19).
- Thirteen years later, Mary had difficulty understanding the mission of her twelve year-old Son when He was found in the temple after having been lost for two days. When they found Him, He was engaged in a most unusual discussion with the temple priests. Jesus asked His mother why she was looking for Him, stating that she should know that He had to be about His Father's business (Lu.2:49).
- Some seventeen years after the temple experience, Mary called on her Son to help at a wedding in Cana of Galilee. Jesus saw in the request an opportunity to begin familiarizing His mother with just who He really is, the Son of God. She was slow to grasp His purpose, so He gave her a mild rebuke (Jn.2:4; see note—Jn.2:3-5 for a more detailed explanation).

Mary had known Jesus as one of her children and as a young man for some thirty years. Throughout these years, she had known Jesus only in a day-to-day family setting, in a day-to-day routine environment. Then He suddenly pulled up stakes, left home, and forsook what was apparently a flourishing carpentry business. The events that occurred from the moment He departed happened so rapidly over the next few months and were so dramatic that Mary was bound to feel overwhelmed and perplexed. She and all the others who were close to Jesus were having to learn that He was not just a man, but the Son of God Himself. (See outline and notes—Mk.3:21 for other unusual acts by Jesus that caused problems for the friends and the family. Mary was bound to be concerned because of what was happening and being said about her Son.)

2 True kinship is more than being related by blood.

3:33

Jesus responded to His family's interference with a probing, puzzling question: *who are my mother and my brothers?* The question made a critical point: true kinship is not just a blood relationship.

33 And he answered them, "Who are my mother and my brothers?"

Jesus is not downgrading the family or human ties to blood relatives (see note—Mt.12:46–47). No one was ever more devoted to the family than Jesus. This is seen in . . .

- His care of Mary throughout His life (see Jn.19:26–27)
- His teaching and the teaching of His disciples throughout Scripture (see Ep.5:22–6:4)
- His impact upon society's treatment of women, children, and the family (see note—Mk.10:5; see Col.3:18–21)
- His own half-brothers who eventually became disciples (see note—Mk.6:3–4)

Jesus is saying that human genes, family blood and traits, are not always enough to create and make a genuine family. A *true family*, a *true kinship* does not automatically exist just because some people have common blood, DNA, and traits. This is clearly seen in the pages of family histories every day. Too many families are in turmoil, divided, and torn apart. Too many families are in constant conflict, ranging from mild verbal attacks to murderous assaults. There is . . .

- parent against child
- child against parent
- husband against wife
- sister against sister
- brother against brother
- relative against relative

Now picture the scene. Jesus is standing before the crowd. He has just been told that His mother and brothers are outside looking for Him. He sees a unique opportunity to teach a much needed lesson. Stretching forth His arms toward the multitude, He cries out, "Who are my mother and my brothers?" He is proclaiming that blood relationships, family genes and traits, do not necessarily create true kinship. There is a relationship that is stronger than the blood relationship, stronger than the family tie.

> **Bear fruits in keeping with repentance. And do not begin to say to yourselves, 'We have Abraham as our father.' For I tell you, God is able from these stones to raise up children for Abraham. (Lu.3:8)**

> **But to all who did receive him, who believed in his name, he gave the right to become children of God, who were born, not of blood nor of the will of the flesh nor of the will of man, but of God. (Jn.1:12–13)**

> **Know then that it is those of faith who are the sons of Abraham. (Ga.3:7)**

> **From whom every family in heaven and on earth is named. (Ep.3:15)**

3:34–35

³⁴ And looking about at those who sat around him, he said, "Here are my mother and my brothers!
³⁵ For whoever does the will of God, he is my brother and sister and mother."

3 True kinship is having a common relationship with God.

There is a level of kinship deeper than a physical, flesh and blood relationship. This kinship is based on a common relationship with God. True kinship is a spiritual relationship.

God is Spirit, and those who would know and follow Him must be in spiritual union with Him. True kinship is a matter of the spirit, heart, and mind (Jn.4:23–24). All who are in *spiritual union* with God become sons and daughters of God and brothers and sisters of Jesus. They comprise the true family of God (2 Co.6:17–18; Ro.8:29). Jesus points out two facts about this spiritual relationship:

a. It is being a disciple of Christ (v.34).

True kinship is based on being a true disciple, a true follower of Christ. Mark notes that, as Jesus made this statement, He was looking at those who were sitting around Him. Matthew says specifically that Jesus was looking at His disciples (Mt.12:49). Jesus is saying that His true family were the disciples, those who had accepted Him as Lord and Master and had dedicated their lives to following Him. It was their acceptance of Him in spirit and heart that bound them together. He is saying that all who follow Him are spiritually united. They constitute a kinship that is based on having the same Lord and Master, a true kinship that will last forever (see Deeper Study # 3–Ac.2:42; notes—Ep.2:11–18; 2:19–22 for discussion).

> **But to all who did receive him, who believed in his name, he gave the right to become children of God. (Jn.1:12)**

For all who are led by the Spirit of God are sons of God. For you did not receive the spirit of slavery to fall back into fear, but you have received the Spirit of adoption as sons, by whom we cry, "Abba! Father!" The Spirit himself bears witness with our spirit that we are children of God, and if children, then heirs—heirs of God and fellow heirs with Christ, provided we suffer with him in order that we may also be glorified with him. (Ro.8:14-17)

But when the fullness of time had come, God sent forth his Son, born of woman, born under the law, to redeem those who were under the law, so that we might receive adoption as sons. And because you are sons, God has sent the Spirit of his Son into our hearts, crying, "Abba! Father!" (Ga.4:4-6)

For through him we both have access in one Spirit to the Father. So then you are no longer strangers and aliens, but you are fellow citizens with the saints and members of the household of God. (Ep.2:18-19)

For he who sanctifies and those who are sanctified all have one source. That is why he is not ashamed to call them brothers. (He.2:11)

b. It is seeking to do God's will (v.35).

True kinship is based on doing the will of God. Jesus had given Himself to do God's will. The disciples had accepted Jesus as their Lord and Master. Therefore, they were committed to do exactly what their Lord did: the will of God. God's will became the objective and drive of their lives. All true disciples of Jesus have the same objective: to do the will of God. Therefore, it is the spiritual commitment to do God's will that binds all genuine believers together.

All who focus their lives on the will of God are bound together spiritually, bound together to do His will. Jesus is saying no greater kinship exists.

THOUGHT 1. The will of God is the law of God as summarized in the Ten Commandments (Ex.20:3-17). Doing God's will should be the driving force of our lives. And it should not be a grievous duty that we grudgingly perform. To the contrary, doing God's will should be the delight of our lives.

I appeal to you therefore, brothers, by the mercies of God, to present your bodies as a living sacrifice, holy and acceptable to God, which is your spiritual worship. Do not be conformed to this world, but be transformed by the renewal of your mind, that by testing you may discern what is the will of God, what is good and acceptable and perfect. (Ro.12:1-2)

For this is the will of God, your sanctification: that you abstain from sexual immorality. (1 Th.4:3)

Give thanks in all circumstances; for this is the will of God in Christ Jesus for you. (1 Th.5:18)

So as to live for the rest of the time in the flesh no longer for human passions but for the will of God. (1 Pe.4:2)

I delight to do your will, O my God; your law is within my heart. (Ps.40:8)

CHAPTER 4

III. THE SON OF GOD'S CONTINUING MINISTRY: JESUS' PARABLES AND HIS AUTHORITY, 4:1–6:6

A. The Parable of the Sower or Farmer: How People Receive the Word of God, 4:1–20

(Mt.13:1–23; Lu.8:4–15)

1. Jesus began a new method of teaching: The parable
a. The setting: By the lakeshore in a boat
b. The crowd: Very large
c. The parable[DS1]

2. The parable: A farmer planted his seed by hand-casting it in the field
a. Sowed some seed that did not take root
1) A portion fell on the hard path: Was eaten by birds
2) A portion fell upon rocky soil:
• The seed sprouted quickly because of the shallow soil

• The plants just as quickly withered because they had no root

b. Sowed other seed that took root, but did not bear fruit: The plants grew up among thorns and choked to death
c. Sowed some seed that bore fruit: Some bore 30 percent and others 60 percent
d. Sowed only a few seeds that bore 100 percent fruit
e. A message heard only by spiritual ears

3. The response to the parable

a. Disciples accept the parable
b. Outsiders reject the parable deliberately
1) Lest they hear, see, and understand
2) Lest they be converted and forgiven

Again he began to teach beside the sea. And a very large crowd gathered about him, so that he got into a boat and sat in it on the sea, and the whole crowd was beside the sea on the land. ² And he was teaching them many things in parables, and in his teaching he said to them: ³ "Listen! Behold, a sower went out to sow. ⁴ And as he sowed, some seed fell along the path, and the birds came and devoured it.

⁵ Other seed fell on rocky ground, where it did not have much soil, and immediately it sprang up, since it had no depth of soil. ⁶ And when the sun rose, it was scorched, and since it had no root, it withered away. ⁷ Other seed fell among thorns, and the thorns grew up and choked it, and it yielded no grain. ⁸ And other seeds fell into good soil and produced grain, growing up and increasing and yielding thirtyfold and sixtyfold and a hundredfold."

⁹ And he said, "He who has ears to hear, let him hear." ¹⁰ And when he was alone, those around him with the twelve asked him about the parables. ¹¹ And he said to them, "To you has been given the secret of the kingdom of God, but for those outside everything is in parables, ¹² so that 'they may indeed see but not perceive, and may indeed hear but

not understand, lest they should turn and be forgiven.'"

¹³ And he said to them, "Do you not understand this parable? How then will you understand all the parables?

¹⁴ The sower sows the word.

¹⁵ And these are the ones along the path, where the word is sown: when they hear, Satan immediately comes and takes away the word that is sown in them.

¹⁶ And these are the ones sown on rocky ground: the ones who, when they hear the word, immediately receive it with joy.

¹⁷ And they have no root in themselves, but endure for a while; then, when tribulation or persecution arises on account of the word, immediately they fall away.

¹⁸ And others are the ones sown among thorns. They are those who hear the word,

¹⁹ but the cares of the world and the deceitfulness of riches and the desires for other things enter in and choke the word, and it proves unfruitful.

²⁰ But those that were sown on the good soil are the ones who hear the word and accept it and bear fruit, thirtyfold and sixtyfold and a hundredfold.'"

4. The meaning of the parable

a. The farmer sows the Word of God
b. Some hear the Word on the hard path
  1) The Word is heard
  2) Satan comes and takes away the Word

c. Some hear the Word on rocky places
  1) The Word is received excitedly

  2) The Word has no root
  3) Trial and testing come
  4) They wither away

d. Some hear the Word among thorns

  1) The Word is only added to life
  2) The world, riches, and possessions choke the Word

e. Some receive the Word on good soil: They bear fruit[DS2]
f. Some—but only a few—bear 100 percent fruit

Division III

The Son of God's Continuing Ministry: Jesus' Parables and His Authority, 4:1–6:6

A. The Parable of the Sower or Farmer: How People Receive the Word of God, 4:1–20

(Mt.13:1–23; Lu.8:4–15)

4:1–20
Introduction

The Parable of the Sower is one of the best known of Jesus' parables. Our Lord taught a number of valuable lessons in this parable, but two stand out.

    The first is the lesson of sowing the seed, the lesson to the messenger of God. The messenger of God is every genuine believer. We are to sow the seed, the Word of God, wherever we are—no matter the difficulty, the opposition, or the discouragement. When Jesus stood before people, He knew the kind of people who sat before Him. He knew . . .

- the hard, closed hearts of the religionists and others
- the shallow, deceptive enthusiasm of the poor and needy and of others
- the worldliness of the well-to-do and of others, how entangled they were in *things* and pleasure

Jesus knew that many would never listen, but He also knew that if He kept sowing the seed faithfully, some would bear fruit. Some soil would be fertile, craving the truth of life and eternity. Therefore, some people would hear the Word, accept it, and bear fruit (v.20). This is the reason Jesus pressed on. He kept sowing, never giving in to discouragement—sowing that some might be saved and bear fruit. Jesus expects us to do the same, to continue on no matter the discouragement or opposition. While many will not receive our message, some soils are fertile, plowed, and ready to receive the seed and to bear fruit.

The second stand-out lesson is that of receiving the seed, the lesson to the hearers of God's Word. The soils, that is, human hearts, vary among people. This variance ranges all the way from hard, pavement-like hearts to soft, plowed hearts. Just what kind of heart people have depends on how they have lived and responded and conditioned themselves throughout life.

The condition of a person's heart determines how they will love God and their neighbor, whether they will be responsive or close-minded. The point is that God holds every individual responsible for the condition of their heart and for how they respond to the gospel.

In this parable Jesus paints the picture of various soils (hearts) and how they receive the seed, the Word of God (see notes—Mt.13:1-9; Lu.8:4-15 for more detailed discussion and application). This is, *The Parable of the Sower or Farmer: How People Receive the Word of God*, 4:1-20.

1. Jesus began a new method of teaching: The parable (vv.1-2).
2. The parable: A farmer planted his seed by hand-casting it in the field (vv.3-9).
3. The response to the parable (vv.10-12).
4. The meaning of the parable (vv.13-20).

4:1-2

Again he began to teach beside the sea. And a very large crowd gathered about him, so that he got into a boat and sat in it on the sea, and the whole crowd was beside the sea on the land.
² And he was teaching them many things in parables, and in his teaching he said to them:

1 Jesus began a new method of teaching: The parable.

Jesus began a new method of teaching—the parable—and He taught from a new platform—a boat. Both demonstrate how important it was to Jesus to make sure His message was heard and understood by the people. He was willing to do whatever He could to be most effective in His ministry.

a. **The setting: By the lakeshore in a boat (v.1a).**

b. **The crowd: Very large (v.1b).**
   The setting for this parable was by the seashore, and the crowd was extremely large. In fact, the multitude was so great that they overflowed the seashore. They pressed in upon Jesus so tightly that He was forced into a boat. It was an intriguing and impressive scene: Jesus teaching from a boat with the sea as His stage, and the people fanned out across the beach.

c. **The parable (v.2).**
   Jesus utilized a new method for teaching the people: using parables. The parable would become one of His most effective tools for conveying spiritual truths (see DEEPER STUDY # 1; outlines and notes—Mt.13:10-17 for a detailed discussion of Christ's reasons for using parables).

DEEPER STUDY # 1

(4:2) **Parable** (Gk. parabole; pronounced *pa-ra-bow-lay'*): literally means placing a thing by the side of something else for the purpose of comparing. The word *comparison* best describes a parable.

1. A parable is a comparison: it is an earthly event pointing out a heavenly truth. It is a comparison between the earthly and the heavenly.

2. A parable is a comparison: the earthly story has to be delved into to discover the heavenly truth. The spiritual point is found only by active thought and effort, by actively *comparing* the physical world with the spiritual world. In fact, the more a person thinks and meditates on a parable, the more he or she usually sees of the truth.

Jesus is the *Master User* of the parable. No teacher ever used the parable so effectively. Why did He use the parable so frequently? (See notes—Mt.13:10-17; Lu.8:9-10 for the reasons and for more discussion.)

2 The parable: A farmer planted his seed by hand-casting it in the field.

The parable Jesus told was a simple story, yet its meaning was profound. However, it was not understood by most (see vv.10-13). It revolved around facts known by practically everyone who was familiar with sowing seed (v.3). Jesus taught five truths in this parable.

a. Sowed some seed that did not take root (vv.4–6).

The farmer sows some seed that *does not take root*. Two kinds of soil bear no root at all. These two soils differ from other soils in that there is *never* any root.

The first soil is the *path*, the *wayside*, the *road* (v.4). These terms speak of the unplowed, packed down areas right outside the plowed field. The path joins the field and may even be a part of the field; but it lies in the corners, the hard to reach areas that cannot be reached with the plow. It is the edge of the field. The seed that falls there cannot penetrate the hard ground, so it ends up being eaten by birds.

The second soil is the *rocky ground*, rocks that lie right under the surface of the ground (vv.5-6). Rocks hold the water and heat longer, plus the soil is shallow; therefore, the seed sprouts quickly. But the plant withers just as quickly because it has no root; the sun scorches and kills it.

b. Sowed other seed that took root but did not bear fruit: The plants grew up among thorns and choked to death (v.7).

The farmer sows some seed that *takes root*, but it does not yield fruit. This is seed that falls among thorns. The thorny soil is part of the field. It has been plowed, but it is deceptive ground. It looks good, but lying right underneath the soil is a mass of thorn roots ready to spring up. The fact that they were not destroyed in the plowing and that they are already in the ground means that they will spring up faster and choke the seed.

c. Sowed some seed that bore fruit: Some bore thirty percent and others sixty percent (v.8a).

The farmer sows some seed that *bears fruit*. This is seed that falls on good soil. This fertile ground yields fruit, and when fruit appears, it increases and grows. This is the significant fact to see in the good soil.

d. Sowed only a few seeds that bore one hundred percent fruit (v.8b).

The farmer sows *only a few seeds that bear one hundred percent fruit*. All seed in the good ground bears fruit, but each plant varies in its degree of fruitfulness. This, too, is significant. Some fruitful plants bear only thirty percent. They are very weak plants, seventy percent unfruitful.

3 "Listen! Behold, a sower went out to sow.
4 And as he sowed, some seed fell along the path, and the birds came and devoured it.
5 Other seed fell on rocky ground, where it did not have much soil, and immediately it sprang up, since it had no depth of soil.
6 And when the sun rose, it was scorched, and since it had no root, it withered away.
7 Other seed fell among thorns, and the thorns grew up and choked it, and it yielded no grain.
8 And other seeds fell into good soil and produced grain, growing up and increasing and yielding thirtyfold and sixtyfold and a hundredfold."
9 And he said, "He who has ears to hear, let him hear."

Other plants bear only sixty percent. They too are weak, being forty percent unfruitful. Only a few plants bear one hundred percent of their potential fruit.

e. A message heard only by spiritual ears (v.9).

Jesus then makes a forceful statement that stresses the importance of the parable: "He who has ears to hear [spiritual ears], let him hear" (v.9). What does this statement mean? *The message of the parable is heard—understood—only by the spiritual.* Luke tells us that Jesus *called out* or *cried* (ephonei), shouted the words, which stressed the importance even more (Lk.8:8). The message was so important, so critical. Jesus wanted all to hear and understand; but He knew, brokenheartedly, that all would not hear.

4:10-12

¹⁰ And when he was alone, those around him with the twelve asked him about the parables.
¹¹ And he said to them, "To you has been given the secret of the kingdom of God, but for those outside everything is in parables,
¹² so that 'they may indeed see but not perceive, and may indeed hear but not understand, lest they should turn and be forgiven.'"

3 The response to the parable.

After the crowd had dispersed, the twelve disciples and a group of other genuine believers asked Jesus about the parable (v.10). The Lord explained His reason for using parables as well as people's twofold response to them.

a. Disciples accept the parable (v.11a).

Those who genuinely follow Jesus understand and accept the parable. They do not just hear the words, but they hear the message, and they hear with their hearts. True disciples are receptive—willing to think and to meditate and to receive the message into their lives. They are willing to do exactly what the parable teaches. Therefore, God reveals the mysteries of His Kingdom to them.

b. Outsiders reject the parable deliberately (vv.11b-12).

Unbelievers hear the parable, but not with spiritual ears. They just hear the words without grasping the spiritual truth. Note that Jesus refers to unbelievers as those *outside* (exo). They are *outsiders* to Christ's followers, *outsiders* to God's kingdom, *outsiders* to the family of God.

Outsiders see Jesus teach and hear His words, but they do not perceive and understand the spiritual truths of the parables. Why do they not perceive or understand? Jesus gives the reason: *lest they should turn and be forgiven* (v.12).

Unbelievers are unwilling to receive what their lives and hearts are taught, unwilling to change their lives, unwilling to repent and be converted. Therefore, they shut their minds, twist the truth, and rationalize their behavior. They reject the truth of the parable deliberately. But note: God will not give His pearls to the swine (Mt.7:6). This is one reason Jesus taught using parables.

Unbelievers experience the law of conditioning. The more they harden their minds and hearts to the truth, the harder they become. They become more and more conditioned against the truth. Their openness and sensitivity to spiritual truth dwindles more and more until it is gone. The law of spiritual conditioning says that the more we receive spiritual truth, the more we increase our capacity to understand and grow in spiritual truth. But the opposite is also true: the more we reject spiritual truth, the more we decrease our sensitivity and become hardened to spiritual truth (see notes—Mt.13:10-17).

THOUGHT 1. There are many who are *outside* . . .
- who are hard-hearted against spiritual things
- whose hearts are shallow or whose minds are superficial. They are rootless, having no depth—usually in all areas of life
- who are worldly-minded, interested in spiritual matters only as a little *extra* added to their lives

For the word of God is living and active, sharper than any two-edged sword, piercing to the division of soul and of spirit, of joints and of marrow, and discerning the thoughts and intentions of the heart. (He.4:2)

For if anyone is a hearer of the word and not a doer, he is like a man who looks intently at his natural face in a mirror. For he looks at himself and goes away and at once forgets what he was like. (Js.1:23-24)

Let their eyes be darkened, so that they cannot see, and make their loins tremble continually. (Ps.69:23)

He sees many things, but does not observe them; his ears are open, but he does not hear. (Is.42:20)

4 The meaning of the parable.

The meaning of the parable is given by Jesus Himself (see outline and notes—Mt.13:1-9 for a discussion of this point). He explained the details of the parable, making the spiritual truths clear to His genuine followers.

a. The farmer sows the Word of God (v.14).

The seed sown by the farmer is the Word of God. Therefore, the farmer is the genuine follower of Christ who spreads His message, shares the gospel, or teaches and preaches God's Word.

The emphasis of the parable is not on the sower, but on the type of ground which receives the seed, that is, the kind of person who receives the Word of God. All four grounds (all four types of persons) hear the Word, but each receive it in a different manner. How each receives the Word depends on the kind of *ground* they are. The following chart shows this:

¹³ And he said to them, "Do you not understand this parable? How then will you understand all the parables?
¹⁴ The sower sows the word.
¹⁵ And these are the ones along the path, where the word is sown: when they hear, Satan immediately comes and takes away the word that is sown in them.
¹⁶ And these are the ones sown on rocky ground: the ones who, when they hear the word, immediately receive it with joy.
¹⁷ And they have no root in themselves, but endure for a while; then, when tribulation or persecution arises on account of the word, immediately they fall away.
¹⁸ And others are the ones sown among thorns. They are those who hear the word,
¹⁹ but the cares of the world and the deceitfulness of riches and the desires for other things enter in and choke the word, and it proves unfruitful.
²⁰ But those that were sown on the good soil are the ones who hear the word and accept it and bear fruit, thirtyfold and sixtyfold and a hundredfold."

The wayside ground . . . . . . is an unplowed heart . . . . . . that results in a hardened life.

The rocky ground . . . . . . is a rootless heart . . . . . . that results in a superficial life.

The thorny ground . . . . . . is a worldly heart . . . . . . that results in a strangled life.

The fruitful ground . . . . . . is an honest and good heart . . . . . . that results in a fruitful life.

b. Some hear the Word on the hard path (v.15).

Jesus explained the seed that fell along the path, beside the road, by the wayside. The wayside ground is an unplowed heart that results in a hardened life. Those on the path do hear the Word of God. They may even be present in church; but they are off to the side, out of the way, not involved. They let their minds wander, thinking little, and involving themselves even less. They are on the outer circle, paying little attention to the warnings and promises of the Word.

Note what happens: before such a person believes, the devil comes and snatches the Word away. It is taken from the person; the person never applies the Word to his or her life, never genuinely receives the truth (see Judas Iscariot and see Herod who enjoyed listening to John the Baptist, Mk.6:20).

'For this people's heart has grown dull, and with their ears they can barely hear, and their eyes they have closed; lest they should see with their eyes and hear with their ears and understand with their heart and turn, and I would heal them.' (Ac.28:27)

> But because of your hard and impenitent heart you are storing up wrath for yourself on the day of wrath when God's righteous judgment will be revealed. (Ro.2:5)

> They have become callous and have given themselves up to sensuality, greedy to practice every kind of impurity. (Ep.4:19)

> But exhort one another every day, as long as it is called "today," that none of you may be hardened by the deceitfulness of sin. (He.3:13)

> Blessed is the one who fears the LORD always, but whoever hardens his heart will fall into calamity. (Pr.28:14)

> He who is often reproved, yet stiffens his neck, will suddenly be broken beyond healing. (Pr.29:1)

c. Some hear the Word on rocky soil (vv.16–17).

The rocky ground is a rootless heart that results in a surface, superficial life. Such people hear the Word and become excited over it. They receive the seed—the Word—profess belief in Christ, and make a profession of faith before the world (v.16). But they fail to count the cost, to consider the commitment, the self-denial, the sacrifice, the study, the learning, the hours and effort required. They do not apply themselves to *learn Christ*; therefore, they do not become rooted and grounded in the Word. They are only surface, superficial believers.

Again, note what happens: when trials and testing come, they wither away (v.17). Their profession is scorched and consumed, burned up by the heat of the trial and temptation. (See John Mark, who at first failed to endure [Ac.13:13] and the people who discovered that following Christ cost too much [Lu.9:57–62].)

> But the one who hears and does not do them is like a man who built a house on the ground without a foundation. When the stream broke against it, immediately it fell, and the ruin of that house was great. (Lu.6:49)

> Jesus said to him, "No one who puts his hand to the plow and looks back is fit for the kingdom of God." (Lu.9:62)

> But now that you have come to know God, or rather to be known by God, how can you turn back again to the weak and worthless elementary principles of the world, whose slaves you want to be once more? (Ga.4:9)

> But my righteous one shall live by faith, and if he shrinks back, my soul has no pleasure in him. (He.10:38)

> For if, after they have escaped the defilements of the world through the knowledge of our Lord and Savior Jesus Christ, they are again entangled in them and overcome, the last state has become worse for them than the first. For it would have been better for them never to have known the way of righteousness than after knowing it to turn back from the holy commandment delivered to them. What the true proverb says has happened to them: "The dog returns to its own vomit, and the sow, after washing herself, returns to wallow in the mire." (2 Pe.2:20–22)

> But I have this against you, that you have abandoned the love you had at first. (Re.2:4–5)

> Remember therefore from where you have fallen; repent, and do the works you did at first. If not, I will come to you and remove your lampstand from its place, unless you repent. (Re.2:4–5)

d. Some hear the Word among thorns (vv.18–19).

The thorns in this scene represent a worldly heart that results in a strangled life. This pictures people who receive the Word and *honestly try* (profess) to live for Christ. Christ and His followers and the church and its activities appeal to them. So they join right in, adding the Word to their lives and even professing Christ as they walk about their daily affairs. But they have a serious problem: the thorns of worldliness. They are unwilling to cut completely loose from the world, unwilling to separate themselves from worldly people and behavior (2 Co.6:17–18). They live a double life, trying to live for Christ and yet still live in the ways of the world. They keep right on growing in the midst of the thorns, giving their minds and attention to the *cares* and *riches* and *pleasures* of this world.

Note what happens: fruit does appear, but it never ripens. It is never able to be harvested. The thorns—the world, riches, possessions, pleasures, prideful ambition—choke the life out of it. The fruit never lives long enough to mature (see the Rich Young Ruler, Lu.18:18f; Ananias and Sapphira, Ac.5:1f; Demas, 2 Ti.4:10).

Therefore I tell you, do not be anxious about your life, what you will eat or what you will drink, nor about your body, what you will put on. Is not life more than food, and the body more than clothing? (Mt.6:25)

But watch yourselves lest your hearts be weighed down with dissipation and drunkenness and cares of this life, and that day come upon you suddenly like a trap. (Lu.21:34)

But those who desire to be rich fall into temptation, into a snare, into many senseless and harmful desires that plunge people into ruin and destruction. (1 Ti.6:9)

e. Some receive the Word on good soil: They bear fruit (v.20a).

The seed that fell on good soil is an honest and pure heart which results in a fruitful life (see DEEPER STUDY # 2). These are people who have a sincere heart; therefore, when they hear the Word, they keep it.

f. Some—but only a few—bear one hundred percent fruit (v.20b).

Of those who bear fruit for the Lord, some are exceptional. Most bear less than their full potential, as represented by *thirtyfold* and *sixtyfold*. But some bear *a hundredfold*. They produce *much fruit* (Jn.12:24; 15:5, 8). Why? Because they give themselves fully to Christ. They are fully devoted to His Word and fully dedicated to Him. They hold nothing back; instead, they die to themselves, take up their crosses, and follow Jesus wholeheartedly. With them, the Lord is especially well-pleased.

Truly, truly, I say to you, unless a grain of wheat falls into the earth and dies, it remains alone; but if it dies, it bears much fruit. (Jn.12:24)

I am the vine; you are the branches. Whoever abides in me and I in him, he it is that bears much fruit, for apart from me you can do nothing. . . . By this my Father is glorified, that you bear much fruit and so prove to be my disciples. (Jn.15:5, 8)

Filled with the fruit of righteousness that comes through Jesus Christ, to the glory and praise of God. (Ph.1:11)

So as to walk in a manner worthy of the Lord, fully pleasing to him: bearing fruit in every good work and increasing in the knowledge of God. (Col.1:10)

DEEPER STUDY # 2

(4:20) **Fruit-Bearing:** note the three steps involved in bearing fruit:
1. Hearing the Word.
2. Receiving the Word.
3. Bringing forth the Word, that is, doing and living the Word.

B. The Parables Dealing with Truth: Truth and Mankind's Duty, 4:21–25

(Mt.5:15–16; 10:26–27; 13:12; 24:29; Lu.8:16–18; 11:33)

1. Share the truth
   a. The fact: Lamps are to be placed on a lampstand
   b. The warning: All things will be revealed; nothing is hidden—except temporarily
   c. The exhortation: A person had better hear
2. Focus on the truth
   a. Pay attention, make sure you hear and understand the truth
   b. The reason: Determines your reward
      1) The reward of being given even more understanding, more truth
      2) The judgment of losing all

21 And he said to them, "Is a lamp brought in to be put under a basket, or under a bed, and not on a stand? 22 For nothing is hidden except to be made manifest; nor is anything secret except to come to light. 23 If anyone has ears to hear, let him hear." 24 And he said to them, "Pay attention to what you hear: with the measure you use, it will be measured to you, and still more will be added to you. 25 For to the one who has, more will be given, and from the one who has not, even what he has will be taken away."

Division III

The Son of God's Continuing Ministry: Jesus' Parables and His Authority, 4:1–6:6

B. The Parables Dealing with Truth: Truth and Mankind's Duty, 4:21–25

(Mt.5:15–16; 10:26–27; 13:12; 24:29; Lu.8:16–18; 11:33)

4:21–25
Introduction

This parable is difficult to grasp. The light reader and surface thinker will not understand what Jesus is saying. This very fact is the point Jesus makes. Grasping and knowing the truth takes time and effort and energy, and each of us has a twofold responsibility toward the truth (see outline and notes—Lu.8:16–18 for more discussion). This is, *The Parables Dealing with Truth: Truth and Mankind's Duty, 4:21–25.*
   1. Share the truth (vv.21–23).
   2. Focus on the truth (vv.24–25).

4:21–23

21 And he said to them, "Is a lamp brought in to be put under a basket, or under a bed, and not on a stand? 22 For nothing is hidden except to be made manifest; nor is anything secret except to come to light. 23 If anyone has ears to hear, let him hear."

1 Share the truth.

Jesus emphasized a simple fact of daily life: light is to be set in the most conspicuous place, where it can best be seen. The lesson to us is clear: truth is to be shared. We have a God-given responsibility to share the truth.

a. The fact: Lamps are to be placed on a lampstand (v.21).

Jesus shared a basic, obvious fact. A candle is to be placed on a candlestick so its light can be seen. The candle or lamp is a symbol, a type of the truth. It stands for the light of the truth.

Light and truth are to be the character, the very nature and behavior of the believer. Believers are to live out the truth. We are to set the candle, the truth in the most conspicuous place in our lives. Through our character and conduct, we are to display the truth for others to see (see outline and notes—Mt.5:15-16 for more discussion).

Light and truth are also to be the witness of the believer. We are to bear verbal witness to the truth. We are commanded by Christ to share the candle—the truth—and its light with others. Again, we are to place the truth in the most conspicuous place.

As Jesus explained, a candle is not placed under a basket. The basket would extinguish its light, and it would no longer be able to fulfill its purpose. It could not give off its light, for its flame and light would no longer exist. However, note something: the candle would still be a candle; but it would be a candle with no purpose—hidden, as it were, under a basket.

Similarly, a candle is not put under a bed. It would carelessly set the bed on fire and destroy it. The candle would be serving the wrong purpose; it would tragically be using its flame and light for the wrong reason. It would still be a candle, but it would be a candle using its flame and light in the wrong way.

THOUGHT 1. God gives the light of the truth to believers for a specific purpose: that we might share it. God wants others to see and know the light, the truth and purpose of life. We must make sure that we do not hide or misuse the light of the truth.

> **You are the light of the world. A city set on a hill cannot be hidden. (Mt.5:14)**

> **For so the Lord has commanded us, saying, 'I have made you a light for the Gentiles, that you may bring salvation to the ends of the earth.' (Ac.13:47)**

> **For at one time you were darkness, but now you are light in the Lord. Walk as children of light. (Ep.5:8)**

> **That you may be blameless and innocent, children of God without blemish in the midst of a crooked and twisted generation, among whom you shine as lights in the world. (Ph.2:15)**

> **For you are all children of light, children of the day. We are not of the night or of the darkness. (1 Th.5:5)**

> **But you are a chosen race, a royal priesthood, a holy nation, a people for his own possession, that you may proclaim the excellencies of him who called you out of darkness into his marvelous light. (1 Pe.2:9)**

b. **The warning: All things will be revealed; nothing is hidden—except temporarily (vv.22-23).**
Jesus issued a sober warning: even if a believer hides the candle and keeps it secret, the day is coming when it will be revealed anyway. All things will be revealed; truth may be hidden, but only temporarily. It is critical to grasp what Jesus is saying here: everything that is hidden *will* be revealed. Anything kept secret *will* be brought to light (see outline and notes—Mt.10:26-27 for more discussion). This can mean two things:
- Light and truth cannot be hid or extinguished or used for the wrong purpose forever. Both light and truth will break forth someday. The bushel will be lifted and the bed consumed (v.21), and the light and truth will be seen and will fulfill their original purpose.
- If we hide or misuse the light and truth given to us, then what we have done will be revealed someday. We cannot hide and misuse the light and truth forever. A day of judgment is coming.

c. **The exhortation: A person had better hear (v.23).**
Jesus exhorted us to grasp what He is saying, to understand it and pay careful attention to it. We cannot ignore our responsibility to share the truth. We will answer to God for what He has committed to us—His truth, His gospel of salvation, His principles for living. Therefore, we had better tune our spiritual ears to what Jesus is saying and take heed to it.

THOUGHT 1. Every individual is given some light, some truth (see Ro.1:20-23; 1 Co.2:12; Jn.8:32; Ro.12:3-8; Ep.4:7; 1 Co.12:7f). We are responsible to use what light and truth we have. We are not to hide or misuse it. God will hold each of us accountable for what light or truth we have, for what He has given us (2 Co.5:10).

So then each of us will give an account of himself to God. (Ro.14:12)

For we must all appear before the judgment seat of Christ, so that each one may receive what is due for what he has done in the body, whether good or evil. (2 Co.5:10)

Therefore do not be ashamed of the testimony about our Lord, nor of me his prisoner, but share in suffering for the gospel by the power of God. (2 Ti.1:8)

But in your hearts honor Christ the Lord as holy, always being prepared to make a defense to anyone who asks you for a reason for the hope that is in you; yet do it with gentleness and respect. (1 Pe.3:15)

On your walls, O Jerusalem, I have set watchmen; all the day and all the night they shall never be silent. You who put the LORD in remembrance, take no rest. (Is.62:6)

The LORD has brought about our vindication; come, let us declare in Zion the work of the LORD our God. (Je.51:10)

4:24-25

²⁴ And he said to them, "Pay attention to what you hear: with the measure you use, it will be measured to you, and still more will be added to you.
²⁵ For to the one who has, more will be given, and from the one who has not, even what he has will be taken away."

2 Focus on the truth.

Jesus emphasized how critical it is that we focus on *what we hear*—the light or truth that God gives us. God is watching us, and He only gives more to those who are faithful with what He has already committed to them.

a. Pay attention, make sure you hear and understand the truth (v.24a).

Jesus urged us to pay careful attention to the truth, to take heed, to make sure we hear the truth. The Lord is still talking about the responsibility of the hearer: the hearer is responsible for *hearing* the truth. We are also responsible for *what* we hear and how we interpret what is being said. All people are responsible for making sure that they *have* the truth, that they possess and know the truth. Each of us is responsible for *what* we hear, possess, and know.

THOUGHT 1. If a person listens to *junk* and, consequently, is filled with *junk*, they are responsible for the *junk*. If they are filled with the knowledge of real truth, then they are also responsible for the truth. We are all accountable for what we allow to enter our hearts and minds. Therefore, Christ warns us to pay attention, to take heed, to take care what we listen to. We need to keep guard, watch, make sure that we hear the truth.

And you will know the truth, and the truth will set you free. (Jn.8:32)

We destroy arguments and every lofty opinion raised against the knowledge of God, and take every thought captive to obey Christ. (2 Co.10:5)

For at one time you were darkness, but now you are light in the Lord. Walk as children of light (for the fruit of light is found in all that is good and right and true). (Ep.5:8–9)

Finally, brothers, whatever is true, whatever is honorable, whatever is just, whatever is pure, whatever is lovely, whatever is commendable, if there is any excellence, if there is anything worthy of praise, think about these things. (Ph.4:8)

Buy truth, and do not sell it; buy wisdom, instruction, and understanding. (Pr.23:23)

b. The reason: Determines your reward (vv.24b–25).

Jesus states why we need to make sure we hear the truth and to pay attention to what we hear. There is a pointedly clear principle that takes effect in every person's life: the measure to which we give ourselves to know the truth determines our reward. The energy, effort, and degree of commitment, the time and depth of thought—all that we give to know the truth—determines our reward (see outline and notes—Mt.13:12 for more discussion).

What is our reward for seeking and pursuing God's truth diligently, for faithfully using the truth we have already been given? The answer is thrilling: *more truth* (v.24b)! Those who give themselves to know the truth will be given *more* truth. We will have the truth, and God will give us more truth (v.25a).

In contrast, those who do not give themselves to know the truth, and those who do not faithfully use the truth God has already given them, will lose all. Everything will be taken away from them (v.25b).

Note the two Scriptural principles that Jesus applies here to our possession of truth:

- The principle of *sowing and reaping* (2 Co.9:6; Ga.6:7). We reap according to what we sow.
- The principle of *stewardship* (Mt.25:14-29). God gives more to those who are faithful with what He has already committed to them. He takes away what He has committed from those who are unfaithful with it.

THOUGHT 1. The commitment, the energy, the effort, the work, the knowledge, the degree to which we give ourselves to the truth (to God)—all determine how much God is able to entrust and give to us. Common sense tells us this.

> Ask, and it will be given to you; seek, and you will find; knock, and it will be opened to you. For everyone who asks receives, and the one who seeks finds, and to the one who knocks it will be opened. (Mt.7:7-8)

> For to everyone who has will more be given, and he will have an abundance. But from the one who has not, even what he has will be taken away. (Mt.25:29)

> Now these Jews were more noble than those in Thessalonica; they received the word with all eagerness, examining the Scriptures daily to see if these things were so. (Ac.17:11, 27)

> Do your best to present yourself to God as one approved, a worker who has no need to be ashamed, rightly handling the word of truth. (2 Ti.2:15)

> Watch yourselves, so that you may not lose what we have worked for, but may win a full reward. (2 Jn.1:8)

> Sow for yourselves righteousness; reap steadfast love; break up your fallow ground, for it is the time to seek the LORD, that he may come and rain righteousness upon you. (Ho.10:12)

THOUGHT 2. God expects every individual to seek after the truth. He abhors laziness, selfishness, indulgence, uselessness, worldliness, and ignorance. He holds us responsible for hearing the truth. He expects us . . .

- ➤ to look around and recognize what He has revealed to us through His creation (Ro.1:8:19-20; Ps.19:1-3: Pr.30:4)
- ➤ to seek more truth and to believe that His Word is truth (Jn.17:17; 2 Ti.3:5-17; 2 Pe.1:20-21; Ps.19:7-11; Pr.30:5)
- ➤ to get up and go hear someone who knows and teaches the truth (2 Ti.1:13)
- ➤ to sit down and study the truth (the Word, Jn.17:17)
- ➤ to learn and know Christ, who is the truth (Jn.1:17; 14:6; see Ep.4:20)

C. The Parable of the Growing Seed:
The Growth of Believers, 4:26–29

1. The parable: Describes the kingdom	26 And he said, "The kingdom of God is as if a man should scatter seed on the ground."
2. The seed is sown by a man	
3. The growth is not of man	27 "He sleeps and rises night and day, and the seed sprouts and grows; he knows not how."
4. The growth is sure and constant, but gradual	28 "The earth produces by itself, first the blade, then the ear, then the full grain in the ear."
5. The growth is consummated and harvested	29 "But when the grain is ripe, at once he puts in the sickle, because the harvest has come."

Division III

The Son of God's Continuing Ministry: Jesus' Parables and His Authority, 4:1–6:6

C. The Parable of the Growing Seed: The Growth of Believers, 4:26–29

4:26–29
Introduction

This parable explains what happens to the fruitful seed in the Parable of the Sower or Soils (Mk.4:1-20). It describes how the seed goes about growing, and the process through which it passes. The seed is the Word, and the ground is the *good ground*, either the believer individually or the church collectively. Four truths are taught about the fruitful seed once it has taken root, but the major point is that growth is sure; it is inevitable. Once the gospel has taken root in a believer's heart, growth will take place. The believer will grow spiritually. This is the great promise of God, the great assurance and confidence, the great hope and encouragement to every believer. This is, *The Parable of the Growing Seed: The Growth of Believers, 4:26-29.*

1. The parable: Describes the kingdom (v.26).
2. The seed is sown by a man (v.26).
3. The growth is not of man (v.27).
4. The growth is sure and constant, but gradual (v.28).
5. The growth is consummated and harvested (v.29).

4:26

26 And he said, "The kingdom of God is as if a man should scatter seed on the ground."

1 The parable: Describes the kingdom.

Jesus is describing one aspect of the kingdom of God in this parable. Once the seed—God's Word, the gospel—is sown, it sprouts and grows. The fruit of the seed—the kingdom (church) and its citizens—will and does grow. The kingdom is looked at in its *present state* here on earth. The kingdom of God is growing: more and more people are being reached for God, and as they are reached, they are growing just as God intends for them to grow (see Deeper Study # 3—Mt.19:23-24 for discussion).

2 The seed is sown by a man.

The growth of God's kingdom involves human hands. The seed has to be sown by a person; there simply is no other way it can be sown. *We* have been entrusted with the sacred duty of sowing the precious seed of the gospel. *We* are the instrument God has chosen to share the gospel with the world.

The farmer sowed his seed on the ground. In the parable, *the ground* represents the people of the earth who need the gospel. We sow the precious seed of the gospel throughout the world (Ac.1:8). God wants us to reach all the people of the world; He wants the entire world to hear His good news. God has sent His followers out into the world to sow the seed of the gospel.

[26] And he said, "The kingdom of God is as if a man should scatter seed on the ground."

Note that the seed is *scattered* or *cast* (Gk. bale; pronounced *ball'-ay*; to throw). The sower takes a handful of seed and scatters it broadly as he walks along. This is how we are to sow the seed of the gospel. As we walk along through life, we are to scatter the seed broadly, sharing the gospel with everyone we meet.

And proclaim as you go, saying, 'The kingdom of heaven is at hand.' . . . What I tell you in the dark, say in the light, and what you hear whispered, proclaim on the housetops. (Mt.10:7, 27)

Go therefore and make disciples of all nations, baptizing them in the name of the Father and of the Son and of the Holy Spirit, teaching them to observe all that I have commanded you. And behold, I am with you always, to the end of the age. (Mt.28:19-20)

And he said to them, "Go into all the world and proclaim the gospel to the whole creation." (Mk.16:15)

But you will receive power when the Holy Spirit has come upon you, and you will be my witnesses in Jerusalem and in all Judea and Samaria, and to the end of the earth. (Ac.1:8)

Go and stand in the temple and speak to the people all the words of this Life. (Ac.5:20)

3 The growth is not of man.

4:27

The sower or farmer plants his seed and then goes about his regular affairs. He sleeps and rises day by day. And while he carries on the routine of his life, the seed germinates, springs up, and grows. The point is this: the seed grows by its own virtue. The seed uses the sun, water, air, and earth to grow; but the power to germinate, to break forth and grow is of the seed itself, by its own virtue. It is not man who makes the seed grow. We do not even know how the mysterious growth takes place. The secret of life and of growth is beyond us. We discover, we invent, we rearrange, we develop; but we do not create, not in the real sense of *creation* (ex nihilo, out of nothing).

[27] "He sleeps and rises night and day, and the seed sprouts and grows; he knows not how."

The same is true with the kingdom of God, with the growth of believers both individually and collectively. Growth is not of man; growth is of God (1 Co.3:7). It is the Spirit of God that takes the gospel and changes a person's heart and causes him or her to grow. It is the Spirit of God that recreates a person spiritually, that causes a person to be *born again* and to grow in grace (see Jn.3:3-8; Ep.2:8-9). We plant the seed; God makes it grow.

But to all who did receive him, who believed in his name, he gave the right to become children of God, Who were born, not of blood nor of the will of the flesh nor of the will of man, but of God. (Jn.1:12-13)

Jesus answered, "Truly, truly, I say to you, unless one is born of water and the Spirit, he cannot enter the kingdom of God." (Jn.3:5)

So neither he who plants nor he who waters is anything, but only God who gives the growth. (1 Co.3:7)

For by grace you have been saved through faith. And this is not your own doing; it is the gift of God. Not a result of works, so that no one may boast. (Ep.2:8-9)

He saved us, not because of works done by us in righteousness, but according to his own mercy, by the washing of regeneration and renewal of the Holy Spirit. (Tit.3:5)

Since you have been born again, not of perishable seed but of imperishable, through the living and abiding word of God. (1 Pe.1:23)

THOUGHT 1. The ground or soil can hinder and slow the process of growth. Seed sown into some ground bears only thirty percent fruit, some only sixty percent fruit. Very few bear one hundred percent fruit (see outlines and notes—Mt.13:8, 23; Mk.4:13–20 for discussion).

4:28

²⁸ "The earth produces by itself, first the blade, then the ear, then the full grain in the ear."

4 The growth is sure and constant, but gradual.

The farmer sows his seed with the confidence that it will grow. Jesus noted that the earth bears fruit *by itself* (automate; pronounced *au-tow-ma'-tay*). Obviously, this Greek word is the source our English word *automatically*. It means spontaneously, of necessity, self-moving. The idea is that the earth brings forth fruit automatically, by its very nature. Note two facts:

- Growth is sure, inevitable. But two conditions are essential. The ground must be "good soil or ground" (Mk.4:20), and the seed must be sown in the ground. If these two conditions exist, then growth is both *inevitable* and unstoppable. Even a small blade of grass will find a crack in the pavement. Nothing can stop the seed from growing (see outline and notes—Ro.8:28–39 for more discussion).

THOUGHT 1. Genuine believers (good ground) can rest assured: we are truly God's children, and God will complete the work of grace in our lives. The grace of God planted in our hearts is unstoppable. Believers' confidence is in God, not in our own flesh and weak efforts. Therefore, there is no reason, no excuse, for being down and discouraged, withdrawn and depressed.

> I am the vine; you are the branches. Whoever abides in me and I in him, he it is that bears much fruit, for apart from me you can do nothing. (Jn.15:5)

> And we know that for those who love God all things work together for good, for those who are called according to his purpose. (Ro.8:28)

> And I am sure of this, that he who began a good work in you will bring it to completion at the day of Jesus Christ. (Ph.1:6)

> For it is God who works in you, both to will and to work for his good pleasure. (Ph.2:13)

> Which is why I suffer as I do. But I am not ashamed, for I know whom I have believed, and I am convinced that he is able to guard until that day what has been entrusted to me. (2 Ti.1:12)

- Growth is constant, but it is gradual, ever so gradual. The seed is sown, and then day after day and night after night passes before the blade ever springs up. Then many more days and nights pass before the ear forms. It takes weeks before the full ear of corn appears. Growth does take place; it is constant—but growth is gradual. It takes time; it does not happen overnight.

THOUGHT 1. Growth is of God, and the believer is to trust and to wait on God for growth. But the trust and waiting are to be active—a working trust and waiting. There is no such thing as inactive faith and waiting—not to God. Faith and waiting on God are active; they both serve and work (see Js.2:14–18).

THOUGHT 2. This glorious truth, the truth of sure growth, of being secure in God's promises, is greatly abused. People have misused this truth . . .

- to say I am secure, no matter what I do, so I can go ahead and live as I wish (see Ro.6:16, 23).
- to say God assures His kingdom and its growth, so there is no need for me to sacrifice to meet the needs of the world (see outlines and notes—Mt.19:16–22; 19:23–26; 19:27–30).
- to say believers and the church will grow without me, therefore neither do I have to go nor do I have to serve.

THOUGHT 3. Growth requires much patience and trust.

> He who supplies seed to the sower and bread for food will supply and multiply your seed for sowing and increase the harvest of your righteousness. (2 Co.9:10)

Rather, speaking the truth in love, we are to grow up in every way into him who is the head, into Christ. (Ep.4:15)

We ought always to give thanks to God for you, brothers, as is right, because your faith is growing abundantly, and the love of every one of you for one another is increasing. (2 Th.1:3)

Practice these things, immerse yourself in them, so that all may see your progress. (1 Ti.4:15)

Like newborn infants, long for the pure spiritual milk, that by it you may grow up into salvation—if indeed you have tasted that the Lord is good. (1 Pe.2:2-3)

But grow in the grace and knowledge of our Lord and Savior Jesus Christ. To him be the glory both now and to the day of eternity. Amen. (2 Pe.3:18)

5 The growth is consummated and harvested.

4:29

Eventually, the seed grows to maturity. The fruit does ripen; the day does come when the corn is *fully grown* and is ready to be harvested. By pointing out this fact, Jesus is teaching at least two truths.

[29] "But when the grain is ripe, at once he puts in the sickle, because the harvest has come."

First, the believer's sowing does bear fruit. Jesus does honor His Word, and it never returns to Him void. As we sow the seed of the gospel, we can be assured of reaping some harvest.

THOUGHT 1. What an encouragement to believers! How we should be challenged to work for our Lord! We are assured of results before we ever labor. God assures that fruit will be borne.

Do you not say, 'There are yet four months, then comes the harvest'? Look, I tell you, lift up your eyes, and see that the fields are white for harvest. Already the one who reaps is receiving wages and gathering fruit for eternal life, so that sower and reaper may rejoice together. (Jn.4:35-36)

For the one who sows to his own flesh will from the flesh reap corruption, but the one who sows to the Spirit will from the Spirit reap eternal life. And let us not grow weary of doing good, for in due season we will reap, if we do not give up. (Ga.6:8-9)

So shall my word be that goes out from my mouth; it shall not return to me empty, but it shall accomplish that which I purpose, and shall succeed in the thing for which I sent it. (Is.55:11)

Sow for yourselves righteousness; reap steadfast love; break up your fallow ground, for it is the time to seek the LORD, that he may come and rain righteousness upon you. (Ho.10:12)

Second, believers themselves are harvested, taken on to heaven when our growth is completed. When we have done all that God wills for us or all that we are going to do, God then escorts us home forever (see DEEPER STUDY # 1—2 Co.5:10; DEEPER STUDY # 1—1 Jn.5:16).

And he will place the sheep on his right, but the goats on the left. (Mt.25:33; see Mt.25:34; Mk.9:41)

And I heard a voice from heaven saying, "Write this: Blessed are the dead who die in the Lord from now on." "Blessed indeed," says the Spirit, "that they may rest from their labors, for their deeds follow them!" (Re.14:13)

The wicked earns deceptive wages, but one who sows righteousness gets a sure reward. (Pr.11:18)

131

D. The Parable of the Mustard Seed:
The Growth of God's Kingdom,[DS1] 4:30–32

(Mt.13:31–32; Lu.13:18–19)

1. The parable describes the kingdom	³⁰ And he said, "With what can we compare the kingdom of God, or what parable shall we use for it?"

2. The seed is sown[DS2]
  a. It is planted in the ground
  b. It is the smallest of all seeds
	³¹ "It is like a grain of mustard seed, which, when sown on the ground, is the smallest of all the seeds on earth,"

3. The seed grows
  a. The reason: It is planted
  b. The result: It is larger than all the plants
	³² "yet when it is sown it grows up and becomes larger than all the garden plants and puts out large branches, so that the birds of the air can make nests in its shade."

4. The birds nest in its shade	

Division III

The Son of God's Continuing Ministry: Jesus' Parables and His Authority, 4:1–6:6

D. The Parable of the Mustard Seed: The Growth of God's Kingdom, 4:30–32

(Mt.13:31–32; Lu.13:18–19)

4:30–32
Introduction

In this parable, Jesus describes the growth and greatness of His kingdom, that is, of Christianity (see DEEPER STUDY # 1). He shows how Christianity begins as the smallest of seeds and grows into the greatest of movements. The message of the parable is a powerful message to individual believers and congregations as well as to the worldwide church. The seed of the gospel begins ever so small, but it grows into the greatest of bushes as it nourishes itself day by day. Mature (grown, v.32) believers and congregations alike provide lodging for the people of a turbulent world. This is, *The Parable of the Mustard Seed: The Growth of God's Kingdom,* 4:30-32.

1. The parable describes the kingdom (v.30).
2. The seed is sown (v.31).
3. The seed grows (v.32).
4. The birds nest in its shade (v.32).

DEEPER STUDY # 1

(4:30-32) **Christianity—Church:** there are two primary interpretations of this parable.

    1. Some say the birds are those in the world who find their lodging in the kingdom (the church, Christianity). The kingdom had a small beginning, but it is now growing into a stately movement. Many in the world, believers and nonbelievers alike, have found help and safety under its branches. Laws and institutions of mercy, justice, and honor have to a large extent sprung forth from this magnificent movement. This interpretation relies heavily on the picture painted by the Old Testament. A great empire is said to be like a tree, and conquered nations are said to be like birds who lodge under its shadow (Eze.17:22-24; 31:1-6; Da.4:14).

2. Others say the birds are the children of the evil one (Satan) who see the protective covering of the kingdom and seek lodging therein.

Neither interpretation need exhaust the meaning. However, two facts should be noted.

1. Jesus was speaking to the multitudes in the first four parables. His purpose was to teach what the kingdom of God is like. It is a mixture of good and evil; that is, it is penetrated by those who are evil. He had just been vindicating His Messiahship to the Pharisees, who were set upon destroying Him (Mt.12:1-50; 12:14). It was the same day that He began to speak in parables. His purpose was to hide mysteries from from those who were not truly believers and to protect Himself from those who would destroy Him (Mt.12:10-17). They were the evil ones who had penetrated the kingdom of God. However, this needed to be known only by the true disciple, not necessarily by those who were evil.

2. The birds are used to describe the evil one in the Parable of the Seed.

1 The parable describes the kingdom.

4:30

Jesus stated clearly that the parable was describing the kingdom of God, that is, the kingdom's *present state* on earth. He revealed how the kingdom, Christianity, was to begin as the smallest movement and grow into the greatest movement.

[30] And he said, "With what can we compare the kingdom of God, or what parable shall we use for it?"

2 The seed is sown.

4:31

Like the two previous parables, this one also begins with the seed being sown. Remember, the seed is God's Word, the gospel.

[31] "It is like a grain of mustard seed, which, when sown on the ground, is the smallest of all the seeds on earth,"

a. It is planted in the ground.

As in the previous parables, the seed is sown on the ground or soil, which represents the earth. This is a significant detail. It is the earth—the world—that needs the seed of the gospel. And God has ordained the good news of His love to be sown on every square inch of the earth (Mk.16:15; Jn.3:16; Ac.1:8; 1 Jn.2:1-2; see DEEPER STUDY # 2—1 Co.15:1-11; notes—Mt.13:31).

> For God so loved the world, that he gave his only Son, that whoever believes in him should not perish but have eternal life. (Jn.3:16)

> But you will receive power when the Holy Spirit has come upon you, and you will be my witnesses in Jerusalem and in all Judea and Samaria, and to the end of the earth. (Ac.1:8)

> For there is no distinction between Jew and Greek; for the same Lord is Lord of all, bestowing his riches on all who call on him. (Ro.10:12)

> Who desires all people to be saved and to come to the knowledge of the truth. (1 Ti.2:4)

> My little children, I am writing these things to you so that you may not sin. But if anyone does sin, we have an advocate with the Father, Jesus Christ the righteous. He is the propitiation for our sins, and not for ours only but also for the sins of the whole world. (1 Jn.2:1-2)

THOUGHT 1. The farmer has to have a commitment of heart, mind, and body to sow the seed. All three are essential. Without any one of the commitments, the sowing does not get done or else it is done haphazardly. He must have . . .

- commitment of heart for motivation
- commitment of mind for planning
- commitment of body for planting

Likewise, we need to be totally committed to sowing the seed of the gospel in every corner of the world. If we are not, the job will not get done. People will never hear of Jesus and of salvation, and they will perish eternally.

'And you shall love the Lord your God with all your heart and with all your soul and with all your mind and with all your strength.' (Mk.12:30)

Jesus said to them, "My food is to do the will of him who sent me and to accomplish his work." Do you not say, 'There are yet four months, then comes the harvest'? Look, I tell you, lift up your eyes, and see that the fields are white for harvest. (Jn.4:34–35)

We must work the works of him who sent me while it is day; night is coming, when no one can work. (Jn.9:4)

How then will they call on him in whom they have not believed? And how are they to believe in him of whom they have never heard? And how are they to hear without someone preaching? (Ro.10:14)

I appeal to you therefore, brothers, by the mercies of God, to present your bodies as a living sacrifice, holy and acceptable to God, which is your spiritual worship. Do not be conformed to this world, but be transformed by the renewal of your mind, that by testing you may discern what is the will of God, what is good and acceptable and perfect. (Ro.12:1–2)

And even if our gospel is veiled, it is veiled to those who are perishing. In their case the god of this world has blinded the minds of the unbelievers, to keep them from seeing the light of the gospel of the glory of Christ, who is the image of God. (2 Co.4:3–4)

THOUGHT 2. The earth is fruitless, empty, barren without the mustard seed of the gospel. Without the God news of salvation through Christ, the world becomes a wasteland.

Who has cleft a channel for the torrents of rain and a way for the thunderbolt, to satisfy the waste and desolate land, and to make the ground sprout with grass? (Jb.38:25–27)

For the nation and kingdom that will not serve you shall perish; those nations shall be utterly laid waste. (Is.60:12; see Joel 1:10–13)

b. **It is the smallest of all seeds.**

The fact that the mustard seed is the smallest of seeds is also significant (see DEEPER STUDY # 2). Just because a seed is small does not discourage or keep the farmer from sowing it. He knows the enormous potential of the seed for growth and fruitfulness, so he plants the tiniest seed. Remember, the power for reproduction and bearing fruit is in the *seed*, not in the farmer. All the farmer has to do is sow the seed. But again, someone *has* to sow the seed if there is to be fruit.

THOUGHT 1. What a lesson for believers and churches! The seed of the gospel, though ever so small, is enormously powerful.

➢ No matter how insignificant or small we may feel in reaching others, we need to sow the gospel.

➢ No matter how insignificant or small we may feel our church witness is, we need to sow the gospel (see note 2—Mk.4:26 for discussion and verses of application).

And he said to them, "Go into all the world and proclaim the gospel to the whole creation." (Mk.16:15)

Jesus said to them again, "Peace be with you. As the Father has sent me, even so I am sending you." (Jn.20:21)

Because of the hope laid up for you in heaven. Of this you have heard before in the word of the truth, the gospel, which has come to you, as indeed in the whole world it is bearing fruit and increasing—as it also does among you, since the day you heard it and understood the grace of God in truth. (Col.1:5–6)

Those who sow in tears shall reap with shouts of joy! He who goes out weeping, bearing the seed for sowing, shall come home with shouts of joy, bringing his sheaves with him. (Ps.126:5–6)

Sow for yourselves righteousness; reap steadfast love; break up your fallow ground, for it is the time to seek the LORD, that he may come and rain righteousness upon you. (Ho.10:12)

(4:31) **Mustard Seed:** it was among the smallest seeds known in Jesus' day. Even though the seed was small, the mustard bush grew as large as some trees. It has been reported that a rider on horseback could find shade under its branches. The fact that such a small seed could produce such a huge bush caused people to use the mustard seed as a proverbial saying to describe smallness.

3 The seed grows.

4:32a

Amazingly, the tiny mustard seed grows into a plant literally thousands of times its size. More than two thousand years have now passed since Jesus walked the earth, and God's kingdom has grown exponentially, as the seed—the gospel of salvation through Christ—has been sown throughout the earth.

32 "yet when it is sown it grows up and becomes larger than all the garden plants and puts out large branches, so that the birds of the air can make nests in its shade."

a. **The reason: it is planted.**

Note the words "when it is sown." Again, the critical point is, the seed has to be sown. In like manner, someone has to sow the seed of the gospel if the kingdom (Christianity) is to continue to grow. *Growth follows sowing. If there is no sowing, there is no growth. This is the law of reproduction, of fruitbearing.* The seed can only grow if it is placed on the ground. Until it makes contact with the soil, it is lifeless.

b. **The result: it is larger than all the plants.**

In time, the small mustard seed grows larger than all the other garden plants. The result of sowing is growth. In dealing with Christianity and the church, the result of sowing is to see the greatest of movements (see notes—Mt.13:32; notes—Mk.4:28 for more discussion).

THOUGHT 1. The growth of a tree from a small seed is nothing compared to the growth of a person who truly comes to know Christ nor to the growth of a church that is truly committed to the mission of Christ (Jn.12:24).

> Therefore let it be known to you that this salvation of God has been sent to the Gentiles; they will listen. (Ac.28:28)

> And in order that the Gentiles might glorify God for his mercy. As it is written, "Therefore I will praise you among the Gentiles, and sing to your name." (Ro.15:9)

> So that in Christ Jesus the blessing of Abraham might come to the Gentiles, so that we might receive the promised Spirit through faith. (Ga.3:14)

> And they sang a new song, saying, "Worthy are you to take the scroll and to open its seals, for you were slain, and by your blood you ransomed people for God from every tribe and language and people and nation." (Re.5:9)

> Of the increase of his government and of peace there will be no end, on the throne of David and over his kingdom, to establish it and to uphold it with justice and with righteousness from this time forth and forevermore. The zeal of the LORD of hosts will do this. (Is.9:7)

> For you will spread abroad to the right and to the left, and your offspring will possess the nations and will people the desolate cities. . . . Behold, you shall call a nation that you do not know, and a nation that did not know you shall run to you, because of the LORD your God, and of the Holy One of Israel, for he has glorified you. (Is.55:3, 5)

4 The birds nest in its shade.

Jesus concluded this parable by pointing out that the birds nest in the mustard tree. Many commentators also point out that birds feast on its seeds. Note the application: the church is a refuge in our weary, sin-cursed world. Think of how the world has been blessed by the presence and work of the church and the influence of the gospel! The very fact that the bush (the church) is present with *so much good* to be feasted upon means that many will come to its shade (see note—Mt.13:32 for discussion).

4:32b

[32] "yet when it is sown it grows up and becomes larger than all the garden plants and puts out large branches, so that the birds of the air can make nests in its shade."

(Mt.13:34–35)

³³ With many such parables he spoke the word to them, as they were able to hear it.

³⁴ He did not speak to them without a parable, but privately to his own disciples he explained everything.

1. To illustrate the Word
2. To teach step by step

3. To be able to apply the lessons in private

Division III

The Son of God's Continuing Ministry: Jesus' Parables and His Authority, 4:1–6:6

E. The Use of Parables by Jesus: Why He Used Parables, 4:33–34

(Mt.13:34–35)

4:33–34
Introduction

The wisest of all teachers used illustrations to convey spiritual truths; more specifically, He used parables (see DEEPER STUDY # 1—Mk.4:2 for a detailed discussion). This passage presents three practical reasons why Jesus used these illustrations in His teaching (see outline and notes—Mt.13:10–17 for a detailed discussion of the reasons Jesus spoke in parables). This is, *The Use of Parables by Jesus: Why He Used Parables,* 4:33–34.

1. To illustrate the Word (v.33).
2. To teach step by step (v.33).
3. To be able to apply the lessons in private (v.34).

4:33

1 To illustrate the Word.

The first reason Jesus used parables was to illustrate the Word. Note the statement, "He spoke the *word* to them." What *word* did He preach? What is meant by *the word*?

³³ With many such parables he spoke the word to them, as they were able to hear it.

> ➤ It is "the Word of the kingdom" (Mt.13:19–20, 22–23; Mk.4:16, 18, 20; Lu.8:15).
> ➤ It is "the Word of God" (Mk.7:13; Lu.3:2; 4:4; 5:1; 8:11, 21; 11:28; 1 Th.2:13).
> ➤ It is "the Word (message) of this salvation" (Ac.13:26).
> ➤ It is simply "the Word" (Ac.17:11; Gal.6:6; Ph.1:14; 1 Th.1:6; 1 Ti.5:17; 2 Ti.4:2; Js.1:21; 1 Pe.2:2, 8).
> ➤ It is "the Word of His grace" (Ac.20:32).
> ➤ It is "the Word of faith" (Ro.10:8).
> ➤ It is "the Word (message) of reconciliation" (2 Co.5:19).
> ➤ It is "the Word of life" (Ph.2:16; 1 Jn.1:1).
> ➤ It is "the Word of the truth" (Col.1:5).
> ➤ It is "the Word of Christ" (Col.3:16).
> ➤ It is "the trustworthy (faithful) Word" (Tit.1:9).
> ➤ It is "the Word of righteousness" (He.5:13).

➤ It is "the Word of exhortation" (He.13:22).

➤ It is "the implanted Word" (Js.1:21).

➤ It is "the prophetic Word confirmed (made sure)" (2 Pe.1:19).

➤ It is "the Word about patient endurance (command to persevere or endure, word of perseverance)" (Re.3:10).

➤ It is called "the Word of their [Christian brothers and sisters] testimony" (Re.12:11).

Jesus used the parable to illustrate the great truths of the Word. What is there about illustrations or parables that caused Jesus to use them so much?

First, stories and pictures are more interesting and tend to *draw* a person's attention more readily.

Second, some experts believe a person thinks only in pictures; others believe abstract thought apart from pictures is possible. No matter, it is certainly easier to see and remember pictures than statements, principles, or rules.

Third, parables usually require more thought to see the comparison between the story and the truth. Parables are not for the lazy and non-thinking person.

4:33

³³ With many such parables he spoke the word to them, as they were able to hear it.

2 To teach step by step.

The second reason Jesus used parables was to teach step by step. He taught the people "as they were able to hear it (understand)." This means at least three things.

First, Jesus drew comparisons from the people's daily lives, from things and events with which they were familiar. Second, Jesus spoke in the language of the people, using simple and plain words. He did not seek to show a superiority over the people: a superior education, vocabulary, speaking ability, or anything else. He never acted above the people; He always spoke to them on their level.

Third, Jesus taught the people *progressively*. He moved them along step by step as they were able to grasp spiritual truth. The point of the spiritual truth was not available to all, but the story itself was understandable to all. It could easily be recalled in the future for spiritual growth if the person was stirred to seek for the truth.

It should always be remembered that the lazy and non-thinking person seldom learns or achieves, and the unbeliever never succeeds spiritually. Matthew discusses this in some detail (see outline and notes—Mt.13:10-11; 13:12; 13:13-15).

4:34

³⁴ He did not speak to them without a parable, but privately to his own disciples he explained everything.

3 To be able to apply the lessons in private.

The third reason Jesus used parables was to enforce the lesson in private. It was now time to give some very special lessons to His close associates, the twelve disciples. They needed to know *the mysteries of the kingdom* (see notes—Mt.13:10-17 for discussion and application).

F. The Authority of Jesus over Nature: Rest and Peace, 4:35–41

(Mt.8:23–27; Lu.8:22–25)

35 On that day, when evening had come, he said to them, "Let us go across to the other side."

36 And leaving the crowd, they took him with them in the boat, just as he was. And other boats were with him.

37 And a great windstorm arose, and the waves were breaking into the boat, so that the boat was already filling.

38 But he was in the stern, asleep on the cushion. And they woke him and said to him, "Teacher, do you not care that we are perishing?"

39 And he awoke and rebuked the wind and said to the sea, "Peace! Be still!" And the wind ceased, and there was a great calm.
40 He said to them, "Why are you so afraid? Have you still no faith?"

41 And they were filled with great fear and said to one another, "Who then is this, that even the wind and the sea obey him?"

1. **Rest and peace are sought after a tiring day**
   a. Jesus was very tired when evening came
   b. Jesus was so fatigued that He left for the other shore without any preparation
   c. Jesus drew others to follow Him also
2. **Rest and peace can be experienced despite a great storm**
   a. The storm struck quickly and the boat filled with water
   b. The storm did not disturb Jesus' rest and peace: He slept
3. **Rest and peace are a concern to Jesus**
   a. The disciples were struck with fear, the fear of drowning
   b. The power of Jesus was demonstrated: He controlled the situation

4. **Rest and peace come through two sources**
   a. Through faith
   b. Through Jesus, His power and His Word, 39

Division III

The Son of God's Continuing Ministry: Jesus' Parables and His Authority, 4:1–6:6

F. The Authority of Jesus over Nature: Rest and Peace, 4:35–41

(Mt.8:23–27; Lu.8:22–25)

4:35–41
Introduction

Why do bad things happen to good people? Why does God allow us to go through painful or frightening situations? These are age-old questions that people—both believers and unbelievers—ask today and will continue to ask as long as time endures.

In this passage, Jesus' disciples encountered a terrifying, life-threatening situation: a fierce storm arose while they were sailing across the Sea of Galilee. What was the purpose of this experience? Why did God allow a storm to develop on the sea with Jesus in the boat? Verse 41 tells us the purpose for this storm. And what a marvelous purpose it was: to stir His people to ask, "Who is this?" Jesus proved again that He is the Messiah! Jesus' calming the storm accomplished three things:

- It demonstrated who He is: the Sovereign Lord who has all power—even power over nature.
- It strengthened His followers' faith, belief in Him as the Messiah and in His personal care as their Savior.
- It gave to all generations a picture of His care and power to deliver through all the storms of life (trials and fearful experiences).

Whatever the storm or trial we face or how terrifying it may be—Jesus is able to deliver us and give us peace. In Jesus' day, few trials could be as terrifying as being caught in a life-threatening storm at sea. In this experience, the Lord has demonstrated His wonderful care and power to deliver us through all the storms of life. This is, *The Authority of Jesus over Nature: Rest and Peace,* 4:35-41.

1. Rest and peace are sought after a tiring day (vv.35-36).
2. Rest and peace can be experienced despite a great storm (vv.37-38).
3. Rest and peace are a concern to Jesus (vv.38-39).
4. Rest and peace come through two sources (vv.40-41).

4:35-36

1 Rest and peace are sought after a tiring day.

³⁵ On that day, when evening had come, he said to them, "Let us go across to the other side." ³⁶ And leaving the crowd, they took him with them in the boat, just as he was. And other boats were with him.

After a long and exhausting day of ministry, Jesus and His disciples needed a break. He instructed the disciples to raise anchor and move to the other side of the Sea of Galilee, where, away from people, they could find some peace and rest.

a. Jesus was very tired when evening came (v.35).
During the evening, Jesus sought rest and peace after a very busy day. He had been teaching all day to a multitude of people. The crowd had been so massive and pressing that they had forced Him offshore into a boat (Mk.4:1). As anyone knows, just being in such a huge throng of people and struggling for space is tiring. It strains and taxes even the strongest and most patient person. An abundance of noise, movement, and other distractions, along with the difficulty of projecting His voice to such a huge crowd made Jesus' task even more exhausting. Imagine our Lord's fatigue, having been responsible for the crowd, controlling and teaching them all day long.

b. Jesus was so fatigued that He left for the other shore without any preparation (v.36a).
Our Lord's exhaustion is seen in the fact that He left immediately for the other shore without making any preparations whatsoever. Note the words, "they took Him . . . just as He was" (v.36). He took no provisions, no change of clothing, and spent no time notifying His family that He would be gone a while—nothing mattered at this moment but rest and peace. He just had to get away. Jesus was so exhausted He even slept through the storm (v.38).

c. Jesus drew others to follow Him also (v.36b).
Mark reported an interesting detail not included by the other Gospel writers: other boats followed Jesus' boat across the Sea. Mark mentions this bit of information to stress Christ's deity, His being the Son of God. People were so drawn to Him and needed what only He can offer so desperately that they would not leave Him alone. Their persistence served another purpose: there would be additional witnesses to the miracle He would perform along the way, other witnesses to His great power and control over nature.

THOUGHT 1. In laboring to the point of exhaustion, Jesus sets a dynamic example. How many of us ever serve the Lord to the point that we just collapse, being unable to even shower or change clothes, being so tired that we even sleep through violent storms? Our Lord's example reminds us that we need to be fully-devoted to ministering to people.

> We must work the works of him who sent me while it is day; night is coming, when no one can work. (Jn.9:4)

> The night is far gone; the day is at hand. So then let us cast off the works of darkness and put on the armor of light. (Ro.13:12)

> Therefore, my beloved brothers, be steadfast, immovable, always abounding in the work of the Lord, knowing that in the Lord your labor is not in vain. (1 Co.15:58)

> Preach the word; be ready in season and out of season; reprove, rebuke, and exhort, with complete patience and teaching. (2Ti.4:2)

THOUGHT 2. At the same time, Jesus set another critical example for us, showing us that there are times when we desperately need rest and peace. At such times, we need to take a break, and we should not allow anything to interfere with our getting the rest and peace we need.

> Now when Jesus heard this, he withdrew from there in a boat to a desolate place by himself. But when the crowds heard it, they followed him on foot from the towns. (Mt.14:13)

> And he said to them, "Come away by yourselves to a desolate place and rest a while." For many were coming and going, and they had no leisure even to eat. (Mk.6:31)

THOUGHT 3. Note those who followed in the other boats. Others had gone away, but these wanted more of Jesus' presence and teaching. They followed Him out of town, booking passage across the lake. Just think what they would have missed if they had turned away and not followed Him. A storm, yes! But they would have also missed experiencing His salvation and power over the storm. They would also have missed the enormous opportunity for growth in learning to trust God more and more.

> For he says, "In a favorable time I listened to you, and in a day of salvation I have helped you." Behold, now is the favorable time; behold, now is the day of salvation. (2 Co.6:2)

> Therefore let everyone who is godly offer prayer to you at a time when you may be found; surely in the rush of great waters, they shall not reach him. (Ps.32:6)

2 Rest and peace can be experienced despite a great storm.

4:37–38a

As Jesus and His disciples crossed the Sea, a furious storm arose. Strangely, our Lord slept through it all, demonstrating that we can experience rest and peace in the midst of life's great storms—the trials and terrifying experiences of life.

37 And a great windstorm arose, and the waves were breaking into the boat, so that the boat was already filling.

38 But he was in the stern, asleep on the cushion. And they woke him and said to him, "Teacher, do you not care that we are perishing?"

a. The storm struck quickly and the boat filled with water (v.37).

Mark reports that a *great* (Gk. megale; pronounced *meh-gah'-lay*) windstorm arose. The idea is a severe storm with . . .

- rolling black clouds thundering and tumbling in upon one another
- fierce gusts of wind slamming into everything standing in the path of the wind's force
- heavy drops of rain falling like pellets

The idea in the Greek is something like the fury of a hurricane. Such violent storms were regular occurrences on the Sea of Galilee (see DEEPER STUDY # 1—Mk.1:16). As the vicious winds whipped the waters, the waves lunged to unmanageable heights and landed in the boat, filling it with water.

> And behold, there arose a great storm on the sea, so that the boat was being swamped by the waves; but he was asleep. (Mt.8:24)

> And as they sailed he fell asleep. And a windstorm came down on the lake, and they were filling with water and were in danger. (Lu.8:23)

b. The storm did not disturb Jesus' rest and peace: He slept (v.38a).

Extraordinarily, while the life-threatening storm and all the resulting turmoil were raging, Jesus was sleeping in the back of the boat! He was, so to speak, at rest—at peace with Himself and with others and undisturbed by the trouble that surrounded Him—including nature itself. Because He was altogether certain of God's care, He was able to rest through the storm (see note—Mt.8:24 for more detailed discussion).

THOUGHT 1. The storms or trials of life often come suddenly and violently upon us. And too often Christ seems to be far away, asleep. What we need during the storms of life are the same rest and peace, trust and confidence in God, that Jesus had.

> Who shall separate us from the love of Christ? Shall tribulation, or distress, or persecution, or famine, or nakedness, or danger, or sword? As it is written, "For your sake we are being killed all the day long; we are regarded as sheep to be slaughtered." No, in all these things we are more than conquerors through him who loved us. For I am sure that neither death nor life, nor angels nor rulers, nor things present nor things to come, nor powers, nor height nor depth, nor anything else in all creation, will be able to separate us from the love of God in Christ Jesus our Lord. (Ro.8:35–39)

> For God gave us a spirit not of fear but of power and love and self-control. (2 Ti.1:7)

> Be merciful to me, O God, be merciful to me, for in you my soul takes refuge; in the shadow of your wings I will take refuge, till the storms of destruction pass by. I cry out to God Most High, to God who fulfills his purpose for me. (Ps.57:1–2)

> Behold, God is my salvation; I will trust, and will not be afraid; for the Lord God is my strength and my song, and he has become my salvation. (Is.12:2)

4:38b–39

[38] But he was in the stern, asleep on the cushion. And they woke him and said to him, "Teacher, do you not care that we are perishing?"
[39] And he awoke and rebuked the wind and said to the sea, "Peace! Be still!" And the wind ceased, and there was a great calm.

3 Rest and peace are a concern to Jesus.

Naturally, the disciples panicked as the boat took on more and more water. Although the roaring winds and raging waves did not awaken the Master, the cries of His followers did. Their (and our) rest and peace are of great concern to Jesus. He not only cares about our physical safety, but also about our troubled souls.

a. The disciples were struck with fear, the fear of drowning (v.38b).

The disciples were seasoned fishermen. They had been caught in storms before, but never in one this fierce and frightening. Understandably, they feared for their lives. They had tried to handle the situation themselves, but it was out of their hands. They assumed Jesus would awaken on His own, as any person normally would; but they were wrong, and they could wait no longer.

Desperate and disturbed by Jesus' non-response, they cried out in fear and frustration. Note their exact words: "Teacher, do You not care that we are perishing?" They confessed they were perishing. They were prideful men, rugged men, men skilled in their profession. They had always handled every situation before, and they had started out handling this storm. But there they stood confessing their *human inability* and their *need* for Christ's help, the help of God Himself (see note—Mt.8:25 for detailed thoughts).

b. The power of Jesus was demonstrated: He controlled the situation (v.39).

Jesus' response to His disciples' plea was dramatic:

➢ He awoke.
➢ He rebuked the wind, and it ceased to rage, totally died down.
➢ He spoke to the sea, and it became completely calm.

The words "peace, be still" (siopa pephimoso) literally mean to *be muzzled*. The use of this word *muzzled* conveys the violence and fury of the storm and stresses the dramatic act of Jesus.

THOUGHT 1. The power of Jesus to control the sea and its storms, to control nature itself, demonstrates three facts (see note 6—Mt.8:26 for more detailed thoughts).

1) Christ is the Son of God, the Sovereign Lord over all nature and life. He not only possesses the authority of God; but, as Mark sets out to prove, He is the Son of God Himself (see Deeper Study # 2—Mk.1:1).

2) Christ can calm any storm of life for us.

> And Jesus came and said to them, "All authority in heaven and on earth has been given to me." (Mt.28:18)
>
> But he said, "What is impossible with man is possible with God." (Lu.18:27)
>
> Now to him who is able to do far more abundantly than all that we ask or think, according to the power at work within us. (Ep.3:20)
>
> Who alone stretched out the heavens and trampled the waves of the sea. (Jb.9:8)
>
> Who stills the roaring of the seas, the roaring of their waves, the tumult of the peoples. (Ps.65:7)

3) Christ can strengthen us to go through any trial.

> No temptation has overtaken you that is not common to man. God is faithful, and he will not let you be tempted beyond your ability, but with the temptation he will also provide the way of escape, that you may be able to endure it. (1 Co.10:13)
>
> Blessed be the God and Father of our Lord Jesus Christ, the Father of mercies and God of all comfort, Who comforts us in all our affliction, so that we may be able to comfort those who are in any affliction, with the comfort with which we ourselves are comforted by God. (2 Co.1:3–4)
>
> But thanks be to God, who in Christ always leads us in triumphal procession, and through us spreads the fragrance of the knowledge of him everywhere. (2 Co.2:14)
>
> The Lord will rescue me from every evil deed and bring me safely into his heavenly kingdom. To him be the glory forever and ever. Amen. (2 Ti.4:18)
>
> For he will deliver you from the snare of the fowler and from the deadly pestilence. (Ps.91:3)

4 Rest and peace come through two sources.

4:40–41

Our Lord had a great lesson to teach His fearful disciples. By preserving this story in God's Holy Word, the Holy Spirit wants us to grasp this lesson as well. It is a lesson that will guide us through all the fierce storms we may face in our lives: rest and peace in the midst of the storm come through faith in Christ and in the power of His Word.

⁴⁰ He said to them, "Why are you so afraid? Have you still no faith?"

⁴¹ And they were filled with great fear and said to one another, "Who then is this, that even the wind and the sea obey him?"

a. Through faith (v.40).

Jesus rebuked His disciples for their fear. Why was the Lord so displeased with the disciples being intensely afraid of the furious storm? The answer is, because it revealed their lack of faith. Not only had they doubted Jesus' power over the storm, they had doubted His care for them. Surely, they struck a painful blow to Jesus' heart when they said, "Do you not care?" (v.38). (See notes and Deeper Study # 2—Mt.8:26 for detailed discussion and thoughts. Also see notes—Mk.11:22-23; note and Deeper Study # 1—Gal.2:15-16.)

THOUGHT 1. We will only have rest and peace when we have faith in our Lord. The opposite of faith is fear. When we are afraid, we reveal that we doubt both our Lord's hand and His heart: His power over our circumstances, and His care for us. When pressed by a threatening situation or crushing circumstances, it is so easy to think that God does not care about us, that if He loved us, He would not allow this to happen. Surely, nothing we could say hurts God more. The Father loves us so much that He gave His Son for us (Jn.3:16; Ro.8:32). The Son loves us so much that He died on the cross for us (Jn.15:13; Ro.5:8). How can we be so faithless as to think that He does not care about us?

He who did not spare his own Son but gave him up for us all, how will he not also with him graciously give us all things? (Ro.8:32)

Since we have the same spirit of faith according to what has been written, "I believed, and so I spoke," we also believe, and so we also speak, knowing that he who raised the Lord Jesus will raise us also with Jesus and bring us with you into his presence. (2 Co.4:13–14)

. . . But I am not ashamed, for I know whom I have believed, and I am convinced that he is able to guard until that day what has been entrusted to me. (2 Ti.1:12)

The Lord is my light and my salvation; whom shall I fear? The Lord is the stronghold of my life; of whom shall I be afraid? (Ps.27:1)

He is not afraid of bad news; his heart is firm, trusting in the Lord. (Ps.112:7)

b. Through Jesus, His power and His Word (v.41).

The disciples were awestruck by the immeasurable, unstoppable power of Jesus' Word. The Lord had merely spoken, and the life-threatening storm had ceased (v.39). The power of Christ's Word provoked great fear in their hearts. *The Bible Knowledge Commentary* explains their fear:

In stilling the storm Jesus assumed the authority exercised only by God in the Old Testament (cf. Pss.89:8–9; 104:5–9; 106:8–9; 107:23–32). That is why the disciples were terrified (lit., "feared a great fear") when they saw that even the forces of nature did obey Him. The verb "terrified" ["filled with great fear" ESV; "feared exceedingly" NKJV; "became very much afraid" NASB]. . . . refers to a reverence that overtakes people in the presence of supernatural power (cf.16:8).[1]

More than ever before, the disciples were convinced that Jesus is truly God. More than ever before they knew what it meant to call Him "Lord." And, more than ever before, they knew that they could trust Him and His Word (see note—Mt.8:27 for discussion).

Come to me, all who labor and are heavy laden, and I will give you rest. (Mt.11:28)

Peace I leave with you; my peace I give to you. Not as the world gives do I give to you. Let not your hearts be troubled, neither let them be afraid. (Jn.14:27)

I have said these things to you, that in me you may have peace. In the world you will have tribulation. But take heart; I have overcome the world. (Jn.16:33)

How God anointed Jesus of Nazareth with the Holy Spirit and with power. He went about doing good and healing all who were oppressed by the devil, for God was with him. (Ac.10:38)

And what is the immeasurable greatness of his power toward us who believe, according to the working of his great might that he worked in Christ when he raised him from the dead and seated him at his right hand in the heavenly places, far above all rule and authority and power and dominion, and above every name that is named, not only in this age but also in the one to come. And he put all things under his feet and gave him as head over all things to the church. (Ep.1:19–22)

For we do not have a high priest who is unable to sympathize with our weaknesses, but one who in every respect has been tempted as we are, yet without sin. Let us then with confidence draw near to the throne of grace, that we may receive mercy and find grace to help in time of need. (He.4:15–16)

---

1 Walvoord and Zuck, *The Bible Knowledge Commentary: An Exposition of the Scriptures by Dallas Seminary Faculty*, (Wheaton, IL: Victor Books, 1983). Digital edition via Wordsearch Bible Software.

CHAPTER 5

G. The Authority of Jesus to Banish Demons:
Hope for the Most Severely Affected,[DS1] 5:1–20

(Mt.8:28-34; Lu.8:26-39)

They came to the other side of the sea, to the country of the Gerasenes.

² And when Jesus had stepped out of the boat, immediately there met him out of the tombs a man with an unclean spirit. ³ He lived among the tombs. And no one could bind him anymore, not even with a chain, ⁴ for he had often been bound with shackles and chains, but he wrenched the chains apart, and he broke the shackles in pieces. No one had the strength to subdue him. ⁵ Night and day among the tombs and on the mountains he was always crying out and cutting himself with stones. ⁶ And when he saw Jesus from afar, he ran and fell down before him.

⁷ And crying out with a loud voice, he said, "What have you to do with me, Jesus, Son of the Most High God? I adjure you by God, do not torment me." ⁸ For he was saying to him, "Come out of the man, you unclean spirit!"

⁹ And Jesus asked him, "What is your name?" He replied, "My name is Legion, for we are many." ¹⁰ And he begged him earnestly not to send them out of the country. ¹¹ Now a great herd of pigs was feeding there on the hillside, ¹² and they begged him, saying, "Send us to the pigs; let us enter them." ¹³ So he gave them permission. And the unclean spirits came out and entered the pigs; and the herd, numbering about two thousand, rushed down the steep bank into the sea and drowned in the sea.

1. **Scene 1: An eerie event at night—on the lakeshore among the tombs, Mk.4:35, 41**
2. **Scene 2: A man hopelessly possessed—without Jesus**
   a. He had an evil spirit

   b. He lived among the tombs[DS2]
   c. He was cut off from society

   d. He was uncontrollable, unrestrained, wild, and violent tempered
   e. He was naked, 15

   f. He repeatedly inflicted wounds upon himself

3. **Scene 3: A man desperately affected by the Son of God**
   a. He worshiped Jesus
   b. He acknowledged the deity of Jesus
   c. He begged not to be tortured

4. **Scene 4: A man miraculously cleansed by Jesus' authority**
   a. Jesus spoke His powerful words
   b. Jesus exposed the man's great need

   c. Jesus showed the nature of evil spirits
      1) Were subject to Christ
      2) Desired a body to indwell and influence

      3) Were destroyers, malicious and violent[DS3]

5. **Scene 5: A people callously rejected Jesus—by begging Him to leave their presence**
   a. A logical reaction: Ran to tell what had happened
   b. A logical investigation: Came to Jesus

   c. A logical account: Told of the healing and also of the pigs

   d. An illogical request: Asked Jesus to leave
   e. A tragic end: Jesus left
6. **Scene 6: A man deliberately commissioned by Jesus**
   a. He requested discipleship
   b. He was sent home to be a witness there[DS4]

   c. He was faithful
   d. He was successful

¹⁴ The herdsmen fled and told it in the city and in the country. And people came to see what it was that had happened.

¹⁵ And they came to Jesus and saw the demon-possessed man, the one who had had the legion, sitting there, clothed and in his right mind, and they were afraid. ¹⁶ And those who had seen it described to them what had happened to the demon-possessed man and to the pigs. ¹⁷ And they began to beg Jesus to depart from their region. ¹⁸ As he was getting into the boat, the man who had been possessed with demons begged him that he might be with him. ¹⁹ And he did not permit him but said to him, "Go home to your friends and tell them how much the Lord has done for you, and how he has had mercy on you." ²⁰ And he went away and began to proclaim in the Decapolis how much Jesus had done for him, and everyone marveled.

Division III

The Son of God's Continuing Ministry: Jesus' Parables and His Authority, 4:1–6:6

G. The Authority of Jesus to Banish Demons: Hope for the Most Severely Affected, 5:1–20

(Mt.8:28–34; Lu.8:26–39)

5:1–20
Introduction

In our society, many downplay satanic and demonic activity. It is a popular source of entertainment and jokes, and many consider it be mythical and fictitious. But the power of Satan and evil spirits is real (see DEEPER STUDY # 1). Demonic activity—influence, oppression, and possession—is just as real today as it was in Jesus' day. Many people are controlled by evil spirits to some degree. Some are extremely controlled by evil; others are just slightly controlled. The Gospels relate a number of true stories of people under the power of demons. The man in the present passage is said to have been possessed by a legion, that is, hordes of demons.

Regardless of what degree an individual is possessed and controlled by evil, no matter how severely affected that person is, Christ can deliver! This is wonderful hope for all—even those held most tightly in the clutch of evil spirits. This is the message of the present passage (also see note—Mt.8:28-34). This is, *The Authority of Jesus to Banish Demons: Hope for the Most Severely Affected,* 5:1-20.

1. Scene 1: An eerie event at night—on the lakeshore among the tombs, Mk.4:35, 41 (v.1).
2. Scene 2: A man hopelessly possessed—without Jesus (vv.2-5).
3. Scene 3: A man desperately affected by the Son of God (vv.6-7).
4. Scene 4: A man miraculously cleansed by the authority of Jesus (vv.8-13).
5. Scene 5: A people callously rejected Jesus—by begging Him to leave their presence (vv.14-18a).
6. Scene 6: A man deliberately commissioned by Jesus (vv.18b-20).

DEEPER STUDY # 1

(5:1-20) **Evil Spirits:** see DEEPER STUDY # 1—Mt.8:28-34.

---

1 Scene 1: An eerie event at night— on the lakeshore among the tombs.

After Jesus calmed the furious storm (Mk.4:35-41), the disciples proceeded across the Sea of Galilee and drifted ashore into the country of the Gerasenes (Gadarenes). The pitch-dark night served as a fitting setting for the eerie episode they encountered. Their boat struck land right in the midst of a seaside graveyard, and as soon as Jesus stepped ashore, a wild-acting man came running out from among the tombs.

5:1

They came to the other side of the sea, to the country of the Gerasenes.

2 Scene 2: A man hopelessly possessed—without Jesus.

This scary man was hopelessly and completely possessed by demons. The purpose of Mark's descriptive account is to show that the man was as possessed with evil as any person can be. He serves as a detailed portrait of the wretched condition of the demon-possessed. Somewhere along the way he had opened the door of his life to demons. He had plunged deeper and deeper into dark, sinful activities and influences until Satan's evil forces took total control of him. But Jesus is God, and, as God, He cares and has the power to deliver even the wildest and most wicked individuals, those held most tightly in the destructive grip of evil spirits (see outline and notes—Mt.8:28-31; Mk.1:23).

5:2-5

[2] And when Jesus had stepped out of the boat, immediately there met him out of the tombs a man with an unclean spirit. [3] He lived among the tombs. And no one could bind him anymore, not even with a chain, [4] for he had often been bound with shackles and chains, but he wrenched the chains apart, and he broke the shackles in pieces. No one had the strength to subdue him. [5] Night and day among the tombs and on the mountains he was always crying out and cutting himself with stones.

a. **He had an evil spirit (v.2).**

The first impression was that the man had an unclean or evil spirit. But as the story unfolds, it is revealed that he was possessed by a horde of demons (v.9). But the point is, some evil, spiritual power dwelt within his body; some alien, foreign, outside power possessed and controlled the wild man. He represents every person who is not spiritual, all who are not possessed and controlled by God and His Spirit (Ro.8:14). Every unbeliever, every person who is not indwelt by God's Spirit, has the potential to end up like this man.

Now the works of the flesh are evident: sexual immorality, impurity, sensuality, idolatry, sorcery, enmity, strife, jealousy, fits of anger, rivalries, dissensions, divisions, envy, drunkenness, orgies,

and things like these. I warn you, as I warned you before, that those who do such things will not inherit the kingdom of God. (Ga.5:19–21)

b. **He lived among the tombs (v.3).**

The demon-controlled man lived among the tombs. These were lofty, vault-like tombs, hewn out of the limestone hills (see Deeper Study # 2). The evil spirits caused the man to dwell in the darkest, most eerie place imaginable, and living in this eerie setting aggravated his condition. He represents every person who loves darkness because their deeds are evil. And he represents every person who dabbles in the dark, dangerous world of what is often referred to as the "black arts," things such as sorcery, witchcraft, black magic, the occult, horoscopes, fortune-telling, and trying to communicate with the dead.

> And this is the judgment: the light has come into the world, and people loved the darkness rather than the light because their works were evil. (Jn.3:19)

c. **He was cut off from society (v.3).**

Living in the tombs, this dangerous man was cut off from the rest of society. He did not live among the living; he lived among the dead. He represents *the living dead*; that is, all people without Christ are "dead in their sins" and are cut off from the *society of God*.

> And you were dead in the trespasses and sins in which you once walked, following the course of this world, following the prince of the power of the air, the spirit that is now at work in the sons of disobedience—among whom we all once lived in the passions of our flesh, carrying out the desires of the body and the mind, and were by nature children of wrath, like the rest of mankind. (Ep.2:1–3)

d. **He was uncontrollable, unrestrained, untamed, wild, and violent tempered (v.4).**

All human efforts to help this pitiful man had failed. He could not be helped, nor controlled, nor tamed. Every attempt to restrain him had failed, for he possessed super-human strength. Even the strongest shackles and chains were no match for the evil powers that controlled him. He represents the uncontrollable evil or depravity of the most wicked and the helplessness of sinful humans to deliver or save themselves (see Ro.1:20–32; 3:10f; Ep.2:8–9; Tit.3:3–7; 2 Pe.2:10–12).

> They were filled with all manner of unrighteousness, evil, covetousness, malice. They are full of envy, murder, strife, deceit, maliciousness. They are gossips, slanderers, haters of God, insolent, haughty, boastful, inventors of evil, disobedient to parents, foolish, faithless, heartless, ruthless. Though they know God's righteous decree that those who practice such things deserve to die, they not only do them but give approval to those who practice them. (Ro.1:29–32)

e. **He was naked (see v.15).**

Mark eventually reveals that the man was naked (v.15). The evil forces that controlled him had stripped him of all decency and all acceptable behavior. He represents the old man—the sinful, spiritually-destitute person—who stands naked before the eyes of God and who desperately needs to be clothed with the righteousness of God and with the garments of the new man—the spiritual person, the new creation in Christ (Ro.13:14; 2 Co.5:17–21; Ga.3:27; Ep.4:24; Col.3:10).

> But put on the Lord Jesus Christ, and make no provision for the flesh, to gratify its desires. (Ro.13:14)

> For as many of you as were baptized into Christ have put on Christ. (Ga.3:27)

f. **He repeatedly inflicted wounds upon himself (v.5).**

The man was a threat to himself and to others, inflicting harm upon himself. He represents all people who have become dangerous, so given over to evil that they are a threat to society. He represents the most dangerous of society who are totally depraved, those so far gone they no longer have respect for human life, even their own; the people whose "mouths are full of cursing and bitterness" and whose "feet are swift to shed blood" (Ro.3:14–15). He represents all who have plunged to the depths of the pit—so deep they can fall no further. He was absolutely hopeless, and no one but God could possibly save him.

But Jesus saved him, and this is the point of this scene in Mark from Christ's life and ministry. By saving the man, Jesus demonstrates that He is God and that, as God, He is able to save the worst of sinners, even those possessed by a pack of demons, even those who have committed the most despicable sins—even those who are totally hopeless.

> As it is written: "None is righteous, no, not one; no one understands; no one seeks for God. All have turned aside; together they have become worthless; no one does good, not even one. Their throat is an open grave; they use their tongues to deceive. The venom of asps is under their lips. Their mouth is full of curses and bitterness. Their feet are swift to shed blood; in their paths are ruin and misery, and the way of peace they have not known. There is no fear of God before their eyes." (Ro.3:10–18)

> The saying is trustworthy and deserving of full acceptance, that Christ Jesus came into the world to save sinners, of whom I am the foremost. (1 Ti.1:15)

> But if we walk in the light, as he is in the light, we have fellowship with one another, and the blood of Jesus his Son cleanses us from all sin. (1 Jn.1:7)

DEEPER STUDY # 2

(5:3) **Tombs—Graveyards:** Jewish cemeteries were always located outside the city or town. This was necessary because Jewish law said that people became temporarily defiled if they touched a grave. Some of the cemeteries were located around limestone hills or mountainous terrain. This enabled people to find caverns or else to hew out tombs in the limestone facing. The tombs were often large enough for a man to stand in (see DEEPER STUDY # 1—Mt.27:65-66).

---

3 Scene 3: A man desperately affected by the Son of God.

5:6–7

The Son of God had fearfully affected this desperate demon-possessed man—desperate to be set free from bondage. The intense, dramatic chain of events that follows depicts a fierce spiritual battle: the man was clearly struggling to be delivered from the evil spirits, while the demons were wrestling to maintain control over him.

> [6] And when he saw Jesus from afar, he ran and fell down before him.
> [7] And crying out with a loud voice, he said, "What have you to do with me, Jesus, Son of the Most High God? I adjure you by God, do not torment me."

a. He worshiped Jesus (v.6).

The man saw Jesus afar off, probably while Jesus was in the boat approaching the shore. When he spied the Savior, he ran to Him and fell down before Him in worship. Note that he ran *to* Jesus, not *from* Him. It seems highly unlikely that the demons would have forced the man to run *to* Jesus. Apparently, the man summoned whatever measure of self-will and self-control he had remaining and ran to Jesus. Before sinners can be helped by the Lord, they must turn to Him for help.

b. He acknowledged the deity of Jesus (v.7a).

c. He begged not to be tortured (v.7b).

The man acknowledged Jesus to be the Son of God, and he begged Jesus not to torment him, that is, not to send him to the abyss or to hell (see Lu.8:31). This detail indicates that the evil spirit was now speaking through the man. No *human* is sent to hell by Jesus—not in this life, not while still living.

Scripture teaches four facts about the devil and his angels (messengers, demons, evil spirits) that should always be kept in mind.

- They believe there is one God, and they tremble (Js.2:19).
- They have nothing to do with Jesus; that is, their nature is entirely different from the clean spirit of Jesus. Evil and evil spirits are diametrically opposed to the purity and holiness of Jesus.

- The Son of God came to destroy the works of the devil. All evil and evil spirits are to be destroyed (1 Jn.3:8; see also He.2:14–15).
- They are doomed to everlasting torment (see Deeper Study # 3—Mt.25:41).

All four of these facts were evident in the behavior of the demon-possessed man. Under the control of evil spirits, he trembled before the Son of God. He was stricken with the purity and holiness of Jesus. He begged Jesus not to doom him—not yet (see note—Mk.1:23–24 for detailed discussion and thoughts).

Note something: the demon knew that Jesus had come to destroy evil. He knew that Jesus was going to cast him out and free the man, despite the man's utter, hopeless depravity. How marvelous the love and power of Jesus, that He frees even the most defiled!

Even as the Son of Man came not to be served but to serve, and to give his life as a ransom for many. (Mt.20:28)

And when Jesus heard it, he said to them, "Those who are well have no need of a physician, but those who are sick. I came not to call the righteous, but sinners." (Mk.2:17)

For the Son of Man came to seek and to save the lost. (Lu.19:10)

5:8–13

⁸ For he was saying to him, "Come out of the man, you unclean spirit!"

⁹ And Jesus asked him, "What is your name?" He replied, "My name is Legion, for we are many."

¹⁰ And he begged him earnestly not to send them out of the country.

¹¹ Now a great herd of pigs was feeding there on the hillside,

¹² and they begged him, saying, "Send us to the pigs; let us enter them."

¹³ So he gave them permission. And the unclean spirits came out and entered the pigs; and the herd, numbering about two thousand, rushed down the steep bank into the sea and drowned in the sea.

4 Scene 4: A man miraculously cleansed by Jesus' authority.

Jesus claimed authority over the evil spirit and ordered it out of the man. The demon yielded to the authority of God's Son, and the man was miraculously delivered.

a. Jesus spoke His powerful words (v.8).

The battle for the man ended when Jesus spoke the word of power to the demon. There was no struggle, no fight, no wrestling. The evil spirit that had so violently destroyed this man's life meekly submitted when the Son of God commanded it to come out of the man.

b. Jesus exposed the man's great need (v.9).

Jesus revealed just how great the man's need was, how *severely affected* by evil he was. Jesus ordered the evil spirit to identify itself. Its name was Legion, referring to the Roman military legion that included over six thousand men. Apparently, the demon who addressed Jesus was the commander over this particular regiment of satanic forces. Think of the dreadful magnitude of this fact: the man was possessed by an army of demons! The point is, the man was as desperate as a person could be, but Jesus' power was more sufficient, eternally so. He is definitely the Son of God. He could cast a legion of evil spirits out of a man.

c. Jesus showed the nature of evil spirits (vv.10–13).

By moving upon Mark to include so many details in his inspired account, the Holy Spirit uses this occasion to teach and warn us about evil spirits. Jesus reveals their destructive nature. We can learn much about demons and how they operate by studying these verses.

First, evil spirits are subject to Jesus (v.10). No evil can stand up to Him. The evil spirit asked to remain in his present country. Apparently, the country and its lifestyle were more evil and more subject to evil than other countries.

Second, evil spirits desire a body to indwell and influence (vv.11-12; see note, pt.5—Mt.8:28-31). They begged to enter the bodies of a herd of pigs. Note the plural noun and pronouns used of the evil spirits and the fact that there were about two thousand pigs (v.13). This again stresses the enormous evil within the man, his desperate, hopeless plight.

Third, evil spirits are malicious and violent; they are destroyers (v.13). As soon as they entered the pigs, they destroyed them (see Deeper Study # 3).

THOUGHT 1. Jesus Christ has the authority to cleanse a person, no matter how wicked and evil.

> But Jesus looked at them and said, "With man this is impossible, but with God all things are possible." (Mt.19:26)
>
> And Jesus came and said to them, "All authority in heaven and on earth has been given to me." (Mt.28:18)
>
> How God anointed Jesus of Nazareth with the Holy Spirit and with power. He went about doing good and healing all who were oppressed by the devil, for God was with him. (Ac.10:38)
>
> Now to him who is able to do far more abundantly than all that we ask or think, according to the power at work within us. (Ep.3:20)

DEEPER STUDY # 3

(5:12-13) **Jesus Christ, Judgment:** the question as to why Jesus would allow a herd of pigs to be killed is discussed in DEEPER STUDY # 2—Mt.8:32.

5 Scene 5: A people callously rejected Jesus—by begging Him to leave their presence.

One would think that the Gerasenes (Gadarenes) would be thrilled that Jesus had come to their country. But they were not. Instead of being grateful that Jesus had come to them, they callously rejected Him and begged Him to leave.

a. A logical reaction: Ran to tell what had happened (v.14).
The keepers of the hogs reacted to the loss by doing what was only logical: they ran into the city to relate what had happened, most likely to the herd owners. The whole herd had been destroyed; it was a huge and devastating financial loss. They had to make sure the fault was not laid at their feet.

14 The herdsmen fled and told it in the city and in the country. And people came to see what it was that had happened.
15 And they came to Jesus and saw the demon-possessed man, the one who had had the legion, sitting there, clothed and in his right mind, and they were afraid.
16 And those who had seen it described to them what had happened to the demon-possessed man and to the pigs.
17 And they began to beg Jesus to depart from their region.
18 As he was getting into the boat, the man who had been possessed with demons begged him that he might be with him.

b. A logical investigation: Came to Jesus (v.15).
In response, the people they told did what was logical: they came to Jesus to investigate the loss. They saw the once-crazy man sitting before Jesus—clothed and in his right mind. They were troubled with fear of Jesus' power, for they had known this demon-controlled man and his hopeless condition. What power this Jesus must have!

THOUGHT 1. When Jesus cleanses people, they come to their *right mind*. They are truly and completely delivered.

c. A logical account: Told of the healing and also of the pigs (v.16).
The eyewitnesses of what had taken place gave their testimony. They told the good news of what had happened to the man, but they also added what had happened to the herd. The locals could not get past the financial loss. They thought more of the world and its money than God meeting people's needs.

d. An illogical request: Asked Jesus to leave (v.17).
Compelled by their fear and their greed, the citizens asked Jesus to leave (Lu.8:37). They were gripped with fear, not fear in the sense of reverence and humility, but a fear of Jesus' power as well as a fear of suffering additional financial loss.

e. A tragic end: Jesus left (v18a).

Jesus did exactly what the people requested Him to do: He left. The Lord will not stay where He is not wanted (Mk.6:11).

THOUGHT 1. Note that Satan got exactly what he wanted. The people rejected Jesus, choosing the riches of the world rather than Him. (Contrast the spirit of Moses, He.11:25–26.)

> For what will it profit a man if he gains the whole world and forfeits his soul? Or what shall a man give in return for his soul? (Mt.16:26)

> Set your minds on things that are above, not on things that are on earth. (Col.3:2)

> Training us to renounce ungodliness and worldly passions, and to live self-controlled, upright, and godly lives in the present age, (Tit.2:12)

> Do not love the world or the things in the world. If anyone loves the world, the love of the Father is not in him. For all that is in the world—the desires of the flesh and the desires of the eyes and pride of life—is not from the Father but is from the world. (1 Jn.2:15–16)

THOUGHT 2. Jesus granted their request: He left them. Jesus will grant our request to be left alone and to go our own way, but the result will be rejection by God (Ps.106:15).

> But whoever denies me before men, I also will deny before my Father who is in heaven. (Mt.10:33)

> And if any place will not receive you and they will not listen to you, when you leave, shake off the dust that is on your feet as a testimony against them. (Mk.6:11)

> For whoever is ashamed of me and of my words in this adulterous and sinful generation, of him will the Son of Man also be ashamed when he comes in the glory of his Father with the holy angels. (Mk.8:38)

> He who loves money will not be satisfied with money, nor he who loves wealth with his income; this also is vanity. (Ec.5:10)

> Why do you spend your money for that which is not bread, and your labor for that which does not satisfy? Listen diligently to me, and eat what is good, and delight yourselves in rich food. (Is.55:2)

5:18b–20

¹⁸ As he was getting into the boat, the man who had been possessed with demons begged him that he might be with him.

¹⁹ And he did not permit him but said to him, "Go home to your friends and tell them how much the Lord has done for you, and how he has had mercy on you."

²⁰ And he went away and began to proclaim in the Decapolis how much Jesus had done for him, and everyone marveled.

6 Scene 6: A man deliberately commissioned by Jesus.

As Jesus was leaving, the delivered man begged to go with Him. But Jesus had another plan for this powerful witness, and He commissioned the man to follow Him by witnessing to those in his home country.

a. He requested discipleship (v.18b).

The restored man was naturally grateful to Jesus for delivering him and immediately wanted to become a Christ-follower. He wanted to join the others who traveled and ministered with Jesus.

b. He was sent home to be a witness there (v.19).

Jesus saw a greater opportunity for this transformed man. He was uniquely qualified to be a dynamic evangelist among his own people, as well as to his community that had rejected Christ. Consequently, Jesus commissioned him to be a disciple at home (see DEEPER STUDY # 4).

c. He was faithful (v.20a).

The man's story ends with two simple details about the rest of his life. First, he was faithful. He obeyed Christ faithfully, proclaiming what Jesus had done throughout the region.

d. He was successful (v.20b).

Second, he was successful. Even though Jesus left the area, but the gospel never left because of this man's witness. He was a walking testimony of the love and power of Jesus Christ. He fulfilled the Great Commission in the region of the world where he lived, and people marveled at his story. No doubt, some—perhaps many—believed.

THOUGHT 1. How fitting that this account immediately follows the parables of Mark 4, for it is truly a real-life illustration of the parables' truths. The delivered man sowed the seed of the gospel in the ground—amongst the people—where he lived. And it brought forth fruit.

After Jesus' death and resurrection, He left this earth, just as He left Gadara. But He left His message behind, just as He did in Gadara. Just as our Lord commissioned the cleansed man to spread the good news, He has commissioned all of us to take His message to every corner of the earth.

When Jesus returned to this area, a crowd of four thousand assembled and stayed three days to hear Him teach (8:1-9). The delivered man had faithfully done what Jesus commanded him to do. Likewise, Jesus is coming back to this earth someday. We are to work faithfully until He comes, sowing the gospel seed in the soil of human hearts. And just as our Lord promised in the parables, and just like this man, if we are faithful, we will be successful.

> **And Jesus came and said to them, "All authority in heaven and on earth has been given to me. Go therefore and make disciples of all nations, baptizing them in the name of the Father and of the Son and of the Holy Spirit, teaching them to observe all that I have commanded you. And behold, I am with you always, to the end of the age." (Mt.28:18–20)**

> **And he said to them, "Go into all the world and proclaim the gospel to the whole creation." (Mk.16:15)**

> **But you will receive power when the Holy Spirit has come upon you, and you will be my witnesses in Jerusalem and in all Judea and Samaria, and to the end of the earth. (Ac.1:8)**

> **Those who sow in tears shall reap with shouts of joy! He who goes out weeping, bearing the seed for sowing, shall come home with shouts of joy, bringing his sheaves with him. (Ps.126:5–6)**

DEEPER STUDY # 4

(5:19) **Witnessing:** Why would Jesus tell this man to proclaim the *good news* when He had instructed the leper not to spread the Word (Mk.1:44)? Jesus had just been forbidden to continue His ministry among the Gadarenes. He needed someone to carry on the work, so He commissioned this new believer.

H. The Approaches That Lay Hold of Jesus' Authority:
How to Approach Jesus,[DS1] 5:21–43

(Mt.9:18–26; Lu.8:40–56)

1. Scene 1: A large crowd gathered around Jesus

2. Scene 2: A ruler's desperate approach
   a. A selfless attitude
   b. A humble attitude
   c. A pleading attitude
   d. An expectant, believing attitude

   e. The result: Jesus granted the desperate request

3. Scene 3: A woman's hopeless approach

   a. A last-resort attitude

   b. A shy, embarrassed, unworthy attitude

   c. An expectant, believing attitude

   d. A confessing attitude
     1) The personal cost to Jesus of serving others

     2) The insensitivity of the apostles

     3) The confession of the woman

   e. The result: Jesus granted the hopeless request

21 And when Jesus had crossed again in the boat to the other side, a great crowd gathered about him, and he was beside the sea. 22 Then came one of the rulers of the synagogue, Jairus by name, and seeing him, he fell at his feet 23 and implored him earnestly, saying, "My little daughter is at the point of death. Come and lay your hands on her, so that she may be made well and live." 24 And he went with him. And a great crowd followed him and thronged about him. 25 And there was a woman who had had a discharge of blood for twelve years, 26 and who had suffered much under many physicians, and had spent all that she had, and was no better but rather grew worse. 27 She had heard the reports about Jesus and came up behind him in the crowd and touched his garment. 28 For she said, "If I touch even his garments, I will be made well." 29 And immediately the flow of blood dried up, and she felt in her body that she was healed of her disease. 30 And Jesus, perceiving in himself that power had gone out from him, immediately turned about in the crowd and said, "Who touched my garments?" 31 And his disciples said to him, "You see the crowd pressing around you, and yet you say, 'Who touched me?'" 32 And he looked around to see who had done it. 33 But the woman, knowing what had happened to her, came in fear and trembling and fell down before him and told him the whole truth. 34 And he said to her, "Daughter, your faith has made you well; go in peace, and be healed of your disease."

³⁵ While he was still speaking, there came from the ruler's house some who said, "Your daughter is dead. Why trouble the Teacher any further?"

³⁶ But overhearing what they said, Jesus said to the ruler of the synagogue, "Do not fear, only believe."

³⁷ And he allowed no one to follow him except Peter and James and John the brother of James.

³⁸ They came to the house of the ruler of the synagogue, and Jesus saw a commotion, people weeping and wailing loudly.

³⁹ And when he had entered, he said to them, "Why are you making a commotion and weeping? The child is not dead but sleeping."

⁴⁰ And they laughed at him. But he put them all outside and took the child's father and mother and those who were with him and went in where the child was.

⁴¹ Taking her by the hand he said to her, "Talitha cumi," which means, "Little girl, I say to you, arise."

⁴² And immediately the girl got up and began walking (for she was twelve years of age), and they were immediately overcome with amazement.

⁴³ And he strictly charged them that no one should know this, and told them to give her something to eat.

4. **Scene 4: A ruler's believing approach**
   a. Not a fearful, despairing attitude
      1) Faced a devastating situation

      2) The answer to the terrible situation: Jesus' challenge to believe and not to fear[DS2]

   b. Not a wailing, whining attitude
      1) The social customs and influences of that day: To express hopelessness

      2) The answer: Jesus' comfort and assurance

   c. Not a sarcastic, skeptical attitude
   d. An obedient attitude: The parents followed Jesus despite the sarcasm

   e. The result: Jesus granted the believer's request

      1) The power of Jesus: Raised the girl from the dead
      2) The amazement of the family

      3) The thoughtfulness of Jesus

Division III

The Son of God's Continuing Ministry: Jesus' Parables and His Authority, 4:1–6:6

H. The Approaches That Lay Hold of Jesus' Authority: How to Approach Jesus, 5:21–43

(Mt.9:18–26; Lu.8:40–56)

5:21–43
Introduction

At some point in our lives, we all will face a desperate situation for which there appears to be no hope. It may be some situation where only God can help: a devastating medical diagnosis, a sudden accident or disaster, the death of a spouse or child, marital unfaithfulness or desertion, loss of employment, a crushing financial loss, or some other overwhelming problem that has no apparent solution.

At such times, how can we lay hold of Jesus and His power? This passage tells us of two desperate people in desperate situations. It gives us the key to approaching Jesus and securing His help when He is our only hope. That key is *faith* (DEEPER STUDY # 1). This is, *The Approaches That Lay Hold of Jesus' Authority: How to Approach Jesus*, 5:21-43.

1. Scene 1: A large crowd gathered around Jesus (v.21).
2. Scene 2: A ruler's desperate approach (vv.22-24).
3. Scene 3: A woman's hopeless approach (vv.25-34).
4. Scene 4: A ruler's believing approach (vv.35-43).

DEEPER STUDY # 1

(5:21-43) **Faith—Believe:** the one thing that lays hold of Jesus and His power is faith (see DEEPER STUDY # 1—Mt.9:18-34; notes—Mk.11:22-23; DEEPER STUDY # 2—Ga.2:16; see Jn.2:24; He.10:38).

5:21

²¹ And when Jesus had crossed again in the boat to the other side, a great crowd gathered about him, and he was beside the sea.

1 Scene 1: A large crowd gathered around Jesus.

After being rejected in Gadara, Jesus crossed back over the Sea of Galilee, apparently near Capernaum, His headquarters. As soon as people learned that He had returned, a large crowd gathered around Him once again. He stayed along the seashore, where the events that follow took place.

5:22-24

²² Then came one of the rulers of the synagogue, Jairus by name, and seeing him, he fell at his feet
²³ and implored him earnestly, saying, "My little daughter is at the point of death. Come and lay your hands on her, so that she may be made well and live."
²⁴ And he went with him. And a great crowd followed him and thronged about him.

2 Scene 2: A ruler's desperate approach.

Jairus, one of the rulers of the synagogue, was in a desperate situation: his daughter was dying (see note—Mt.9:18-19). He turned to the right place, to the right Person. In desperate times, we should always turn to Jesus. Our loving Lord sees and answers all who come to Him. Jarius' attitude teaches us how we should approach Jesus when we are desperate for His help.

a. **A selfless attitude (v.22a).**

In approaching Jesus, Jairus displayed a selfless attitude.

Jairus was a ruler, one of the most important men in the community. The Jewish rulers were already violently opposed to Jesus and were publicly expressing their opposition. By coming to Jesus, Jairus was running the risk of provoking the hostility of his peers and of being censored. He could have easily lost his position and profession.

Notice that Jairus himself approached Jesus. Why would he leave his dying daughter's side to seek Jesus' help instead of sending someone else? Could it be that even they of his own household feared approaching Jesus because of the heated opposition? Jairus would most likely not have left his daughter's side if there had been another person willing to come to Jesus.

The point is that Jairus was desperate for help. He knew that no ordinary person could help him. But he had heard of Jesus' supernatural power. Therefore, he set aside everything—profession, friends, family—he forgot self completely; and he went to Jesus for help.

> All these things my hand has made, and so all these things came to be, declares the LORD. But this is the one to whom I will look: he who is humble and contrite in spirit and trembles at my word. (Is.66:2)

b. A humble attitude (v.22b).

Jairus had a humble attitude. He pushed and shoved his way through the crowd as rapidly as he could. When he caught his first glimpse of Jesus, his pace quickened; and when he finally reached Jesus, he "fell at His feet." This is humility at its height. The ruler—a man of position and power—humbled himself and willingly . . .

- laid aside all his pride and dignity
- laid aside his family and friends in all their prejudice and opposition
- laid aside his profession with all its security, fame, and authority

> **Whoever humbles himself like this child is the greatest in the kingdom of heaven. (Mt.18:4)**

> **But he gives more grace. Therefore it says, "God opposes the proud but gives grace to the humble." . . . Humble yourselves before the Lord, and he will exalt you. (Js.4:6, 10)**

c. A pleading attitude (v.23a).

Jairus cast himself at the mercy of Jesus. He *implored, begged, entreated, pleaded* for Jesus to help him. All of these words translate the Greek word *parakalei*, which means to call to one's side for help. But he did not call casually; he pled with Jesus *earnestly* (Gk. polla), which means "much," "greatly," "with deep intensity." The ruler pleaded and begged Jesus from the bottom of his heart, with everything in him, to help him.

> **When he calls to me, I will answer him; I will be with him in trouble; I will rescue him and honor him. (Ps.91:15)**

> **Then you shall call, and the Lᴏʀᴅ will answer; you shall cry, and he will say, 'Here I am.' If you take away the yoke from your midst, the pointing of the finger, and speaking wickedness. (Is.58:9)**

> **Call to me and I will answer you, and will tell you great and hidden things that you have not known. (Je.33:3)**

d. An expectant, believing attitude (v.23b).

Jarius had a little daughter twelve years old, and she was dying, or "at the point of death." But he had great faith. Note what he said: if Jesus would come and lay His hands upon her, she would be healed and live. Jarius approached Jesus with an expectant, believing attitude.

> **And whatever you ask in prayer, you will receive, if you have faith. (Mt.21:22)**

> **If you ask me anything in my name, I will do it. (Jn.14:14)**

e. The result: Jesus granted the desperate request (v.24).

The result and the impact of Jarius' attitude was powerful. Jesus granted his request: He went with the Jewish ruler to help the man's dying daughter.

THOUGHT 1. Desperation—a selfless, humble, pleading, believing desperation—gets the Lord's help. Jesus meets the need of the desperate who come to Him with . . .

- a selfless attitude
- a humble attitude
- a pleading attitude
- a believing attitude

3 Scene 3: A woman's hopeless approach.

As Jesus was en route to Jairus' house, a hopeless woman approached Him (see note—Mt.9:20–22). The hopeless approach always lays hold of Jesus. Jesus senses the touch of the hopeless and always helps the hopeless who come to Him. A hopeless approach involves four attitudes.

5:25–34

²⁵ And there was a woman who had had a discharge of blood for twelve years,

²⁶ and who had suffered much under many physicians, and had spent all that she had, and was no better but rather grew worse.

²⁷ She had heard the reports about Jesus and came up behind him in the crowd and touched his garment.

²⁸ For she said, "If I touch even his garments, I will be made well."

²⁹ And immediately the flow of blood dried up, and she felt in her body that she was healed of her disease.

³⁰ And Jesus, perceiving in himself that power had gone out from him, immediately turned about in the crowd and said, "Who touched my garments?"

³¹ And his disciples said to him, "You see the crowd pressing around you, and yet you say, 'Who touched me?'"

³² And he looked around to see who had done it.

³³ But the woman, knowing what had happened to her, came in fear and trembling and fell down before him and told him the whole truth.

³⁴ And he said to her, "Daughter, your faith has made you well; go in peace, and be healed of your disease."

a. A last-resort attitude (vv.25–26).

The woman had been hemorrhaging uncontrollably for twelve years. By Jewish law she was considered unclean, so unclean that she was to be divorced by her husband (Le.15:25–27). No one could touch her nor touch anything she had touched. She was to be totally cut off from society and religious worship. She had tried everything she knew. She had seen "many physicians" and "spent all that she had," and yet she "grew worse." There was nowhere else to turn except to Jesus. He was her last resort (see note—Mt.9:20–22 for more details about her condition).

Come to me, all who labor and are heavy laden, and I will give you rest. (Mt.11:28)

THOUGHT 1. When all else fails, there is Jesus. However, most people try all else before Jesus. Nevertheless, He loves us, and He cares for us—enormously so. We should turn to Jesus, for He is always waiting for us—waiting even if we turn to Him as a last resort.

THOUGHT 2. A person who has been brought to the point of helplessness and hopelessness can be helped. When there is no hope anywhere else, there is hope in Christ.

THOUGHT 3. There is no need to reach the point of hopelessness; no need to reach the *end of our ropes*; no need to become utterly depressed. Circumstances should never be allowed to destroy us, not to the point of utter hopelessness. Nevertheless, many reach that point. The one thing to remember is that Jesus does care and will never turn away from the hopeless. He opens His arms to all who come—even to the hopeless.

Casting all your anxieties on him, because he cares for you. (1 Pet.5:7)

We are afflicted in every way, but not crushed; perplexed, but not driven to despair; persecuted, but not forsaken; struck down, but not destroyed. (2 Co.4:8–9)

b. A shy, embarrassed, unworthy attitude (v.27).

The woman elbowed her way through the crowd and came up behind Jesus. She wanted to touch the Lord without being seen or noticed. Why? She was embarrassed and felt unworthy. Her hemorrhaging was a personal, intimate matter for her, something she did not want to be known and discussed. She was considered unclean; therefore, she felt unworthy to approach Jesus.

THOUGHT 1. It is the sense of unworthiness and hopelessness that touches the Savior's heart, not any tendency of being shy or fearing embarrassment. Shyness and embarrassment are only *attitudes that create* a sense of unworthiness and hopelessness. Jesus accepts any of the hopeless who truly come to Him, no matter what causes their sense of unworthiness.

THOUGHT 2. Embarrassing matters, personal matters, secret matters—all are understood by Christ. He wishes no one to suffer ridicule or shame. He will accept the shy, quiet approach that comes to Him.

THOUGHT 3. Personal, embarrassing matters that we all wish to keep secret can sometimes cause serious problems that have the potential to drive us to the point of hopelessness. Even a shy, embarrassed attitude that approaches Jesus will be acceptable. A sense of unworthiness and hopelessness touches His heart.

> The Spirit of the Lord is upon me, because he has anointed me to proclaim good news to the poor. He has sent me to proclaim liberty to the captives and recovering of sight to the blind, to set at liberty those who are oppressed. (Lu.4:18)
>
> The LORD is near to the brokenhearted and saves the crushed in spirit. (Ps.34:18)
>
> The sacrifices of God are a broken spirit; a broken and contrite heart, O God, you will not despise. (Ps.51:17)

c. An expectant, believing attitude (vv.28–29).

The hopeless woman believed what she had heard about Jesus (v.27). She believed that Jesus loved and cared and would make her whole. Her faith was so strong that she was convinced that if she could somehow get close enough to Him to just touch His clothes, she would be healed (v.28). She came to Jesus expecting to be healed. Deep in her heart she believed that He had the power to make her whole.

THOUGHT 1. The same expectant, believing attitude is essential for any person to come to Christ, whether hopeless or not. We must believe in the gospel and in the power of Jesus to make us whole.

> And saying, "The time is fulfilled, and the kingdom of God is at hand; repent and believe in the gospel." (Mk.1:15)
>
> And Jesus said to him, "'If you can'! All things are possible for one who believes." (Mk.9:23)
>
> For I am not ashamed of the gospel, for it is the power of God for salvation to everyone who believes, to the Jew first and also to the Greek. (Ro.1:16)

d. A confessing attitude (vv.30–33).

Jesus had made it easy for the sick woman to approach Him. He had allowed her to be healed without embarrassment, but it was not enough to believe in secret. She needed to be brought to the point of confessing her faith.

The woman's healing had come at a cost to Jesus (v.30). Spiritual power had flowed out from Him into the woman. This expenditure of power must have sapped His physical strength, for Jesus felt His energy drain from His body. He turned and asked the pressing throng surrounding Him, "Who touched Me?"

THOUGHT 1. Imagine the enormous amounts of power that flowed out from Jesus from the day of His baptism to the cross! Imagine the fathomless flow of energy that flowed from the cross, covering believers of all generations. It is incomprehensible! Yet it is a fact—a fact that proclaims the love of the Son of God. He poured out all the power within His eternal being for mankind.

> So that Christ may dwell in your hearts through faith—that you, being rooted and grounded in love, may have strength to comprehend with all the saints what is the breadth and length and height and depth, and to know the love of Christ that surpasses knowledge, that you may be filled with all the fullness of God. Now to him who is able to do far more abundantly than all that we ask or think, according to the power at work within us. (Ep.3:17-20)

The disciples were unaware of what it cost Jesus to heal the woman. They were insensitive to the spiritual energy He was exerting (vv.31-32). They were totally unaware of what Jesus was doing:

➢ "He Himself took our infirmities, and bore our sicknesses" (Mt.8:17 NKJV; see Is.53:4).

➢ He was teaching that public confession of Him was essential.

The disciples' insensitivity made them somewhat surprised at Jesus' question, "Who touched me?" He was completely surrounded by a mass of people. In their surprise, they asked Him why He was asking such a question. How could He possibly expect not to be touched?

As Jesus surveyed those around Him, the woman confessed that it was she who had touched the Master (v.33). She had approached the Lord *being unclean* and had not requested permission to touch Him. But she had still been healed. Now she felt that she must respond to His question and identify herself lest He rebuke her and reject her faith. Perhaps she feared that somehow her healing might be reversed if she did not confess that she had touched Him. So trembling with fear, she fell down before Jesus and publicly confessed what had happened. It was difficult and embarrassing, but she did it.

> So everyone who acknowledges me before men, I also will acknowledge before my Father who is in heaven. (Mt.10:32)

> And I tell you, everyone who acknowledges me before men, the Son of Man also will acknowledge before the angels of God. (Lu.12:8)

e. **The result: Jesus granted the hopeless request (v.34).**

The result is glorious. Jesus granted the request of the hopeless woman. The fear and trembling were taken away, and she was flooded with peace. And she was made whole, both physically and spiritually.

> And to the centurion Jesus said, "Go; let it be done for you as you have believed." And the servant was healed at that very moment. (Mt.8:13)

> Then he touched their eyes, saying, "According to your faith be it done to you." And their eyes were opened. . . . (Mt.9:29–30)

> And Jesus said to him, "'If you can'! All things are possible for one who believes." (Mk.9:23)

> Peace I leave with you; my peace I give to you. Not as the world gives do I give to you. Let not your hearts be troubled, neither let them be afraid. (Jn.14:27)

5:35–43

> Because, if you confess with your mouth that Jesus is Lord and believe in your heart that God raised him from the dead, you will be saved. For with the heart one believes and is justified, and with the mouth one confesses and is saved. (Ro.10:9–10)

[35] While he was still speaking, there came from the ruler's house some who said, "Your daughter is dead. Why trouble the Teacher any further?"
[36] But overhearing what they said, Jesus said to the ruler of the synagogue, "Do not fear, only believe."
[37] And he allowed no one to follow him except Peter and James and John the brother of James.
[38] They came to the house of the ruler of the synagogue, and Jesus saw a commotion, people weeping and wailing loudly.
[39] And when he had entered, he said to them, "Why are you making a commotion and weeping? The child is not dead but sleeping."
[40] And they laughed at him. But he put them all outside and took the child's father and mother and those who were with him and went in where the child was.
[41] Taking her by the hand he said to her, "Talitha cumi," which means, "Little girl, I say to you, arise."
[42] And immediately the girl got up and began walking (for she was twelve years of age), and they were immediately overcome with amazement.
[43] And he strictly charged them that no one should know this, and told them to give her something to eat.

4 Scene 4: A ruler's believing approach.

The focus of the narrative suddenly shifts back to Jarius. The Jewish ruler received earth-shattering news, but with Jesus' encouragement, his faith held fast. Jarius demonstrates the believing approach. This approach always lays hold of Jesus. Jesus knows when a person truly believes. A believing approach involves one simple attitude, but there are also several attitudes that it does not involve.

a. **Not a fearful, despairing attitude (vv.35–37).**

Faith banishes fear and despair. A fearful, despairing attitude reveals an unbelieving heart. Jarius faced the most devastating situation, the indescribable tragedy that parents cannot bear to even imagine. While Jesus was still talking with the woman, someone came from Jairus' home with unbearable news: his daughter had died. Think of the trauma—how Jairus felt. How anxious he must have felt with the pushing and shoving and slow movement of the crowd. How nervous he must have become as Jesus stopped to help the hemorrhaging woman. If Jesus had just hurried, He could have reached his daughter in time. Naturally, Jairus was devastated, crushed, fearful, and despairing. Now it was too late. He was helpless; all hope was gone. The worst had come to pass.

As soon as the awful news was delivered—before Jarius could even react—Jesus spoke to him. Our loving Lord's challenge to the devastated dad is the answer to all our terrible situations: "Do not fear, only believe" (see DEEPER STUDY # 2).

b. Not a wailing, whining attitude (vv.38–39).

Loud, excessive mourning was a part of Jewish culture. In fact, it was a business; grieving families hired professional mourners to bewail their departed loved ones. *The New American Commentary* notes that the *Mishna* prescribes "that for a burial 'even the poorest in Israel should hire not less than two flutes and one wailing woman.'"[1] Being a ruler, Jairus was no doubt a man of means. When word spread that his little girl was gravely ill, the mourners likely lingered outside his door, jockeying for position, hoping to be hired.

But when Jesus arrived at the house and saw the commotion—the manufactured mourning—He rebuked the wailers. Note that Jesus was not scolding the family for grieving and weeping. Jesus Himself wept when His dear friend Lazarus died (Jn.11:35). He was rebuking the faithless attitude that dominated the scene. Believing has nothing to do with such an attitude. Society and others may engage in and encourage wailing and whining—excessive, attention-seeking demonstrations of hopeless sorrow. They may feel and say that nothing can be done now, that all one can do is to bear up under the weight and tragedy of the loss.

However, the answer to any circumstance, mild or tragic, is not hopelessness. The answer is Jesus' *comfort* and *assurance*. Even if the circumstance is death, Jesus comforts and assures: "Why are you making a commotion and weeping? The child is not dead, but sleeping" (v.39).

It is critical that we understand what Jesus was saying. The little girl *was* dead, physically speaking. But her lifeless physical state was only temporary, like sleep. Her body rested in death to *rise again!* Jesus was teaching that death is like sleep for the believer. Our physical bodies rest only for that season of death until they are raised in victory, awakened to live forevermore (1 Co.15:12-58; 1 Th.4:13-18). We have the hope—the promise, the assurance—of the resurrection, which is a living fact, a certain event that is to take place in God's timing. In addition, we have the hope of eternal life, of never dying, of being transported into the very presence of God immediately upon passing from this life (Jn.5:24-29; 11:25-26; 2 Co.5:8; see DEEPER STUDY # 1—2 Ti.4:18). Truly, we grieve when our loved ones die in Christ, but not like those who have no hope. The Word of the Lord comforts and assures us by these glorious truths (see outline and notes—1 Th.4:13-18 for detailed discussion).

> **Truly, truly, I say to you, whoever hears my word and believes him who sent me has eternal life. He does not come into judgment, but has passed from death to life. Truly, truly, I say to you, an hour is coming, and is now here, when the dead will hear the voice of the Son of God, and those who hear will live. (Jn.5:24–25)**

> **Jesus said to her, "I am the resurrection and the life. Whoever believes in me, though he die, yet shall he live, And everyone who lives and believes in me shall never die. Do you believe this?" (Jn.11:25–26)**

> **But we do not want you to be uninformed, brothers, about those who are asleep, that you may not grieve as others do who have no hope. (1 Th.4:13)**

> **The Lord will rescue me from every evil deed and bring me safely into his heavenly kingdom. To him be the glory forever and ever. Amen. (2 Ti.4:18)**

c. Not a sarcastic, skeptical attitude (v.40a).

The mourners laughed Jesus to scorn (see note, pt.5—Mt.9:23-26 for a detailed discussion and thoughts). Jesus did not bother to rebuke them any further. Instead, he took Jarius and his wife away from the commotion, away from the faithlessness and hopelessness. Sarcasm and skepticism have no place with faith.

---

1 H. Danby, trans., *The Mishnah* (London: Oxford University Press, 1933). As cited in *The New American Commentary* (Volume 23: Mark), via Wordsearch digital edition.

d. An obedient attitude: The parents followed Jesus despite the sarcasm (v.40b).

Faith displays an obedient attitude, an attitude that believes and follows Jesus. The grieving parents did exactly as Jesus said: they removed the guests and followed Jesus into the room where their dead daughter lay. They obeyed Him despite others' scorn and skepticism.

THOUGHT 1. A believing faith often requires bearing abuse, scorn, and persecution to follow Jesus. Conquering the impossible requires great faith, and often it requires standing all alone against everyone else.

> So that . . . I may hear of you that you are standing firm in one spirit, with one mind striving side by side for the faith of the gospel, and not frightened in anything by your opponents. This is a clear sign to them of their destruction, but of your salvation, and that from God. For it has been granted to you that for the sake of Christ you should not only believe in him but also suffer for his sake. (Ph.1:27–29)

e. The result: Jesus granted the believer's request (vv.41–43).

Jesus granted faith-filled Jarius' request. In a vivid demonstration of His great love and amazing power, the Lord of life raised Jairus' daughter from the dead (v.41). He showed just how much He cared for the man and the family who approached Him in belief and trust.

The family, of course, was amazed, as anyone would be (v.42). But note the *thoughtfulness* of Jesus. He told the family to tell no one what had really happened in order to protect them from an immediate onrush of sightseers. And He showed genuine tenderness by telling them to give their daughter something to eat (v.43).

THOUGHT 1. *Stubborn faith* is desperately needed by many parents on behalf of their children. However, note what must precede stubborn faith: a desperate faith that forgets and denies self and that seeks Jesus no matter the cost. Difficult cases require both a desperate faith and a stubborn faith. It is such faith that receives the *great* reward.

> He said to them, "Because of your little faith. For truly, I say to you, if you have faith like a grain of mustard seed, you will say to this mountain, 'Move from here to there,' and it will move, and nothing will be impossible for you." (Mt.17:20; see Mt.21:21)

> And Jesus answered them, "Have faith in God." Truly, I say to you, whoever says to this mountain, 'Be taken up and thrown into the sea,' and does not doubt in his heart, but believes that what he says will come to pass, it will be done for him. Therefore I tell you, whatever you ask in prayer, believe that you have received it, and it will be yours. (Mk.11:22–24)

> But Jesus on hearing this answered him, "Do not fear; only believe, and she will be well." (Lu.8:50)

> And they rose early in the morning and went out into the wilderness of Tekoa. And when they went out, Jehoshaphat stood and said, "Hear me, Judah and inhabitants of Jerusalem! Believe in the LORD your God, and you will be established; believe his prophets, and you will succeed." (2 Chr.20:20)

THOUGHT 2. Jesus' instruction to give the regenerated girl something to eat is a picture of the need of new believers. When we who are spiritually dead are made alive—saved, born again, raised to "walk in newness of life" (Ro.6:1; Ep.2:1)—we immediately need spiritual nourishment. That nourishment comes from God's Word. Our Lord expects us to intentionally, conscientiously help every new believer get established in God's Word, that they may grow in grace and in the knowledge of Christ and all that He wants for them.

> But he answered, "It is written, 'Man shall not live by bread alone, but by every word that comes from the mouth of God.'" (Mt.4:4)

> For though by this time you ought to be teachers, you need someone to teach you again the basic principles of the oracles of God. You need milk, not solid food, for everyone who lives on milk is unskilled in the word of righteousness, since he is a child. But solid food is for the mature, for those who have their powers of discernment trained by constant practice to distinguish good from evil. Therefore let us leave the elementary doctrine of Christ and go on to maturity, not laying again a foundation of repentance from dead works and of faith toward God. (He.5:12–6:1)

Like newborn infants, long for the pure spiritual milk, that by it you may grow up into salvation. (1 Pe.2:2)

Your words were found, and I ate them, and your words became to me a joy and the delight of my heart, for I am called by your name, O Lord, God of hosts. (Je.15:16)

DEEPER STUDY # 2

(5:36) **Faith—Fear:** fear is the opposite of belief. Believing God eliminates fear. Believing that God actually cares and will deliver us through any and all circumstances of life erases fear. If God does care, there is nothing to fear. However, if one does not believe that God cares, then fear is present. Why? Because there is no one beyond humans to help, and human help is limited—very limited. There are many times in life when other people's help is not enough, or even close to being enough. Therefore, for the unbelieving person, there are all kinds of things to fear: unfortunate circumstances, bad health, accidents, loneliness, death, and the loss of anything and everything—family, profession, friends, business, home, to name a few.

CHAPTER 6

I. The Rejection of Jesus' Authority:
Why Jesus Is Rejected,[DS1] 6:1-6

(Mt.13:54-58; Lu.4:16-30)

1. **Jesus was in His hometown, Nazareth**

   a. He entered the synagogue
   b. He taught: The people were amazed
2. **Some people questioned Jesus' source of authority**
   a. He lacked proper credentials and education

   b. He was from humble, human beginnings[DS2]

3. **Some people were offended by Jesus: They thought of Him only as one of their own**

4. **Some people blocked others from receiving God's power**

5. **Some people were gripped with unbelief—shockingly so**

He went away from there and came to his hometown, and his disciples followed him. ² And on the Sabbath he began to teach in the synagogue, and many who heard him were astonished, saying, "Where did this man get these things? What is the wisdom given to him? How are such mighty works done by his hands?" ³ Is not this the carpenter, the son of Mary and brother of James and Joses and Judas and Simon? And are not his sisters here with us?" And they took offense at him. ⁴ And Jesus said to them, "A prophet is not without honor, except in his hometown and among his relatives and in his own household." ⁵ And he could do no mighty work there, except that he laid his hands on a few sick people and healed them. ⁶ And he marveled because of their unbelief. And he went about among the villages teaching.

Division III

The Son of God's Continuing Ministry: Jesus' Parables and His Authority, 4:1–6:6

I. The Rejection of Jesus' Authority: Why Jesus Is Rejected, 6:1–6

(Mt.13:54–58; Lu.4:16–30)

6:1–6
Introduction

While multitudes throughout Galilee embraced Jesus' ministry, His hometown was harsh with Him. Most of His neighbors could never accept the fact that He was the Messiah. The fact that a person who grew up among them could really be the true Messiah, the Son of God, was beyond their comprehension (see DEEPER STUDY # 1). Some were envious and jealous of the prominence and esteem He had achieved. Unacceptance, unbelief, and rumors about

Him were widespread among His own people, and their unbelief led them to do some terrible things:

➢ Some in the city tried to kill Him.
➢ Some friends and neighbors considered Him insane, so they went after Him to take Him home (Mk.3:20-21; Lu.4:16-30).
➢ His family was extremely embarrassed by His claims and the wild rumors surrounding Him (Mk.3:31-32).

The most severe critics of most people's lives and work are those who have always known them. This reality certainly proved true for Jesus. This is, *The Rejection of Jesus' Authority: Why Jesus Is Rejected,* 6:1-6.

1. Jesus was in His hometown, Nazareth (vv.1-2).
2. Some people questioned Jesus' source of authority (vv.2-3).
3. Some people were offended by Jesus: They thought of Him only as one of their own (vv.3-4).
4. Some people blocked others from receiving God's power (v.5).
5. Some people were gripped with unbelief—shockingly so (v.6).

DEEPER STUDY # 1

(6:1-6) **Jesus Christ, Childhood and Early Life:** see note—Mt.2:12-23 for detailed discussion.

---

1 Jesus was in His hometown, Nazareth.   6:1–2b

a. He entered the synagogue (v.2a).

b. He taught: The people were amazed (v.2b.)

Jesus left Capernaum and returned to Nazareth, the city where He had grown up as a child and young man (v.1). The hometown folks did not flock to Him like people elsewhere had. From all indications, He had no opportunity to preach and teach until the Sabbath. When the Sabbath came, He entered the synagogue and began to teach. His teaching was powerful, extremely impressive—so much so that many were amazed at the ability and the force of what the *hometown boy* had to say.

He went away from there and came to his hometown, and his disciples followed him.
² And on the Sabbath he began to teach in the synagogue, and many who heard him were astonished, saying, "Where did this man get these things? What is the wisdom given to him? How are such mighty works done by his hands?"

THOUGHT 1. Jesus was perfectly obedient to the Father (He.5:8). He lived and moved and had His being in the Father. This, of course, is the key to our power in life and ministry. *Powerful living, powerful preaching,* and *powerful teaching* all come from the presence of God Himself.

But you will receive power when the Holy Spirit has come upon you, and you will be my witnesses in Jerusalem and in all Judea and Samaria, and to the end of the earth. (Ac.1:8)

And what is the immeasurable greatness of his power toward us who believe, according to the working of his great might that he worked in Christ when he raised him from the dead and seated him at his right hand in the heavenly places. (Ep.1:19-20)

Now to him who is able to do far more abundantly than all that we ask or think, according to the power at work within us. (Ep.3:20)

For God gave us a spirit not of fear but of power and love and self-control. Therefore do not be ashamed of the testimony about our Lord, nor of me his prisoner, but share in suffering for the gospel by the power of God. (2 Ti.1:7-8)

2 Some people questioned Jesus' source of authority.

As impressive as Jesus' teaching was, the people would not believe. They were skeptical of Him and His ministry, looking for some basis to criticize Him and hinder His acceptance. They could find no fault with Jesus' powerful teaching, so they questioned His source of authority. They cited two primary reasons for their doubts.

6:2c–3a

² And on the Sabbath he began to teach in the synagogue, and many who heard him were astonished, saying, "Where did this man get these things? What is the wisdom given to him? How are such mighty works done by his hands?

³ Is not this the carpenter, the son of Mary and brother of James and Joses and Judas and Simon? And are not his sisters here with us?" And they took offense at him.

a. **He lacked proper credentials and education (v.2c).**
   Jesus did not have a rabbi's credentials and education. He had no formal training. His wisdom could not be denied; neither could the mighty works which He had done elsewhere be denied. The people even recognized that His wisdom and power were a *given* wisdom and power, but they could not understand from where and from whom He had received these.

Their question was a good one; it was the right question to ask. It showed that they were thinking about Jesus, but they were making a mistake. Why? Because they were unwilling to acknowledge that He had personally come from God (see note, pt.1—Mt.13:54–56; Lu.4:16–21; Jn.10:30–38 for more discussion and applications).

b. **He was from humble, human beginnings (v.3a).**
Jesus did not have an impressive family background like most of the rabbis (Ph.3:5). He was a mere working man, a carpenter. His family had offered him no social or educational advantage. They were just common, ordinary people, none of whom had ever achieved anything significant in society's eyes; yet, here He was teaching as a great rabbi (see DEEPER STUDY # 2; note, pt.2—Mt.13:54–56 for a detailed discussion).

THOUGHT 1. The basic problem with Jesus' neighbors was rooted in envy and jealousy. They begrudged Jesus the honor and esteem that was being given Him by so many. He had become far more famous than any of them, and most of them had held so much more advantage and promise as children. They were simply unwilling to admit that Jesus was really who He claimed to be (see Lu.4:16–24). They resented His claims, resented them so much that they became stiff-necked, giving themselves over to obstinate unbelief.

> They said to him therefore, "Where is your Father?" Jesus answered, "You know neither me nor my Father. If you knew me, you would know my Father also." (Jn.8:19)

> Then I said, "These are only the poor; they have no sense; for they do not know the way of the LORD, the justice of their God." (Je.5:4)

> But they do not know the thoughts of the LORD; they do not understand his plan, that he has gathered them as sheaves to the threshing floor. (Mi.4:12)

THOUGHT 2. God abhors envy, people resenting gifts given to others. God bestows gifts as He wills to help humanity in its desperate plight. He expects the gifts to be used, and He expects all to encourage one another in the use of those gifts.

> For who sees anything different in you? What do you have that you did not receive? If then you received it, why do you boast as if you did not receive it? (1 Co.4:7)

> Love is patient and kind; love does not envy or boast; it is not arrogant. (1 Co.13:4)

> Let us not become conceited, provoking one another, envying one another. (Ga.5:26)

DEEPER STUDY # 2

(6:3) **Jesus Christ—Accusations Against:** Jesus was not just being rejected; He was being sneered at and despised (Is.53:3). Contrary to the skeptics' claims, He had not come *from* such a humble place as Nazareth, but He had come from God *to* Nazareth—come to seek and to save those who had been His neighbors.

> Have this mind among yourselves, which is yours in Christ Jesus, who, though he was in the form of God, did not count equality with God a thing to be grasped, but emptied himself, by taking the form of a servant, being born in the likeness of men. And being found in human form, he humbled himself by becoming obedient to the point of death, even death on a cross. (Ph.2:5-8)

> For to us a child is born, to us a son is given; and the government shall be upon his shoulder, and his name shall be called Wonderful Counselor, Mighty God, Everlasting Father, Prince of Peace. (Is.9:6)

> But you, O Bethlehem Ephrathah, who are too little to be among the clans of Judah, from you shall come forth for me one who is to be ruler in Israel, whose coming forth is from of old, from ancient days. (Mi.5:2)

3 Some people were offended by Jesus: They thought of Him only as one of their own.

Many of the people of Jesus' hometown *took offense* or *were offended* (eskandalizonto) at Him. The Greek noun (*skandalon*) from which this verb is derived originally referred to "the trigger of a trap on which the bait is placed, and which, when touched by the animal, springs and causes it to close causing entrapment."[2] The bait Satan used to lure the people of Nazareth into the trap of unbelief was the fact that, physically speaking, Jesus was one of their own. Tragically, they eagerly took the bait.

[3] "Is not this the carpenter, the son of Mary and brother of James and Joses and Judas and Simon? And are not his sisters here with us?" And they took offense at him.

[4] And Jesus said to them, "A prophet is not without honor, except in his hometown and among his relatives and in his own household."

> He was in the world, and the world was made through him, yet the world did not know him. He came to his own, and his own people did not receive him. (Jn.1:10-11)

> For, being ignorant of the righteousness of God, and seeking to establish their own, they did not submit to God's righteousness. (Ro.10:3)

> They are darkened in their understanding, alienated from the life of God because of the ignorance that is in them, due to their hardness of heart. (Ep.4:18)

Jesus identified three groups who were offended at and dishonored Him (v.4; see note—Mt.13:57 for a detailed discussion):

- "His hometown" or "His own country": the people of Nazareth, who attempted to kill Him (see outline and notes—Lu.4:16-30).
- "His relatives": friends and neighbors, and perhaps extended family, who thought Him insane (see outline, notes, and DEEPER STUDY # 1—Mk.3:20-21).
- "His own household": immediate family members who were embarrassed by His claims and the neighbors' talk (see outline and notes—Mk.3:31-32).

THOUGHT 2. Christ earnestly tried to reach all three of these groups during His lifetime. Every believer is responsible to reach out to the same three segments of society with the gospel. We should go about every day of our lives conscious of the fact that we will be held accountable for how faithfully we reach out to them.

> He first found his own brother Simon and said to him, "We have found the Messiah" (which means Christ). (Jn.1:41)

> . . . I have great sorrow and unceasing anguish in my heart. For I could wish that I myself were accursed and cut off from Christ for the sake of my brothers, my kinsmen according to the flesh. (Ro.9:2-3)

---

2 Spiros Zodhiates, ed., *The Complete Word Study Dictionary New Testament*, (Chattanooga, TN: AMG Publishers, 1992), via Wordsearch digital edition.

So you, son of man, I have made a watchman for the house of Israel. Whenever you hear a word from my mouth, you shall give them warning from me. If I say to the wicked, O wicked one, you shall surely die, and you do not speak to warn the wicked to turn from his way, that wicked person shall die in his iniquity, but his blood I will require at your hand. (Eze.33:7-8)

6:5

⁵ And he could do no mighty work there, except that he laid his hands on a few sick people and healed them.

4 Some people blocked others from receiving God's power.

The people who arrogantly and enviously rejected Jesus blocked God's power for the whole community. Their obstinate unbelief, questioning, rumors, and repulsion toward Jesus, kept most away. Only a few sick individuals were healed.

THOUGHT 1. A person's unbelief affects and influences others. It keeps others away from Christ. What an awful judgment—a terrible accounting—awaits those who keep their own family and friends and neighbors from coming to Jesus or from following Jesus!

> But whoever causes one of these little ones who believe in me to sin, it would be better for him to have a great millstone fastened around his neck and to be drowned in the depth of the sea. (Mt.18:6)

> But woe to you, scribes and Pharisees, hypocrites! For you shut the kingdom of heaven in people's faces. For you neither enter yourselves nor allow those who would enter to go in. (Mt.23:13)

> Therefore let us not pass judgment on one another any longer, but rather decide never to put a stumbling block or hindrance in the way of a brother. (Ro.14:13)

> Whoever loves his brother abides in the light, and in him there is no cause for stumbling. (1 Jn.2:10)

6:6

⁶ And he marveled because of their unbelief. And he went about among the villages teaching.

5 Some people were gripped with unbelief—shockingly so.

Jesus was astounded by the obstinate unbelief of so many of His neighbors. Nothing they saw Him do or heard Him say moved them; they were gripped with unbelief—shockingly so (see note—Mt.13:58). They had Jesus' presence, His wisdom, and the testimony of His mighty works. They had His power to help them in all their need, yet they stayed away from His meetings. They would not come to Him. In pride, they refused to trust and believe Him. The situation amazed Jesus. Their unbelief was mindboggling, but He had to accept their rejection. He could not force Himself upon them, so He left town and ministered in the villages surrounding Nazareth.

THOUGHT 1. Unbelief is shocking. It is astounding to think that any person would ever reject the salvation of Christ—the salvation that delivers us from sin, death, and judgment to come. By rejecting Christ, one also rejects the abundant life that He offers us now (Jn.10:10), all that He wants to do to enrich and enhance our present lives (see Ga.5:22-23; DEEPER STUDIES 4, 5—Mt.1:21; note—2 Co.3:17-18; DEEPER STUDY # 1—Ep.1:7; Ro.8:28-39).

> For this people's heart has grown dull, and with their ears they can barely hear, and their eyes they have closed, lest they should see with their eyes and hear with their ears and understand with their heart and turn, and I would heal them. (Mt.13:15)

> They say to God, 'Depart from us! We do not desire the knowledge of your ways.' (Jb.21:14)

A. The Sending Out of the Disciples, 6:7–13

(Mt.9:35–10:42; Lu.9:1–6)

⁷ And he called the twelve and began to send them out two by two, and gave them authority over the unclean spirits.

⁸ He charged them to take nothing for their journey except a staff—no bread, no bag, no money in their belts—
⁹ but to wear sandals and not put on two tunics.
¹⁰ And he said to them, "Whenever you enter a house, stay there until you depart from there.
¹¹ And if any place will not receive you and they will not listen to you, when you leave, shake off the dust that is on your feet as a testimony against them."
¹² So they went out and proclaimed that people should repent.
¹³ And they cast out many demons and anointed with oil many who were sick and healed them.

1. **Jesus equipped the disciples**
   a. He called them to Him
   b. He sent them out two by two
   c. He gave them authority
2. **Jesus instructed the disciples**
   a. They were to live in utter simplicity and humility

   b. They were to show stability and discipline

   c. They were to reject any who were not hospitable and receptive: As a warning of terrible judgment to come

   d. They were to preach repentance

   e. They were to minister to the demon-possessed and the sick

Division IV

The Son of God's Training Ministry: Jesus' Intensive Preparation of the Disciples, 6:7–8:26

A. The Sending Out of the Disciples, 6:7–13

(Mt.9:35–10:42; Lu.9:1–6)

6:7–13
Introduction

In every realm of life, a person needs to be equipped before initiating a project or endeavor. To a great degree, our success depends on how well-equipped we are. This is certainly true of people in the business world and in various professional vocations. It is also true of God's servants and disciples. We must be equipped by God as we go forth to carry out our ministry for the Lord. When Jesus sent out His disciples, He equipped them fully for the work He was assigning them to do. Likewise, our Lord will equip us for anything and everything He calls us to do. This is, *The Sending Out of the Disciples*, 6:7–13.

1. Jesus equipped the disciples (v.7).
2. Jesus instructed the disciples (vv.8–13).

1 Jesus equipped the disciples.

Christ did not send His disciples out unprepared and unequipped. For some time now, He had been training them for the work He had for them to do.

6:7

⁷ And he called the twelve and began to send them out two by two, and gave them authority over the unclean spirits.

a. He called them to Him.

This passage begins by reporting that Jesus *called* (proskaleitai, pronounced *pros-ka-lay'-tigh*) the twelve disciples. This Greek compound word means "to call toward." The middle voice indicates that Christ called them toward or to Himself. Appropriately, some English translations (including the NASB and CSB) translate the word as "summoned."³ Some time previous to this, Jesus had called His disciples to Himself for a specific purpose: "that they might be with Him and He might [later] send them out to preach" (Mk.3:13-14; see note—Mk.3:14-15 for a detailed discussion).

This was the very method Christ used to equip His disciples: the method of *attachment* or *discipleship*. Christ simply called these men to *be with Him*: to walk and associate with Him, to follow and live in His presence. By being *"with Him,"* they would see how He walked with God and ministered to people. They would begin to absorb and assimilate His very character and behavior. They would begin to be like Him, and in becoming like Him, they would begin to follow Him and to serve Him more and more (see note—Mt.28:19-20 for a detailed discussion on Christ's method of discipleship).

b. He sent them out two by two.

The time had come for Jesus to send His disciples out to preach (Mk.3:14). So, He summoned them once again and sent them out two by two. Why did the Lord send them out in pairs? There are at least two reasons:

First, for their protection; in order that every word would be established (confirmed, upheld) by the testimony of two witnesses (Mt.18:16).

Second, for their encouragement and support (Ec.4:9-12). Two would provide company for each other and be able to more easily face trials together. They could strengthen and help each other.

c. He gave them authority.

Christ gave His disciples great power. Note that power over unclean spirits is all that is mentioned here (see Mk.3:15). However, the Lord also gave them the authority to heal the sick and to preach the kingdom of God (see Mt.10:1; Deeper Study # 3—Mk.3:15; Lu.9:1-2). Why then, does Mark mention only the power over evil spirits?

The first reason is, Mark is writing to the Gentiles, a people who . . .

- did not glorify God as God
- were not thankful to God
- had become futile in their thinking
- had foolish and darkened hearts
- claimed to be wise, but were fools
- changed the glory of God into images resembling humans and birds and animals and creeping creatures
- were unclean through the lusts of their own hearts
- dishonored their own bodies among themselves
- exchanged the truth of God for a lie
- worshiped and served the creature more than the Creator
- were given over to vile and degrading passions
- turned to unnatural—lesbian and homosexual—acts and relationships
- did not see fit to acknowledge God

---

3   In Mark 3:13, the ESV translates this exact same Greek word (*proskaleitai*) as "called to Him."

- had debased or depraved minds
- did things that are degrading and immoral (see Ro.1:21–28)

Very simply and clearly stated, Mark was writing to a people filled with all kinds of evil, a people *subject* to being controlled by all kinds of evil spirits. Gentile society needed to be aware of the unclean spirits among them and their need to be cleansed of such uncleanness and evil. Therefore, Mark focused on the disciples' authority over unclean spirits.

> **They were filled with all manner of unrighteousness, evil, covetousness, malice. They are full of envy, murder, strife, deceit, maliciousness. They are gossips, slanderers, haters of God, insolent, haughty, boastful, inventors of evil, disobedient to parents, foolish, faithless, heartless, ruthless. (Ro.1:29–31)**

The second reason is, Mark focused on the central purpose of Christ: to conquer the *spirit of evil* and to *destroy the works of the devil*, especially in people's hearts and lives.

> **Now is the judgment of this world; now will the ruler of this world be cast out. (Jn.12:31)**

> **He disarmed the rulers and authorities and put them to open shame, by triumphing over them in him. (Col.2:15)**

> **Whoever makes a practice of sinning is of the devil, for the devil has been sinning from the beginning. The reason the Son of God appeared was to destroy the works of the devil. (1 Jn.3:8)**

2 Jesus instructed the disciples.

6:8–13

The disciples' training also included instruction. As the Lord sent them out, He gave them five specific instructions.

a. They were to live in utter simplicity and humility (vv.8–9).

Christ instructed the twelve to live simply and humbly. They were to travel light, depending totally on God for their needs. Jesus' exact instructions define this command:

➤ They were to take a staff (walking stick) only.
➤ They were to take no bag, nor wallet, no food, and no money in their belts.
➤ They were to wear sandals for protection and coolness and comfort for walking.
➤ They were not to wear two coats, for this would display extravagant and wasteful living.

⁸ He charged them to take nothing for their journey except a staff—no bread, no bag, no money in their belts—
⁹ but to wear sandals and not put on two tunics.
¹⁰ And he said to them, "Whenever you enter a house, stay there until you depart from there.
¹¹ And if any place will not receive you and they will not listen to you, when you leave, shake off the dust that is on your feet as a testimony against them."
¹² So they went out and proclaimed that people should repent.
¹³ And they cast out many demons and anointed with oil many who were sick and healed them.

THOUGHT 1. The whole idea is that the servant of God is to live simply and humbly, just as ordinary people live. As Christ's servants, we are not to be extravagant and flamboyant, worldly and materialistic-minded, indulgent and flashy. There are four critical reasons for this instruction:

1) The Lord's servants are to "seek . . . and set [our] minds" on heavenly things, not earthly things (Col.3:1–2). We are to be *heavenly minded*, so that people will know there is a far better life and land than what this earth offers (see He.11:13–16, 24–26).

> **For those who live according to the flesh set their minds on the things of the flesh, but those who live according to the Spirit set their minds on the things of the Spirit. For to set the mind on the flesh is death, but to set the mind on the Spirit is life and peace. (Ro.8:5–6)**

2) The Lord's servants are to focus on *preaching the gospel and ministering* to people, not on material things such as money, land, clothes, the best food, buying and selling, and accumulating possessions.

> **Preach the word; be ready in season and out of season; reprove, rebuke, and exhort, with complete patience and teaching. (2 Ti.4:2)**

3) The Lord's servants (as we labor and serve) are to demonstrate trust in God for our needs, so that others might learn to depend on God (Mt.6:24–34).

> But seek first the kingdom of God and his righteousness, and all these things will be added to you. (Mt.6:33)

4) The Lord's servants are to teach and depend on God's people to be used of God to meet their needs (see Mt.10:9–10).

> Do you not know that those who are employed in the temple service get their food from the temple, and those who serve at the altar share in the sacrificial offerings? In the same way, the Lord commanded that those who proclaim the gospel should get their living by the gospel. (1 Co.9:13–14)

b. They were to show stability and discipline (v.10).

When the disciples entered a town and found a host, they were to remain with that host and not be moving about from place to place. They were not to seek more comfort and luxury after they came to know a place. Nor were they to offend their hosts by causing them to think their accommodations were unsatisfactory.

THOUGHT 1. There are several good reasons for this instruction (see note—Mt.10:11 for the kind of host to seek). Favoring some hosts over others would . . .
- indicate favoritism and cause jealousy
- indicate a selfish and materialistic mindset and would lead to the questioning of the disciple's commitment
- distract from the disciple's purpose and ministry
- hurt and often alienate the first host and others in the congregation

c. They were to reject any who were not hospitable and receptive: As a warning of terrible judgment to come (v.11).

Jesus instructed His disciples to move on from places where they were not wanted. If a household or town rejected them and their message, they were to shake the dust off their feet and move on. The disciples' rejection of those who rejected the gospel would point them to the frightening fact that God will reject all who reject His Son. His terrible judgment awaits them (see note, pts. 3, 4—Mt.10:12-15 for a detailed discussion).

d. They were to preach repentance (v.12).

The disciples were not to preach their own message or ideas, not what they thought or believed. They were God's heralds, messengers and representatives of the King. They were given the message of the King, and it was the King's message—and only the King's message—that they were to proclaim. Mark reports that they were faithful to this command; they preached God's message of repentance.

THOUGHT 1. God's message was—and is—that people should repent. Every human being needs to turn from sin and self to Christ, from unbelief to faith, from sin to righteousness (see DEEPER STUDY # 1—Ac.17:29–30).

> No, I tell you; but unless you repent, you will all likewise perish. (Lu.13:3)

> And Peter said to them, "Repent and be baptized every one of you in the name of Jesus Christ for the forgiveness of your sins, and you will receive the gift of the Holy Spirit." (Ac.2:38)

> Repent therefore, and turn back, that your sins may be blotted out. (Ac.3:19)

> Let the wicked forsake his way, and the unrighteous man his thoughts; let him return to the LORD, that he may have compassion on him, and to our God, for he will abundantly pardon. (Is.55:7)

> Cast away from you all the transgressions that you have committed, and make yourselves a new heart and a new spirit! Why will you die, O house of Israel? (Eze.18:31)

e. They were to minister to the demon-possessed and the sick (v.13).

Jesus called His disciples to minister to both body and soul. They were to liberate the soul from evil spirits, delivering those who were obviously gripped in the bondage of sin and shame. They were also to minister to the sick, those who were suffering and hurting. Mark reports that they fulfilled this work as well.

Note that they anointed the sick with oil. This is the anointing spoken of in *James* (see note—Js.5:14-15). Oil is a symbol of the Holy Spirit, of His presence. The oil helps the sick person to focus and concentrate on the presence of the Holy Spirit and His power. It is often difficult for a sick person to focus and concentrate. This is especially true when people are hurting and suffering, racked with excruciating pain. It is also true of those with short attention spans. The oil—its presence and placement on the body—helps the sick person focus and concentrate on the Holy Spirit, His presence and power.

Oil is also a symbol of God's care, comfort, and joy, of His mercy to us. It is the oil of gladness. Therefore, oil actually focuses the attention on and stirs the sick person to believe in God's mercy, filling the sufferer's heart with gladness.

> **Is anyone among you sick? Let him call for the elders of the church, and let them pray over him, anointing him with oil in the name of the Lord. (Js.5:14)**

> **You have loved righteousness and hated wickedness. Therefore God, your God, has anointed you with the oil of gladness beyond your companions. (Ps.45:7; He.1:9)**

B. The Death of John the Baptist:
The Immoral vs. the Righteous, 6:14–29

(Mt.14:1–14; Lu.9:7–9)

1. The opinions about Jesus spread as the disciples preached, vv.7, 30f
   a. Herod: Thought Jesus was John the Baptist risen from the dead

   b. Other people: Thought Jesus was Elijah or a prophet

2. Herod's reaction to Jesus: A guilty conscience
   a. Because of several illegal acts
      1) Imprisoning and executing a just man
      2) Stealing his half-brother's wife

      3) Committing adultery

   b. Because of an inadequate religion

   c. Because of a partying, drunken spirit

   d. Because of seeking social approval

3. Salome's reaction to Herod: Weakness of character
   a. Immodest, seductive behavior, v. 22
   b. Immature dependence on her mother,

4. Herodias' reaction to John: A vengeful spirit, v. 19

¹⁴ King Herod heard of it, for Jesus' name had become known. Some said, "John the Baptist has been raised from the dead. That is why these miraculous powers are at work in him."
¹⁵ But others said, "He is Elijah." And others said, "He is a prophet, like one of the prophets of old."
¹⁶ But when Herod heard of it, he said, "John, whom I beheaded, has been raised."

¹⁷ For it was Herod who had sent and seized John and bound him in prison for the sake of Herodias, his brother Philip's wife, because he had married her.
¹⁸ For John had been saying to Herod, "It is not lawful for you to have your brother's wife."
¹⁹ And Herodias had a grudge against him and wanted to put him to death. But she could not,
²⁰ for Herod feared John, knowing that he was a righteous and holy man, and he kept him safe. When he heard him, he was greatly perplexed, and yet he heard him gladly.
²¹ But an opportunity came when Herod on his birthday gave a banquet for his nobles and military commanders and the leading men of Galilee.
²² For when Herodias's daughter came in and danced, she pleased Herod and his guests. And the king said to the girl, "Ask me for whatever you wish, and I will give it to you."
²³ And he vowed to her, "Whatever you ask me, I will give you, up to half of my kingdom."
²⁴ And she went out and said to her mother, "For what should I ask?" And she said, "The head of John the Baptist."
²⁵ And she came in immediately with haste to the king and asked, saying, "I want you to give me at once the head of John the Baptist on a platter."

²⁶ And the king was exceedingly sorry, but because of his oaths and his guests he did not want to break his word to her.

²⁷ And immediately the king sent an executioner with orders to bring John's head. He went and beheaded him in the prison

²⁸ and brought his head on a platter and gave it to the girl, and the girl gave it to her mother.

²⁹ When his disciples heard of it, they came and took his body and laid it in a tomb.

5. **Herod's reaction to his conscience: Feared people more than God**

6. **John's reaction to Jesus: Was courageous and loyal to the end—martyrdom**

Division IV

The Son of God's Training Ministry: Jesus' Intensive Preparation of the Disciples, 6:7–8:26

B. The Death of John the Baptist: The Immoral vs. the Righteous, 6:14–29

(Mt.14:1–14; Lu.9:7–9)

6:14-29
Introduction

The preaching of the disciples throughout Galilee reached the ears of Herod. The news of Jesus troubled him, apparently causing some spiritual conviction. Why? The sordid reason is revealed in this passage. This is, *The Death of John the Baptist: The Immoral vs. the Righteous, 6:14–29*.

1. The opinions about Jesus spread as the disciples preached, vv.7, 30f (vv.14–15).
2. Herod's reaction to Jesus: A guilty conscience (vv.16–23).
3. Salome's reaction to Herod: Weakness of character (vv.24–25).
4. Herodias' reaction to John: A vengeful spirit, v.19 (v.25).
5. Herod's reaction to his conscience: Feared people more than God (vv.26–28).
6. John's reaction to Jesus: Was courageous and loyal to the end—martyrdom (v.29).

1 The opinions about Jesus spread as the disciples preached.

6:14-15

As the disciples preached the gospel throughout the region, various opinions about Jesus spread like wildfire (see v.7, 30f). Herod heard all about what was going on. He heard about a man called Jesus who preached righteousness and who worked enormous miracles.

¹⁴ King Herod heard of it, for Jesus' name had become known. Some said, "John the Baptist has been raised from the dead. That is why these miraculous powers are at work in him."

¹⁵ But others said, "He is Elijah." And others said, "He is a prophet, like one of the prophets of old."

a. **Herod: Thought Jesus was John the Baptist risen from the dead (v.14).**

When the troubled king heard about Jesus and His miracles, he was perplexed. He had known only one man who was so righteous that he was able to do mighty works, and that was John. Therefore, Herod concluded that John the Baptist had been raised from the dead, that is, raised in the body of Jesus Christ.

b. **Other people: Thought Jesus was Elijah or a prophet (v.15).**

Others believed and told Herod that it was not John, but Elijah or one of the other prophets (see note—Mk.8:28 for discussion). As will be seen, Herod refused to believe it was anyone other than John the Baptist.

6:16-23

¹⁶ But when Herod heard of it, he said, "John, whom I beheaded, has been raised."

¹⁷ For it was Herod who had sent and seized John and bound him in prison for the sake of Herodias, his brother Philip's wife, because he had married her.

¹⁸ For John had been saying to Herod, "It is not lawful for you to have your brother's wife."

¹⁹ And Herodias had a grudge against him and wanted to put him to death. But she could not,

²⁰ for Herod feared John, knowing that he was a righteous and holy man, and he kept him safe. When he heard him, he was greatly perplexed, and yet he heard him gladly.

²¹ But an opportunity came when Herod on his birthday gave a banquet for his nobles and military commanders and the leading men of Galilee.

²² For when Herodias's daughter came in and danced, she pleased Herod and his guests. And the king said to the girl, "Ask me for whatever you wish, and I will give it to you."

²³ And he vowed to her, "Whatever you ask me, I will give you, up to half of my kingdom."

2 Herod's reaction to Jesus: A guilty conscience.

Herod lived a life of gross sin, immorality, and murder—including the murder of God's prophet, John the Baptist. Consequently, the news about Jesus pierced Herod's conscience. He could not escape the guilt of his wicked life, especially when a righteous person appeared on the scene.

a. **Because of several illegal acts (vv.16-18).**

Herod's conscience was raw because he had committed several illegal acts, including murder. He had imprisoned and executed a just and innocent man, John the Baptist, because John had been preaching against the kind of life Herod was living. Herod was married to the daughter of Aretas, King of the Nabataean Arabs. On a trip to Rome, he had visited his half-brother and was deeply attracted to his wife, Herodias. He seduced her and talked her into returning with him. Herod's own wife discovered his plans and fled to her father, King Aretas. Herod committed two serious sins. He put away his own wife (her life was probably threatened), and he stole the wife of his half-brother. John had preached boldly against such immorality, and he had confronted Herod directly about his adultery (see DEEPER STUDIES 1, 2—Mt:14:1-14 for detailed discussion and thoughts).

b. **Because of an inadequate religion (vv.19-20).**

Herodias wanted John executed, but Herod refused out of respect to John or fear of him. He kept John alive for a little over a year. Herod had a sensitive conscience; he was not totally hardened against the truth of righteousness. He recognized something in John, something that drew him and caused him to want to hear what John had to say, and apparently, he even tried to observe and do some of the things John preached. These details reveal that Herod had an inclination toward religion, an interest and even a certain amount of belief in God and in righteousness. In spite of his despicable deeds, his heart had not yet grown totally cold to what was right. However, Herod's "form of godliness" (2 Ti.3:5) was inadequate. As every genuine believer knows, religion is *never* adequate. Only a personal relationship with God suffices and meets the need of the human soul. Herod was inconsistent, loving the world and its things more than God and His righteousness.

> Therefore go out from their midst, and be separate from them, says the Lord, and touch no unclean thing; then I will welcome you, and I will be a father to you, and you shall be sons and daughters to me, says the Lord Almighty. (2 Co.6:17-18)

> Do not love the world or the things in the world. If anyone loves the world, the love of the Father is not in him. For all that is in the world—the desires of the flesh and the desires of the eyes and pride of life—is not from the Father but is from the world. (1 Jn.2:15-16)

c. **Because of a partying, drunken spirit (v.21).**

Herod had a guilty conscience because of his partying, drunken spirit. An example of this is seen in the event recorded in this passage. He apparently followed the Greek custom of celebrating special events with lavish feasts, heavy drinking, and suggestive and passionate dancing (see note—Mt.14:6-8 for detailed discussion).

THOUGHT 1. What a scene! So much like our day and time; in fact, so much like so many generations! Believers ought to avoid such indulgences of the flesh.

> Do not present your members to sin as instruments for unrighteousness, but present yourselves to God as those who have been brought from death to life, and your members to God as instruments for righteousness. (Ro.6:13)

d. Because of seeking social approval (vv.22-23).

Herod had a guilty conscience because he sought social approval above godly honor and respect. Under the influence of alcohol, he was stirred with such lust for his stepdaughter (Herodias' daughter) that he offered her anything, even half his kingdom (v.23). Herod's marred judgment and foolishness were seen in this *reckless offer* to his stepdaughter.

When the stepdaughter demanded John's beheading, Herod feared what his dinner guests would think if he did not keep His word (vv.25-27). He was foolish to think that he had to keep a wicked and dishonorable oath or else lose favor with his friends and associates (see DEEPER STUDY # 1—Mt.14:1-14 for detailed discussion).

THOUGHT 1. Today we see people using parties and drinking events to seek social approval. Too often social approval is sought by reckless and foolish behavior—ranging from too much drink, suggestive movement of the body in dance, suggestive conversation; and, as in Herod's case, all of these.

THOUGHT 2. Why does so much irresponsible, loose, and sinful behavior take place at drinking and dancing events?
- ➤ A person needs social approval and acceptance.
- ➤ A person has low self-esteem and needs to fit in.
- ➤ A person fears disapproval, unacceptance, and rejection.
- ➤ Inhibitions, modesty, and good sense are compromised by the effects of alcohol.
- ➤ Impure thoughts and lust are provoked by sensuous dancing.

> But watch yourselves lest your hearts be weighed down with dissipation and drunkenness and cares of this life, and that day come upon you suddenly like a trap. (Lu.21:34)

> You adulterous people! Do you not know that friendship with the world is enmity with God? Therefore whoever wishes to be a friend of the world makes himself an enemy of God. (Js.4:4)

3 Salome's reaction to Herod: Weakness of character.

6:24-25

Although Herod's stepdaughter's name is not mentioned in the Gospels, the historian Josephus reported that her name was Salome.[1] The two acts mentioned in this one scene from her life reveal her weak character.

24 And she went out and said to her mother, "For what should I ask?" And she said, "The head of John the Baptist."

25 And she came in immediately with haste to the king and asked, saying, "I want you to give me at once the head of John the Baptist on a platter."

a. Immodest, seductive behavior (v.22).

Salome danced at Herod's birthday party. Make no mistake about it: her dance was not performed for artistic purposes. No doubt scantily clad, she danced seductively for the carnal pleasure of Herod's drunken, leering guests. Salome's dance borders on the incredible because she was of the royal family. The fact that she would dance so suggestively is a sad picture of her character.

---

1 William Whiston, Tr., *The Complete Works of Flavius Josephus*, (Grand Rapids, MI: Baker Publishing Group, 1974), via Wordsearch digital edition.

THOUGHT 1. So many women—and men—in today's society dress immodestly and behave suggestively. Married and unmarried alike dress and behave inappropriately for the purpose of inciting sexual desire. Even many young girls—underage girls—dress to draw attention and lustful glances. And their parents think nothing of it! On another note, think of the unfathomable amount of pornography that is easily accessible through the Internet, of the sheer number of people who stoop to such shameful debauchery. Or of the serious problem of teenagers and preteens taking nude pictures of themselves with their cell phones and other devices.

More than ever, parents must warn their children and watch them carefully. They must stay aware of their children's activities and regularly check their computers, phones, and other devices. They must be strong and adamant, refusing to give in to pressure and protests from their children and from society. And, more than ever, pastors must diligently proclaim the principles of God's Word to their congregations, being faithful to warn their people of the dangers of immodesty and immorality and to teach them the blessings of holiness.

> For this is the will of God, your sanctification: that you abstain from sexual immorality; that each one of you know how to control his own body in holiness and honor, not in the passion of lust like the Gentiles who do not know God; that no one transgress and wrong his brother in this matter, because the Lord is an avenger in all these things, as we told you beforehand and solemnly warned you. For God has not called us for impurity, but in holiness. Therefore whoever disregards this, disregards not man but God, who gives his Holy Spirit to you. (1 Th.4:3–8)

> Likewise also that women should adorn themselves in respectable apparel, with modesty and self-control, not with braided hair and gold or pearls or costly attire. (1 Ti.2:9)

b. **Immature dependence on her mother (vv.24–25).**

These verses imply that Salome's shameful behavior was instigated by her mother, Herodias. This wicked woman was willing to vulgarly display and degrade—and possibly even prostitute—her daughter in order to get revenge on John the Baptist. Salome's age is not known, but the Greek word used for *girl* (korosio, v.22) indicates that she was a young woman of marriageable age. To have danced in the manner she did supports this, as does Herod's offer to her. She was of age, personally responsible for her decisions. But note how heavily influenced she was by her mother, both in dancing and in seeking what to ask as a reward. She was immature in both spirit and personal responsibility, did not have the fortitude to make right decisions, and was easily led into irresponsible and sinful behavior, lacking self-esteem and a strong spirit.

> He did what was evil in the sight of the LORD and walked in the way of his father and in the way of his mother and in the way of Jeroboam the son of Nebat, who made Israel to sin. He served Baal and worshiped him and provoked the LORD, the God of Israel, to anger in every way that his father had done. (1 K.22:52–53)

> He also walked in the ways of the house of Ahab, for his mother was his counselor in doing wickedly. (2 Chr.22:3)

> But have stubbornly followed their own hearts and have gone after the Baals, as their fathers taught them (Je.9:14)

> And I said to their children in the wilderness, 'Do not walk in the statutes of your fathers, nor keep their rules, nor defile yourselves with their idols. I am the LORD your God; walk in my statutes, and be careful to obey my rules.' (Eze.20:18–19)

THOUGHT 1. Salome is a picture of so many today who lack self-esteem and a strong spirit, of many who sense a great need to fit in. Therefore, they neither think for nor stand up for themselves. Instead, they give in to the immoral and sinful suggestions and lusts of others.

> Therefore go out from their midst, and be separate from them, says the Lord, and touch no unclean thing; then I will welcome you, and I will be a father to you, and you shall be sons and daughters to me, says the Lord Almighty. (2 Co.6:17–18)

> You shall not fall in with the many to do evil, nor shall you bear witness in a lawsuit, siding with the many, so as to pervert justice. (Ex.23:2)

4 Herodias' reaction to John: A vengeful spirit.

Herodias' spirit was vengeful toward John (vv.19, 24). Her bitterness and her desire to humiliate John are clearly seen (vv.18–19). John's preaching against immorality angered her tremendously. She wanted him dead, and apparently, she plotted this whole event, hoping to trap Herod into executing John. Herodias' life is a picture of vengeance and its causes.

6:24–25

> She *wanted to live as she wished* and not be told how to live by anyone else—not by the king nor by the righteous and certainly not by God.

> She *wanted to sin without interference* and without being reminded of it. She wanted everything and everyone that reminded her that she was sinning removed out of her presence.

> She *ignored God*, His law and demand for accountability. She ignored the message of God and His righteousness. She ignored the fact that she had to meet God after death.

24 And she went out and said to her mother, "For what should I ask?" And she said, "The head of John the Baptist."
25 And she came in immediately with haste to the king and asked, saying, "I want you to give me at once the head of John the Baptist on a platter."

And just as it is appointed for man to die once, and after that comes judgment. (He.9:27)

Whoever says he is in the light and hates his brother is still in darkness. (1 Jn.2:9)

Everyone who hates his brother is a murderer, and you know that no murderer has eternal life abiding in him. (1 Jn.3:15)

5 Herod's reaction to his conscience: Feared people more than God.

6:26–28

Herod's reaction to Salome's request was one of regret. He had a guilty conscience because of his fear of what other people—his guests—might say (v.26). Herod had made a foolish promise. Now he was faced with going back on a wicked oath or breaking one of God's major laws: "Thou shalt not kill." His pride prevented him from confessing his error. He feared being shamed and embarrassed by a woman's tantrums before his guests and being the object of ridicule in their jokes. He knew what he *should* do, but in *pride and weakness* before other people, he buckled under to commit a terrible sin (see DEEPER STUDY # 1—Mt.14:1–14 for a detailed discussion).

26 And the king was exceedingly sorry, but because of his oaths and his guests he did not want to break his word to her.
27 And immediately the king sent an executioner with orders to bring John's head. He went and beheaded him in the prison
28 and brought his head on a platter and gave it to the girl, and the girl gave it to her mother.

Do not be conformed to this world, but be transformed by the renewal of your mind, that by testing you may discern what is the will of God, what is good and acceptable and perfect. (Ro.12:2)

6 John's reaction to Jesus: Was courageous and loyal to the end—martyrdom.

6:27, 29

The corrupt, cowardly king complied with the grisly request of his vulgar stepdaughter. John was courageous and loyal to Christ to the end. He was executed because he stood firm for God and God's truth. He preached righteousness while suffering in Herod's rat- and roach-infested prison for over a year until he was savagely slain as a martyr for the cause of righteousness (see notes—Mt.14:10–14 for detailed discussion and application).

27 And immediately the king sent an executioner with orders to bring John's head. He went and beheaded him in the prison
29 When his disciples heard of it, they came and took his body and laid it in a tomb.

THOUGHT 1. God give us the backbone and conviction of John the Baptist! Those who refuse to compromise God's truth are being increasingly persecuted by a vile society that despises God's commands and righteousness. Even some churches, denominations, and ministers have forsaken the clear teaching of God's Word in areas relating to sex and sexuality. Most tragic, many believers throughout the world are being slain because they refuse to deny Christ.

More than ever, we must resolve to stand courageously and loyally for Christ and His Word. And we must not fail to pray for our brothers and sisters in Christ across the earth who risk their lives by being faithful to our Lord.

> . . . whether I come and see you or am absent, I may hear of you that you are standing firm in one spirit, with one mind striving side by side for the faith of the gospel, and not frightened in anything by your opponents. This is a clear sign to them of their destruction, but of your salvation, and that from God. (Ph.1:27–28)

> Do not fear what you are about to suffer. Behold, the devil is about to throw some of you into prison, that you may be tested, and for ten days you will have tribulation. Be faithful unto death, and I will give you the crown of life. (Re.2:10)

> The LORD is on my side; I will not fear. What can man do to me? (Ps.118:6)

> Behold, God is my salvation; I will trust, and will not be afraid; for the LORD GOD is my strength and my song, and he has become my salvation. (Is.12:2)

(Lu.9:10; Jn.6:1–4)

³⁰ The apostles returned to Jesus and told him all that they had done and taught.

³¹ And he said to them, "Come away by yourselves to a desolate place and rest a while." For many were coming and going, and they had no leisure even to eat.

³² And they went away in the boat to a desolate place by themselves.

³³ Now many saw them going and recognized them, and they ran there on foot from all the towns and got there ahead of them.

³⁴ When he went ashore he saw a great crowd, and he had compassion on them, because they were like sheep without a shepherd. And he began to teach them many things.

1. **The setting: The disciples returned from their mission**
   a. Reported what they had done
   b. Reported what they had taught
2. **The 1st danger: Not taking enough time to rest**
   a. The disciples were working long and hard days
   b. The disciples were pressed by the crowds
   c. The disciples left to rest

3. **The 2nd danger: Taking too much time to rest when people are seeking help**

4. **The 3rd danger: Losing sight of people who are as sheep without a shepherd**
   a. Jesus saw the people and had compassion
   b. Jesus began to teach them

Division IV

The Son of God's Training Ministry: Jesus' Intensive Preparation of the Disciples, 6:7–8:26

C. The Need for Rest and Its Dangers, 6:30–34

(Lu.9:10; Jn.6:1–4)

6:30–34
Introduction

Each of us needs rest, relaxation, and time alone with God. However, when we are seeking to rest, we need to be aware that some serious dangers confront us. This passage reveals three of those dangers. This is, *The Need for Rest and Its Dangers,* 6:30–34.

1. The setting: The disciples returned from their mission (v.30).
2. The first danger: Not taking enough time to rest (vv.31–32).
3. The second danger: Taking too much time to rest when people are seeking help (v.33).
4. The third danger: Losing sight of people who are as sheep without a shepherd (v.34).

1 The setting: The disciples returned from their mission.

a. **Reported what they had done.**

b. **Reported what they had taught.**

Earlier in this chapter, Jesus sent the disciples out in pairs to preach and to minister (vv.7–12). The disciples returned from their mission and reported to Jesus concerning what they had done and what they had taught. How they had lived and ministered and what they had taught were both of vital interest to Christ. He had given them precise instructions in both areas. Their report would reveal their obedience to Him, the degree of commitment and effectiveness of each disciple. Jesus needed to know, for the salvation of the world depended on their lives and teaching. He was soon to leave all in their hands.

6:30

³⁰ The apostles returned to Jesus and told him all that they had done and taught.

THOUGHT 1. We are accountable to Christ both for how we live and for what we teach. We are to be obedient to Christ—living exactly as He has said and teaching exactly what He has said to teach. Every disciple is held accountable to the Lord (2 Co.5:10; He.13:17).

We need to be careful to live and teach so that we can confidently share anything with the Lord, so that we have nothing to be ashamed of. We should be ever mindful of the fact that the Lord sees and knows everything we say and do. Nothing can be hidden from Him.

So then each of us will give an account of himself to God. (Ro.14:12)

Each one's work will become manifest, for the Day will disclose it, because it will be revealed by fire, and the fire will test what sort of work each one has done. If the work that anyone has built on the foundation survives, he will receive a reward. If anyone's work is burned up, he will suffer loss, though he himself will be saved, but only as through fire. (1 Co.3:13–15)

For we must all appear before the judgment seat of Christ, so that each one may receive what is due for what he has done in the body, whether good or evil. (2 Co.5:10)

Obey your leaders and submit to them, for they are keeping watch over your souls, as those who will have to give an account. Let them do this with joy and not with groaning, for that would be of no advantage to you. (He.13:17)

O Lord, you have searched me and known me! You know when I sit down and when I rise up; you discern my thoughts from afar. You search out my path and my lying down and are acquainted with all my ways. Even before a word is on my tongue, behold, O Lord, you know it altogether. (Ps.139:1–4)

The eyes of the Lord are in every place, keeping watch on the evil and the good. (Pr.15:3)

6:31–32

³¹ And he said to them, "Come away by yourselves to a desolate place and rest a while." For many were coming and going, and they had no leisure even to eat.
³² And they went away in the boat to a desolate place by themselves.

2 The First Danger: Not taking enough time to rest.

When we need rest, the first danger is in not taking time to rest. Jesus knows this, and He ordered His weary disciples to take a vacation—to get away from their work and rest.

a. **The disciples were working long and hard days (v.31a).**
The disciples were extremely tired from diligently carrying out the Lord's mission, preaching and ministering. Every day was long and hard, and they had become exhausted.

b. **The disciples were pressed by the crowds (v.31b).**
Since returning, the demanding crowds surrounding Jesus were pressing on the disciples. It seemed that there was never enough time to minister to all the people who came for help. The disciples barely had time to make their reports, much less rest and meditate. Therefore, Jesus suggested they go apart into a desert place and rest for a while. Note several things:

➤ Both the work of the ministry and the demands of the crowd taxed the disciples' energy.

➤ The disciples' bodies naturally required some relief from pressure and rest from labor.

➤ The disciples' spirits needed some extended time alone with God in meditation, study, and prayer. They had to receive from God in order to share the presence and message of God. To receive from God, they had to be still and listen to Him. They had to be recharged from spending time in God's presence before they would have the power and energy to minister to others.

➤ The disciples needed a quiet place to get alone with God—not a place where they would be accessible to others.

➤ The Lord cared about them; He cared about their exhaustion. They had poured themselves into His mission and into the lives of needy people. He knew they needed rest and rekindling, refuge and consoling, relaxation and worship. Because He had compassion on them, He instructed them to get away from their work and from the crowds to rest.

THOUGHT 1. It is not work alone that makes us tired. The weight of responsibility creates pressure and taxes our energy. Just the presence of a demanding crowd was a constant reminder to the disciples that they were responsible to work. Likewise, simply being near our responsibilities makes it hard to get relief from them. For this reason, we all need times when we get completely away from our responsibilities to rest and be refreshed. We need to take vacations and days off in order that we can continue to fulfill our responsibilities.

> The LORD is my shepherd; I shall not want. He makes me lie down in green pastures. He leads me beside still waters. (Ps.23:1–2)

> And I say, "Oh, that I had wings like a dove! I would fly away and be at rest; yes, I would wander far away; I would lodge in the wilderness; Selah." (Ps.55:6–7)

> To whom he has said, "This is rest; give rest to the weary; and this is repose"; yet they would not hear. (Is.28:12)

c. **The disciples left to rest (v.32).**
The weary disciples obeyed the Lord's command. They boarded their boat and sailed away to a quiet place where they could be alone and rest.

> Come to me, all who labor and are heavy laden, and I will give you rest. (Mt.11:28)

> And he said, "My presence will go with you, and I will give you rest." (Ex.33:14)

> Six days you shall work, but on the seventh day you shall rest. In plowing time and in harvest you shall rest. (Ex.34:21)

3 The second danger: Taking too much time to rest when people are seeking help.

6:33

The second danger is taking too much time to rest when people need our help. People have serious—and at times, desperate—needs. Therefore, we must take only the time needed to rest our bodies and spirits, no more, no less.

33 Now many saw them going and recognized them, and they ran there on foot from all the towns and got there ahead of them.

As the disciples sailed away for a break, a dramatic scene unfolded. The people could see where Jesus and the disciples were heading, so they began to run by foot around the lake. As they ran, they spread the news that Jesus was nearby. All along the way, more and more people joined the procession around the lake. By the time they reached the place where Jesus' boat was to dock, the crowd had grown to five thousand men, not counting women and children.

The disciples needed rest. They knew it and Jesus knew it, yet the demanding crowd would not leave them alone. They were interfering and keeping the disciples from their much-needed rest. The disciples became irritated and soon wanted the people sent away (vv.35–36). However, Jesus knew something. The disciples had gotten some rest coming across the lake. The sea, their familiar territory, had relaxed them a great deal. That was sufficient to carry the disciples through another session of ministry. It was a matter of just how exhausted the human body *really* was versus the needs of the people. Jesus prioritized the needs of the people.

THOUGHT 1. There is a time to minister, just as there is a time to spend alone with God. There is a time to work, just as there is a time to pray. There is a time to get up and get to it just as there is a time to rest and relax. God's servants must learn to balance the two. We have to find a way to meet our need for rest while making sure that our people's needs are met. Through His actions here, Jesus taught us that there are times when we need to delay our rest in order to meet others' needs.

THOUGHT 2. Unfortunately, many have the problem of resting and relaxing too much instead of working too much. Some even spend too much time in what they call Bible study, prayer, and fellowship with God and neglect ministering to others. While on this earth, fellowship with God is primarily to prepare us to go out and minister. Again, balance is the key.

> We must work the works of him who sent me while it is day; night is coming, when no one can work. (Jn.9:4)

> For we cannot but speak of what we have seen and heard. (Ac.4:20)

> For if I preach the gospel, that gives me no ground for boasting. For necessity is laid upon me. Woe to me if I do not preach the gospel! (1 Co.9:16)

> For Zion's sake I will not keep silent, and for Jerusalem's sake I will not be quiet, until her righteousness goes forth as brightness, and her salvation as a burning torch. (Is.62:1)

> If I say, "I will not mention him, or speak any more in his name," there is in my heart as it were a burning fire shut up in my bones, and I am weary with holding it in, and I cannot. (Je.20:9)

6:34

³⁴ When he went ashore he saw a great crowd, and he had compassion on them, because they were like sheep without a shepherd. And he began to teach them many things.

4 The third danger: Losing sight of people who are as sheep without a shepherd.

a. Jesus saw the people and had compassion.

b. Jesus began to teach them.

As the boat approached the shore, Jesus stood in the boat and watched the multitude clamoring for space on the seashore. He needed rest, and the disciples needed rest even more. But He was not annoyed or irritated with the people. To the contrary, He was moved with intense compassion, because the people were like sheep without a shepherd. He could not turn from them. He could not send them away despite the need for rest. He could do only one thing. He had to meet their need; He had to teach them, so He began "to teach them many things."

Why did Jesus see the people as "sheep without a shepherd?" What does this mean? (See notes—Jn.10:1-6; 10:11-18. See Is.53:6.)

First, sheep without a shepherd are bewildered and wander about, not knowing where they are or where they are going. They get lost ever so easily and cannot find their way back to the flock. So it is with people. People without the shepherd, the Lord Jesus Christ, are bewildered. They do not know where they have come from, where they are going, nor why they are where they are. They wander about, getting lost in place after place, never finding the way to true life (see note and DEEPER STUDY # 1—Lu.15:4).

> When he saw the crowds, he had compassion for them, because they were harassed and helpless, like sheep without a shepherd. (Mt.9:36)

> Jesus said to him, "I am the way, and the truth, and the life. No one comes to the Father except through me." (Jn.14:6)

> For you were straying like sheep, but have now returned to the Shepherd and Overseer of your souls. (1 Pe.2:25)

> My people have been lost sheep. Their shepherds have led them astray, turning them away on the mountains. From mountain to hill they have gone. They have forgotten their fold. (Je.50:6)

They wandered over all the mountains and on every high hill. My sheep were scattered over all the face of the earth, with none to search or seek for them. (Eze.34:6)

6:30–34

Second, sheep without a shepherd go hungry. They do not have adequate nourishment. They cannot find sufficient food to live. So it is with people. People without the Shepherd, the Lord Jesus Christ, go spiritually hungry. They do not have the Shepherd of God to feed and inspire their souls nor to satisfy their inner longings for peace, love, and joy (Ga.5:22-23). They have only themselves to depend on as they seek to meet their craving for life. They have only themselves in seeking the answer to . . .

- purpose
- direction
- assurance
- loneliness
- emptiness
- disturbance
- depression
- sickness
- death

Jesus said to them, "I am the bread of life; whoever comes to me shall not hunger, and whoever believes in me shall never thirst. . . . I am the living bread that came down from heaven. If anyone eats of this bread, he will live forever. And the bread that I will give for the life of the world is my flesh." (Jn.6:35, 51)

Third, sheep without a shepherd cannot find shelter or safety. The sheep are exposed to all the dangers of the wilderness (see note 3—Lu.15:4). So it is with people. People without the Shepherd, the Lord Jesus Christ, are exposed to all that is within the world, and they are doomed. They are doomed because, like wild beasts, the temptations and trials of the world, attack at every opportunity and destroy all who wander about (see outlines and notes—Jn.10:1-18; DEEPER STUDY # 3—10:27-29 for more discussion and application).

Be sober-minded; be watchful. Your adversary the devil prowls around like a roaring lion, seeking someone to devour. (1 Pe.5:8)

Be merciful to me, O God, be merciful to me, for in you my soul takes refuge; in the shadow of your wings I will take refuge, till the storms of destruction pass by. (Ps.57:1)

He who dwells in the shelter of the Most High will abide in the shadow of the Almighty. (Ps.91:1; see Ps.61:1-4; 91:1-6)

(Mt.14:15–21; Lu.9:11–17; Jn.6:1–15)

1. **Two attitudes toward human need**
   a. Individual responsibility: The disciples wanted the people sent away, wanted to be responsible only for their own welfare

   b. Corporate responsibility: Jesus wanted the disciples to feel responsible

2. **Six attitudes toward resources**
   a. Questioning our ability to give
   b. Checking to see what we can give

   c. Organizing to use what resources we have

   d. Being thankful for what we have and can give
   e. Giving what we have

   f. Being careful in the handling of resources

35 And when it grew late, his disciples came to him and said, "This is a desolate place, and the hour is now late.
36 Send them away to go into the surrounding countryside and villages and buy themselves something to eat."
37 But he answered them, "You give them something to eat." And they said to him, "Shall we go and buy two hundred denarii worth of bread and give it to them to eat?"
38 And he said to them, "How many loaves do you have? Go and see." And when they had found out, they said, "Five, and two fish."
39 Then he commanded them all to sit down in groups on the green grass.
40 So they sat down in groups, by hundreds and by fifties.
41 And taking the five loaves and the two fish, he looked up to heaven and said a blessing and broke the loaves and gave them to the disciples to set before the people. And he divided the two fish among them all.
42 And they all ate and were satisfied.
43 And they took up twelve baskets full of broken pieces and of the fish.
44 And those who ate the loaves were five thousand men.

Division IV

The Son of God's Training Ministry: Jesus' Intensive Preparation of the Disciples, 6:7–8:26

D. The Attitudes Toward Human Need and Resources, 6:35–44

(Mt.14:15–21; Lu.9:11–17; Jn.6:1–15)

6:35–44
Introduction

The feeding of five thousand is the *only miracle* recorded by all four Gospel writers. This fact sets it apart from all of Jesus' other miracles, emphasizing its importance.

The reason this miracle is so critical is because it has to do with what is so close to God's heart: human need. Christ deals with our attitudes toward human need. He is concerned with how we handle our resources, with how we go about meeting the needs that confront us. The lesson is powerful (see outline and notes—Mt.14:15–21; Lu.9:10–17; Jn.6:1–15). The apostles were deeply affected by this miracle. It made a dramatic and lasting impact upon them, as it should on us. This is, *The Attitudes Toward Human Need and Resources*, 6:35-44.

1. Two attitudes toward human need (vv.35-37).
2. Six attitudes toward resources (vv.37-44).

(6:35-44) **Another Outline:** What Christ Does with What Is Given to Him.
1. He thanks God for it (v.41).
2. He blesses it (v.41).
3. He breaks it (v.41).
4. He multiplies it (v.41).
5. He feeds with it (v.42).
6. He supplies more than enough (v.43).

1 Two attitudes toward human need.

Christ had been teaching for many hours, and now it was late afternoon, probably after 3 p.m. The disciples were still exhausted and in need of rest. They came to Jesus and reminded Him that there was little time left in the day for them to rest. They suggested that Jesus send the multitude away to buy food *for themselves*. But Jesus said, "No, you give them food to eat." Two attitudes toward human need are pictured in these words.

> [35] And when it grew late, his disciples came to him and said, "This is a desolate place, and the hour is now late.
> [36] Send them away to go into the surrounding countryside and villages and buy themselves something to eat."
> [37] But he answered them, "You give them something to eat." And they said to him, "Shall we go and buy two hundred denarii worth of bread and give it to them to eat?"

a. **Individual responsibility: The disciples wanted the people sent away, wanted to be responsible only for their own welfare (vv.35-36).**

Neither the disciples nor Jesus had invited the crowd. The disciples and Jesus were trying to get away from the crowds in order to get some much needed rest. The crowd was interfering with their plans; therefore, the disciples sensed no responsibility for the crowd. They wanted to get rid of the people so they could be free to do as they wished. Their attitude was: "They are responsible for themselves, so send them away to fend for themselves."

b. **Corporate responsibility: Jesus wanted the disciples to feel responsible (v.37a).**

Jesus was saying very simply, "You give them food. They are hungry, and they are your neighbors, part of your world. You are responsible for your world and the people in it. If you know of people who have need, then you are responsible to help them. They may be irresponsible. They may not have been invited, and they may be interfering with your plans; but they have need, and you know about their need. So, meet it. Feed them."

THOUGHT 1. Too many try to escape their responsibility for the world. When looking at or hearing about the poor and hungry, lonely and depressed, problem-centered and burdened, too many say: "Send them away. They got themselves into this mess because they were irresponsible or sinful. If they wanted to be diligent and responsible, they could. I'm too busy to become involved with such shiftless and irresponsible people."

Such an attitude misses the whole point of Christ. We are responsible for our world, no matter the condition. We are responsible for our neighbors. In fact, the worse off a neighbor is, the more we are responsible to help. The cause of their condition does not matter: whether sin and shame, or clear and understandable circumstances.

➢ If their condition is sin and shame, then we are to share the gospel and teach them how to live and work responsibly.
➢ If their condition is due to clear and understandable circumstances, then we are to help restore them to a place of responsibility and self-worth.

> **Brothers, if anyone is caught in any transgression, you who are spiritual should restore him in a spirit of gentleness. Keep watch on yourself, lest you too be tempted. (Ga.6:1)**

2 Six attitudes toward resources.

It takes resources to meet human needs. In consideration of this, a fact needs to be acknowledged: every person has something to give. Each of us can help and do something to meet a need when a need confronts us. The problem is neither a lack of resources nor a lack of ability or money or time. The problem is attitude—attitude toward the resources we have.

6:37-44

37 But he answered them, "You give them something to eat." And they said to him, "Shall we go and buy two hundred denarii worth of bread and give it to them to eat?"
38 And he said to them, "How many loaves do you have? Go and see." And when they had found out, they said, "Five, and two fish."
39 Then he commanded them all to sit down in groups on the green grass.
40 So they sat down in groups, by hundreds and by fifties.
41 And taking the five loaves and the two fish, he looked up to heaven and said a blessing and broke the loaves and gave them to the disciples to set before the people. And he divided the two fish among them all.
42 And they all ate and were satisfied.
43 And they took up twelve baskets full of broken pieces and of the fish.
44 And those who ate the loaves were five thousand men.

a. Questioning our ability to give (v.37b).

The disciples questioned their ability to give. Jesus had just said, "Give them something to eat." The disciples were shocked and even disturbed with the order, for the crowd was enormous and the task *impossible*. They were already upset over the presence and burden of the crowd. Irritated, the disciples fired back at Jesus, "Shall we go and buy two hundred denarii of bread, and give it to them to eat?" Two hundred denarii amounted to about six months' wages for the disciples. They did not have the money to buy enough food for the massive crowd, so Jesus' command sounded ridiculous to them. There was no way they could buy enough food to meet the need of the crowd. However, the disciples overlooked two realities.

First, the disciples overlooked the reality that they *did have something*. The need of the crowd in this instance was for food, and the disciples had food for themselves (or at least enough money to buy food for themselves). Yet, they did not think to mention this fact. They were thinking only of what excess, what above their own needs they had to give.

Second, the disciples overlooked the power of God. They did not think of how much God loved and cared for these people as well as for them. They did not realize that God will meet the needs of any and all, if only they will put what they have at His disposal. They failed to consider that God's power can take little and multiply it.

THOUGHT 1. The widow's mite is an excellent application for this point. We all have *something* to give.

> And he sat down opposite the treasury and watched the people putting money into the offering box. Many rich people put in large sums. And a poor widow came and put in two small copper coins, which make a penny. And he called his disciples to him and said to them, "Truly, I say to you, this poor widow has put in more than all those who are contributing to the offering box. For they all contributed out of their abundance, but she out of her poverty has put in everything she had, all she had to live on." (Mk.12:41-44)

> Give, and it will be given to you. Good measure, pressed down, shaken together, running over, will be put into your lap. For with the measure you use it will be measured back to you. (Lu.6:38)

> Honor the LORD with your wealth and with the firstfruits of all your produce. (Pr.3:9)

b. Checking to see what we can give (v.38).

In response to the disciples' impatience, Jesus remained cool, instructing them to see how much food they had. The disciples checked and reported that they had five loaves of bread and two fish.

Naturally, the disciples considered their resources insufficient and therefore insignificant. Why? Because they had so little. There was no possibility their resources could ever meet the need. In fact, two fish and five loaves of bread could not even make a dent in the hunger of five thousand men, not to mention the women and children present! From the disciples' perspective, it was impossible for their resources to do any good whatsoever. And, in the natural realm, they were right.

However, Jesus did not ask the disciples to feed all five thousand men with what they had. He asked them to determine *what resources they had* to give. They were to look at what they themselves could give, not at how the whole task could be done with what they had. Their eyes and perspective were to be on using what they had, not on the mammoth impossibility of the task. This is a critical point, and we need to carefully consider it when looking at the vast needs of the world.

THOUGHT 1. We need to discover and consider every resource, every single thing we can give, no matter how small and insignificant it may be. Every single thing can be used by God to help meet a need.

THOUGHT 2. The needs of those in our community, much less our world, can be overwhelming. They can swamp and easily discourage us. In response, we need to focus on what Christ is teaching. Set your eyes on what you can give and do, not on the greatness of the need or the impossibility of the task. Check up on yourself. Find out what resources you have and can give to *help* meet the need.

> So the disciples determined, every one according to his ability, to send relief to the brothers living in Judea. (Ac.11:29)

> On the first day of every week, each of you is to put something aside and store it up, as he may prosper, so that there will be no collecting when I come. (1 Co.16:2)

> Every man shall give as he is able, according to the blessing of the LORD your God that he has given you. (De.16:17)

c. **Organizing to use what resources we have (vv.39–40).**
The hour was late. Darkness was rapidly approaching. Distributing food to approximately fifteen thousand people—perhaps more—was a legitimate challenge. But Jesus had a plan. He organized the people into groups—perhaps small circles or rows—leaving room for the disciples to walk between them to distribute the food. We need to carefully note this important step.

THOUGHT 1. Our resources, whatever we give and do, should be used in an organized fashion. Organization, arrangement, and orderliness are always God's will in the meeting of needs and the handling of resources.

> But all things should be done decently and in order. (1 Co.14:40)

d. **Being thankful for what we have and can give (v.41a).**
What Jesus did was impressive. He took the five loaves and two fish in His hands, and He looked up to heaven and gave thanks for it. It was small; it was insignificant. It looked like it would do little, like it would be insignificant; but our Lord took it anyway and *looked up to heaven and blessed it.*

THOUGHT 1. What a tremendous lesson on what our attitude toward our resources should be! No resource, no gift, no ability is too small. We should always thank God for whatever resource(s) we have, no matter how insignificant, unimpressive, or seemingly insufficient.

> The earth is the LORD's and the fullness thereof, the world and those who dwell therein. (Ps.24:1)

> For every beast of the forest is mine, the cattle on a thousand hills. (Ps.50:10)

> The silver is mine, and the gold is mine, declares the LORD of hosts. (Hag.2:8)

e. **Giving what we have (vv.41b–42).**
After giving thanks, Jesus took the food and gave it to the disciples to set before the people (v.41b). Then the miracle happened! The power of God—a power superseding anything we can ask or think—went to work (Ep.3:20). The resource was multiplied; all the people were fed and

were filled (v.42). Note that the people were not merely given a snack to tide them over. They ate until their hunger was satisfied, until they did not *want* any more food.

THOUGHT 1. At least two lessons are visible in this act of Christ.

1) We are to give what we have, no matter how small. We *are* to take what we have and give it to meet the need.

> But give as alms those things that are within, and behold, everything is clean for you. (Lu.11:41)

> Sell your possessions, and give to the needy. Provide yourselves with moneybags that do not grow old, with a treasure in the heavens that does not fail, where no thief approaches and no moth destroys. (Lu.12:33)

> In all things I have shown you that by working hard in this way we must help the weak and remember the words of the Lord Jesus, how he himself said, "It is more blessed to give than to receive." (Ac.20:35)

> As for the rich in this present age, charge them not to be haughty, nor to set their hopes on the uncertainty of riches, but on God, who richly provides us with everything to enjoy. They are to do good, to be rich in good works, to be generous and ready to share, thus storing up treasure for themselves as a good foundation for the future, so that they may take hold of that which is truly life. (1 Ti.6:17–19)

2) Christ is *The Perfect Provider, The Perfect Supplier*. He takes what we give and multiplies it to meet the need. He also multiplies its purpose, meaning, and significance.

> But seek first the kingdom of God and his righteousness, and all these things will be added to you. (Mt.6:33)

> Each one must give as he has decided in his heart, not reluctantly or under compulsion, for God loves a cheerful giver. And God is able to make all grace abound to you, so that having all sufficiency in all things at all times, you may abound in every good work. As it is written, "He has distributed freely, he has given to the poor; his righteousness endures forever." He who supplies seed to the sower and bread for food will supply and multiply your seed for sowing and increase the harvest of your righteousness. (2 Co.9:7–10)

f. **Being careful in the handling of resources (vv.43–44).**

Very simply, Christ teaches that resources are not to be wasted. They are to be used day after day. When there is more than enough to meet one need, what is left over is to be gathered up to use elsewhere.

THOUGHT 1. Note three lessons.

1) There is no room in Christ's economy for extravagance. When there is more than what is needed, the excess is to be saved for another need.

2) There is no room for wasting. No resource is to be wasted; it is to be used elsewhere.

3) There is no room for resources to be stored and banked; there is not any excuse for allowing resources to lie around unused. All resources—abilities or money—are to be used to meet needs as long as needs exist (see notes—Mt.19:21–22; 19:23–26).

> For if the readiness is there, it is acceptable according to what a person has, not according to what he does not have. For I do not mean that others should be eased and you burdened, but that as a matter of fairness your abundance at the present time should supply their need, so that their abundance may supply your need, that there may be fairness. As it is written, "Whoever gathered much had nothing left over, and whoever gathered little had no lack." (2 Co.8:12–15)

(Mt.14:22–33; Jn.6:16–21)

45 Immediately he made his disciples get into the boat and go before him to the other side, to Bethsaida, while he dismissed the crowd.

46 And after he had taken leave of them, he went up on the mountain to pray.

47 And when evening came, the boat was out on the sea, and he was alone on the land.

48 And he saw that they were making headway painfully, for the wind was against them. And about the fourth watch of the night he came to them, walking on the sea. He meant to pass by them,

49 but when they saw him walking on the sea they thought it was a ghost, and cried out,

50 for they all saw him and were terrified. But immediately he spoke to them and said, "Take heart; it is I. Do not be afraid."

51 And he got into the boat with them, and the wind ceased. And they were utterly astounded,

52 for they did not understand about the loaves, but their hearts were hardened.

1. **Lesson 1: Crowd excitement is not always wise (Jesus made His disciples leave, Jn.6:15)**

2. **Lesson 2: Prayer after service is most wise**

3. **Lesson 3: Crying for help in time of need is wise**

   a. Their struggle was long[DS1]

   b. Their cry was desperate

   c. Their fear was horrifying

4. **Lesson 4: Receiving the presence of Jesus is wise[DS2]**
   a. His presence erases fear
   b. His presence calms the storm

5. **Lesson 5: Remembering and trusting the power of Jesus is wise**

Division IV

The Son of God's Training Ministry: Jesus' Intensive Preparation of the Disciples, 6:7–8:26

E. Five Wise Lessons for Service, 6:45–52

(Mt.14:22–33; Jn.6:16–21)

6:45–52
Introduction

As we serve and live for the Lord, there may be times when He leads us in ways that we do not understand. There may be times when His will does not seem logical or does not make sense to us. And there may be times when the Lord calls us to do something we do not want to do or to go someplace we do not want to go. Or, He may call us to do something at a time when we do not want to do it or when it is not convenient for us.

This passage records such an occasion in the lives and ministry of Jesus' disciples. Jesus had to make His disciples leave the remote, isolated place where they had come to rest and go back across the Sea of Galilee to Bethsaida. *Made* (Gk. enankasen) means constrained, compelled, forced. The fact that Jesus had to make the disciples get in the boat and go implies that they argued with Him about it and possibly even refused. Why did Jesus overrule them and make them go?

First, right after Jesus had fed the crowd, they wished to take Him by force and make Him king (Jn.6:15). Jesus knew the popular view of Messiahship. People viewed that the Messiah was to lead Israel in revolt against the Roman conquerors and free the people, establishing the government of theocracy, that is, the rule and reign of God over all the earth (see notes—Mt.1:1; Deeper Study # 1—Mk.1:18; Deeper Study # 3—3:11; notes—11:1-6; 11:2-3; Deeper Study # 1—11:5; Deeper Study # 2—11:6; Deeper Study # 1—12:16; note—Lu.7:21-23). The disciples were caught up in the excitement of this prospect. Christ had to send them across the lake and disperse the crowd in order to prevent an immediate uprising.

Second, it was time for Jesus to move on. Others needed His ministry. He wanted the disciples to make use of what little daylight there was in crossing the lake.

Third, and so important to see, Jesus needed time alone for prayer.

Fourth, Christ wanted the disciples to learn five lessons for service—lessons that would prove invaluable in their ministry to the world (see outlines and notes—Mt.14:22-33; Jn.6:16-21). The Holy Spirit moved upon Mark (as well as Matthew and John) to record this episode so that we too would learn these vital lessons. This is, *Five Wise Lessons for Service*, 6:45-52.

1. Lesson 1: Crowd excitement is not always wise (Jesus made His disciples leave, Jn.6:15) (v.45).
2. Lesson 2: Prayer after service is most wise (v.46).
3. Lesson 3: Crying for help in time of need is wise (vv.47-49).
4. Lesson 4: Receiving the presence of Jesus is wise (vv.50-51).
5. Lesson 5: Remembering and trusting the power of Jesus is wise (v.52).

6:45

⁴⁵ Immediately he made his disciples get into the boat and go before him to the other side, to Bethsaida, while he dismissed the crowd.

1 Lesson 1: Crowd excitement is not always wise (Jesus made His disciples leave, Jn.6:15).

The first lesson is that crowd excitement is not always wise. The crowd had been fed miraculously. They were extremely excited, for they thought Jesus was surely the Messiah. He could always feed them and meet their needs, no matter what their needs were. They wanted to take Him by force and make Him king (see Jn.6:14-15). Of course, the authorities would never allow a revolt; they would crush the people. But the people were not thinking. They wanted to act now, whether wise or unwise.

➢ Fleshy emotions were running wild.
➢ Selfish desires were dominating.
➢ Rationality and thoughtfulness were lacking.
➢ Spiritual insight was completely absent.

Jesus could not allow the disciples to be caught up in the excitement and unwise desires of the crowd. God's will had to be done, and His will was the cross, an eternal kingdom, not a worldly kingdom that enhances this life only. God wants people to live now, yes, but He also wants people to live eternally. Jesus knew this. And He also knew that people could live forever *only by the cross, only by a spiritual rebirth* made possible by the death of the Son of God (Jn.3:16; Ep.1:7; 1 Pe.2:24; 3:18). Jesus had to do God's will. He had to get the disciples away from the crowd and their carnal excitement lest the disciples be ill-affected.

THOUGHT 1. Impulsive excitement is often stirred by wrong motives, objectives, and a lack of self-control. Excitement due to wrong motives and desires can lead to several problems:

➢ Carnal and unwise action and behavior without thought or understanding.

➢ Stimulation or exaltation of the flesh.

➢ Ignoring thoughtful prayer and God's will.

When a crowd of people is excited, others are often incited to follow along without thinking. Their flesh is stimulated, excited, tingling, and often craving. They give way to their urge and act in their own flesh and strength. In doing so, they ignore God, giving no consideration whatsoever to seeking God's will. This was the danger with the disciples, and it is often the danger confronting us.

The answer, of course, is what Jesus did with the disciples: getting away from the crowd and its worldly and carnal motives and excitement.

> **Therefore go out from their midst, and be separate from them, says the Lord, and touch no unclean thing; then I will welcome you, and I will be a father to you, and you shall be sons and daughters to me, says the Lord Almighty. (2 Co.6:17–18)**

> **Take no part in the unfruitful works of darkness, but instead expose them. (Ep.5:11)**

THOUGHT 2. We must be surrendered to walk in God's will and way, not in the will and way of a worldly crowd.

> **I appeal to you therefore, brothers, by the mercies of God, to present your bodies as a living sacrifice, holy and acceptable to God, which is your spiritual worship. Do not be conformed to this world, but be transformed by the renewal of your mind, that by testing you may discern what is the will of God, what is good and acceptable and perfect. (Ro.12:1–2)**

> **You adulterous people! Do you not know that friendship with the world is enmity with God? Therefore whoever wishes to be a friend of the world makes himself an enemy of God. (Js.4:4)**

2 Lesson 2: Prayer after service is most wise.

6:46

The second lesson is that it is wise to enter into a period of prayer after a time of successful ministry (see note—Mt.14:22–23 for discussion). Jesus had been teaching the crowd and ministering to them. In the eyes of the world, He could not have been more successful. The results of His service and ministry were phenomenal. He had a large successful ministry. The crowds were huge, well into the thousands. People were literally running and clamoring to get to Him (see Mk.6:33). He had the recognition, esteem, praise, and honor of the crowd. And He was the reason for their excitement and motivation. They were motivated enough to even make Him king.

> 46 And after he had taken leave of them, he went up on the mountain to pray.

But at the height of Jesus' popularity, He dismissed the people, sent them away. Why? So He could get alone "to pray." God, not the crowds, was His . . .

- source
- rest
- excitement
- deliverance
- strength
- motivation
- object of worship
- source of renewal

Jesus had to get alone with God. The word for *pray* (Gk. proseuchasthai; pronounced *pros-yoo'-kas-tigh*) is a descriptive word. It means to pray fervently, to pour one's whole heart and total being out to God. Jesus was totally dependent on God, not on the crowds. The crowds could give Him nothing, whereas God the Father could give Him everything. Why was Jesus so driven to pray?

First, He was exhausted. He needed God's presence and rest.

Second, He was tempted. He needed God's strength and deliverance (see note—Mt.14:22–23).

Third, He was drained spiritually. He needed to worship God and to be renewed.

Fourth, He was weary of people's worldly excitement and motives. He needed God's excitement and motivation.

> Watch and pray that you may not enter into temptation. The spirit indeed is willing, but the flesh is weak. (Mt.26:41)

> And he told them a parable to the effect that they ought always to pray and not lose heart. (Lu.18:1)

> Pray without ceasing. (1 Th.5:17)

> Seek the LORD and his strength; seek his presence continually! (1 Chr.16:11)

6:47–50a

47 And when evening came, the boat was out on the sea, and he was alone on the land.
48 And he saw that they were making headway painfully, for the wind was against them. And about the fourth watch of the night he came to them, walking on the sea. He meant to pass by them,
49 but when they saw him walking on the sea they thought it was a ghost, and cried out,
50 for they all saw him and were terrified. But immediately he spoke to them and said, "Take heart; it is I. Do not be afraid."

3 Lesson 3: Crying for help in time of need is wise.

The third lesson is that it is wise to cry out to God for help in our time of need. A storm came up while the disciples were crossing the lake. Three things are stressed about the disciples in the storm.

a. Their struggle was long (v.48).

The disciples did everything in their power to survive the storm. Their toil was long. The Sea of Galilee was only four to six miles across. They had been rowing against a headwind for some six to nine hours and had progressed only about three miles (see DEEPER STUDY # 1).

b. Their cry was desperate (v.49).

The disciples were all rowing furiously to save their lives, when Jesus came walking toward them on the water. Thinking He was a ghost, they cried out in desperation. *Cried out* (anekraxan, pronounced *on-a-krox'-on)* means screamed or shrieked loudly.

c. Their fear was horrifying (v.50a).

The disciples screamed out of sheer terror. They were physically exhausted and mentally drained from fighting the storm all night. Their lives were at stake; they were struggling for survival. All of a sudden, out of nowhere, they saw a figure, what they thought to be a ghost, walking on the water. They were scared, perhaps bordering on going into shock—perhaps thinking that the death angel, or a premonition of their death, was at hand.

THOUGHT 1. Note two significant points.

1) The disciples desperately needed help. They did exactly what they needed to do to get help: they cried out to Jesus.

> Casting all your anxieties on him, because he cares for you. (1 Pe.5:7)

> In distress you called, and I delivered you; I answered you in the secret place of thunder; I tested you at the waters of Meribah. Selah. (Ps.81:7)

> Call to me and I will answer you, and will tell you great and hidden things that you have not known. (Je.33:3)

2) The disciples were doing God's will when the storm came. They were doing exactly what Christ had told them to do, that is, cross the lake and get ready to minister there. The storm was part of God's will. They had to learn . . .

- to confess their need for Him before He could help
- to endure against the storms of life
- to trust Him through all, no matter how terrifying

DEEPER STUDY # 1

(6:48) A Day's Timetable: Hebrew time parameters are presented in the Gospels of Matthew, Mark, and Luke, and the Book of Acts. Sunrise (6 a.m.) was the beginning of the day. The first hour was 7 a.m. and so on. Scripture sometimes refers to a watch. Both the day and the night were divided into four watches each. A watch was three hours long. The first watch of the day was 6 a.m. to 9 a.m. The fourth watch of the night mentioned above was 3 a.m. to 6 a.m. The disciples had been rowing between six and nine hours and had advanced only three miles. The Gospel of John uses Roman time, with the hours beginning at 12 noon (p.m.) and 12 midnight (a.m.). Note that twenty-first century time is the same as Roman time.

4 Lesson 4: Receiving the presence of Jesus is wise.

The fourth lesson is that receiving the presence of Jesus is wise. It was an eerie, stormy night. The disciples were terrified and cried out for help. All of a sudden, a voice from the body walking on the water shouted out (see DEEPER STUDY # 2). Recognizing the voice, the disciples realized it was Jesus and were encouraged. The presence of Jesus made all the difference.

⁵⁰ for they all saw him and were terrified. But immediately he spoke to them and said, "Take heart; it is I. Do not be afraid."
⁵¹ And he got into the boat with them, and the wind ceased. And they were utterly astounded,

a. **His presence erases fear (v.50b).**

The presence of Jesus erased the panicked disciples' fears. Once they heard His voice, they knew they were safe and secure. Jesus cared about them and had the power to take care of them all. Specifically, it was Jesus' words that calmed their troubled hearts. When Jesus told them to take courage and not be afraid, they trusted Him and were strengthened.

b. **His presence calms the storm (v.51).**

When Jesus got into the boat with the disciples, the wind stopped raging. The disciples stood amazed (beyond measure) in the presence of the Lord.

THOUGHT 1. Receiving the presence of Jesus Christ takes care of all problems and trials. He gives the strength to row through all the storms of life, no matter their turbulence and severity.

> Teaching them to observe all that I have commanded you. And behold, I am with you always, to the end of the age. (Mt.28:20)
>
> But the Lord stood by me and strengthened me, so that through me the message might be fully proclaimed and all the Gentiles might hear it. So I was rescued from the lion's mouth. (2 Ti.4:17)
>
> When he calls to me, I will answer him; I will be with him in trouble; I will rescue him and honor him. (Ps.91:15)
>
> Fear not, for I am with you; be not dismayed, for I am your God; I will strengthen you, I will help you, I will uphold you with my righteous right hand. (Is.41:10)

THOUGHT 2. Think: What if the disciples had been forced to face the storm alone? What if we had to face the storms of life alone? Which storm would drown the breath of life out of us? Which storm would send us reeling into eternity, having to meet God *unprepared*?

> Peace I leave with you; my peace I give to you. Not as the world gives do I give to you. Let not your hearts be troubled, neither let them be afraid. (Jn.14:27)
>
> Do not be anxious about anything, but in everything by prayer and supplication with thanksgiving let your requests be made known to God. and the peace of God, which surpasses all understanding, will guard your hearts and your minds in Christ Jesus. (Ph.4:6-7)

Then the Lord knows how to rescue the godly from trials, and to keep the unrighteous under punishment until the day of judgment. (2 Pe.2:9)

For he will deliver you from the snare of the fowler and from the deadly pestilence. (Ps.91:3)

Even to your old age I am he, and to gray hairs I will carry you. I have made, and I will bear; I will carry and will save. (Is.46:4)

THOUGHT 3. It is through God's Word that He gives us comfort, peace, and hope.

For whatever was written in former days was written for our instruction, that through endurance and through the encouragement of the Scriptures we might have hope. (Ro.15:4)

Remember your word to your servant, in which you have made me hope. . . . Those who fear you shall see me and rejoice, because I have hoped in your word. (Ps.119:49, 74)

DEEPER STUDY # 2

(6:50) **"I Am"—Jesus Christ, Names—Titles**: Jesus identified Himself to the disciples, saying, "It is I." Most literally translated, Jesus said, *"I am"* (ego eimi). This is the great name of God, the Self-Existent One, the Supreme One of the Universe (see note—Jn.6:20-21; Jn.8:58).

6:52

52 for they did not understand about the loaves, but their hearts were hardened.

5 Lesson 5: Remembering and trusting the power of Jesus is wise.

The fifth lesson is that we are wise when we remember and trust Jesus' power. The disciples should not have been so amazed at Jesus' calming the storm. (They had already witnessed Him calm a storm; see Mk.4:35-41.) They had just witnessed the miracle of Christ's feeding of five thousand men with just a little food. Christ was unquestionably God. And God not only cared about people, He could do anything for people—even control all of nature. How could they forget so easily? The answer: "their hearts were hardened" (v.52). A hardened heart is attached to the earth. It cannot break loose from the earth; it cannot see anything beyond the ordinary and explainable. It is slow to see anything beyond natural law controlling the world. The hardened heart may hope that God exists; it may even say that God exists, but it cannot truly believe that there is a real God who is actively controlling the world. Profession is easy; living in complete trust in God is difficult.

THOUGHT 1. The disciples were as so many are: they had spiritual experience after experience, but they were attached to the earth. Therefore, they grew hard and callous, and they became dull to spiritual truth. Their spiritual understanding was always needing a boost.

'For this people's heart has grown dull, and with their ears they can barely hear, and their eyes they have closed; lest they should see with their eyes and hear with their ears and understand with their heart and turn, and I would heal them.' (Ac.28:27)

No one understands; no one seeks for God. (Ro.3:11)

Always learning and never able to arrive at a knowledge of the truth. (2 Ti.3:7)

They have neither knowledge nor understanding, they walk about in darkness; all the foundations of the earth are shaken. (Ps.82:5)

Son of man, you dwell in the midst of a rebellious house, who have eyes to see, but see not, who have ears to hear, but hear not, for they are a rebellious house. (Eze.12:2)

THOUGHT 2. A spiritual mind and constant prayer are the answer to hardness of heart (see v.46).

Do not be conformed to this world, but be transformed by the renewal of your mind, that by testing you may discern what is the will of God, what is good and acceptable and perfect. (Ro.12:2)

We destroy arguments and every lofty opinion raised against the knowledge of God, and take every thought captive to obey Christ. (2 Co.10:5)

To put off your old self, which belongs to your former manner of life and is corrupt through deceitful desires, and to be renewed in the spirit of your minds, and to put on the new self, created after the likeness of God in true righteousness and holiness. (Ep.4:22–24)

(Mt.14:34–36)

1. **Step 1: Recognizing Jesus**

2. **Step 2: Acknowledging our need and believing that Jesus can help**

3. **Step 3: Asking unashamedly and unreservedly for Jesus' help**

⁵³ When they had crossed over, they came to land at Gennesaret and moored to the shore. ⁵⁴ And when they got out of the boat, the people immediately recognized him ⁵⁵ and ran about the whole region and began to bring the sick people on their beds to wherever they heard he was.

⁵⁶ And wherever he came, in villages, cities, or countryside, they laid the sick in the marketplaces and implored him that they might touch even the fringe of his garment. And as many as touched it were made well.

Division IV

The Son of God's Training Ministry: Jesus' Intensive Preparation of the Disciples, 6:7–8:26

F. The Steps to Healing, 6:53–56

(Mt.14:34–36)

6:53–56
Introduction

Immediately after making the bitter waters of Marah sweet, God revealed Himself to His people as *Jehovah-Rapha*, the LORD who heals (Ex.15:26). He can heal us both spiritually and physically (Ps.103:3; Is.53:5; Js.5:14-16). In this passage, Mark gives a brief account of many who were healed. He presents the necessary steps for both spiritual and physical healing. If a person wishes to be healed by Christ, he or she must take the same three steps (see outline and notes—Mt.14:34-36, for a more detailed discussion). This is, *The Steps to Healing, 6:53-56.*

1. Step 1: Recognizing Jesus (vv.53-54).
2. Step 2: Acknowledging our need and believing that Jesus can help (v.55).
3. Step 3: Asking unashamedly and unreservedly for Jesus' help (v.56).

6:53–54

⁵³ When they had crossed over, they came to land at Gennesaret and moored to the shore.
⁵⁴ And when they got out of the boat, the people immediately recognized him

1 Step 1: Recognizing Jesus.

When Jesus arrived at Gennesaret, the people *recognized* (Gk. epignontes) Him; that is, they easily and clearly identified Him; they knew exactly who He was. The idea is that people *knew Him by experience.* Some had been touched and healed by Jesus before; others had witnessed Him touch and heal members of their family, friends, and strangers. They were excited that Jesus had come to their land. He was now present, at hand, reachable, available to make them and their loved ones whole.

Moreover, the people knew that Jesus cared about the sick and that He had the power to make them whole. There was just something different about Jesus. His interest and care in people and His power to help them were unique. He was so humble and meek, yet so authoritative and strong. The presence of God was unquestionably within Him in a most unique way.

THOUGHT 1. Jesus has come to earth. He has come to our land, and He is available and able to make us whole.

> **Teaching them to observe all that I have commanded you. And behold, I am with you always, to the end of the age. (Mt.28:20)**
>
> **For the Son of Man came to seek and to save the lost. (Lu.19:10)**
>
> **For God so loved the world, that he gave his only Son, that whoever believes in him should not perish but have eternal life. For God did not send his Son into the world to condemn the world, but in order that the world might be saved through him. (Jn.3:16-17)**
>
> **The thief comes only to steal and kill and destroy. I came that they may have life and have it abundantly. (Jn.10:10)**
>
> **Seek the LORD while he may be found; call upon him while he is near; let the wicked forsake his way, and the unrighteous man his thoughts; let him return to the LORD, that he may have compassion on him, and to our God, for he will abundantly pardon. (Is.55:6-7)**

2 Step 2: Acknowledging our need and believing that Jesus can help.

The second step to healing is acknowledging our need and believing Jesus can help. The people not only came to Jesus themselves, they ran through the whole region and brought their families and friends to Jesus. They even spread the word about Jesus to strangers. The picture is very descriptive. All who "recognized Jesus" (v.54) cared deeply for all the people throughout their region who needed Jesus' help. Their care and love were intense. No inconvenience was too great; no burden nor pain too much to bear; no distance too far. Wherever they heard Jesus was, they carried the sick to Him. The picture is that of running to and fro. If Jesus was not where they went, they picked the sick back up and carried them on to the next village or town, searching for Him until they found Him.

> 55 and ran about the whole region and began to bring the sick people on their beds to wherever they heard he was.

What would cause such intense seeking after Jesus? What would stir people to sacrifice their own time and comfort to transport others to Jesus?

First, the people knew they had great need. They were sick and needed to be made whole. They acknowledged their need. They did not try to hide their disease or injury.

Second, the people believed Jesus could help; they believed He could make them whole. There was no chance they were going to miss this opportunity.

THOUGHT 1. The same two things are true about us.

1) We have the need to be made whole . . .

- spiritually
- mentally
- emotionally
- physically
- racially
- socially
- nationally
- internationally

> **As it is written: "None is righteous, no, not one; no one understands; no one seeks for God. All have turned aside; together they have become worthless; no one does good, not even one. Their throat is an open grave; they use their tongues to deceive. The venom of asps is under their lips." (Ro.3:10-13)**

For the wages of sin is death, but the free gift of God is eternal life in Christ Jesus our Lord. (Ro.6:23)

We know that we are from God, and the whole world lies in the power of the evil one. (1 Jn.5:19; see Ro.3:10–18 for a descriptive picture of man's desperate need. Also see Ro.1:18–32.)

2) We must believe that Jesus can help us. He can, but we *must believe* that He can before He will heal us and before the world will come to Him for help.

And when Jesus heard it, he said to them, "Those who are well have no need of a physician, but those who are sick. I came not to call the righteous, but sinners." (Mk.2:17)

And Jesus said to him, "'If you can'! All things are possible for one who believes." (Mk.9:23)

Because, if you confess with your mouth that Jesus is Lord and believe in your heart that God raised him from the dead, you will be saved. For with the heart one believes and is justified, and with the mouth one confesses and is saved. (Ro.10:9–10)

6:56

[56] And wherever he came, in villages, cities, or countryside, they laid the sick in the marketplaces and implored him that they might touch even the fringe of his garment. And as many as touched it were made well.

3 Step 3. Asking unashamedly and unreservedly for Jesus' help.

These people asked unashamedly and unreservedly for Jesus' help. They begged Jesus to let them touch Him, to simply touch "the fringe (border, hem, end, edge) of His garment" (see DEEPER STUDY # 1—Mt.14:36). Note that they implored Jesus, begged Him, entreated Him. This fact points to three essential attitudes necessary to be made whole:

- A sense of need: sensing our need for Christ's help so much that we implore Him, asking and begging in desperation if needed.
- A sense of humility: sensing that our need is really desperate and beyond human help. We must sense the desperation so deeply that we humble ourselves, earnestly asking Christ to make us whole. Spectators and curiosity seekers who might be looking on just do not matter. We are willing to humble ourselves, no matter what other people may say, in order to have our need met.
- A belief in Christ's power and willingness to make us whole: believing so much that we ask and beg Him to make us whole through and through.

A wonderful fact concludes this passage: all who touched Jesus were made whole. Touching Jesus brought healing to their whole being (see note—Mt.14:36). Jesus did not refuse nor shun anyone, no matter how deformed, abnormal, diseased, unattractive, dirty, immoral, or sinful the person was.

THOUGHT 1. Jesus loves everyone, and He sees the need within every individual and longs to meet that need. He takes everyone who reaches out to Him by the hand and pulls them to His heart—joyfully receiving people and making them whole through and through.

But to all who did receive him, who believed in his name, he gave the right to become children of God. (Jn.1:12)

All that the Father gives me will come to me, and whoever comes to me I will never cast out. (Jn.6:37)

If you ask me anything in my name, I will do it. (Jn.14:14)

If my people who are called by my name humble themselves, and pray and seek my face and turn from their wicked ways, then I will hear from heaven and will forgive their sin and heal their land. (2 Chr.7:14. Note how this verse includes all three points in this note.)

CHAPTER 7

G. The Emptiness of (Man-Made) Tradition, Ritual, Ceremony, Works, 7:1–13

(see Mt.15:1–9)

Now when the Pharisees gathered to him, with some of the scribes who had come from Jerusalem,

² they saw that some of his disciples ate with hands that were defiled, that is, unwashed.

³ (For the Pharisees and all the Jews do not eat unless they wash their hands properly, holding to the tradition of the elders,

⁴ and when they come from the marketplace, they do not eat unless they wash. And there are many other traditions that they observe, such as the washing of cups and pots and copper vessels and dining couches.)

⁵ And the Pharisees and the scribes asked him, "Why do your disciples not walk according to the tradition of the elders, but eat with defiled hands?"

⁶ And he said to them, "Well did Isaiah prophesy of you hypocrites, as it is written, 'This people honors me with their lips, but their heart is far from me;'"

⁷ "'in vain do they worship me, teaching as doctrines the commandments of men.'"

⁸ "You leave the commandment of God and hold to the tradition of men."

⁹ And he said to them, "You have a fine way of rejecting the commandment of God in order to establish your tradition!

¹⁰ For Moses said, 'Honor your father and your mother'; and, 'Whoever reviles father or mother must surely die.'

¹¹ But you say, 'If a man tells his father or his mother, "Whatever you would have gained from me is Corban"' (that is, given to God)—

¹² then you no longer permit him to do anything for his father or mother,"

¹³ "thus making void the word of God by your tradition that you have handed down. And many such things you do."

1. **Tradition can be placed before need**

   a. The religionists found fault with Jesus' disciples: Eating with unwashed, unclean hands
     1) The tradition of cleanliness explained

     2) The tradition illustrated

   b. The charge against the disciples was brought to Jesus

2. **Tradition can be hypocritical honor**

3. **Tradition can be empty, worthless worship**

4. **Tradition can be man-made commands**

5. **Tradition can be kept before the commands of God**

   a. The people twisted God's commands[DS1]

   b. The religionists insisted on obedience to tradition

6. **Tradition can nullify the Word of God or make the Word of God ineffective**[DS2, 3]

Division IV

The Son of God's Training Ministry: Jesus' Intensive Preparation of the Disciples, 6:7–8:26

G. The Emptiness of (Man-Made) Tradition, Ritual, Ceremony, Works, 7:1–13

(see Mt.15:1–9)

7:1–13
Introduction

Neither mankind nor religion can survive being institutionalized, that is, being based and focused on tradition, ritual, ceremony, and works. For either to survive, people's hearts must be focused on acceptance and reconciliation, approval and redemption, peace and love, humility and giving, joy and hope. Instead of being guided by religious tradition, we function best when we . . .

- accept each other and are reconciled to God in Christ (together)
- approve each other and are redeemed
- live in peace and love
- experience the joy and hope of Christ
- walk humbly and live a life of service

These are the precepts revealed and emphasized by God in His holy Word. Religion must be based and built upon truth, God's truth as revealed in His holy Word. In this passage, Jesus warns His disciples about the dangers of basing religion on human traditions rather than divine truth. We need to study the passage carefully and teach it faithfully, for it is of critical importance for the destiny of both humanity and religion. This is, *The Emptiness of (Man-made) Tradition, Ritual, Ceremony, Works, 7:1–13.*

1. Tradition, can be placed before need (vv.1–5).
2. Tradition can be hypocritical honor (v.6).
3. Tradition can be empty, worthless worship (v.7).
4. Tradition can be man-made commands (v.8).
5. Tradition can be kept before the commands of God (vv.9–12).
6. Tradition can nullify the Word of God or make the Word of God ineffective (v.13).

7:1–5

Now when the Pharisees gathered to him, with some of the scribes who had come from Jerusalem,
² they saw that some of his disciples ate with hands that were defiled, that is, unwashed.
³ (For the Pharisees and all the Jews do not eat unless they wash their hands properly, holding to the tradition of the elders,
⁴ and when they come from the marketplace, they do not eat unless they wash. And there are many other traditions that they observe, such as the washing of cups and pots and copper vessels and dining couches.)
⁵ And the Pharisees and the scribes asked him, "Why do your disciples not walk according to the tradition of the elders, but eat with defiled hands?"

1 Tradition can be placed before need.

This scene unfolds as a fact-finding commission of Jewish leaders—religionists—came from Jerusalem to investigate Jesus, to see exactly what was going on. News of His preaching and healing, as well as of His conflicts with local authorities, was constantly reaching the Jerusalem leaders. They had already sent one fact-finding commission to confront Jesus, and their report had not been good. They had accused Jesus of healing and casting out demons by Beelzebub. They had also accused Him of breaking the Sabbath law. Previously, a fact-finding commission had been sent to investigate John the Baptist. His preaching and baptism and his priesthood had also been considered suspect (see notes—Mt.3:7–10; Jn.1:19).

The whole country was astir with news of Jesus' claims and unbelievable miracles. People were stirred up, dangerously so. Some had even suggested forcefully establishing Christ as king (Jn.6:15). All this resulted in another commission being sent out to investigate Jesus.

a. The religionists found fault with Jesus' disciples: Eating with unwashed, unclean hands (v.2).

When the commission arrived, they immediately saw the disciples breaking one of their traditions. The disciples were eating with unwashed and unclean hands. Of course, what they meant was not that the disciples had bad manners, nor that they were practicing poor hygiene. They meant the disciples were unclean in the eyes of God. Why? Because the disciples had not washed their hands as a sign to God that they were offering themselves and their food to God. The traditional ceremony of washing one's hands before meals (as a sign of thanksgiving to God) had been broken. The disciples were ceremonially unclean.

Mark explains and illustrates this tradition (vv.3-4). The Law of Moses prescribed washing before handling some items. The purpose was to instill within the people respect for the holiness of God and His temple, and the need for people to be *spiritually clean* before approaching Him or handling His affairs. But some religionists had added to God's Word. They had taken the law of God, including the laws of cleansing, and had added thousands and thousands of rules and regulations. There was a rule governing practically everything a person did, so many rules that no one could conceivably keep them. Instead of pointing a person to God and to the need for the cleansing of the heart, the rules caused a person to concentrate on the rules themselves and the keeping of them. The rules became the center and focus of attention, not God.

b. The charge against the disciples was brought to Jesus (v.5).

In the case at hand, the rule being broken was that of washing the hands before eating a meal. The disciples had violated the tradition of the elders and had embarrassed the religious faithful of their day. In the eyes of the investigating committee, they were unclean in the sight of God. They had broken a tradition of the elders, and there was no excuse for it, not if they were disciples of a true rabbi. A true rabbi would be teaching his disciples the traditions of the elders, not ignoring and violating them. Thus, the commission brought their charge to Jesus. They confronted Him about His disciples' failure to obey their tradition.

2 Tradition can be hypocritical honor.

7:6

Jesus took charge of the situation and turned the religionists' accusation against them. He quoted from Scripture, applying Isaiah's words to their spiritual condition (Is.29:13; see 1 S.15:22; 16:7). His words were strong and forceful: He called them "hypocrites" (see DEEPER STUDY # 2—Mt.23:13). They honored God with their lips, but their heart was far from Him. Their tradition was nothing more than *hypocritical*. It was meaningless and unacceptable to God.

> [6] And he said to them, "Well did Isaiah prophesy of you hypocrites, as it is written, 'This people honors me with their lips, but their heart is far from me;'"

THOUGHT 1. Hypocrites give lip service while keeping their hearts far from God. They acknowledge God and attend worship, but their efforts are unacceptable to God. Some—such as the Scribes and Pharisees—are *religiously deceived.* They study Scripture, pray, witness, help the needy, and keep the rules. They would even fight to maintain religious tradition. Yet, Jesus says they are hypocrites. Why? Because their heart is not God's. They refuse to personally accept Jesus as the Son of God, the Messiah and Savior of the world. Therefore, they do not know God personally, not in the depths of their hearts (Jn.14:6). They adhere to their traditions rather than the truth of God's Word. Because of this, their religious efforts are meaningless and unacceptable to God.

> They profess to know God, but they deny him by their works. They are detestable, disobedient, unfit for any good work. (Tit.1:16)

> Knowing that you were ransomed from the futile ways inherited from your forefathers, not with perishable things such as silver or gold, but with the precious blood of Christ, like that of a lamb without blemish or spot. (1 Pe.1:18-19)

For, speaking loud boasts of folly, they entice by sensual passions of the flesh those who are barely escaping from those who live in error. They promise them freedom, but they themselves are slaves of corruption. For whatever overcomes a person, to that he is enslaved. (2 Pe.2:18-19)

By this you know the Spirit of God: every spirit that confesses that Jesus Christ has come in the flesh is from God, and every spirit that does not confess Jesus is not from God. This is the spirit of the antichrist, which you heard was coming and now is in the world already. (1 Jn.4:2-3)

7:7

[7] "'in vain do they worship me, teaching as doctrines the commandments of men.'"

3 Tradition can be empty, worthless worship.

Following tradition rather than truth results in empty, worthless worship. Jesus declared that the religionists worshiped *in vain* (Gk. matain)—futilely, pointlessly, without purpose or beneficial result. As Jesus said, they truly did not know what (Whom) they were worshiping (Jn.4:22). Those who emphasize traditions over truth worship, but with an empty heart. Jesus taught that true worship must be *in spirit and in truth*: not only *in spirit*, but *in truth* as well (Jn.4:24). A person who denies Christ or denies God's Word cannot truly worship God (Jn.14:6; 17:17). They may worship; but their worship is empty, worthless, unacceptable. The religionists of Jesus' day were professing religion with their lips, but denying Christ, God's Son, in their hearts (see vv.17-20).

7:8

[8] "You leave the commandment of God and hold to the tradition of men."

4 Tradition can be man-made commands.

Religionists teach tradition as God's commandment. They teach their tradition as they practice it or proclaim it. Tradition is man's *idea* of what should be or what should not be done. Some traditions are good; however, they are not to be taught as though they are the commandments of God. As important as some traditions may seem to be, they are not as important as God's Word. God has revealed all of His commandments and everything He expects of us in His Word. It is dangerous to add to God's body of revealed truth—the Scripture (Jn.17:17; 2 Co.2:10-12; Re.22:18-19).

See to it that no one takes you captive by philosophy and empty deceit, according to human tradition, according to the elemental spirits of the world, and not according to Christ. (Col.2:8)

Preach the word; be ready in season and out of season; reprove, rebuke, and exhort, with complete patience and teaching. (2 Ti.4:2)

Not devoting themselves to Jewish myths and the commands of people who turn away from the truth. (Tit.1:14; see Jn.17:17)

7:9-12

[9] And he said to them, "You have a fine way of rejecting the commandment of God in order to establish your tradition!
[10] For Moses said, 'Honor your father and your mother'; and, 'Whoever reviles father or mother must surely die.'
[11] But you say, 'If a man tells his father or his mother, "Whatever you would have gained from me is Corban"' (that is, given to God)—
[12] then you no longer permit him to do anything for his father or mother,"

5 Tradition can be kept before the commands of God.

Jesus made another serious charge against the religionists. He said they broke God's law *in order to keep* their traditions (v.9). They prioritized keeping their traditions before keeping God's commands. He proceeded to give an example of this, citing God's command to honor one's parents (v.10).

a. The people twisted God's commands (v.11).

Jesus explained how the religionists allowed the people to twist God's commands to their benefit. God's law commands people to honor their parents. Jesus' teaching here clearly establishes that honoring our parents includes taking care of and providing for them when they can no longer take care of and provide for themselves.

However, Jewish religious leaders taught that if a person's parents needed help, and the person had made a financial commitment to the temple, they should neglect providing for their parents in order to fulfill that commitment, if necessary. Once they vowed to give a gift to the temple, they could never back out of the vow, even if they later needed the gift to take care of their parents. They justified the neglecting of their parents' by declaring their money to be *corban*—the Hebrew word for offerings to God (see Deeper Study # 1). "One merely declared something 'korban,' and it was technically set aside for temple use. In theory it may have been dedicated to the temple, but in practice the offeror kept the 'gift' for his own use. Thus *corban* was a loophole used to avoid [financial] responsibility."[1]

b. The religionists insisted on obedience to tradition (v.12).

By forbidding people to use money supposedly committed to the temple to care for their parents, Jewish leaders demanded that people obey tradition over God's law. By pointing this out, Jesus was saying, "I am not the law breaker, the hypocrite. You are. You are the ones who are breaking God's law. You put your own rule above the law of God." (Several notes should be read at this point to see the background of this conflict. See notes—Mt.12:1-8; note and Deeper Study # 1—12:10; Deeper Study # 1—Mk.7:11; Deeper Study # 1—Lu.6:2.)

> You leave the commandment of God and hold to the tradition of men. (Mk.7:8)

> Little children, yet a little while I am with you. You will seek me, and just as I said to the Jews, so now I also say to you, 'Where I am going you cannot come.' A new commandment I give to you, that you love one another: just as I have loved you, you also are to love one another. (Jn.13:33-34)

> And this is his commandment, that we believe in the name of his Son Jesus Christ and love one another, just as he has commanded us. (1 Jn.3:23)

> And the Lord said: "Because this people draw near with their mouth and honor me with their lips, while their hearts are far from me, and their fear of me is a commandment taught by men." (Is.29:13)

Deeper Study # 1

(7:11) **Corban:** a gift dedicated to God. When a person gave a gift or left an estate to God, they simply pronounced the words, "My goods are corban." It was an official statement that was legally binding. Once the statement was made, the goods belonged to the temple. The problem arose when the religious leaders went too far in encouraging such gifts and estates. They tried to secure the vow even from those who had parents or family members that needed help. In such cases, a person was evading the most basic duty: caring for their family members (see Ex.20:12; 21:17).

6 Tradition can nullify the Word of God or make the Word of God ineffective.

7:13

Jesus charged the religionists with setting aside God's Word for tradition, thereby nullifying God's Word (see Deeper Studies 2, 3). God's law was no longer in effect; man-made tradition overruled it. Jesus was attacking the fact that so many religionists put their traditions first while neglecting and ignoring God's Word (see notes—Mt.12:1-8; note and Deeper Study # 1—12:10).

13 "thus making void the word of God by your tradition that you have handed down. And many such things you do."

---

1 Thoralf Gilbrant, Ralph W. Harris, eds., *The Complete Biblical Library Greek-English Dictionary*, (Springfield, MO: World Library Press, 1990), via Wordsearch digital edition.

Religious traditions may be described as institutional or personal. Institutional traditions are such things as rituals, rules, regulations, schedules, forms, services, procedures, organizations—anything that gives order and security to the persons involved.

Personal traditions are such things as frequency of church attendance, prayers, habits, ceremonies, practices which people use (somewhat superstitiously) to keep themselves feeling religiously secure.

> He answered them, "And why do you break the commandment of God for the sake of your tradition?" (Mt.15:3)

> For freedom Christ has set us free; stand firm therefore, and do not submit again to a yoke of slavery. (Ga.5:1)

> If with Christ you died to the elemental spirits of the world, why, as if you were still alive in the world, do you submit to regulations? (Col.2:20)

> But deal only with food and drink and various washings, regulations for the body imposed until the time of reformation. But when Christ appeared as a high priest of the good things that have come, then through the greater and more perfect tent (not made with hands, that is, not of this creation) he entered once for all into the holy places, not by means of the blood of goats and calves but by means of his own blood, thus securing an eternal redemption. For if the blood of goats and bulls, and the sprinkling of defiled persons with the ashes of a heifer, sanctify for the purification of the flesh, how much more will the blood of Christ, who through the eternal Spirit offered himself without blemish to God, purify our conscience from dead works to serve the living God. Therefore he is the mediator of a new covenant, so that those who are called may receive the promised eternal inheritance, since a death has occurred that redeems them from the transgressions committed under the first covenant. (He.9:10–15)

DEEPER STUDY # 2

(7:13) **Making void or of no effect, invalidating, nullifying** (akurountes): to make ineffective; to annul; to deprive of value, authority, and power.

DEEPER STUDY # 3

(7:13) **Word of God:** see notes and DEEPER STUDY # 1—1 Th.2:13; notes—2 Th.2:13; 2 Ti.3:16; note and DEEPER STUDIES 1, 2—2 Pe.1:19-21. See also Ac.17:11; 20:32; 1 Pe.2:2-3.

¹⁴ And he called the people to him again and said to them, "Hear me, all of you, and understand:

¹⁵ There is nothing outside a person that by going into him can defile him, but the things that come out of a person are what defile him."

¹⁷ And when he had entered the house and left the people, his disciples asked him about the parable.

¹⁸ And he said to them, "Then are you also without understanding? Do you not see that whatever goes into a person from outside cannot defile him,

¹⁹ since it enters not his heart but his stomach, and is expelled?" (Thus he declared all foods clean.)

²⁰ And he said, "What comes out of a person is what defiles him.

²¹ For from within, out of the heart of man, come evil thoughts, sexual immorality, theft, murder, adultery,

²² coveting, wickedness, deceit, sensuality, envy, slander, pride, foolishness."

²³ "All these evil things come from within, and they defile a person."

1. **Jesus called the crowd together and shared a parable**
   a. The importance stressed: Listen and understand
   b. The parable shared

   c. The disciples' request for the parable to be explained

2. **Explanation 1: The thing that enters the body neither defiles it nor makes a person unclean**

   a. It does not enter the heart
   b. It enters the digestive tract

3. **Explanation 2: The thing that comes out of the heart does defile a person**[DS1]
   a. The progression and growth of sin[DS2]
   b. The sins listed[DS3-15]

4. **Explanation 3: The source of evil is the heart**

Division IV

The Son of God's Training Ministry: Jesus' Intensive Preparation of the Disciples, 6:7–8:26

H. The Things That Defile and Make a Person Unclean 7:14–23

(Mt.15:10–20; Lu.11:37–41)

7:14–23
Introduction

The truth of this passage is one of the most startling Jesus ever taught. It shook the world of His day, and it has disturbed and gnawed at people's minds and consciences ever since. It revolutionizes humanity's idea of evil and wrongdoing, of just what evil is and what causes it. It knocks the props out from under man's system of religion and morality. It lays people bare before God, making them totally dependent on God for salvation and life. This is, *The Things That Defile and Make a Person Unclean*, 7:14–23.

1. Jesus called the crowd together and shared a parable (vv.14–17).

2. Explanation 1: The thing that enters the body neither defiles it nor makes a person unclean (vv.18–19).
3. Explanation 2: The thing that comes out of the heart does defile a person (vv.20–22).
4. Explanation 3: The source of evil is the heart (v.23).

7:14–17

¹⁴ And he called the people to him again and said to them, "Hear me, all of you, and understand:
¹⁵ There is nothing outside a person that by going into him can defile him, but the things that come out of a person are what defile him."
¹⁷ And when he had entered the house and left the people, his disciples asked him about the parable.

1 Jesus called the crowd together and shared a parable.

After Jesus' confrontation with the Scribes and Pharisees, He called the people together again to teach them a critical truth. Apparently, the people had heard what Jesus had said to the Pharisees about their tradition, and He wanted them to understand exactly what He was saying.

a. The importance stressed; Listen and understand (v.14).
Jesus challenged the people to do two things:
- To listen carefully to Him, to give Him their full attention.
- To make sure they fully understood what He was saying.

What Jesus was about to teach was of supreme importance. It was critical that they grasp its truth and apply it to their lives.

b. The parable shared (v.15).
Jesus shared a parable revolving around eating and digesting food. Simply stated, the meaning of the parable is as follows: people are not defiled by what enters their bodies, but by what comes out of their hearts. Immediately after presenting the brief parable, the Lord once again stressed the importance of understanding it (v.16: KJV, NKJV, NASB[1]).

c. The disciples' request for the parable to be explained (v.17).
The disciples did not understand the parable. Later, when they were alone with Jesus, they asked Him to explain it.

THOUGHT 1. It is not enough for us to hear what Christ is saying, we must understand. If we do not understand some part of Scripture, we should follow the disciples' example and seek help in understanding.

> And beginning with Moses and all the Prophets, he interpreted to them in all the Scriptures the things concerning himself. . . . Then he opened their minds to understand the Scriptures. (Lu.24:27, 45)

> Declare these things; exhort and rebuke with all authority. Let no one disregard you. (Tit.2:15)

> They read from the book, from the Law of God, clearly, and they gave the sense, so that the people understood the reading. (Ne.8:8)

---

1 The earliest manuscripts from which the ESV, CSB, NIV, and a number of other modern English Bible translations are translated do not include verse 16.

2 Explanation 1: The thing that enters the body neither defiles it nor makes a person unclean.

a. It does not enter the heart (v.19a).

b. It enters the digestive tract (v.19b).

Jesus explained that what we eat and drink is not what defiles us, not spiritually (v.18). What we eat and drink does not enter the heart; it enters the stomach—the digestive tract—and passes out of the body (v.19). Therefore, food and drink, or eating with unwashed hands, or doing any other outward thing cannot defile a person—not *spiritually*. The disciples were not defiled—as the Pharisees claimed—because they ate with unwashed hands (vv.2-4).

18 And he said to them, "Then are you also without understanding? Do you not see that whatever goes into a person from outside cannot defile him,
19 since it enters not his heart but his stomach, and is expelled?" (Thus he declared all foods clean.)

There is a difference in the physical and the spiritual; there is no connection between what we eat physically and spirituality. That is not to say that excessive eating and a lack of self-control are not wrong. Harmful and excessive appetites come *out of the heart*. But when it comes to the items themselves, the food and drink, there is no merit or value, no morality or virtue to them—not within themselves. It is *what we do with the things*, what our heart does, that makes us either good or bad, spiritual or carnal.

THOUGHT 1. When *formal* or *outward religion* is outlined like Christ shares in this passage, the foolishness of holding such a position is really seen.

> For the kingdom of God is not a matter of eating and drinking but of righteousness and peace and joy in the Holy Spirit. (Ro.14:17)

> For neither circumcision counts for anything nor uncircumcision, but keeping the commandments of God. (1 Co.7:19)

> Food will not commend us to God. We are no worse off if we do not eat, and no better off if we do. (1 Co.8:8)

> You observe days and months and seasons and years! I am afraid I may have labored over you in vain. (Ga.4:10-11)

> Having the appearance of godliness, but denying its power. Avoid such people. (2 Ti.3:5)

3 Explanation 2: The thing that comes out of the heart does defile a person.

a. The progress and growth of sin (v.21).

b. The sins listed (vv.21-22).

What *does* defile us, Jesus explained, is that which comes out of our hearts (v.20; see DEEPER STUDY # 1). Note what Jesus is saying here: "It is not outward things that defile a person. It is the heart that defiles a person." The human heart is corrupt; therefore, we corrupt ourselves. We are not *made spiritually unclean* by outward things; we are

20 And he said, "What comes out of a person is what defiles him.
21 For from within, out of the heart of man, come evil thoughts, sexual immorality, theft, murder, adultery,
22 coveting, wickedness, deceit, sensuality, envy, slander, pride, foolishness."

spiritually unclean because of our polluted heart, because we are corrupt within. *It is our defiled heart that causes us to do unclean things.* Sin proceeds and grows out of our corrupt human heart (see DEEPER STUDY # 2). Jesus proceeded to list a number of sins that naturally flow out of people's depraved hearts (see DEEPER STUDIES 3-15—Mk.7:21-22 for discussion[2]).

---

2 The order of the sins listed as well as where the verses are divided varies between manuscripts. Consequently, they vary between Bible translations. They are listed in the Deeper Studies according to the order and in which verse they are listed in the ESV.

DEEPER STUDY # 1

(7:19-20) **Heart** (Gk. kardia): in the Bible the word "heart" refers to both the major organ of the body (Le.17:11) and to the most important part of a person, that is, to our innermost being. The heart is the central part, the very center of a person's life. It is the most vital part of our being.

The heart is every person's inward life. It lies deep within, containing the *hidden person* or the real person (1 Pe.3:4); that is, the heart is what we really are, our true character. The heart determines what we do, our behavior, whether good or depraved (Mt.15:18; Mk.7:21-23).

1. The heart is the source of our rational being: reasoning (Mk.2:6), understanding (Mt.13:15), thinking (Mt.9:4).

2. The heart is the source of our emotional being: joy (Jn.16:22; Ep.5:19), affections (Lu.24:32), desires (Mt.5:28).

3. The heart is the source of our spiritual being: conscience (Ac.2:37), will (Ro.6:17), faith (Mk.11:23; Ro.10:10), evil (Mt.15:18; Mk.7:21-23; see Je.17:9).

DEEPER STUDY # 2

(7:21) **Sin:** note the progression of sin in our lives. (1) It begins in human nature: "within, out of the heart." (2) It develops in the human mind: in "evil thoughts." (3) It is expressed in human acts: "adulteries, fornications. . . ."

DEEPER STUDY # 3

(7:21) **Evil Thoughts** (dialogismoi hoi kakoi): thoughts and imaginations and ideas and concepts that are base, wrong, wicked, immoral, unjust, reprehensible; thoughts that are not what they should be; thoughts that are not moral, clean, and pure; thoughts that are not just and equitable; thoughts that are not uplifting and edifying; thoughts that are not spiritual, but carnal (see Mt.5:28; Ro.8:6; 2 Co.10:5; Ph.4:8). Evil thoughts are a sin against all the commandments (Ex.20:1f).

> But Jesus, knowing their thoughts, said, "Why do you think evil in your hearts?" (Mt.9:4)

> For although they knew God, they did not honor him as God or give thanks to him, but they became futile in their thinking, and their foolish hearts were darkened. (Ro.1:21)

> The Lord saw that the wickedness of man was great in the earth, and that every intention of the thoughts of his heart was only evil continually. (Ge.6:5)

> The thoughts of the wicked are an abomination to the Lord, but gracious words are pure. (Pr.15:26)

> The devising of folly is sin, and the scoffer is an abomination to mankind. (Pr.24:9)

DEEPER STUDY # 4

(7:21) **Sexual immorality or Fornication** (porneiai; pronounced *por-nay'-eye*): sexual immorality includes all forms and kinds of immoral and sexual acts. It includes *every* sexual vice, from premarital sex and adultery to homosexual sex acts and pornography.

> Flee from sexual immorality. Every other sin a person commits is outside the body, but the sexually immoral person sins against his own body. (1 Co.6:18)

> But sexual immorality and all impurity or covetousness must not even be named among you, as is proper among saints. (Ep.5:3)

> Put to death therefore what is earthly in you: sexual immorality, impurity, passion, evil desire, and covetousness, which is idolatry. (Col.3:5)
>
> For this is the will of God, your sanctification: that you abstain from sexual immorality. (1 Th.4:3)

DEEPER STUDY # 5

(7:21) **Theft** (klopi): to cheat and steal; to take wrongfully from another person, either legally or illegally.

> Let the thief no longer steal, but rather let him labor, doing honest work with his own hands, so that he may have something to share with anyone in need. (Ep.4:28)
>
> Not pilfering, but showing all good faith, so that in everything they may adorn the doctrine of God our Savior. (Tit.2:10)
>
> You shall not steal. (Ex.20:15)
>
> You shall not steal; you shall not deal falsely; you shall not lie to one another. (Le.19:11)

DEEPER STUDY # 6

(7:21) **Murder** (phonoi): to kill, to take the life of another. Murder is a sin against the sixth commandment.

> He said to him, "Which ones?" And Jesus said, "You shall not murder, You shall not commit adultery, You shall not steal, You shall not bear false witness." (Mt.19:18)
>
> For the commandments, "You shall not commit adultery, You shall not murder, You shall not steal, You shall not covet," and any other commandment, are summed up in this word: "You shall love your neighbor as yourself." Love does no wrong to a neighbor; therefore love is the fulfilling of the law. (Ro.13:8–10)
>
> Everyone who hates his brother is a murderer, and you know that no murderer has eternal life abiding in him. (1 Jn.3:15)
>
> You shall not murder. (Ex.20:13)

DEEPER STUDY # 7

(7:21) **Adultery** (moicheiai; pronounced *moi-kay'-eye*): sexual unfaithfulness to husband or wife. Jesus added that it includes looking on a woman or a man to lust after her or him. Looking with lustful thoughts and imagining sex with anyone other than your spouse, whether in person, or through magazines, books, or anywhere else, is adultery. It is committing the act within the heart (see notes—Mt.5:28; DEEPER STUDY # 5—19:9 for discussion). Adultery is a sin against the seventh commandment.

> You have heard that it was said, 'You shall not commit adultery.' But I say to you that everyone who looks at a woman with lustful intent has already committed adultery with her in his heart. (Mt.5:27–28)
>
> Or do you not know that the unrighteous will not inherit the kingdom of God? Do not be deceived: neither the sexually immoral, nor idolaters, nor adulterers, nor men who practice homosexuality, nor thieves, nor the greedy, nor drunkards, nor revilers, nor swindlers will inherit the kingdom of God. (1 Co.6:9–10)
>
> They have eyes full of adultery, insatiable for sin. They entice unsteady souls. They have hearts trained in greed. Accursed children! (2 Pe.2:14)
>
> You shall not commit adultery. (Ex.20:14)

DEEPER STUDY # 8

(7:22) **Coveting or Covetousness** (pleonexiai; pronounced *pleh-on-ex-ay'-eye*): to lust for more and more; to have a starving appetite for something; to have a love of possessing (2 Pe.2:14); to crave after and for. It means to crave and grasp after possessions, pleasure, power, fame. Covetousness lacks restraint. It lacks the ability to discriminate. It wants to have in order to spend in pleasure and luxury. Covetousness is an insatiable lust and craving of the flesh that cannot be satisfied. It is an intense appetite for gain, a passion for the pleasure that things can bring. It is a lust and craving so deep that a person finds their happiness in things instead of in God. It is a form of idolatry (Ep.5:5).

> And he said to them, "Take care, and be on your guard against all covetousness, for one's life does not consist in the abundance of his possessions." (Lu.12:15)

> For you may be sure of this, that everyone who is sexually immoral or impure, or who is covetous (that is, an idolater), has no inheritance in the kingdom of Christ and God. (Ep.5:5)

> Put to death therefore what is earthly in you: sexual immorality, impurity, passion, evil desire, and covetousness, which is idolatry. (Col.3:5)

> You shall not covet your neighbor's house; you shall not covet your neighbor's wife, or his male servant, or his female servant, or his ox, or his donkey, or anything that is your neighbor's. (Ex.20:17)

DEEPER STUDY # 9

(7:22) **Wickedness** (poneriai; pronounced *pon-ay-ree'-eye*): to be depraved, to be actively evil, to do mischief, to trouble others and cause harm, to be malicious, to be dangerous and destructive. It is malice, hatred, and ill-will. It is an active wickedness, a desire within the heart to do harm and to corrupt people. It is actually pursuing others in order to seduce them or to harm them.

> For we ourselves were once foolish, disobedient, led astray, slaves to various passions and pleasures, passing our days in malice and envy, hated by others and hating one another. (Tit.3:3)

> For there is no truth in their mouth; their inmost self is destruction; their throat is an open grave; they flatter with their tongue. (Ps.5:9)

> The wicked plots against the righteous and gnashes his teeth at him. (Ps.37:12)

> For they cannot sleep unless they have done wrong; they are robbed of sleep unless they have made someone stumble. (Pr.4:16)

DEEPER STUDY # 10

(7:22) **Deceit** (dolos): to bait, to snare, to mislead, to beguile, to be crafty and deceitful, to mislead or give a false impression by word, act, or influence. It is conniving and twisting the truth to get one's own way. A person plots and deceives, doing whatever has to be done in order to get what they want.

> Their throat is an open grave; they use their tongues to deceive. The venom of asps is under their lips. (Ro.3:13)

> Do not lie to one another, seeing that you have put off the old self with its practices. (Col.3:9)

> You destroy those who speak lies; the LORD abhors the bloodthirsty and deceitful man. (Ps.5:6)

> No one who practices deceit shall dwell in my house; no one who utters lies shall continue before my eyes. (Ps.101:7)

> Everyone deceives his neighbor, and no one speaks the truth; they have taught their tongue to speak lies; they weary themselves committing iniquity. (Je.9:5)

> The heart is deceitful above all things, and desperately sick; who can understand it? (Je.17:9)

DEEPER STUDY # 11

(7:22) **Sensuality, Lewdness, or Self-indulgence** (aselgeia; pronounced *ah-sel'-gay-ah*): filthiness, indecency, shamelessness. A chief characteristic of this behavior is open and shameless indecency. It means unrestrained evil thoughts and behavior. It is giving in to brutish and lustful desires, a readiness for any pleasure. It is a person who knows no restraint, a person who has sinned so much they no longer care what people say or think. It is something far more distasteful than just doing wrong. Those who misbehave usually try to hide their wrong, but the lewd do not care who knows about their exploits or shame. They want; therefore, they seek to take and gratify. Decency and opinion do not matter. When they initially begin to sin, they do as all do: they misbehave in secret. But eventually, the sin gets the best of them—to the point that they no longer care who sees or knows. They become the slave of a master—the master being the habit. People become the slaves of such things as unbridled lust, wantonness, licentiousness, outrageousness, shamelessness, insolence (Mk.7:22), wanton manners, filthy words, indecent body movements, immoral handling of males and females (Ro.13:13), carnality, gluttony, and sexual immorality (1 Pe.4:3; 2 Pe.2:2, 18; see also 2 Co.12:21; Ga.5:19; Ep.4:19; 2 Pe.2:7).

> And the men likewise gave up natural relations with women and were consumed with passion for one another, men committing shameless acts with men and receiving in themselves the due penalty for their error. (Ro.1:27)

> They have become callous and have given themselves up to sensuality, greedy to practice every kind of impurity. (Ep.4:19)

> For the time that is past suffices for doing what the Gentiles want to do, living in sensuality, passions, drunkenness, orgies, drinking parties, and lawless idolatry. (1 Pe.4:3)

> For certain people have crept in unnoticed who long ago were designated for this condemnation, ungodly people, who pervert the grace of our God into sensuality and deny our only Master and Lord, Jesus Christ . . . just as Sodom and Gomorrah and the surrounding cities, which likewise indulged in sexual immorality and pursued unnatural desire, serve as an example by undergoing a punishment of eternal fire. (Jude 4, 7)

DEEPER STUDY # 12

(7:22) **Envy or Evil Eye** (ophthalmos poneros): to look where one should not; to lust after what one should not; to envy, covet, crave or desire by looking; to use the eye in an evil way; to satisfy one's lusts and desires by looking.

> You have heard that it was said, 'You shall not commit adultery.' But I say to you that everyone who looks at a woman with lustful intent has already committed adultery with her in his heart. (Mt.5:27–28)

> Your eye is the lamp of your body. When your eye is healthy, your whole body is full of light, but when it is bad, your body is full of darkness. (Lu.11:34)

> I will not set before my eyes anything that is worthless. I hate the work of those who fall away; it shall not cling to me. (Ps.101:3)

DEEPER STUDY # 13

(7:22) **Slander or Blasphemy** (blasphemia): to insult, revile, speak evil of God or another person (see DEEPER STUDY # 4—Mt.9:3).

> Truly, I say to you, all sins will be forgiven the children of man, and whatever blasphemies they utter, but whoever blasphemes against the Holy Spirit never has forgiveness, but is guilty of an eternal sin. (Mk.3:28–29)

> Among whom are Hymenaeus and Alexander, whom I have handed over to Satan that they may learn not to blaspheme. (1 Ti.1:20)

Are they not the ones who blaspheme the honorable name by which you were called? (Js.2:7)

Whoever blasphemes the name of the Lord shall surely be put to death. All the congregation shall stone him. The sojourner as well as the native, when he blasphemes the Name, shall be put to death. (Le.24:16)

DEEPER STUDY # 14

(7:22) **Pride** (huperephania; pronounced *hu-per-ay-phon-ee'-ah*): self-exaltation, conceit, arrogance, haughtiness, putting oneself above others, looking down on others, scorn, contempt. It means to lift one's head above another, to hold contempt for another, to compare oneself with others. Pride can be hidden in the heart as well as openly displayed. God resists the proud (Pr.3:24; Js.4:6; 1 Pe.5:5).

Live in harmony with one another. Do not be haughty, but associate with the lowly. Never be wise in your own sight. (Ro.12:16)

For all that is in the world—the desires of the flesh and the desires of the eyes and pride of life—is not from the Father but is from the world. (1 Jn.2:16)

Pride goes before destruction, and a haughty spirit before a fall. (Pr.16:18)

Haughty eyes and a proud heart, the lamp of the wicked, are sin. (Pr.21:4)

DEEPER STUDY # 15

(7:22) **Foolishness** (aphrosune; *ah-phro-soo'-nay*): moral senselessness, folly, recklessness, thoughtlessness. It is a person who acts foolishly in morals and duty, behavior and thought.

And the Lord said to him, "Now you Pharisees cleanse the outside of the cup and of the dish, but inside you are full of greed and wickedness. You fools! Did not he who made the outside make the inside also?" (Lu.11:39–40)

The fool says in his heart, "There is no God." They are corrupt, doing abominable iniquity; there is none who does good. (Ps.53:1)

Whoever trusts in his own mind is a fool, but he who walks in wisdom will be delivered. (Pr.28:26)

Dead flies make the perfumer's ointment give off a stench; so a little folly outweighs wisdom and honor. (Ec.10:1)

7:23

²³ "All these evil things come from within, and they defile a person."

4 Explanation 3: The source of evil is the heart.

Jesus reemphasized the lesson that the source of evil is the heart. The problem of evil is from within, not from without; it is internal, not external. Evil comes from the heart (spirit), not the body. Consider the news reports of any city on any given day. Notice the evil things reported, and keep in mind that those accounts are only reporting one particular city's daily evil—and only the misdeeds bad enough to make the news. Multiply that evil, including unreported evil, by every city of any size. Just think of all the evil that is being done every day. Think of evil words and evil treatment and evil thoughts—all evil things done in every location (Mk.7:21-22)—and one has a picture of what Jesus meant. The human heart is our problem. It is from the heart that *these evil things* come. Human beings know better. They have more intelligence than to allow so much evil in their lives and homes and communities. We simply cannot control the heart.

Individuals and society as a whole make three fatal mistakes when dealing with problems of the heart.

First, they judge evil to be external only. They judge only the sinful act, only the deed. In the eyes of society, a person would be considered perfect if they never did bad—never broke the law and never did the forbidden thing. People are considered good if they *seldom* do bad—*seldom* break the law or *seldom* do the wrong thing (for example, breaking the speed limit or taking supplies from an office).

Second, they fail to see (or confess) that evil arises from the heart, from within. They do not consider that evil things come from an evil heart. Therefore, they put little if any restraint on lust and inward thoughts. People seldom think beyond the act; they seldom dig into the reason for the lust and thought; they seldom give any attention to the heart. The result: society still grapples and always will have to grapple with the problem and tragedy of evil.

Third, they fail to see and acknowledge that the human heart needs to be changed, that is, converted. Society refuses to face up to the fact that a new heart is what is needed. Somehow a person needs to be reborn.

> **And to be renewed in the spirit of your minds, and to put on the new self, created after the likeness of God in true righteousness and holiness. (Ep.4:23-24)**

> **Do not lie to one another, seeing that you have put off the old self with its practices and have put on the new self, which is being renewed in knowledge after the image of its creator. (Col.3:9-10)**

> **Since you have been born again, not of perishable seed but of imperishable, through the living and abiding word of God. (1 Pe.1:23)**

(Mt.15:21–28)

1. **Step 1: Taking care of our own body and spirit**
   a. Jesus entered the land of the Gentiles
   b. Jesus needed rest and sought quiet in a house
2. **Step 2: Allowing interruptions of our privacy or schedule by the rejected**

3. **Step 3: Conversing with the rejected**
   a. Listening to the cry of the rejected.

   b. Stressing to the rejected the need for humility: The Jews (children) were to receive the gospel first; the Gentiles (dogs) were to receive it later[DS1]
   c. Leading the rejected (a Gentile) to endure and believe

4. **Step 4: Meeting the needs of the rejected**

²⁴ And from there he arose and went away to the region of Tyre and Sidon. And he entered a house and did not want anyone to know, yet he could not be hidden.
²⁵ But immediately a woman whose little daughter had an unclean spirit heard of him and came and fell down at his feet.
²⁶ Now the woman was a Gentile, a Syrophoenician by birth. And she begged him to cast the demon out of her daughter.
²⁷ And he said to her, "Let the children be fed first, for it is not right to take the children's bread and throw it to the dogs."
²⁸ But she answered him, "Yes, Lord; yet even the dogs under the table eat the children's crumbs."
²⁹ And he said to her, "For this statement you may go your way; the demon has left your daughter."
³⁰ And she went home and found the child lying in bed and the demon gone.

Division IV

The Son of God's Training Ministry: Jesus' Intensive Preparation of the Disciples, 6:7–8:26

I. The Steps to Caring for the Rejected, 7:24–30

(Mt.15:21–28)

7:24–30
Introduction

World history is littered with prejudice and discrimination. In many ways, little progress has truly been made in this tragic area. Whether based on race, nationality, gender, religion, or some other factor, prejudice and discrimination continue to infect our world. Nevertheless, prejudice and discrimination are wrong. The rejected are to be reached out to and helped.

The rejected are always *cut off* by society, excluded from walking in the midst of society. They are unaccepted and ostracized. Why? Because society wraps its acceptable biases and behavior around itself and secludes itself from those who act differently. Society has little time to deal with those who differ and sometimes even fears them. But this must not be. Society must allow its seclusion to be interrupted—face up to the differences and needs of the rejected; converse and discuss the differences with them; and then work to meet their needs.

In this passage, Jesus encounters a woman who had been discriminated against by Jewish society. In her coming to Jesus, she demonstrates steps that the rejected can take in order to receive help. The rejected woman approaches Jesus humbly (v.25); discusses her need with Him (vv.26-28); perseveres in asking for help (v.28); confesses her humble status or need (v.28); and then she receives help (vv.29-30). Jesus, in turn, demonstrates how we should treat those who are discriminated against.

This is a vital passage, for it foreshadows the spread of the gospel worldwide and God's great desire for all barriers between different groups of people to be broken down (see outline and notes—Ep.2:11-22). This is, *The Steps to Caring for the Rejected*, 7:24-30.

1. Step 1: Taking care of our own body and spirit (v.24).
2. Step 2: Allowing interruptions of our privacy or schedule by the rejected (v.25).
3. Step 3: Conversing with the rejected (vv.26-28).
4. Step 4: Meeting the needs of the rejected (vv.29-30).

1 Step 1: Taking care of our own body and spirit.

7:24

a. Jesus entered the land of the Gentiles.
b. Jesus needed rest and sought quiet in a house.

Jesus and the disciples had yet to get the rest they so sorely needed (6:31). Once again, Jesus attempted to get that rest. This time, He deliberately withdrew to the borders of Gentile country, hoping to find quiet and time to prepare both Himself and His disciples for the days ahead. The only place He could find freedom from the crowds and from His opponents was in the northern area that bordered Gentile territory. No Jew was likely to enter Gentile areas. Therefore, the Lord went to the region of Tyre and Sidon.

Tyre was the capital of Phoenicia (see note, *Tyre*—Ac.21:1-3). It was immediately north of Judea, and Sidon was immediately north of its border. Apparently, multitudes of people had flocked to Jesus from these Gentile areas. His fame had already spread as far away as Tyre and Sidon (Mk.3:8). Jesus hoped to find peace and quiet in a private house, but as Mark points out, He could not hide from the people—both desperate and curious—who untiringly sought Him.

THOUGHT 1. In order to serve God effectively, we have to take care of both our bodies and our spirits. There is a time to labor, and there is a time to seek rest and God's presence. Note: Jesus wanted to be alone. He did not want anyone to know where He was. Seeking rest and God's presence are essential if we are to serve in the power of God. Jesus' stay in Gentile country was apparently about six months long. Imagine being in God's presence on a spiritual retreat for much of a six-month period (see notes—Mk.7:31; see Mt.15:29).

²⁴ And from there he arose and went away to the region of Tyre and Sidon. And he entered a house and did not want anyone to know, yet he could not be hidden.

2 Step 2: Allowing interruptions of our privacy or schedule by the rejected.

7:25–26a

A woman with a desperate need heard where Jesus was, and she rushed to the house where He was staying. *Jesus did not refuse to see her.* Instead, He allowed His privacy and plans to be interrupted in order to help her.

This woman had two strikes against her in finding help from society. First, she had a daughter with an unclean spirit (v.25). In the ancient world, when a person had an evil spirit, the whole family was feared and therefore shunned. Both the daughter and mother knew rejection and the deep emotions that come with it.

²⁵ But immediately a woman whose little daughter had an unclean spirit heard of him and came and fell down at his feet.
²⁶ Now the woman was a Gentile, a Syrophoenician by birth. And she begged him to cast the demon out of her daughter.

Second, the mother was a Greek, a Syrophoenician or Canaanite by race (v.26a). She was from one of the seven nations mentioned in the Old Testament that were driven out of the land of Canaan. These nations and the Jews were bitter, ancestral enemies. They despised each other. In approaching Jesus, she knew that she was coming to a Jew who was assumed to be her enemy.

But note a significant fact: Jesus let her come to Him; He did not stop her. Others rejected her and her daughter, having nothing to do with them. The two stood alone in the world, rejected by all. Jesus needed rest and time alone with God, and the disciples objected to her (Mt.15:23). But Jesus allowed her to interrupt Him. She was as rejected as a person could be, but Jesus received her.

> Come to me, all who labor and are heavy laden, and I will give you rest. (Mt.11:28)

> Then children were brought to him that he might lay his hands on them and pray. The disciples rebuked the people, but Jesus said, "Let the little children come to me and do not hinder them, for to such belongs the kingdom of heaven." (Mt.19:13–14)

> Even as the Son of Man came not to be served but to serve, and to give his life as a ransom for many. (Mt.20:28)

7:26b–28

²⁶ Now the woman was a Gentile, a Syrophoenician by birth. And she begged him to cast the demon out of her daughter.

²⁷ And he said to her, "Let the children be fed first, for it is not right to take the children's bread and throw it to the dogs."

²⁸ But she answered him, "Yes, Lord; yet even the dogs under the table eat the children's crumbs."

3 Step 3: Conversing with the rejected.

Remember, our Lord is setting an example as to how we should treat those who are discriminated against. First, He welcomed the rejected woman, and, now, He conversed with her. He made a concentrated attempt to understand her and her needs.

a. Listening to the cry of the rejected (vv.26b–27a).

The rejected woman *begged* or *asked* (erota) Christ to help her demon-possessed daughter. The Greek verb is in the imperfect tense, which means she *kept on begging and begging.* Jesus listened to her cry and responded. *Said* (elegen, v.27a) is also in the imperfect tense, meaning He *kept on saying.* This fact implies that our loving Lord kept on listening and listening to what the woman was saying to Him. He carried on a two-way conversation with her.

It is important to understand what was happening. The woman had only a *limited* concept of Jesus, of who He was. She had apparently heard that the Jews expected a Messiah, a son of the great King David, who was to work miracles for them. And she had heard about Jesus, that He was delivering people from their sicknesses and healing them. But seeing Jesus only as a miracle worker and healer was an inadequate concept of Him. It prohibited Him from working. What the woman needed was to grow in her understanding of just who Jesus really was. Her greatest need was not the Messiah's help for her daughter. Her greatest need was salvation—both for herself and her daughter—the salvation that comes only through faith in the Messiah.

How gracious is our Lord! He listened to the cry of this rejected woman. He knew her heart, what was in it, every thought. He knew what she needed in order to be brought around to understanding His true Messiahship. So, He began to lead her step by step to understand His Lordship and to confess her faith with a humble and worshipful spirit.

b. Stressing to the rejected the need for humility: The Jews (children) were to receive the gospel first; the Gentiles (dogs) were to receive it later (v.27b).

Jesus stressed the need for humility to the rejected. He said two things to the woman—two statements that are often thought to be harsh because they are misunderstood. What He said needs to be clearly understood.

First, Jesus said, "Let the children be fed or filled first" (v.27b). What did Jesus mean by this? He was saying, "The Jews, the first children of God, must first be reached." There was no rejection whatsoever in this statement to the woman. It was merely a statement of fact. Jesus had come primarily to the house of Israel while on earth. He had to concentrate His ministry if He were to achieve His purpose. But why make this statement to the woman? There were apparently two reasons:

➢ The woman needed to learn persistence, humility, and trust.

➢ The woman needed to learn that there was only one true religion and one true Messiah. She was Greek from a proud pagan society. She had been and probably was presently a worshiper of false gods; therefore, she was undeserving of being heard by the true Messiah, the only living and true God of the universe. She had recognized Jesus as the Son of David, as the miracle worker of the Jews who was delivering them from their diseases. But she needed to recognize something else: that He is the *only Messiah* and the *only hope* for all people. No other religion, no other gods could do anything for her or for anyone else. He alone was her hope. He alone was to be the Lord and Master whom she was to worship. She had to learn the same lesson that the Samaritan woman at the well had to learn: salvation is of the Jews (Jn.4:22; see note—Mt.15:21-28).

Second, Jesus said, "It is not right to take the children's bread and throw it to the dogs" (v.27c). These words could be interpreted as harsh except for one thing: Jesus never spoke harshly or rejected anyone who came to Him with a desperate need and had the potential of trusting Him as Lord. So, whatever happened, we know that Jesus was not being harsh to the woman, nor was He rejecting her.

What, then, did Jesus mean by this seemingly unkind, harsh statement? Again, Jesus had to move the woman forward in faith and in understanding who He is: the Lord and Master of *everyone's* life, not just of the Jews. He was not just the Son of David. He had to teach her that salvation was of the Jews, and that He was that Salvation—the Savior and Master of all people, both Jew and Gentile. He was telling her that it was not right to take the bread of the gospel that belonged to the true worshipers of God and give it to the *dogs*, that is, those who worshiped false gods.

The woman was Greek; she was of a proud people with a rich heritage, but Greeks despised the Jews. She was a worshiper of false gods, a heathen, an outsider, a sinner; and He was the Messiah, the Savior and Lord of all people. He was leading her to make the critical decision that determines every person's eternal destiny, the decision to either accept or reject Jesus as Savior and Lord. Was she willing to humble herself, surrendering to Him as the Master of her life?

c. **Leading the rejected (a Gentile) to endure and believe (v.28).**
Jesus led the rejected woman to persist in calling on Him and to believe. Incisively and with great spiritual insight, she saw and confessed that she was nothing spiritually: she was like *a dog*. However, a family's dog was allowed to eat the crumbs that fell from the family's table (see DEEPER STUDY # 1).

Note that the woman now called Jesus *Lord* and now worshiped Him as Lord. She called Him "Lord" before, but now she did the one essential thing: she worshiped Him as Lord (see Mt.15:22). She believed in Him and confessed Him as Master of her life (Ro.10:9-10).

> Not everyone who says to me, 'Lord, Lord,' will enter the kingdom of heaven, but the one who does the will of my Father who is in heaven. (Mt.7:21; see 7:21-23)

> Because, if you confess with your mouth that Jesus is Lord and believe in your heart that God raised him from the dead, you will be saved. For with the heart one believes and is justified, and with the mouth one confesses and is saved. . . . For "everyone who calls on the name of the Lord will be saved." (Ro.10:9-10, 13)

DEEPER STUDY # 1

(7:27) **Dog:** was usually a symbol of dishonor—referring to the wild scavenging dogs of the streets. Calling people *dogs* in Jesus' day was a common practice. Paul called the Judaizers who hounded and persecuted believers *dogs* (Ph.3:2). Jews sometimes called Gentiles *dogs* as a term of contempt and insult. A Gentile was a *Gentile dog*, an *infidel dog*, or a *Christian* *dog.* However, note this: the word for dog used by Jesus is not the dog of the street (*kuon*), but of the house, a pet (*kunarion*). This, as well as the tone of His voice, apparently took any contemptuous sting out of the word. This seems clear by the woman's persistence in seeking help. Jesus' use of the word was evidently to stir and test her sincerity and persistence (see notes—Mt.15:26-27; 15:28).

7:29-30

²⁹ And he said to her, "For this statement you may go your way; the demon has left your daughter."

³⁰ And she went home and found the child lying in bed and the demon gone.

4 Step 4: Meeting the needs of the rejected.

Jesus rewarded the woman's confession. He answered her prayer and met her need. *From a distance,* our omnipotent Lord cast the devil out of her daughter.

One thing rises above all others in the experience of this desperate mother. She believed Jesus could meet her need, and she would not let Him go until He did this for her. Her belief was so strong she would not quit despite being met with apparent rebuff and being told that she was undeserving (see notes—Mt.15:23-24; Mk.7:25). There is no way to accurately describe her except as a woman of great faith.

> **And I tell you, ask, and it will be given to you; seek, and you will find; knock, and it will be opened to you. (Lu.11:9)**

Imagine this also: she believed Jesus' power could overcome space and time. Her daughter was back home. The woman had no visible confirmation that her daughter had been delivered, yet she went on her way. She simply took Jesus at His Word. What enormous faith!

But note a crucial point. Her faith in Jesus' power, as great as it was, was not enough. Her faith alone was not what caused Jesus to answer her prayer; it was her personal humility (surrender) and worship of Him as Lord. Jesus answers the prayer of and exercises His power on behalf of those who surrender (humble) themselves to Him and worship Him as Lord.

> **Even as the Son of Man came not to be served but to serve, and to give his life as a ransom for many. (Mt.20:28)**

> **If you ask me anything in my name, I will do it. (Jn.14:14)**

> **For we do not have a high priest who is unable to sympathize with our weaknesses, but one who in every respect has been tempted as we are, yet without sin. Let us then with confidence draw near to the throne of grace, that we may receive mercy and find grace to help in time of need. (He.4:15-16)**

J. The Verdict Sought For Our Service: Doing Everything Well, 7:31-37

(Mt.15:29-31)

³¹ Then he returned from the region of Tyre and went through Sidon to the Sea of Galilee, in the region of the Decapolis.

³² And they brought to him a man who was deaf and had a speech impediment, and they begged him to lay his hand on him.

³³ And taking him aside from the crowd privately, he put his fingers into his ears, and after spitting touched his tongue.

³⁴ And looking up to heaven, he sighed and said to him, "Ephphatha," that is, "Be opened."

³⁵ And his ears were opened, his tongue was released, and he spoke plainly.

³⁶ And Jesus charged them to tell no one. But the more he charged them, the more zealously they proclaimed it.

³⁷ And they were astonished beyond measure, saying, "He has done all things well. He even makes the deaf hear and the mute speak."

1. Jesus looked after His own personal needs and the needs of His loved ones (the disciples)
2. Jesus listened to the people's pleas for help
3. Jesus was considerate of the people's feelings and conditions: Took the man aside, alone
4. Jesus trusted God for the power to help the man
5. Jesus sought no personal applause or praise
6. Jesus' works demanded a verdict: "He has done all things well"

Division IV

The Son of God's Training Ministry: Jesus' Intensive Preparation of the Disciples, 6:7-8:26

J. The Verdict Sought for Our Service: Doing Everything Well, 7:31-37

(Mt.15:29-31)

7:31-37
Introduction

After witnessing Jesus heal a man who could neither hear nor speak, the people made a remarkable statement about Him, saying, "He has done all things well" (v.37). This was the verdict of this particular crowd, but it was not and never has been the verdict of every individual. Every person has to make a decision about Jesus, has to pass judgment on Jesus. A verdict is required.

The day is coming when God is going to pronounce *His* verdict, *His* judgment on every human being. We are all determining exactly what God's verdict will be. How? By the way we live.

The verdict Christ wants pronounced on every one of us is, "He (she) has done all things well." He wants to be able to say to each of us, "Well done, good and faithful servant" (Mt.25:21). How can we be assured of such a verdict by the Lord? Jesus shows us how in this passage. This is, *The Verdict Sought for Our Service: Doing Everything Well*, 7:31-37.

1. Jesus looked after His own personal needs and the needs of His loved ones (the disciples) (v.31).
2. Jesus listened to the people's pleas for help (v.32).
3. Jesus was considerate of the people's feelings and conditions of others: Took the man aside, alone (v.33).
4. Jesus trusted God for the power to help the man (vv.34-35).
5. Jesus sought no personal applause or praise (v.36).
6. Jesus' works demanded a verdict: "He has done all things well" (v.37).

7:31

³¹ Then he returned from the region of Tyre and went through Sidon to the Sea of Galilee, in the region of the Decapolis.

1 Jesus looked after His own personal needs and the needs of His loved ones (the disciples).

This is a strange verse, for Jesus was in Tyre, and He wanted to go to Galilee, which is to the south. However, the verse says He traveled north, from Tyre to Sidon. Why would He go north to Sidon if He wished to go south to Galilee? Probably for two reasons. First, He needed a period of quietness before facing the opposition and storm that awaited Him in Galilee and beyond. Second, the disciples also needed a long period of quiet training.

Jesus' appointment with the cross was rapidly approaching. The end was drawing nearer and nearer. The Gentile area was the only place He could be free from the crowds and have some quiet time with the disciples (see note—Mt.15:21-22). He and His disciples needed to be prepared for the end. Apparently, the disciples had six months or more of uninterrupted and intensive training at the feet of Jesus (see notes—Mt.15:21-22; 16:21-28; 17:22; note—Mt.15:29 for more detailed discussion).

THOUGHT 1. There are times when we need quiet—freedom from crowds and from the hustle and bustle of daily responsibilities. However, rest does not mean inactivity. Even when resting, we should be meeting with God, preparing ourselves for whatever lies ahead.

> Now therefore stand still that I may plead with you before the LORD concerning all the righteous deeds of the LORD that he performed for you and for your fathers. (1 S.12:7)

> Hear this, O Job; stop and consider the wondrous works of God. (Jb.37:14)

> Be angry, and do not sin; ponder in your own hearts on your beds, and be silent. Selah (Ps.4:4)

> Be still, and know that I am God. I will be exalted among the nations, I will be exalted in the earth! (Ps.46:10)

THOUGHT 2. Imagine six months of training on the death and resurrection of Christ. How supreme is its importance!

> For God so loved the world, that he gave his only Son, that whoever believes in him should not perish but have eternal life. (Jn.3:16)

> For I delivered to you as of first importance what I also received: that Christ died for our sins in accordance with the Scriptures, that he was buried, that he was raised on the third day in accordance with the Scriptures. (1 Co.15:3-4)

> He himself bore our sins in his body on the tree, that we might die to sin and live to righteousness. By his wounds you have been healed. (1 Pe.2:24)

2 Jesus listened to the people's pleas for help.

After six or so months, Jesus returned to the Sea of Galilee in the district of Decapolis (v.31). Some friends brought a deaf man to Him, and, as is so often the case with deafness, the man also had a speech impediment.

When the sounds of nature sang forth, the man could not hear their beauty. When people carried on conversations, he could not participate. When strangers spoke loudly in an attempt to help him hear, it only added to his embarrassment. He could not verbally express his feelings and desires. He could only sit in stone silence.

> [32] And they brought to him a man who was deaf and had a speech impediment, and they begged him to lay his hand on him.

Jesus was tender toward all who had need. When the man's friends begged Jesus to help by touching the man, He listened to their earnest plea. Jesus felt compassion for him, and then He responded. He did exactly what He should do: "He did all things well" (v.37).

THOUGHT 1. We should listen to people's pleas for help. Listening is part of "doing all things well." Listening demonstrates a *Christ-centered, compassionate heart*, a heart that belongs to a sensitive, godly servant of the Lord.

> **For I was hungry and you gave me food, I was thirsty and you gave me drink, I was a stranger and you welcomed me. I was naked and you clothed me, I was sick and you visited me, I was in prison and you came to me. (Mt.25:35–36)**
>
> **Be merciful, even as your Father is merciful. (Lu.6:36)**
>
> **We who are strong have an obligation to bear with the failings of the weak, and not to please ourselves. (Ro.15:1)**

3 Jesus was considerate of the people's feelings and conditions of others: Took the man aside, alone.

Out of sensitivity to the impaired man's feelings, Jesus took the man aside, out of the presence of the others. The man had suffered embarrassment all his life because he could not participate in conversation or activities with others. No

> [33] And taking him aside from the crowd privately, he put his fingers into his ears, and after spitting touched his tongue.

doubt, some had made fun of him and had been impatient with him. Life had been cruel to him. He knew what embarrassment really was. Most likely, he was shy and reserved, perhaps even withdrawn. He had experienced embarrassment even standing there before Jesus. Jesus responded tenderly. He *considered* the man's feelings; therefore, He took him aside from the crowd.

THOUGHT 1. Doing all things well requires consideration. Consideration, tenderly reacting to the feelings of others, is always to be the way of the believer.

> **Bear one another's burdens, and so fulfill the law of Christ. (Ga.6:2)**
>
> **For we do not have a high priest who is unable to sympathize with our weaknesses, but one who in every respect has been tempted as we are, yet without sin. Let us then with confidence draw near to the throne of grace, that we may receive mercy and find grace to help in time of need. (He.4:15–16)**
>
> **As a father shows compassion to his children, so the LORD shows compassion to those who fear him. (Ps.103:13)**

After taking the man aside, Jesus did an unusual thing. He put His fingers into the man's ears and put some of His own saliva on the man's tongue. Why? The man could not hear what Jesus was saying. He needed to know that it was Jesus who alone had the power to heal him. The saliva and fingers were signs that the power came through Jesus' body, from within His very being. Jesus Christ, His power alone, was the man's source of healing. The man needed to know this beyond any question. He could not hear, so some symbolic act had to be used.

The scene must have been dramatic for this man. He saw it all; and, standing there face to face with Jesus, his attention must have been glued to Jesus' every act. The man's faith was bound to be stirred enormously when Jesus touched His stammering tongue and placed His fingers into his feeble ears. A tremendous sense of expectancy surely surged through his body.

THOUGHT 1. The source of the man's healing was Jesus. Jesus used whatever was at His disposal to show this. Every person needs to be shown that Jesus is the source of healing, the source of being made whole. We should use everything at our disposal to proclaim Jesus as the only source of deliverance (salvation).

> Therefore he had to be made like his brothers in every respect, so that he might become a merciful and faithful high priest in the service of God, to make propitiation for the sins of the people. For because he himself has suffered when tempted, he is able to help those who are being tempted. (He.2:17–18)

7:34–35

³⁴ And looking up to heaven, he sighed and said to him, "Ephphatha," that is, "Be opened."
³⁵ And his ears were opened, his tongue was released, and he spoke plainly.

4 Jesus trusted God for power to help the man.

Jesus trusted God for the power to heal the man. He demonstrated His dependence on His Father through three distinct acts.

First, Jesus looked up to heaven. (Remember the man could not hear.) Very simply, Jesus was demonstrating a point—a point that must always be made: the power to make a person whole comes from God above. People must look up to heaven, to God, for deliverance.

Note a significant point: Jesus indicated in this act that He is *the Mediator* who stands between God and humans. The source of power is God, and God's power is brought to us by the Mediator, Jesus Christ.

Second, Jesus *sighed* (Gk. estenaxen); that is, He groaned in grief and empathy. The feeling and struggles caused by the man's infirmities touched Jesus; He sympathized with his weakness. And He was probably thinking of all humanity, of the crowd in all its infirmity and sin (see He.4:15). He had just looked up to heaven and felt the great gap between heaven and earth, the enormous difference between heaven's perfection and earth's sin and corruption. Jesus was bound to groan under the strain of such a spiritual ache—an ache for all people to be made whole.

Third, Jesus exerted the power of God and healed the man. He simply said, *"Ephphatha,"* an Aramaic word which, as Mark explained, means "be opened." Jesus opened the man's ears and loosed his tongue, and the man was able to hear and speak clearly.

THOUGHT 1. The miracle powerfully demonstrated two things.
1) That Jesus is the Messiah, the Son of God Himself. Isaiah had predicted the Messiah would perform such miracles (Is.35:5–6).

> "Whoever blasphemes the name of the Lord shall surely be put to death. All the congregation shall stone him. The sojourner as well as the native, when he blasphemes the Name, shall be put to death. The Spirit of the Lord is upon me, because he has anointed me to proclaim good news to the poor. He has sent me to proclaim liberty to the captives and recovering of sight to the blind, to set at liberty those who are oppressed, to proclaim the year of the Lord's favor." And he rolled up the scroll and gave it back to the attendant and sat down. And the eyes of all in the synagogue were fixed on him. And he began to say to them, "Today this Scripture has been fulfilled in your hearing." (Lu.4:17–21)

> How God anointed Jesus of Nazareth with the Holy Spirit and with power. He went about doing good and healing all who were oppressed by the devil, for God was with him. (Ac.10:38)

2) Jesus' tender consideration for the needs and feelings of others—a strong lesson for every believer.

> Even as the Son of Man came not to be served but to serve, and to give his life as a ransom for many. (Mt.20:28)

Jesus said to them again, "Peace be with you. As the Father has sent me, even so I am sending you." (Jn.20:21)

Remember those who are in prison, as though in prison with them, and those who are mistreated, since you also are in the body. (He.13:3)

5 Jesus sought no personal applause or praise.

Jesus sought no personal honor from performing this compassionate miracle. He charged everyone to keep the miracle quiet, to tell no one. The Greek word for *charged* or *commanded* (diesteilato; pronounced *dee-es-teel'-ah-tow*) is strong. It speaks of a firm order. The order was clearly given.

[36] And Jesus charged them to tell no one. But the more he charged them, the more zealously they proclaimed it.

The reason is not known, but there is a lesson on humility in the charge. Jesus was not after people's applause or praise. He did not perform miracles for that reason. All that He was and all that He had done was to help people and point them to God. People were lost and perishing, and He had come to seek and save the lost, not to win their applause (see Lu.19:10).

THOUGHT 1. Jesus taught two lessons here.

1) A lesson on humility.

It shall not be so among you. But whoever would be great among you must be your servant, and whoever would be first among you must be your slave. (Mt.20:26-27)

Do nothing from selfish ambition or conceit, but in humility count others more significant than yourselves. Let each of you look not only to his own interests, but also to the interests of others. (Ph.2:3-4)

2) A lesson on witnessing. The healed man and his friends were forbidden to share their glorious experience, but they could not keep quiet. They were so full of the presence of God and His power, they just had to bear witness. How much more the disciples! They surely learned the importance of being filled with God and His power for witnessing.

But you will receive power when the Holy Spirit has come upon you, and you will be my witnesses in Jerusalem and in all Judea and Samaria, and to the end of the earth. (Ac.1:8)

For we cannot but speak of what we have seen and heard. (Ac.4:20)

That is, in Christ God was reconciling the world to himself, not counting their trespasses against them, and entrusting to us the message of reconciliation. Therefore, we are ambassadors for Christ, God making his appeal through us. We implore you on behalf of Christ, be reconciled to God. (2 Co.5:19-20)

6 Jesus' works demanded a verdict: "He has done all things well."

Jesus healed a multitude of people at that time (Mt.15:30-31). The people were astonished *beyond measure* (huperperissos); that is, they were overwhelmed by what Jesus had done and how He had done it. Consequently, they pronounced the verdict: "He has done all things well," the very verdict Christ

[37] And they were astonished beyond measure, saying, "He has done all things well. He even makes the deaf hear and the mute speak."

was after. The people desperately needed to focus their attention on *the Mediator and the power of God* to make people whole.

For there is one God, and there is one mediator between God and men, the man Christ Jesus. who gave himself as a ransom for all, which is the testimony given at the proper time. (1 Ti.2:5-6)

Consequently, he is able to save to the uttermost those who draw near to God through him, since he always lives to make intercession for them. (He.7:25)

CHAPTER 8

K. The Need for Spiritual Food, Compassion, and Evangelism, 8:1–9

(Mt.15:32–39)

1. **The need for spiritual food**
   a. Crowds followed Jesus
   b. Crowds hungered spiritually: Had gone without food for two to three days
2. **The need for compassion**[DS1]
   a. Compassion involves seeing people's needs

   b. Compassion involves using all available resources

   c. Compassion involves being organized
   d. Compassion involves giving and using all we have to meet people's needs
   e. Compassion involves giving thanks to God for what we have

   f. Compassion involves saving and preserving

3. **The need for evangelism, for moving on to reach others**

In those days, when again a great crowd had gathered, and they had nothing to eat, he called his disciples to him and said to them,

² "I have compassion on the crowd, because they have been with me now three days and have nothing to eat. ³ And if I send them away hungry to their homes, they will faint on the way. And some of them have come from far away."

⁴ And his disciples answered him, "How can one feed these people with bread here in this desolate place?" ⁵ And he asked them, "How many loaves do you have?" They said, "Seven." ⁶ And he directed the crowd to sit down on the ground. And he took the seven loaves, and having given thanks, he broke them and gave them to his disciples to set before the people; and they set them before the crowd. ⁷ And they had a few small fish. And having blessed them, he said that these also should be set before them.

⁸ And they ate and were satisfied. And they took up the broken pieces left over, seven baskets full. ⁹ And there were about four thousand people. And he sent them away.

Division IV

The Son of God's Training Ministry: Jesus' Intensive Preparation of the Disciples, 6:7–8:26

K. The Need for Spiritual Food, Compassion, and Evangelism, 8:1–9

(Mt.15:32–39)

8:1–9
Introduction

Another time. Another place. Same miracle.

Many skeptics assume that Jesus' feeding of four thousand in this passage is an additional telling of the feeding of five thousand recorded earlier (Mk.6:35-44). They claim that the vast difference in details shows that the Bible contains errors and contradictions.

To the contrary, the different details are evidence that these are two different events—the same miracle performed at a different time, in a different place, for different people. Mark's record clearly establishes that these were two different events when he quotes Jesus referring to them as two separate events (vv.19-20).

What was Jesus' purpose in performing the same miracle a second time?

First, as always, our Lord was demonstrating His Messiahship in order to drive the truth more and more deeply into the hearts and minds of the disciples. The disciples were slow to understand the truth about Jesus, who He is and how much He loved them. In spite of everything they had witnessed, their faith was weak (vv.17-21).

Second, in a most direct way, Jesus was teaching His disciples that they were to minister to the needy, no matter who the needy were. When Jesus fed the five thousand, the multitude was made up primarily of Jews. In this event, He was ministering primarily, if not totally, to Gentiles (see notes—Mt.15:21-22; 15:29). The Jews considered the Gentiles to be heathen, lost, and despised by God. Jewish prejudice against the Gentiles ran deep. But Jesus had come to save all people, not just Jews. The disciples desperately needed to learn this truth, for they would need to minister to all people, regardless of race, after His return to the Father.

In a very simple yet forceful demonstration, Jesus revealed that the *whole world* has three great needs. This is, *The Need for Spiritual Food, Compassion, and Evangelism,* 8:1-9.

1. The need for spiritual food (v.1).
2. The need for compassion (vv.2–8).
3. The need for evangelism, for moving on to reach others (v.9).

1 The need for spiritual food.

8:1

On another occasion, a large crowd gathered to hear Jesus teach. They stayed for three days—not three hours, but three *days.* Naturally, they were hungry. The rumble of so many empty stomachs was no doubt noticeable throughout the crowd! But these people were willing to stay so long and go without food because they had a greater hunger, a deeper

> In those days, when again a great crowd had gathered, and they had nothing to eat, he called his disciples to him and said to them,

hunger. They were spiritually starved; they craved the Bread of Life and the milk of God's Word (Mt.4:4; Jn.6:33, 35, 48, 51; 1 Pe.2:2). They needed *spiritual* food.

a. Crowds followed Jesus.

This crowd was exceedingly large. Four thousand ate (v.9). This is an interesting number. The event occurred on the other side of the Sea of Galilee in Decapolis, a land heavily populated by Gentiles. These were the very people who had rejected Jesus earlier and had requested Him to leave their area after He had healed the demoniac (Mk.5:1-20). What brought about this significant change? The answer is probably found in Jesus' instructions to the healed demoniac.

The demoniac had requested to follow Jesus, but Jesus had told him to remain in his own country to witness. Evidently, his witness had borne great fruit and prepared the people for Jesus' return. What a lesson to us on the importance of witnessing!

b. Crowds hungered spiritually: Had gone without food for two to three days.

The crowd was so hungry for *spiritual* food, they had gone without *physical* food for three days. A few folks may have brought some provision, but by now all the food had been eaten. The people craved the Word of God. The word of Jesus was esteemed more highly than "necessary food" (Jb.23:12).

> Blessed are those who hunger and thirst for righteousness, for they shall be satisfied. (Mt.5:6)

> Jesus said to them, "I am the bread of life; whoever comes to me shall not hunger, and whoever believes in me shall never thirst." (Jn.6:35)

> And now I commend you to God and to the word of his grace, which is able to build you up and to give you the inheritance among all those who are sanctified. (Ac.20:32)

> Like newborn infants, long for the pure spiritual milk, that by it you may grow up into salvation—if indeed you have tasted that the Lord is good. (1 Pe.2:2–3)

8:2–8

² "I have compassion on the crowd, because they have been with me now three days and have nothing to eat.
³ And if I send them away hungry to their homes, they will faint on the way. And some of them have come from far away."
⁴ And his disciples answered him, "How can one feed these people with bread here in this desolate place?"
⁵ And he asked them, "How many loaves do you have?" They said, "Seven."
⁶ And he directed the crowd to sit down on the ground. And he took the seven loaves, and having given thanks, he broke them and gave them to his disciples to set before the people; and they set them before the crowd.
⁷ And they had a few small fish. And having blessed them, he said that these also should be set before them.
⁸ And they ate and were satisfied. And they took up the broken pieces left over, seven baskets full.

2 The need for compassion.

Jesus' disciples needed to learn to have compassion for *all* people (see DEEPER STUDY # 1). Unfortunately, the disciples looked upon many of these people as outcasts. They were Gentiles, aliens from God's chosen race. They were even considered enemies by many Jews. There was nothing attractive or appealing about them in the eyes of the disciples. The disciples . . .

- had no compassion for them
- did not observe them at all
- were not concerned for them
- had no thought of helping them

Jesus had to teach His disciples compassion. He had already discussed this need with them (Mt.9:36–38). Now He tried to stir their compassion for the lost and outcast, regardless of who they were or where they were from. He did this by demonstrating just what compassion involves.

a. Compassion involves seeing people's needs (vv.2–3).
Jesus had looked at and observed the people, and in doing so, He had seen their need. The disciples should have also looked and observed, but they had not. They were too prejudiced and too prideful. They felt the Gentile people were beneath them, not worthy of their time and effort. Therefore, the disciples never observed the people's needs. They should have, for Jesus had just taught the same lesson (Mk.6:35–44); but their prejudice and pride blinded their eyes and hearts, even from the truth they had just been taught. Their hardheartedness shows the great need for Jesus to repeat the same truths over and over.

THOUGHT 1. Looking at and observing people are essential in order to see need, and seeing need is essential to stir compassion. Compassion is kindled by seeing and observing or studying people's needs. If we never expose ourselves to people's needs, we will never experience compassion.

> And he said to them, "The harvest is plentiful, but the laborers are few. Therefore pray earnestly to the Lord of the harvest to send out laborers into his harvest." (Lu.10:2)

> Do you not say, 'There are yet four months, then comes the harvest'? Look, I tell you, lift up your eyes, and see that the fields are white for harvest. (Jn.4:35)
>
> Brothers, my heart's desire and prayer to God for them is that they may be saved. (Ro.10:1)

b. Compassion involves using all available resources (vv.4–5; see note—Mk.6:37–44).
Needs can never be met apart from resources. The disciples wondered about the resources, where enough bread could be secured to feed so many; and they asked Jesus about the matter, offering every objection and excuse.

➢ The place was a wilderness, a desolate place, beyond reach (v.4).
➢ Their resources were too meager (v.5).
➢ The multitude and the need were too great (vv.1, 9).

THOUGHT 1. Too many use the same excuses to keep from becoming involved. Too many needs go unmet because of such flimsy excuses.

THOUGHT 2. Note two significant points.
1) The disciples overlooked the resources they had.
2) Jesus did not ask the disciples to discuss how they could meet so great a need. He told them to check on what resources *they had*. What resources others had and just how God was going to meet the need should not have been their concern. Their concern should have been see-ing just what they could do.

> In all things I have shown you that by working hard in this way we must help the weak and remember the words of the Lord Jesus, how he himself said, 'It is more blessed to give than to receive.' (Ac.20:35)
>
> Contribute to the needs of the saints and seek to show hospitality. (Ro.12:13)
>
> So then, as we have opportunity, let us do good to everyone, and especially to those who are of the household of faith. (Ga.6:10)
>
> They are to do good, to be rich in good works, to be generous and ready to share, thus stor-ing up treasure for themselves as a good foundation for the future, so that they may take hold of that which is truly life. (1 Ti.6:18–19)

c. Compassion involves being organized (v.6a).
Jesus did not meet the people's needs in a disorderly, haphazard way. He did not pass out the food randomly. Instead, He directed the people to sit down, organizing them to receive the provision (see note, pt.3—Mk.6:37–44 for discussion).

d. Compassion involves giving and using all we have to meet people's needs (v.6b).
All seven loaves were *given to Jesus*, then Jesus *took all* seven loaves and *used all* seven to meet the need. Nothing was held back. All the resources available were used to meet the need. True compassion will always give generously, and then take all and use all that is given to meet needs.

THOUGHT 1. How often we hold back, store up, even deceive, lie, and cheat when managing our resources—just to keep from having to give. Christ teaches that we are to freely give our resources to meet the needs of a desperate world. Then we are to make sure that all we gave is *taken and used* in meeting the needs. Such is *true compassion*.

> But lay up for yourselves treasures in heaven, where neither moth nor rust destroys and where thieves do not break in and steal. (Mt.6:20)
>
> Sell your possessions, and give to the needy. Provide yourselves with moneybags that do not grow old, with a treasure in the heavens that does not fail, where no thief approaches and no moth destroys. (Lu.12:33)
>
> So therefore, any one of you who does not renounce all that he has cannot be my disciple. (Lu.14:33)
>
> So the disciples determined, every one according to his ability, to send relief to the brothers living in Judea. (Ac.11:29)

e. **Compassion involves giving thanks to God for what we have (v.6c).**

Jesus "gave thanks" (v.6) and "blessed" (v.7) the resources. The point is striking. What the disciples had to give was small, really insignificant in meeting such a mammoth need, and what Jesus held in His hands was so meager it was impossible to meet the need. Yet Christ gave thanks for the meager resource, for what He held in His hands.

THOUGHT 1. The resource had been given to be used; therefore, Jesus was able to use it despite its smallness. If it had not been given, it would not have been used. And most tragically, the need would not have been met. Christ is forever thankful for the resource given to Him, no matter how small; and He is able to use the resource to meet the need—no matter how insignificant the resource and no matter how mammoth the need may seem.

f. **Compassion involves saving and preserving (v.8).**

Jesus taught us that resources given to Him are precious and are to be handled carefully. He ordered the disciples to collect everything that had not been eaten. Nothing is to be wasted. Whatever is not used in meeting one need is to be used in meeting another need (see note, pt.6—Mk.6:37–44).

Deeper Study # 1

(8:2) **Compassion:** see note 2 and Deeper Study # 2—Mt.9:36.

8:9

⁹ And there were about four thousand people. And he sent them away.

3 The need for evangelism, for moving on to reach others.

After the people were filled—both spiritually and physically—Jesus sent them on their way. Remember this crowd had hungered for the Word of God, hungered for spiritual food, even putting the spiritual needs before the physical. Now Jesus sent them away. Essentially, He sent them away as a group, as a body of people who had hungered spiritually and had been fed. As they went, they would certainly bear witness to their glorious experience of having been fed by Jesus, both spiritually and physically. They would go on from this place to evangelize others, as would Jesus.

THOUGHT 1. Christ has sent us, too, to proclaim that He alone can feed the hungering human soul. Certainly there is a time to sit at the feet of Jesus and be fed, but there is also a time to be sent away, to go out carrying the glorious message that He feeds the hungering heart, that He is the Bread of Life.

> But they went away and spread his fame through all that district. (Mt.9:31)

> "Return to your home, and declare how much God has done for you." And he went away, proclaiming throughout the whole city how much Jesus had done for him. (Lu.8:39)

> Jesus said to them again, "Peace be with you. As the Father has sent me, even so I am sending you." (Jn.20:21)

> And what you have heard from me in the presence of many witnesses entrust to faithful men, who will be able to teach others also. (2 Ti.2:2)

> I will recount the steadfast love of the LORD, the praises of the LORD, according to all that the LORD has granted us, and the great goodness to the house of Israel that he has granted them according to his compassion, according to the abundance of his steadfast love. (Is.63:7)

(Mt.16:1–4)

¹⁰ And immediately he got into the boat with his disciples and went to the district of Dalmanutha. ¹¹ The Pharisees came and began to argue with him, seeking from him a sign from heaven to test him.

¹² And he sighed deeply in his spirit and said, "Why does this generation seek a sign? Truly, I say to you, no sign will be given to this generation." ¹³ And he left them, got into the boat again, and went to the other side.

1. They confronted Jesus in disbelief
   a. Jesus crossed the lake
   b. Jesus entered Dalmanutha[DS1]
   c. Religionists confronted Him
2. They sought a sign
   a. They were blind to His works
   b. Their motive: To trick Him
3. They grieved the Lord[DS2]
4. They received no sign from the Lord

5. They were left behind by the Lord

Division IV

The Son of God's Training Ministry: Jesus' Intensive Preparation of the Disciples, 6:7–8:26

L. The Fault of the Spiritually Blind, 8:10–13

(Mt.16:1–4)

8:10–13
Introduction

Spiritual blindness is a problem for every generation. In fact, most people are spiritually blind (2 Co.4:4). Many seek some sort of "sign" that God is real, but their eyes are shut to the evidence God has already given—to the presence, mercy, care, and gifts of God to humanity.

God is easily seen by people who openly and honestly seek the truth. He is seen in the world and happenings of life, in the merciful actions that often occur in life, in the care and love often experienced, and in the gifts of goodness to help a person get along in an antagonistic world. Yet, so few look for God and give thanks to Him for all He is and does. Instead, so many people choose rather to reject a personal God and to attribute the happenings and things of life to their own efforts (humanism). Why? There is one clear reason: if people acknowledge a personal God, they have to surrender their lives to that God. Therefore, people challenge God: "If there be a God, prove yourself, show yourself, give us a sign." However, these faithless people expect no sign, and even if they saw one, they would deny it—all because they are spiritually blind to the truth.

Jesus, in this passage, discusses skeptical, unbelieving people who seek signs. This is, *The Fault of the Spiritually Blind*, 8:10-13.

1. They confronted Jesus in disbelief (vv.10–11).
2. They sought a sign (v.11).
3. They grieved the Lord (v.12).
4. They received no sign from the Lord (v.12).
5. They were left behind by the Lord (v.13).

1 They confronted Jesus in disbelief.

a. Jesus crossed the lake (v.10a).

b. Jesus entered Dalmanutha (v.10b).

c. Religionists confronted Him (v.11a).

Immediately after feeding the four thousand and dismissing them, Jesus crossed the lake (Sea of Galilee) to the west side and to the lands close to Dalmanutha (see Deeper Study # 1). As

8:10–11a

¹⁰ And immediately he got into the boat with his disciples and went to the district of Dalmanutha.
¹¹ The Pharisees came and began to argue with him, seeking from him a sign from heaven to test him.

soon as He stepped off the boat, the Jewish religious leaders confronted Him. Note that Mark mentions only the Pharisees. Matthew says the Sadducees had joined forces with them in an attempt to discredit Jesus before the people (Mt.16:1). In so doing, they revealed their spiritual blindness (see note—Mt.12:1-8; note and Deeper Study # 1—12:10; Deeper Study # 4—12:24; notes—12:31-32; 15:1-20; Deeper Study # 2—15:6-9).

Deeper Study # 1

(8:10) **Dalmanutha:** this was a city next to Magdala (Magadan) on the west coast of the lake or Sea of Galilee. Both cities were in the Decapolis district (see Mt.15:39).

8:11

¹¹ The Pharisees came and began to argue with him, seeking from him a sign from heaven to test him.

2 They sought a sign.

The religious leaders demanded that Jesus give them a sign from heaven to prove His claims and to validate His miracles as being done in God's power and not Satan's. In so doing, they were trying to set a trap for Jesus. However, instead of catching Jesus, they snared themselves, revealing their spiritual blindness.

a. They were blind to His works.

A sharp difference exists between people's natural and spiritual senses. The *natural senses can be sharp and discerning*. People are skillful in drawing conclusions from their observations and experiences of the natural world. Weather is an example. However, when it comes to the *spiritual senses, people are dead and undiscerning*. They neither observe nor experience the spiritual world, not really. The signs of the times are an example of this fact.

The people of Jesus' day had signs to point them toward the Messiah. They lived in critical times, times that foretold of the Messiah's coming. A thoughtful and genuinely spiritual person could see the signs. Some did, such as Simeon and Anna (Lu.3:25f). Consider some of the signs God had given to identify the Messiah:

➢ The scepter, that is, the lawgiver, had come from Judah (Mt.1:2).
➢ The weeks or ages predicted by Daniel were closing out (see Deeper Study # 1—Mt.24:15).
➢ The predicted return of Elijah, fulfilled in the Messiah's forerunner (John the Baptist), who had come and proclaimed the Messiah to be Jesus (Mt.3:1-12).
➢ The baby Jesus had been born in Bethlehem (Mt.2:1).
➢ Many throughout the world were expecting the coming of some great person, some Messiah (Mt.1:18).
➢ Many godly Jews were looking for the coming of the Messiah, God's great Deliverer of Israel (Lu.2:25f).

In addition to all these, and even more convincing, were the miracles Jesus had publicly performed. The message and works of Jesus were great evidence, phenomenal miracles given by God to substantiate His claims (see note and Deeper Study # 1—Jn.14:11). However, Jewish religious leaders and many others were blind to Christ's miraculous works.

THOUGHT 1. The people of our generation and every generation since Christ have had signs that testify that God exists and that Jesus was—and is—God's Son, the Messiah, the Savior of the world, the Lord of the universe.

- There are the signs of the natural world, the marvels of which are being revealed every day. But people refuse to acknowledge the Creator to whom creation points (see Ro.1:20; see Ro.1:18–32).
- There are the privileges of life, the beauty of the world, and the experience of God's daily mercy. But people ascribe them all to natural happenings or to the laws of nature or to humanistic ability and evolution.
- There is the Old Testament. But people, while perhaps appreciating some of its history, reject its prophetic promises of God's Messiah and salvation.
- There is conscience or consciousness of sin (inner thought). But people deny sin. They deny it even while experiencing guilt and wondering deep within what the truth really is.
- There is Jesus Christ and His claim to be the Messiah, the very Son of God. But people reject and deny His claim. They reject and deny it while extolling the morality and value of all else He taught.
- There is the death and resurrection of Christ, and its enormous effect on so many down through the generations. But people deny a substitutionary death in behalf of the sinful human race, and they deny the resurrection despite all the evidence validating it.
- There are the changed lives of teeming thousands who proclaim that *the living Lord* has saved them from destruction and indwells their being. And there is the historical record and daily increasing number of people who lay down their lives rather than deny Christ. But people attribute such change and commitment to psychological causes.

He was in the world, and the world was made through him, yet the world did not know him. He came to his own, and his own people did not receive him. But to all who did receive him, who believed in his name, he gave the right to become children of God. (Jn.1:10–12)

And they will do these things because they have not known the Father, nor me. (Jn.16:3)

He was with the proconsul, Sergius Paulus, a man of intelligence, who summoned Barnabas and Saul and sought to hear the word of God. (Ac.13:7)

None of the rulers of this age understood this, for if they had, they would not have crucified the Lord of glory. (1 Co.2:8)

In their case the god of this world has blinded the minds of the unbelievers, to keep them from seeing the light of the gospel of the glory of Christ, who is the image of God. (2 Co.4:4)

He was despised and rejected by men, a man of sorrows and acquainted with grief; and as one from whom men hide their faces he was despised, and we esteemed him not. (Is.53:3)

b. Their motive: To trick Him.

The motive of the religious leaders was not open and honest, nor was it the motive of people genuinely seeking the truth. They were out to *test* or to trick Jesus, to disprove His claim and discredit Him before the people. Their motive was to show Him to be an imposter (see notes—Mt.12:1-8; DEEPER STUDY # 1—12:10; DEEPER STUDIES 3, 4—12:24; notes—12:31-32; 15:1-20; DEEPER STUDY # 2—15:6-9).

In many cases, the reason people are intelligent and discerning within the natural world yet ignorant and blind to the spiritual world is their motive. Their motive is to discredit the spiritual world, whether by denying and disproving its existence or by minimizing its influence and authority.

If people truly admit the existence of a spiritual world or of a Savior, then they are forced to make a choice. They must either surrender and follow that Savior as Lord, or they must reject that Savior and await condemnation. Unbelieving people do not want to be put into such a position. They do not want to live with a sense, a constant nagging, of being condemned, nor do they want to change their lifestyle. So they close their minds and say they will believe only if God gives them a personal sign, a miraculous sign, a sign from heaven. And all the while, they expect no sign and are convinced there will be none.

Again, there are already plenty of signs. It is a very simple matter to see God and the spiritual world behind the physical world. Any thinking individual who is *open and honest and seeking the truth* will be touched by God. There is not a chance that God will not open the honest person's eyes and heart so that individual can see and know. Such an honest and seeking person can clearly see that the world shows a Supreme Designer, a Supreme Intelligence and Force, an eternal purpose, a first cause (see outlines and notes—Ro.1:19-23). To all who believe the light God has already given, *God will give more light.*

The problem is that the natural man—the sin nature—seeks justification for its worldly motives, desires, and lifestyle. Those enslaved to their sin nature do not want to change their life and desires. They want to do their own thing, to control their own destiny. In fact, a person's morality, desires, motives, and lifestyle determine their beliefs. Those enslaved to their sin nature want to justify themselves, prove themselves and their thoughts to be right. They do not want to discover a heavenly world and a spiritual Lord who would demand righteousness and love, total giving and sacrifice. They do not want to be under a Lord who requires a total commitment to meeting the needs of a desperate world. They do not want to turn from sin and selfishness. They do not want to change.

> And he said to all, "If anyone would come after me, let him deny himself and take up his cross daily and follow me. For whoever would save his life will lose it, but whoever loses his life for my sake will save it." (Lu.9:23-24)

> So therefore, any one of you who does not renounce all that he has cannot be my disciple. (Lu.14:33)

> Let all the house of Israel therefore know for certain that God has made him both Lord and Christ, this Jesus whom you crucified. (Ac.2:36)

> Therefore God has highly exalted him and bestowed on him the name that is above every name, so that at the name of Jesus every knee should bow, in heaven and on earth and under the earth. (Ph.2:9-10)

8:12a

12 And he sighed deeply in his spirit and said, "Why does this generation seek a sign? Truly, I say to you, no sign will be given to this generation."

3 They grieved the Lord.

Jesus was deeply grieved by the religious leaders' blindness, just as He is grieved by spiritual blindness today (see DEEPER STUDY # 2). There is no excuse for spiritual blindness. Evidence after evidence, sign after sign, work after work can clearly be seen by the *honest, thinking* person. Yet people continue to deceive themselves, and they do it knowingly.

Every person knows that God exists; they know down deep within the quiet recesses of their heart. Scripture clearly states this truth:

> For the wrath of God is revealed from heaven against all ungodliness and unrighteousness of men, who by their unrighteousness suppress the truth. For what can be known about God is plain to them, because God has shown it to them. (Ro.1:18-19)

Yet the spiritually blind outwardly deny this knowledge, deceiving themselves. Such is obstinate unbelief, and obstinate unbelief is both irrational and inexcusable.

> For although they knew God, they did not honor him as God or give thanks to him, but they became futile in their thinking, and their foolish hearts were darkened. Claiming to be wise, they became fools. (Ro.1:21-22)

Jesus faced a tragic fact. The men who were standing before Him were spiritually blind, but they were not ordinary secular men. They were religious men who knew God's Word and who had the enormous evidence of Christ's life and miracles before their very eyes. Yet they chose to keep their lives in their own hands and to deny the Son of God who loved them and came to save them. This fact grieved Jesus tremendously.

THOUGHT 1. Obstinate unbelief grieves the Lord—terribly so.

> And do not grieve the Holy Spirit of God, by whom you were sealed for the day of redemption. (Ep.4:30)

> Do not quench the Spirit. (1 Th.5:19)

Therefore I was provoked with that generation, and said, 'They always go astray in their heart; they have not known my ways.' (He.3:10)

THOUGHT 2. There have always been unbelievers even among religious leaders. Acts of social justice—the care and ministry of enough food, clothing, housing, peace, security, happiness, health—have always attracted some to the service of Christ. Christ taught social justice and care, and what He taught is to be done. But He also taught that existence is eternal. He taught that people must be delivered from sin and corruption, born again spiritually so that they might inherit eternal life instead of dying and being separated from God eternally (see DEEPER STUDY # 1—He.9:27).

Truly, truly, I say to you, whoever hears my word and believes him who sent me has eternal life. He does not come into judgment, but has passed from death to life. (Jn.5:24)

Since therefore the children share in flesh and blood, he himself likewise partook of the same things, that through death he might destroy the one who has the power of death, that is, the devil, and deliver all those who through fear of death were subject to lifelong slavery. (He.2:14–15)

DEEPER STUDY # 2

(8:12) **Sighed Deeply** (anastenazas): means to groan, to sigh in grief. Jesus felt both grief and indignation from the bottom of His heart. He was stirred to the depths, to the very core of His being by the Jewish leaders' unbelief. Therefore, He groaned within His spirit (see notes—Ep.4:30; DEEPER STUDY # 1—1 Th.5:19; see also DEEPER STUDY # 1—Mk.3:5; notes—Heb.3:10; Ps.95:10; Is.54:6).

4 They received no sign from the Lord.

8:12b

Jesus refused to give the faithless Pharisees the sign they asked for. The spiritually blind receive no sign from the Lord. There are seven reasons why "no sign [was] given to this generation."

12 And he sighed deeply in his spirit and said, "Why does this generation seek a sign? Truly, I say to you, no sign will be given to this generation."

First, the Jews refused to look at the signs of the times (chose to be spiritually blind) because they were wicked and adulterous (v.38; Mt.12:39; 16:4). There were never enough signs or evidences to convince them, to change their lives, nor to lead them to turn to God (see note—Mt.12:38-40).

And this is the judgment: the light has come into the world, and people loved the darkness rather than the light because their works were evil. (Jn.3:19)

He said to him, 'If they do not hear Moses and the Prophets, neither will they be convinced if someone should rise from the dead.' (Lu.16:31)

Second, the Jews were totally unjustified in seeking additional signs from Jesus. There had been sign after sign, miracle after miracle, work after work—enough to lead any sincere person to the firm belief that Jesus is truly the Son of God (Mk.15:39; see Ac.2:22).

Third, the Jews just did not believe. In fact, they did not want to believe. The result, of course, was what always happens to willful unbelievers: they became obstinate in their unbelief (see DEEPER STUDY # 4—Mt.12:24; note—12:31-32).

Fourth, the Jews did not understand the love and the faith of God, that is, the true religion of God. They failed to see what God was after: faith and love, not signs and works. God wants people to simply believe and love Him because of who He is and because of what He has done, and continues to do, for humanity. The true religion of God is not a religion of works and signs, but of faith and love in Christ Jesus, His own Son (see DEEPER STUDY # 2—Jn.2:24; DEEPER STUDY # 1—4:22; note—4:48-49; DEEPER STUDY # 1—Ro.4:1-25; note—4:5: Ac.2:22).

Fifth, the Jews sought a sign because they were an evil and adulterous generation. The reason was simple. They were apostates, going after the false gods of works and signs instead of seeking the God of faith and love. In seeking signs and works, they were committing spiritual adultery, turning from God and His Messiah to the false gods of signs and works. (Note: It is human reason that seeks signs and works and proofs. The spirit that God gives every person seeks belief and trust and love—the spiritual qualities that bind life together and make sense of life in all its facets.)

Sixth, the Jews wanted signs of their own choosing, not the signs God had chosen to give. People are always wanting God to deal with them through some . . .

- spectacular sign
- brilliant sight
- astounding truth
- irrefutable argument
- miraculous experience
- unbelievable deliverance

Seventh, God's great concern is not "signs from heaven," signs outside man. God's great concern is meeting people in their lives and hearts where they really need Him if they are to live abundantly and eternally. God wants to meet people in their sickness and sorrow, corruption and death. Meeting people in the areas of their need is an irrefutable sign given to every generation.

THOUGHT 1. What is said of the religionists of Jesus' generation can be said of every generation of unbelievers. Unbelievers do not receive signs—not from the Lord. But believers do receive signs, the signs of having their needs met.

> **Blessed are those who hunger and thirst for righteousness, for they shall be satisfied. (Mt.5:6)**

> **But whoever drinks of the water that I will give him will never be thirsty again. The water that I will give him will become in him a spring of water welling up to eternal life. (Jn.4:14)**

> **On the last day of the feast, the great day, Jesus stood up and cried out, "If anyone thirsts, let him come to me and drink." (Jn.7:37)**

> **They feast on the abundance of your house, and you give them drink from the river of your delights. (Ps.36:8; see Ps.23:1f)**

> **And the LORD will guide you continually and satisfy your desire in scorched places and make your bones strong; and you shall be like a watered garden, like a spring of water, whose waters do not fail. (Is.58:11)**

8:13

¹³ And he left them, got into the boat again, and went to the other side.

5 They were left behind by the Lord.

Note the force of the words, "He left them." They refused to believe despite all the evidence. Jesus had no choice. The decision was theirs. He had to turn and leave them. Because of their obstinate unbelief, the spiritually blind are left behind by the Lord. They will spend eternity tragically—and unnecessarily—separated from the Lord.

> **But whoever denies me before men, I also will deny before my Father who is in heaven. (Mt.10:33)**

> **For whoever is ashamed of me and of my words in this adulterous and sinful generation, of him will the Son of Man also be ashamed when he comes in the glory of his Father with the holy angels. (Mk.8:38)**

> **If we endure, we will also reign with him; if we deny him, he also will deny us. (2 Ti.2:12)**

> **Who is the liar but he who denies that Jesus is the Christ? This is the antichrist, he who denies the Father and the Son. No one who denies the Son has the Father. Whoever confesses the Son has the Father also. (1 Jn.2:22–23)**

> **But as for the cowardly, the faithless, the detestable, as for murderers, the sexually immoral, sorcerers, idolaters, and all liars, their portion will be in the lake that burns with fire and sulfur, which is the second death. (Re.21:8)**

(Mt.16:5–12)

¹⁴ Now they had forgotten to bring bread, and they had only one loaf with them in the boat.

¹⁵ And he cautioned them, saying, "Watch out; beware of the leaven of the Pharisees and the leaven of Herod."

¹⁶ And they began discussing with one another the fact that they had no bread.

¹⁷ And Jesus, aware of this, said to them, "Why are you discussing the fact that you have no bread? Do you not yet perceive or understand? Are your hearts hardened?

¹⁸ Having eyes do you not see, and having ears do you not hear? And do you not remember?

¹⁹ When I broke the five loaves for the five thousand, how many baskets full of broken pieces did you take up?" They said to him, "Twelve."

²⁰ "And the seven for the four thousand, how many baskets full of broken pieces did you take up?" And they said to him, "Seven."

²¹ And he said to them, "Do you not yet understand?"

1. **The disciples' neglect**
   a. They forgot to take bread
   b. Jesus used their forgetfulness to teach a needed lesson

2. **The evil (yeast) of religionists and world leaders: Beware of their evil**[DS1, 2]

3. **The danger in dealing with religionists and world leaders**

   a. Danger 1: Being spiritually blind and hard-hearted—a concern with material things, with the bread of this world

   b. Danger 2: Not seeing and understanding the Lord's provision

      1) The feeding of five thousand

      2) The feeding of four thousand

   c. Danger 3: Grieving the Lord's heart

Division IV

The Son of God's Training Ministry: Jesus' Intensive Preparation of the Disciples, 6:7–8:26

M. The Evil and Danger of Religionists and World Leaders, 8:14–21

(Mt.16:5–12)

8:14–21
Introduction

In every generation, some world leaders pose a threat to people. And, as strange as it may seem, some religious leaders do as well. Jesus taught this, and we need to take heed and beware of both religious and world leaders who can do people harm. Just what Jesus meant is clearly seen and explained in this event. This is, *The Evil and Danger of Religionists and World Leaders*, 8:14–21.

1. The disciples' neglect (v.14).
2. The evil (yeast) of religionists and world leaders: Beware of their evil (v.15).
3. The danger in dealing with religionists and world leaders (vv.16–21).

1 The disciples' neglect.

After dealing with Jewish religious leaders, Jesus boarded the boat, and He and the disciples set sail again across the Sea of Galilee (v.13). The disciples suddenly remembered something: they had forgotten to bring food, and they had only one loaf of bread in the boat. Jesus saw in their forgetfulness the chance to teach a much-needed lesson on the evil and dangers of errant religious leaders and ungodly world leaders.

8:14

¹⁴ Now they had forgotten to bring bread, and they had only one loaf with them in the boat.

8:15

¹⁵ And he cautioned them, saying, "Watch out; beware of the leaven of the Pharisees and the leaven of Herod."

2 The evil (yeast) of religionists and world leaders: Beware of their evil.

Using the loaf of bread as an illustration, Jesus described the evil of religionists (as represented by the Pharisees) and ungodly world leaders (as represented by Herod) as leaven. The disciples completely misunderstood what Jesus was saying. Apparently, they thought Jesus meant one of three things:

- ➢ They may have thought He was rebuking them for having forgotten to take bread.
- ➢ They may have thought He was warning them not to eat the "bread" of the religionists or world leaders. The Pharisees were very strict in the kind of leaven that was to be used in bread. They used the rule governing leaven to stress ceremonial cleanliness. The disciples thought Jesus was saying they were to become involved neither in the external stress of religion nor in the indulgence of the world.
- ➢ They may have thought He meant they were not to sit down with the religionists and world leaders (fellowship) and eat their "leaven" and bread; that is, they were not to fellowship with them.

What did Jesus mean by the leaven of the Pharisees and of Herod or world leaders? (Matthew uses *Sadducees* instead of *Herod*. Most Herodians, followers of Herod, were Sadducees. See Deeper Study # 2—Mt.22:16; Deeper Study # 2—Ac.23:8.)

First, the leaven of the Pharisees (religionists) was their doctrine or teaching (Mt.16:12) and their hypocrisy, deception, and play-acting (Lu.12:1). Like leaven (yeast), Pharisees *fermented and soured* everyone they touched (see Deeper Study # 2—Ac.23:8).

The Pharisees believed in a personal God and in the Scripture as God's Word to humanity, but they added to God's Word (see Deeper Study # 1—Lu.6:2). They added rules and regulations, rituals and ceremonies which put undue restrictions on people's lives. This led people to think that their good behavior and their religious rituals and ceremonies made them acceptable to God. In other words, they were depending on good works for righteousness.

The expansion of rules and ceremonies led to a religion of social respectability, to an external religion. If the people were socially respectable and did all the right things, then they were judged acceptable to God.

This expansion also led to an attitude and an air of self-righteousness. If the people kept the rules and regulations, they naturally felt righteous and sometimes demonstrated it. There was a dependence upon self, upon keeping the right rules and thereby being righteous.

Second, the leaven of the Sadducees involved both religion and politics. The Sadducees or Herodians were the liberal-minded of their day. They took away from God's Word, denying all Scripture except the Pentateuch, the first five books of the Old Testament.

In addition, the Sadducees were free thinkers and rationalists who were secular and materialistic-minded. Therefore, they were willing to collaborate with the Romans in doing away with Jewish culture and instituting Roman and Greek culture. Because of this, Rome placed their leaders in the governing positions (the Sanhedrin) and gave them wealth. Their worldly-mindedness, secular philosophy, and liberal theology were always a threat to the people (see note—Mt.16:1-12).

Jesus gave a double warning in regard to these two groups: "Watch out (take heed), beware." This stressed the supreme importance of guarding against the leaven of both religionists and world leaders (see Deeper Studies 1, 2).

> Beware of false prophets, who come to you in sheep's clothing but inwardly are ravenous wolves. (Mt.7:15)

> In vain do they worship me, teaching as doctrines the commandments of men. (Mt.15:9)

> And from among your own selves will arise men speaking twisted things, to draw away the disciples after them. (Ac.20:30)

> Now the Spirit expressly says that in later times some will depart from the faith by devoting themselves to deceitful spirits and teachings of demons. (1 Ti.4:1-2)

> For there are many who are insubordinate, empty talkers and deceivers, especially those of the circumcision party. They must be silenced, since they are upsetting whole families by teaching for shameful gain what they ought not to teach. (Tit.1:10-11)

> But false prophets also arose among the people, just as there will be false teachers among you, who will secretly bring in destructive heresies, even denying the Master who bought them, bringing upon themselves swift destruction. (2 Pe.2:1)

Deeper Study # 1

(8:15) **Watch Out or Take Heed** (Gk. horao): to see, behold, discern, and acquaint oneself by closely observing and experiencing. Two things are needed for a person to "take heed": active thought and a discerning mind. The thing to be watched out for must be actively observed, thought through, and discerned.

In the present passage, the charge is a *present imperative*. The disciple is to watch out for leaven beginning right now, and continue to watch out, always observing and discerning.

Deeper Study # 2

(8:15) **Beware** (blepo): to see, perceive, grasp, and understand in order to watch out for something; to turn the mind upon an object and consider and keep a watchful eye on it; to guard and protect against something.

Again, the charge is a *present imperative*. The person is to begin immediately to beware and to continue watching, always looking out for danger.

3 The danger in dealing with religionists and world leaders.

Jesus issued the double warning about dealing with religionists and world leaders because the dangers they present are subtle and ever so serious. He pointed out these dangers through a series of questions to His disciples.

a. Danger 1: Being spiritually blind and hard-hearted—a concern with material things (vv.16-17).

The disciples failed to grasp what Jesus was saying. They thought Jesus was only talking about actual bread, physical bread. This reveals the first danger: spiritual blindness and hardness of heart, being concerned with material and earthly things—bread (v.16).

Note that Jesus does nothing but ask questions through the rest of this passage. His questions point out the failure of the disciples. They fail . . .

16 And they began discussing with one another the fact that they had no bread.

17 And Jesus, aware of this, said to them, "Why are you discussing the fact that you have no bread? Do you not yet perceive or understand? Are your hearts hardened?

18 Having eyes do you not see, and having ears do you not hear? And do you not remember?

19 When I broke the five loaves for the five thousand, how many baskets full of broken pieces did you take up?" They said to him, "Twelve."

20 "And the seven for the four thousand, how many baskets full of broken pieces did you take up?" And they said to him, "Seven."

21 And he said to them, "Do you not yet understand?"

- to reason (v.17)
- to perceive (v.17)
- to understand (v.17)
- to have soft hearts (v.17)

- to see (v.18)
- to hear (v.18)
- to remember (v.18)

What Jesus is doing is rebuking such preoccupation with earthly matters. He calls it distrust, a lack of faith (Mt.16:8). The Lord's followers are to be primarily concerned with spiritual matters, not with earthly affairs. Guarding one's mind and soul against the leaven of the Pharisees and ungodly world leaders is to be the believer's constant concern, not worrying and caring for earthly things. Our thoughts must be immersed in the truth so that we may remain in the truth and not be misled spiritually (Mt.15:19; Ro.8:5-7; 2 Co.10:3-5; Ep.4:23-34). The leaven, the false teaching of religionists and world leaders, is the great threat to human survival. If believers are blind to this fact, then the world is doomed.

THOUGHT 1. We face the same danger today: spiritual blindness and hardness. Too many are attached to the world and its things, its possessions and pleasures. The world and its god (the devil) blind people's minds so they cannot see the truth (2 Co.4:4). As a result people are dying, and they are doomed to perish eternally.

> For this people's heart has grown dull, and with their ears they can barely hear, and their eyes they have closed; lest they should see with their eyes and hear with their ears and understand with their heart and turn, and I would heal them. (Ac.28:27)

> Do not be conformed to this world, but be transformed by the renewal of your mind, that by testing you may discern what is the will of God, what is good and acceptable and perfect. (Ro.12:2)

> "Therefore go out from their midst, and be separate from them," says the Lord, "and touch no unclean thing; then I will welcome you, and I will be a father to you, and you shall be sons and daughters to me, says the Lord Almighty." (2 Co.6:17-18)

> For my people are foolish; they know me not; they are stupid children; they have no understanding. They are 'wise'—in doing evil! But how to do good they know not. . . . Hear this, O foolish and senseless people, who have eyes, but see not, who have ears, but hear not. (Je.4:22, 5:21)

b. **Danger 2: Not seeing and understanding the Lord's provision (vv.18-20).**
The disciples had just witnessed two extraordinary events. They had seen a crowd of people hungering for the Lord's Word, hungering so much that they had gone without food for three days. Then, they had seen the Lord miraculously feed all four thousand of them with just seven loaves of bread (see outline and notes—Mk.8:1-9).
➤ Yet, having eyes, they did not see what had really happened (v.18a).
➤ Yet, having ears, they did not hear what had really happened (v.18b).
➤ Yet, they did not remember what Jesus had done (v.18c).

On two separate occasions, the disciples had witnessed Jesus miraculously feed a great multitude of people with a handful of food (vv.19-20). Each time, Christ had supplied more than what was needed to feed the hungry crowds; each time, they had gathered the leftover food. Yet, they could not see the message behind the miracles. They had failed to make the connection between the people's hunger for God's Word and the fact that Jesus alone could give them God's Word. They did not grasp the people's hunger for bread and the fact that Jesus alone could give them bread from heaven, the energy and power of His very being. They had failed to see and understand that Jesus Christ is "the Bread of Life," the only "Bread" that can satisfy mankind's spiritual hunger. He is the abundant provision for our spiritual need. World and religious leaders can never satisfy our need (see note—Jn.6:1-71; see outline and notes—Jn.6:30-36 for application).

> Jesus said to them, "I am the bread of life; whoever comes to me shall not hunger, and whoever believes in me shall never thirst." (Jn.6:35)

> Truly, truly, I say to you, whoever believes has eternal life. I am the bread of life. Your fathers ate the manna in the wilderness, and they died. This is the bread that comes down from heaven, so

that one may eat of it and not die. I am the living bread that came down from heaven. If anyone eats of this bread, he will live forever. And the bread that I will give for the life of the world is my flesh. (Jn.6:47–51)

Why do you spend your money for that which is not bread, and your labor for that which does not satisfy? Listen diligently to me, and eat what is good, and delight yourselves in rich food. (Is.55:2)

c. Danger 3: Grieving the Lord's heart (v.21).

Clearly, the Lord was grieved when He asked the disciples how they could not understand the truth. All that the Lord had pointed out caused agony to His soul. He grieved deeply over . . .

* spiritual blindness
* hardness of heart
* materialistic and carnal minds
* not seeing and understanding His provision

The issues of leaven—true and false doctrine, real and hypocritical behavior—are of supreme importance. The issue of Jesus' being the Bread of Life—the real truth, the true doctrine, the only way to true satisfaction—is of eternal importance. At first, the disciples failed to get the point and make the connection, and they grieved the Lord deeply. How many have grieved Him since that day? (See note—Ep.4:30; Deeper Study # 1—1 Th.5:19.)

O Jerusalem, Jerusalem, the city that kills the prophets and stones those who are sent to it! How often would I have gathered your children together as a hen gathers her brood under her wings, and you were not willing! (Lu.13:34)

And he said to them, "O foolish ones, and slow of heart to believe all that the prophets have spoken!" (Lu.24:25)

Jesus said to him, "I am the way, and the truth, and the life. No one comes to the Father except through me. If you had known me, you would have known my Father also. From now on you do know him and have seen him." Philip said to him, "Lord, show us the Father, and it is enough for us." Jesus said to him, "Have I been with you so long, and you still do not know me, Philip? Whoever has seen me has seen the Father. How can you say, 'Show us the Father'?" (Jn.14:6–9)

1. **Jesus cared about the man's friends: Did what they requested**

2. **Jesus cared about the man's handicap**
3. **Jesus cared about the man's beliefs: He believed that saliva had healing properties**

4. **Jesus cared enough about the man to continue helping him: Healed in stages to strengthen the man's faith**

5. **Jesus cared about the man's family**

22 And they came to Bethsaida. And some people brought to him a blind man and begged him to touch him.

23 And he took the blind man by the hand and led him out of the village, and when he had spit on his eyes and laid his hands on him, he asked him, "Do you see anything?"

24 And he looked up and said, "I see people, but they look like trees, walking."

25 Then Jesus laid his hands on his eyes again; and he opened his eyes, his sight was restored, and he saw everything clearly.

26 And he sent him to his home, saying, "Do not even enter the village."

Division IV

The Son of God's Training Ministry: Jesus' Intensive Preparation of the Disciples, 6:7–8:26

N. The Necessity for Caring, 8:22–26

8:22–26
Introduction

Shortly after confronting spiritual blindness (vv.10–13), Jesus healed a man who was physically blind. Of the four Gospel writers, Mark alone tells the story of this blind man. The emphasis of the account is caring for others. Jesus experienced deep feelings all throughout the encounter. In every detail, Christ's intense care for this sightless man is apparent. Out of concern and anguish over the man's suffering and how it affected his family and friends, Jesus used the whole experience to teach His followers to care deeply about others and their needs. This is, *The Necessity for Caring*, 8:22–26.

1. Jesus cared about the man's friends: Did what they requested (v.22).
2. Jesus cared about the man's handicap (v.23).
3. Jesus cared about the man's beliefs: He believed that saliva had healing properties (vv.23–24).
4. Jesus cared enough about the man to continue helping him: Healed in stages to strengthen the man's faith (v.25).
5. Jesus cared about the man's family (v.26).

8:22

22 And they came to Bethsaida. And some people brought to him a blind man and begged him to touch him.

1 Jesus cared about the man's friends: Did what they requested.

The blind man's friends cared for him deeply, for they brought him to Jesus. They earnestly interceded for the man, begging Jesus to touch him. They cared enough to want him well and to do something about it. Apparently, he had been blind all of his life, so the friends would have been accustomed to his blindness, to his daily routine year after year. However, here they were—years later—still caring, still hoping, still praying, and still wanting their friend made whole. When the opportunity to help him arose, they sprang into action, displaying deep and genuine care, and Jesus took notice of this.

The friends believed that Jesus could heal the blind man. It was primarily their faith that led Jesus to act. Jesus cared about the man's friends, and He demonstrated His care for them by doing what they requested.

> **THOUGHT 1.** This is a strong lesson on *intercession*. We are to care enough to bring people to Christ and to pray (beg) for Christ to help them. Genuine care for another person includes both of these. It is not just enough to pray for people to be saved. If we truly care about them, we will do everything in our power to bring them to Jesus.
>
> > One of the two who heard John speak and followed Jesus was Andrew, Simon Peter's brother. He first found his own brother Simon and said to him, "We have found the Messiah" (which means Christ). He brought him to Jesus. Jesus looked at him and said, "You are Simon the son of John. You shall be called Cephas" (which means Peter). (Jn.1:40–42)
> >
> > For God is my witness, whom I serve with my spirit in the gospel of his Son, that without ceasing I mention you (Ro.1:9)
> >
> > I do not cease to give thanks for you, remembering you in my prayers (Ep.1:16)
> >
> > Epaphras, who is one of you, a servant of Christ Jesus, greets you, always struggling on your behalf in his prayers, that you may stand mature and fully assured in all the will of God (Col.4:12)
> >
> > We give thanks to God always for all of you, constantly mentioning you in our prayers. (1 Th.1:2)
> >
> > Moreover, as for me, far be it from me that I should sin against the Lord by ceasing to pray for you, and I will instruct you in the good and the right way. (1 S.12:23)

> **THOUGHT 2.** Jesus cares deeply for *friends* who care. He cares enough to receive and listen and act in their behalf. Both the caring person and the intercessor receive the care of Christ.
>
> > But it shall not be so among you. But whoever would be great among you must be your servant, and whoever would be first among you must be slave of all. (Mk.10:43–44)
> >
> > Bear one another's burdens, and so fulfill the law of Christ. . . . So then, as we have opportunity, let us do good to everyone, and especially to those who are of the household of faith. (Ga.6:2, 10)

2 Jesus cared about the man's handicap.

8:23

Imagine standing in the blind man's shoes at this scene. He had never seen anything before. Surrounding him and Jesus was a throng of people along with the noise that comes from such a massive crowd. Surely, the man was at the same time excited, nervous, and somewhat bewildered; and the barrage of noise weakened his concentration. Because Jesus cared about the man and his handicap, He was sensitive to

> ²³ And he took the blind man by the hand and led him out of the village, and when he had spit on his eyes and laid his hands on him, he asked him, "Do you see anything?"

his feelings. He perceived that the man needed to be taken aside, away from the crowd so that he could more easily focus his attention and concentrate upon Jesus. Furthermore, the Lord discerned that the man's eyes needed to be opened slowly, lest he be stunned and bewildered with the sudden sight of everything rushing in upon his mind.

Jesus knew everything about this man. He knew all the problems and difficulties that the man's blindness had caused, and He knew all that the man needed to be perfectly healed. Jesus cared for the man's handicap, so He took the blind man by the hand and led him out of town. He was ever so sensitive to the blind man's needs.

THOUGHT 1. We are to care for the people who are handicapped . . .

- understanding their problems and difficulties
- being sensitive to their special needs
- doing all we can to bring them to Christ and to see that they receive help or healing

> Let love be genuine. Abhor what is evil; hold fast to what is good. Love one another with brotherly affection. Outdo one another in showing honor. (Ro.12:9-10)

> We who are strong have an obligation to bear with the failings of the weak, and not to please ourselves. (Ro.15:1)

> I was eyes to the blind and feet to the lame. I was a father to the needy, and I searched out the cause of him whom I did not know. (Jb.29:15-16)

8:23

²³ And he took the blind man by the hand and led him out of the village, and when he had spit on his eyes and laid his hands on him, he asked him, "Do you see anything?"

3 Jesus cared about the man's beliefs: He believed that saliva had healing properties.

Think about something: one of the first things most people do when they burn or cut their finger is put it in their mouth. The saliva seems to ease the pain. With that in mind, we can understand how people of Jesus' day believed spittle or saliva had some healing properties. And we can see why Jesus did what He did: He placed saliva on the man's eyes and put His hands on the man. Jesus focused the man's attention on the healing power of both the saliva and His hands. The touch of both would mean so much more than just spoken words, and the touch of both would stir the man's faith more readily.

The point is, Jesus cared about the man's belief in the healing power of saliva. Jesus met the man *where he was*. The Lord wisely began where the man was in his beliefs and led him on into the essential belief that healing comes through the Lord Himself, through His touch. This sensitive approach may also have calmed the man's fears or anxiety.

> For we do not have a high priest who is unable to sympathize with our weaknesses, but one who in every respect has been tempted as we are, yet without sin. Let us then with confidence draw near to the throne of grace, that we may receive mercy and find grace to help in time of need. (He.4:15-16)

> Casting all your anxieties on him, because he cares for you. (1 Pe.5:7)

THOUGHT 1. Note three principles our Lord taught us about caring for and helping people.
  1) We are to care for people even when their beliefs are wrong.
  2) We should begin where people are in dealing with them. We can begin with the faith they already have and move them on to more belief in Christ.
  3) We must always lead people to the essential belief: the power to be made whole comes only through the Lord Himself.

8:24-25

²⁴ And he looked up and said, "I see people, but they look like trees, walking."
²⁵ Then Jesus laid his hands on his eyes again; and he opened his eyes, his sight was restored, and he saw everything clearly.

4 Jesus cared enough about the man to continue helping him: Healed in stages to strengthen the man's faith.

So far as is known, this is the only miracle Jesus performed in stages. After spitting on the blind man's eyes and touching him, Jesus asked if he saw anything (v.23). The man replied that he saw people walking around, but they looked like trees (v.24). The man's sight was not completely healed. He saw only faintly, dimly. His eyes were foggy. He saw people, but he did not see them clearly. Extremely excited, the man most likely blurted out whatever crossed his mind first, so he said they looked like trees.

At that point, Jesus placed His hands on the man's eyes again (v.25). This time, the man's sight was restored completely, and he saw clearly.

Why did Jesus heal the man in stages? Apparently, the man's faith was weak and needed to be strengthened, but not all at once. Greater hope and desire needed to be stirred within him. The man needed to grow more spiritually, grow more in faith, before he could be healed. This seems to be indicated by his having his friends ask Jesus to touch him, instead of asking Jesus himself. *His friends* seem to be the ones with firm faith and confidence in Jesus.

The point is, Jesus cared enough to keep after the man's need. He did not ignore the man or turn from him just because his faith was weak. Jesus did not leave the man or let him go. He stayed right with him, doing all that was necessary to meet the man's need.

THOUGHT 1. Note a critical point. A person is not always led to Christ immediately, and faith often grows in stages. No Christian is ever *mature in Christ* immediately. A person grows in Christ step by step and stage by stage (2 Pe.3:18; 2 Th.1:3; 1 Pe.2:2–3).

The crucial point for believers and churches to grasp can be simply stated: we must *care enough* to keep after people's needs. We must care enough to keep after . . .

- witnessing
- visiting
- ministering
- feeding and clothing
- teaching and instructing
- loving

> Therefore, my beloved brothers, be steadfast, immovable, always abounding in the work of the Lord, knowing that in the Lord your labor is not in vain. (1 Co.15:58)

> And let us not grow weary of doing good, for in due season we will reap, if we do not give up. (Ga.6:9)

> Remember those who are in prison, as though in prison with them, and those who are mistreated, since you also are in the body. (He.13:3)

5 Jesus cared about the man's family.

8:26

Jesus told the man not to go back into the town of Bethsaida. Apparently, he lived either in the countryside or in some surrounding town. Why did Jesus tell the man not to enter the town, but instead to go home? The reason seemed to be that Jesus cared for the whole family and was sensitive to their feelings and hopes. Since the man was from out of town, Jesus wanted the man to go home immediately to share the glorious news with his family. They all deserved to share in the joy. They should be the first to know.

[26] And he sent him to his home, saying, "Do not even enter the village."

THOUGHT 1. Sensitivity to a person's family is essential. The feelings and hopes of family members matter greatly.

> In the same way husbands should love their wives as their own bodies. He who loves his wife loves himself. (Ep.5:28)

> Only take care, and keep your soul diligently, lest you forget the things that your eyes have seen, and lest they depart from your heart all the days of your life. Make them known to your children and your children's children. (De.4:9)

> And these words that I command you today shall be on your heart. You shall teach them diligently to your children, and shall talk of them when you sit in your house, and when you walk by the way, and when you lie down, and when you rise. . ... You shall write them on the doorposts of your house and on your gates. (De.6:6–7, 9)

V. The Son of God's Closing Ministry: Jesus Teaches the Idea of God's Messiahship, Not Man's Messiahship, 8:27–9:50

A. The Great Confession of Peter: Who Jesus Is, 8:27–30

(see Mt.16:13–20; Lu.9:18–21)

1. The setting: Jesus in Caesarea Philippi[DS1]
   a. He visited the villages
   b. He questioned the people's belief about Him
2. The confession of people: He is a great man

3. The confession of His disciples: He is the Christ

4. The need: To personally learn about God's Messiah before sharing the message

27 And Jesus went on with his disciples to the villages of Caesarea Philippi. And on the way he asked his disciples, "Who do people say that I am?"

28 And they told him, "John the Baptist; and others say, Elijah; and others, one of the prophets."
29 And he asked them, "But who do you say that I am?" Peter answered him, "You are the Christ."
30 And he strictly charged them to tell no one about him.

Division V

The Son of God's Closing Ministry: Jesus Teaches the Idea of God's Messiahship, not Man's Messiahship, 8:27–9:50

A. The Great Confession of Peter: Who Jesus Is, 8:27–30

(see Mt.16:13–20; Lu.9:18–21)

8:27–9:50
DIVISION OVERVIEW

Most people do not object to the idea of a Messiah, that is, a deliverer, savior, provider, and protector. Most want a leader who is going to bring about a perfect society that will provide social justice and plenty for everyone—a savior who fits into the wants and passions and power structures of their world. People want their bellies full, their bodies clothed and housed and their urges satisfied. They want the *good things* of this world. If a deliverer can give these, then people are usually ready and willing to accept him.

When Jesus came, people rejected Him because He was not the deliverer *they* wanted Him to be. Jesus deliberately set out to make sure that the disciples saw Him as *God's* Messiah and not what people desired the Messiah to be. He had to make sure they understood *God's* way of salvation and deliverance, that God was concerned with victory over death and a life that lasted eternally, not just for seventy or so years on this earth. *God's* Messiah and salvation was not humanity's way of power and pleasure; it was not living for the present and leaving the future to take care of itself (see notes—Mt.1:1; Deeper Study # 2—1:18; Deeper Study # 3—3:11; notes—11:1-6; 11:2-3; Deeper Study # 1—11:5; Deeper Study # 2—11:6; Deeper Study # 1—12:16; note—22:42).

In mere days, Jesus would be facing the cross, and He still had much to teach His disciples. It was time for them to learn that He was building a church—an assembly of people who would be confessing Him to be the Messiah. The present passage highlights the most important confession ever made, a confession offered in response to the most critical question ever asked. Every person must answer this question, and their answer determines their eternal destiny. This is, *The Great Confession of Peter: Who Jesus Is,* 8:27-30.

1. The setting: Jesus in Caesarea Philippi (v.27).
2. The confession of people: He is a great man (v.28).
3. The confession of His disciples: He is the Christ (v.29).
4. The need: To personally learn about God's Messiah before sharing the message (v.30).

1 The setting: Jesus in Caesarea Philippi.

8:27

a. **He visited the villages.**

b. **He questioned the people's belief about Him.**

> [27] And Jesus went on with his disciples to the villages of Caesarea Philippi. And on the way he asked his disciples, "Who do people say that I am?"

Jesus left Bethsaida and traveled into the villages of Caesarea Philippi (see DEEPER STUDY # 1). As He was traveling along the road between villages, He asked the key question of life—the question that when answered determines a person's eternal destiny (v.29). But first, leading up to this question, He asked His disciples, "Who do people say that I am?"

DEEPER STUDY # 1

(8:27) **Caesarea Philippi:** the city had a rich religious history. It had once been the center of Baal worship with at least fourteen temples in and around the city. It was believed to have within its borders the cavern in which the Greek god of nature, Pan, was born. In the beginning of its history, the city was so identified with this god that it was named after the god, being called Panias. One of its most beautiful structures was the gleaming white marble temple built for the worship of Caesar. Herod the Great had built the temple in honor of Caesar when Caesar had given him authority over an additional country. But it was Herod's son Philip who adorned the temple with the magnificence for which it became known worldwide. It was also Philip who changed the name of the city from Panias to Caesarea, or "Caesar's town." He added his own name also, calling the city Caesarea Philippi.

The city proclaimed far and wide the worship of Caesar and of the gods of one's choice, that is, the worship of all except the One true and living God. It was against this dramatic yet terrible background that Jesus asked the pointed question, "But who do you say that I am?" (emphatic Greek translation). It was also against this background of religious pluralism that Peter made his great discovery and confession: Jesus is the Christ, the real Messiah.

2 The confession of people: He is a great man.

8:28

> [28] And they told him, "John the Baptist; and others say, Elijah; and others, one of the prophets."

The various confessions of people shortchanged Jesus. Most saw Jesus only as a great man, a man who was highly esteemed and respected. Their confessions revealed that they considered Him one of the greatest of men, but note a crucial point: these *professions* were not only untrue, they were dangerous. They contained only half-truths, and people were deceived and misled by them.

Some said Jesus was John the Baptist. They professed Jesus to be a great spirit of righteousness, a spirit that was willing to be martyred for its faith. Herod and others thought this (Mt.14:1-2). Upon hearing of Jesus' marvelous works, Herod fancied that either John had come back from the dead or else his spirit indwelt this man, Jesus.

The common people also saw some similarity between John and Jesus: both were doing a great work for God; both were divinely chosen and gifted by God; and both proclaimed the kingdom of God and prepared people for it. Therefore, when some looked at Jesus and His ministry, they thought Jesus was not the Messiah Himself, but the reincarnation of the one who had claimed to be the promised forerunner of the Messiah (Mal.4:5).

Some said Jesus was Elijah, considered to be the greatest prophet and teacher of all time. For generations, many had predicted that the prophesied forerunner of the coming Messiah would be Elijah (Mal.4:5). Even today, Jews expect Elijah to return ahead of the Messiah. In the celebration of the Passover, they always leave a chair vacant for him to occupy. Elijah had also been used by God to miraculously feed a widow woman and her son (1 K.17:14); therefore, the people connected Elijah's miracle and Jesus' feeding of the multitude.

Some said Jesus was one of the prophets. They professed Jesus to be a great prophet sent for their day and time. He was thought to be one of the great prophets brought back to life or one in whom the spirit of a great prophet dwelt (see De.18:15, 18).

THOUGHT 1. The same false confessions about Christ exist in every generation.
1) He was only a great man of righteousness who was martyred for His great faith. As such He leaves us a great example of how to live and stand up for what we believe.
2) He was one of the greatest teachers and prophets of all time.
3) He was only a great man who revealed some very important things to us about God and religion. As such He can make a significant contribution to every person in their search for God.
4) He was only a great man, a prophet sent to the people (Jews) of His day from whom we can learn by studying His life.

> "Is not this the carpenter, the son of Mary and brother of James and Joses and Judas and Simon? And are not his sisters here with us?" And they took offense at him. (Mk.6:3)

> He was in the world, and the world was made through him, yet the world did not know him. He came to his own, and his own people did not receive him. (Jn.1:10–11)

> They said to him therefore, "Where is your Father?" Jesus answered, "You know neither me nor my Father. If you knew me, you would know my Father also." (Jn.8:19)

> Who is the liar but he who denies that Jesus is the Christ? This is the antichrist, he who denies the Father and the Son. No one who denies the Son has the Father. Whoever confesses the Son has the Father also. (1 Jn.2:22–23)

> And every spirit that does not confess Jesus is not from God. This is the spirit of the antichrist, which you heard was coming and now is in the world already. (1 Jn.4:3)

8:29

3 The confession of His disciples: He is the Christ.

²⁹ And he asked them, "But who do you say that I am?" Peter answered him, "You are the Christ."

Jesus proceeded to ask His disciples a second question, the question that is the key question of life, the question that determines where every person spends eternity: "Who do you say that I am?" Led by Peter, the disciples confessed that Jesus is the Christ, the Messiah, the God-sent Savior and Deliverer of the human race. Note three facts about Jesus' question and the disciples' answer.

First, the word *asked* or *said* (Gk. eperota) is in the imperfect tense, which means that Jesus kept on asking them. It may suggest that they did not answer Jesus immediately. The question, "Who do you say that I am?" was extremely pointed and direct. The answer required concentrated thought and correct belief and genuine confession.

Second, the question asked is emphatic in the Greek. Translated most literally, it is, "But you, who do you say that I am?" The emphasis is on the individual and the individual's answer to the question. Every individual's answer to the question is critical; it is all important. It determines the person's eternal destiny.

Third, the answer given was unwavering and concise: "You are the Christ," that is, the promised Messiah, the Son of the living God. (See Mt.16:16 for the full confession. Remember Mark was Peter's disciple, and Mark's writing shows the humility of Peter. He usually de-emphasizes the facts surrounding Peter.)

The confession is momentous, arising from a personal conviction. It is both the faith-produced confession that saves the soul and the confession that lays the foundation for the church. The very life and survival of a person's soul and of the church as a whole rest upon this simple, yet profound conviction. Jesus is . . .

- ➤ the Christ: the Messiah; the anointed One of God (see DEEPER STUDY # 1—Mt.1:18 for discussion)
- ➤ the Son of God: of the same being, the same substance; One with the Father (see notes—Jn.1:1-2; 1:34; Ph.2:6)
- ➤ living: the source and being of life; possessing the source, energy, and power of life within Himself (see DEEPER STUDY # 2—Jn.1:4; note—1:4-5; DEEPER STUDY # 1—17:2-3; see also Jn.5:26; 1 Th.1:9 for discussion and application).

4 The need: To personally learn about God's Messiah before sharing the message.

8:30

Jesus instructed the disciples not to share their confession with anyone else—not now. Why? Because they were just beginning to learn what God's idea of the Messiah really meant. They needed to personally understand the truth about Christ and be accurate in their understanding of that truth before they proceeded to share the message. They could do irreparable harm by spreading a false concept of the Messiah. Therefore, Jesus had to protect them against this error.

[30] And he strictly charged them to tell no one about him.

THOUGHT 1. Confession is just the beginning of our spiritual journey. There is much to study and learn about Christ after coming to know Him personally. Note two considerations.

1) We must be accurate in what we study. We must make sure we learn the truth and not error (see outline and notes—Mk.8:15).
2) We must be accurate in what we share, making certain that we share the truth. This necessitates time to study and grow before we begin sharing.

> Now these Jews were more noble than those in Thessalonica; they received the word with all eagerness, examining the Scriptures daily to see if these things were so. (Ac.17:11)

> Do your best to present yourself to God as one approved, a worker who has no need to be ashamed, rightly handling the word of truth. (2 Ti.2:15)

> Like newborn infants, long for the pure spiritual milk, that by it you may grow up into salvation—if indeed you have tasted that the Lord is good. (1 Pe.2:2-3; see also Ac.20:32; 2 Ti.2:15; 2 Pe.3:18)

B. The First Prediction of Death:
God's Messiah vs. Man's Messiah, 8:31–33

(Mt.16:21–23; Lu.9:22)

1. The way of God's Messiah
a. Involves suffering and death
b. Involves resurrection from the dead

2. The way of man's messiah
a. Involves rejecting God's Messiah
b. Involves following the way of Satan
c. Involves setting the mind on worldly things, not on the things of God

³¹ And he began to teach them that the Son of Man must suffer many things and be rejected by the elders and the chief priests and the scribes and be killed, and after three days rise again. ³² And he said this plainly. And Peter took him aside and began to rebuke him. ³³ But turning and seeing his disciples, he rebuked Peter and said, "Get behind me, Satan! For you are not setting your mind on the things of God, but on the things of man."

Division V

The Son of God's Closing Ministry: Jesus Teaches the Idea of God's Messiahship, not Man's Messiahship, 8:27–9:50

B. The First Prediction of Death: God's Messiah vs. Man's Messiah, 8:31–33

(Mt.16:21–23; Lu.9:22)

8:31–33
Introduction

Mankind's way of thinking and God's way of thinking could not be more different. Scripture clearly states this:

> **For as the heavens are higher than the earth, so are my ways higher than your ways and my thoughts than your thoughts. (Is.55:9)**

Human wisdom and God's wisdom vary radically. We can only understand God's wisdom with the help of God's Spirit:

> **Yet among the mature we do impart wisdom, although it is not a wisdom of this age or of the rulers of this age, who are doomed to pass away. But we impart a secret and hidden wisdom of God, which God decreed before the ages for our glory. None of the rulers of this age understood this, for if they had, they would not have crucified the Lord of glory. But, as it is written, "What no eye has seen, nor ear heard, nor the heart of man imagined, what God has prepared for those who love him"—these things God has revealed to us through the Spirit. For the Spirit searches everything, even the depths of God. For who knows a person's thoughts except the spirit of that person, which is in him? So also no one comprehends the thoughts of God except the Spirit of God. Now we have received not the spirit of the world, but the Spirit who is from God, that we might understand the things freely given us by God. And we impart this in words not taught by human wisdom but taught by the Spirit, interpreting spiritual truths to those who are spiritual. The natural person does not accept the things of the Spirit of God, for they are folly to him, and he is not able to understand them because they are spiritually discerned. (1 Co 2:6–14)**

As Jesus, for the first time, teaches His disciples frankly about His death, the conflict between humanity's thinking and God's thinking is strikingly clear. The subject of the conflict is the most critical subject in all the world: the atoning death of God's Son, the Messiah. This is, *The First Pre-diction of Death: God's Messiah vs. Man's Messiah,* 8:31-33.

1. The way of God's Messiah (v.31).
2. The way of man's messiah (vv.32-33).

1 The way of God's Messiah.

The disciples had just made the profound confession that Jesus is the Christ, the Messiah, the Son of the living God. At this point, Jesus launched a new stage in their training. The statement "He began to teach them" is significant. Matthew says, "From that time"; that is, from the time of their profound confession that Jesus is beyond question the Messiah—something significant happened. Jesus began to indoctrinate them into the way of God's Messiah, for God's Messiah was not man's messiah (see note—Mk.8:27-9:50).

> 31 And he began to teach them that the Son of Man must suffer many things and be rejected by the elders and the chief priests and the scribes and be killed, and after three days rise again.

a. Involves suffering and death.

Jesus revealed with a powerful thrust that He was going to be killed. Never before had this happened. Never again would it happen. History would be made. "Jerusalem, the city that kills the prophets" (Mt.23:37) would now commit the ultimate crime: Jerusalem would kill God's own Son.

Jesus had been telling His disciples about His death for some time. But they had not understood. First, the idea of a suffering Messiah differed radically from their own idea of the Messiah (see notes—Mt.1:1; Deeper Study # 2—1:18; Deeper Study # 3—3:11; notes—11:1-6; 11:2-3; Deeper Study # 1—11:5; Deeper Study # 2—11:6; Deeper Study # 1—12:16; note—Lu.7:21-23). And second, the revelation had been veiled in pictures and symbols.

> **Jesus answered them, "Destroy this temple, and in three days I will raise it up." (Jn.2:19)**

> **And as Moses lifted up the serpent in the wilderness, so must the Son of Man be lifted up. (Jn.3:14)**

> **I am the living bread that came down from heaven. If anyone eats of this bread, he will live forever. And the bread that I will give for the life of the world is my flesh. (Jn.6:51)**

The difference now was that Jesus no longer spoke in pictures and symbols. He told them in simple and direct words (see Mt.20:18-20; Lu.18:31-33). A new stage in the revelation of God's plan for the world was now to take place: God's Son was to die for the sins of the world. God's plan for saving the world was to take place through a suffering Messiah, not a conquering Messiah. God's Messiah was not going to deliver a materialistic world into the hands of His followers. To the contrary, He was going to die, and His death was going to usher in the kingdom of God, making it possible for His followers to live eternally in the very presence of God Himself (see Deeper Study # 3—Mt.19:23-24; see Jn.3:16; 5:24f).

The words "must suffer" are strong. *Must* (Gk. dei) means it is an absolute, non-negotiable necessity (see Deeper Study # 2—Ac.2:23 for more discussion). It was absolutely necessary by the very nature of the case for Jesus to suffer. God is love and humanity is corrupt, so God, in love, must provide salvation for the sinful human race. But God is also just, so He must provide salvation in such a way that justice will be done. The penalty must be paid; death must be carried out. Some *Ideal Man* must die for all people so that His *Ideal Death* can stand for and cover all people (see notes, *Son of Man*—Jn.1:51; *Justification*—Ro.5:1). There is only one Ideal Man: Jesus, the Son of God. The Son of God must become the Son of Man, the Ideal Man:

> ➢ He must live a perfect life providing for the world the Ideal Righteousness or Ideal Life.
> ➢ He must die, providing for the world the Ideal Death.
> ➢ He must arise from the dead, providing for the world the Ideal Resurrection.

The words "suffer many things" include much more than just the sufferings involved with Jesus' death. This is often overlooked. Scripture clearly states that, even though Christ was a Son, He learned obedience through suffering (He.5:8). However, the point is not seen unless one acknowledges the truth of the word *Son,* that is, Jesus' deity. Jesus is *the Son of God* who left the very presence of God. He left heaven with all the majesty and splendor, glory and worship, praise and honor due Him. He is *the Son of Heaven*, but He became the Son of a woman. He belonged in heaven, but He was present on earth. He had ruled in the perfect, incorruptible world, but He was now a servant in this imperfect and corruptible world. Every sight, sound, touch, taste—every experience and awareness was a world of distance from what He had known. He suffered through every moment and through every experience. Every experience drained "virtue" out of Him, for He always had before His face the truth and glory of heaven and the sin and corruption of earth. From the time He came to this earth to His final breath, the spotless Son of God "suffered many things."

b. Involves resurrection from the dead.

Jesus also revealed that, after being dead three days, He would rise again. Jesus' prediction of His resurrection is clear to us because we can look back on it. But it was never clear to His disciples. Why? Very simply, it was to be a new experience. Perhaps the disciples believed somewhat like Martha, that there was to be a future resurrection of all people (Jn.11:24-26). Such a belief was an expression of the hope that is within every person, the hope to continue on in some form of existence—an easier belief to accept. Even today, to think of an immediate resurrection, to think of a person's arising from the dead, is difficult. Just think how hard it would have been for the disciples to grasp this concept more than two thousand years ago. The idea of the Messiah's dying and arising from the dead would be almost unimaginable to those who had not been taught the truth.

Exactly what the disciples thought Jesus meant when He spoke of His resurrection is not known. The fact that they did not fully understand is clear from the fact that their spirits were crushed when He was killed. But some of His followers seemed to grasp more of a real bodily resurrection than others. This is clear by an immediate remembrance of His words after His resurrection. For example, John did believe immediately (Jn.20:8-9); Mary Magdalene was shown that He had risen (Mt.28:6). However, others were slower to understand and believe (Mk.16:11; Jn.20:24-25).

> To this day I have had the help that comes from God, and so I stand here testifying both to small and great, saying nothing but what the prophets and Moses said would come to pass: that the Christ must suffer and that, by being the first to rise from the dead, he would proclaim light both to our people and to the Gentiles. (Ac.26:22-23)

> For I delivered to you as of first importance what I also received: that Christ died for our sins in accordance with the Scriptures that he was buried, that he was raised on the third day in accordance with the Scriptures. (1 Co.15:3-4)

> And he died for all, that those who live might no longer live for themselves but for him who for their sake died and was raised. (2 Co.5:15)

> For Christ also suffered once for sins, the righteous for the unrighteous, that he might bring us to God, being put to death in the flesh but made alive in the spirit. (1 Pe.3:18)

8:32-33

³² And he said this plainly. And Peter took him aside and began to rebuke him.

³³ But turning and seeing his disciples, he rebuked Peter and said, "Get behind me, Satan! For you are not setting your mind on the things of God, but on the things of man."

2 The way of man's messiah.

Jesus' disciples could not accept the idea that the Messiah would be killed. Note the word *plainly* or *openly* (parresia). It means bluntly, unmistakably, frankly. Again, Jesus no longer spoke of His death in pictures and symbols. His meaning was crystal clear. He was going to be killed. This reality shook the disciples, so much so that Peter rebuked Christ for saying such a thing. They could only view the Messiah from *man's* perspective, what the people thought the Messiah would do.

What the people expected the Messiah to be and what God's Messiah actually was (and still is) were not the same. Note three truths about the way of man's messiah.

a. Involves rejecting God's Messiah (v.32).

The natural person—the unspiritual person, the person without God's Spirit—does not receive the things of God's Spirit (1 Co.2:14). Therefore, the natural person rejects God's Messiah. He rebels at the idea of the cross. He wants another way other than the cross. This is what Peter was doing: rebelling against the idea that *God's Son* was to die, that His blood was to be shed for the sins of the world (1 Pe.2:24). Peter could accept Jesus as *the Son of the living God*, but not as the Suffering Savior. Such an idea was repulsive and unacceptable to him. Therefore, he tried to stop the idea by doing two things.

First, "Peter *took* Him *aside*" (proslabomenos). The Greek rendering is stronger than what the English communicates. It means *caught hold*. Peter took hold and grabbed Jesus. Peter bodily took Jesus aside for a private conversation.

Second, Peter "began to *rebuke* (epitiman) Him." This Greek word also suggests stronger action than any English equivalent. It is not just a wish, but a forcible attempt to stop the idea of the Suffering Savior: Peter said, "This must not and cannot happen to you." *God forbid* is the equivalent idea. Peter was out to stop the cross. He was urging Jesus to be the Messiah of power, fame, and sensation that the Jews were expecting (see notes—Mk.8:27-9:50; 8:30; Mt.1:1; Deeper Study # 2—1:18; Deeper Study # 3—3:11; notes—11:1-6; 11:2-3; Deeper Study # 1—11:5; Deeper Study # 2—11:6; Deeper Study # 1—12:16; note—Lu.7:21-23). Peter was urging Jesus to follow human schemes instead of God's way. And by such, he was tempting Jesus with the very same compromises that Satan used to tempt Jesus, the compromises of power, fame, and sensations (Mt.4:1-11). Peter was zealous for God, but He was mistaken and ignorant in his zeal. He did not understand that God was planning to save the world through the death of His Son (see note, pt.3—v.31).

Peter's behavior is the way of the world. It is the natural, carnal mind. People simply rebel and recoil against the idea of a suffering Savior who dies for the sins of the world, a suffering Savior who demands the same sacrifice and denial of His followers. Such an idea is unacceptable and repulsive (1 Co.1:23).

THOUGHT 1. The natural person's idea of God and of God's plan for humanity is seen in three concepts.

1) Some think the path of life is an indulgent love. God is seen as a giving, loving, indulgent *grandfather type* of person. He is seen as One who tolerates (and rewards by accepting) even the worst behavior, no matter how much human suffering and devastation is wrought by the hands of a person. To think of the cross and the blood of Christ as an emblem of suffering is repulsive. The cross is viewed only as an emblem of love, not of sin and shame. The way of love is thought to be the path of life that people are to follow.

2) Some think that comfort and pleasure are the path of life and God's way. God again is viewed only as an indulgent *grandfather type*. His will for people is to have *the good life* of things: comfort and pleasure, ease and plenty, health and leisure. And again, the cross is only an emblem of love and care for the world, not of suffering and sacrifice and self-denial. Its shame and pain and agony and its purpose of reconciling a world lost in sin and depravity are denied.

> **And as for what fell among the thorns, they are those who hear, but as they go on their way they are choked by the cares and riches and pleasures of life, and their fruit does not mature. (Lu.8:14)**

> **And I will say to my soul, "Soul, you have ample goods laid up for many years; relax, eat, drink, be merry." (Lu.12:19)**

> **But she who is self-indulgent is dead even while she lives. (1 Ti.5:6)**

> **Now therefore hear this, you lover of pleasures, who sit securely, who say in your heart, "I am, and there is no one besides me; I shall not sit as a widow or know the loss of children" (Is.47:8-9)**

3) Some feel that triumph, victory, power, and reigning supreme are God's way. This was the idea of most Jews in Christ's day. It was Peter's concept of the Messiah (see notes—Mt.1:1; Deeper Study # 2—1:18; Deeper Study # 3—3:11; notes—11:1-6; 11:2-3; Deeper Study # 1—11:5;

DEEPER STUDY # 2—11:6; DEEPER STUDY # 1—12:16; note—Lu.7:21-23). Applying humanity's ideas to their own emotional and mental state of being, as well as to their physical and material being, is revealing. The ideas show how some view the concepts of *Self-Image, Self-Improvement*, and *Personal Development* as being God's plan and path for humanity. Again, the idea of suffering and sacrifice and self-denial is rejected.

> **But Jesus called them to him and said, "You know that the rulers of the Gentiles lord it over them, and their great ones exercise authority over them. It shall not be so among you. But whoever would be great among you must be your servant, and whoever would be first among you must be your slave," (Mt.20:25-27)**

> **How can you believe, when you receive glory from one another and do not seek the glory that comes from the only God? (Jn.5:44)**

> **For all that is in the world—the desires of the flesh and the desires of the eyes and pride of life—is not from the Father but is from the world. (1 Jn.2:16)**

> **For you say, I am rich, I have prospered, and I need nothing, not realizing that you are wretched, pitiable, poor, blind, and naked. (Re.3:17)**

> **Man in his pomp will not remain; he is like the beasts that perish. (Ps.49:12)**

b. Involves following the way of Satan (v.33a).

Christ's response to Peter was startling. He abruptly turned to Peter before Peter could say anything else and stopped him in his tracks. He charged Peter with being Satan, with being under the authority of Satan, with speaking for Satan. He had become as Satan, an adversary against God's plan for His Son and for the salvation of the world.

The natural person—the person without the Spirit—follows the way of Satan. The literal meaning of the name "Satan" is *Adversary* (see DEEPER STUDY # 1—Re.12:9). Calling Peter "Satan" was stern, yet such sternness was necessary. Peter was tempting Christ with the very same temptation Jesus had faced in the wilderness (see notes—Mt.4:8-10). All the world's glory that could be His may have flashed across His mind. Once again, people were suggesting a path forward without the cross. How this must have cut the heart of Jesus! This time the temptation was coming from one of His own disciples. When people refuse to accept God's plan for life, they become an adversary to God, whether they know it or not. They oppose God's will. In essence they say that they know what is best; they are *wiser* than God. Think! When people do not accept God's plan for life, the crux of what they say to God is, "The cross is not necessary. Jesus' death to save the world is a useless plan. It is not needed."

This is what Peter was doing and saying. He was opposing God's plan for life, that is, opposing the salvation of the world through the death of God's Son. Although Peter surely did not intend it, he was saying that he was wiser than God.

> **You are of your father the devil, and your will is to do your father's desires. He was a murderer from the beginning, and does not stand in the truth, because there is no truth in him. When he lies, he speaks out of his own character, for he is a liar and the father of lies. (Jn.8:44)**

> **And [Paul] said [to Elymas, the magician], "You son of the devil, you enemy of all righteousness, full of all deceit and villainy, will you not stop making crooked the straight paths of the Lord?" (Ac.13:10)**

> **In which you once walked, following the course of this world, following the prince of the power of the air, the spirit that is now at work in the sons of disobedience. (Ep.2:2)**

> **By this it is evident who are the children of God, and who are the children of the devil: whoever does not practice righteousness is not of God, nor is the one who does not love his brother. (1 Jn.3:10)**

c. Involves setting the mind on worldly things, not on the things of God (v.33b).

The natural man sets his or her mind on material things, not on the things of God. Peter did not have his mind, his thinking, in line with God's mind and thoughts. His ideas were different from God's ideas. Peter's thoughts were worldly and self-pleasing, definitely not spiritual and certainly not pleasing to God. He was using human reasoning, not God's reasoning. The death of God's Son through the shedding of His blood for the sins of the world was distasteful to Peter. In his mind, such a concept was unfit for God.

Jesus' words to Peter regarding His death revealed Peter's true nature and humanity's true nature, a nature that uses natural and carnal reasoning instead of spiritual reasoning.

> For those who live according to the flesh set their minds on the things of the flesh, but those who live according to the Spirit set their minds on the things of the Spirit. For to set the mind on the flesh is death, but to set the mind on the Spirit is life and peace. For the mind that is set on the flesh is hostile to God, for it does not submit to God's law; indeed, it cannot. (Ro.8:5-7)

> Now this I say and testify in the Lord, that you must no longer walk as the Gentiles do, in the futility of their minds. (Ep.4:17)

> For many, of whom I have often told you and now tell you even with tears, walk as enemies of the cross of Christ. Their end is destruction, their god is their belly, and they glory in their shame, with minds set on earthly things. (Ph.3:18-19)

> And you, who once were alienated and hostile in mind, doing evil deeds, he has now reconciled in his body of flesh by his death, in order to present you holy and blameless and above reproach before him. (Col.1:21-22)

> O Jerusalem, wash your heart from evil, that you may be saved. How long shall your wicked thoughts lodge within you? (Je.4:14)

THOUGHT 1. Jesus was tempted to bypass God's will for His life. And note: the temptation came from a disciple. We are often tempted to bypass God's will, and unfortunately, the temptation often comes from friends! They may mean well; they may want to save us from the difficult path of trouble, sorrow, and trials. Nevertheless, their suggestion to bypass the cross is not of God. It is of Satan.

THOUGHT 2. Note Peter's testimony after Jesus' death and resurrection.

> Blessed be the God and Father of our Lord Jesus Christ! According to his great mercy, he has caused us to be born again to a living hope through the resurrection of Jesus Christ from the dead, to an inheritance that is imperishable, undefiled, and unfading, kept in heaven for you. (1 Pe.1:3-4)

> Knowing that you were ransomed from the futile ways inherited from your forefathers, not with perishable things such as silver or gold, but with the precious blood of Christ, like that of a lamb without blemish or spot. . . . who through him are believers in God, who raised him from the dead and gave him glory, so that your faith and hope are in God. (1 Pe.1:18-19, 21)

> He himself bore our sins in his body on the tree, that we might die to sin and live to righteousness. By his wounds you have been healed. (1 Pe.2:24)

> For Christ also suffered once for sins, the righteous for the unrighteous, that he might bring us to God, being put to death in the flesh but made alive in the spirit. (1 Pe.3:18)

> Since therefore Christ suffered in the flesh, arm yourselves with the same way of thinking, for whoever has suffered in the flesh has ceased from sin. (1 Pe.4:1)

CHAPTER 9

C. The Issues of God and the Issues of Men, 8:34–9:1

(Mt.16:24-28; Lu.9:23-27)

<table>
<tr><td>

1. Jesus spoke to all, to the people and to His disciples
2. The issue of discipleship: Indulging self vs. denying self[DS1, 2, 3]
3. The issue of life: Saving life vs. losing life

4. The issue of value: Gaining the world vs. saving the soul

5. The issue of the Messiah: Being ashamed of Christ vs. confessing Christ

6. The issue of death: Tasting death vs. seeing God's kingdom

</td><td>

[34] And calling the crowd to him with his disciples, he said to them, "If anyone would come after me, let him deny himself and take up his cross and follow me."
[35] "For whoever would save his life will lose it, but whoever loses his life for my sake and the gospel's will save it."
[36] "For what does it profit a man to gain the whole world and forfeit his soul?
[37] For what can a man give in return for his soul?"
[38] "For whoever is ashamed of me and of my words in this adulterous and sinful generation, of him will the Son of Man also be ashamed when he comes in the glory of his Father with the holy angels."
And he said to them, "Truly, I say to you, there are some standing here who will not taste death until they see the kingdom of God after it has come with power."

</td></tr>
</table>

Division V

The Son of God's Closing Ministry: Jesus Teaches the Idea of God's Messiahship, not Man's Messiahship, 8:27–9:50

C. The Issues of God and the Issues of Men, 8:34–9:1

(Mt.16:24-28; Lu.9:23-27)

8:34–9:1
Introduction

Just as God's thoughts and ways differ from those of sinful human beings, the issues that matter to God and the issues that matter to most people differ radically. However, the genuine Christ-follower is not like most people. The true disciple of Christ adopts the issues of God as their own. They live by a different set of principles, a different set of priorities; they live as Christ lived. This passage, which shows just how much the issues of God differ from the issues of mankind, serves as a warning to every person. This is, *The Issues of God and the Issues of Men*, 8:34–9:1.

1. Jesus spoke to all, to the people and to His disciples (v.34).
2. The issue of discipleship: Indulging self vs. denying self (v.34).
3. The issue of life: Saving life vs. losing life (v.35).
4. The issue of value: Gaining the world vs. saving the soul (vv.36-37).

5. The issue of the Messiah: Being ashamed of Christ vs. confessing Christ (v.38).
6. The issue of death: Tasting death vs. seeing God's kingdom (v.9:1).

1 Jesus spoke to all, to the people and to His disciples.

This episode from the ministry of Christ involves the people as well as the disciples. He had a critical lesson for all the people, a requirement that separates genuine believers from those who merely profess to believe.

2 The issue of discipleship: Indulging self vs. denying self.

Jesus addressed the issue of discipleship, of truly following Him. What He said was blunt and to the point. Being a Christ-follower boils down to one primary requirement: you must deny yourself. There is a life of self-indulgence, and there is a life of self-denial (Ro.12:1-2; 2 Co.6:17-18; 1 Jn.2:15-16). The disciple of Christ chooses a life of self-denial. A person has to make a choice between . . .

> 34 And calling the crowd to him with his disciples, he said to them, "If anyone would come after me, let him deny himself and take up his cross and follow me."

• loving comfort and ease	or	honoring commitment and discipline
• loving wealth and property	or	respecting work and compassion
• loving recognition and fame	or	living in a spirit of humility and sacrifice
• loving position and power	or	offering service and ministry
• loving pleasure and indulgence	or	loving righteousness and self-control

The question is, how do we go about making the right choice? Jesus gave four guiding criteria:

> ➤ We must *will to come* after Him—desire willingly to follow Him (see DEEPER STUDY # 1).
> ➤ We must *deny ourselves* (see DEEPER STUDY # 2).
> ➤ We must *take up our cross* (see DEEPER STUDY # 1—Lu.9:23).
> ➤ We must *follow Christ* (see DEEPER STUDY # 3).

DEEPER STUDY # 1

(8:34) **Would or Desires, Wishes, Wants** (Gk. thelei; pronounce *thay-lay'*): to design, purpose, resolve, determine. It is a deliberate willing, a deliberate choice, a determined resolve to follow Christ. If a person really desires and deliberately chooses to "come after" Christ, then he or she has to do the three things mentioned in this verse: deny oneself, take up one's cross, and follow Jesus. Note, the choice is voluntary. It is not forced upon anyone. It is the individual who wills and chooses; therefore, it is the individual who must act and do these three things.

DEEPER STUDY # 2

(8:34) **Deny** (aparneomai; pronounced *ap-ar-neh'-oh-my*): to disown, disregard, forsake, renounce, reject, refuse, restrain, disclaim, do without. It means to subdue, to disregard oneself and one's interest. Very simply, it means to say "no." But note: the call is not to say "no" to some behavior or thing, but instead say "no" to *self*. We are to *deny self*. This means much more than just being negative, that is, giving up something and doing without something. It means that we are to act positively, to say "yes" to Christ and "no" to self. It means to let Christ rule and reign in your heart and life, to let Christ have His way completely. Of course, if you allow Christ to rule in your life, all negative as well as positive behavior is taken care of. In the Greek, the verb tense carries the deeper meaning of a person entering a new state or condition. It means *let him at once begin* to "deny self."

DEEPER STUDY # 3

(8:34) **Follow** (akolootheo; pronounced ah-kol-oo-theh'-oh): to be a follower or companion, to be a disciple. It has the idea of seeking to be in union with and in the likeness of. It is following Christ, seeking to be just like Him. Again, this is not passive behavior, but an active commitment and walk. It is energy and effort, action and work. It is going after Christ with zeal and energy, struggling and seeking to follow in His footsteps no matter the cost. Note that His steps lead to death before they lead to glory (Mt.16:21).

8:35

[35] "For whoever would save his life will lose it, but whoever loses his life for my sake and the gospel's will save it."

3 The issue of life: Saving life vs. losing life.

Jesus made a perplexing statement. If a person wishes to save their life, they must first lose it. What did He mean? How is this possible? The key is found in two phrases.

The first phrase is: "for my sake." "Whoever loses his life *for my sake* . . . will save it." The person who abandons this life, who sacrifices and gives all that they are and have for Christ, will save their life. But the person who *keeps* their life, that is, what they have, and *seeks* more and more of this life will lose their life completely and eternally.

The person "who would save their life," who . . .

- seeks to please self and others and denies Christ, will lose eternal life
- seeks to be more and more comfortable and secure beyond what is necessary and neglects Christ, will lose eternal life
- seeks to gain wealth, power, and fame, and who compromises Christ, will lose eternal life
- seeks the thrills, excitement, and stimulation of this world and ignores Christ, will lose eternal life

As said above, the person who *loses* their life for Christ, who sacrifices and gives all for Christ, saves their life and saves it eternally. The person who *keeps* their life and what they have for self will lose their life and lose it eternally. The call of Christ is just what He says: a life of denial that takes up the cross and follows in His steps.

> And I will say to my soul, 'Soul, you have ample goods laid up for many years; relax, eat, drink, be merry.' But God said to him, 'Fool! This night your soul is required of you, and the things you have prepared, whose will they be?' (Lu.12:19–20)

> Why do you spend your money for that which is not bread, and your labor for that which does not satisfy? Listen diligently to me, and eat what is good, and delight yourselves in rich food. (Is.55:2)

The second phrase is: "and the gospel's [sake]." In view of the full context of the verse, "Whoever loses his life for . . . the gospel's [sake], will save it." The person who abandons this life, who sacrifices and gives all they are and have for the gospel will save their life. But the person who keeps their life and all that they are and have and tries to keep self and family from facing from the suffering and needs of this world—at the expense of souls—that person will lose their life.

The person who saves his life . . .	The person who gives his life . . .
• who lies around in the comforts of home . . . will lose his life	• who becomes an explorer and pioneer for Christ . . . will save his life
• who spends all he has on himself and his family . . . will lose his life	• who sacrifices and gives to the gospel . . . will save his life
• who takes all his time for his own affairs and desires . . . will lose his life	• who gives of his time for the gospel (visiting, teaching, sharing, witnessing, ministering) . . . will save his life

> **And everyone who has left houses or brothers or sisters or father or mother or children or lands, for my name's sake, will receive a hundredfold and will inherit eternal life. (Mt.19:29)**

> **I was a stranger and you did not welcome me, naked and you did not clothe me, sick and in prison and you did not visit me. (Mt.25:43)**

> **For we who live are always being given over to death for Jesus' sake, so that the life of Jesus also may be manifested in our mortal flesh. (2 Co.4:11)**

> **But if anyone has the world's goods and sees his brother in need, yet closes his heart against him, how does God's love abide in him? (1 Jn.3:17)**

> **And when you eat and when you drink, do you not eat for yourselves and drink for yourselves? (Zec.7:6)**

4 The issue of value: Gaining the world vs. saving the soul.

8:36–37

Jesus proceeded to address the value of the soul. The Greek word translated *soul* (psuche; pronounced *psoo-kay'*) is the same Greek word translated *life* (v.35). Jesus used the word *life* in two senses. There are *two stages, two beings, two existences* to the same life: the life that exists on this earth and the life that will exist beyond this earth. Once a person (life) is born into this world, they will exist forever. It is just a matter of where they go after life in this world: to be with God or to be apart from God.

> [36] "For what does it profit a man to gain the whole world and forfeit his soul?
> [37] For what can a man give in return for his soul?"

No person can gain the whole world. But what if you could? All the pleasure and wealth and power and fame are *nothing* compared with your soul. The value of the soul far outweighs the value of *everything* in this world for three primary reasons.

First, everything in this world fades and passes away. A person possesses something but for a short time:

- A person may choose money and possessions instead of helping to meet the needs of the world. But money and possessions can be held only for a short time.
- A person may choose position and power instead of giving their life where it would do the most good. But position and power are held only for a short time.
- A person may choose freedom and pleasure instead of home and family. But freedom and pleasure last only for a short time.
- A person may choose the world and comfort instead of God and His church. But the world and comfort do not satisfy, and they last only for a short time.

> **For we brought nothing into the world, and we cannot take anything out of the world. (1 Ti.6:7)**

> **For "All flesh is like grass and all its glory like the flower of grass. The grass withers, and the flower falls." (1 Pe.1:24)**

> **A voice says, "Cry!" And I said, "What shall I cry?" All flesh is grass, and all its beauty is like the flower of the field. (Is.40:6)**

Second, everything in the world cannot be used all at once. Everything sits, is unused most of the time. Most of the time clothes, cars, and other possessions sit unused. Power goes unused, and popularity and fame are not thought of.

Third, the human soul is eternal; it never dies, never ceases to exist. It will live forever, either with or apart from God.

> Whoever believes in the Son has eternal life; whoever does not obey the Son shall not see life, but the wrath of God remains on him. (Jn.3:36)

> Whoever loves his life loses it, and whoever hates his life in this world will keep it for eternal life. (Jn.12:25)

> For the one who sows to his own flesh will from the flesh reap corruption, but the one who sows to the Spirit will from the Spirit reap eternal life. (Ga.6:8)

Therefore, the human soul is of more value than the whole world.

> Do not love the world or the things in the world. If anyone loves the world, the love of the Father is not in him. For all that is in the world—the desires of the flesh and the desires of the eyes and pride of life—is not from the Father but is from the world. And the world is passing away along with its desires, but whoever does the will of God abides forever. (1 Jn.2:15–17)

> Man in his pomp will not remain; he is like the beasts that perish. (Ps.49:12)

8:38

[38] "For whoever is ashamed of me and of my words in this adulterous and sinful generation, of him will the Son of Man also be ashamed when he comes in the glory of his Father with the holy angels."

5 The issue of the Messiah: Being ashamed of Christ vs. confessing Christ.

A true disciple of Christ is not ashamed of Him, not ashamed to confess Him openly (see note—Mt.10:32-33). He or she is neither ashamed of Christ nor *His words*—the gospel and Jesus' teachings.

Many who profess to believe in Christ are actually ashamed of Him. Some fear what others will say. They fear being ridiculed by peers: talked about, questioned, avoided, sneered at, abused, persecuted. Therefore, they deny Christ. They deny Him by their words, by their actions, and by their silence.

The fact is, the world makes it difficult to confess Christ. Why? The world is an *adulterous and sinful* place. And every generation passes down its adulterous and sinful behavior. Few ever want to confess (follow) the true and living God. God's insistence on the denial of self and the giving of all one is and has is too high a price for most people. Most want to keep some control over their lives and much of their wealth for themselves. Most are unwilling to give themselves fully to God (that is, to the gospel) and to the demanding love that *the needs of this desperate world require.*

Jesus reminded us that the day of the Messiah's glory is coming, a day when His glory will be revealed to all. It will be a day of glory and splendor, of triumph and victory, a day when all will see Him as He really is: the true Messiah, the Son of the living God.

The day of judgment—of shame and of being ashamed—is also coming. All who are ashamed of the Messiah in this world will be ashamed of their behavior where it really counts—before God Himself. The person will see Christ standing with God, and Christ will be ashamed of the person and of the selfish life the person has lived. All who professed to know Christ but were not genuinely born again will hear those fateful and terrifying words, "I never knew you: depart from me" (Mt.7:23; see Mt.25:41-46).

> And then will I declare to them, 'I never knew you; depart from me, you workers of lawlessness.' (Mt.7:23)

> But the one who denies me before men will be denied before the angels of God. (Lu.12:9)

> But he will say, 'I tell you, I do not know where you come from. Depart from me, all you workers of evil!' (Lu.13:27)

9:1

And he said to them, "Truly, I say to you, there are some standing here who will not taste death until they see the kingdom of God after it has come with power."

6 The issue of death: Tasting death vs. seeing God's kingdom.

Finally, there is the issue of death, that is, tasting death versus seeing God's kingdom. Jesus concluded this teaching with a word of hope and encouragement to all who choose to take up the cross and follow Him. He said that some who heard His voice that day would live to see the kingdom of God come with power. Scholarly opinion varies as to what Jesus meant by this statement. Obviously, it is not a reference to the Lord's second coming, for all the disciples did die before Jesus' return. A strong possibility is that it refers to the Lord's victory over death and hell which took place on the cross and in the resurrection. Or it may refer to the rule and reign of God's kingdom that takes place within the heart of the believer, to the rule and reign of the Holy Spirit when the Holy Spirit came on the Day of Pentecost to take residence within the believer. It may also be a reference to the gospel's spread throughout the known world and the firm establishment of the church in spite of Satan's fierce, determined efforts to stop it (see notes—Mt.16:28, pt.4; DEEPER STUDY # 3—19:23-24; see Jn.8:52; Heb.2:9).

THOUGHT 1. Spiritually speaking, a person either tastes death or sees God's kingdom with power.

- Most people walk in death.

    So Jesus said to them, "Truly, truly, I say to you, unless you eat the flesh of the Son of Man and drink his blood, you have no life in you." (Jn.6:53)

    For anything that becomes visible is light. Therefore it says, "Awake, O sleeper, and arise from the dead, and Christ will shine on you." (Ep.5:14)

    But she who is self-indulgent is dead even while she lives. (1 Ti.5:6)

    And to the angel of the church in Sardis write: "The words of him who has the seven spirits of God and the seven stars. 'I know your works. You have the reputation of being alive, but you are dead.'" (Re.3:1)

- Some people experience the saving power of God's kingdom (see note, pt.1—Mt.19:23-24).

    It was fitting to celebrate and be glad, for this your brother was dead, and is alive; he was lost, and is found. (Lu.15:32)

    The Jews said to him, "Now we know that you have a demon! Abraham died, as did the prophets, yet you say, 'If anyone keeps my word, he will never taste death.'" (Jn.8:52)

    And you, who were dead in your trespasses and the uncircumcision of your flesh, God made alive together with him, having forgiven us all our trespasses. (Col.2:13)

    But we see him who for a little while was made lower than the angels, namely Jesus, crowned with glory and honor because of the suffering of death, so that by the grace of God he might taste death for everyone. (He.2:9)

D. The Transfiguration:
A Glimpse of Heaven's Glory, 9:2–13

(Mt.17:1–13; Lu.9:28–36)

1. **The setting: Jesus took three disciples all alone up a high mountain**[DS1]
2. **The transfiguration strengthened Jesus**[DS2]

   a. His transfiguration
      1) Jesus' appearance changed
      2) Jesus' clothing began to shine brilliantly
   b. His companions
      1) The great prophet Elijah
      2) The great lawgiver, Moses
3. **The transfiguration strengthened the disciples**
   a. Helped their shattered faith
   b. Gave them a taste of glory
   c. Struck them with awesome fear

   d. Made them witnesses of God's approval[DS3]

4. **The transfiguration gave a unique opportunity to discuss God's Messiahship**
   a. Jesus charged the disciples to tell no one about the experience until after His resurrection

   b. The disciples discussed the resurrection: Why must Elijah come first?

   c. Jesus revealed three facts to the disciples
      1) Elijah was to come first
      2) Scripture did say that the Messiah must suffer and die
      3) Elijah had already come: He was John the Baptist

² And after six days Jesus took with him Peter and James and John, and led them up a high mountain by themselves. And he was transfigured before them,

³ and his clothes became radiant, intensely white, as no one on earth could bleach them.

⁴ And there appeared to them Elijah with Moses, and they were talking with Jesus.

⁵ And Peter said to Jesus, "Rabbi, it is good that we are here. Let us make three tents, one for you and one for Moses and one for Elijah."

⁶ For he did not know what to say, for they were terrified.

⁷ And a cloud overshadowed them, and a voice came out of the cloud, "This is my beloved Son; listen to him."

⁸ And suddenly, looking around, they no longer saw anyone with them but Jesus only.

⁹ And as they were coming down the mountain, he charged them to tell no one what they had seen, until the Son of Man had risen from the dead.

¹⁰ So they kept the matter to themselves, questioning what this rising from the dead might mean.

¹¹ And they asked him, "Why do the scribes say that first Elijah must come?"

¹² And he said to them, "Elijah does come first to restore all things. And how is it written of the Son of Man that he should suffer many things and be treated with contempt?

¹³ But I tell you that Elijah has come, and they did to him whatever they pleased, as it is written of him."

Division V

The Son of God's Closing Ministry: Jesus Teaches the Idea of God's Messiahship, not Man's Messiahship, 8:27–9:50

D. The Transfiguration: A Glimpse of Heaven's Glory, 9:2–13

(Mt.17:1–13; Lu.9:28–36)

9:2–13
Introduction

When Jesus returns to earth, every eye will see Him in all His glory (Re.1:7). But when He came to earth the first time, only three men had the holy privilege of seeing God's Son as He truly is. Jesus selected Peter, James, and John to accompany Him to the mountain where He was transfigured. For a splendid, sacred moment, a measure of the glory that was inside of Jesus—glory that He largely set aside when He became a man—came to the outside.

The purpose of the transfiguration was to reveal heaven's glory. Heaven's glory would strengthen Jesus to bear the cross and strengthen the disciples in believing that Jesus was God's Messiah (see note—Mt.17:1–13; Lu.9:28–36). A close study of the transfiguration will strengthen the faith of any of us in our Lord. And a strengthened faith will enable us to bear the cross of our own calling. This is *The Transfiguration: A Glimpse of Heaven's Glory*, 9:2–13.

1. The setting: Jesus took three disciples all alone up a high mountain (v.2).
2. The transfiguration strengthened Jesus (vv.2–4).
3. The transfiguration strengthened the disciples (vv.5–7).
4. The transfiguration gave a unique opportunity to discuss God's Messiahship (vv.8–13).

(9:2–13) **Another Outline**: The Transfiguration—Some Strange Events.

1. Jesus transfigured (v.3).
2. Elijah and Moses talking with Jesus (v.4).
3. The exhilaration of the experience (vv.5–6).
4. God's voice (v.7).
5. Sudden silence (v.8).
6. A restriction: "Tell no one" (v.9).
7. A statement: Jesus was to arise from the dead (vv.9b–10).
8. A discussion of Messiahship (vv.11–13).

1 The setting: Jesus took three disciples all alone up a high mountain.

9:2

Jesus took only three disciples—Peter, James, and John—to the mountain with Him. Why did He not take the other disciples as well? The answer is not given. It is only speculation to guess (see DEEPER STUDY # 1).

² And after six days Jesus took with him Peter and James and John, and led them up a high mountain by themselves. And he was transfigured before them,

---

DEEPER STUDY # 1

(9:2) **Disciples, Inner Circle:** Peter, James, and John apparently formed an inner circle around Jesus. Jesus revealed more to these three men than to the other disciples. They were with Him when He raised Jairus' daughter, when He was in the Garden of Gethsemane, and here on the mount of transfiguration. Why were these three chosen to receive these additional revelations?

We do not know the full answer. What we do know is, each was being chosen for a very special ministry role or call. They were not aware of it yet, but they were to fill unique positions in the ministry of the early church.

1. Peter was to be the leader of the early church, the one who was to open the door of the gospel to both Jew and Gentile after Pentecost (Ac.2:1f; 10:1f).

2. James was called to be an apostle and to be martyred for his faith in Christ (Ac.12:2).

3. John was to receive *The Revelation* from God to close out the Scripture.

9:2-4

² And after six days Jesus took with him Peter and James and John, and led them up a high mountain by themselves. And he was transfigured before them,
³ and his clothes became radiant, intensely white, as no one on earth could bleach them.
⁴ And there appeared to them Elijah with Moses, and they were talking with Jesus.

2 The transfiguration strengthened Jesus.

As Jesus' appointment with the cross drew near, our blessed Savior needed to be strengthened. He was about to face the full weight of all that was involved in dying for the sins of the world. The pressure of bearing God's judgment for *all* the sins of the world was beginning to press in upon Him. He needed additional strength, encouragement, and assurance from God the Father in a very special way. Therefore, the Father gave Jesus two very special experiences.

a. **His transfiguration (vv.2-3).**

When Jesus, Peter, James, and John reached the top of the tall mountain, the Lord was *transfigured* (Gk. metamorphothe; pronounced *me-ta-mor-foe'-thay*; see DEEPER STUDY # 2). It is easy to see that the English word "metamorphosis" comes from this Greek word. This is the word used of the transformation of the lowly caterpillar to a glorious butterfly. Think of a butterfly bursting out of its silken shell, and that will give you a mere glimpse of the radiant glory of Jesus bursting through His shell of human flesh and bones.

Jesus' appearance changed right before the dazzled disciples' eyes (v.3). Luke reports that even our Lord's face looked different (Lu.9:29). His clothing shone brilliantly as His glory glowed through it. His garment was a shade of pure white beyond anything man could produce.

b. **His companions (v.4).**

Two saints from heaven visited Jesus during this occasion: Moses, the great lawgiver, and Elijah, the great prophet. Why did Moses and Elijah appear with Jesus? There seem to be two reasons.

First, to discuss Jesus' death (Lu.17:31). Jesus needed to be strengthened to bear the weight and pressure of the cross. This indescribably heavy burden is seen in the Garden of Gethsemane experience and in His cry on the cross (see note—Mt.27:46-49; Lu.22:39-46).

Second, the presence of Moses and Elijah affirm that Jesus is the true Messiah, the Son of God, the One who is superior to the law and the prophets. Moses represented the law; and Elijah, who was considered the greatest of the prophets, represented the prophets. These two men were honoring and ministering to Jesus. They were symbolizing that the law and the prophets found their fulfillment in Jesus. Jesus is the One of whom the law and the prophets spoke; He is the One to whom the law and the prophets pointed. The old covenant was now to be fulfilled and superseded by Jesus who was to usher in the new covenant (see Mt.9:16-17; see also outline and notes—2 Co.3:6-18; He.9:15-22).

DEEPER STUDY # 2

(9:2-3) **Transfigured** (metamorphoo): a change into another form; a transformation; a change of countenance; a complete change. Note how the Gospel writers describe what happened.

> And he was transfigured before them, and his face shone like the sun, and his clothes became white as light. (Mt.17:2)

> And his clothes became radiant, intensely white, as no one on earth could bleach them. (Mk.9:3)

> And as he was praying, the appearance of his face was altered, and his clothing became dazzling white. (Lu.9:29)

Apparently, *the glory* of Christ's Godly nature was allowed to shine through His body. "The glory which [He] had with the Father before the world existed" emanated through His body right through His clothes (Jn.17:5). Peter says, "We were eyewitnesses of His majesty" (2 Pe.1:16). In John's vision of Jesus in *The Revelation*, he compares the glory of Christ to the sun shining at full strength (Re.1:16). The Scripture says:

> Who alone has immortality, who dwells in unapproachable light, whom no one has ever seen or can see. To him be honor and eternal dominion. Amen. (1 Ti.6:16)

> This is the message we have heard from him and proclaim to you, that God is light, and in him is no darkness at all. (1 Jn.1:5)

> Covering yourself with light as with a garment, stretching out the heavens like a tent. (Ps.104:2)

Two things need to be noted.

1. *Radiant, shining,* or *dazzling* (stilbonta) is a Greek participle, which means the shining is active. The transfiguration was a real, active experience. It was no illusion, no dream; it was not of the imagination. It was not a reflection of the sun's shining off some rock, glass, or lake. The "shining" was the glory of the Lord's inner nature, of His Godly nature actively shining right through His being.

2. The *full* glory of the Godhead was not shining through Jesus. No person could ever stand in the full glory of the Lord's presence, not in our present physical bodies. As Scripture says, the Lord Jesus dwells in unapproachable light (1 Ti.6:14–16). Apparently, God allowed only a small degree of Christ's glory, only what the three disciples could bear, to shine through the body and clothing of Jesus.

The transfiguration is, of course, a mystery to us. But we should remember that it is a mystery cloaked in the fullness of the Godhead. And God's glory is so brilliant, there is no need for a sun (Re.21:23; 22:5). The glory of the Supreme Being who stands behind the universe in His unlimited presence and power is bound to be beyond description and thought (see Ep.3:20).

3 The transfiguration strengthened the disciples.

Imagine the range of strong emotions that overwhelmed Peter, James, and John when they suddenly saw Jesus standing in His glory with Moses and Elijah! This wondrous experience strengthened the three leaders of the disciples for the dark, difficult day that was rapidly approaching.

[5] And Peter said to Jesus, "Rabbi, it is good that we are here. Let us make three tents, one for you and one for Moses and one for Elijah."

[6] For he did not know what to say, for they were terrified.

[7] And a cloud overshadowed them, and a voice came out of the cloud, "This is my beloved Son; listen to him."

a. Helped their shattered faith (v.5a).

The transfiguration strengthened the disciples' shattered faith. The disciples were crushed because Jesus had recently told them that He was going to Jerusalem to die (Mk.8:31). All of their expectations concerning the Messiah had been demolished. However, the transfiguration made them eyewitnesses to the brilliant splendor and radiance of the Messiah's glory and to God's voice of approval. They also saw that the law and the prophets, as represented in Moses and Elijah, found their fulfillment in Him. Therefore, their spirits were bolstered in the firm conviction that Jesus was indeed God's Messiah.

b. Gave them a taste of glory (v.5b).

The transfiguration gave the disciples a taste of glory. Three privileged disciples were tasting some of heaven's joy, peace, security, fulfillment, and perfection. They did not want to leave this hallowed ground.

Hoping to extend the stay of the heavenly guests and the glorious experience, Peter offered to build three tents (tabernacles, shelters) for Jesus and the two prophets. The *tents* (skenas) which Peter offered to build were booths made of branches and grass which could be quickly constructed, the kind often set up by travelers on their stops along the road night by night.

Concerning building these tents, Matthew adds that Peter said, "If you wish" (Mt.17:4). Peter, even in a moment as glorious as this, would not act against his Lord's will. Seeing the glory of Jesus brought Peter to a place of full submission to His Lordship.

c. Struck them with awesome fear (v.6).

The transfiguration struck the disciples with awe-inspiring fear (v.6). The disciples' experience can be applied to the future, to the appearance of believers before God in the great Day of Redemption, the day when our bodies are at last redeemed and we stand in the presence of the Lord (Ep.4:30). In fact, that is just what happened to Peter, James, and John. They found themselves in God's presence. Our experience in the Day of Redemption will undoubtedly be very much like what they experienced.

➢   We will experience the Shekinah glory, see its full manifestation upon Christ.
➢   We will hear the voice of God proclaiming Christ to be His Son, expressing perfect approval of His redemptive work, and rejoicing that He has been heard and is to be heard throughout all eternity.
➢   We will fall upon our faces, prostrate before Christ in awe and adoration and worship.
➢   We will experience the Lord's intercessory work. We will feel the Lord's hand reaching out to touch us and to lift us up. And we will stand in the Lord's righteousness and perfection, living in a state of glory forever.
➢   We will witness and experience the Lord's preeminence throughout all eternity.

d. Made them witnesses of God's approval (v.7).

The disciples witnessed God's approval of Christ. A cloud moved over them, and the very voice of God thundered out of the cloud, declaring that Jesus is His Son (see Deeper Study # 3; note—Mt.17:8).

THOUGHT 1. We must often get alone with Christ in order to have our strength renewed.

So we do not lose heart. Though our outer self is wasting away, our inner self is being renewed day by day. (2 Co.4:16)

But they who wait for the LORD shall renew their strength; they shall mount up with wings like eagles; they shall run and not be weary; they shall walk and not faint. (Is.40:31)

Listen to me in silence, O coastlands; let the peoples renew their strength; let them approach, then let them speak; let us together draw near for judgment. (Is.41:1)

Fear not, for I am with you; be not dismayed, for I am your God; I will strengthen you, I will help you, I will uphold you with my righteous right hand. (Is.41:10)

DEEPER STUDY # 3

(9:7) **Cloud:** the cloud enveloped both Jesus and the three disciples. The cloud and the voice of God terrified the disciples and caused them to fall immediately on their faces, prostrate and unable to look up (Mt.17:6). As mortal men they were paralyzed in fear. Note three facts.

1. The cloud was "a bright cloud" (Mt.17:5). This was the Shekinah glory, the cloud that symbolized God's presence. It was the cloud that guided Israel out of Egypt and that rested upon the tabernacle (Ex.40:34–38) and above the Mercy Seat in the Most Holy Place. God

dwells in unapproachable light upon which no man can look (1 Ti.6:16). Peter later called it the "majestic" or "excellent glory" (2 Pe.1:17).

2. The "bright cloud" overshadowing Jesus is in contrast to the dark and threatening cloud that overshadowed the giving of the old covenant to Moses, that is, the law (Ex.19:18; 20:21). There is a point to be made here. The law (Old Covenant) was dark and threatening (see DEEPER STUDY # 2—Ga.3:10); the New Covenant (the love and grace of Christ) is bright and is given to save and bless, not to threaten and condemn (He.12:18-24; see also He.8:6-13).

3. In the Greek text, the voice speaking literally says, "This is My Son, the Beloved One." Note the two facts stressed. Jesus is God's Son, and He is the Beloved One. The idea is that Jesus is the "only begotten Son" who was to be given for the world (Jn.3:16).

4 The transfiguration gave a unique opportunity to discuss God's Messiahship.

The transfiguration provided a unique opportunity for the three disciples to discuss God's Messiahship. They talked about what they had seen and what Jesus had told them was coming—His death and resurrection.

a. **Jesus charged the disciples to tell no one about the experience until after His resurrection (vv.9–10a).**

As the disciples and Jesus journeyed back down the mountain, Jesus instructed the three to remain silent about the transfiguration until after He had "risen from the dead" (v.9). Imagine what a difficult instruction this would be to follow. Imagine seeing what they had seen and not being able to tell anybody about it. Yet, they kept the matter to themselves (v.10a). How could they dare not obey Jesus after seeing His glory and hearing the voice of the Father announce that Jesus is His Son?

8 And suddenly, looking around, they no longer saw anyone with them but Jesus only.

9 And as they were coming down the mountain, he charged them to tell no one what they had seen, until the Son of Man had risen from the dead.

10 So they kept the matter to themselves, questioning what this rising from the dead might mean.

11 And they asked him, "Why do the scribes say that first Elijah must come?"

12 And he said to them, "Elijah does come first to restore all things. And how is it written of the Son of Man that he should suffer many things and be treated with contempt?

13 But I tell you that Elijah has come, and they did to him whatever they pleased, as it is written of him."

b. **The disciples discussed the resurrection: Why must Elijah come first (vv.10b–11)?**

The disciples did not understand what Jesus was saying about rising from the dead. They had just witnessed His glory and seen Moses and Elijah with Him. They thought that the appearance of Elijah meant that He was going to set up His kingdom *now* and that He would reign in glory from this point forward. The Scribes said that Elijah had to come before the Messiah would set up His kingdom. Why, then, did Elijah leave? The disciples asked Jesus what all these things meant.

c. **Jesus revealed three facts to the disciples (vv.12–13).**

Christ answered the disciples and corrected the view that the Scribes had always taught. Jesus explained what the Scripture actually teaches about the subject.

First, Scripture does teach that Elijah must come first and restore or prepare all things (v.12a).

Second, Scripture also teaches that the Messiah must die. And it is this fact that they were overlooking (v.12b; Jn.10:11, 15, 17–18).

Third, Elijah had already come. The prophecy was fulfilled in John the Baptist (v.13; Lu.1:16–17).

THOUGHT 1. Jesus Christ is the Messiah, the Son of God. Belief in Him is absolutely essential.

The woman said to him, "I know that Messiah is coming (he who is called Christ). When he comes, he will tell us all things." Jesus said to her, "I who speak to you am he." (Jn.4:25–26)

And we have believed, and have come to know, that you are the Holy One of God. (Jn.6:69; see Jn.11:25–27)

I told you that you would die in your sins, for unless you believe that I am he you will die in your sins. (Jn.8:24)

But Saul increased all the more in strength, and confounded the Jews who lived in Damascus by proving that Jesus was the Christ. (Ac.9:22; see Ac.17:2–3)

Everyone who believes that Jesus is the Christ has been born of God, and everyone who loves the Father loves whoever has been born of him. (1 Jn.5:1)

(Mt.17:14–21; Lu.9:37–42)

14 And when they came to the disciples, they saw a great crowd around them, and scribes arguing with them.

15 And immediately all the crowd, when they saw him, were greatly amazed and ran up to him and greeted him.

16 And he asked them, "What are you arguing about with them?"

17 And someone from the crowd answered him, "Teacher, I brought my son to you, for he has a spirit that makes him mute.

18 And whenever it seizes him, it throws him down, and he foams and grinds his teeth and becomes rigid. So I asked your disciples to cast it out, and they were not able."

19 And he answered them, "O faithless generation, how long am I to be with you? How long am I to bear with you? Bring him to me."

20 And they brought the boy to him. And when the spirit saw him, immediately it convulsed the boy, and he fell on the ground and rolled about, foaming at the mouth.

21 And Jesus asked his father, "How long has this been happening to him?" And he said, "From childhood.

22 And it has often cast him into fire and into water, to destroy him. But if you can do anything, have compassion on us and help us."

23 And Jesus said to him, "'If you can'! All things are possible for one who believes."

24 Immediately the father of the child cried out and said, "I believe; help my unbelief!"

25 And when Jesus saw that a crowd came running together, he rebuked the unclean spirit, saying to it, "You mute and deaf spirit, I command you, come out of him and never enter him again."

1. **Spiritual immaturity belittles and shames**
   a. The crowd gathered
   b. The teachers of the law argued with the disciples
   c. The crowd rushed up to Jesus—overwhelmed with wonder[DS1]

   d. Jesus drew attention away from the humiliated disciples
   e. The cause of the embarrassment
      1) The desperate need of a sick child[DS2]

      2) The weak faith of a concerned father, v. 23
      3) The powerless ministry of the disciples[DS3]

2. **Spiritual immaturity grieves the Lord**
   a. The faithlessness of people

   b. The pitiful condition of a person's need

   c. The desperate plight of loved ones

3. **Spiritual immaturity must be acknowledged to receive God's blessings**
   a. Acknowledged by faith
   b. Acknowledged by humility and by crying for help
   c. Result: Spiritual blessings are secured by Jesus' word and power

4. Spiritual immaturity can be conquered: Spiritual power is available

    a. By seeking the Lord
    b. By prayer and fasting[DS4, 5]

²⁶ And after crying out and convulsing him terribly, it came out, and the boy was like a corpse, so that most of them said, "He is dead."

²⁷ But Jesus took him by the hand and lifted him up, and he arose.

²⁸ And when he had entered the house, his disciples asked him privately, "Why could we not cast it out?"

²⁹ And he said to them, "This kind cannot be driven out by anything but prayer."

Division V

The Son of God's Closing Ministry: Jesus Teaches the Idea of God's Messiahship, not Man's Messiahship, 8:27–9:50

E. The Problem of Spiritual Immaturity and Powerlessness, 9:14–29

(Mt.17:14–21; Lu.9:37–42)

9:14–29
Introduction

Satan is extremely powerful, far more powerful than we are. Many people never seem able to overcome his hold on their lives, not completely. They face temptations they cannot resist. They remain a captive to the particular sins that so easily ensnare them (He.12:1). They cannot tear down some stronghold the enemy has established in their lives (2 Co.10:4). They never are able to appropriate God's power to give them victory over Satan and his spiritual forces, nor to give them victory over their flesh.

Similarly, many minister without God's power. As sincere as they may be in serving God, preaching or teaching His Word, and trying to help others, nothing happens.

Others are powerless in prayer. They pray, asking God for specific things, for help for themselves and others, yet it seems their prayers are in vain.

This passage presents examples of all the above: a boy, possibly a young man, who was a slave to evil; the disciples, whose ministry was powerless; a father whose prayers and seeking of help for his son had all proved futile. And, this passage identifies the problem and presents the solution. This is, *The Problem of Spiritual Immaturity and Powerlessness, 9:14–29.*

1. Spiritual immaturity belittles and shames (vv.14–18).
2. Spiritual immaturity grieves the Lord (vv.19–22).
3. Spiritual immaturity must be acknowledged to receive God's blessings (vv.23–27).
4. Spiritual immaturity can be conquered: Spiritual power is available (vv.28–29).

1 Spiritual immaturity belittles and shames.

The event described in this passage is an embarrassing one for those involved. At the root of the embarrassment is spiritual immaturity. As the details reveal, spiritual immaturity belittles and shames.

a. The crowd gathered (v.14a).

After descending from the mountain where Jesus was transfigured, Jesus, Peter, James, and John reunited with the rest of the disciples. Something out of the ordinary was going on, for a large crowd was gathered around them.

b. The teachers of the law argued with the disciples (v.14b).

As Jesus and the three drew closer, they found the Scribes arguing with the disciples. Most likely, the Scribes were questioning and belittling their credentials to minister. The Scribes' and Pharisees' method was to ridicule and shame anybody who challenged their traditions, opinions, or authority. By discrediting and humiliating the disciples, they hoped to discredit Jesus in the eyes of the people (see notes—Mt.12:1-8; note and DEEPER STUDY # 1—12:10).

> ¹⁴ And when they came to the disciples, they saw a great crowd around them, and scribes arguing with them.
> ¹⁵ And immediately all the crowd, when they saw him, were greatly amazed and ran up to him and greeted him.
> ¹⁶ And he asked them, "What are you arguing about with them?"
> ¹⁷ And someone from the crowd answered him, "Teacher, I brought my son to you, for he has a spirit that makes him mute.
> ¹⁸ And whenever it seizes him, it throws him down, and he foams and grinds his teeth and becomes rigid. So I asked your disciples to cast it out, and they were not able."

c. The crowd rushed up to Jesus—overwhelmed with wonder (v.15).

When the crowd saw Jesus approaching, their attention shifted immediately from the disturbance created by the Scribes to the Lord. They were "greatly amazed" and ran to meet Him (see DEEPER STUDY # 1).

d. Jesus drew attention away from the humiliated disciples (v.16).

When Jesus reached the Scribes and the disciples, He asked the Scribes what they were questioning. Note how Jesus had stepped into the scene. He drew attention away from the disciples' humiliation. He delivered them from the embarrassment being cast upon them.

e. The cause of the embarrassment (vv.17–18).

Before the Scribes could answer Jesus, someone else spoke up (v.17a). It was the desperate father of a needy son. He willingly stepped forward and assumed responsibility for the incident.

The entire scene was embarrassing, not only for the disciples, but also for the father and his helpless son. First, the son's affliction caused embarrassment (v.17; see DEEPER STUDY # 2). He was possessed by an unclean spirit; consequently, he was isolated from and rejected by society. Because of society's reaction, families were embarrassed whenever a loved one was afflicted by a demon. Just imagine this scene. The son and father were right in the midst of a shameful experience. Questioning and ridicule had become the norm. Imagine their embarrassment in being the focus of this crowd's attention. Most likely, they had gone quietly to the disciples for help and ended up being a public spectacle.

The father's weak faith brought additional embarrassment (vv.18). The disciples were unable to heal the boy because of weak faith—both theirs and the father's. Jesus confronted the father's faithlessness, and the desperate dad confessed it and asked for Jesus' help (vv.23-24). His skepticism is understandable. His son had been afflicted since he was a little boy, and nobody had been able to help. On this occasion, he brought his tormented son to Jesus' disciples for help but, in his heart, he expected nothing to change.

The powerless disciples heaped embarrassment on top of embarrassment (v.18). The very persons who should have been able to help were the disciples. Nine disciples were there when the man first came for help, yet not a single one of them was able to help. They all lacked the power to overcome the demon that possessed the boy (DEEPER STUDY # 3).

THOUGHT 1. *A lack of power* affects the testimony of believers (see DEEPER STUDY # 3).

THOUGHT 2. Remember this critical fact: the world uses the lives of believers to judge not only their testimonies but also Christ Himself. The world tries to discredit Christ because of the powerlessness of believers.

THOUGHT 3. Note the three causes of embarrassment in this passage: a weak faith, a powerless ministry, and the son's affliction. An illness (whether due to natural causes or brought on by immorality, drunkenness, or some other sinful behavior that destroys or brings injury to the body) can be a source of embarrassment. Those suffering from illnesses should never be made to feel embarrassed. Instead, they should be loved, prayed for, and encouraged.

We need to also remember that there is no excuse for a believer's living a sinful life, a life so sinful that one's faith becomes weak, ministry becomes powerless, or one's body contracts a disease as the result of sin.

> And he did not do many mighty works there, because of their unbelief. (Mt.13:58)

> Jesus immediately reached out his hand and took hold of him, saying to him, "O you of little faith, why did you doubt?" (Mt.14:31)

> He said to them, "Why are you so afraid? Have you still no faith?" (Mk.4:40)

> I know, O LORD, that the way of man is not in himself, that it is not in man who walks to direct his steps. (Je.10:23)

DEEPER STUDY # 1

(9:15) **Greatly Amazed** (Gk. exethambethe; pronounced *ex-e-tham-bay'-thay*): to be filled with wonder. What amazed the people when they saw Jesus?

1. Perhaps Jesus retained some of the glory of the transfiguration (see Ex.34:29 when Moses came down from the mountain after having been with God). The people may have seen a glow, a majestic countenance, about Jesus.

2. Perhaps Jesus came at such an opportune time that the people were amazed to see Him, as though His timing was destined. He arrived just when His disciples needed help.

3. Perhaps Jesus walked with a renewed demeanor, a more authoritative and decisive countenance than before. Just coming from the transfiguration was bound to instill a renewed confidence and authority within Him.

4. Perhaps the people had witnessed or heard about Jesus' miracles and held Him in awe.

DEEPER STUDY # 2

(9:17-18) **Evil Spirits:** whether the son's illness was caused by the evil spirit or whether he was both afflicted with a disease and with a demon is unclear. The description of his condition in Mark sounds similar to what is known today as epilepsy (Mt.17:15; Mk.9:17-18; Lu.9:39). If so, the demon possession in particular seems to have heightened and aggravated the condition, perhaps causing some suicidal tendencies (Mt.17:15; Mk.9:22). Throughout the Gospels this seems to be one of the major works of evil spirits: to *heighten and aggravate* existing conditions.

On the other hand, the father's description of his son's condition indicates that, at least from his perspective, the son's seizures were the direct result of demonic power (v.18). The text states clearly that the seizure suffered by the boy at the scene was caused directly by the demon (vv.20, 26).

Luke's account states that Jesus "rebuked the unclean spirit and healed the boy" (Lu.9:42). Whether this speaks of one act described in two ways—healing the boy by rebuking the evil spirit—or of two separate acts—rebuking the evil spirit *and* healing the boy of the disease—is unclear. Matthew's account seems to say that the boy was healed *when* Jesus cast out the demon (Mt.17:18). Mark mentions only that Jesus cast out the unclean spirit (Mk.9:25).

Whatever the case, the tormented boy was completely restored by the power of our loving, merciful Lord.

Note the description of the three Gospels. Luke's description is especially interesting because it is the description of a physician.

Mark 9:17-18	Luke 9:39	Mt.17:15
A spirit that makes him mute	A spirit (evil)	A demon (v.18)
It seizes Him	Seizes him	Epilectic
It throws him down	Cries out	Suffers terribly (severely)
He foams	Convulses him	Falls into the fire
He grinds (gnashes) his teeth	Foams	Falls into the water
He becomes rigid	Shatters (bruises, mauls) him	

DEEPER STUDY # 3

(9:18) **Power, Lack of:** Why do the servants of God fail? Why do they often lack power? Why does their faith weaken? This experience of the disciples reveals much about spiritual failure and lack of power.

1. A sense that Christ is far away and out of reach makes one ineffective. The indwelling presence and power of Christ are just not felt—not to the extent that they need to be available. In the above situation Christ was absent, but His power was still available. The disciples were just not all that aware of His power.

2. The lack of leadership causes the faith and loyalty of some to weaken. The nine disciples apparently had no leader to stand forth as a champion of faith and power.

3. Uncompromising unbelief can weaken one's trust (v.16). This was true of the Scribes' unbelief and questioning. They distracted and sapped the disciples' faith and power.

4. An atmosphere of questioning and unbelief often affects the faith and power of a person's life. A terrible atmosphere of unbelief and distrust in God was created by everyone present: the man's questionable belief (v.22), the Scribes' questioning (v.16), the disciples' lack of faith and power, and the people's disturbance over the whole affair.

What happens when the servants of God have *no power*? What are the results of a powerless life and ministry?

➤ No power causes embarrassment and shame.
➤ No power causes the world to question and ridicule and belittle.
➤ No power questions the deity (validity) of Christ and God.
➤ No power causes the questioning of God and His ability to deliver.

Christ provides the solution to no power. Power comes (1) through seeking and (2) through prayer and fasting (vv.28-29).

2 Spiritual immaturity grieves the Lord.

The Lord was grieved by the situation around Him. A young boy was tormented by a demon, and nobody was spiritually mature enough to help him. Jesus confronted the problem, calling those standing before Him a "faithless (unbelieving) generation."

9:19–22

¹⁹ And he answered them, "O faithless generation, how long am I to be with you? How long am I to bear with you? Bring him to me."
²⁰ And they brought the boy to him. And when the spirit saw him, immediately it convulsed the boy, and he fell on the ground and rolled about, foaming at the mouth.
²¹ And Jesus asked his father, "How long has this been happening to him?" And he said, "From childhood.
²² And it has often cast him into fire and into water, to destroy him. But if you can do anything, have compassion on us and help us."

a. The faithlessness of people (v.19).
Christ rebuked the generation standing before Him, especially the powerless disciples; but in all honesty, the Lord was rebuking every generation, for every generation has proven to be faithless. Having no faith saddened and brought sorrow to the Lord's heart. He expressed His sorrow through two rhetorical questions: "How long will I be with you? How long will I bear with you?"

Who is being rebuked? Who is faithless? To whom is Christ speaking? The answer is clearly seen. There was not a single person present who helped the desperate child: not the father, not the crowd, not the disciples, and not even the questioning religionists.

➢ The father was unbelieving.
➢ The crowd was unspiritual and worldly.
➢ The disciples were ineffective and powerless.
➢ The religionists were self-centered and critical.

> And he looked around at them with anger, grieved at their hardness of heart, and said to the man, "Stretch out your hand." He stretched it out, and his hand was restored. (Mk.3:5)

> Therefore I was provoked with that generation, and said, 'They always go astray in their heart; they have not known my ways.' (He.3:10)

> For forty years I loathed that generation and said, "They are a people who go astray in their heart, and they have not known my ways." (Ps.95:10)

b. The pitiful condition of a person's need (v.20).
The son was helpless, under the power of an evil spirit that caused him to have violent convulsions (see notes—Mk.1:23-24; 5:6-7). This spirit had tried repeatedly to destroy the boy, driving him to attempt to take his own life (v.22). The sight of the boy in such a pitiful condition touched and grieved the heart of Christ.

c. The desperate plight of loved ones (vv.21–22).
Jesus also grieved because of the father's grief. Jesus cared for the father just as much as He cared for the son. The father was hurting in his heart. It was his love for the son that drove him to seek Jesus in the first place. Jesus knew this, and Jesus knew something else. The father's faith was weak and needed strengthening, so Jesus asked the father about the history of the boy's illness (v.21). But note: Jesus was not interested so much in the boy's case history as He was in getting the father . . .

• to focus on his desperate need
• to focus on Jesus who stood before him
• to focus on Jesus who alone could meet his need
• to focus on Jesus so much that his faith would be stirred

Jesus' purpose was accomplished: the man's attention was focused on the Lord and on his son's case history. The man said two significant things to Jesus (v.22):
• "If you can do anything . . . help us."
• "Have compassion on us, and help us."

The man lacked personal knowledge and faith in Jesus' power, but He cried for the compassion of Jesus—in the off-chance Jesus really did have the power to help. There was no way Jesus would turn away from the man's cry for mercy (see Lu.18:13).

THOUGHT 1. Jesus sees and has mercy on brokenhearted souls. In spite of the man's lack of faith, Jesus still had compassion on him. How comforting and assuring it is that He still cares about us even when our faith is weak!

> The LORD is near to the brokenhearted and saves the crushed in spirit. (Ps.34:18)

> Because he holds fast to me in love, I will deliver him; I will protect him, because he knows my name. When he calls to me, I will answer him; I will be with him in trouble; I will rescue him and honor him. (Ps.91:14–15)

THOUGHT 2. The same three things that grieved Christ should grieve the heart of every believer. We should be grieved to the point that we act and minister just as Christ did.

3 Spiritual immaturity must be acknowledged to receive God's blessings.

9:23–27

The father revealed his spiritual immaturity—his weak faith—by questioning whether Jesus could help his demon-possessed son. He had to acknowledge his spiritual weakness before he would receive the blessing of the Lord's help.

a. Acknowledged by faith (vv.23–24a).

Spiritual immaturity must be acknowledged by *faith*. The father's faith was immature. Jesus threw the father's words—"if You can"—back to him. The Lord was saying, "The question is not, 'If *I* can,' but 'If *you* can—if you can believe.' All things are possible for the person who believes."

Jesus was teaching the desperate father the vital principle of prayer and faith. All things are possible to the Son of God. God's power is available, but we must trust in God's power. We must have unwavering faith in God.

> And whatever you ask in prayer, you will receive, if you have faith. (Mt.21:22; see note—Mk.11:22–23)

> And without faith it is impossible to please him, for whoever would draw near to God must believe that he exists and that he rewards those who seek him. (He.11:6)

> But let him ask in faith, with no doubting, for the one who doubts is like a wave of the sea that is driven and tossed by the wind. For that person must not suppose that he will receive anything from the Lord; he is a double-minded man, unstable in all his ways. (Js.1:6–8)

b. Acknowledged by humility and by crying for help (v.24b).

The man acknowledged his spiritual immaturity by *humbling himself and crying for help*. The man was weak, but his need was desperate. He *accepted* the Lord's Word . . .

- about his being weak (sinful) and needing help personally
- about his lack of faith being the problem

The man responded in humility and cried out, most likely with tears, "Lord I believe; help my unbelief." Note that he cried out for Jesus to help him *even* in his faith. He needed help even in his believing; but he did one thing right—he cried out with all his heart and being, *confessing* that he needed help.

> For we do not have a high priest who is unable to sympathize with our weaknesses, but one who in every respect has been tempted as we are, yet without sin. Let us then with confidence draw near to the throne of grace, that we may receive mercy and find grace to help in time of need. (He.4:15–16)

> Likewise, you who are younger, be subject to the elders. Clothe yourselves, all of you, with humility toward one another, for "God opposes the proud but gives grace to the humble." (1 Pe.5:5)

23 And Jesus said to him, "'If you can'! All things are possible for one who believes."
24 Immediately the father of the child cried out and said, "I believe; help my unbelief!"
25 And when Jesus saw that a crowd came running together, he rebuked the unclean spirit, saying to it, "You mute and deaf spirit, I command you, come out of him and never enter him again."
26 And after crying out and convulsing him terribly, it came out, and the boy was like a corpse, so that most of them said, "He is dead."
27 But Jesus took him by the hand and lifted him up, and he arose.

As a father shows compassion to his children, so the Lord shows compassion to those who fear him. (Ps.103:13)

For thus says the One who is high and lifted up, who inhabits eternity, whose name is Holy: "I dwell in the high and holy place, and also with him who is of a contrite and lowly spirit, to revive the spirit of the lowly, and to revive the heart of the contrite." (Is.57:15)

c. Result: Spiritual blessings are secured by Jesus' Word and power (vv.25–27).

When the desperate father confessed his need and cried out to Jesus for help, the Lord graciously restored his tortured boy. When Jesus saw the crowd running toward them, he rebuked the demon and healed the boy (v.25). This detail reveals that Jesus had apparently pulled the father and boy to the side to help the father's concentration and to shield them from further embarrassment (see note, pt.1—Lu.9:14-18).

Jesus healed the boy by the power of His Word. It was His Word that broke the devil's authority and hold over the boy. *Rebuked* (epetimesen) is a strong word, authoritative, even severe. Satan cannot stand before God's Word. Christ has disarmed the rulers and authorities (principalities and powers) of evil (Col.2:15).

The evil spirit made one last effort to disrupt and discredit the power of Christ (v.26). The evil spirit (as so often happens) apparently attempted to kill the boy, causing him to have the most severe seizure yet. The onlookers thought the boy was dead. Jesus took the boy by the hand and lifted him up, and the boy arose, being healed.

Some scholars think the boy *was* dead; that the demon, in its final attempt, succeeded in destroying him. Whether the boy actually died, Mark's description suggests the idea of resurrection. The second and third verbs in v.27 ["lifted" and "arose"] are often used in connection with resurrection. The account has much in common with the raising of Jairus's daughter (5:41-42).[1]

9:28-29

28 And when he had entered the house, his disciples asked him privately, "Why could we not cast it out?"

29 And he said to them, "This kind cannot be driven out by anything but prayer."

4 Spiritual immaturity can be conquered: Spiritual power is available.

Later, after the crowd had dispersed and the disciples were alone with Jesus, the disciples asked why they could not cast out the evil spirit that possessed the boy. In response, the Lord taught them the secrets to conquering spiritual immaturity and receiving God's power.

a. By seeking the Lord (v.29; 17–18).

Immaturity can be conquered by *seeking spiritual power*. The disciples sought to know why they failed. They wanted to know the cause. Remember: Jesus had already given them power over evil spirits, and they had already exercised such power. They could not understand why they had failed when they had been successful before (Mk.3:14-15; see Lu.9:1; 10:17). They sought the Lord and His help.

b. By prayer and fasting (v.29).

Immaturity can be conquered by *prayer and fasting* (see Deeper Studies 4, 5). Jesus pointed to one thing: the disciples were not living close enough to God. They were not praying and fasting enough, not seeking Him enough, not putting Him before food and other things. They were taking time for other things, but not taking time for God. Spiritual maturity—a faith strong enough to overcome the power of Satan—comes only through prayer and fasting.

---

1 James A. Brooks. *The New American Commentary: An Exegetical and Theological Exposition of Holy Scripture (Mark),* (Nashville: Holman Reference, 1991). Via Wordsearch digital edition.

THOUGHT 1. We need to depend on God so much that, when necessary, we are willing to set aside food and everything else in order to seek Him. Our hearts must sometimes crave God and His power so desperately that we put seeking Him above eating and everything else in our lives.

> And I tell you, ask, and it will be given to you; seek, and you will find; knock, and it will be opened to you. (Lu.11:9)
>
> If you ask me anything in my name, I will do it. (Jn.14:14)
>
> But from there you will seek the LORD your God and you will find him, if you search after him with all your heart and with all your soul. (De.4:29)
>
> I love those who love me, and those who seek me diligently find me. (Pr.8:17)
>
> You will seek me and find me, when you seek me with all your heart. (Je.29:13)

DEEPER STUDY # 4

(9:29) **Prayer:** see note—Mt.7:7-11; see Ep.6:18.

DEEPER STUDY # 5

(9:29) **Fasting:** see note—Mt.6:16-18.

F. The Second Prediction of Death:
Intensive Training on the Death of Christ, 9:30–32

(Mt.17:22–23; Lu.9:43–45)

1. The preparation: Jesus got alone with His disciples

2. The lesson: Jesus taught His disciples that He was to die and then arise[DS1, 2]

3. The response: The disciples could not accept a literal interpretation of the facts, rejecting what they did not wish to see

30 They went on from there and passed through Galilee. And he did not want anyone to know,
31 for he was teaching his disciples, saying to them, "The Son of Man is going to be delivered into the hands of men, and they will kill him. And when he is killed, after three days he will rise."
32 But they did not understand the saying, and were afraid to ask him.

Division V

The Son of God's Closing Ministry: Jesus Teaches the Idea of God's Messiahship, not Man's Messiahship, 8:27–9:50

F. The Second Prediction of Death: Intensive Training on the Death of Christ, 9:30–32

(Mt.17:22–23; Lu.9:43–45)

9:30–32
Introduction

This passage presents a turning point in the life and ministry of Jesus. He redirected His focus from ministering to the crowds to teaching His disciples. The thrust of this passage is Christ's death and resurrection (see outline and notes—Mk.8:31-33; 10:32-34; Mt.16:21-23; 17:22-23; 20:17-19). Because of its enormous importance, Jesus drilled the truth of His death and resurrection into His disciples. It was critical that they understand His approaching death and resurrection. Likewise, it is absolutely essential that every individual grasp the death and resurrection of Jesus.

➢ A person's eternal destiny depends on their grasping the truth.
➢ The fate of the Christian message depends on believing the truth.
➢ The fate of the world, moral truth and justice, depends on people's grasping and believing the truth.

This is, *The Second Prediction of Death: Intensive Training on the Death of Christ, 9:30-32.*
1. The preparation: Jesus got alone with His disciples (v.30).
2. The lesson: Jesus taught His disciples that He was to die and then arise (v.31).
3. The response: The disciples could not accept a literal interpretation of the facts, rejecting what they did not wish to see (v.32).

1 The preparation: Jesus got alone with His disciples.

Jesus left the area of Caesarea Philippi in the north country where He was safe and headed toward Galilee from where He was to go into Jerusalem. *This was a pivotal point in Jesus' ministry.* The cross and His impending death were looming larger before Him with each passing day (see Mk.8:31-33). As the Lord and His disciples passed through Galilee, they moved about quietly, for Jesus did not want people to know they were in the area. They intentionally avoided the crowds as they moved gradually closer to Jerusalem and the cross.

9:30

30 They went on from there and passed through Galilee. And he did not want anyone to know,

Why did Jesus travel secretly? Why did He not want to minister to the crowds along the way? Jesus needed to concentrate on His disciples, to drill into them the fact that He had to die and arise from the dead. He had to continue repeating and reiterating His death and resurrection because it was contrary to all their hopes and expectations. It was different from all they had ever heard or been taught. The Messiah was thought to be a Messiah of power and sovereign rule, not a Messiah who had to suffer and die in order to save sinful humanity (see notes—Mt.1:1; DEEPER STUDY # 2—1:18; DEEPER STUDY # 3—3:11; notes—11:1-6; 11:2-3; DEEPER STUDY # 1—11:5; DEEPER STUDY # 2—11:6; DEEPER STUDY # 1—12:16; notes—22:42; Lu.7:21-23).

2 The lesson: Jesus taught His disciples that He was to die and then arise.

9:31

Jesus *was teaching* or *taught* (edidasken) His disciples about His impending death and resurrection. The Greek tense is imperfect, expressing that He continued to teach them, kept right on teaching them. As they traveled, He taught them continuously, perhaps pulling one to the side, then another, then two, then four or five, then the whole group. He taught and taught, drilling the fact of His death and resurrection into them.

31 for he was teaching his disciples, saying to them, "The Son of Man is going to be delivered into the hands of men, and they will kill him. And when he is killed, after three days he will rise."

Delivered or *being betrayed* (paradidotai) means to be delivered over and into death. It is a direct reference to His betrayal (see notes—Mt.26:20-25; 27:3-5; Mk.14:10-11; Lu.22:4-6; Jn.13:18; 13:21-26). Someone would turn Him over to authorities who sought to execute Him. It also implies the fact that His death was determined, ordained, set in the plan and counsel of God. Note how this truth is declared throughout Scripture:

- God delivered Christ up to be betrayed.

  This Jesus, delivered up according to the definite plan and foreknowledge of God, you crucified and killed by the hands of lawless men. (Ac.2:23)

  He who did not spare his own Son but gave him up for us all, how will he not also with him graciously give us all things? (Ro.8:32)

- Christ delivered Himself up to be crucified.

  Who gave himself for our sins to deliver us from the present evil age, according to the will of our God and Father. (Ga.1:4)

  And walk in love, as Christ loved us and gave himself up for us, a fragrant offering and sacrifice to God. (Ep.5:2)

  Husbands, love your wives, as Christ loved the church and gave himself up for her. (Ep.5:25)

  Who gave himself for us to redeem us from all lawlessness and to purify for himself a people for his own possession who are zealous for good works. (Tit.2:14)

  By this we know love, that he laid down his life for us, and we ought to lay down our lives for the brothers. (1 Jn.3:16)

Eventually, Jesus named the man who would deliver Him to His enemies. The betrayal would be by *Judas* who identified Him for the *elders, chief priests,* and *Scribes*; they in turn would deliver Him to the *Gentiles* (or Romans) for execution (Mt.20:19; see DEEPER STUDY # 1—Mt.16:21). In preaching to the Jews right after Pentecost, Peter openly condemned the Jews for being responsible for Jesus' death (Ac.2:23).

Jesus repeated and repeated the fact of His death for at least five reasons (also see DEEPER STUDIES 1, 2).

First, to enforce that He was *dying as a willing sacrifice* and not as a hopeless martyr or as a mistaken man who thought He was the Messiah.

> **I am the good shepherd. The good shepherd lays down his life for the sheep. (Jn.10:11)**

> **Just as the Father knows me and I know the Father; and I lay down my life for the sheep. . . . For this reason the Father loves me, because I lay down my life that I may take it up again. No one takes it from me, but I lay it down of my own accord. I have authority to lay it down, and I have authority to take it up again. This charge I have received from my Father. (Jn.10:15, 17–18)**

Second, to stress that He was *dying to redeem humanity* just as God willed.

> **And are justified by his grace as a gift, through the redemption that is in Christ Jesus, whom God put forward as a propitiation by his blood, to be received by faith. This was to show God's righteousness, because in his divine forbearance he had passed over former sins. (Ro.3:24–25)**

> **In him we have redemption through his blood, the forgiveness of our trespasses, according to the riches of his grace. (Ep.1:7)**

> **Who gave himself for us to redeem us from all lawlessness and to purify for himself a people for his own possession who are zealous for good works. (Tit.2:14)**

> **He entered once for all into the holy places, not by means of the blood of goats and calves but by means of his own blood, thus securing an eternal redemption. (He.9:12)**

> **Knowing that you were ransomed from the futile ways inherited from your forefathers, not with perishable things such as silver or gold, but with the precious blood of Christ, like that of a lamb without blemish or spot. (1 Pe.1:18–19)**

> **And they sang a new song, saying, "Worthy are you to take the scroll and to open its seals, for you were slain, and by your blood you ransomed people for God from every tribe and language and people and nation." (Re.5:9)**

Third, to assure that His death was deliberately planned under the purpose of God and that He was willingly dying to fulfill that purpose.

> **This Jesus, delivered up according to the definite plan and foreknowledge of God, you crucified and killed by the hands of lawless men. (Ac.2:23)**

> **He who did not spare his own Son but gave him up for us all, how will he not also with him graciously give us all things? (Ro.8:32)**

Fourth, to keep the disciples from thinking that the Messiah, the Son of God, could never die (see note, pt.2—Mk.9:31).

Fifth, to drill His death into the disciples so that they could better understand the truth after His resurrection.

DEEPER STUDY # 1

(9:31) **Jesus Christ, Death:** Jesus Christ was killed for two reasons (see note, *Death*—Mt.17:23 for discussion). This note includes most of the New Testament passages dealing with the death of Christ (see note and DEEPER STUDY # 1—Ac.1:3; DEEPER STUDIES 2, 3—2:23; DEEPER STUDY # 2—Ro.3:24; notes—5:1; 5:6–7; 5:6–11; 6:1–10; 7:4; DEEPER STUDY # 2—8:3; note—8:31-33.)

DEEPER STUDY # 2

(9:31) **Jesus Christ, Resurrection:** God raised Christ for several reasons (See note, *Resurrection*—Mt.17:23 for discussion. This note includes most of the New Testament passages dealing with the resurrection of Christ. See note and DEEPER STUDY # 1—Ac.1:3; DEEPER STUDY # 4—2:24.)

3 The response: The disciples could not accept a literal interpretation of the facts, rejecting what they did not wish to see.

Jesus stressed His death and resurrection repeatedly to the disciples. He meant what He said: He was to die, and He was to arise from the dead. They did not fully understand what Jesus was saying, and they did not want to understand because they were afraid of the truth. The disciples were just not able to fathom the realities of the future that loomed ahead. They rejected what they did not want to believe. Their confusion and rejection were understandable:

[32] But they did not understand the saying, and were afraid to ask him.

> ➤ They had been taught all their lives that the Messiah was coming to free them from all oppression and suffering (see notes—Lu.3:24-31).
> ➤ Jesus had taught them that the kingdom was at hand, ready to be established now. How could it be established if He were to literally die? They failed to see the various stages of the kingdom (see DEEPER STUDY # 3—Mt.19:23-24).
> ➤ They had been with Jesus for only mere months. *A complete reversal and unlearning of beliefs takes time.* They had not had enough time to sit at Jesus' feet, not enough time to accept and understand the literal truth of His death and resurrection.

Apparently, the disciples spiritualized Christ's death and resurrection. They clearly saw a new demeanor about Him as He quickened His pace and set His face toward Jerusalem. They could tell that something was pending, something that seemed to draw Christ forward with more determination than ever before. They knew that for many months now, He had been concentrating on teaching them and sharing the truth of His death and resurrection. However, it was all a mystery to them; it was a puzzle (see notes—Mt.17:22; Mk.9:30, outline note 1). By death and resurrection, did He mean . . .

- that He had to *die to self,* being shamed and discredited by the leaders, before He would become riled enough to *rise up and establish the kingdom*?
- that He had to *die to self,* rejecting the present order of things (present religion and government), before He could *rise up* and restore things to some higher level or state?
- that the conflict of freeing Israel from her enemies would be so severe that it would be like a death and the victory which would take three days would be like a resurrection from the dead?

The disciples just did not understand. They certainly did not want to accept the fact that their Lord would be literally killed. So, they went along with the desire of their flesh and refused to accept what He literally said.

> And he said, "Are you also still without understanding?" (Mt.15:16)
>
> And he said to them, "O foolish ones, and slow of heart to believe all that the prophets have spoken!" (Lu.24:25)
>
> For this people's heart has grown dull, and with their ears they can barely hear, and their eyes they have closed; lest they should see with their eyes and hear with their ears and understand with their heart and turn, and I would heal them. (Ac.28:27)
>
> They have neither knowledge nor understanding, they walk about in darkness; all the foundations of the earth are shaken. (Ps.82:5)
>
> But they do not know the thoughts of the LORD; they do not understand his plan, that he has gathered them as sheaves to the threshing floor. (Mi.4:12)

G. The Disciples' Terrible Ignorance of Messiahship:
A Problem of Ambition, 9:33–37

(Mt.18:1–4; Lu.9:46–48)

1. **Ambition can cause disputes, arguments**
   a. The disciples argued
   b. Jesus questioned what they were arguing about
2. **Ambition can shame**

3. **Ambition needs guidance**
4. **Ambition is a virtue if it is directed toward the right goal: To serve**

5. **Ambition for service proves a person's discipleship**
   a. The illustration: Welcoming a child in Jesus' name
   b. The lesson: Proves a person's discipleship
      1) Proves a person has received Christ
      2) Proves a person has received God

³³ And they came to Capernaum. And when he was in the house he asked them, "What were you discussing on the way?"

³⁴ But they kept silent, for on the way they had argued with one another about who was the greatest.
³⁵ And he sat down and called the twelve. And he said to them, "If anyone would be first, he must be last of all and servant of all."
³⁶ And he took a child and put him in the midst of them, and taking him in his arms, he said to them,

³⁷ "Whoever receives one such child in my name receives me, and whoever receives me, receives not me but him who sent me."

Division V

The Son of God's Closing Ministry: Jesus Teaches the Idea of God's Messiahship, not Man's Messiahship, 8:27–9:50

G. The Disciples' Terrible Ignorance of Messiahship: A Problem of Ambition, 9:33–37

(Mt.18:1–4; Lu.9:46–48)

9:33–37
Introduction

We live in a world where people are tirelessly striving to be better than others, to attain more than others, whether it be power, position, popularity, prestige, or possessions. In the world's eyes, these are the things that constitute greatness.

But in Christ's kingdom, greatness is something different, something that is achieved in an unlikely way: through service to others.

On more than one occasion, the disciples argued over who should hold the highest position in Christ's kingdom (see outlines and notes—Mt.18:1–2; 20:20–28; Lu.22:24–30). Their desire was for recognition and honor in an earthly kingdom. Jesus had to reeducate them in their thinking.

This same reeducation is needed by all people. All have the same needs for some . . .

- recognition
- position
- prestige
- money
- authority
- esteem
- challenge
- physical satisfaction

There is nothing wrong with these needs. They are human and legitimate and must be met, but people so often allow their hearts to be overtaken with selfishness. They become prideful, covetous, worldly, ambitious, envious, and hurtful, some even to the point of destroying and killing in order to fulfill their fleshly desires (see Js.4:1-3).

Christ wants to change our ambitions and reeducate our concept of greatness. May God grant us the grace to grasp the lesson of this passage and apply it daily to our lives. This is, *The Disciples' Terrible Ignorance of Messiahship: A Problem of Ambition,* 9:33-37.

1. Ambition can cause disputes, arguments (v.33).
2. Ambition can shame (v.34).
3. Ambition needs guidance (v.35).
4. Ambition is a virtue if it is directed toward the right goal: To serve (v.35).
5. Ambition for service proves a person's discipleship (vv.36-37).

1 Ambition can cause disputes, arguments.

9:33

Jesus had returned to Capernaum, His headquarters, and entered the home which was so often opened to Him. As the disciples traveled with Him, their selfish ambitions had surfaced, creating obvious tension.

> [33] And they came to Capernaum. And when he was in the house he asked them, "What were you discussing on the way?"

a. The disciples argued.

The disciples had been disputing among themselves and may have been continuing to argue after entering the house. The English Standard Version (ESV) and New American Standard Bible (NASB) translate the Greek word *dialogizesthe* as "discussing." But this attempt at translation comes short of expressing the spirit of their conversation. They were definitely arguing (v.34).

b. Jesus questioned what they were arguing about.

Jesus knew about the dispute, and He knew what they were arguing about. But, apparently, the disciples were not aware that He knew. Jesus could do only one thing: continue to teach them. He simply turned and asked, "What were you arguing about along the way?"

Imagine how Jesus' heart must have been cut to the core. He had just been teaching them about His sacrificial death. Here He was, about to stand face-to-face with the cross, and the disciples were arguing over which of them should be the greatest.

THOUGHT 1. How often we have heard about the cross, and yet how easily we forget.
1) Many have heard time after time and have never responded. This deeply cuts the heart of Christ.
2) Many have heard and have responded, yet they continue to pursue their worldly ambitions, seeking the things of the world: power, position, wealth, property, fame. This also grieves Christ.

THOUGHT 2. People who pursue the world soon forget the cross. They forget that they were cleansed from their sins (2 Pe.1:9).

2 Ambition can shame.

9:34

The disciples kept quiet and said nothing in response to Jesus. They knew they had done wrong and were ashamed and embarrassed. They had been arguing over who should be the greatest in Jesus' government. Their selfish ambition had led them to quarrel and divide, and they were ashamed.

> [34] But they kept silent, for on the way they had argued with one another about who was the greatest.

The disciples were not arguing about who would be the greatest in quality or character, but in name and position. They were thinking in terms of power, fame, wealth, position, and name (see notes—Mt.1:1; Deeper Study # 1—1:18; Deeper

STUDY # 3—3:11; notes—11:1-6; 11:2-3; DEEPER STUDY # 1—11:5; DEEPER STUDY # 2—11:6; DEEPER STUDY # 1—12:16; note—Lu.7:21-23 for a picture of their concept of the Messiah).

The disciples sensed that Jesus was about to set up His kingdom, about to assume His throne, and they were looking forward to becoming top officials in His kingdom. Jesus had already honored three of them in special ways (Peter, James, and John, Mt.17:1-13). And one of them in particular had been distinguished (Peter, Mt.16:17-19). They wondered who among them would be the highest-ranking leaders in the Lord's kingdom, as they were all apparently gripped with jealousy, envy, ambition, and some rivalry.

Remember that the disciples had misinterpreted Jesus' words that He must die and arise again. They spiritualized His words instead of taking them at face value (see notes—Mk.9:32; Mt.17:22). Apparently, they connected the thought of "rising from the dead" with the setting up of His kingdom, and they began to argue over the top positions of leadership.

The disciples did not yet understand what the kingdom was. They still saw an earthly, temporal kingdom and not a spiritual, eternal kingdom. This passage shows just how far away they were from understanding God's idea of the Messiah (see points above; note—Mk.10:35-37).

THOUGHT 1. Ambition that leads to argument and division is wrong. Just as the disciples had to answer to Christ, we must all give an account both of our words and our lives. We must answer to Christ for failing to live and serve in unity with other believers. Those who seek to further themselves by disputing and causing division with other believers will stand before Christ ashamed and embarrassed.

> For by your words you will be justified, and by your words you will be condemned. (Mt.12:37)

> Whoever exalts himself will be humbled, and whoever humbles himself will be exalted. (Mt.23:12)

> For we must all appear before the judgment seat of Christ, so that each one may receive what is due for what he has done in the body, whether good or evil. (2 Co.5:10)

> And just as it is appointed for man to die once, and after that comes judgment. (He.9:27)

> And now, little children, abide in him, so that when he appears we may have confidence and not shrink from him in shame at his coming. (1 Jn.2:28)

> There are six things that the LORD hates, seven that are an abomination to him: haughty eyes, a lying tongue, and hands that shed innocent blood, a heart that devises wicked plans, feet that make haste to run to evil, a false witness who breathes out lies, and one who sows discord among brothers. (Pr.6:16-19)

9:35

³⁵ And he sat down and called the twelve. And he said to them, "If anyone would be first, he must be last of all and servant of all."

3 Ambition needs guidance.

Jesus "*sat down* and called the twelve." In Jesus' day, when a rabbi was ready to give a profound lesson, he sat down before his pupils. The disciples had slipped into gross error and committed a serious sin, the sin of pride. They needed to be corrected and taught the truth. Their ambition needed to be instructed and guided in the right direction.

> Do your best to present yourself to God as one approved, a worker who has no need to be ashamed, rightly handling the word of truth. But avoid irreverent babble, for it will lead people into more and more ungodliness. (2 Ti.2:15-16)

> For the commandment is a lamp and the teaching a light, and the reproofs of discipline are the way of life. (Pr.6:23)

> Whoever loves discipline loves knowledge, but he who hates reproof is stupid. (Pr.12:1)

> Whoever ignores instruction despises himself, but he who listens to reproof gains intelligence. (Pr.15:32)

4 Ambition is a virtue if it is directed toward the right goal: To serve.

Ambition is a virtue. It is not wrong to desire greatness, to desire to make a contribution. Jesus did not rebuke the disciples' ambition. What He did was to steer their ambition, their energy and motive and efforts, in the right direction.

The way to greatness is service, humble service. If we wish to be great, then we need to actively seek to serve others. No matter our position or level of authority, we are to serve; we are to actively work for the sake and benefit of others. Our ambition must not be to lead for the sake of holding position and authority and receiving honor from other people.

> 35 And he sat down and called the twelve. And he said to them, "If anyone would be first, he must be last of all and servant of all."

To be great, our ambition must be to use our gifts and abilities to serve others, helping and ministering to them in every way possible. People who are truly great do not build their own prestige. Great people build the lives and better the welfare of others.

> For by the grace given to me I say to everyone among you not to think of himself more highly than he ought to think, but to think with sober judgment, each according to the measure of faith that God has assigned. . . . Live in harmony with one another. Do not be haughty, but associate with the lowly. Never be wise in your own sight. (Ro.12:3, 16)

> Do nothing from selfish ambition or conceit, but in humility count others more significant than yourselves. Let each of you look not only to his own interests, but also to the interests of others. (Ph.2:3–4)

> For the wicked boasts of the desires of his soul, and the one greedy for gain curses and renounces the LORD. (Ps.10:3)

5 Ambition for service proves a person's discipleship.

In this passage, Jesus teaches His disciples—and us—the basic principle of being a disciple. It is a principle He modeled throughout His earthly life, and, most vividly and powerfully, through His death. Genuine disciples of Christ are not ambitious for greatness, but for serving others.

> 36 And he took a child and put him in the midst of them, and taking him in his arms, he said to them,
> 37 "Whoever receives one such child in my name receives me, and whoever receives me, receives not me but him who sent me."

a. The illustration: Welcoming a child in Jesus' name (v.36).

Jesus illustrated His point. He took a child into His arms, receiving and gathering the child unto Himself. And then He drove His point home.

b. The lesson: Proves a person's discipleship (v.37).

Jesus said that the very qualities that are necessary to *receive* a child are the qualities that are to characterize the believer's life. We are to treat all people as we would when we receive a child into our arms. Note the qualities present when a person receives and gathers up a child into their arms.

First, receiving a child requires humility. In matters of adult life, many consider a child useless, unable to contribute. They overlook and fail to consider the great contributions a child makes to an adult. A child requires and teaches the spirit of love, caring, forgiveness, courage, trust, and on and on. A person who serves a child must be humble.

Second, receiving a child requires courage. A child is a great responsibility. When we receive a child, we undertake the child's care and welfare. A person who serves a child must be courageous.

Third, receiving a child requires faith and trust. A person has to believe the child will respond and learn, not rebel and reject. A person who serves a child must believe and trust.

Fourth, receiving a child requires patience and endurance. A person has to be patient and persevering in teaching and training. The child is sometimes slow to learn. A person who serves a child must be patient.

Fifth, receiving a child requires forgiveness. A child fails and fails often, making the same mistake time and again. A person who serves a child must be forgiving.

Jesus was teaching that a child has needs. Thus, it is with society. All people have needs. Just as we receive a little child, so we must receive all people. Just as we serve and treat a little child, so we must serve and treat all. An ambition for this type of loving service is the proof of our discipleship.

To all who aspire to Christ-like service, Jesus made a wonderful promise. If we receive a child, a person in need, we receive Him; and if we receive Him, we receive God (see Mt.25:34f).

Even as the Son of Man came not to be served but to serve, and to give his life as a ransom for many. (Mt.20:28)

In all things I have shown you that by working hard in this way we must help the weak and remember the words of the Lord Jesus, how he himself said, 'It is more blessed to give than to receive.' (Ac.20:35)

We who are strong have an obligation to bear with the failings of the weak, and not to please ourselves. (Ro.15:1)

Have this mind among yourselves, which is yours in Christ Jesus, who, though he was in the form of God, did not count equality with God a thing to be grasped, but emptied himself, by taking the form of a servant, being born in the likeness of men. And being found in human form, he humbled himself by becoming obedient to the point of death, even death on a cross. (Ph.2:5–8)

Humble yourselves before the Lord, and he will exalt you. (Js.4:10)

For thus says the One who is high and lifted up, who inhabits eternity, whose name is Holy: "I dwell in the high and holy place, and also with him who is of a contrite and lowly spirit, to revive the spirit of the lowly, and to revive the heart of the contrite." (Is.57:15)

(Lu.9:49–50)

³⁸ John said to him, "Teacher, we saw someone casting out demons in your name, and we tried to stop him, because he was not following us."

³⁹ But Jesus said, "Do not stop him, for no one who does a mighty work in my name will be able soon afterward to speak evil of me."

⁴⁰ For the one who is not against us is for us.

⁴¹ For truly, I say to you, whoever gives you a cup of water to drink because you belong to Christ will by no means lose his reward."

1. **The setting: The disciples felt guilt for rejecting a man**
   a. A man who was ministering in Jesus' name
   b. A man who was not in their group
2. **The instruction of Jesus: Receive him**
   a. Basis 1: A person who works a miracle in Jesus' name will not say anything bad about Him
   b. Basis 2: A person who is not against Christ is for Christ
   c. Basis 3: A person who shows kindness in Jesus' name to the followers of Christ will receive a reward

Division V

The Son of God's Closing Ministry: Jesus Teaches the Idea of God's Messiahship, not Man's Messiahship, 8:27–9:50

H. The Basis for Tolerance, 9:38–41

(Lu.9:49–50)

9:38–41
Introduction

Jesus had just taught a lesson on ambition and service. Now He teaches a lesson on tolerance and accepting the ministry of others. The lesson is greatly needed, for within the body of Christ today, many sincere believers oppose other sincere believers and do not accept their ministries.

Jesus' words in verse 37 stirred John to share about a man's ministering in Jesus' name. John saw immediately that Jesus seemed to be saying that people were to be accepted and cared for in His name—no matter who they were. In response to John's account of rejecting a fellow minister, Jesus gave the basis for receiving the ministries of others. While the epistles give more detailed guidelines, Christ's teachings here lay the foundation for unity amidst diversity within the body of Christ. This is, *The Basis for Tolerance*, 9:38–41.

1. The setting: The disciples felt guilt for rejecting a man (vv.38–39).
2. The instruction of Jesus: Receive Him (vv.39–41).

9:38–39

1 The setting: The disciples felt guilt for rejecting a man.

Jesus had just said that His followers were to be open-armed in receiving people (v.37). These words stirred feelings of guilt within John. He and the other disciples had seen a man ministering in Jesus' name, and they had stopped him. Why? Note John's words: "He *was not following us.*" The disciples stopped him because he . . .

³⁸ John said to him, "Teacher, we saw someone casting out demons in your name, and we tried to stop him, because he was not following us."

³⁹ But Jesus said, "Do not stop him, for no one who does a mighty work in my name will be able soon afterward to speak evil of me."

- was not one of them, of their group
- was not of their inner circle
- was unattached, had not been called and ordained by their Leader (Christ)
- had not been taught by their Teacher (Christ)
- could not have been as strong and firm in his beliefs as they were
- did not stand with them; in their minds, their way was the only way
- may not have done things the same way as the disciples

However, this man had somehow been influenced by the Lord. He knew about the Lord and had a strong faith in the Lord's name. He had given himself to the ministry and was ministering to people. In fact, he was ministering to the most difficult cases, to the demon-possessed. And note: ministering to the demon-possessed was the ministry which was difficult for the disciples to perform (see vv.14–29). The disciples may have been jealous of his success.

Although this man professed Christ and was ministering *in the name of Christ,* the apostles rebuked and stopped him. What he was doing was unacceptable to them. But John felt guilt over the matter, and he was honest enough to confess his intolerance and ask Jesus about the matter.

THOUGHT 1. Why do some individuals, churches, denominations, and other Christian groups oppose other Christians and their ministries? Why are they intolerant of others who are seeking to win people to Christ, help others, and establish God's kingdom?

1. Loyalty to an organization or to a leader can cause intolerance. If they are not a part of our organization or a follower of our leader, we often deem them unacceptable.
2. Conviction of our own position and belief can cause intolerance. If they do not agree with our position or belief in its entirety, if they differ in their interpretation of non-essential doctrines, they are often deemed unacceptable.
3. The desire for submission can cause intolerance. If they question or oppose us or our organization and its acts, we often deem them unacceptable.
4. A sense of authority and self-exaltation can cause intolerance. We can think too highly of ourselves, feeling that we are the great defenders of the truth, the only ones who are right. Therefore, if they question or oppose our position or acts, we often deem them unacceptable.
5. Jealousy and envy can cause intolerance. Who a person is (spiritually, physically, mentally) and what that person has (position, gifts, recognition) are often secretly desired or coveted. Therefore, the person is often deemed unacceptable. The same is true with churches and Christian groups that may be larger and have more influence.
6. A sense of pride and arrogance, of being better than others, can cause intolerance. A person who is poor, disadvantaged, unemployed, uneducated, single, and a myriad of other conditions can be deemed unacceptable.

THOUGHT 2. The disciples made several gross errors.
1) They set themselves up as judges of others.
2) They were too narrow, too exclusive.
3) They denied another the right to serve.
4) They wrecked a servant's ministry.
5) They kept many from ever being helped.
6) They taught intolerance.

THOUGHT 3. Intolerance has wrecked many lives and churches. Intolerance causes strife and division, hurt and pain. It shames and ruins and paralyzes both individuals and churches. It fails to grant the great desire and prayer of Jesus:

> **And I am no longer in the world, but they are in the world, and I am coming to you. Holy Father, keep them in your name, which you have given me, that they may be one, even as we are one. . . . I do not ask for these only, but also for those who will believe in me through their word, that they may all be one, just as you, Father, are in me, and I in you, that they also may be in us, so that the world may believe that you have sent me. The glory that you have given me I have given to them, that they may be one even as we are one, I in them and you in me, that they may become perfectly one, so that the world may know that you sent me and loved them even as you loved me. (Jn.17:11, 20–23)**

2 The instruction of Jesus: Receive Him.

Jesus instructed the disciples not to stop someone who is ministering in His name (v.39). Jesus Christ Himself said that we are to not oppose another's ministry *if* they meet certain conditions. Jesus proceeded to give three bases for receiving—not opposing—another's ministry.

[39] But Jesus said, "Do not stop him, for no one who does a mighty work in my name will be able soon afterward to speak evil of me.

[40] For the one who is not against us is for us.

[41] For truly, I say to you, whoever gives you a cup of water to drink because you belong to Christ will by no means lose his reward."

a. Basis 1: A person who works a miracle in Jesus' name will not say anything bad about Him (v.39).

First, we are to receive those who do not speak evil of Christ. The emphasis of this point seems to be on the phrase "speaking evil of Christ." A person who truly ministers "in [Christ's] name" will not speak evil of Christ. Therefore, those who do not speak evil of Christ show that they are ministering in His name and are to be accepted.

But the opposite is also true. Those who speak evil of Christ show that they are an enemy of Christ and are not to be accepted.

> Some indeed preach Christ from envy and rivalry, but others from good will. The latter do it out of love, knowing that I am put here for the defense of the gospel. The former proclaim Christ out of selfish ambition, not sincerely but thinking to afflict me in my imprisonment. What then? Only that in every way, whether in pretense or in truth, Christ is proclaimed, and in that I rejoice. Yes, and I will rejoice. (Ph.1:15-18)

b. Basis 2: A person who is not against Christ is for Christ (v.40).

Second, we are to receive those who are not against Christ and His disciples. Note that Jesus uses the word "us." A person's attitude toward both Christ *and His disciples* (church) is to be observed. People's attitude toward believers reveals their attitude toward Christ. In Christ's eyes He and His people are one. To stand against His followers is to stand against Him. To mistreat His followers is to mistreat Him. To speak evil of His followers is to speak evil of Him.

> Whoever receives you receives me, and whoever receives me receives him who sent me. (Mt.10:40)

> The one who hears you hears me, and the one who rejects you rejects me, and the one who rejects me rejects him who sent me. (Lu.10:16)

> And I have other sheep that are not of this fold. I must bring them also, and they will listen to my voice. So there will be one flock, one shepherd. (Jn.10:16)

We are to consider people's actions—nothing else: not their appearance, education, credentials, group, or label. If people have a spirit of faith, love, joy, peace, forgiveness, unity, and worship, we are to accept them. They do not stand against Christ. But if they have a spirit of unbelief, disturbance, unforgiveness, or divisiveness, they are against Christ and His followers. Therefore, we should not accept them. They are "against us."

> Whoever is not with me is against me, and whoever does not gather with me scatters. (Lu.11:23)

> Thus, sinning against your brothers and wounding their conscience when it is weak, you sin against Christ. (1 Co.8:12)

c. Basis 3: A person who shows kindness in Jesus' name to the followers of Christ will receive a reward (v.41).

Third, we are to receive those who show kindness to the followers of Christ. Giving a cup of water in a hot country like Palestine was a common sight. But note: Christ is talking about giving "in His name." If a person does something for a believer "because he or she belongs to Christ," then that person will be rewarded. And the idea is that they will be rewarded greatly. The whole point is helping, giving to a person "because he or she belongs to Christ."

Many people help and give to others. They help and give because . . .

- it is the custom and practice
- it is the respectable thing to do
- they wish to receive recognition and honor
- they would be embarrassed not to give
- they are touched by the need

All who give and help God's people because of the fact that they "belong to Christ" will be rewarded. The reward is promised for a specific act, the act of helping a person because he or she "belongs to Christ."

The reward is given for the most simple and humble of acts, the giving of water to a thirsty believer. Anyone would give a drink of water, yet so simple an act done for one of Christ's followers will be greatly rewarded.

THOUGHT 1. No gift, no service is too small. God notices all. What an encouragement! What a challenge to use what we have and all we have for Christ and His followers! We will not lose our reward (1 Co.15:58; 2 Co.5:10). Our reward is sure; it is guaranteed!

> And everyone who has left houses or brothers or sisters or father or mother or children or lands, for my name's sake, will receive a hundredfold and will inherit eternal life. (Mt.19:29)

> Then the King will say to those on his right, 'Come, you who are blessed by my Father, inherit the kingdom prepared for you from the foundation of the world. For I was hungry and you gave me food, I was thirsty and you gave me drink, I was a stranger and you welcomed me, I was naked and you clothed me, I was sick and you visited me, I was in prison and you came to me.' . . . And the King will answer them, 'Truly, I say to you, as you did it to one of the least of these my brothers, you did it to me.' (Mt.25:34–36, 40)

THOUGHT 2. The criteria given by our Lord for accepting others' ministries are clear. No individual, church, denomination, or group of churches can single-handedly fulfill the Great Commission. We need each other—all who believe in Christ and His Word. Each of us needs to examine our attitude toward others who truly minister in Jesus' name, who are outside of our circle, or may differ from us in some non-essential ways.

> The glory that you have given me I have given to them, that they may be one even as we are one, I in them and you in me, that they may become perfectly one, so that the world may know that you sent me and loved them even as you loved me. (Jn.17:22–23)

> For you are still of the flesh. For while there is jealousy and strife among you, are you not of the flesh and behaving only in a human way? For when one says, "I follow Paul," and another, "I follow Apollos," are you not being merely human? What then is Apollos? What is Paul? Servants through whom you believed, as the Lord assigned to each. I planted, Apollos watered, but God gave the growth. So neither he who plants nor he who waters is anything, but only God who gives the growth. He who plants and he who waters are one, and each will receive his wages according to his labor. For we are God's fellow workers. You are God's field, God's building. (1 Co.3:3–9)

> Because there is one bread, we who are many are one body, for we all partake of the one bread. (1 Co.10:17)

> Here there is not Greek and Jew, circumcised and uncircumcised, barbarian, Scythian, slave, free; but Christ is all, and in all. (Col.3:11)

⁴² "Whoever causes one of these little ones who believe in me to sin, it would be better for him if a great millstone were hung around his neck and he were thrown into the sea."

⁴³ "And if your hand causes you to sin, cut it off. It is better for you to enter life crippled than with two hands to go to hell, to the unquenchable fire."

⁴⁵ "And if your foot causes you to sin, cut it off. It is better for you to enter life lame than with two feet to be thrown into hell."

⁴⁷ "And if your eye causes you to sin, tear it out. It is better for you to enter the kingdom of God with one eye than with two eyes to be thrown into hell,

⁴⁸ 'where their worm does not die and the fire is not quenched.'"

⁴⁹ "For everyone will be salted with fire."

⁵⁰ "Salt is good, but if the salt has lost its saltiness, how will you make it salty again? Have salt in yourselves, and be at peace with one another."

1. **The terrible sin of causing others to sin**
   a. The unimaginable sin: Causing "little ones" to sin
   b. The better alternative: To drown yourself[DS1, 2]
2. **The terrible sins of the hands**
   a. The better alternative: To cut off your hand
   b. The reason: Sins of the hand condemn you to hell
   c. The tragedy: Hell is punishment, and it is forever
3. **The terrible sins of the feet**
   a. The better alternative: To cut off your foot
   b. The reason: Sins of the feet condemn you to hell
   c. The tragedy: Hell is punishment, and it is forever
4. **The terrible sins of the eyes**
   a. The better alternative: To pluck out your eye
   b. The reason: Sins of the eye condemn you to hell
   c. The tragedy: Hell is punishment, and it is forever
5. **The terrible surety of judgment upon everyone**
6. **The challenge to preserve yourself from sin**
   a. Search yourself
   b. Be salted: Be pure and useful and at peace with one another

Division V

The Son of God's Closing Ministry: Jesus Teaches the Idea of God's Messiahship, not Man's Messiahship, 8:27–9:50

I. The Terrible Tragedy of Sin, 9:42–50

9:42–50
Introduction

We live in a sinful world, full of terrible, evil behavior. No one can walk out into the world without facing temptation after temptation and pull after pull to look, touch, taste—to experience the *pleasurable life* of physical gratification, earthly comfort, and personal fulfillment. We are tempted, seduced, and influenced at every turn, and we cannot escape (see Ro.3:9–18).

For all have sinned and fall short of the glory of God. (Ro.3:23)

We know that we are from God, and the whole world lies in the power of the evil one. (1 Jn.5:19)

In this passage, Christ stresses just how terrible sin is, and He warns the sinner. Every one of us is personally responsible for our sin. The fact of a sinful world does not lessen our personal responsibility. We cannot blame the world, society, or others, for each of us has a free will. In addition, we have the knowledge of much good, and we have the inner desire to do good (at least initially). We also have examples of goodness, and we can choose to do good. We can even work to overcome our weaknesses. And, most of all, we have God, who provides a way to escape temptation (1 Co.10:13). Therefore, we are *personally* responsible for choosing to sin and for how our sin affects others. Every sin becomes a stumbling block to others! As Jesus teaches here, the person who sins and places a stumbling block for others to fall over faces eternal punishment that is severe beyond our imagination. This is, *The Terrible Tragedy of Sin*, 9:42-50.

1. The terrible sin of causing others to sin (v.42).
2. The terrible sins of the hands (vv.43-44).
3. The terrible sins of the feet (vv.45-46).
4. The terrible sins of the eyes (vv.47-48).
5. The terrible surety of judgment upon everyone (v.49).
6. The challenge to preserve yourself from sin (v.50).

9:42

[42] "Whoever causes one of these little ones who believe in me to sin, it would be better for him if a great millstone were hung around his neck and he were thrown into the sea."

1 The terrible sin of causing others to sin.

Christ warned against the terrible sin of causing others to sin or stumble, of actually leading others to sin (see note—Mt.18:5-10 for more discussion). The warning revolved around the child He was still holding in His arms (vv.36-37).

a. The unimaginable sin: Causing "little ones" to sin.

The *little ones* are identified by Christ. They are those who "believe in me." He is speaking about sinning against children but also about sinning against a new believer. Christ often called the believers little ones and described the believer as a little child (see note—Mt.18:5-10). Believers are children of God. A little one is any little child, any *new beginner* in the faith, and any person who has a *child-like faith and spirit in Christ*.

Christ seems to be saying that the most terrible sin of all is leading another person to sin. Indeed, there is no sin any worse than leading another person astray. It is the worst conceivable sin. How do we cause others to sin?

- By leading them into sin and teaching them to sin. "Oh, come on, no one will know. It's not going to hurt you."
- By example, things that we do. Example is not a direct vocal suggestion. We are not necessarily aware that "the child" sees or is observing us; nevertheless, he sees and learns from what we do. He thinks to himself: "If it's all right for him, then it must be all right for me."
- By overlooking or passing over wrong; by giving soft names to it; by considering some sins to be merely minor sins. "Oh, that's all right. There's not that much to it. It isn't going to hurt anyone. Don't pay any attention to it. Just forget it."
- By ridiculing or poking fun at, or by joking and sneering at a person's attempt to do right. "Oh, don't be a fanatic. You and your religion."
- By looking at, touching, and tasting some things that are socially acceptable; but that are sinful to God. They are harmful, habit forming, and physically stimulating when they should not be.
- By persecuting and threatening "a child" or a believer. The threat can range all the way from loss of promotion, job, friendship, or acceptance to imprisonment and death.

b. The better alternative: To drown yourself.

The terribleness of this sin is stressed by the better alternative Christ gives. A person would be better off to hang a huge stone about his neck and cast himself into the sea than to lead another person to sin (see DEEPER STUDIES 1, 2).

> And he said to his disciples, "Temptations to sin are sure to come, but woe to the one through whom they come! It would be better for him if a millstone were hung around his neck and he were cast into the sea than that he should cause one of these little ones to sin." (Lu.17:1-2)

> Therefore let us not pass judgment on one another any longer, but rather decide never to put a stumbling block or hindrance in the way of a brother. . . . For if your brother is grieved by what you eat, you are no longer walking in love. By what you eat, do not destroy the one for whom Christ died. . . . It is good not to eat meat or drink wine or do anything that causes your brother to stumble. (Ro.14:13, 15, 21)

> Give no offense to Jews or to Greeks or to the church of God. (1 Co.10:32)

> We put no obstacle in anyone's way, so that no fault may be found with our ministry. (2 Co.6:3)

> Whoever loves his brother abides in the light, and in him there is no cause for stumbling. (1 Jn.2:10)

DEEPER STUDY # 1

(9:42) **Millstone** (Gk. mulikos or mulos onikos): literally, the millstone of a donkey. The word *onos* is the word for a donkey. The word *mulos* is the word for the millstone that the donkey pulled around to grind the grain. Thus, the millstone Christ spoke of is the huge millstone, not the small hand millstone used by the women to grind a little grain at a time. Note: the very fact that Christ chose the huge millstone to demonstrate His point shows how severe this sin is. The person would be held to the bottom of the sea by the most awful and terrible weight. The sin of leading a child astray is the worst possible sin; therefore, its condemnation will be awful and terrible.

DEEPER STUDY # 2

(9:42) **Death—Drowning:** drowning was a form of capital punishment used by the Romans, but never by the Jews. The Jews saw drowning as a symbol of *utter destruction and annihilation*, of being in the very depths of death. They feared it. Even the Romans reserved it only for the worst criminals.

Note something: Christ *added to the fear* of His audience. He painted the picture of a stone around the offender's neck. Why? So that the body could never rise to the top and be properly buried. But He went even further to add to the fear—He pictured the huge millstone, not the small one. Why did He want to strike such intense fear into the heart of His hearers, laying additional stress upon the fear? The answer is clear: the sin of leading another person astray is terrible, and the offender must know the fate that is awaiting him.

2 The terrible sins of the hands.

Christ mentioned the terrible sins of the hand (see note—Mt.18:7-9). The hand can cause a person to sin. If something is *forbidden or unwise* or if it should be *given or let go*, the hand can sin by . . .

- touching
- clutching
- holding
- grabbing
- pointing
- stroking
- striking

⁴³ "And if your hand causes you to sin, cut it off. It is better for you to enter life crippled than with two hands to go to hell, to the unquenchable fire."

9:43-44

a. The better alternative: To cut off your hand (v.43a).

Jesus said there is a better alternative than sinning with one's hand: cutting it off. This is strong language, very descriptive, and radical in its point. Jesus used stark language to make a critical point. But honesty and thought are called for in seeing the point of Christ. What is more horrible than taking one's hand and leading "a little one" to sin and being a stumbling block to their life and salvation? What is more horrible than dooming another to what Christ calls *hell fire*? What is more horrible than doing the same with one's self? If God really loves the human race and hell-fire is real, then descriptive and radical language is needed to awaken sinful people to the truth.

b. The reason: Sins of the hand condemn you to hell (v.43b).

Sinning condemns a person to hell, and many sins are committed with the hand. Christ stated this fearful truth unequivocally and very plainly (see Deeper Study # 2—Mt.5:22).

c. The tragedy: Hell is punishment, and it is forever (vv.43c–44).

Hell is a place of unquenchable fire (v.43c). Christ said, "Their worm does not die, and the fire is not quenched" (vv.44, 46, 48).[1] The point of this statement relates both to punishment and duration of punishment. The punishment will be just like the punishment inflicted by a worm and fire, and it will be forever.

By "worm" Christ meant one of two things:

- There is a "worm" in hell that afflicts people; therefore, it can be called "their worm." This is, of course, a picture of something in hell that preys upon people, wounds them, and inflicts a biting, gnawing, and consuming pain. And note, it "does not die"; it never ends.
- There is a "worm" within people in hell. It is a "worm" within, a worm created by their own sinfulness, a worm within that bites, gnaws, and consumes them. Perhaps the worm is memory and conscience that never leaves people alone. It disturbs and reminds them of what they have missed and lost (see Lu.16:19–31). Note that the punishment is forever. Both worm and fire are forever.

THOUGHT 1. In many ways, the hand determines our destiny. We reap the results of what we do with our hands, both spiritually and physically.

> Therefore go out from their midst, and be separate from them, says the Lord, and touch no unclean thing; then I will welcome you, and I will be a father to you, and you shall be sons and daughters to me, says the Lord Almighty. (2 Co.6:17–18)

9:45–46

[45] "And if your foot causes you to sin, cut it off. It is better for you to enter life lame than with two feet to be thrown into hell."

- standing
- running
- jumping
- walking

- pointing
- dancing
- turning
- kicking

3 The terrible sins of the feet.

Christ mentioned the terrible sins of the feet (see note—Mt.18:7-9). Like our hands, our feet can cause us to sin. If something is *forbidden or unwise* or if it should be *avoided*, our feet can sin by . . .

a. The better alternative: To cut off your foot (v.45a).

Jesus said there is a better alternative than sinning with the foot: cutting it off (see note, pt.2—vv.43–44 for discussion). Again, Jesus is using stark language to make a critical point, to convey the awfulness of eternal punishment in hell.

---

1 The textual manuscripts from which many modern English Bibles (ESV, CSB, NIV, and others) are translated do not include verses 44 and 46. They do include this specific statement (v.48), but not its repetition by Christ.

b. The reason: Sins of the feet condemn you to hell (v.45b).

Some sins are committed with the feet. The punishment for sin is eternal separation from God in hell (see Deeper Study # 2—Mt.5:22).

c. Hell is punishment, and it is forever (vv.45c–46).

Once again Jesus emphasized the terrifying truth that hell is a place of never-ending punishment (see note, pt.c—vv.43c–44).

> **THOUGHT 1.** The believer is to walk even as Christ walked.
>
> **Look carefully then how you walk, not as unwise but as wise. (Ep.5:15)**
>
> **Therefore, as you received Christ Jesus the Lord, so walk in him. (Col.2:6)**
>
> **Whoever says he abides in him ought to walk in the same way in which he walked. (1 Jn.2:6)**

4 The terrible sins of the eyes.

Christ proceeded to speak about the terrible sins of the eyes (see note—Mt.18:7-9). Just as with our feet and hands, some sins are committed with our eyes. If something is *forbidden or unwise* or if it should be *avoided or not observed*, our eyes can sin by . . .

- looking
- staring
- focusing
- glancing
- opening
- scanning

⁴⁷ "And if your eye causes you to sin, tear it out. It is better for you to enter the kingdom of God with one eye than with two eyes to be thrown into hell,
⁴⁸ 'where their worm does not die and the fire is not quenched.'"

a. The better alternative: To pluck out your eye (v.47a).

Jesus said it is better to tear out your eye than to go on sinning with it. Note that the alternative in this case is the kingdom of God instead of life. The eye is one of *the doors* into the mind and heart of every person. What we look at and focus on is of extreme importance. Sight can lead to a spirit of lust (sinful desires) quicker than any other single thing: the lust for . . .

- the world and excitement
- material goods and possessions
- illicit affairs and relationships
- recognition and fame
- money and wealth

Every person knows the importance of sight, of being able to see. Most people would rather lose any other sense than to lose the sense of sight. Because of the enormous need for sight and the power of the eye, Christ stacked it up against the kingdom of God. It would be better to enter the kingdom of God with one eye, than to allow an eye to sin and doom you to hell.

b. The reason: Sins of the eye condemn you to hell (v.47b).

For a third time, Christ says the very same thing. Sin—including the sins committed with our eyes—condemns people to hell (see Deeper Study # 2—Mt.5:22).

c. The tragedy: Hell is punishment, and it is forever (vv.47c–48).

(See note, pt.c—vv.43c-44 for discussion.)

> **THOUGHT 1.** Scripture's warnings about the eye are pointed.
>
> **But I say to you that everyone who looks at a woman with lustful intent has already committed adultery with her in his heart. (Mt.5:28)**
>
> **For all that is in the world—the desires of the flesh and the desires of the eyes and pride of life—is not from the Father but is from the world. (1 Jn.2:16)**
>
> **Whoever winks the eye causes trouble, and a babbling fool will come to ruin. (Pr.10:10)**
>
> **All things are full of weariness; a man cannot utter it; the eye is not satisfied with seeing, nor the ear filled with hearing. (Ec.1:8)**

One person who has no other, either son or brother, yet there is no end to all his toil, and his eyes are never satisfied with riches, so that he never asks, "For whom am I toiling and depriving myself of pleasure?" This also is vanity and an unhappy business. (Ec.4:8)

[49] "For everyone will be salted with fire."

5 The terrible surety of judgment upon everyone.

Every person is going to be judged. Every thought we have entertained, every word we have spoken, and every deed we have done will be judged.

Jesus said that everybody will be salted or seasoned with fire. "Salted with fire" probably means everyone will be tried with fire:

> Now if anyone builds on the foundation with gold, silver, precious stones, wood, hay, straw—each one's work will become manifest, for the Day will disclose it, because it will be revealed by fire, and the fire will test what sort of work each one has done. If the work that anyone has built on the foundation survives, he will receive a reward. If anyone's work is burned up, he will suffer loss, though he himself will be saved, but only as through fire. (1 Co.3:12–15)

Everything we have done will be set afire. The wood, hay, and straw will be burned. Why? Because they are . . .

- impure
- worthless and unusable
- unpleasing

But the gold, silver, and precious stones will endure the fire and be proven incorruptible. Why? Because they are . . .

- pure
- beneficial and usable
- pleasing

"Seasoned with salt" (NKJV) probably means that every work will be preserved, no matter what sort they are.[2] If the works are good, they will be preserved forever in the kingdom of God. But if the works are bad, they will be preserved forever in hell. There will be no end to the eternal state that is coming after God's plan for this world is complete.

> For the Son of Man is going to come with his angels in the glory of his Father, and then he will repay each person according to what he has done. (Mt.16:27)

> Everyone who comes to me and hears my words and does them, I will show you what he is like: he is like a man building a house, who dug deep and laid the foundation on the rock. And when a flood arose, the stream broke against that house and could not shake it, because it had been well built. But the one who hears and does not do them is like a man who built a house on the ground without a foundation. When the stream broke against it, immediately it fell, and the ruin of that house was great. (Lu.6:47–49)

> And if you call on him as Father who judges impartially according to each one's deeds, conduct yourselves with fear throughout the time of your exile. (1 Pe.1:17)

> And I saw the dead, great and small, standing before the throne, and books were opened. Then another book was opened, which is the book of life. And the dead were judged by what was written in the books, according to what they had done. (Re.20:12)

> Behold, I am coming soon, bringing my recompense with me, to repay each one for what he has done. (Re.22:12)

> I the LORD search the heart and test the mind, to give every man according to his ways, according to the fruit of his deeds. (Je.17:10)

---

2 "Every sacrifice will be seasoned with salt" is not included in the manuscripts from which many newer Bible versions (including the ESV) are translated.

6 The challenge to preserve yourself from sin.

Christ concluded this critical, sobering message with a challenge: we all need to preserve ourselves from sin. Salt is a preservative. That which has been salted is good, beneficial, and useful (see note, *Salt*—Mt.5:13 for a detailed discussion of this point).

a. Search yourself.

Jesus' challenge is to search yourself and your deeds. Evaluate your "*saltiness*," your purity and usefulness. Cleanse your life of everything that is not pure and useful.

> 50 "Salt is good, but if the salt has lost its saltiness, how will you make it salty again? Have salt in yourselves, and be at peace with one another."

b. Be salted: Be pure and useful and at peace with one another.

Be sure to be salted; that is, pure and useful in all your words and works. When our lives are salted—preserved from sinful words and deeds—we will live in peace with other people. We will put off the sins of our sinful nature and put on the nature of Christ, fulfilling His Great Commandment to love others.

> A new commandment I give to you, that you love one another: just as I have loved you, you also are to love one another. By this all people will know that you are my disciples, if you have love for one another. (Jn.13:34–35)

> Let all bitterness and wrath and anger and clamor and slander be put away from you, along with all malice. Be kind to one another, tenderhearted, forgiving one another, as God in Christ forgave you. (Ep.4:31–32)

In conclusion, note what brought about this great lesson from Christ: the arguing among the disciples (vv.33–37) and the intolerance shown toward a man's ministering in the Lord's name (vv.38–41).

THOUGHT 1. An important detail in Jesus' teaching establishes that He is obviously speaking figuratively, not literally, when He says to cut off your hand or foot and pluck out your eye. Note the detail: each of these nouns—"hand," "foot," "eye"—is *singular*, not plural. If Jesus were speaking literally, if He meant that people should literally maim themselves in order to avoid sinning, cutting off only *one* hand or foot and tearing out only *one* eye does not solve the problem. A person can commit the same sins with the remaining hand, foot, or eye.

The point of Jesus' extreme illustrations and this message itself is a serious one: we need to understand the terribleness of our sin and deal with it. If we do not deal with it, God will. We will face His judgment and punishment.

> No, I tell you; but unless you repent, you will all likewise perish. (Lu.13:3)

> But God shows his love for us in that while we were still sinners, Christ died for us. Since, therefore, we have now been justified by his blood, much more shall we be saved by him from the wrath of God. (Ro.5:8–9)

> For the wages of sin is death, but the free gift of God is eternal life in Christ Jesus our Lord. (Ro.6:23)

> But if we judged ourselves truly, we would not be judged. But when we are judged by the Lord, we are disciplined so that we may not be condemned along with the world. (1 Co.11:31–32)

> But if we walk in the light, as he is in the light, we have fellowship with one another, and the blood of Jesus his Son cleanses us from all sin. If we say we have no sin, we deceive ourselves, and the truth is not in us. If we confess our sins, he is faithful and just to forgive us our sins and to cleanse us from all unrighteousness. If we say we have not sinned, we make him a liar, and his word is not in us. (1 Jn.1:7–10)

CHAPTER 10

VI. THE SON OF GOD'S LAST PUBLIC MINISTRY: JESUS DEALS WITH SOME SPECIAL ISSUES, 10:1–52

A. The Issue of Divorce, 10:1–12

(Mt.19:1-12. See Mt.5:31-32; Lu.16:18; 1 Co.7:10-16)

1. Jesus began to minister in Judea
   a. The crowds gathered to hear Jesus teach

   b. The Pharisees gathered to ask Jesus a trick question: Is divorce legal?[DS1]

      1) Jesus asked what their law said

      2) The Pharisees replied: The law grants divorce

2. Jesus saw divorce as hardness of heart

3. Jesus saw marriage as God's way since creation
4. Jesus saw marriage as the most precious bond, a bond that cleaves and unites
5. Jesus saw marriage as the closest human bond—as two becoming one flesh
6. Jesus saw marriage as a divine, spiritual bond wrought by God
7. Jesus saw divorce and remarriage as adultery[DS2]

And he left there and went to the region of Judea and beyond the Jordan, and crowds gathered to him again. And again, as was his custom, he taught them.

² And Pharisees came up and in order to test him asked, "Is it lawful for a man to divorce his wife?"

³ He answered them, "What did Moses command you?"

⁴ They said, "Moses allowed a man to write a certificate of divorce and to send her away."

⁵ And Jesus said to them, "Because of your hardness of heart he wrote you this commandment."

⁶ "But from the beginning of creation, 'God made them male and female.'"

⁷ "'Therefore a man shall leave his father and mother and hold fast to his wife,'"

⁸ "'and the two shall become one flesh.' So they are no longer two but one flesh."

⁹ "What therefore God has joined together, let not man separate."

¹⁰ And in the house the disciples asked him again about this matter.

¹¹ And he said to them, "Whoever divorces his wife and marries another commits adultery against her,

¹² and if she divorces her husband and marries another, she commits adultery."

Division VI

The Son of God's Last Public Ministry: Jesus Deals with Some Special Issues, 10:1–52

A. The Issue of Divorce, 10:1–12

(Mt.19:1–12. See Mt.5:31–32; Lu.16:18; 1 Co.7:10–16)

10:1–12
Introduction

Marriage and divorce are often extremely controversial issues within societies heavily influenced by Christian teaching. Opinions vary, and interpretations differ. There is always the closed view that says divorce is never allowed by God no matter the cruelty and meanness that may exist within the marriage. And there is always the more open view that says divorce is allowed if the rift between a couple is not reconciled and causes more damage than good.

The former view says Jesus gave a complete exposition on marriage and divorce; the latter says He gave guidelines. The former sometimes treats divorce in such a spirit that it appears to be the unpardonable sin; the latter sometimes treats it in such a spirit that it appears to be the escape route to do as one likes (ranging from minor selfish acts to sinful fleshly pleasures).

In Jesus' day the two schools of thought were the conservative Shammai School and the liberal Hillel School (see DEEPER STUDY # 1—Mt.19:1–12 for discussion). As in every generation, some within each school would have nothing to do with anyone who held another opinion. A person's view became a litmus test of fellowship.

It was because of these strong feelings that the religionists (Pharisees) thought they could entrap and discredit Jesus with the subject of divorce. No matter what He said, a great number of people would differ, and they would stop supporting His ministry. He would be discredited, and His ministry would be destroyed.

There is always a reluctance to express a different opinion when a great number hold a particular position. Every generation and every society have issues about which sincere believers disagree. However, divorce is an issue faced in every generation. The issues of marriage and divorce need to be addressed, no matter the different opinions and practices of society. Why?

Divorces have been abundant in every generation. Many of the people involved desperately need help. Their faith, hope, security, children—their whole lives have been drastically affected. If God's people do not open their hearts to them, then a great opportunity to reach them and help them grow in Christ is missed.

Even today, many marriages (perhaps most) are experiencing some serious difficulty. Hardness and cruelty, ranging from mild withdrawal to physical abuse, tear away at the bond created by marriage commitment. Sometimes it is the fault of one; sometimes it is the fault of both. In either case, a great need exists. Again, if God's people do not reach out to help, a great opportunity is lost for Christ.

Note what Jesus did. He did not hesitate to speak up and teach, and the issue was as controversial in His day as it has been in most generations. As we deal with the critical issues of marriage and divorce, we need to follow our Lord's example—and His teaching. This is, *The Issue of Divorce*, 10:1–12 (also see outlines and notes—Mt.5:31–32; 1 Co.7:1–16; Ep.5:22–33).

1. Jesus began to minister in Judea (vv.1-4).
2. Jesus saw divorce as hardness of heart (v.5).
3. Jesus saw marriage as God's way since creation (v.6).
4. Jesus saw marriage as the most precious bond, a bond that cleaves and unites (v.7).
5. Jesus saw marriage as the closest human bond—as two becoming one flesh (v.8).
6. Jesus saw true marriage as a divine, spiritual bond wrought by God (v.9).
7. Jesus saw divorce and remarriage as adultery (vv.10-12).

1 Jesus began to minister in Judea.

This chapter marks the beginning of Jesus' ministry in Judea. Mark 1-9 have covered the Galilean ministry of Jesus; now, chapters 10-15 cover Jesus' Judean ministry. It should be noted that Mark does not give an account of many events that took place between these two ministries. The omit-

10:1-4

And he left there and went to the region of Judea and beyond the Jordan, and crowds gathered to him again. And again, as was his custom, he taught them.

² And Pharisees came up and in order to test him asked, "Is it lawful for a man to divorce his wife?"

³ He answered them, "What did Moses command you?"

⁴ They said, "Moses allowed a man to write a certificate of divorce and to send her away."

ted section is usually called the **travel-narrative** or travel-ministry. It is covered in detail in Luke 9-18. Matthew also gives isolated events of the travel-ministry.

a. The crowds gathered to hear Jesus teach (v.1).

The crowds flocked to Jesus, and, as He always did, the Lord taught them and healed them (Mt.19:2). The success of the Lord's ministry was phenomenal. During the few months of His ministry, it seemed the whole country was flocking to Him. This, of course, provoked the leaders, both civil and religious (see notes—Mt.12:1-8; note and Deeper Study # 1—12:10; Deeper Study # 2—Mk.3:22).

b. The Pharisees gathered to ask Jesus a trick question: Is divorce legal (vv.2-4)?

The leaders of Jerusalem again sent an investigating committee to discredit Jesus before the people. The Jewish leaders (Sanhedrin) were convinced they must break the people away from Jesus. He seemed to be undermining Jewish religion and leading the people away from their control. And there was always the danger that the Roman authorities would clamp down on the apparent disturbance caused by this so-called Messiah. They feared the Romans would remove them from power and replace them with more capable leaders.

These concerns prompted the investigating committee to confront Jesus. This time, they questioned Him about divorce, and they were thoroughly convinced that Jesus could not answer without entrapping Himself.

Jesus responded by turning the question back to the Pharisees, asking them what their law said (v.3). They replied that the law permits divorce (v.4; see Deeper Study # 1).

Deeper Study # 1

(10:2-4) **Marriage—Divorce—Schools of Thought—Shammai—Hillel:** the Pharisees came to Jesus tempting Him, trying to discredit Him. They asked if it was lawful for a man to divorce his wife. Matthew adds, "for any cause" (Mt.19:3).

There was a background to this question. The society of Jesus' day was very loose morally—even Jewish society. Marriage was considered nothing more than a piece of paper: if it worked, fine; if it did not work, fine. One could always divorce (see notes—Mt.5:31).

There were two positions or schools of thought on divorce. Moses had said that any man could divorce his wife if "she finds no favor in his eyes, because he has found some indecency [or uncleanness] in her" (De.24:1).

1. The school of Shammai said that the words "some indecency" meant adultery only. A wife could be as loose and as mean as Jezebel, but she was not to be divorced unless she committed adultery.

2. The school of Hillel said that the words "some indecency" meant anything that was not pleasing to the man. A person should remember that women were counted as nothing but *property* to be possessed by men. They had no rights whatsoever, except as a man might wish to give. Of course, the position followed by society was the position that allowed human nature to run loose. Women were abused: neglected, used, discarded, and violated. They had no rights whatsoever. They were nothing but chattel, property of men, very often considered of less value than other property (whether animals or land or other possession). Therefore, divorce ran rampant in Jesus' day.

The Pharisees wished to draw Jesus in the controversy between the conservative (Shammai) and liberal view (Hillel). They were simply asking Him if He agreed with the school of Hillel which held that a man could lawfully divorce his wife for any cause. No matter which position Jesus took, He would offend and stir up a large number of people, becoming embroiled in a contentious controversy. He answered as follows.

1. "God made them [Adam and Eve] male and female" (v.6). He did not make them males and females as He did animals. But He made *one male* and *one female*. Each one was made for the other. They were not made for anyone else, for there was no one else.

2. The man is to hold fast to [be joined to, cleave to] his wife and create a new family distinct from the family of his parents (v.7). He says, "a man," not men, and "his wife," not wives. Note that a man leaves his father and mother. The union between husband and wife is to gain primacy over the union between parent and child. The union is wrought by God and appointed by God; therefore, marriage is a divine institution. Just as parents and children are not to divorce one another, neither are the husband and wife to divorce each other.

3. The man and his wife are no longer two; they are molded into "one flesh" (v.8). What is it that makes them one flesh? Holding fast or cleaving to each other. They are one body, one flesh, one person. They are not joined to two or three or four other persons, but they cleave only to one other person.

4. They have been joined together by God; Consequently, no human should separate what God has joined together (v.9). Neither one of them nor anyone else is to step in between the two and cause separation.

2 Jesus saw divorce as hardness of heart.

Jesus answered that the law only permitted divorce because of the hardness of men's hearts. The Old Testament (Moses) *did not command* divorce if two people were not compatible and did not get along. The Old Testament *only granted a divorce*. It legally accommodated the desires of men who refused to live within God's will for marriage. It *never approved of* nor *recommended* divorce.

> [5] And Jesus said to them, "Because of your hardness of heart he wrote you this commandment."

The ancient world treated women as nothing more than chattel property. A man could secure as many wives as he wished (polygamy), and he could discard them *whenever*, *wherever*, and *however* he wished. He could *kick a wife out* and dispose of her as he wished. Most men's hearts were hard in their treatment of women and in their attitude toward marriage and divorce. Many had . . .

- a total disdain for morality
- a total defiance against marital law
- a total disregard of God's will for marriage
- a total insensitivity to women's rights in marriage

The Old Testament (Moses) law was not a loose law, not in the ancient world. It required a *written contract of divorce*, which was unpracticed and unheard of in most societies. It required some time and some thought before a divorce could be issued, and a man could no longer get rid of his wife without involving a third party in the matter. Some official had to approve and write up *the certificate of divorce*.

The law of the Old Testament (Moses) taught that a written contract of divorce . . .

- could check the breakdown of the family to some degree
- would give time for a person to think about the consequences of divorce
- did proclaim that there was a higher law than a man's own whims, urges, and desires; if nothing else, a man had to seek a contract of divorce from a higher authority

It is critical to understand that Jesus *saw divorce as hardness of heart*. This, He said, was the reason the law of Moses permitted a certificate of divorce. Note that Jesus is saying three things about the Old Testament law on divorce:

First, divorce is a concession, not the will of God.

Second, divorce is allowed only because the man's heart was hard, that is, sinful.

Third, divorce was not the purpose of God and it was never His will (see Deeper Study # 4—Mt.19:8 for detailed discussion and application of this point).

10:6

⁶ "But from the beginning of creation, 'God made them male and female.'"

3 Jesus saw marriage as God's way since creation.

Jesus saw marriage as God's way—since creation. From the very beginning of human existence, God joined the male and female together. What Jesus was saying is that creation is the root basis, the very foundation for marriage. He pointed out three truths in His simple statement.

- The *creative* truth: Jesus said that God did not make man and woman plural. He did not make them males and females. He made one male and one female—each made for the other. They were not made for *any* other, for there was no one else—just Adam and Eve.
- The *spiritual* truth: Jesus was saying that male and female were created distinctively from animals. Animals were created *en masse,* to be together with any and many. But male and female were created differently and distinctively. They were created one male and one female, created as spiritual beings, created for a much higher purpose than animals. Since there were not others like them, they were sharing their purpose together in constant fellowship with God. Note: they were sharing their purpose with no other, for there was no other.
- The *logical* truth: reason alone says that if God created all other animals *en masse,* and then turned around and created one male and one female, then the male and female belonged to each other. They were created to be together, one with one, even as animals were created to be together *en masse.*

10:7

⁷ "'Therefore a man shall leave his father and mother and hold fast to his wife,'"

4 Jesus saw marriage as the most precious bond, a bond that cleaves and unites.

Jesus saw marriage as the most precious bond, the bond that holds the husband and wife together. God made the *two* genders—male *and* female—for *this* reason ("therefore," ESV) or cause. Note the clear, specific truths Jesus taught.

First, a man (one) is to hold fast (be joined, cleave) to his wife and create a new family distinct from the family of his parents. Jesus said, "a man," not men, and "his wife," not wives.

Second, a man leaves his father and mother. The union between husband and wife is to gain primacy over the union between parent and child. *Leaving* is a permanent act; *holding fast* (cleaving, being joined) is also a permanent act.

Third, *holding fast* means more than being close and intimate. It is stronger than the closeness that exists between parent and child, for it causes a husband and wife to leave parents. By *holding fast,* Jesus meant a spiritual union that could be brought about and given only by God (see Deeper Study # 2—Mt.19:5). Therefore, marriage becomes the most precious bond that can be known between human beings. Marriage becomes a divine institution.

Fourth, just as parents and children are not to divorce one another, so husband and wife are not to divorce one another. Note that father, mother, and child comprise a unit, a family. Jesus said father and mother are there when the child leaves, and the child (man) leaves to "hold fast to his wife." There is no thought, not even a hint of separation in this statement. It is unquestionably a statement of God's purpose for father, mother, and child. The structure of the family is the means by which humans are to carry out the purposes of God on earth. Divorce, tearing down the structure of the family, is not the purpose of God. Father, mother, and child—the structure of a family—is the purpose of God.

Fifth, the relationship between father and mother is to be closer, more intimate, and longer than that between parent and child. The day comes when the child leaves the parent, and the parents are left with each other—alone. This says much to husband and wife: they must not neglect their lives together. The day comes when they are alone, by themselves.

5 Jesus saw marriage as the closest human bond—as two becoming one flesh.

Jesus saw marriage as the closest of human bonds—as two becoming one flesh—one person. Jesus had just said that a man is to "hold fast to his wife." This is a powerful statement. *Hold fast to, be joined to, or cleave to* (Gk. proskollethesetai pros; pronounced *pros-kol-lay'-thay-seh-tah-ee pros*) means to be glued to. When two objects are glued together, the result is *one* object. Likewise, *cleaving*, when spiritually brought by God, molds two people into one person. As the husband and wife cleave, as they become more and more spiritually united by God, they become more and more meshed into one being. Each grows into the very being of the other spouse. They become one body, one flesh, one person.

8 "'and the two shall become one flesh.' So they are no longer two but one flesh."

The husband and wife are not joined to two or three or four other persons. They can *hold fast* or *cleave* only under God and only to one other person.

The power of God is enormous to a couple who will obey Him. God can cause their cleaving to bind them so close together that they are as one person.

6 Jesus saw true marriage as a divine, spiritual bond wrought by God.

Jesus saw true marriage as a divine, spiritual bond brought about by God. He said that a man and woman who choose to cleave to each other—marry each other—are not merely joined together by human decision or decree; they are joined together by *God*. Therefore, marriage is intended to be something more than what is often thought or pictured: it does not just involve a civil contract, embracing, or sexual union. "What God has joined together" speaks of a spiritual dimension to marriage, a spiritual union.

9 "What therefore God has joined together, let not man separate."

Spouses who are *obedient* to Christ by holding fast or cleaving to each other, not only physically but spiritually, are the ones who become one flesh in every way and the ones whom God can truly join together. A civil contract does not bind people together spiritually—neither does embracing—neither does sex. When a couple does not obey Christ, they never enjoy life and marriage the way God intends for them to be. Only God can bind a couple together spiritually, and He does so because a couple is obedient to Him. He rewards and blesses obedience, not disobedience.

Jesus stated firmly that a man and woman who marry are joined together by God. No one is to separate what God joins together. Neither wife nor husband nor anyone else is to step in between the two and cause separation.

The apostle Paul, by inspiration of the Holy Spirit, explained more deeply the spiritual dimension of marriage. Marriage is to be a bond so closely and spiritually bound together that it mirrors the spiritual union between Christ and His church, between Christ and the believer (see outline and notes—Ep.5:22-33; Col.3:18-21;1 Co.6:19).

Husbands, love your wives, as Christ loved the church and gave himself up for her. (Ep.5:25)

7 Jesus saw divorce and remarriage as adultery.

Later, in private, the disciples asked Jesus more questions about divorce. Jesus replied that He saw divorce and remarriage as adultery (see DEEPER STUDY # 2). In a discussion of this point, Matthew covers Jesus' teaching much more thoroughly. For this reason, Matthew should always be studied in looking at divorce and remarriage (see outline and notes—Mt.19:9–12).

10:10–12

¹⁰ And in the house the disciples asked him again about this matter.

¹¹ And he said to them, "Whoever divorces his wife and marries another commits adultery against her,

¹² and if she divorces her husband and marries another, she commits adultery."

DEEPER STUDY # 2

(10:10–12) **Fornication—Adultery:** a person, especially a Christian believer, needs to think about the real meaning of adultery. Adultery is the turning away from a spouse to another person. Many people would never think of turning away from their spouse to a third person, yet they readily and willingly turn toward self and toward other things. God said that the backslidden nation, Israel, committed adultery against Him, and that He sent her away with a certificate of divorce (Je.3:8). Many people have done just as Israel did. They have refused to surrender to God; they have lived in a backslidden state; they have committed spiritual adultery against God. As a result of turning away from God, they have turned more and more away from their spouse and in many cases from their children.

Day by day many people mistreat their spouse and children by . . .
- being mean and ugly
- being nagging and mentally cruel
- being neglectful and unthoughtful
- being physically abusive and life-threatening
- being deliberately withdrawn and separated

And the truth of the matter is that many mistreat spouses and family out of selfishness. Some are cruel; others sadistic. Some are critical; others sarcastic; still others demonic and hellish. Some are mentally abusive; others physically abusive, even to the point of murdering spouse and children—the unthinkable.

Only God knows the truth about a marriage. A husband or a wife can use his or her personality to present a front to the world. Yet within the heart there can be such a hardness toward his or her spouse, such an unwillingness to truly cleave or hold fast that God simply cannot join them together as one flesh. Hardness, very simply, wrecks a marriage by causing one spouse to turn away and separate from the other spouse. If the spouses are not together, then they are separate, not cleaving. There can be no cleaving if the two are not together. And as pointed out earlier, cleaving is the blessing and the gift of God. Cleaving is only possible as each allows God to *join them together* into the spiritual union of marriage.

(Mt.19:13-15; Lu.18:15-17)

13 And they were bringing children to him that he might touch them, and the disciples rebuked them.

14 But when Jesus saw it, he was indignant and said to them, "Let the children come to me; do not hinder them, for to such belongs the kingdom of God.

15 Truly, I say to you, whoever does not receive the kingdom of God like a child shall not enter it."

16 And he took them in his arms and blessed them, laying his hands on them.

1. **The issue regarding children**[DS1]
   a. They are totally dependent
   b. They can cause frivolous pride in their parents
   c. They can interfere with work
2. **The truth about children and Jesus**[DS2]
   a. They are invited to Jesus[DS3]
   b. They are citizens of God's kingdom[DS4]

   c. They illustrate how a person receives the kingdom[DS5]

   d. They are received and blessed by Jesus[DS6]
   e. They respond to Jesus[DS7]

Division VI

The Son of God's Last Public Ministry: Jesus Deals with Some Special Issues, 10:1–52

B. The Issue of Children and the Truth About Children and Jesus, 10:13–16

(Mt.19:13-15; Lu.18:15-17)

10:13–16
Introduction

"Jesus loves the little children, all the children of the world," says the Sunday school song. Nothing ever written by human beings is truer. In this passage, our Lord demonstrated His love for children.

This event involving children follows directly after the question about divorce (also see Mt.19:13). The family as a whole is being discussed: the husband, wife, and children.

Children are a joy, but many people look upon them as problems or a nuisance. And tragically, children are sometimes neglected, ignored, oppressed, and even abused.

In this passage, Jesus pulls no punches. It is one of the times He became extremely angry, filled and moved with indignation. Jesus is the great defender of children, and every man and woman needs to heed His words about them. This is, *The Issue of Children and the Truth About Children and Jesus*, 10:13–16

1. The issue regarding children (v.13).
2. The truth about children and Jesus (vv.14–16).

1 The issue regarding children.

This scene was both touching and tragic. Some parents, tenderly and with hope, were bringing their children to Jesus (see DEEPER STUDY # 1). Why? That He might simply *touch*

10:13

13 And they were bringing children to him that he might touch them, and the disciples rebuked them.

them. The parents were hoping that Jesus would touch their children, and in touching, their children would be blessed.

But this was not the only scene. The disciples were rebuking the parents for bringing the children. *Rebuked* (Gk. epitimao) is a strong word: it means actively hindering and reproving. The disciples were actually holding the parents and pushing them back, trying to stop them from bringing their children to Jesus. Why? Very simply, the disciples saw a problem with children. They looked upon children just as many others look upon them: they felt the children could contribute nothing to the adult world. In adult affairs, children were deemed useless, unimportant, a nuisance; therefore, they should not disturb the adults when they were busy at work. They felt Jesus was too busy and His work was too important to be disturbed. The disciples, just like so many adults, saw the following problems with children.

a. They are totally dependent.

Children are totally dependent. These children were so young they had to be brought to Jesus. The disciples felt they could contribute nothing significant. They were too young, too helpless, too dependent. Therefore, their place was off to the side somewhere. They should not be bothering the Lord right now. Their parents should have known this and should have been more respectful.

b. They can cause frivolous pride in their parents.

Parents often have a frivolous pride over their children. The disciples may have thought the parents just wanted to show off their children and have Jesus make over them. Frivolous pride often aggravates busy people, especially when they are interrupted by parents who merely want to show off their children. The disciples felt that the children were not important enough to be allowed to interfere, certainly not right now.

c. They can interfere with work.

The disciples felt the children were interfering with Jesus' important work. At times children do interrupt work, sometimes important work. They distract, causing a person to lose their thought; they require attention and help. The disciples felt the children were not important enough to be allowed to interrupt at this time.

DEEPER STUDY # 1

(10:13) **Were Bringing; Brought** (prosphero): to bring to; to bring unto. It is the word used in connection with offerings. The idea is that whatever is brought is being brought as an offering. It is a dedication to God (see Mt.5:23–24).

10:14–16

[14] But when Jesus saw it, he was indignant and said to them, "Let the children come to me; do not hinder them, for to such belongs the kingdom of God.
[15] Truly, I say to you, whoever does not receive the kingdom of God like a child shall not enter it."
[16] And he took them in his arms and blessed them, laying his hands on them.

2 The truth about Jesus and children.

Jesus saw how the disciples were treating the children, and He was indignant or displeased (see DEEPER STUDY # 2). Children are not a problem—not to Jesus, not ever. And, as He demonstrated here, He becomes extremely angry when adults treat children as if they are a problem. He wanted His disciples to learn this, so He taught them five simple truths about children.

a. They are invited to Jesus (v.14a).

Jesus firmly ordered the disciples to stop hindering the children from coming to Him. Children are to be invited to Jesus, never discouraged nor forbidden to come to Him (see DEEPER STUDY # 3).

b. They are citizens of God's kingdom (v.14b).

What an intriguing—and beautiful statement our Savior made in regard to children: the kingdom of God belongs to them. Children are citizens of God's kingdom (see Deeper Study # 4).

c. They illustrate how a person receives the kingdom (v.15).

The openness and willing faith of children illustrates how people are to receive the kingdom. If we—adults—wish to enter God's kingdom, we must come as children (see Deeper Study # 5). Every man and woman needs to meditate on this statement and take it to heart.

d. They are received and blessed by Jesus (v.16a).

No child should ever hesitate to come to Jesus, nor should they wonder what kind of reception they will receive. Jesus welcomes every child with open arms. He is always available to receive them and bless them (see Deeper Study # 6). How critical it is that we teach children this assuring truth.

e. They respond to Jesus (v.16b).

Imagine the joy in these little ones' hearts and the beaming smiles on their faces when Jesus took them in His arms. Children respond to Jesus. We must encourage them to come to Jesus while their hearts are tender and open to Him (see Deeper Study # 7).

DEEPER STUDY # 2

(10:14) **Indignant; Displeased:** (aganaktesen; pronounced *ay-gan-ahk-tay'-sen*): to be moved with indignation; to feel pain; to grieve; to be displeased, sore displeased, and much displeased (see 2 Co.7:11).

The word is very strong, expressing deep, even violent emotion. The Lord was moved with indignation toward the disciples for what they were doing. Note two facts indicated by this experience.

1. Strong indignation against sin and injustice is sometimes justified.

2. Not being moved with indignation toward sin and injustice is sometimes a gross wrong.

DEEPER STUDY # 3

(10:14) **Children:** Jesus said let the children come and forbid them not. *Hinder* or *forbid* (koluete; *ko-loo'-eh-teh*) means to prevent or to restrain. The tense is a *present imperative*, a continuous command: stop hindering, stop preventing the children from coming to Me. In this case His own disciples were hindering the children, continuously preventing their coming to Jesus. No wonder He was moved with indignation. Note four observations.

1. Jesus called for and received children. They were welcome, even when they were so little they had to be brought. They may have been too little to understand, but Jesus was big enough to bless them and see to it that the blessing remained upon them. He is, after all, God; and as God He is omnipotent, all-powerful, and able to exercise His power as He wills. In no way will He ever reject children.

2. Jesus rebuked those who stopped and disregarded the children. He said that such action was wrong. We are not to stop little children from coming to Christ. Contrariwise, we are to bring them to Him. He is God; and as God He is providential, doing as He wills; therefore, He is the One who determines whom He will bless. No person determines it for Him. Despite their tender age and lack of reason, children are not to be kept from coming to Him. No obstacle is to be put in their way.

3. The benefits of bringing children to Christ are innumerable. Just a few major benefits are as follows:
   a. They learn love: that they are loved by God and by all who trust God, no matter how evil some in the world may act. They are even taught to love those who do wrong.
   b. They grow, learning power and triumph: that God will help His followers through all trials and temptations. They learn there is a supernatural power available to help, a power to help when mother and dad and loved ones have done all they can.
   c. They grow, learning hope and faith: that no matter what happens, no matter how great a trial, they can still trust God and hope in Him. God has provided a very special strength to carry them through the trials of life (no matter how painful); and He has provided a very special place called heaven where He will carry them and their loved ones who trust Him when they face death.
   d. They grow, learning the truth of life and service: that God has given them the privilege of life and of living in a beautiful earth and universe. The evil and bad that exist in the world are caused by evil and bad people. But despite such evil, they are to appreciate and to serve life and the beautiful earth. They are to continue to work, making the greatest contribution they can to both life and the earth.
   e. They grow, learning trust and endurance: that life is full of temptations and pitfalls which can easily rob them of joy, destroying their lives and the fulfillment of their purpose. The way to escape temptations and pitfalls is to follow Christ and cling to Him, enduring in His work and purpose.
   f. They grow, learning peace: that there is an inner peace despite the turbulent waters of this world, and that peace is knowing and trusting Christ.
4. Parents do not bring their children to Christ for several reasons.
   a. Some parents (in civilized as well as uncivilized parts of the world) are not aware of the only living and true God. Therefore, they are blind; they simply do not know. Christians have failed to take the gospel to the whole world.
   b. Some parents have heard the truth, but they have rejected Christ. They are agnostics or atheists, or else they love the world and the things of the world more than they love the news of the living God who gives eternal life. They do not care about anything beyond the comfort of self and the benefits of this world.
   c. Some parents do believe, at least mentally, but they are complacent and lethargic. They are not concerned enough to come to Christ nor to bring their children to Christ.
   d. Some parents are believers, but unfortunately they are immature and inconsistent in their Christian life. Their own Christian life and worship are weak and neglected, so their children are taught that Christ is not really all that important.
   e. Some parents are not willing to influence and mold their child's thinking spiritually. They want their children to make their own choices. They are willing to teach them what foods to eat and books to read and anything else that will teach them how to care for themselves physically and materially. But they leave the care of the spiritual up to them after they become adults.

There are two great errors with all five of the above reasons.

First, the philosophy underlying every one of the reasons is false. Any parent who does not bring their child to Christ is following a false philosophy of life and is not facing reality.

> I told you that you would die in your sins, for unless you believe that I am he you will die in your sins. (Jn.8:24)

> Jesus said to him, "I am the way, and the truth, and the life. No one comes to the Father except through me." (Jn.14:6)

> For there is one God, and there is one mediator between God and men, the man Christ Jesus. (1 Ti.2:5)

> And without faith it is impossible to please him, for whoever would draw near to God must believe that he exists and that he rewards those who seek him. (He.11:6)

Second, children's minds are molded by those they are with, whether the loose and immoral or the disciplined and moral. If the child's mind is not molded by *godly parents*, it will be molded by the worldliness of the parents and the carnality of those who walk in selfish and corrupt ways.

> Prompted by her mother, she said, "Give me the head of John the Baptist here on a platter." (Mt.14:8)
>
> I am reminded of your sincere faith, a faith that dwelt first in your grandmother Lois and your mother Eunice and now, I am sure, dwells in you as well. (2 Ti.1:5)
>
> He did what was evil in the sight of the LORD and walked in the way of his father and in the way of his mother and in the way of Jeroboam the son of Nebat, who made Israel to sin. (1 K.22:52)
>
> He walked in the way of Asa his father and did not turn aside from it, doing what was right in the sight of the LORD. (2 Chr.20:32)
>
> He also walked in the ways of the house of Ahab, for his mother was his counselor in doing wickedly. (2 Chr.22:3)
>
> And he did what was right in the eyes of the LORD, according to all that his father Amaziah had done. (2 Chr.26:4)

DEEPER STUDY # 4

(10:14) **Children:** children are citizens of God's kingdom. Jesus said, "to such [little children] belongs the kingdom of God." What Jesus meant was at least two things.

1. Little children are citizens of God's kingdom, at least until they are able to reason and make decisions between right and wrong, that is, the age of accountability.
2. Little children show what a person must be like to enter the kingdom of God. The nature, character, and traits that are essential to get into heaven are seen in little children.
   a. Little children are dependent and trusting. They are totally dependent. They know little and can do little in taking care of themselves. To them, *big people*, especially mommy and daddy, know everything and can do everything. Children are also trusting. They trust everyone. Anyone can take the child into their arms. The child has not learned to suspect the world. Everyone is a friend; no one is an enemy, and few are strangers.
   b. Little children are responsive and submissive. They respond to an adult. They will come, go, pick up, do whatever is suggested to them. They will drop whatever they are doing, surrender whatever is occupying their thoughts and behavior, and respond.
   c. Little children are obedient and learning. They will do exactly what they are asked to do, and they will learn by it. They are ever learning what they see and are told, whether good or bad.
   d. Little children are humble and forgiving. They are not interested in prominence, fame, power, wealth, or position. They do not push themselves forward. Generally speaking, they do not want to sit around in the midst of a group of adults. They have not been taught to think in terms of self-importance, not yet. Children also forgive and forget. (We must remember Christ is talking about the child in a normal, healthy environment. He is not talking about an abusive environment. In other teachings, He condemned the abuse or mistreatment of children.)

DEEPER STUDY # 5

(10:15) **Children:** children illustrate exactly how a person receives the Kingdom of God. Note the strong words of Jesus about the terrible end of the person who does not come to God with the mindset of a child. A person has to approach God and receive God's kingdom

(His rule, reign, and authority) into their life just like a little child, or else they will not enter the eternal kingdom of God (see DEEPER STUDY # 5—Mt.19:23-24).

What did Jesus mean by receiving the kingdom as a little child? (See note, Conversion—Mt.18:3 for a clear illustration of this.)

1. Children trust and depend on Jesus: (a) They sense the warmth, tenderness, care, and love of Jesus; and (b) they listen to the call (message, gospel) of Jesus. They trust what they hear and depend on Jesus to take care of them now and forever.

> Truly, truly, I say to you, whoever hears my word and believes him who sent me has eternal life. He does not come into judgment, but has passed from death to life. (Jn.5:24)

> But I have calmed and quieted my soul, like a weaned child with its mother; like a weaned child is my soul within me. (Ps.131:2)

2. Children more eagerly respond and surrender to Jesus. They are ready and willing to respond to Jesus. They are more likely willing to give up what they are doing, to surrender whatever is occupying their thoughts, behavior, and time, in order to receive Jesus. They want the kingdom of God in their heart (God's rule and reign), and they want to enter the eternal kingdom of God someday in the future.

> The Spirit himself bears witness with our spirit that we are children of God, and if children, then heirs—heirs of God and fellow heirs with Christ, provided we suffer with him in order that we may also be glorified with him. (Ro.8:16-17)

> But when the fullness of time had come, God sent forth his Son, born of woman, born under the law, to redeem those who were under the law, so that we might receive adoption as sons. And because you are sons, God has sent the Spirit of his Son into our hearts, crying, "Abba! Father!" So you are no longer a slave, but a son, and if a son, then an heir through God. (Ga.4:4-7)

3. Children are obedient to Jesus and are ever learning of Him. They listen and do exactly what Jesus says, even if it is difficult and requires self-denial. They do it simply because Jesus asks them to do it. They do not act independently or behave selfishly.

> If you keep my commandments, you will abide in my love, just as I have kept my Father's commandments and abide in his love. . . . You are my friends if you do what I command you. (Jn.15:10, 14)

> Therefore be imitators of God, as beloved children. (Ep.5:1)

> And have you forgotten the exhortation that addresses you as sons? "My son, do not regard lightly the discipline of the Lord, nor be weary when reproved by him." For the Lord disciplines the one he loves, and chastises every son whom he receives. (He.12:5-6; see v.5-10)

4. Children are humble and forgiving (see note, pt.2—Mk.10:14).

> Blessed are the peacemakers, for they shall be called sons of God. (Mt.5:9)

> But not so with you. Rather, let the greatest among you become as the youngest, and the leader as one who serves. (Lu.22:26)

> Let all bitterness and wrath and anger and clamor and slander be put away from you, along with all malice. Be kind to one another, tenderhearted, forgiving one another, as God in Christ forgave you. (Ep.4:31-32)

> He has told you, O man, what is good; and what does the LORD require of you but to do justice, and to love kindness, and to walk humbly with your God? (Mi.6:8)

DEEPER STUDY # 6

(10:16) **Children:** children are received and blessed by Jesus. Note how Jesus took the children up in His arms, put His hands on them, and blessed them. The scene is warm, full of genuine care and truth that we often overlook. It is not so much that we come and touch God as it is that He comes and touches us. It is not so much that we take hold of God as it is that we are taken hold of by Him (Ph.3:12-13).

> But to all who did receive him, who believed in his name, he gave the right to become children of God, who were born, not of blood nor of the will of the flesh nor of the will of man, but of God. (Jn.1:12–13)

> All that the Father gives me will come to me, and whoever comes to me I will never cast out. (Jn.6:37)

> I love those who love me, and those who seek me diligently find me. (Pr.8:17)

God's blessing is not so much due to how rational and capable *we are* as it is to *His purpose and will*. God can choose to touch and bless whom He wills, and He demonstrates beyond all question that He chooses to touch and bless the children brought to Him.

DEEPER STUDY # 7

(10:16) **Children:** children respond to Jesus. They have nothing to give but themselves, and they are ready to give themselves. Their little hearts are tender and responsive to authority. They look to others to provide, teach, protect, and care for them. They are ready to respond; all they need is for someone to present the warmth and tenderness and love of Jesus.

> But when the chief priests and the scribes saw the wonderful things that he did, and the children crying out in the temple, "Hosanna to the Son of David!" they were indignant. (Mt.21:15. See note—Mt.21:15–16 for an excellent example of this point.)

> And he said to them, "Why were you looking for me? Did you not know that I must be in my Father's house?" (Lu.2:49)

> And how from childhood you have been acquainted with the sacred writings, which are able to make you wise for salvation through faith in Christ Jesus. (2 Ti.3:15)

> Now the boy Samuel continued to grow both in stature and in favor with the LORD and also with man. (1 S.2:26)

> Joash was seven years old when he began to reign, and he reigned forty years in Jerusalem. His mother's name was Zibiah of Beersheba. And Joash did what was right in the eyes of the LORD all the days of Jehoiada the priest. (2 Chr.24:1–2)

> Josiah was eight years old when he began to reign, and he reigned thirty-one years in Jerusalem. And he did what was right in the eyes of the LORD, and walked in the ways of David his father; and he did not turn aside to the right hand or to the left. (2 Chr.34:1–2)

C. The Rich Young Ruler:
The Issue of Eternal Life, 10:17–22

(Mt.19:16–22; Lu.18:18–23)

1. **Fact 1: Seeking Jesus is not enough to receive eternal life**
   a. A rich young man eagerly sought out Jesus
   b. His concern: He sought eternal life
2. **Fact 2: To praise Jesus is not enough to receive eternal life**

3. **Fact 3: To be respectable is not enough to receive eternal life**
   a. The laws of respectability

   b. The respectable character of the young ruler
4. **Fact 4: Being loved by Jesus is not enough to receive eternal life**
5. **Fact 5: Following Christ is required to receive eternal life**
   a. The command: Total and sacrificial surrender, the abandonment of all
   b. The result: The requirement was too heavy—he went away sad and grieved

¹⁷ And as he was setting out on his journey, a man ran up and knelt before him and asked him, "Good Teacher, what must I do to inherit eternal life?"

¹⁸ And Jesus said to him, "Why do you call me good? No one is good except God alone."

¹⁹ "You know the commandments: 'Do not murder, Do not commit adultery, Do not steal, Do not bear false witness, Do not defraud, Honor your father and mother.'"

²⁰ And he said to him, "Teacher, all these I have kept from my youth."

²¹ And Jesus, looking at him, loved him, and said to him, "You lack one thing: go, sell all that you have and give to the poor, and you will have treasure in heaven; and come, follow me."

²² Disheartened by the saying, he went away sorrowful, for he had great possessions.

Division VI

The Son of God's Last Public Ministry:
Jesus Deals with Some Special Issues, 10:1–52

C. The Rich Young Ruler: The Issue of Eternal Life, 10:17–22

(Mt.19:16–22; Lu.18:18–23)

10:17–22
Introduction

Worldly success cannot bring satisfaction, not true inner satisfaction and peace. Those who achieve prosperity, position, and power find that these alone are not enough to appease their souls. They long for something more, something that will permanently fill the void in their hearts.

This passage acquaints us with such a man. He is known as "the rich young ruler," because of the combined picture gleaned from all three Gospels:

➢ He was rich (Mt.19:22; Mk.10:22; Lu.18:23).
➢ He was young (Mt.19:20).
➢ He was a ruler (Lu.18:18).

Truly, this man was rare among the young people of his day. The fact that he had already been placed in a position of leadership reveals that he was conscientious, responsible, dependable, and was very mature for his age.

But of even greater importance, he was eagerly seeking eternal life, something more than the success he had achieved at such an unusually young age. Spiritual matters are often shunned by many young people, but this fellow was concerned about his soul.

The dominant theme of the young man's encounter with Jesus is his sincerity, his desperate search for eternal life. Jesus takes the man's desperation and shocks the world. Desperation, sincerity, eagerness, and seeking eternal life are not enough. Inheriting eternal life takes much more than sincerely desiring to possess it. In seeking eternal life, people have a problem that must be overcome. This is, *The Rich Young Ruler: The Issue of Eternal Life*, 10:17-22.

(Note: For a full understanding of the teachings and commentary of this passage, it is necessary to also read the outlines and commentary for 10:23-27 and 10:28-31.)

1. Fact 1: Seeking Jesus is not enough to receive eternal life (v.17).
2. Fact 2: To praise Jesus is not enough to receive eternal life (v.18).
3. Fact 3: To be respectable is not enough to receive eternal life (vv.19-20).
4. Fact 4: Being loved by Jesus is not enough to receive eternal life (v.21).
5. Fact 5: Following Christ is required to receive eternal life (vv.21-22).

1 Fact 1: Seeking Jesus is not enough to receive eternal life.

10:17

Picture the striking scene Mark describes. After Jesus' confrontation with the Pharisees and His correction of the disciples, he journeyed on toward Jerusalem (v.32). Suddenly, a man dashed toward the Lord and knelt at His feet.

> [17] And as he was setting out on his journey, a man ran up and knelt before him and asked him, "Good Teacher, what must I do to inherit eternal life?"

a. A rich young man eagerly sought out Jesus.

This man sought Jesus with a sense of urgency and desperation seldom seen. Note what the details of this verse reveal about him:

- The man was *eager*, ever so eager: he *ran* to Jesus.
- The man was *humble*: he cast himself to the ground, kneeling before Jesus, showing extreme reverence. He esteemed Jesus ever so highly. He bowed the knee to Him.
- The man was *respectful*: he addressed Jesus as "Good Teacher," which was the proper and courteous address to a revered rabbi or teacher.

b. His concern: He sought eternal life.

The desperate man was *concerned* about his spiritual welfare. He immediately came to the point for which he had so eagerly and diligently sought Jesus, asking what he had to do to inherit eternal life.

The young man demonstrated how we should seek eternal life. He did exactly what we should do when we wish for anything: seek it. We are to *seek* eternal life as the rich young ruler did. But in seeking eternal life, something is critical. We must go to the right *source*. This is exactly what the rich young man did: he approached Jesus, the Source of eternal life; and he asked, confessing his need.

Note two observations about the young man's seeking eternal life.

First, he believed that eternal life existed, that there was such a thing as eternal life. He believed that there was something beyond this life and this world. He believed there was life in another world, and he was sincerely eager (perhaps desperate) to receive it. It was for this reason and this reason alone that he ran to Jesus and knelt before Him.

Second, he did a rare thing. He openly confessed his eager concern for eternal life. Few of the rich would ever confess such a concern openly as he did, and few of the young would ever consider it important enough at their early stage of life. He had an urgent need, and he knew it and openly confessed it. He was seeking for inner peace and a sense of completeness, fulfillment, and satisfaction.

2 Fact 2: To praise Jesus is not enough to receive eternal life.

The young man had praised and honored Jesus as much as a person could. He had eagerly sought and reverenced Jesus, not only kneeling before Him but also casting himself on the dust of the ground before Jesus. He addressed Jesus with as high a title as a person could address a revered teacher. He could not praise Jesus more. But note a critical truth: the man's praise and honor of Jesus were not enough.

10:18

¹⁸ And Jesus said to him, "Why do you call me good? No one is good except God alone."

The rich man called Jesus "Good Teacher" or *good Rabbi*, not "Lord" or "Christ"—the Messiah. He was acknowledging that Jesus was an honorable person to be highly regarded. But he conceived Jesus to be *only* a highly regarded teacher. He did not consider Jesus to be the divine Son of God. He conceived Jesus to be but a mere man, not God. He thought Jesus was a man who had achieved unusual moral goodness and by such had become a *good teacher*, one capable of teaching the great truths of God and life (see note, pt.1—Lu.18:18-23 for another idea and more discussion).

Jesus had to correct this gross error. He attempted to correct it by asking the man why he called Him good, because only God is good. Jesus was saying to the young man, "No person is good, not in comparison to God, not good enough to ever stand before God in righteousness. *If I am but a mere man*, a good teacher, then I am not truly 'good' and do not have the words to eternal life. *But if I am God*, then you can address me as 'good,' and I do have the words to eternal life."

Note two insights into Jesus' statement:

- Jesus directly answered the earnest young man's question: He told him how to receive eternal life. Therefore, Jesus was claiming to be God.
- Jesus was correcting the young man. He spoke these words forcefully. Jesus would not have the young man thinking of Him only as a man, no matter how preeminent a teacher the young man thought Him to be. He is God, God's very own Son; and He is to be known and called the Son of God. Therefore, Jesus tried to lead the young man to acknowledge and honor Him as God. It was the only way the young man could ever receive eternal life.

Simon Peter answered him, "Lord, to whom shall we go? You have the words of eternal life." (Jn.6:68)

I told you that you would die in your sins, for unless you believe that I am he you will die in your sins. (Jn.8:24)

Jesus said to him, "I am the way, and the truth, and the life. No one comes to the Father except through me. If you had known me, you would have known my Father also. From now on you do know him and have seen him." (Jn.14:6-7)

And there is salvation in no one else, for there is no other name under heaven given among men by which we must be saved. (Ac.4:12)

For there is one God, and there is one mediator between God and men, the man Christ Jesus, who gave himself as a ransom for all, which is the testimony given at the proper time. (1 Ti.2:5-6)

10:19-20

¹⁹ "You know the commandments: 'Do not murder, Do not commit adultery, Do not steal, Do not bear false witness, Do not defraud, Honor your father and mother.'"
²⁰ And he said to him, "Teacher, all these I have kept from my youth."

3 Fact 3: To be respectable is not enough to receive eternal life.

The young man had asked, "What *good deed* must I do?" (Mt.19:16). He had a religion of *works*, not of faith. He thought people could secure eternal life for themselves by being good. He felt that if he could just keep some great rule or law and live a moral, clean life, then God would accept him. He believed that his acts of morality and good works piled up a balance sheet that made him acceptable to God. But he was mistaken. To be respectable and to do good works are not enough to gain eternal life.

a. The laws of respectability (v.19).

Jesus again had to correct the man; He had to strike directly at the root of the problem. Jesus knew that the man was failing to love his neighbor as himself (this will be brought out later). So Jesus told the young man very simply, "You know the commandments"; and He proceeded to quote five of the Ten Commandments, the five laws of respectability that had to do with his duty toward his neighbor (Ex.20:12-16).

b. The respectable character of the young ruler (v.20).

The man made the extraordinary claim that he had kept all five of the commandments that Jesus quoted. He, of course, had not kept them perfectly, not in God's eyes, not in the spirit in which God intended them to be kept. As Jesus would reveal, he was not generous enough with others and not giving and helping like he should be. Jesus was now ready to show him and lead him to do this. In summary, here is what Jesus had said to the rich young ruler: keep the commandments dealing with your neighbor—the ones especially needed by rulers and the rich—the ones so often misunderstood and neglected by such people.

But the rich young ruler misunderstood God's law: he had a tragic sense of self-righteousness. He thought some commandments were more important than others. And he thought that his record of keeping God's law and building up a balance sheet with God should secure God's acceptance.

THOUGHT 1. The young man, "*What must I do* to inherit eternal life?" It is not any *good thing* that we do, nor is it all the *good things* that we do that give us eternal life.

> For I tell you, unless your righteousness exceeds that of the scribes and Pharisees, you will never enter the kingdom of heaven. (Mt.5:20)

> On that day many will say to me, 'Lord, Lord, did we not prophesy in your name, and cast out demons in your name, and do many mighty works in your name?' And then will I declare to them, 'I never knew you; depart from me, you workers of lawlessness.' (Mt.7:22–23)

> Yet we know that a person is not justified by works of the law but through faith in Jesus Christ, so we also have believed in Christ Jesus, in order to be justified by faith in Christ and not by works of the law, because by works of the law no one will be justified. (Ga.2:16)

> For by grace you have been saved through faith. And this is not your own doing; it is the gift of God, not a result of works, so that no one may boast. (Ep.2:8–9)

> Who saved us and called us to a holy calling, not because of our works but because of his own purpose and grace, which he gave us in Christ Jesus before the ages began. (2 Ti.1:9)

> But when the goodness and loving kindness of God our Savior appeared, he saved us, not because of works done by us in righteousness, but according to his own mercy, by the washing of regeneration and renewal of the Holy Spirit. (Tit.3:4–5)

4 Fact 4: Being loved by Jesus is not enough to receive eternal life.

Scripture says specifically that Jesus loved this sincere young man. The Lord's eyes penetrated into the man's innermost being and sensed a deep, deep longing and earnestness. The man's longing and ache for eternal life touched Jesus deeply. Jesus was drawn to the man and loved him in a very, very special sense.

²¹ And Jesus, looking at him, loved him, and said to him, "You lack one thing: go, sell all that you have and give to the poor, and you will have treasure in heaven; and come, follow me."

But note the crucial point: the love of Jesus for this man's soul—even the very, very special love of Jesus for a person—was not enough to save the man. Jesus' piercing look also discerned what it was this kept this earnest young man from believing in Him unto eternal life. The man still lacked one thing, and Jesus brought that one thing to the surface.

THOUGHT 1. When Christ looks at us, He sees us through eyes of love. The love of Christ is great, and it is touching and encouraging. But it is not enough. The Lord's love does not automatically save us, not by itself, not against our will.

O Jerusalem, Jerusalem, the city that kills the prophets and stones those who are sent to it! How often would I have gathered your children together as a hen gathers her brood under her wings, and you were not willing! (Mt.23:37)

Because I have called and you refused to listen, have stretched out my hand and no one has heeded. (Pr.1:24)

10:21-22

²¹ And Jesus, looking at him, loved him, and said to him, "You lack one thing: go, sell all that you have and give to the poor, and you will have treasure in heaven; and come, follow me."
²² Disheartened by the saying, he went away sorrowful, for he had great possessions.

5 Fact 5: Following Christ is required to receive eternal life.

The fifth fact to know about eternal life is critical: following Christ is required to receive eternal life. *Giving everything*—fully surrendering himself to Christ—was the one thing this man was lacking, the one thing that causes so many to miss out on eternal life.

In this man's case, he was trusting in his money, and he loved his money and possessions more than he loved God. Jesus knew that the wealthy fellow needed to let go of his riches and trust Him fully. He also knew that the young man needed to give God his heart.

Again, Jesus knew exactly what this young man needed. In spite of the man's moral goodness, the Lord knew that the particular sin that enslaved him was greed and materialism (v.21). He was hoarding his wealth instead of distributing it. God had given wealth to him that he might be able to help others, but he was failing to love and help his neighbor as he should (Ep.4:28).

What *this* young man needed to hear was just what Jesus said. He needed to repent of his sin—in his case, the sin of greed. His repentance would be evident if he was willing to sell everything he had and give the proceeds to the poor and leave his prosperous lifestyle behind to follow Jesus.

a. **The command: Total and sacrificial surrender, the abandonment of all (v.21).**

At this point, it is critical to note the fact that Jesus called this young man to sell all that he had and give it to the poor. In doing so, he would be showing that money and possessions were no longer his god, and he would be freed up from his earthly responsibilities to follow Christ. "He needed to give up that which was the idol of his heart so he could attain true wealth. He needed to renounce anything which would keep him from an unconditional life of discipleship to Christ."[1]

Jesus called for a sacrificial surrender, a commitment that required the young man to surrender all to follow Him. In our dedicated efforts to protect the glorious truth that people are saved by grace and grace alone, we often forget and neglect a great truth: Christ calls the sinner to *follow Him,* and *to truly follow Christ we must surrender everything to Him.* To follow Christ is to deny self completely—*all that we are and all that we have* (see DEEPER STUDY # 1—Lu.9:23; see outline and notes—Mk.10:29-30 for a thorough discussion of what this means).

When we deny ourselves and surrender all we are and have to the Lord, we demonstrate that we have genuine saving faith. The reward for surrendering all to Christ is rich: we receive treasure in heaven (Mt.6:19-20; Lu.12:33). To deny self, *to give all we are and have in following Jesus,* is a hard saying, but Christ commands it. Our attempt to soften it does not annul His commandment (see DEEPER STUDY # 1—Ro.3:3). One cannot deal honestly with what Jesus says here without acknowledging that Jesus connects eternal life with giving up all and following Him. This does not mean that salvation is earned by doing so. Salvation is entirely by grace, through faith. It is not the result of works (Ep.2:8-9). But genuine saving faith is a faith *that* works. If it is not accompanied by works, it is not genuine saving faith; it is dead (Ep.2:10; Ph.2:12; Js.2:14-20). "Authentic, eternal life can only come through absolute obedience to and dependence on Jesus."[2]

1 Thoralf Gilbrant, Ralph W. Harris, Stanley M. Horton, eds., *The Complete Biblical Library Commentary* (Matthew-John and Harmony), (Tulsa, OK: Harrison House, 2017). Via Wordsearch digital edition.
2 Ibid.

b. The result: The requirement was too heavy—he went away sad and grieved (v.22).

The rich young ruler was unwilling to obey Christ. What Christ called for was too much; he was not willing to surrender all—to repent and make a commitment to follow Christ—in order to receive eternal life. He went away sad and grieved, for his wealth was more important to him than eternal life. As far as we know, today, the man is in hell.

The rich young ruler rejected Jesus for three reasons:

First, he rejected Christ because of his unbelief: he was not willing to entrust his life to Jesus. There was some lack of belief that the Man Jesus standing before him was really God, therefore, the young man would not trust the Lord. "The way to eternal life [is] in turning from trust in self-attainments and earthly securities to trust in Jesus."[3]

Second, he rejected Christ because of his self-righteousness and pride: his concept of religion was keeping laws and doing good in order to secure God's acceptance. He felt that he, as well as other people, had the power and goodness to make God approve and accept him.

Third, he rejected Christ because of his love of the world: he was rich and was unwilling to give up the comfort and possessions he had obtained to follow Christ. He made the fatal mistake that so many make with wealth, power, and fame. He loved the things of the world more than he loved the Lord. Therefore, he was not willing to follow Christ's command to help the needy. He preferred hoarding and extravagance, living sumptuously and comfortably to helping those who were so desperately needful. He loved the things of the world more than he loved the hope of eternal life. He loved the position, recognition, esteem, and power of the world more than he loved Christ.

Now, note a critical point: the subject of *giving up all* is a sensitive subject, so sensitive that the words of Christ are seldom taken or preached at face value. The words of the Lord are *watered down* to mean no more than an ideal in a person's mind—an ideal that is left up to every person to decide within their own selfish, deceptive, and corrupt hearts. Is the person *willing* to surrender all? Then their willingness is said to be acceptable to God. The fact that they do not commit all to Christ, that they refuse Christ's command to take up the cross and follow Him, is said not to matter. However, the critical point seldom crosses people's minds: Christ calls all who desire eternal life to a total commitment to Him. "He was declaring that nothing must come between a person and devotion to God. Some people may have to give up money. Others may have to abandon a cherished dream. Still others may have to surrender family."[4] In this young man's case, it was money, power, and prestige.

It is also critical to see that this surrender is carried out through serving and ministering to others. Jesus called the rich young man to give what he had been blessed with in life to help others (see DEEPER STUDY # 1). When we love our neighbor as ourselves, then we show that we truly love God. If we do not love and minister to our neighbor (above self), then, in reality, we do not love God (1 Jn.4:20).

THOUGHT 1. The young man had a serious flaw—the very same flaw that exists within so many today: he did not believe heaven was glorious enough to *merit the giving up* of his possessions.

> And he said to all, "If anyone would come after me, let him deny himself and take up his cross daily and follow me." (Lu.9:23)

> Sell your possessions, and give to the needy. Provide yourselves with moneybags that do not grow old, with a treasure in the heavens that does not fail, where no thief approaches and no moth destroys. (Lu.12:33)

---

3 John F. Walvoord and Roy B. Zuck, eds., *The Bible Knowledge Commentary: An Exposition of the Scriptures by Dallas Seminary Faculty* (New Testament Edition), (Wheaton, IL: Victor Books, 1983). Via Wordsearch digital edition.

4 Rodney L. Cooper, Max Anders (ed.), *Holman New Testament Commentary (Mark)*, (Nashville: Holman Reference, 2000). Via Wordsearch digital edition.

(10:21) **Giving—Helping Others—Covetousness:** Jesus' command to give to the poor is for all. The God of all people *can never justify keeping and storing and banking and hoarding and even holding back as long as a single need exists and is going unmet.*

If all people are truly God's by creation, then God is bound to expect all needs to be met; and He is bound to hold accountable the person who has and keeps, stores and banks, hoards and holds back. The point is easily understood by honest and thinking people who truly ponder the issue. The thinking and honest person sees both the single person and the masses . . .

- who are starving
- who are without clothes, housing, medicine, treatment, education, and skills
- who are lost from God and doomed eternally because they have never heard the gospel

Imagine the millions who have never heard about Christ even once. When the thinking person sees the picture and is honest, he or she can no longer refuse to accept Jesus' words at face value. Yet, so many do not think and so many refuse to be honest. So, they continue to *spiritualize and idealize what Jesus was saying* to this young man. Why? Do we fear the strictness of what Christ says? Do we fear the reaction of people? Do we fear what we will have to give up? Do we lack the faith within to trust God? (See outline, notes, and DEEPER STUDY # 1—Mt.10:28; note—Mk.10:23-27 for more discussion.)

Scripture is clear: God expects us to work so that we can have enough to help others (Ep.4:28). God gives us *a talent* to use in taking care of our own needs, but after our needs are met, the talent entrusted to us is to be used to help others in their need. We are to help as we are able, but we are to be *honest* about our ability to help.

> And Zacchaeus stood and said to the Lord, "Behold, Lord, the half of my goods I give to the poor. And if I have defrauded anyone of anything, I restore it fourfold." (Lu.19:8)

> In all things I have shown you that by working hard in this way we must help the weak and remember the words of the Lord Jesus, how he himself said, 'It is more blessed to give than to receive.' (Ac.20:35)

> Let the thief no longer steal, but rather let him labor, doing honest work with his own hands, so that he may have something to share with anyone in need. (Ep.4:28)

> As for the rich in this present age, charge them not to be haughty, nor to set their hopes on the uncertainty of riches, but on God, who richly provides us with everything to enjoy. They are to do good, to be rich in good works, to be generous and ready to share. (1 Ti.6:17-18)

> Do not neglect to do good and to share what you have, for such sacrifices are pleasing to God. (He.13:16)

> Whoever has a bountiful eye will be blessed, for he shares his bread with the poor. (Pr.22:9)

(Mt.19:23–26; Lu.18:24–27)

²³ And Jesus looked around and said to his disciples, "How difficult it will be for those who have wealth to enter the kingdom of God!"

²⁴ And the disciples were amazed at his words. But Jesus said to them again, "Children, how difficult it is to enter the kingdom of God!

²⁵ "It is easier for a camel to go through the eye of a needle than for a rich person to enter the kingdom of God."

²⁶ And they were exceedingly astonished, and said to him, "Then who can be saved?"

²⁷ Jesus looked at them and said, "With man it is impossible, but not with God. For all things are possible with God."

1. **The rich face the perils of wealth**
   a. Wealth can be dangerous[DS1, DS2]
   b. Wealth can keep a person from God's kingdom[DS3]

2. **The rich face great difficulty spiritually**

3. **The rich are set on a pedestal by the world**

4. **The rich have only one hope—God alone**
   a. God alone can save
   b. God alone judges

Division VI

The Son of God's Last Public Ministry: Jesus Deals with Some Special Issues, 10:1–52

D. The Issue of Wealth and Its Dangers, 10:23–27

(Mt.19:23–26; Lu.18:24–27)

10:23–27
Introduction

Jesus took the rich young ruler's rejection of heaven and warned all people about the problem and dangers of wealth. Wealth is fraught with pitfalls, both for those who are seeking to be rich and for those who are already rich. The dangers are many, and they are entangling and enslaving, so much so that Jesus stated that it is extremely difficult for a rich person to be saved.

The words are strong; the idea is shocking. Yet Jesus must be truthful, for He loves and cares for all people. He must warn all people: it is extremely difficult for a rich person to enter heaven. The dangers which face the rich are real and terrible, so the warning must be real and truthful. This is, *The Issue of Wealth and Its Dangers*, 10:23-27.

1. The rich face the perils of wealth (vv.23-24).
2. The rich face great difficulty spiritually (v.25).
3. The rich are set on a pedestal by the world (v.26).
4. The rich have only one hope—God alone (v.27).

1 The rich face the perils of wealth.

This passage is tied to the rich young ruler. Imagine the scene: as the rich young ruler turned and walked away from Jesus, Jesus perhaps stood for the longest of times watching the young man fade into the distance. Jesus was heartbroken and thoughtful, for the young man had so much potential.

10:23–24

²³ And Jesus looked around and said to his disciples, "How difficult it will be for those who have wealth to enter the kingdom of God!"
²⁴ And the disciples were amazed at his words. But Jesus said to them again, "Children, how difficult it is to enter the kingdom of God!

But the perils of wealth had seized his selfish soul. Quickly, full of energy and authority, perhaps even bordering on anger (against the enslaving power of wealth), Jesus "looked around" and made an earth-shaking statement: "How hard it is for the wealthy to enter the kingdom of God."

a. Wealth can be dangerous (v.23a).

The rich young ruler is a vivid, tragic illustration of the fact that having riches can be dangerous (see DEEPER STUDIES 1, 2). For this reason, Scripture strongly warns those who desire to be rich as well as those who love money (1 Ti.6:9–10).

One of the reasons Jesus' statement was so shocking was that, in Jewish culture of that time, wealth was viewed as a sign of God's favor and blessing on the righteous—just as it is by many today. While this is sometimes true, more often than not, it is not true. The reality of life in our world is, many wicked people are wealthy, and many of the world's godliest people have little of this world's money and possessions.

b. Wealth can keep a person from God's kingdom (vv.23b–24).

The most terrible peril of wealth is that it so easily keeps a person from coming into the kingdom of God. Money and possessions pose a serious problem and an eternal danger for those ensnared by the love of wealth. Again, the rich young ruler's love of possessions kept him from being saved.

The disciples were shocked when Jesus stated that it is difficult for the rich to be saved (v.24). Therefore, He said it again. Greek manuscripts differ on exactly what Jesus said the second time. Accordingly, some translations (including the KJV and NKJV) say, "for those who trust in riches" (see DEEPER STUDY # 3). Certainly, one of the most dangerous perils of wealth is trusting in one's riches (1 Ti.6:17).

DEEPER STUDY # 1

(10:23) **Riches—Wealth** (Gk. chremata): money, things, properties, possessions—what one has and uses—material things or goods. It means all the things which a person has, all the things that have value and are worth something in this world. Jesus chose a word that is applicable to every generation and every person who has possessions or has things of value.

DEEPER STUDY # 2

(10:23) **Riches—Wealth:** Who are the rich? Realistically, in comparison to what the vast majority of the world has, *the rich person is anyone who has anything to put back beyond meeting the true needs of their own family.* This is exactly what Christ and the Bible say time and again (see also Mk.12:41–44; Lu.21:1–4; Ac.4:34–35; etc.).

Again, *the rich person is any person who has anything beyond basic needs.* Christ commands us to give to meet the needs of those in desperate need, holding back nothing. This is often the great complaint against Christians, that we do not believe what Christ says. The evidence of our unbelief is seen in Christ's insistence that we give what we have to feed the starving and to meet the desperate needs of the world, and yet we refuse to obey Him. Gandhi, the great leader of India's independence, is said to have never embraced Christianity for this very reason: because Christians live lives of hypocrisy. Many, if not most,

Christians do not follow the teachings of Christ; they do not give as Christ commands to meet the desperate needs of the world. How many others have rejected Christ because of our hypocrisy?

> Jesus said to him, "If you would be perfect, go, sell what you possess and give to the poor, and you will have treasure in heaven; and come, follow me." (Mt.19:21)

> And a second is like it: You shall love your neighbor as yourself. (Mt.22:39)

> Instead, seek his kingdom, and these things will be added to you. Fear not, little flock, for it is your Father's good pleasure to give you the kingdom. Sell your possessions, and give to the needy. Provide yourselves with moneybags that do not grow old, with a treasure in the heavens that does not fail, where no thief approaches and no moth destroys. For where your treasure is, there will your heart be also. (Lu.12:31-34)

> And Zacchaeus stood and said to the Lord, "Behold, Lord, the half of my goods I give to the poor. And if I have defrauded anyone of anything, I restore it fourfold." (Lu.19:8)

> Let the thief no longer steal, but rather let him labor, doing honest work with his own hands, so that he may have something to share with anyone in need. (Ep.4:28)

> Keep your life free from love of money, and be content with what you have, for he has said, "I will never leave you nor forsake you." (He.13:5)

DEEPER STUDY # 3

(10:24) **Wealth—Materialism—Worldliness:** rich people tend to trust in riches (money and things). Jesus made this statement because of the things that *pulled* the rich young ruler away. Wealth can pull a person away from receiving heaven and eternal life. There is a lure, an attraction, a force, a power, a pull that reaches out to draw any person who looks at or possesses wealth. There are pulls so forceful that they will enslave and doom any rich person that fails to turn and embrace God. There are three reasons for this.

1. Rich people tend to trust in the world and in their riches. Their wealth attaches them to the world. Wealth enables them to buy things that . . .

- make them comfortable
- please their taste
- stir their ego
- inflate their self-image

- expand their experience
- challenge their mental pursuit
- stimulate their flesh

If people center their life on the things of the world, their attention is on the world, not on God. They tend to become wrapped up in securing more and in protecting what they have. They give little time and thought to heavenly matters. Wealth and the things it can provide can and usually do consume the rich.

2. A rich person's trust will more than likely not be in the most valuable, that is, in God. Wealth leads people to trust themselves, their abilities, their energy and efforts. Wealth creates the *big I* (see vv.17, 20). The wealthy are usually looked up to, esteemed, honored, and envied. Wealth brings position, power, and recognition. It boosts *ego*, making a person self-sufficient and independent in this world. As a result, there is a tendency for the rich to feel they are truly independent and self-sufficient, that they need nothing. And in such an atmosphere and world of thought, God is forgotten. People forget that there are things that money cannot buy and events from which money cannot save. Peace, love, joy—all that really matters within the human spirit can never be bought. Neither can money save a person from disaster, disease, accident, death, and on and on.

3. Many rich people tend to hoard, to be selfish with *most* of their money. They trust in their riches, keeping *most* of everything for themselves (see note, pt.2—Mt.19:23).

> And I will say to my soul, "Soul, you have ample goods laid up for many years; relax, eat, drink, be merry." But God said to him, 'Fool! This night your soul is required of you, and the things you have prepared, whose will they be?' (Lu.12:19-20)

But those who desire to be rich fall into temptation, into a snare, into many senseless and harmful desires that plunge people into ruin and destruction. For the love of money is a root of all kinds of evils. It is through this craving that some have wandered away from the faith and pierced themselves with many pangs. (1 Ti.6:9–10)

As for the rich in this present age, charge them not to be haughty, nor to set their hopes on the uncertainty of riches, but on God, who richly provides us with everything to enjoy. (1 Ti.6:17)

If I have made gold my trust or called fine gold my confidence, if I have rejoiced because my wealth was abundant or because my hand had found much . . . this also would be an iniquity to be punished by the judges, for I would have been false to God above. (Jb.31:24–25, 28)

See the man who would not make God his refuge, but trusted in the abundance of his riches and sought refuge in his own destruction! (Ps.52:7)

Whoever trusts in his riches will fall, but the righteous will flourish like a green leaf. (Pr.11:28)

10:25

[25] "It is easier for a camel to go through the eye of a needle than for a rich person to enter the kingdom of God."

2 The rich face great difficulty spiritually.

Jesus said that it is extremely difficult for a rich person to enter into the kingdom of God. It is so difficult that Jesus said that it is easier for a camel to pass through the eye of a needle.

Various interpretations of "camel" and "needle" have been offered in an attempt to soften Jesus' words. For example, some have said that Jesus was speaking of a small gate in the wall surrounding Jerusalem that sat right beside the large gate. At night the large gate was closed to protect the city from thieves and enemies, and the small gate was used. The small gate is said to have been called "The Needle's Eye" because it was so small that it was difficult for even a single person to pass through. Others have said that the Greek word Jesus used was *kamilos* (a ship's rope or cable) not *kamelos* (camel). Note that the only difference between the two words is the second vowel. Three considerations need to be noted about these interpretations.

First, there is no doubt that Jesus meant a literal needle. He as much as said so: "With man this is impossible" (v.27). What He did was use a proverbial expression illustrating a perceived *impossibility*. Most if not all cultures have sayings that express the impossibility of some things. The camel was the largest animal among the Jews, so Jesus simply used a well-known proverb among the Jews or else created one. It should also be pointed out that when Jesus chose to speak in parables, He chose the most common and ordinary concepts to express His meaning.

Second, attempts to soften the Lord's point are just that: attempts to soften. But nothing can be softened with Jesus' statement, "With man this is impossible." No person, not even the rich man himself, can save a rich person. The danger of riches is very real and terrible. Wealth entangles and enslaves a person so much that it is extremely difficult for many rich people to let go and give their wealth to help the desperate needs of the world. Many just cannot accept the fact that they are to give what they have earned to others (Ep.4:28). It is so difficult not to live in personal luxury and build large estates. Big and fancy meals, full and fashionable wardrobes, luxurious and massive homes, the latest and most expensive automobiles—so much is so difficult to let go. It is the ego that refuses to let go.

Third, attempts to soften the interpretation of Christ's saying are just as difficult to accept as the most literal interpretation. How does a camel trying to get through a tiny gate made only for a man soften anything? It still would be impossible. And how is the idea of threading a needle with a ship's cable any more palatable? Again, we're dealing with an impossible scenario.

THOUGHT 1. Many rich people will not enter the kingdom of God. Why? Scripture spells out the reasons in clear terms.

1) Riches and worldliness can choke the Word of God out of a person's life.

But the cares of the world and the deceitfulness of riches and the desires for other things enter in and choke the word, and it proves unfruitful. (Mk.4:19)

2) Riches can give people a sense of false security.

> And I will say to my soul, "Soul, you have ample goods laid up for many years; relax, eat, drink, be merry." But God said to him, 'Fool! This night your soul is required of you, and the things you have prepared, whose will they be?' (Lu.12:19-20)

3) Riches bring a flood of temptations and snares upon a person.

> But those who desire to be rich fall into temptation, into a snare, into many senseless and harmful desires that plunge people into ruin and destruction. (1 Ti.6:9)

4) Riches can cause people to be highminded (conceited, proud, arrogant, haughty).

> As for the rich in this present age, charge them not to be haughty, nor to set their hopes on the uncertainty of riches, but on God, who richly provides us with everything to enjoy. (1 Ti.6:17)

> A rich man's wealth is his strong city, and like a high wall in his imagination. (Pr.18:11)

5) Riches tend to make people forget God.

> And when your herds and flocks multiply and your silver and gold is multiplied and all that you have is multiplied, then your heart be lifted up, and you forget the LORD your God, who brought you out of the land of Egypt, out of the house of slavery. (De.8:13-14)

6) Riches often strengthen a person's wickedness.

> See the man who would not make God his refuge, but trusted in the abundance of his riches and sought refuge in his own destruction! (Ps.52:7)

3 The rich are set on a pedestal by the world (v.26).

Like some today, Jews considered wealth a special blessing from God. It was the measure of a person's spiritual standing with God. This is the concept of *natural religion*. Throughout history a person who has been rich in wealth, intellect, talents, or personality has been thought to be especially blessed by God and to have all things easier.

> 26 And they were exceedingly astonished, and said to him, "Then who can be saved?"

Note that the disciples were astonished twice—beyond imagination (vv.24, 26). Why? Because they failed to see that riches are two things to a person: a test from God, and a responsibility for the person to prove just how responsible they will be to God and to others in meeting their desperate needs (see note—Js.1:9-11).

Jesus says something diametrically opposed to what the disciples and everyone else in Judaism had always thought. As with people in succeeding generations, even those in the church, Jews had always been taught . . .

- ➤ that prosperity (wealth, comfort, and things) is God's blessing
- ➤ that a person receives and has because God is blessing them
- ➤ that prosperity is the reward of righteousness and obedience
- ➤ that God blesses a person with the things of this earth if they are righteous and obedient

But in this passage, Jesus was saying the very opposite: a wealthy person would most likely never enter heaven; prosperity posed such a dangerous threat to a person that eternal doom was almost assured. The disciples knew that God would never put a person in such a precarious, dangerous position. They knew that Jesus was attacking the world's most cherished and ardent belief: be good (righteous) and you will be blessed by God with material things, the things of *this* world (see note—Ep.1:3 for a discussion of God's blessings).

The disciples were shocked, thoroughly dismayed. They asked Jesus who *could* be saved, a seemingly logical question. The vast majority of people were threatening their own eternal destiny. They were dooming themselves. Since prosperity was not the reward (sign) for righteousness, and the rich would not enter heaven, then that meant that the poor, too, were doomed; for they were spending most of their time in dreaming of and seeking prosperity.

The idea that prosperity is the reward for righteousness, that God blesses people with the things of this earth if they are righteous and obedient, is so prevalent a view that a comment is needed at this point.

God's concern is spiritual blessings, not material blessings. God does promise us the necessities of life (food, clothing, shelter) if we seek Him first (Mt.6:33; see 6:25-34). And God can, if He chooses, bless any of us with whatever He wishes so that we may be able to help meet others' needs, both physical and spiritual. But just because a person is prosperous does not mean they are righteous, and just because a person is righteous does not mean they are going to be blessed materially. Righteousness and prosperity have nothing to do with each other. Jesus made this clear when He stressed how hard it is for a rich person to go to heaven.

For many, if not most people, wealth is *seldom* a good thing. As Jesus teaches in this passage, wealth is fraught with dangers that make it extremely difficult for the rich to enter heaven. Yet the whole world, rich and poor alike, believer and non-believer, puts their primary attention on dreaming of being wealthy and getting more and more.

Wealth is secured by people themselves, by their own energy and effort. People secure wealth by dreaming of how to make it (a clear vision, perspective), and by having the initiative to make it (acting and timing). People may trust God to help them secure wealth, but they may also choose to have nothing to do with God and secure wealth on their own. There is a sense in which a person's strength and mind are from God, but that has nothing to do with a personal, active relationship with God. Many, if not most rich people control their own lives and go about securing their treasure on this earth *without God* (Mt.6:21).

On the other hand, people may trust God to bless them so that they may help others, and God may choose to bless them financially. But God's choosing to bless them is for the purpose of helping others, not to hoard and live above what is needed (extravagantly and sumptuously). In fact, what Jesus teaches is that the rich are to live sacrificially in order to meet the desperate needs of a starving, doomed, and dying world. May God grant that we never forget this (see notes and DEEPER STUDIES 1, 2—Mt.19:23; note—Mk.12:42; outline—Lu.21:1-4).

THOUGHT 1. One of the most tragic and dangerous tendencies of many people is to set the rich (the powerful, the athletic, the gifted) up on a pedestal. Scripture is clear: a person's hope and security must not be placed in other people.

It is better to take refuge in the LORD than to trust in princes. (Ps.118:9)

Stop regarding man in whose nostrils is breath, for of what account is he? (Is.2:22)

Thus says the LORD: "Cursed is the man who trusts in man and makes flesh his strength, whose heart turns away from the LORD." (Je.17:5)

10:27

[27] Jesus looked at them and said, "With man it is impossible, but not with God. For all things are possible with God."

4 The rich have only one hope—God alone.

Like all other people, the rich face an eternity without God. The only hope for the rich—just as it is for all other people—is God. God alone can save. Rich people must turn to God and away from the world. No person can save them, not themselves nor any other human being. What is impossible with man is possible with God. God can save any person—even those for whom it is the hardest to be saved. Consider how the power of God—and only the power of God—can break through to the rich person's heart and reach him or her.

Nobody has the strength or know-how to break the power of *seeking things* that holds sway over them. The natural urge within people is to seek more and more comfort and ease and possessions. Nobody has the power to break that *natural urge*. The entanglements are too pleasing and enslaving.

In addition, nobody can re-create a person's soul; nobody can change the soul of another person so that they seek heavenly things and set their hearts on things above, rather than things on the earth (Col.3:1-2). No philosophy, no psychology, no medicine, no education, no politics, no social movement can change the human soul.

The rich—like everyone else—must turn to God and His power. God is the only hope for a rich person the same as He is for any other person. Only God can break a wealthy person's enslavement to this earth—only God can convert, change, turn, and save the rich individual from the danger and doom of wealth.

THOUGHT 1. Four practical steps will help a rich person—or anybody—who struggles with the love of money and possessions.
1) Listen and heed immediately the inner voice, the pricking of conscience to give one's life and possessions to God. Turn immediately to God. Never turn away.
2) Study God's Word for direction—every day—and talk to and trust God to keep one's heart free from the lure and deception of possessions.
3) Use one's wealth to help meet the desperate needs of others. *Realize, know, and acknowledge that the vast majority* of the world is hungry, hurting, and needing help—desperately so; and that God expects us to use what we have *to meet those needs, not to hoard and live extravagantly in the midst of so much need.*
4) Develop a strong desire for heaven, knowing that our sojourn on earth is ever so short, as brief as the lily of the field.

THOUGHT 2. Christ does not force anybody to be saved. He lets every person make his or her own decision. He let the rich young ruler walk away to his own eternal doom. Likewise, He lets us walk away if we choose. He does not violate our free will. He does not make us robots that do only what He programs us to do. We must choose to repent, believe in Him, and be saved.

THOUGHT 3. Money and possessions cannot take care of us. Money and gadgets have no life. They are material things. They cannot look after us; we have to look after them. But not so with God. God can take care of and look after our welfare, both now and eternally.

> **For nothing will be impossible with God. (Lu.1:37)**

> **For no one can lay a foundation other than that which is laid, which is Jesus Christ. (1 Co.3:11)**

> **As for the rich in this present age, charge them not to be haughty, nor to set their hopes on the uncertainty of riches, but on God, who richly provides us with everything to enjoy. They are to do good, to be rich in good works, to be generous and ready to share, thus storing up treasure for themselves as a good foundation for the future, so that they may take hold of that which is truly life. (1 Ti.6:17-19)**

> **I know that you can do all things, and that no purpose of yours can be thwarted. (Jb.42:2)**

E. The Issue of Rewards:
What a Person Receives for Following Christ, 10:28–31

(Mt.19:27–30; Lu.18:28–30)

1. **Peter wondered if the disciples'**
   sacrifice would be rewarded
2. **A person receives a hundred times**
   what they give up
   a. Whether housing or family
   b. Whether property or wealth
3. **A person receives persecution**
4. **A person receives eternal life**

5. **A person receives an immediate**
   warning and also assurance

28 Peter began to say to him, "See, we have left everything and followed you."
29 Jesus said, "Truly, I say to you, there is no one who has left house or brothers or sisters or mother or father or children or lands, for my sake and for the gospel,
30 who will not receive a hundredfold now in this time, houses and brothers and sisters and mothers and children and lands, with persecutions, and in the age to come eternal life."
31 "But many who are first will be last, and the last first."

Division VI

The Son of God's Last Public Ministry: Jesus Deals with Some Special Issues, 10:1–52

E. The Issue of Rewards: What a Person Receives for Following Christ, 10:28–31

(Mt.19:27–30; Lu.18:28–30)

10:28–31
Introduction

The idea of rewards in heaven is foreign to many; it is rejected by others, feeling the idea of God's rewarding people is self-serving and greedy. They feel rewards of rank and position, of possession and levels of responsibility have no place in a perfect world. However, Christ Himself endured the cross *"for the joy* that was set before Him" (He.12:2). And Scripture says that Moses valued the reproach of Christ over the treasures of Egypt (He.11:26; see He.11:1-40). Scripture abounds with the teaching of rewards "in the age to come" (v.30).

The point of this passage is rewards. Our Lord is just, and He will not unrighteously overlook all we do for Him (He.6:10). Jesus deals with the issue of rewards, of just what a true disciple will receive both in this world and in the age to come (see notes—Lu.16:10-12; Jn.4:36-38). This is, *The Issue of Rewards: What a Person Receives for Following Christ, 10:28-31.*

1. Peter wondered if the disciples' sacrifice would be rewarded (v.28).
2. A person receives a hundred times what they give up (vv.29-30).
3. A person receives persecution (v.30).
4. A person receives eternal life (v.30).
5. A person receives an immediate warning and also assurance (v.31).

10:28

28 Peter began to say to him, "See, we have left everything and followed you."

1 Peter wondered if the disciples' sacrifice would be rewarded.

Peter had just been shocked. He had seen a rich young man with enormous potential turn and walk away from Jesus.

The man had rejected Jesus because he was unwilling to forsake all he had, unwilling to forsake his wealth and use it to meet the needs of the world. Then Peter had heard Jesus give an earth-shaking discussion on riches—just how difficult it is for people with riches to enter heaven.

The demand sounded hard and rigid. Peter was stunned. He felt he and the disciples *had* given all. He was almost sure they were holding nothing back, but he wanted to make *absolutely sure.* Anyone would need assurance after what Jesus had just said. Few sell everything and give it all away, and few (rich or poor) control their dreams and urges to have more (see note—Mt.19:25). The disciples, as all honest people, knew this. They also knew the extreme demands Jesus was making to be a true follower of His. They, unlike so many of us in our attempts to soften His words, understood exactly what He was saying. The extremity of His words was shocking. They could not see how anyone could be saved. And the answer Jesus gave to their question about salvation said nothing to give them personal assurance. He said that it *is* impossible with men, but also that everything is possible with God (v.27; Mt.19:26).

The disciples sensed a deep need for assurance. Had they done enough, given up enough? They thought so, were almost sure they had, but had they? Peter, somewhat meekly, noted that the disciples *had* left everything to follow Jesus. They had surrendered all to Him. Then, Peter asked the question festering in the disciples' hearts: "What will we have?" (Mt.19:27). Jesus used Peter's question to teach a wonderful truth. They, His own dear apostles, and all who follow Him thereafter, can rest assured: all who give all they are and have to follow Christ will be enormously rewarded.

Peter, speaking on behalf of all the disciples, was able to honestly say to the Lord, to His face, "We have left everything." What a glorious testimony! Just think about these men. They had given up everything for Christ's sake and the gospel's (v.29). They had left family, friends, businesses, professions, wealth—left all in order to meet the needs of a desperate world. It should be noted that they readily met the needs of their families (see Mt.8:14). Even Jesus saw to the care of His mother (Jn.19:26-27). Leaving all does not mean the desertion or shirking of one's responsibility. It means centering one's life and possessions upon Christ and using all one is and has to serve Him and to meet the needs of the world. It means putting Christ first (Mt.6:33).

The disciples had followed Jesus and His gospel; they had not followed some other self-proclaimed Messiah or false message (see Ga.1:6-9). They believed that Jesus was the true Messiah, the Son of the living God; and they had committed their lives and possessions, all they were and had to Him and His gospel.

Leaving all and following Christ represent the foundation for reward. Any person who leaves all and follows Christ can expect a reward. This is the wonderful truth Jesus was about to teach His disciples. They were uneasy because of what had just happened to the rich young ruler and because of Jesus' comments about the incident. Jesus wanted to assure them. They were very dear to Him because they had left all and were following Him. He wanted them to know they would be rewarded and rewarded abundantly.

2 A person receives a hundred times what they give up.

10:29–30a

Jesus made an astounding promise. *True disciples* will be abundantly rewarded; in fact, they will receive a hundred times what they give up and sacrifice. But note the crucial point: what is given is given *for Christ's sake, and the gospel's.* The person's motive has to be that they are giving for Christ and the spread of the gospel. They are sacrificing and giving what they have for the Lord and His cause. They are doing their part, all that they can, to accomplish the mission of redemption and the helping of mankind.

29 Jesus said, "Truly, I say to you, there is no one who has left house or brothers or sisters or mother or father or children or lands, for my sake and for the gospel,

30 who will not receive a hundredfold now in this time, houses and brothers and sisters and mothers and children and lands, with persecutions, and in the age to come eternal life."

a. Whether housing or family (v.29a).

How does a person give up home and family to serve Christ? First, when some people choose to follow Christ wholeheartedly, they are rejected by family. In some cases, parents, spouses, or other family members will throw them out of the house, especially when these family members adhere to other religions or to no religion at all. Or they no longer welcome the converted Christians into their homes. As men and women turn to Jesus for salvation or set out to serve Jesus, their families often reject them and turn them out.

Second, believers take all they are and have, including family and home, and use it for Christ's sake and for the gospel. All *true disciples* serve Jesus, putting Him first. The house and family are given to Him, that is, centered around Him and used for Him. The home and family are known . . .

➢ as a place where He is honored
➢ as a place that is dedicated entirely to Him
➢ as a place that is used to spread the gospel

There is also the aspect of serving Jesus away from home and family. The disciple has to sacrifice, to leave home and family to serve Jesus out in the world through witnessing, ministering, preaching, doing whatever God has called that person to do. This often involves being away from home and family for extended periods of time (for example: evangelists, missionaries, even ministers who are on call day and night). The twelve disciples exemplify this. Jesus called them to leave their homes and families for extended periods to travel and minister with Him.

Now, note the glorious promise of Christ. The true disciples who give up their homes and families for Christ's sake and the gospel's will receive a hundredfold reward (v.30a). They will receive . . .

• a spiritual bond and kinship with a much larger family, the family of God in both heaven and earth, both now and throughout eternity (see outline and notes, *Brotherhood*—Mt.12:46-50; Lu.8:19-21)
• a fellowship and communion, a very present and practical help when needed through the local church, the fellowship of believers within their own community (see notes and DEEPER STUDIES 1-5—Ac.2:42)
• the presence of the Spirit of God who communes with and directs them day by day

THOUGHT 1. Believers need to make sure that they are in a local church or fellowship that is truly centered on Christ and His gospel. Not every church is.

THOUGHT 2. Every church needs to search its heart and make sure that it honors Christ and His gospel, that it does have the warm heart and spiritual bond, the open arms and strong fellowship, that are needed among God's people.

> For where two or three are gathered in my name, there am I among them. (Mt.18:20)

> And they devoted themselves to the apostles' teaching and the fellowship, to the breaking of bread and the prayers. (Ac.2:42)

> So we, though many, are one body in Christ, and individually members one of another. (Ro.12:5)

> That which we have seen and heard we proclaim also to you, so that you too may have fellowship with us; and indeed our fellowship is with the Father and with his Son Jesus Christ. (1 Jn.1:3)

> I am a companion of all who fear you, of those who keep your precepts. (Ps.119:63)

> Then those who feared the LORD spoke with one another. The LORD paid attention and heard them, and a book of remembrance was written before him of those who feared the LORD and esteemed his name. (Mal.3:16)

b. Whether property or wealth (vv.29b–30a).

Many believers will be called to give up their property and wealth to serve Christ. Some will be called to give up their careers and businesses to relocate, perhaps even to go to another part of the world. Many who have successful careers will be called to give up large salaries or profits and live on far, far less income. They will be called to sell what property and possessions they have accumulated in order to support themselves in full-time ministry. Or they may be called to use their financial savings to meet their current and future needs.

Others will give their wealth directly to the work of the Lord. They will sell property and possessions to meet a need in their local church or in some other realm of the Lord's work. We must not forget that the Lord does not call all of His disciples to vocational ministry. He calls most to serve Him *through* their vocation. The work of Christ is accomplished because of those who earn money in the world and give it to the Lord (Lu.16:9). In His wisdom, the Lord blesses some with the talent and opportunity to own a profitable business in order that they can give much to His work.

The point is, we are to give all we are and have to Christ, surrender everything to Him to be used as He sees fit. When He calls us to make a specific sacrifice to Him and His work, we are to obey Him without hesitation or fear. How can we do this? How can we give so sacrificially without hesitation or fear?

The answer to this ever so critical question is, we must believe the promise of our Lord (v.30a). Christ promises to give *lands* back to those who have given up lands. *Lands* represents any material possessions or wealth. The promise of being *blessed materially*, of receiving a hundredfold is astounding to the world, but not to the believer. The believer understands what Jesus is saying. Jesus is laying down God's principle of money, of finances, of riches, of possessions, of material goods, of giving, of stewardship—whatever we wish to call the *things* of this world that we value (see DEEPER STUDY # 1—Mk.10:23). The principle is simple. It can be stated several ways:

➤ True disciples seek the kingdom of God and His righteousness first, and then all the necessities of life are given to them (Mt.6:33). They simply give all they are and have to the kingdom of God, and God sees to it that they have what is needed to take care of their necessities. The idea is a present experience, a continuous process. They keep on giving of themselves and what they have, and God keeps on giving to them.

➤ True disciples work so that they may have enough to give to others. Their very purpose for working is not only to take care of their own needs but also to earn enough to help others (Ep.4:28). Again, the idea is a continuous process. They work and earn and give to others, so God continues to give to them so that they can continue to spread the gospel and help others.

➤ True disciples give all they are and have to meet the needs of a desperate world. God sees to it that the generous believer receives more (2 Co.9:6-12). But what the believer receives is not given to keep and store up. God replenishes the believer so that the believer can continue to reach and help the world. True disciples keep on giving, and God keeps on giving to them, so that Christ-followers, as long as they live, can continue to spread the gospel and meet the needs of the world.

The whole idea is that Christ's disciples never see an end to what they receive from God. The giving and receiving goes on and on, never ending.

There is another idea behind what Jesus was saying: the idea of security and confidence and assurance. Those who seek God first, who give all they are and have, are assured of being taken care of—always. God promises His children that they will always have food, clothing, and shelter—if they truly seek God first. A price tag cannot be put on such assurance, confidence, and security. It is invaluable, more than a hundredfold. As long as the true disciples remain on earth, until God is ready to take them home to heaven, they are assured of God's taking care of them. And then on top of all this, there is life eternal, the glorious experience of living forever in all the majesty and glory of God and serving Him forever.

But seek first the kingdom of God and his righteousness, and all these things will be added to you. (Mt.6:33; see Mt.6:25-34)

And God is able to make all grace abound to you, so that having all sufficiency in all things at all times, you may abound in every good work. (2 Co.9:8)

And my God will supply every need of yours according to his riches in glory in Christ Jesus. (Ph.4:19)

You shall serve the LORD your God, and he will bless your bread and your water, and I will take sickness away from among them. (Ex.23:25)

They feast on the abundance of your house, and you give them drink from the river of your delights. (Ps.36:8)

Bring the full tithe into the storehouse, that there may be food in my house. And thereby put me to the test, says the LORD of hosts, if I will not open the windows of heaven for you and pour down for you a blessing until there is no more need. (Mal.3:10)

10:30b

[30] "who will not receive a hundredfold now in this time, houses and brothers and sisters and mothers and children and lands, with persecutions, and in the age to come eternal life."

3 A person receives persecution.

The true disciple also receives the reward of persecution. This statement is shocking. How can persecution be considered a reward? Peter tells us:

If you are insulted for the name of Christ, you are blessed, because the Spirit of glory and of God rests upon you. (1 Pe.4:14)

The words "insulted [reproached, reviled, ridiculed] for the name of Christ" mean that a believer suffers for righteousness; that is, he or she is persecuted or abused for Christ. When a disciple suffers for Christ, God's Spirit—the Spirit of glory—rests upon that person. Persecuted Christ-followers are given a very *special closeness*, a oneness with Christ that is beyond imagination, unexplainable (Ac.7:54-60). The Holy Spirit infuses them with a deep, *intense consciousness* of the Lord's presence, a consciousness so deep that it cannot be experienced apart from some severe experience of suffering.

In suffering for Christ, the disciple also experiences a very special identification with Christ. For as the Lord suffered on behalf of the disciple, so now the disciple suffers on behalf of the Lord. There is a sense in which the disciple's sufferings "fill up" the sufferings of Christ and complete the sufferings of Christ for the church (see note—Col.1:24).

These two experiences, gaining a deeper consciousness of the Lord's presence and experiencing a special identification with Christ and His suffering, are gained only through suffering. They make suffering a privilege and a joy for us as disciples, for we suffer even as our Lord suffered (Mt.10:24-25; Ac.5:41). Truly, enduring persecution on behalf of Christ is a reward, an indescribably rich reward!

Blessed are you when others revile you and persecute you and utter all kinds of evil against you falsely on my account. Rejoice and be glad, for your reward is great in heaven, for so they persecuted the prophets who were before you. (Mt.5:11-12)

For it has been granted to you that for the sake of Christ you should not only believe in him but also suffer for his sake. (Ph.1:29)

Indeed, all who desire to live a godly life in Christ Jesus will be persecuted. (2 Ti.3:12)

For to this you have been called, because Christ also suffered for you, leaving you an example, so that you might follow in his steps. (1 Pe.2:21)

But even if you should suffer for righteousness' sake, you will be blessed. Have no fear of them, nor be troubled. (1 Pe.3:14)

10:30c

[30] "who will not receive a hundredfold now in this time, houses and brothers and sisters and mothers and children and lands, with persecutions, and in the age to come eternal life."

4 A person receives eternal life.

The true disciple receives eternal life. Eternal life begins at the moment we repent and believe in Christ unto salvation. We begin to enjoy the abundant life that Christ came to give us here and now (Jn.10:10). The *full* abundance of this life is experienced only by those who give all they are and have to Him.

As joyous and fulfilling as this abundant life is, Christ not only promises to reward His disciples in this life. He promises to reward them "in the age to come"; that is, throughout eternity or eternal life. Imagine the reward: to *live forever in a perfect state of being*. Imagine the heavens and earth being made into "a new heaven and earth," being made perfect and eternal. Living forever in that *perfect world* is what Christ promises to the true disciple, the one who gives all they have and are for Christ's sake, and the gospel's (see notes and Deeper Study # 1—Mt.19:28; Deeper Study # 2—Jn.1:4; Deeper Study # 1—Jn.17:2-3).

However, the reward of dedicated disciples will be far richer throughout eternity than it will be for those who never fully followed Christ. Paul wrote of those who, though believers, were not dedicated followers of Christ. Their works will not survive the penetrating judgment of Christ. Their works will be consumed, burnt up like wood, hay, and straw in a fire. They will be saved—they will have eternal life—but that is all they will have. Christ's dedicated disciples will receive a reward (1 Co.3:12-15). Everything about this reward and all it entails is not revealed in Scripture. But one thing is certain: eternal life will be more joyous and abundant for them than it will be for those "who will be saved, but only as through fire" (1 Co.3:15).

> And Jesus, looking at him, loved him, and said to him, "You lack one thing: go, sell all that you have and give to the poor, and you will have treasure in heaven; and come, follow me." (Mk.10:21)

> Truly, truly, I say to you, whoever hears my word and believes him who sent me has eternal life. He does not come into judgment, but has passed from death to life. (Jn.5:24)

> Now if anyone builds on the foundation with gold, silver, precious stones, wood, hay, straw—each one's work will become manifest, for the Day will disclose it, because it will be revealed by fire, and the fire will test what sort of work each one has done. If the work that anyone has built on the foundation survives, he will receive a reward. If anyone's work is burned up, he will suffer loss, though he himself will be saved, but only as through fire. (1 Co.3:12–15)

5 A person receives an immediate warning and also assurance.

Jesus both assured and warned the disciples by stating a sobering truth: God is going to reverse the order of people in eternity. Many who are first in this world are going to be placed last, and they are going to be last forever, for all eternity. But many who are last are going to be placed *first* by God forever.

> [31] "But many who are first will be last, and the last first."

God is going to place every person exactly where they belong. He is going to rectify injustices. No matter what the esteem and rank are on earth, if a person belongs last, God is going to place them last. If the person belongs first, God is going to place them first. They will be judged, assigned, and honored according to God's and heaven's standards, not man's earthly standards. And Christ actually says that "many" changes are coming. The idea is that the majority of people will be switched from their earthly social standing. In God's eyes, some of the dearest, most repentant, heartbroken, and diligent people are now last; but He is going to exalt them to be ever so near and close to Him. This is an integral aspect of the devoted disciple's reward.

> He has brought down the mighty from their thrones and exalted those of humble estate (Lu.1:52)

> Woe to you who are full now, for you shall be hungry. Woe to you who laugh now, for you shall mourn and weep. (Lu.6:25)

> But Abraham said, 'Child, remember that you in your lifetime received your good things, and Lazarus in like manner bad things; but now he is comforted here, and you are in anguish.' (Lu.16:25)

> For we must all appear before the judgment seat of Christ, so that each one may receive what is due for what he has done in the body, whether good or evil. (2 Co.5:10)

> But it is God who executes judgment, putting down one and lifting up another. (Ps.75:7)

F. The Third Prediction of Death:
The Issue of Christ's Death, 10:32–34

(Mt.20:17–19; Lu.18:31–34)

1. **Jesus' iron determination: Was set on His purpose—to die**
2. **Jesus' amazing drawing power: Many followed**
3. **Jesus' thoughtful consideration: Took the disciples aside to explain His death**
4. **Jesus' magnificent love and courage**
   a. He will be betrayed to the Jews and condemned
   b. He will be handed over to the Gentiles, tortured and killed

5. **Jesus' great purpose**
   a. To die
   b. To arise

³² And they were on the road, going up to Jerusalem, and Jesus was walking ahead of them. And they were amazed, and those who followed were afraid. And taking the twelve again, he began to tell them what was to happen to him, ³³ saying, "See, we are going up to Jerusalem, and the Son of Man will be delivered over to the chief priests and the scribes, and they will condemn him to death and deliver him over to the Gentiles. ³⁴ And they will mock him and spit on him, and flog him and kill him. And after three days he will rise."

Division VI

The Son of God's Last Public Ministry: Jesus Deals with Some Special Issues, 10:1–52

F. The Third Prediction of Death: The Issue of Christ's Death, 10:32–34

(Mt.20:17–19; Lu.18:31–34)

10:32–34
Introduction

For the third time, Mark stresses the death and resurrection of Christ. This passage gives a striking portrait of Jesus and deals straightforwardly with the issue of His death. Christ was constantly drilling this fact into His disciples. (See outline and notes—Mk.8:31-33; 9:30-32; Mt.16:21-23; 17:22-23; 20:17-19. These passages should be studied along with this passage. The notes at Matthew 17:22-23 includes most of the New Testament passages on the death and resurrection of Christ.)

Jesus wants us, just He did the twelve disciples, to have a firm understanding of His sacrificial death and victorious resurrection. It is only when we fully grasp all that the cross and the empty grave mean that we can truly live in the fullness of their power. This is, *The Third Prediction of Death: The Issue of Christ's Death*, 10:32-34.

1. Jesus' iron determination: Was set on His purpose—to die (v.32).
2. Jesus' amazing drawing power: Many followed (v.32).
3. Jesus' thoughtful consideration: Took the disciples aside to explain His death (v.32).
4. Jesus' magnificent love and courage (v.33).
5. Jesus' great purpose (v.34).

1 Jesus' iron determination: Was set on His purpose—to die.

Jesus had set the course for Jerusalem. As He walked along, He became engrossed in thought—the thought of the cross that lay ahead. As He had said earlier, He came to earth for a specific purpose: to lay down His life as the sacrifice for the sinful human race. He referred to this purpose as "a baptism to be baptized with," and He was compelled to accomplish it (Lu.12:50). The time had now come. He was to go up to Jerusalem for the last time, go up to receive the baptism, the immersing of the cross. As He walked along thinking about the cross, He became so engrossed that He seems to have lost awareness of all around Him. God gave Him a spirit of determination, a determination so strong that He unconsciously quickened His pace and moved out far ahead of the disciples, so far that it perplexed the twelve. However, the point to see is the iron determination of Jesus. He was determined to face the cross. The cross lay right ahead of Him, yet it held so much meaning that He set His course to bear it. He was driven, constrained, pressed, compelled, determined (an iron determination) to bear the sufferings of the cross. Why?

> 32 And they were on the road, going up to Jerusalem, and Jesus was walking ahead of them. And they were amazed, and those who followed were afraid. And taking the twelve again, he began to tell them what was to happen to him,

- The cross was the way to save the world.

  For God so loved the world, that he gave his only Son, that whoever believes in him should not perish but have eternal life. (Jn.3:16)

  And I, when I am lifted up from the earth, will draw all people to myself. (Jn.12:32)

  He himself bore our sins in his body on the tree, that we might die to sin and live to righteousness. By his wounds you have been healed. (1 Pe.2:24)

  For Christ also suffered once for sins, the righteous for the unrighteous, that he might bring us to God, being put to death in the flesh but made alive in the spirit. (1 Pe.3:18)

- The cross was the way to please His Father (see note—Ep.5:2).

  I can do nothing on my own. As I hear, I judge, and my judgment is just, because I seek not my own will but the will of him who sent me. (Jn.5:30)

  "Now is my soul troubled. And what shall I say? 'Father, save me from this hour'? But for this purpose I have come to this hour. Father, glorify your name." Then a voice came from heaven: "I have glorified it, and I will glorify it again." (Jn.12:27–28)

  But I do as the Father has commanded me, so that the world may know that I love the Father. Rise, let us go from here. (Jn.14:31)

  I glorified you on earth, having accomplished the work that you gave me to do. (Jn.17:4)

- The cross was the way to assure His own joy.

  Looking to Jesus, the founder and perfecter of our faith, who for the joy that was set before him endured the cross, despising the shame, and is seated at the right hand of the throne of God. (He.12:2)

2 Jesus' amazing drawing power: Many followed.

Once again, the amazing *drawing power* of Jesus is seen. As He journeyed toward Jerusalem, He was not only followed by the twelve, but also by a number of others. Mark reports that, as these people observed Jesus, they were "amazed" and "afraid." We cannot be sure if the ones who were afraid were His apostles or some of the others following Him. In either case, the reaction was amazement and fear. There were at least two reasons for these reactions.

> 32 And they were on the road, going up to Jerusalem, and Jesus was walking ahead of them. And they were amazed, and those who followed were afraid. And taking the twelve again, he began to tell them what was to happen to him,

First, Jesus' behavior was unusual. He usually walked along with the disciples, utilizing every moment as a teaching opportunity. It was His practice not to lose a moment, other than when He needed to be alone for meditation and prayer. When the disciples saw His striding out ahead of them, they knew something serious and unusual was occupying His mind. His pace and His preoccupation amazed and perplexed them.

Second, Jesus' depth of thought and serious, foreboding countenance amazed and perplexed them. They marveled that He could be so lost in thought that He would become oblivious to all around Him. He seemed to be focused on some event that lay right before Him in Jerusalem. Whatever it was, He had to get there.

The disciples could tell by Jesus' unusual actions that apparently something dreadful was about to happen. They had no idea what it was. Therefore, they were *bewildered, apprehensive,* and *hesitant* to move on. They were gripped with both amazement and fear. Yet note something: despite their lack of understanding along with their fear, they followed right behind Jesus. They did not withdraw nor forsake Him. Why? Because they were drawn to Him through love. Jesus was their life. He had done so much for them; He was their all—all there was worth following. And they were thoroughly convinced that He was the true Messiah. They knew that to follow Him would be well worthwhile.

THOUGHT 1. Many do not understand the behavior (sinless nature) or the depth of thought (teachings) of Christ. In such cases Christ demands the same response He demanded of the disciples: faith. He expects us to follow Him even when we may not understand.

THOUGHT 2. The love of Jesus drew the disciples to Him. They loved Him because He loved them. It was love that kept them following after Him, even when they feared and did not understand.

> For the love of Christ controls us, because we have concluded this: that one has died for all, therefore all have died; and he died for all, that those who live might no longer live for themselves but for him who for their sake died and was raised. (2 Co.5:14–15)

> There is no fear in love, but perfect love casts out fear. For fear has to do with punishment, and whoever fears has not been perfected in love. (1 Jn.4:18)

10:32c

[32] And they were on the road, going up to Jerusalem, and Jesus was walking ahead of them. And they were amazed, and those who followed were afraid. And taking the twelve again, he began to tell them what was to happen to him,

3 Jesus' thoughtful consideration: Took the disciples aside to explain His death.

Jesus became aware of the disciples' bewilderment and fear, revealing His thoughtful consideration for these men who had forsaken all to follow Him. They were distressed, caught in the dark and unable to see what lay ahead. They needed His help. They needed to be prepared for the onrushing tragedy. They were hard to teach and slow to learn. Jesus had already informed them of His impending death and of God's concept of the Messiah. Of necessity, He had to consider the disciples and their slowness and dullness of heart and continue to teach them until they grasped God's Messiahship. As always, He took them aside from the rest of the people to meet their need (see notes—Lu.18:31-34).

THOUGHT 1. Note three important lessons.
1) Jesus will always meet our need, no matter how small or large.
2) It is not Jesus' will for us to be bewildered or gripped by fear.
3) We must, however, remember that we are to walk by faith. Therefore, it is not God's purpose for us to know all things.

> For God gave us a spirit not of fear but of power and love and self-control. (2 Ti.1:7)

> But my righteous one shall live by faith, and if he shrinks back, my soul has no pleasure in him. But we are not of those who shrink back and are destroyed, but of those who have faith and preserve their souls. (He.10:38-39)

> Even though I walk through the valley of the shadow of death, I will fear no evil, for you are with me; your rod and your staff, they comfort me. (Ps.23:4)

Therefore we will not fear though the earth gives way, though the mountains be moved into the heart of the sea. (Ps.46:2)

Behold, God is my salvation; I will trust, and will not be afraid; for the LORD GOD is my strength and my song, and he has become my salvation. (Is.12:2)

4 Jesus' magnificent love and courage.

The great love of Jesus is seen in many things, but the true essence of His love is seen in one supreme act: His *willingness* to be sacrificed for the human race.

Jesus knew exactly what lay ahead of Him in Jerusalem. As He walked and talked with the twelve, He explained what would happen when they reached their destination.

[33] saying, "See, we are going up to Jerusalem, and the Son of Man will be delivered over to the chief priests and the scribes, and they will condemn him to death and deliver him over to the Gentiles.

[34] And they will mock him and spit on him, and flog him and kill him. And after three days he will rise."

a. He will be betrayed to the Jews and condemned (v.33a).

Jesus told the twelve that He would be delivered to the Jews and condemned. *Delivered* or *betrayed* or *handed over* (Gk. paradothesetai, *par-ah-dah-thay'-seh-tie*) means that He would be delivered over to the authority of the Jews for trial and punishment. This event was determined, ordained, set in the plan and counsel of God (Ac.2:23). Now, it was *right before His face*, ready to take place.

Jesus had already named the men who would kill Him (see DEEPER STUDY # 1—Mt.16:21). The betrayal would be by *Judas,* who would identify Him for the *elders, chief priests,* and *Scribes*; and they in turn would deliver Him to the *Gentiles* (or Romans) for execution (Mt.20:19).

Peter, in preaching to the Jews right after Pentecost, charged the Jews with Christ's death, saying bluntly that *they* killed Him by the hands of the lawless Gentiles and Romans (Ac.2:23).

The fact that Jesus was being condemned by the Jews, the people who had been chosen to bring salvation to the world, must have cut Him deeply. He came to His own people, but their rejection of Him as the Son of God and their Messiah surely broke His heart (Jn.1:11).

b. He will be handed over to the Gentiles, tortured and killed (v.33b-34).

Jesus forewarned the twelve that He would be delivered to the Gentiles and tortured and killed. Note that the prosecutors of Jesus were named. They were to be the leaders among the Jews: the chief priests and Scribes and elders (see DEEPER STUDY # 1—Mt.16:21; note—1 Th.2:15-16). But note, they were to be only the prosecutors, not the executioners. They were forbidden by law to execute anyone (Jn.18:31). They had to deliver Jesus over to the Gentiles for execution.

Strong symbolism is seen in the facts that both Jew and Gentile (the world) are guilty of the death of God's Son, and that Jesus was to bear the sins of both Jew and Gentile (the world) in His death. He was to reconcile both to God (see outline and notes—Ep.2:14-15; 2:16-17).

Jesus was to be delivered to the Gentiles for torture and execution. Note the four forms of torture mentioned (v.34):

- *Mockery*: to ridicule, scorn, insult, humiliate, defy, jeer.
- *Spitting*: a sign of utter contempt (see DEEPER STUDY # 1—Mk.14:65).
- *Flogging* or *scourging*: to beat with a rod or a whip weighted with either jagged metal or bone chips. Thirty-nine or forty lashes were inflicted. The whole purpose of scourging was to inflict severe pain.
- *Killing* (crucifixion): see DEEPER STUDY # 1—Mt.27:26-44 for the terrible suffering of the cross.

Jesus bore the sins of the entire human race, suffering the ultimate degree of pain. He suffered pain in an absolute sense.

First, our Savior suffered *mentally*. While He was being tortured, His mind was bound to be upon why He was suffering. He was thinking about the sin of mankind and the problem sin had caused God. Imagine the world's sin—all of it, the enormity and awfulness of it—consuming His mind. He was suffering mentally to the ultimate degree.

Second, Christ suffered *spiritually*. His heart was being broken. Those whom He loved so much were committing a sin so horrendous it defied imagination. They were rebelling against God so much that they were *killing God's own Son*.

In addition, and even more terrible, His own Father was to turn His back upon Him. He was to be separated from God, bearing the condemnation of sin for mankind (see notes—Mt.27:46-49; Mk.15:34). He was beginning to bear and was going to bear spiritual pain in an absolute sense (2 Co.5:21; 1 Pe.2:24; see Is.53:4-7 for a descriptive account of His bearing our sin).

Third, Jesus suffered *physically*. His physical pain would be more severe because of the mental and spiritual pressure He was having to bear at the same time. There is also truth to the fact that the more ridicule within a persecutor's heart, the more he tortures his victim (see the crown of thorns, royal robe, and excessive mockery of the soldiers). The fact that Jesus claimed to be the Son of God provoked the persecutors to inflict more scorn and torture.

THOUGHT 1. Magnificent is the glorious love of Christ—His *willingness* to bear so much for us!

> I am the good shepherd. The good shepherd lays down his life for the sheep. (Jn.10:11)

> For this reason the Father loves me, because I lay down my life that I may take it up again. No one takes it from me, but I lay it down of my own accord. I have authority to lay it down, and I have authority to take it up again. This charge I have received from my Father. (Jn.10:17-18)

> Who gave himself for our sins to deliver us from the present evil age, according to the will of our God and Father. (Ga.1:4)

> By this we know love, that he laid down his life for us, and we ought to lay down our lives for the brothers. (1 Jn.3:16)

> And from Jesus Christ the faithful witness, the firstborn of the dead, and the ruler of kings on earth. To him who loves us and has freed us from our sins by his blood. (Re.1:5)

10:34

³⁴ "And they will mock him and spit on him, and flog him and kill him. And after three days he will rise."

5 Jesus' great purpose.

a. To die.

b. To arise.

The events Jesus foretold would fulfill His great purpose for coming to earth and becoming a man. He came to die and rise again.

> He himself bore our sins in his body on the tree, that we might die to sin and live to righteousness. By his wounds you have been healed. (1 Pe.2:24)

The summit of pain was experienced in the sufferings and death of Jesus Christ. He suffered pain to the ultimate degree, in an absolute sense. Yet in the midst of such terrible suffering, there is something that is very precious—a thought, a truth that should be very, very precious to us. It is this: *Jesus' death was dear to His heart*—dear despite the terrible suffering He was to endure. In a way unknown to mankind and which can never be completely understood by humans, Jesus set His heart and face toward the cross. He was consumed and fixated with the cross. Why? Because the cross was the focus of God's purpose throughout all eternity.

The cross was dear to Jesus' heart because it was His Father's will. In dying, He could please His Father, and pleasing His Father was the supreme objective of His life (see note—Ep.5:2).

> No one takes it from me, but I lay it down of my own accord. I have authority to lay it down, and I have authority to take it up again. This charge I have received from my Father. (Jn.10:18)

> And walk in love, as Christ loved us and gave himself up for us, a fragrant offering and sacrifice to God. (Ep.5:2)

In addition, the cross was dear to Jesus' heart because it was the means by which He was to gain many brothers and sisters (see note—Ro.8:28-39).

> For those whom he foreknew he also predestined to be conformed to the image of his Son, in order that he might be the firstborn among many brothers. (Ro.8:29)

> But when the fullness of time had come, God sent forth his Son, born of woman, born under the law, to redeem those who were under the law, so that we might receive adoption as sons. And because you are sons, God has sent the Spirit of his Son into our hearts, crying, "Abba! Father!" (Ga.4:4–6)

The cross was also dear to the Savior's heart because through death He was to be made "the founder" (captain, author, source) of our salvation.

> But we see him who for a little while was made lower than the angels, namely Jesus, crowned with glory and honor because of the suffering of death, so that by the grace of God he might taste death for everyone. For it was fitting that he, for whom and by whom all things exist, in bringing many sons to glory, should make the founder of their salvation perfect through suffering. (He.2:9–10)

Moreover, the cross was dear to Jesus' heart because by His death He was to destroy the power of the devil over humanity, that is, death.

> Since therefore the children share in flesh and blood, he himself likewise partook of the same things, that through death he might destroy the one who has the power of death, that is, the devil, and deliver all those who through fear of death were subject to lifelong slavery. (He.2:14–15)

And the cross was dear to Christ's heart because by the cross He was to reconcile all people, reconcile us both to God and to one another (see outline and notes—Ep.2:13–18).

> But now in Christ Jesus you who once were far off have been brought near by the blood of Christ. For he himself is our peace, who has made us both one and has broken down in his flesh the dividing wall of hostility . . . and might reconcile us both to God in one body through the cross, thereby killing the hostility. (Ep.2:13–14, 16)

But there is another reason—a glorious reason—the cross was dear to the heart of our blessed Lord: because through death He would arise and return to His former glory which He had with the Father before the foundation of the world (Jn.17:1–5; see notes, *Resurrection*—Mt.17:23; note and DEEPER STUDY # 1—Ac.1:3; DEEPER STUDY # 4—2:24). He could never know the glories of resurrection, and we could never know the power of His resurrection, apart from the cross. For all these reasons and more, the cross is dear to every blood-washed believer, to every individual who, in their repentant and believing heart, has been to Calvary. Truly, we glory in the cross (Ga.6:14).

> I glorified you on earth, having accomplished the work that you gave me to do. And now, Father, glorify me in your own presence with the glory that I had with you before the world existed. . . . Father, I desire that they also, whom you have given me, may be with me where I am, to see my glory that you have given me because you loved me before the foundation of the world. (Jn.17:4–5, 24)

> But far be it from me to boast except in the cross of our Lord Jesus Christ, by which the world has been crucified to me, and I to the world. (Ga.6:14)

G. The Issue of Ambition, 10:35–45

(Mt.20:20–28; Lu.22:24–47)

1. The deceitfulness of selfish ambition
   a. A secret approach, v.41
   b. An open-ended request

2. The possible motives for ambition
   a. Favoritism and wealth
   b. Power and social status
   c. Love, faith, loyalty

3. The great price of ambition[DS1]
   a. The cup: Sacrifice and suffering
   b. The baptism: Immersed, dying to self

   c. The prophecy: The certainty of paying the price[DS2, 3]

4. The exclusive right of God regarding ambition

5. The potential conflict among people with ambition

6. The meaning and greatness of good ambition
   a. Not to rule, not to exercise authority

   b. To be a servant

   c. To be a slave, a bond-slave

7. The supreme example of ambition
   a. Supreme humiliation
   b. Supreme mission
   c. Supreme price[DS4]

35 And James and John, the sons of Zebedee, came up to him and said to him, "Teacher, we want you to do for us whatever we ask of you."
36 And he said to them, "What do you want me to do for you?"
37 And they said to him, "Grant us to sit, one at your right hand and one at your left, in your glory."
38 Jesus said to them, "You do not know what you are asking. Are you able to drink the cup that I drink, or to be baptized with the baptism with which I am baptized?"
39 And they said to him, "We are able." And Jesus said to them, "The cup that I drink you will drink, and with the baptism with which I am baptized, you will be baptized,"
40 "but to sit at my right hand or at my left is not mine to grant, but it is for those for whom it has been prepared."
41 And when the ten heard it, they began to be indignant at James and John.
42 And Jesus called them to him and said to them, "You know that those who are considered rulers of the Gentiles lord it over them, and their great ones exercise authority over them.
43 But it shall not be so among you. But whoever would be great among you must be your servant,
44 and whoever would be first among you must be slave of all."
45 "For even the Son of Man came not to be served but to serve, and to give his life as a ransom for many."

Division VI

The Son of God's Last Public Ministry: Jesus Deals with Some Special Issues, 10:1-52

G. The Issue of Ambition, 10:35-45

(Mt.20:20-28; Lu.22:24-47)

10:35-45
Introduction

Jesus was on His way to Jerusalem to meet a destiny foretold since man first sinned (Ge.3:15). On this visit to Israel's capital, the crisis of His death followed by His resurrection would take place. The Lord had just shared the fact of the crisis again (vv.17-19). For months it had consumed His attention and private teachings to the disciples (Mt.16:13-20; 16:21-28; 17:1-13; 17:22; 17:24-27; 20:17). There was no question in the disciples' minds: this visit to Jerusalem was the fateful event for which they had long looked. Jesus was about to free Israel and set up His kingdom on earth, or so they thought.

We who live today know what Jesus meant by His death and resurrection. He was to die for our sins and be raised again to impart new life to us. But the disciples did not grasp this. Jesus had not yet died and been raised from the dead. To them, He was speaking of an earthly and material kingdom. Therefore, if He was about to set up His kingdom, now was the time to seize the positions of power in His kingdom. Now was the time to secure the positions of rule and authority (see notes—Mt.1:1; DEEPER STUDY # 1—1:18; DEEPER STUDY # 3—3:11; notes—11:1-6; 11:2-3; DEEPER STUDY # 1—11:5; DEEPER STUDY # 2—11:6; DEEPER STUDY # 1—12:16; note—Lu.7:21-23).

This is what James and John were doing. They were assuring themselves of key positions in Jesus' government (see outlines and notes—Mt.18:1-4; Lu.22:24-30). The drama that follows reveals the selfish, competitive hearts of human beings, even among followers of Christ. Jesus ends the bickering by pointing them—and us—to the greatest ambition of all. This is, *The Issue of Ambition*, 10:35-45.

1. The deceitfulness of selfish ambition (vv.35).
2. The possible motives for ambition (vv.36-37).
3. The great price of ambition (vv.38-39).
4. The exclusive right of God regarding ambition (v.40).
5. The potential conflict among people with ambition (v.41).
6. The meaning and greatness of good ambition (vv.42-44).
7. The supreme example of ambition (v.45).

1 The deceitfulness of selfish ambition.

Selfish ambition is a fruit of pride, which is the root of all sins. As James' and John's behavior reveals, it leads to deceit, underhandedness, and manipulation.

10:35

³⁵ And James and John, the sons of Zebedee, came up to him and said to him, "Teacher, we want you to do for us whatever we ask of you."

a. A secret approach.

James and John were aware that the other disciples were also ambitious for position, so they wanted to get the upper hand on their fellow followers of Christ (see Lu.9:46). Matthew adds that they persuaded their mother to go with them (Mt.20:20-21). Their mother, Salome, was probably Mary's sister—Jesus' aunt. Most likely, James and John felt she would add weight to their request. At the very least, her presence would remind Jesus of their family relationship and subtly pressure Him to grant their request in order to please His mother. The ambition that was gripping their heart was not healthy ambition; it was evil ambition. And evil ambition is sneaky. It tries to get an inside track, the upper hand, by hook or by crook. It uses any means whatsoever, including the use and misuse of people, even loved ones (Salome).

b. An open-ended appeal.

Brimming with sinful selfishness, the Sons of Thunder brazenly attempted to manipulate Jesus into granting their request. As we might say, they asked Jesus to give them a blank check: they made an unlimited appeal, asking Jesus to give them whatever they asked for. Again, they were being sneaky. They tried to get a commitment before they revealed their request. They were so inflamed with pride that they thought they could trap the all-wise Son of God into granting the desire of their selfish souls. Surely they sensed that their desire was wrong and evil; but blinded by the lust for honor, position, power, wealth, and recognition, they subdued the sense of conscience.

THOUGHT 1. Wrong or evil ambition is *always deceitful* and *sneaky*. When people want something they should not have and are determined to get it anyway, they become sneaky and manipulative. They will sneak to get the things of the world that satisfy their flesh. And, sadly, they will use and misuse other people, reducing those who love them most to mere pawns in their grab for power, pleasure, money, or whatever it is they crave.

> **Whoever exalts himself will be humbled, and whoever humbles himself will be exalted. (Mt.23:12)**

> **For such persons do not serve our Lord Christ, but their own appetites, and by smooth talk and flattery they deceive the hearts of the naive. (Ro.16:18)**

> **Deceit is in the heart of those who devise evil, but those who plan peace have joy. (Pr.12:20)**

> **Though you soar aloft like the eagle, though your nest is set among the stars, from there I will bring you down, declares the LORD. (Ob.4)**

10:36-37

³⁶ And he said to them, "What do you want me to do for you?"

³⁷ And they said to him, "Grant us to sit, one at your right hand and one at your left, in your glory."

2 The possible motives for ambition.

Before committing Himself, Jesus wisely asked James and John what they wanted (v.36). They wasted no time in coming to the point: "Grant us the top positions in your *glory*"—the kingdom or government they thought Christ was going to set up when they arrived at Jerusalem (v.37). The two men were extremely ambitious. They wanted to be the top ministers of state in Christ's government.

What needs to be noted is that ambition can be good or bad. The determining factor is motive. One's motive makes ambition either good or bad. The ambition of James and John exposes several possible motives. Each one touches a sensitive spot within every person and urges each of us to examine the motives of our hearts (see note, *Ambition*—Mt.20:20-21).

a. Favoritism and wealth (v.37a).

James and John may have been motivated by favoritism and wealth. Along with Peter, they formed an inner circle around Christ (see DEEPER STUDY # 1—Mk.9:2). They apparently had some feeling that they were special, the favorites of Christ; therefore, they were due the top positions.

Zebedee, the father of James and John, was apparently wealthy. He owned a fishing business large enough to furnish fish for the palace (see note—Mk.1:20; Jn.18:15-18). Consequently, they were better off financially than some of the other disciples. They may have felt their wealth made them more qualified for the positions, for wealth did carry weight with monarchs of their day, and they knew it. Or, they may have been simply acting as selfish, pampered young men seeking more.

THOUGHT 1. Feeling special, as though one is a favorite of God, is a common sin—a sin of pride. How many of us have felt we are one of God's specials or favorites? How often have we felt this way?

THOUGHT 2. The inner circle, or the multi-gifted, often feel as though they are the special ones of God or of the church. Some often feel as though they are due special favors.

> So Peter opened his mouth and said: "Truly I understand that God shows no partiality." (Ac.10:34)

> Pride goes before destruction, and a haughty spirit before a fall. (Pr.16:18) (Remember James' and John's desertion of Christ at the cross.)

THOUGHT 3. Wealth can make a person self-centered. It can pamper and make one selfish. It can cause a person to expect more attention, more honor, more recognition, more favor. Those who have wealth often want more. And they set out to get more, whether wise or unwise, whether right or wrong. The wisdom and righteousness of having wealth are determined by a person's motive and true need.

> But the cares of the world and the deceitfulness of riches and the desires for other things enter in and choke the word, and it proves unfruitful. (Mk.4:19)

> But those who desire to be rich fall into temptation, into a snare, into many senseless and harmful desires that plunge people into ruin and destruction. (1 Ti.6:9)

b. Power and social status (v.37b).

James and John were obviously motivated by a thirst for power, position, influence, and authority. It is the very thing for which they asked. They wanted to be right next to Jesus in the top two positions of His government.

Social status is one of the perks of such high-ranking positions. James and John already had a measure of social standing. They were somewhat wealthy and were accepted within the palace and were personally known by the High Priest (see notes—Mk.1:20; Jn.18:15–18). Being the new king's right- and left-hand men would move them instantly to the top rung of the social ladder.

Social standing often makes people feel that they are entitled to more—more position, more recognition, a higher seat. Social standing can also make us feel that we are better or above others. Perhaps James and John had a tinge of both feelings.

THOUGHT 1. People want position, and they think in terms of position and influence. Within the business world, they want positions that assure influence and reward. Within the church, some want positions of leadership and of influence. People seldom think in terms of service or in terms of how they can help the company or the church. Too often their thoughts are on the honor, the reward, the influence, the position they will receive.

THOUGHT 2. How many seek to be next to the boss, the pastor, the leader, or the teacher, seeking to coax favor; seeking to be recognized as knowing them well and as being favored by them?

> Live in harmony with one another. Do not be haughty, but associate with the lowly. Never be wise in your own sight. (Ro.12:16)

> Let no one seek his own good, but the good of his neighbor. . . . just as I try to please everyone in everything I do, not seeking my own advantage, but that of many, that they may be saved. (1 Co.10:24, 33)

> For you know the grace of our Lord Jesus Christ, that though he was rich, yet for your sake he became poor, so that you by his poverty might become rich. (2 Co.8:9)

> Let each of you look not only to his own interests, but also to the interests of others. (Ph.2:4)

c. Love, faith, and loyalty (v.37c).

We must not overlook the reality that James and John were motivated, to some degree, by love, faith, and loyalty. On some level, James and John wanted to be next to Jesus out of hearts of love and loyalty to Him. When ambition is rooted in the Lord and steeped in love and loyalty toward Him, it is *always right and healthy.* Their stooping to deceit and manipulation proves that their motives were not entirely pure. Nevertheless, even though their love and loyalty to

Christ do not seem to be the dominant force in their ambition, they were no doubt a factor. Consider the following observations:

➤ They definitely believed Jesus: His Word, His promises, His kingdom, His power. They were showing loyalty to Christ by expressing confidence in His power to usher in the kingdom of God. They were asking for positions in His kingdom. They knew He was the true Messiah, the Son of the living God who was to become the King of kings and Lord of lords.

➤ They definitely wanted the positions because they wanted to be next to Christ. To them He *deserved* the kingdom and the honor. He deserved it because He had done so much and was going to do so much for them and for the people of God.

"For the Father himself loves you, because you have loved me and have believed that I came from God. I came from the Father and have come into the world, and now I am leaving the world and going to the Father." His disciples said, "Ah, now you are speaking plainly and not using figurative speech! Now we know that you know all things and do not need anyone to question you; this is why we believe that you came from God." (Jn.16:27–30)

Grace be with all who love our Lord Jesus Christ with love incorruptible. (Ep.6:24)

Though you have not seen him, you love him. Though you do not now see him, you believe in him and rejoice with joy that is inexpressible and filled with glory. (1 Pe.1:8)

10:38–39

[38] Jesus said to them, "You do not know what you are asking. Are you able to drink the cup that I drink, or to be baptized with the baptism with which I am baptized?"

[39] And they said to him, "We are able." And Jesus said to them, "The cup that I drink you will drink, and with the baptism with which I am baptized, you will be baptized,"

3 The great price of ambition.

Jesus was straightforward, pulling no punches with these two ambitious men. The Lord told them bluntly that they did not understand what they were asking for (v.38). Those who occupy such positions in Christ's kingdom must pay a great price.

a. The cup: Sacrifice and suffering (v.38a).

Those who reign with Christ must be willing to drink of the same cup He drank of, the cup of suffering and sacrifice (see Mt.26:39; Jn.18:11). Jesus is asking the ambitious believer, "Are you able to go through the terrible experience I have to suffer? Can you drink the cup of my terrible agony, of my inward agony and pain?"

b. The baptism: Immersed, dying to self (v.38b).

Those who reign with Christ must be willing to be baptized with the same baptism with which He was baptized. Baptism is a picture of death (Ro.6:4; Col.2:12). We must die to self just as Jesus did, desiring God's will over our own will, even if it means excruciating suffering (Mt.26:39). Jesus is asking the ambitious disciple, "Are you able to die to self? Can you be immersed in the Father's will? Can you bear the baptism of my terrible sufferings?" (see DEEPER STUDY # 1).

c. The prophecy: The certainty of paying the price (v.39).

James and John accepted the Lord's challenge, and they responded immediately, very positively, saying, "We are able." Of course, they did not know what they were saying, not fully, for they did not truly grasp what Jesus was saying. Nevertheless, at this particular moment they were willing to die for Christ in Jerusalem if necessary.

In response to their profession, Jesus prophesied that one day they *would* have to drink His cup and be baptized with His baptism. They *would* face suffering and death; they *would* pay the price associated with their ambition (see DEEPER STUDIES 2, 3).

THOUGHT 1. The same challenge is issued to every person who desires to follow Christ. The cross precedes the crown. Before we can reign with Him, we must suffer with Him (2 Ti.2:12). We are to drink the Lord's cup and be baptized with His baptism.

1) We are to suffer for His sake, to labor and serve to the point of exhaustion in getting the gospel out and in ministering to a lost world.

2) We are to bear persecution, if necessary, to fulfill His mission. In essence, we are to deny self, do whatever is necessary (see Deeper Study # 1; notes and Deeper Study # 1—Lu.9:23).

> If we endure, we will also reign with him; if we deny him, he also will deny us. (2 Ti.2:12)

> But rejoice insofar as you share Christ's sufferings, that you may also rejoice and be glad when his glory is revealed. (1 Pe.4:13)

> Do not fear what you are about to suffer. Behold, the devil is about to throw some of you into prison, that you may be tested, and for ten days you will have tribulation. Be faithful unto death, and I will give you the crown of life. (Re.2:10)

THOUGHT 2. We should follow the example of James and John. We should accept the Lord's challenge . . .

- accept it immediately, not hesitating at all
- accept it even though we may not fully understand what it involves

> So therefore, any one of you who does not renounce all that he has cannot be my disciple. (Lu.14:33)

THOUGHT 3. There is a price to pay for ambition. If we really want to achieve, we must get to it, and getting to it takes time and work. It involves sacrifice and pain, sweat and tears, isolation and loneliness, and often involves sacrificing our social lives and many other activities. In all honesty, few are willing to pay such a price.

> And he said to all, "If anyone would come after me, let him deny himself and take up his cross daily and follow me. For whoever would save his life will lose it, but whoever loses his life for my sake will save it." (Lu.9:23-24)

> If anyone comes to me and does not hate his own father and mother and wife and children and brothers and sisters, yes, and even his own life, he cannot be my disciple. Whoever does not bear his own cross and come after me cannot be my disciple. (Lu.14:26-27)

> For if you live according to the flesh you will die, but if by the Spirit you put to death the deeds of the body, you will live. (Ro.8:13)

> And those who belong to Christ Jesus have crucified the flesh with its passions and desires. (Ga.5:24)

> Indeed, I count everything as loss because of the surpassing worth of knowing Christ Jesus my Lord. For his sake I have suffered the loss of all things and count them as rubbish, in order that I may gain Christ. (Ph.3:8)

DEEPER STUDY # 1

(10:38-39) **Cup—Baptism:** there is a difference between drinking the cup of suffering and being baptized with suffering. The cup refers more to what we take into ourselves and bear within ourselves. It is more internal suffering, inward agony. The baptism refers more to what is put upon us from the outside. It is more external suffering.

The cup means drinking the bitterness and agony of trials, pain, hurt, sorrow, heartbreak, suffering, disappointment, and tears (see Christ's experience in the Garden of Gethsemane, Mt.26:36-46; His sufferings, Mt.20:19; 27:46-49; and John's experience on Patmos, Rev.1:9; see Introduction—Date).

The baptism of suffering means being immersed in the rapids of affliction, rejection, abuse, ridicule, opposition, persecution, and, if required, martyrdom.

The Christian believer who truly lives and witnesses for Christ will drink His cup and be baptized with His baptism. Just think for a moment. Christ calls for *all we are and have* in order to help people and to carry the message of salvation to a lost world. If we should be serious and give *all we are and have,* just imagine the cost to us. That is how different we would be from the world. Imagine the world's reaction to us. That is the reason Jesus and the apostles met with so much opposition so often. They gave *all they were and had* and lived so differently. They lived for God instead of living for self and the world. Therefore, the world could not understand them. Some ignored and others ridiculed, abused, persecuted, and even killed them. They had the Lord's cup and baptism of suffering and sacrifice to bear. And so do all who truly follow Christ. (See outlines and notes—Mt.10:16-42; 19:23-30. See also Mt.19:29; Ro.8:16-17; Ph.1:28; 2 Ti.3:12; 1 Pe.2:21; 4:1-5; 5:10.)

DEEPER STUDY # 2

(10:39) **James:** was killed by Herod. He was the first apostle to drink the cup of martyrdom.

DEEPER STUDY # 3

(10:39) **John:** lived to be approximately one hundred years old. Just how John died is unknown; however, he drank the cup and was baptized with suffering in a most distressful way.

1. He witnessed the sufferings of Jesus' death.
2. He lived through the murder and deaths of all the other apostles.
3. He lived a long life of banishment and exile on the island of Patmos (see Introduction, *Revelation*—Date).

10:40

[40] "but to sit at my right hand or at my left is not mine to grant, but it is for those for whom it has been prepared."

4 The exclusive right of God regarding ambition.

Jesus said that the positions James and John requested were not His to grant. They are for those for whom they have been prepared. With this statement, Jesus declared two truths.

First, Jesus said that some *will sit* on His right and some on His left hand. God is preparing to bestow such honor upon some. This fact points toward degrees of glory or levels of rewards in heaven.

Second, Jesus said that the right to reign with Him is to be determined by God alone (that is, His absolute justice). It is the Father's prerogative, His exclusive right. He also makes a distinction between the *great*, who only commit themselves to minister and the *first* (greatest), who commit themselves to be *bond-slaves* (vv.43-44; see note—Mt.20:23-28).

> If anyone serves me, he must follow me; and where I am, there will my servant be also. If anyone serves me, the Father will honor him. (Jn.12:26)

> If I then, your Lord and Teacher, have washed your feet, you also ought to wash one another's feet. (Jn.13:14)

> For you were bought with a price. So glorify God in your body. (1 Co.6:20)

> For he who was called in the Lord as a bondservant is a freedman of the Lord. Likewise he who was free when called is a bondservant of Christ. (1 Co.7:22)

> Knowing that from the Lord you will receive the inheritance as your reward. You are serving the Lord Christ. (Col.3:24)

10:41

[41] And when the ten heard it, they began to be indignant at James and John.

5 The potential conflict among people with ambition.

James' and John's selfish ambition caused conflict with the other ten disciples. How did the others hear what James and John had done? Knowing human nature, we can speculate as to what probably transpired. They probably saw the two approach Jesus from off in the distance. They saw them bow before Him (Mt.20:20). Such was most unusual because of their daily association with Him. They knew something unusual was happening. When James and John returned, the ten most likely asked what was going on. Of course, James and John would have been hesitant to reveal the truth. But, as would be expected, this only stirred the disciples' curiosity and cross-examination more. They pressed and pressed the issue until James and John had to confess to their evil and ugly plot.

The ten were indignant with James and John. Tempers flared, and arguments followed. What right did they have to do such a thing? Why did these two deserve a higher position than any of them? Jealousy, envy, pride, self-centeredness, and bitterness bred within the heart of each against the two. Perhaps even hatred was being expressed. One thing is certain. The band of disciples was threatened; their cohesiveness and the very work of the Lord was at stake. A division beyond repair was possible because of James' and John's selfishness and sneakiness.

THOUGHT 1. Selfish ambition can cause some terrible things among people. It can cause . . .

- jealousy
- hatred
- suffering
- envy
- sneakiness
- divisiveness

- bitterness
- conflict
- death
- anger
- self-centeredness
- destruction

Whoever exalts himself will be humbled, and whoever humbles himself will be exalted. (Mt.23:12)

How can you believe, when you receive glory from one another and do not seek the glory that comes from the only God? (Jn.5:44)

Whoever loves transgression loves strife; he who makes his door high seeks destruction. (Pr.17:19)

It is not good to eat much honey, nor is it glorious to seek one's own glory. (Pr.25:27)

6 The meaning and greatness of good ambition.

10:42–44

Jesus did not find fault with ambition as a whole. There is good ambition just as there is bad ambition. But Jesus was quite clear about the difference between the two. One is of the world, the other of God. Note what He essentially says in these verses: godly ambition, ambition that is good and healthy, is an ambition that does not seek to rule and to exercise authority.

The world's view of ambition is far from what Jesus taught. Most people are caught up to some degree in *worldly* ambition, seeking more and more. Few are void of worldly ambition.

The world views ambition as an *internal* thing. Those believing this way believe people should have some degree of freedom to seek what they wish. They should be allowed some recognition, some position, some influence, some fame, some wealth, some gadgets, some vehicles, some machines. They should be allowed to fulfill their ambition, seeking and securing whatever they desire.

From the world's perspective, ambition is also an *external* thing. A person's ambition (greatness) is judged successful by . . .

42 And Jesus called them to him and said to them, "You know that those who are considered rulers of the Gentiles lord it over them, and their great ones exercise authority over them.

43 But it shall not be so among you. But whoever would be great among you must be your servant,

44 and whoever would be first among you must be slave of all."

- one's wealth
- one's home
- one's vehicles
- one's gadgets
- one's position

- one's influence
- one's recognition
- one's social standing
- one's fame
- one's authority

The Lord's view of ambition, however, stands in utter contrast to the world's perspective. In God's eyes and kingdom, greatness is the exact opposite of what the world deems it to be. It is critical that we grasp Jesus' description of greatness.

345

a. Not to rule, not to exercise authority (v.42).

Godly ambition or greatness is not exercising lordship and authority over people. It is not desiring the chief positions. Godly ambition is not self-centered and selfish, not worldly-minded.

However, godly ambition does desire greatness. Christ acknowledges and seems to commend the ambition for greatness (v.43). But there is a crucial point to note: the greatness desired must focus on Christ if it is to be godly ambition. A person becomes great by doing what Christ says. The greatness sought *must not* be greatness for oneself, but the greatness that accompanies doing what the Son of God says. It is greatness due to obedience, due to doing what Christ has revealed.

b. To be a servant (v.43).

True greatness is achieved through service to others. Those ambitious for true greatness seek to serve rather than to be served (v.45). This type of ambition looks for people to help and for ways to help them, whether at work, home, play, or church. It is always seeking those who need encouragement, care, attention, company, food, clothing, shelter, money. It seeks for the sake of ministering (see Mt.25:34–40).

c. To be a slave, a bond-slave (v.44).

Godly ambition (greatness) leads us to become the *slave of all. Slave* (Gk. doulos) means a bond-slave (see note—Ro.1:1). Christ made a significant distinction between the terms *great* and *first* (protos). Note the difference:

➤   The "great" are they who "serve."

➤   The "first" are they who are "slaves" or *bond-slaves.*

What Jesus was saying is that among His disciples, *they who serve or minister are great*, but they who are *bond-slaves are the greatest*. The idea of serving is that of occasional service, whereas the bond-slave is a person who is bound to the Lord every moment of life, always serving—regardless of hour or call or difficulty.

The idea of degrees of service is unquestionably in mind. Not every believer serves with the same fervor or commitment. The idea of degrees of reward for works is also conveyed by our Lord's teaching.

What Christ means is this: a person is to be a minister and a servant. True greatness is not found in being a lord or a master, but in ministering and serving others. Godly ambition and greatness are represented in a person's becoming a *minister and a servant by nature*. He or she assumes the role of a servant, of a bond-slave (see notes—Ro.1:1).

> And whoever gives one of these little ones even a cup of cold water because he is a disciple, truly, I say to you, he will by no means lose his reward. (Mt.10:42)

> But not so with you. Rather, let the greatest among you become as the youngest, and the leader as one who serves. (Lu.22:26)

> If I then, your Lord and Teacher, have washed your feet, you also ought to wash one another's feet. (Jn.13:14)

> Rendering service with a good will as to the Lord and not to man. (Ep.6:7)

> The reward for humility and fear of the Lord is riches and honor and life. (Pr.22:4)

> He has told you, O man, what is good; and what does the Lord require of you but to do justice, and to love kindness, and to walk humbly with your God? (Mi.6:8)

10:45

45 "For even the Son of Man came not to be served but to serve, and to give his life as a ransom for many."

7 The supreme example of ambition.

The Lord Jesus Christ is the supreme example of godly ambition, the ambition that makes a person truly great. He set His face like a flint to accomplish His purpose. The dear Savior modeled this type of ambition in three ways.

a. The supreme humiliation.

Our Lord modeled humility by committing the supreme act of humiliation. This is the act of coming to earth: "The Son of Man *came.*" The incarnation is the Son of God becoming man. To most people, mankind is the summit of creation on this earth. But within the span and scope of the universe and before God, mankind is nothing—not to an honest and thinking person. We are as a microbe on a speck of sand floating through what seems to be infinite space and lasting only about seventy years or so if we can.

In all reality, for God to become a member of so low a race of beings is unimaginable. It is the most humiliating act possible (Ph.2:6–8).

b. The supreme mission.

Jesus modeled service by coming on the supreme mission: "[He] came not to be served, but to serve." He was treated as the lowest by the people to whom He came. Impossible, yet true! They gave Him no place to lay His head (Mt.8:20; Lu.9:58), and only three years after publicly announcing that He had come to save them, they killed Him. Now note: Jesus is the King of kings and Lord of lords, yet He secured His kingdom by becoming a minister and a servant to all. He did not "lord it" over people. He ministered to and served people willingly. Because He became the servant to all, God has now highly exalted Him (Ph.2:7, 9–11).

c. The supreme price.

Our blessed Savior modeled sacrifice by paying the supreme price: "[He gave] His life as a ransom for many" (see Deeper Study # 4).

> And whoever gives one of these little ones even a cup of cold water because he is a disciple, truly, I say to you, he will by no means lose his reward. (Mt.10:42)

> Have this mind among yourselves, which is yours in Christ Jesus, who, though he was in the form of God, did not count equality with God a thing to be grasped, but emptied himself, by taking the form of a servant, being born in the likeness of men. And being found in human form, he humbled himself by becoming obedient to the point of death, even death on a cross. Therefore God has highly exalted him and bestowed on him the name that is above every name, so that at the name of Jesus every knee should bow, in heaven and on earth and under the earth, and every tongue confess that Jesus Christ is Lord, to the glory of God the Father. (Ph.2:5–11)

DEEPER STUDY # 4

(10:45) **Ransom for many** (lutron anti pollon): a ransom in exchange (pollon) for many, a ransom for many, a ransom for the release of many.

Ransom is a means of setting loose in the Old Testament. It is the setting loose (ransom) of a life (Ex.21:30); it is the ransom price, the redemptive price for something, for example: a slave (Le.19:20), some land (Le.25:24), a captive (Is.45:13).

The Greek word for ransom (lutron) is significant. There is no question that the idea of *exchange* is present. Christ gave His life in *exchange*, as a substitute for many. The word is used two other times in the New Testament, in the equivalent passage in Mt.20:28 and in 1 Ti.2:6. In 1 Ti.2:6 the words are a substitutionary "ransom for all" (antilutron huper panton). In the Greek *huper* is the preposition for the idea of substitution. It is a substitution in behalf of all.

> And he died for all, that those who live might no longer live for themselves but for him who for their sake died and was raised. . . . For our sake he made him to be sin who knew no sin, so that in him we might become the righteousness of God. (2 Co.5:15, 21)

> He has no need, like those high priests, to offer sacrifices daily, first for his own sins and then for those of the people, since he did this once for all when he offered up himself. (He.7:27)

> Nor was it to offer himself repeatedly, as the high priest enters the holy places every year with blood not his own, for then he would have had to suffer repeatedly since the foundation of the world. But as it is, he has appeared once for all at the end of the ages to put away sin by the sacrifice of himself. (He.9:25–26)

> And by that will we have been sanctified through the offering of the body of Jesus Christ once for all. (He.10:10)

> He himself bore our sins in his body on the tree, that we might die to sin and live to righteousness. By his wounds you have been healed. (1 Pe.2:24; see 1 Co.5:7; Ep.5:2)

H. The Steps for Getting Help:
Blind Bartimaeus, 10:46–52

(Mt.20:29-34; Lu.18:35-43)

1. **Step 1: Gaining access to Jesus**
   a. Jesus came to Jericho
   b. The disciples and the crowd followed Jesus
   c. A blind man sat by the road begging
2. **Step 2: Believing the reports about Jesus**
3. **Step 3: Acknowledging personal need**[DS1]
4. **Step 4: Being persistent in seeking Jesus**[DS2]

5. **Step 5: Eagerly expecting to receive Jesus' help**
   a. Jesus stopped and then called to the man
   b. The man threw aside his cloak and rushed to Jesus
6. **Step 6: Requesting precisely what is needed**

7. **Step 7: Experiencing the power of Jesus and following Him**

⁴⁶ And they came to Jericho. And as he was leaving Jericho with his disciples and a great crowd, Bartimaeus, a blind beggar, the son of Timaeus, was sitting by the roadside.
⁴⁷ And when he heard that it was Jesus of Nazareth, he began to cry out and say, "Jesus, Son of David, have mercy on me!"
⁴⁸ And many rebuked him, telling him to be silent. But he cried out all the more, "Son of David, have mercy on me!"
⁴⁹ And Jesus stopped and said, "Call him." And they called the blind man, saying to him, "Take heart. Get up; he is calling you."
⁵⁰ And throwing off his cloak, he sprang up and came to Jesus.
⁵¹ And Jesus said to him, "What do you want me to do for you?" And the blind man said to him, "Rabbi, let me recover my sight."
⁵² And Jesus said to him, "Go your way; your faith has made you well." And immediately he recovered his sight and followed him on the way.

Division VI

The Son of God's Last Public Ministry: Jesus Deals with Some Special Issues, 10:1–52

H. The Steps for Getting Help: Blind Bartimaeus, 10:46–52

(Mt.20:29-34; Lu.18:35-43)

10:46-52
Introduction

Bartimaeus needed help and needed it desperately. As we read his story, there is no question but that his blindness is a picture of the blindness, darkness, and needs of a world that reels in desperation for help. The need may be physical, mental, emotional, or spiritual; it may be some problem with the mind, some desperate loneliness, or some tragic sin. Whatever it is, this passage teaches how to get the help from the Lord we so desperately need. This is, *The Steps for Getting Help: Blind Bartimaeus,* 10:46-52.

1. Step 1: Gaining access to Jesus (v.46).
2. Step 2: Believing the reports about Jesus (v.47).
3. Step 3: Acknowledging personal need (v.47).

4. Step 4: Being persistent in seeking Jesus (v.48).
5. Step 5: Eagerly expecting to receive Jesus' help (vv.49–50).
6. Step 6: Requesting precisely what is needed (vv.51–52).
7. Step 7: Experiencing the power of Jesus and following Him (v.52).

1 Step 1: Gaining access to Jesus.

10:46

With great determination, Jesus traveled on toward Jerusalem, where He would meet with the fate for which the Father sent Him to our sinful world. Along the way, He continued to teach His disciples, and He—the Servant (v.45)—stopped to help a blind man who strategically gained access to Him.

> 46 And they came to Jericho. And as he was leaving Jericho with his disciples and a great crowd, Bartimaeus, a blind beggar, the son of Timaeus, was sitting by the roadside.

a. Jesus came to Jericho.

The route to Jerusalem took Jesus through Jericho. In those days, Jericho was one of the most important cities of Palestine. One of the world's main commercial roads ran right through the city, north to south. The city was only about seventeen miles from Jerusalem, and it is thought to be the oldest city in the world.

b. The disciples and the crowd followed Jesus.

The disciples continued to travel with Jesus, and they were followed by a large crowd of people. Some of these people may have been following Jesus for quite some time (v.32). However, it was the Passover season, which means that thousands of pilgrims were making their way to Jerusalem. Most likely, many others joined the crowd following Jesus at Jericho.

c. A blind man sat by the road begging.

The pilgrims were passing right through Jericho. Blind Bartimaeus knew this, and he also knew that religious people were more sensitive to the needs of helpless people who had to beg for a living. It is also possible that Bartimaeus had heard that Jesus was in Jericho (see Lu.18:35-43). If so, he knew that his best chance to find Jesus would be to station himself at the city limits where Jesus would be passing as He left the city. Whatever the case, Bartimaeus had to beg for a living, so he sat by the highway, appealing to the multitudes who passed by on their way to Jerusalem.

THOUGHT 1. Those who desire Jesus' help must seek Him. They must go where they know Jesus is, where Jesus passes by. They must go where they can hear Jesus' word, or they may never hear how they can have eternal life.

> For everyone who asks receives, and the one who seeks finds, and to the one who knocks it will be opened. (Lu.11:10)

> Seek the LORD while he may be found; call upon him while he is near. (Is.55:6)

2 Step 2: Believing the reports about Jesus.

10:47

The second step to getting the Lord's help is believing the reports about Jesus. Sitting there, Bartimaeus heard all kinds of noises coming from the people passing by—the noises of individuals, of groups, of whole caravans. He heard the noise of feet tramping along, of animals, of conversation, of laughter, of play among children. He heard all kinds of talking:

> 47 And when he heard that it was Jesus of Nazareth, he began to cry out and say, "Jesus, Son of David, have mercy on me!"

serious, jovial, commercial, vain, rude, off-colored, religious. But then something happened: the size of the crowd and the noises and talk changed. The passersby became a throng, a multitude of people; and the noises and talk were about Jesus, the One for whom he had hoped and longed.

Bartimaeus had been blind for years, maybe all his life, with no hope of ever seeing. Apparently, he was a beggar with no one to care for him. But then the most glorious event of his life happened. He heard about One called Jesus of Nazareth, who was claiming to be the true Messiah.

He heard that this Jesus had been performing miracles, healing the sick and afflicted. Perhaps for the first time in his life, hope swelled up in him. He knew there was a possibility that he might be healed and enabled to see. From the very first day that he had heard about Jesus, he had hoped and longed for the chance when Jesus might pass by. Why? Because he *believed the testimonies* about Jesus.

Note another fact. Sitting there by the road as Jesus passed by, Bartimaeus had no way to know it was Jesus. He could not see Him. He could only hear people walking and talking. When he heard people talking about Jesus, he believed it was He. Bartimaeus believed and trusted what he was hearing.

THOUGHT 1. People must believe the reports, the testimonies about Jesus before they can receive His help. All Bartimaeus ever had was what he heard. He had never seen or been around Jesus. He only knew the reports people were sharing: Jesus is the Messiah, the Son of David. And he believed the testimonies.

> Truly, truly, I say to you, whoever hears my word and believes him who sent me has eternal life. He does not come into judgment, but has passed from death to life. (Jn.5:24)

> But these are written so that you may believe that Jesus is the Christ, the Son of God, and that by believing you may have life in his name. (Jn.20:31)

But before people can believe in Jesus' power to help them, they must hear about Him. They must hear our testimonies of what He has done for us. We have an eternally-important responsibility to talk about Jesus as we journey through life, faithfully sharing our testimony with others (see Ro.10:14.) How can people believe in Jesus if they never hear about Him?

> For "everyone who calls on the name of the Lord will be saved." How then will they call on him in whom they have not believed? And how are they to believe in him of whom they have never heard? And how are they to hear without someone preaching? And how are they to preach unless they are sent? As it is written, "How beautiful are the feet of those who preach the good news!" (Ro.10:13–15)

> Who has believed what he has heard from us? And to whom has the arm of the LORD been revealed? (Is.53:1)

> The Spirit of the Lord GOD is upon me, because the LORD has anointed me to bring good news to the poor; he has sent me to bind up the brokenhearted, to proclaim liberty to the captives, and the opening of the prison to those who are bound; to proclaim the year of the LORD's favor, and the day of vengeance of our God; to comfort all who mourn. (Is.61:1–2)

10:47

[47] And when he heard that it was Jesus of Nazareth, he began to cry out and say, "Jesus, Son of David, have mercy on me!"

3 Step 3: Acknowledging personal need.

The third step to getting help from the Lord is acknowledging your need. As soon as Bartimaeus heard that it was Jesus, he instantly began shouting out to attract Jesus, creating as much noise as he could above the crowd and its noises.

The point is, Bartimaeus acknowledged his need, and he confessed it publicly. He did not approach Jesus secretly or quietly by asking someone close by to appeal to Jesus on his behalf. He accepted the fact that he had a desperate need. He wanted Jesus' help no matter what. Therefore, He unashamedly cried out to Jesus, referring to the Lord as the "Son of David" (see DEEPER STUDY # I). Certainly, this did not express a complete concept of all that Jesus is. But it was a title that conveyed the blind man's faith in what He had heard about Jesus, that He was the Messiah. Bartimaeus approached Jesus as his hope, his savior, his deliverer, his leader. He used what knowledge he had of Jesus and cried out to Him.

Blind Bartimaeus cried out to Jesus for mercy, not for anything else. He was blind, and he was a beggar, yet he did not cry for housing or clothing or food. He cried for his most basic need to be met—for mercy.

THOUGHT 1. Nobody has a complete concept—a thorough understanding—of Jesus when they first come to Him. Nobody truly understands Jesus until after they are saved and have received the Holy Spirit into their lives and learned of Christ. We must come to Christ believing what we *do* know about Him, in unwavering faith that He is God's Son, the only Savior and Lord. And we must come believing the truth about ourselves, that we are hopelessly and helplessly lost, and that we stand in utter need of His mercy.

> But the tax collector, standing far off, would not even lift up his eyes to heaven, but beat his breast, saying, 'God, be merciful to me, a sinner!' I tell you, this man went down to his house justified, rather than the other. For everyone who exalts himself will be humbled, but the one who humbles himself will be exalted. (Lu.18:13-14)

> For godly grief produces a repentance that leads to salvation without regret, whereas worldly grief produces death. (2 Co.7:10)

> This poor man cried, and the LORD heard him and saved him out of all his troubles. (Ps.34:6)

> The sacrifices of God are a broken spirit; a broken and contrite heart, O God, you will not despise. (Ps.51:17)

> All these things my hand has made, and so all these things came to be, declares the LORD. But this is the one to whom I will look: he who is humble and contrite in spirit and trembles at my word. (Is.66:2)

> And rend your hearts and not your garments. Return to the LORD your God, for he is gracious and merciful, slow to anger, and abounding in steadfast love; and he relents over disaster. (Joel 2:13)

DEEPER STUDY # 1

(10:47) **Son of David:** see notes—Mt.1:1; DEEPER STUDY # 1—1:18; DEEPER STUDY # 3—3:11; notes—11:1-6; 11:2-3; DEEPER STUDY # 1—11:5; DEEPER STUDY # 2—11:6; DEEPER STUDY # 1—12:16; note—Lu.7:21-23.

4 Step 4: Being persistent in seeking Jesus.

10:48

The fourth step to getting the Lord's help is persisting and persevering after Jesus (see DEEPER STUDY # 2). Many among the crowd tried to hush Bartimaeus, but he was desperate and determined and in dead earnest. He would not be discouraged, silenced, nor stopped. He repeatedly cried to the top of his lungs: "Son of David, have mercy on me!"

48 And many rebuked him, telling him to be silent. But he cried out all the more, "Son of David, have mercy on me!"

The point is that Bartimaeus persevered. He had a desperate need, and he would not stop seeking to have his need met. The voices raised against him were "many," but his faith in Jesus was stronger. He believed Jesus could really help him. His faith stood against all the voices of *discouragement* and against the feelings of so many that it was *useless* to cry out to Jesus.

THOUGHT 1. Perseverance is the answer to desperate need—persevering prayer and persevering faith (see note and DEEPER STUDY # 1—Mt.7:7; note and DEEPER STUDY # 1—Lu.11:5-10 for discussion).

Worldly voices will rise up against us, attempting to pull us away, to tell us that it is useless to pray. Naysayers will try to convince us that our need is too desperate to be met and to encourage us to try the world's way instead. But we must be steadfast in our faith and prayers, refusing to be deterred or discouraged from believing in the mercy and power of God.

> For everyone who asks receives, and the one who seeks finds, and to the one who knocks it will be opened. (Mt.7:8)

> And he told them a parable to the effect that they ought always to pray and not lose heart. (Lu.18:1)

> But from there you will seek the LORD your God and you will find him, if you search after him with all your heart and with all your soul. (De.4:29)

> You will seek me and find me, when you seek me with all your heart. (Je.29:13)

(10:48) **Persistence—Perseverance:** persistence always grabs the Lord's attention (see outline and notes—Mt.7:7-11; see Lu.18:1). Note Jesus' question (v.51). He already knew what the blind man wanted. He had probably heard him as well, but He wanted the blind man to experience persistence. Why does Christ teach perseverance instead of just meeting our needs immediately? There are at least five reasons.

1. Having to persevere sharpens, increases, and grows our faith. It teaches endurance, experience (victorious living), and hope (Ro.5:2-4).

2. Having to persevere sharpens and makes us more aware of our minds. It gives us more time for thought and meditation and for the searching of the truth about ourselves and our needs. It focuses in on real needs.

3. Having to persevere teaches us to pray and to seek God more. It creates more awareness of our helplessness and our need for His presence and help. It necessitates more fellowship and deep communion with Him.

4. Having to persevere involves us more in His work and worship. It creates a sense within us of having a greater part. This is not a need on God's part, but a need on our part. Serving Him is a great privilege which He allows us.

5. Having to persevere allows more time for a greater number of people to be reached with God's power. Perseverance is a greater witness for God. When God answers and moves, more people are stirred to observe God's working.

5 Step 5: Eagerly expecting to receive Jesus' help.

The fifth step to getting the Lord's help is eagerly expecting to receive His help. The two acts in these verses—the first by Jesus and the second by Bartimaeus—are significant.

10:49-50

⁴⁹ And Jesus stopped and said, "Call him." And they called the blind man, saying to him, "Take heart. Get up; he is calling you."
⁵⁰ And throwing off his cloak, he sprang up and came to Jesus.

a. **Jesus stopped and then called to the man (v.49).**
Mark reports that Jesus stopped or stood still. The crowd must have been huge, for Jesus had to send for the man. Jesus *stopped* . . .
  - because of the man's need: He could not reach Jesus by himself
  - because the man had persisted in crying despite the many who were opposing him
  - because Jesus never turned away from a person who cried for help

All that the Father gives me will come to me, and whoever comes to me I will never cast out. (Jn.6:37)

The Lord is not slow to fulfill his promise as some count slowness, but is patient toward you, not wishing that any should perish, but that all should reach repentance. (2 Pe.3:9)

b. **The man threw aside his cloak and rushed to Jesus (v.50).**
Bartimaeus cast aside his coat, cast aside all impediments. This was an interesting act. This blind man wanted nothing to hinder him from reaching Jesus as quickly as he could. All in one motion, he cast aside the hindrances, sprang to his feet, and rushed toward Jesus. The emphasis here is on his eagerness to reach Jesus and allowing nothing to hinder him.

THOUGHT 1. What a lesson for us! How few are so eager! How many hang on to that which hinders and hampers and keeps them from reaching Christ?

To put off your old self, which belongs to your former manner of life and is corrupt through deceitful desires. (Ep.4:22)

Therefore, since we are surrounded by so great a cloud of witnesses, let us also lay aside every weight, and sin which clings so closely, and let us run with endurance the race that is set before us. (He.12:1)

Beloved, I urge you as sojourners and exiles to abstain from the passions of the flesh, which wage war against your soul. (1 Pe.2:11)

If iniquity is in your hand, put it far away, and let not injustice dwell in your tents. (Jb.11:14)

Let the wicked forsake his way, and the unrighteous man his thoughts; let him return to the LORD, that he may have compassion on him, and to our God, for he will abundantly pardon. (Is.55:7)

6 Step 6: Requesting precisely what is needed.

The sixth step to getting help from the Lord is requesting precisely what you need. Bartimaeus knew exactly what he needed and had no difficulty stating his need. He did not waver at all. He was not like many who are vague in their prayers and requests. He asked for exactly what he needed, briefly and to the point.

51 And Jesus said to him, "What do you want me to do for you?" And the blind man said to him, "Rabbi, let me recover my sight."
52 And Jesus said to him, "Go your way; your faith has made you well." And immediately he recovered his sight and followed him on the way.

And whatever you ask in prayer, you will receive, if you have faith. (Mt.21:22)

Whatever you ask in my name, this I will do, that the Father may be glorified in the Son. If you ask me anything in my name, I will do it. (Jn.14:13–14)

Until now you have asked nothing in my name. Ask, and you will receive, that your joy may be full. (Jn.16:24)

Before they call I will answer; while they are yet speaking I will hear. (Is.65:24)

Call to me and I will answer you, and will tell you great and hidden things that you have not known. (Je.33:3)

However, Bartimaeus needed to make a personal confession to Jesus. Jesus, of course, knew what Bartimaeus needed; but the Lord's knowing about the man's need was not enough. The man had to make a personal confession to Jesus.

So everyone who acknowledges me before men, I also will acknowledge before my Father who is in heaven, but whoever denies me before men, I also will deny before my Father who is in heaven. (Mt.10:32–33)

In addition, Bartimaeus needed to confess his faith in Jesus' power for the sake of the others standing there. They needed to know that it was faith in Jesus that saved the man.

Because, if you confess with your mouth that Jesus is Lord and believe in your heart that God raised him from the dead, you will be saved. For with the heart one believes and is justified, and with the mouth one confesses and is saved. . . . For "everyone who calls on the name of the Lord will be saved." (Ro.10:9–10, 13)

Bartimaeus addressed Jesus as *Rabboni* (pronounced rob'-boo-nee), which means *my Master*. It is a title that conveys personal reverence, respect, and submission. Note the possessive "my." Bartimaeus' heart reached out to Jesus, desiring to belong to Him.

And he said to all, "If anyone would come after me, let him deny himself and take up his cross daily and follow me." (Lu.9:23)

Bartimaeus prayed a specific request and he received a specific answer: "Your faith has made you well" (see notes—Mk.11:22-23; DEEPER STUDY # 1—Jn.2:24; notes—Ro.10:16–17; Heb.11:1; DEEPER STUDY # 1—11:6).

Consequently, he is able to save to the uttermost those who draw near to God through him, since he always lives to make intercession for them. (He.7:25)

And without faith it is impossible to please him, for whoever would draw near to God must believe that he exists and that he rewards those who seek him. (He.11:6)

Commit your way to the LORD; trust in him, and he will act. (Ps.37:5)

Trust in the LORD with all your heart, and do not lean on your own understanding. (Pr.3:5)

Trust in the LORD forever, for the LORD GOD is an everlasting rock. (Is.26:4)

7 Step 7: Experiencing the power of Jesus and following Him.

10:52

⁵² And Jesus said to him, "Go your way; your faith has made you well." And immediately he recovered his sight and followed him on the way.

The seventh step to getting help from the Lord is following Jesus. This scene in Mark 10 is a very tender scene. Note that Jesus told Bartimaeus to go on his way. But Bartimaeus did not go, not after his Master had touched him. Instead, He followed Jesus on the road to Jerusalem. Bartimaeus clung to Jesus. Nothing was going to pry him away. The way he chose for his life was the way of Christ. His choice is evidence of genuine saving faith.

THOUGHT 1. There are several lessons here.

1) There is a heart of appreciation, of being grateful and thankful.

> Giving thanks to the Father, who has qualified you to share in the inheritance of the saints in light. (Col.1:12)

> And let the peace of Christ rule in your hearts, to which indeed you were called in one body. And be thankful. (Col.3:15)

> And you shall eat and be full, and you shall bless the LORD your God for the good land he has given you. (De.8:10)

2) There is the idea of genuineness of conversion. He followed through.

> And he said to all, "If anyone would come after me, let him deny himself and take up his cross daily and follow me." (Lu.9:23)

3) There is the idea of growing, wanting to learn more and more about the Savior.

> Come to me, all who labor and are heavy laden, and I will give you rest. Take my yoke upon you, and learn from me, for I am gentle and lowly in heart, and you will find rest for your souls. For my yoke is easy, and my burden is light. (Mt.11:28–30)

4) There is the testimony of loyalty and faithfulness.

> Therefore, my beloved brothers, be steadfast, immovable, always abounding in the work of the Lord, knowing that in the Lord your labor is not in vain. (1 Co.15:58)

CHAPTER 11

VII. THE SON OF GOD'S LAST JERUSALEM MINISTRY: JESUS' WARNING AND CONFLICT WITH RELIGIONISTS, 11:1–12:44

A. The Triumphal Entry: A Dramatic Warning, Jesus Is the Messiah,[DS1] 11:1–11

(Mt.21:1–11; Lu.19:28–40; Jn.12:12–19)

Now when they drew near to Jerusalem, to Bethphage and Bethany, at the Mount of Olives, Jesus sent two of his disciples

2 and said to them, "Go into the village in front of you, and immediately as you enter it you will find a colt tied, on which no one has ever sat. Untie it and bring it.

3 If anyone says to you, 'Why are you doing this?' say, 'The Lord has need of it and will send it back here immediately.'"

4 And they went away and found a colt tied at a door outside in the street, and they untied it.

5 And some of those standing there said to them, "What are you doing, untying the colt?"

6 And they told them what Jesus had said, and they let them go.

7 And they brought the colt to Jesus and threw their cloaks on it, and he sat on it.

8 And many spread their cloaks on the road, and others spread leafy branches that they had cut from the fields.

9 And those who went before and those who followed were shouting, "Hosanna! Blessed is he who comes in the name of the Lord!

10 Blessed is the coming kingdom of our father David! Hosanna in the highest!"

11 And he entered Jerusalem and went into the temple. And when he had looked around at everything, as it was already late, he went out to Bethany with the twelve.

1. **Scene 1: The peaceful entry—Jesus came in on a colt**[DS2]

   a. The painstaking details the disciples were to follow
      1) To secure a colt that had never been ridden

      2) To answer the owner's question[DS3]

   b. The details followed exactly as Jesus instructed

   c. The homage paid by the disciples[DS4]

2. **Scene 2: The triumphal entry—Jesus came to save now (Hosanna!)**

   a. The people's concept: A national hero—Hosanna! ("Save now!")[DS5, 6]

   b. The Lord's meaning: He came to bring spiritual peace[DS7, 8]

3. **Scene 3: The investigation of the situation (temple scene)—Jesus came obediently**
4. **Scene 4: The seclusion at Bethany—Jesus prepared spiritually**

Division VII

The Son of God's Last Jerusalem Ministry:
Jesus' Warning and Conflict with Religionists, 11:1–12:44

A. The Triumphal Entry: A Dramatic Warning, Jesus Is the Messiah, 11:1–11

(Mt.21:1–11; Lu.19:28–40; Jn.12:12–19)

11:1–12:44
DIVISION OVERVIEW

Three significant points need to be made about Jesus' ministry in Jerusalem.

1. The first three Gospels (*Matthew, Mark, Luke*) say little about Jesus' ministry in Jerusalem. The present passage is the first mention of a specific visit. The three synoptic Gospels give only hints that Jesus was ever in Jerusalem, hints such as . . .

- His lament over Jerusalem (Mt.23:37); this indicates He had been in the city and made appeal after appeal to the people
- His warm family-like relationship with Martha and her sister and brother, Mary and Lazarus; their home was His home when in Jerusalem (see note—Jn.11:1–3)
- His friendship with Nicodemus and Joseph of Arimathea; they were both involved in His burial, indicating a close friendship probably developed in several meetings (see note—Mt.27:57-60; see Jn.19:38-42)

The first three Gospels concentrate on Jesus' ministry in Galilee. It is the fourth Gospel, the Gospel of *John*, that covers Jesus' ministry in Judea and Jerusalem. John tells us that Jesus was in Jerusalem quite often, especially during the great feasts (see Jn.2:13f; 5:1f; 7:1–10f; esp. v.10 to get an idea of His ministry in Jerusalem).

2. When Jesus visited Jerusalem, His ministry differed entirely from His Galilean ministry. In Galilee, Jesus taught many subjects; but in Jerusalem, He focused only on one theme: His Messiahship. He spent His time proclaiming strongly that He was, beyond any question, the Messiah. There was a strategic reason for this. Jerusalem was the capital of Palestine, and the temple itself was there. Jerusalem was the hub and center of Jewish life and worship. The population of Jerusalem and the surrounding suburbs and cities (for example, Bethphage and Bethany) ranged in the hundreds of thousands. Jericho, a city of sizeable population, was only about seventeen miles away. The temple required over twenty thousand priests alone, not counting the Levite helpers who must have numbered even more. If there was any place where Jesus would proclaim His Messiahship, it would be in Jerusalem. Jerusalem was a city that held every sort of person who had been born and who was yet to be born. Jerusalem was to hear the truth of God's Son and of God's great love for the world. The people of Jerusalem and all born thereafter were to be left without excuse.

> O Jerusalem, Jerusalem, the city that kills the prophets and stones those who are sent to it! How often would I have gathered your children together as a hen gathers her brood under her wings, and you were not willing! (Mt.23:37)

3. Note the following visits to Jerusalem.
   a. John 2:13f: Jesus cleansed the temple proclaiming it to be "My Father's house" (Jn.2:16). He proclaimed that He was the Son of Man (Jn.3:14) and God's only begotten Son (Jn.3:16).
   b. John 5:1f: Jesus healed a man on the Sabbath, a man who had been sick for thirty-eight years. Then He proclaimed that He had the right to break the Sabbath law because He was the Son of the Father. He was equal with God in every sense of the word (Jn.5:1–16; 5:17–30).
   c. Jn.7:1–10f: Jesus declared that God was His Father (Jn.9:28, 36, 38, 49, 54) and that He was: sent of God (Jn.7:16-17, 28-29; 8:18, 26, 29, 42), the Source of life (Jn.7:37–39), the Light of the World (Jn.8:12; 9:5), the Messiah (Jn.8:24, 28), the Spokesman of God

(Jn.8:26-28, 40), the Son of God (Jn.9:35-37), the Son of Man (Jn.8:28), the great "I Am" (Jn.8:58), the Great Shepherd of Life (Jn.10:1-42), and on and on (see the verses in Jn.10-21).

11:1-11
Introduction

There is no louder declaration of our Lord's Messiahship than the triumphal entry. Jesus was deliberately proclaiming that He was "the Son of the living God" (Mt.16:16). But the triumphal entry, which occurred at the outset of Jesus' final week, served an additional purpose (see DEEPER STUDY # 1). Jesus was *dramatically warning* the people that they must change their concept of Messiahship. He was not coming as the *national hero* to save the world physically and materially by overthrowing the Roman and Gentile governments. He was coming as the *King of Peace* to save the world spiritually and eternally. Spiritual and eternal salvation must occur first, then He would return to bring deliverance from oppressive governments and eternal peace as a conquering king. He had to come first as the King of Peace; then He would come as the King of Conquest. This is, *The Triumphal Entry: A Dramatic Warning, Jesus Is the Messiah,* 11:1-11.

1. Scene 1: The peaceful entry—Jesus came in on a colt (vv.1-7).
2. Scene 2: The triumphal entry—Jesus came to save now (Hosanna) (vv.8-10).
3. Scene 3: The investigation of the situation (temple scene)—Jesus came obediently (v.11).
4. Scene 4: The seclusion at Bethany—Jesus prepared spiritually (v.11).

DEEPER STUDY # 1

(11:1-11) **Jesus Christ, Last Week—Holy Week—Palm Sunday:** this was the beginning of Jesus' last week before His death. He had spent the night before in Bethany with Martha, Mary, and Lazarus (Jn.12:1f). The last week of our Lord's life has been known as Holy Week from the earliest times by Christians everywhere. The triumphal entry was the first event of the week, taking place on the first day. It is called Palm Sunday.

1 Scene 1: The peaceful entry—Jesus came in on a colt.

11:1-7

As Jesus neared Jerusalem, He sent two of His disciples on an important assignment: to secure a colt—a young donkey—for Him to ride into Jerusalem. Christ's riding into Jerusalem on the colt would symbolize that He came in peace (see DEEPER STUDY # 2; outline and notes—Jn.12:14 for discussion). But perhaps more important, it would fulfill a specific prophecy concerning the Messiah.

a. The painstaking details the disciples were to follow (vv.2-3).

The disciples' assignment involved painstaking details that Jesus insisted be followed. They were to go to a certain village, where they were to secure an unbroken colt they would find tied near the entrance to the village (v.2). They were to answer the owner's questions by simply stating that the Lord needs it and will return it when His purpose for it is finished (v.4; see DEEPER STUDY # 3).

Christ had a crucial reason for making such detailed preparations to enter Jerusalem. He was deliberately fulfilling a prophecy of Zechariah:

Now when they drew near to Jerusalem, to Bethphage and Bethany, at the Mount of Olives, Jesus sent two of his disciples

² and said to them, "Go into the village in front of you, and immediately as you enter it you will find a colt tied, on which no one has ever sat. Untie it and bring it.

³ If anyone says to you, 'Why are you doing this?' say, 'The Lord has need of it and will send it back here immediately.'"

⁴ And they went away and found a colt tied at a door outside in the street, and they untied it.

⁵ And some of those standing there said to them, "What are you doing, untying the colt?"

⁶ And they told them what Jesus had said, and they let them go.

⁷ And they brought the colt to Jesus and threw their cloaks on it, and he sat on it.

Rejoice greatly, O daughter of Zion! Shout aloud, O daughter of Jerusalem! Behold, your king is coming to you; righteous and having salvation is he, humble and mounted on a donkey, on a colt, the foal of a donkey. (Zec.9:9)

This prophecy was an announcement to Jerusalem that her King was coming. But it also served as a warning that Israel's King—the Messiah—would not be what the nation expected Him to be. His entrance into Jerusalem would depict this. Note the details of Zechariah's prophecy.

First, Israel's King was coming, just as Jerusalem had expected. The people were correct in this part of their expectation. But there was danger in their expectation, the danger of being so fervent in their own expectations and ideas that they missed what really happened. Their King came, but He came quite differently than anticipated.

THOUGHT 1. What a lesson for us! We must guard against reading into Scripture what is not there, especially in looking toward the return of our Lord. We must not dictate *how* Jesus is to return; we must not add to what God has revealed in His Word.

Second, Israel's King would come humbly and lowly. The Messiah was coming in meekness, not as a reigning monarch. He was coming to win people's hearts and lives spiritually and eternally, not physically and materially (see notes—Mk.11:1-11; Ep.1:3; see Mt.11:29).

Third, Israel's King would come riding the foal of a donkey. The Messiah was coming not as a conqueror riding a white stallion, but as a king of peace, riding a young colt. He was coming to save the world peacefully, to reconcile the world to the God of love and reconciliation, not to the God of hate and retaliation and war. He was not going to kill people and overthrow their governments (the Romans and Gentiles). He was coming to win people's hearts and lives through the glorious news (gospel) that God loves and reconciles (see outline and notes—Ep.2:13-18).

Again, note the prophecy and the careful preparation Christ made to fulfill the prophecy. This says something: Christ was dramatizing His Messiahship so clearly that people could not fail to see and understand that He was God's Messiah. This was God's will, prophesied generations before Christ came. God wanted His Son to proclaim His Messiahship so clearly that the people could not mistake what He was doing. God wanted the world to know that He was bringing peace to earth through His Son, Jesus Christ.

> **Because of the tender mercy of our God, whereby the sunrise shall visit us from on high to give light to those who sit in darkness and in the shadow of death, to guide our feet into the way of peace. (Lu.1:78-79)**

> **And suddenly there was with the angel a multitude of the heavenly host praising God and saying, "Glory to God in the highest, and on earth peace among those with whom he is pleased!" (Lu.2:13-14)**

> **As for the word that he sent to Israel, preaching good news of peace through Jesus Christ (he is Lord of all). (Ac.10:36)**

> **For the kingdom of God is not a matter of eating and drinking but of righteousness and peace and joy in the Holy Spirit. (Ro.14:17)**

> **For he himself is our peace, who has made us both one and has broken down in his flesh the dividing wall of hostility. (Ep.2:14)**

> **And through him to reconcile to himself all things, whether on earth or in heaven, making peace by the blood of his cross. (Col.1:20)**

b. The details followed exactly as Jesus instructed (vv.4-6).

The disciples followed Jesus' instructions to the most minute detail. They found the specific colt of which Jesus had spoken, untied it, and answered questions exactly as Jesus had instructed them to.

c. The homage paid by the disciples (v.7).

The disciples put their cloaks on the young donkey's back to serve as a saddle for their Lord. This was an act of respect and honor (see DEEPER STUDY # 4). Note an important detail: Jesus

DEEPER STUDY # 2

(11:1-7) **Donkey—Colt:** in ancient days the colt was a noble animal. It was used as a beast of service to carry people's burdens. But more significantly, it was used by kings and their emissaries. When they entered a city in peace, they rode a colt to symbolize their peaceful intentions (see the judges of Israel and the chieftains throughout the land, Jud.5:10; 10:4). This differed dramatically from a conquering king. When a king entered a city as a conqueror, he rode a stallion.

Jesus was dramatically demonstrating two things for the people. First, He was unquestionably the promised king, the Savior of the people; but second, He was not coming as the conquering king. He was not coming as a worldly potentate, in pomp and ceremony; not coming as the leader of an army to kill, injure, and maim. The people must change their concept of the Messiah. He was coming as the Savior of peace, the Savior of all people. He was coming to show the human race that God is the God of love and reconciliation.

1. The colt was a symbol of peace. Jesus came to bring peace, as pointed out in the above discussion.

2. The colt symbolized service. It was a noble animal, a service animal used to carry burdens. Jesus came upon the colt symbolizing that He came to serve people, to bear their burdens for them.

3. This particular colt symbolized sacredness. It had never been ridden before (v.2). Animals and things used for sacred or religious purposes had to have never been used before (Nu.19:2; De.21:3; 1 S.6:7). This detail points to the sacredness of the event. It pictures for everyone Jesus deliberately proclaiming that *He is the sacred hope*, the promised Messiah of the people.

DEEPER STUDY # 3

(11:3-6) **The Owner of the Colt**: see note, *Prophecy—Mt.21:2-5*.

DEEPER STUDY # 4

(11:7) **Homage to Jesus—Obedience:** Christ deliberately received the homage (reverence, recognition) of the disciples. They did exactly what He asked despite the uncertainty of the matter. They probably had no money to buy or rent the animal, and they were to be questioned about why they wanted the animal; yet they obeyed, not questioning or doubting.

Note the other act of homage. There was no saddle for their Lord. They cared about Him and His comfort, so they took their own outer garments and threw them across the animal. By following Christ, the two men would have accepted a life of poverty, so they would have little clothing. It cost them to use their clothing for such a humble act. The clothing would become soiled and smelly. Nevertheless, they cared and they worshiped through this act.

The point is that Christ was now unmistakably claiming the dignity and rights of a king. He was not washing feet now, nor portraying Himself as the servant of people; He was deliberately accepting the people's homage and reverence.

But note something of critical importance. In claiming the dignity and rights of a king, He was doing it in the most humble practice of His day: entering the city as a king of peace riding a young colt instead of the conqueror's stallion. He was disclaiming all ideas of an earthly and material kingdom. He had come to save Jerusalem and the world through peace, not war.

2 Scene 2: The triumphal entry—Jesus came to save now (Hosanna!).

Mark reports that "many" lined the road as Jesus rode into Jerusalem (v.8). Matthew describes it as a "very great multitude" or "a very large crowd" (Mt.21:8). We are led to imagine an enormous crowd of thousands lining the roadway as Christ was helped atop the colt to begin His triumphal entry into Jerusalem. Several facts point toward this conclusion.

11:8-10

⁸ And many spread their cloaks on the road, and others spread leafy branches that they had cut from the fields.
⁹ And those who went before and those who followed were shouting, "Hosanna! Blessed is he who comes in the name of the Lord!
¹⁰ Blessed is the coming kingdom of our father David! Hosanna in the highest!"

First, two million pilgrims or more gathered in Jerusalem every year for the Passover Feast (see DEEPER STUDY # 1—Mt.26:2). Thousands upon thousands were strict followers of Judaism, believing in the Jewish Messiah.

Second, the news had spread throughout the city and surrounding area concerning the miracles Christ had performed—a concentration of miracles for some days now which included the raising of Lazarus from the dead (Jn.11:1f; 11:55-56). The very atmosphere was electric with the exciting news that Jesus was God's promised Messiah. Multitudes had heard that He was in Bethany and Bethphage (Mk.14:1-9). A large crowd had turned around from Jerusalem to meet Him (Jn.12:17-19). A multitude of people had already been traveling with Him (Mt.21:29). In addition, a multitude of citizens in Bethany and Bethphage had begun gathering around Him (Mk.14:1-9; Jn.12:1f). The whole picture points to literally thousands searching for Jesus and rushing out to welcome Him when they heard He was coming. Crowds were both ahead of Jesus and behind Him as He entered the Holy City (v.9; Mt.21:9).

a. The people's concept: A national hero—Hosanna! ("Save now!") (v.9).

The excited crowd shouted, "Hosanna!" as they cheered Jesus along the way (v.9). This word indicated that they believed Christ was coming to save now. They were proclaiming Jesus to be the Messiah, the Son of David, who was coming to deliver them from the bondage of Roman and Gentile rule (see DEEPER STUDIES 5, 6). They viewed Jesus as a national hero, a military conqueror and a political deliverer.

b. The Lord's meaning: He came to bring spiritual peace (v.10).

Jesus' entry meant something completely different than the people thought. As explained previously, by riding the colt, Jesus was proclaiming that *He had come to save now*, but to save by bringing peace *spiritually*, not militarily.

Nevertheless, Jesus deliberately received the homage of the people. Apparently, the multitude had begun to gather since early morning, excitedly looking for the One who had raised Lazarus from the dead. John tells us this. In fact, he says there were so many people that the Pharisees said, "The world has gone after Him" (Jn.12:17-19). Again, there was . . .

➤ the crowd of disciples already accompanying Him
➤ the pilgrims on their way to the Passover Feast who had joined His caravan
➤ the residents of Bethany and Bethphage who had heard of His presence and the miracles
➤ those who were already in Jerusalem, citizens and pilgrims who rushed out searching for Him

The multitudes received Jesus as their king. This was shown by two acts that were always done for kings when they entered a city. They stripped off their cloaks and cut down tree branches, and they spread both out on the roadway before Him (v.8). They wished to honor and pay Jesus the homage given to a king. They wished to show Him that they received Him as the promised king of Israel. In addition, they received Him as their Messiah, the Son of David who came in the name of the Lord (vv.9-10: see DEEPER STUDIES 7, 8; see notes—Mt.21:8-9).

Nathanael answered him, "Rabbi, you are the Son of God! You are the King of Israel!" (Jn.1:49)

For God so loved the world, that he gave his only Son, that whoever believes in him should not perish but have eternal life. (Jn.3:16)

Then Pilate said to him, "So you are a king?" Jesus answered, "You say that I am a king. For this purpose I was born and for this purpose I have come into the world—to bear witness to the truth. Everyone who is of the truth listens to my voice." (Jn.18:37)

For he says, "In a favorable time I listened to you, and in a day of salvation I have helped you." Behold, now is the favorable time; behold, now is the day of salvation. (2 Co.6:2)

Which he will display at the proper time—he who is the blessed and only Sovereign, the King of kings and Lord of lords. (1 Ti.6:15)

For the grace of God has appeared, bringing salvation for all people, training us to renounce ungodliness and worldly passions, and to live self-controlled, upright, and godly lives in the present age. (Tit.2:11-12)

DEEPER STUDY # 5

(11:9) **Hosanna:** means "save now," or "save, we pray" (see Ps.118:25).

DEEPER STUDY # 6

(11:9) **Blessed . . . of the Lord:** means blessed is He who is sent by God to save His people; blessed is He who is sent with the authority of God.

DEEPER STUDY # 7

(11:10) **Kingdom of David:** see notes—Mt.1:1; DEEPER STUDY # 1—2:18; DEEPER STUDY # 3—3:11; notes—11:1-6; 11:2-3; DEEPER STUDY # 1—11:5; DEEPER STUDY # 2—11:6; DEEPER STUDY # 1—12:16; note—Lu.7:21-23.

DEEPER STUDY # 8

(11:10) **In the Highest:** means "God save, we pray" or "You who are in the Highest, save now through Him whom You have sent."

3 Scene 3: The investigation of the situation (temple scene)—Jesus came obediently.

Upon arriving in Jerusalem, Jesus went to the temple. This symbolized that Jesus came obediently. The scene was descriptive. Upon entering the temple, He "looked around"—investigated the situation there. He stood there, perhaps off to the side someplace where He had the vantage point of seeing all that was happening. Evening was approaching, and He was tired. He stood all alone. The point to see is that He was doing God's will. It took great courage to stand there. The Jewish authorities were seeking some opportunity to take His life, and they were upset more than ever now, for He had not discouraged the homage of the people (see Lu.19:39).

> 11 And he entered Jerusalem and went into the temple. And when he had looked around at everything, as it was already late, he went out to Bethany with the twelve.

➤ The Romans sensed that a popular uprising might be brewing.
➤ The Jewish Herodians (ruling party) feared being blamed and replaced by the Romans.
➤ The Pharisees were stirred to new depths of envy and malice.

But despite all, Jesus had to be courageous; He had to stand there. It was God's will. He had to investigate the situation, investigate God's house. He had to prepare all things for the salvation of God's people. He had come obediently; He had come to obey God.

> Jesus said to them, "My food is to do the will of him who sent me and to accomplish his work." (Jn.4:34)

> I can do nothing on my own. As I hear, I judge, and my judgment is just, because I seek not my own will but the will of him who sent me. (Jn.5:30)

> But I do as the Father has commanded me, so that the world may know that I love the Father. Rise, let us go from here. (Jn.14:31)

> Although he was a son, he learned obedience through what he suffered. (He.5:8)

THOUGHT 1. Two lessons in this point stand out.

1) We are to obey, no matter the threat and opposition.
2) We should investigate before entering into any situation that is threatening or involves corruption (see note—Mk.11:15–19).

11:11b

¹¹ And he entered Jerusalem and went into the temple. And when he had looked around at everything, as it was already late, he went out to Bethany with the twelve.

4 Scene 4: The seclusion at Bethany—Jesus prepared spiritually.

After leaving the temple, Jesus separated Himself from the crowd and went to Bethany. This symbolized that Christ prepared spiritually. He retired for the night in the surrounding area of Bethany. No doubt, He spent a good deal of time alone in prayer. Much lay ahead of Him in this last week of His life. He knew it, sensing every detail and emotion He was to experience. He needed the strong hand of His Father upholding Him. He needed to prepare spiritually. (See note, *Preparation*—Lu.21:37, where we are told that Jesus spent the nights of His last week in prayer on the Mount of Olives.)

> But he would withdraw to desolate places and pray. (Lu.5:16)

> In these days he went out to the mountain to pray, and all night he continued in prayer to God. (Lu.6:12)

B. The Fig Tree Cursed:
A Warning Against a Fruitless Life, 11:12–14

(Mt.21:17-20)

¹² On the following day, when they came from Bethany, he was hungry.

¹³ And seeing in the distance a fig tree in leaf, he went to see if he could find anything on it. When he came to it, he found nothing but leaves, for it was not the season for figs.

¹⁴ And he said to it, "May no one ever eat fruit from you again." And his disciples heard it.

1. Jesus had need

2. Jesus saw potential
3. Jesus examined the tree

4. Jesus condemned the tree (profession) that does not bear fruit

Division VII

The Son of God's Last Jerusalem Ministry: Jesus' Warning and Conflict with Religionists, 11:1–12:44

B. The Fig Tree Cursed: A Warning Against a Fruitless Life, 11:12–14

(Mt.21:17–20)

11:12–14
Introduction

For many people, including some Bible scholars, this episode from Jesus' life is viewed as a problem. Many say that Jesus' cursing the fig tree was contrary to His character. They say He would never lash out at a tree just for not bearing fruit, especially when it was not even time for the figs to be ripe (v.13). But two things always need to be remembered.

First, God is both kind and severe. Scripture teaches us to behold both the kindness or goodness and severity of God (Ro.11:22). We are to stress both the kindness *and severity* of God, not just His kindness. God is love, but He is also pure and just. He demonstrates care and forgiveness, but He also holds people responsible and accountable. God is not an indulgent Father who is never severe. He is not weak and foolish in dealing with His children, winking at and never judging their unfruitfulness. Unfruitfulness and sin lead to destruction, and God is not *a bad Father* who is going to allow His children to destroy themselves. God is good to people. He judges unfruitfulness so that others will bear fruit.

Second, Jesus always acted either to teach people or to save and help people. While Jesus certainly does not need to be defended for cursing the fig tree, those for whom His action presents a problem should keep some things in mind. First, the fig tree was His; He created it, and He owned it. He could use it however He wished. In this case, His purpose was to use it to illustrate a spiritual truth. In addition, it was a plant, an inanimate object. Plants and trees are destroyed all the time for all sorts of purposes. There is nothing wrong or unjust with destroying a plant.

In regard to it not being the season for figs, the *Focus on the Bible Commentary* offers a valuable insight:

> *This seems at first sight to pose a major difficulty, as it would appear to make the judgment quite inappropriate, even irrational. A little knowledge of the development of fig trees in the Holy Land throughout the year, however, helps us to understand. Two months or so before the fig harvest the leaves appear on*

the trees. At the same time, little 'pages' (the word appears, incidentally, as part of the name 'Bethphage', v.1), small green fruit, normally appear with the leaves. They are edible although not particularly pleasant to taste.[1]

In the cursing of the fig tree, Jesus was teaching a lesson about Israel. The fact that Jesus' encounter with the fruitless tree is sandwiched between His surveying of what was going on in the temple (v.11) and Jesus' cleansing of—judgment on—the temple reveals this (vv.15-19). Furthermore, the very next day after Jesus cleansed the temple, the fig tree had dried up completely—in twenty-four hours' time (vv.20-21)—and the disciples observed it the morning after the temple episode. Both immediately before and after Jesus judged the abuse of the temple, He used the fig tree as an object lesson.

In addition, throughout the Old Testament, the fig tree is a symbol of Israel. Jesus' lesson seems to be nothing less than the visual acting out of Old Testament prophecies in regard to Israel's judgment by God (Je.8:13; Joel 1:7; Mi.7:1). "The fact that this particular fig tree had luxuriant foliage, but bore no fruit portrayed exactly what Jesus had seen in Jerusalem."[2]

In cursing the fig tree, Jesus was also teaching each of us a much needed lesson—a lesson that shouts loudly, "*Be fruitful!* Guard against profession without bearing fruit." "Just because we look good, because our leaves are large and shiny, does not mean that we are bearing fruit pleasing to God."[3] It is this lesson that serves as the focus of the commentary. This is, *The Fig Tree Cursed: A Warning Against a Fruitless Life*, 11:12-14.

1. Jesus had need (v.12).
2. Jesus saw potential (v.13).
3. Jesus examined the tree (v.13).
4. Jesus condemned the tree (profession) that does not bear fruit (v.14).

11:12

[12] On the following day, when they came from Bethany, he was hungry.

1 Jesus had need.

Jesus had spent the night in Bethany. Matthew says He was walking into Jerusalem "in the morning." It was early morning before most had arisen from bed (see DEEPER STUDY # 1—Mt.21:18). Most likely, Jesus had been up praying for some time. He needed to be spiritually prepared; He needed very special strength as He faced the cross.

The Lord left Bethany before breakfast. He was hungry; He had a need. And His need painted a picture of His craving for fruit—much fruit in the lives of His people. Christ wants people, and He wants fruitful people. This is His hunger, His craving, His longing.

> The thief comes only to steal and kill and destroy. I came that they may have life and have it abundantly. (Jn.10:10)
>
> I am the vine; you are the branches. Whoever abides in me and I in him, he it is that bears much fruit, for apart from me you can do nothing. By this my Father is glorified, that you bear much fruit and so prove to be my disciples. (Jn.15:5, 8)
>
> But what fruit were you getting at that time from the things of which you are now ashamed? For the end of those things is death. But now that you have been set free from sin and have become slaves of God, the fruit you get leads to sanctification and its end, eternal life. (Ro.6:21-22)
>
> Likewise, my brothers, you also have died to the law through the body of Christ, so that you may belong to another, to him who has been raised from the dead, in order that we may bear fruit for God. (Ro.7:4)
>
> Through him then let us continually offer up a sacrifice of praise to God, that is, the fruit of lips that acknowledge his name. (He.13:15)

---

1 Geoffrey Grogan. *Focus on the Bible Commentary: Mark*, (Geanies House, Scotland, UK: Christian Focus Publications, 1999). Via Wordsearch digital edition.

2 R. Kent Hughes, ed. *Preaching the Word Commentary: Mark*, (Wheaton, IL: Crossway Books, 2015). Via Wordsearch digital edition.

3 Ibid.

2 Jesus saw potential.

Jesus saw the potential of the flourishing fig tree from a great distance away. The tree was so full of foliage (despite the early date) that it appeared to be fully developed. This, of course, meant that there were figs on the tree; for the fig tree puts forth its buds before its leaves. The tree should have had fruit even if not ripe. It was a natural expectation. The full foliage, fruitful appearance was openly professed. Note four correlations to those who profess salvation:

> [13] And seeing in the distance a fig tree in leaf, he went to see if he could find anything on it. When he came to it, he found nothing but leaves, for it was not the season for figs.

➢ The leafy appearance indicated fruit. So it is with people who profess: their profession indicates fruit.

➢ The leafy appearance indicated healthiness, the lack of disease. Profession indicates that the disease of sin has been taken care of, sprayed, and destroyed.

➢ The leafy appearance, the full foliage, stirred expectation. Jesus expected fruit to be present. He expected His hunger to be satisfied by the fruit of the tree. Profession stirs expectation among all who observe, especially among those who are close.

➢ The leafy appearance, the full foliage, necessitated fruit. Profession necessitates that fruitfulness follow. If there is no fruit, then profession is empty and good for nothing. It may as well not exist (see Mt.5:13; Jn.15:6).

So you also outwardly appear righteous to others, but within you are full of hypocrisy and lawlessness. (Mt.23:28)

Having the appearance of godliness, but denying its power. Avoid such people. (2 Ti.3:5)

They profess to know God, but they deny him by their works. They are detestable, disobedient, unfit for any good work. (Tit.1:16)

3 Jesus examined the tree.

When Jesus came to the fig tree, He examined it closely, but He found *nothing*—no fruit whatsoever. Despite its foliage and appearance, the tree was barren and destitute. It *appeared fruitful*, presented itself to be fruitful; but after inspection, the tree had nothing *but leaves* (emphasis on appearance). This fact presents two warnings for all who profess Christ.

First, the appearance of full foliage attracted attention. It was the very appearance of the tree that drew Jesus. Thus it is with profession. Christ is definitely attracted to any person who professes Him. He comes to the person desiring to love, help, and fellowship with him or her.

Second, the appearance of full foliage invited inspection. Jesus was hungry for the fruit. When He arrived, He looked and looked, but found no fruit. So it is with people. Christ craves fruit from those who claim to know Him. If a person professes Him, Christ is going to draw near and inspect that person. All who profess Christ are inviting Christ to inspect them, and Christ will inspect; in fact, He will inspect a person who professes much quicker than someone who does not profess. The professing hypocrite is much more accountable than those who make no pretensions of knowing Christ.

For nothing is hidden except to be made manifest; nor is anything secret except to come to light. (Mk.4:22)

So then each of us will give an account of himself to God. (Ro.14:12)

Each one's work will become manifest, for the Day will disclose it, because it will be revealed by fire, and the fire will test what sort of work each one has done. (1 Co.3:13)

For God will bring every deed into judgment, with every secret thing, whether good or evil. (Ec.12:14)

4 Jesus condemned the tree (profession) that does not bear fruit.

Standing there, Jesus saw no fruit. The tree had life; it was existing. It had the sap to produce a rich foliage of leaves; but

> [14] And he said to it, "May no one ever eat fruit from you again." And his disciples heard it.

the sad fact was, despite all the appearance of fruit-bearing, the tree had none. Its very purpose for existing was to bear fruit, but it did not.

The tree had an empty profession. So do all who claim to believe but do not bear fruit for Christ. Their profession is empty. Their lives do not match their profession. They lack life, behavior, works, purity, holiness, faith, love, and on and on. There is no distinction between them and the world.

In addition, the tree had an unfulfilled purpose. So do people who profess Christ but continue in their own worldly pursuits, forgetting God's purpose entirely. Many who profess Christ spend their time, energy, and money to pursue their own desires and ambitions instead of God's will and purpose.

Finally, the tree had been deceiving instead of serving. So do those who merely profess Christ. They profess to serve, and perhaps do show a little service; but their commitment is to self, family, business, property, society—to an innumerable list of things. Service to God is only an *addition* to everything else. God is not the true Lord of those who merely profess. Mere professing reveals no intention of serving the Lord. Those who only profess look upon God as merely *being there*, along with everything else. God is but one part of their lives, not the center and focus of their hearts, not the one for whom they live.

> **Even now the axe is laid to the root of the trees. Every tree therefore that does not bear good fruit is cut down and thrown into the fire. (Mt.3:10)**
>
> **So, every healthy tree bears good fruit, but the diseased tree bears bad fruit. (Mt.7:17)**
>
> **Every branch in me that does not bear fruit he takes away, and every branch that does bear fruit he prunes, that it may bear more fruit. (Jn.15:2)**
>
> **But if it bears thorns and thistles, it is worthless and near to being cursed, and its end is to be burned. (He.6:8)**
>
> **For their vine comes from the vine of Sodom and from the fields of Gomorrah; their grapes are grapes of poison; their clusters are bitter (De.32:32)**

C. The Temple Cleansed:
A Warning to Those Who Abuse God's Temple, 11:15–19

(Mt.21:12–16; Lu.19:45–46; Jn.2:13–16)

¹⁵ And they came to Jerusalem. And he entered the temple and began to drive out those who sold and those who bought in the temple, and he overturned the tables of the money-changers and the seats of those who sold pigeons.

¹⁶ And he would not allow anyone to carry anything through the temple.

¹⁷ And he was teaching them and saying to them, "Is it not written, 'My house shall be called a house of prayer for all the nations'? But you have made it a den of robbers."

¹⁸ And the chief priests and the scribes heard it and were seeking a way to destroy him, for they feared him, because all the crowd was astonished at his teaching.

¹⁹ And when evening came they went out of the city.

1. **Jesus entered the temple**
2. **Jesus drove some out of the temple**
   a. Those who commercialized or secularized religion
   b. Those who desecrated God's house
   c. Those who affected the atmosphere of prayer
   d. Those who shut people out: Was for all nations
   e. Those who changed the purpose of the temple
3. **Jesus caused a reaction by proclaiming the truth about the temple**
   a. Some sought to persecute and kill Him
   b. Some were amazed
4. **Jesus left when the leaders rejected the truth**

Division VII

The Son of God's Last Jerusalem Ministry:
Jesus' Warning and Conflict with Religionists, 11:1–12:44

C. The Temple Cleansed: A Warning to Those Who Abuse God's Temple, 11:15–19

(Mt.21:12–16; Lu.19:45–46; Jn.2:13–16)

11:15–19
Introduction

The cleansing of the temple took place the day after Christ's triumphal entry into Jerusalem. The scene was this: teeming thousands had lined the roadway for Jesus' triumphal entry. As He rode along to the shouts of welcome from the multitudes, He was led right up to the steps of the temple. He entered the temple and looked around, observing all that was going on (v.11). He stood off to the side watching all the corruption. After some time, heartbroken and weary, He left, returning to Bethany to spend Sunday night. When He arose on Monday morning, He returned to the temple and cleansed it of those who profaned its sacredness.

Four facts should be noted about the temple during this last week of our Lord's life.

First, Jesus was ending His ministry in the temple, His Father's house of prayer, the place where God's presence dwelled in a very special way. Jesus was about to complete His life on earth—a glorious ministry fulfilling the will of God perfectly. The night before, as He had stood off by Himself in the temple observing all that was taking place, His thoughts must have been very contemplative. He was probably meditating on His Father, His life now about completed, the great sacrifice He was to pay for humanity's sins, the corruption of the temple taking place all around Him, the worshiping that should be taking place, and so much more. His heart was probably drawn ever so close to God, yet it was broken and deeply saddened. Right before Him was a picture of the terrible sin for which He was to die. The temple itself, the place where people should be able to draw close to God, was corrupted by greedy, deceitful men. It had become anything but a house of prayer. It was a place for commercialism, for people's greed.

Second, Jesus was revealing who He was by cleansing the temple. He was proclaiming to all generations that He had the right to determine how the temple was to be used and to purge it of corruptions. As God's Son, the temple was His dwelling place, the place where the worship of God was to be especially known.

Third, in cleansing the temple, Jesus was revealing how people are to treat and use the House of God.

Fourth, Jesus began and ended His ministry by cleansing the temple. The two cleansings were separate events which marked the opening and closing of His ministry. The importance of the temple as God's house of prayer and worship was thereby demonstrated.

When our Lord entered Jerusalem, He did not go up to the palace of a king, nor to the courts of the rulers; but He went up to the temple, to the House of God. Our Lord's kingdom was not of this world; it was not a physical kingdom. It was of heaven; it was a spiritual kingdom. His authority and rule were in the temple of God and in people's hearts. Therefore, He went up to the temple of God to cleanse it and to teach us how God's house is to be used. This is, *The Temple Cleansed: A Warning to Those Who Abuse God's Temple,* 11:15–19.

1. Jesus entered the temple (v.15).
2. Jesus drove some out of the temple (vv.15–17).
3. Jesus caused a reaction by proclaiming the truth about the temple (v.18).
4. Jesus left when the leaders rejected the truth (v.19).

11:15

¹⁵ And they came to Jerusalem. And he entered the temple and began to drive out those who sold and those who bought in the temple, and he overturned the tables of the money-changers and the seats of those who sold pigeons.

1 Jesus entered the temple.

An understanding of the layout of the temple is needed in order to see what was happening in this event. Perched atop Mt. Zion, it is thought to have covered about thirty acres of land. The temple consisted of two parts, the temple building itself and the temple precincts or courtyards. The Greek language has two different words to distinguish which is meant.

The temple building (*naos*) was a small, ornate structure which sat in the center of the temple property. It was called the Holy Place or Holy of Holies, and only the High Priest could enter its walls; but even he could enter only once during the year, on the Day of Atonement.

The temple precincts (*hieron*) consisted of four courtyards which surrounded the temple building, each decreasing in importance to the Jewish mind. It is critical to remember that great walls separated the courts from each other.

The Court of the Priests was first. Only the priests were allowed to enter this court. Within the courtyard stood the great furnishings of worship: the Altar of Burnt Offering, The Brazen Laver, the Seven-Branched Lampstand, the Altar of Incense, and the Table of Showbread.

The Court of the Israelites was next. This was a huge courtyard where Jewish worshipers met together for joint services on the great feast days. It was also where worshipers handed over their sacrifices to the priests.

The Court of the Women was the third courtyard. Women were usually limited to this area except for worship. They could, however, enter the Court of the Israelites when they came to make sacrifice or worship in a joint assembly on a great feast day.

The Court of the Gentiles was the last courtyard. It covered a vast space, surrounding all the other courtyards, and was the place of worship for all Gentile converts to Judaism.

When Jesus entered the temple, it was the Court of the Gentiles that He had entered. It is what was taking place in this court, the outer court, that is the center of Jesus' anger.

THOUGHT 1. Note two significant points.

1) Great barriers are built between people in their worship. Imagine the huge walls (barriers) separating people from God and the various courtyards favoring Jewish men before women and all Jews before any Gentile. Imagine the self-righteousness, pride, self-centeredness, prejudice, envy, and jealousy. Where is love, care, ministry, evangelism, and a sense of human need in such a scheme of religion? Every generation of believers must search their hearts for any sign of prejudice and division and purge their hearts of such sins.

2) Christ cleansed the *outer court*, not the *inner court*. It was not just the worship center that was *set apart* to God; it was the worship precincts as well. All thirty acres were hallowed ground and were to be treated as such. This is a warning to the church that needs to be heeded (see note—1 Co.3:17).

2 Jesus drove some out of the temple.

Jesus expelled five different groups of people from God's House. Remember that this whole scene took place in the court of the Gentiles. There were five offenses, five defilements or corruptions going on there that were so offensive to Jesus that He drove the people committing them out of the temple.

15 And they came to Jerusalem. And he entered the temple and began to drive out those who sold and those who bought in the temple, and he overturned the tables of the money-changers and the seats of those who sold pigeons.

16 And he would not allow anyone to carry anything through the temple.

17 And he was teaching them and saying to them, "Is it not written, 'My house shall be called a house of prayer for all the nations'? But you have made it a den of robbers."

a. **Those who commercialized or secularized religion (v.15).** First, Jesus cast out those who commercialized and secularized religion. The outer court of the temple, the court of the Gentiles, was the place where Gentiles worshiped. But it was tragically abused. It had become nothing more than a commercial marketplace owned, and in many cases operated, by the priests. It was used for the selling and buying of sacrificial animals which included oxen and sheep as well as smaller doves and pigeons. It was used for the inspection of the animals' purity, and it was also used for the exchanging of foreign currencies. Every Passover season found thousands of pilgrims from all nations traveling great distances to come to the temple. It was usually impossible for a pilgrim to bring his own animal for sacrifice; but if he did, he had to get it by the inspector, which often cost a fee. The holy system of sacrifices had been reduced to a business that enriched the priests at the expense of the worshipers. The bickering back and forth created an atmosphere of utter chaos that apparently gave off the sound of a human volcanic uproar (see note, pt.2—Ep.2:14-15).

Hundreds of thousands of animals were sold at the great feasts; and, unfortunately, the High Priest and other priests were often in the middle of the commercialism. It was this commercialism and secularism of religion that Jesus struck out against (see DEEPER STUDY # 1—Mt.21:12-16 for detailed discussion and thoughts).

> You shall keep my Sabbaths and reverence my sanctuary: I am the LORD. (Le.19:30)

> But the LORD is in his holy temple; let all the earth keep silence before him. (Hab.2:20)

b. **Those who desecrated God's house (v.16).** Second, Jesus cast out those who desecrated God's house. People were using the temple grounds as a thoroughfare (v.16). The temple and its grounds were so large that the entrances had become a shortcut from one section of town to another, especially if one were carrying a heavy load. Jesus was forbidding such disrespect and desecration of God's house.

THOUGHT 1. Note how hallowed the temple was to Jesus. He forbade people to walk across its outer courtyard, even if they were carrying a heavy load and had to travel a much longer route. This should speak loudly and clearly to the church in every generation. God expects His church and its grounds or courtyards to be held in the highest respect and esteem.

Then he said, "Do not come near; take your sandals off your feet, for the place on which you are standing is holy ground." (Ex.3:5)

A God greatly to be feared in the council of the holy ones, and awesome above all who are around him? (Ps.89:7)

c. Those who affected the atmosphere of prayer (v.17a).

Jesus also cast out those who diminished the atmosphere of prayer within the temple. The temple was more than just a building and grounds. It was a "house of prayer." This is exactly what Jesus said about the temple:

- The temple is "My house." "My" is possessive. Christ possesses the temple. He is the Lord, the Owner of it. Any who are within its walls are either His guests or His servants. No one has the right to mistreat someone else's house. The guest and servant are to respect the property of the Owner.
- "My house shall be called a house of prayer." The purpose of the Lord's house is prayer. It is to be used for prayer *so much* that it becomes known as "the house of prayer." Prayer is to be its distinctiveness, its function, the very thing for which it is known (communing with God, sharing, praising, requesting, giving thanks, listening, and worshiping).
- "My house shall be called a house of prayer *for all nations*." The temple is to be the same in all nations: a house of prayer. No nation, no people is to use it for any other purpose. Within all nations, God's house is to be used for prayer and to be known as "a house of prayer."

THOUGHT 1. The atmosphere for prayer is hindered by . . .

- noise
- other religious activities
- secular activities
- personal barriers
- disturbed spirits
- divisive spirits
- spiritual unpreparedness
- religious barriers

God is spirit, and those who worship him must worship in spirit and truth. (Jn.4:24)

Ascribe to the LORD the glory due his name; bring an offering and come before him! Worship the LORD in the splendor of holiness. (1 Chr.16:29)

Oh come, let us worship and bow down; let us kneel before the LORD, our Maker! (Ps.95:6)

Exalt the LORD our God; worship at his footstool! Holy is he! (Ps.99:5)

d. Those who shut people out: Was for all nations (v.17b).

Jesus cast out those who shut people out of the temple. The temple was to be a house of prayer for *all* nations. Neither the Gentiles nor anyone else were to be excluded. Jewish women and Gentiles were to have as much access to the inner court of worship as Jewish men (see Is.56:7).

The Court of the Gentiles was to have an atmosphere of prayer as much as any other court of the temple. There were no *sections for worship* within the temple, not in the Lord's mind. *All the temple* and its courtyards were for prayer and worship.

THOUGHT 1. This is a critical lesson—a lesson that God has sought to teach people and nations down through the years. There is no caste system, social crust, superior race, or inferior race. There is to be no discrimination. There is not a *better person* or *worse person* or *favorite person* or *special person*, not in God's eyes.

For God so loved the world, that he gave his only Son, that whoever believes in him should not perish but have eternal life. (Jn.3:16)

So Peter opened his mouth and said: "Truly I understand that God shows no partiality." (Ac.10:34)

THOUGHT 2. Every person is to have access to God's house. No one is to be barred nor ignored in the temple. The temple (church) is to be opened wide for all, and all are to know that it is *God's house of prayer* for each one. Every person is to know they can pray therein, being welcomed, comforted, and put at ease. This includes . . .

- the poor
- the destitute
- the widower
- the widow
- the dirty
- the smelly
- the divorced
- the sick

- the ragged
- the sinner
- the child
- the handicapped
- the hungry
- the orphan
- the elderly

e. Those who changed the purpose of the temple (v.17c).

Lastly, Jesus cast out those who altered the purpose of the temple. Tragically, it was the priests themselves who committed this offense. It is not known just when, but at some point in history the priests decided to take advantage of the worshipers' need for sacrificial animals and supplies. The priests saw how they could reap some of the profit for the welfare of the temple and for themselves. They began to set up booths within the Court of the Gentiles for the convenience of the pilgrims and to help defray the cost of the temple and to meet their own needs.

Note a crucial point that issues a severe warning to God's people: the people were sold items that were necessary for their worship. They were not just items that would *help them* in their spiritual growth and their worship, but they were items that were absolutely necessary. They had to have the items.

Now think for a moment. If the items were necessary for their worship and growth, what was wrong with what the priests did? Note exactly what Scripture says: Jesus drove out those who bought and sold "in the temple" (v.15). The buying and selling of the items for worship and growth was necessary and good, *but not within the temple.* It was to be done outside the temple walls, off the temple grounds. The temple was not the place for commercialism.

> **And he told those who sold the pigeons, "Take these things away; do not make my Father's house a house of trade." (Jn.2:16)**

> **What! Do you not have houses to eat and drink in? Or do you despise the church of God and humiliate those who have nothing? What shall I say to you? Shall I commend you in this? No, I will not. (1 Co.11:22)**

> **Guard your steps when you go to the house of God. To draw near to listen is better than to offer the sacrifice of fools, for they do not know that they are doing evil. (Ec.5:1)**

> **For the sons of Judah have done evil in my sight, declares the Lᴏʀᴅ. They have set their detestable things in the house that is called by my name, to defile it. (Je.7:30)**

> **Her prophets are fickle, treacherous men; her priests profane what is holy; they do violence to the law. (Zep.3:4)**

3 Jesus caused a reaction by proclaiming the truth about the temple.

As would be expected, Jesus' cleansing of the temple was not well-received. The Jewish religious leaders were infuriated, but the common people had a different reaction to Jesus' proclaiming the truth.

[18] And the chief priests and the scribes heard it and were seeking a way to destroy him, for they feared him, because all the crowd was astonished at his teaching.

a. Some sought to persecute and kill Him.

The chief priests and Scribes were so enraged they began to persecute Jesus. In fact, they sought to *destroy* (apolesousin) Him. The Greek word means to completely overthrow, to disable. This violent reaction was, of course, from those who were abusing and desecrating the temple. They wanted to immediately stamp out Jesus' influence. They feared what He was doing would catch on, forcing them to stop their profitable activities within the temple. The only way they saw to stamp out His influence was to get rid of Him.

THOUGHT 1. How many today would be *gotten rid of* if they really sought to cleanse the church of the abusers and secular activities often allowed and promoted within its walls?

> For the love of money is a root of all kinds of evils. It is through this craving that some have wandered away from the faith and pierced themselves with many pangs. (1 Ti.6:10)

> Your gold and silver have corroded, and their corrosion will be evidence against you and will eat your flesh like fire. You have laid up treasure in the last days. (Js.5:3)

> Better is a little with righteousness than great revenues with injustice. (Pr.16:8)

> Like the partridge that gathers a brood that she did not hatch, so is he who gets riches but not by justice; in the midst of his days they will leave him, and at his end he will be a fool. (Je.17:11)

b. Some were amazed.

The crowd—the common people who had traveled to Jerusalem to worship—were astonished at what Jesus was teaching by His radical action. They were amazed by His boldness and fearlessness to proclaim the truth, as well as by the authority He displayed. They wanted God's house cleaned up, and they embraced Jesus for, at least for that day, ridding the temple of corruption and greed.

> Blessed are those who hunger and thirst for righteousness, for they shall be satisfied. (Mt.5:6)

> O Lord, all my longing is before you; my sighing is not hidden from you. (Ps.38:9)

> My soul yearns for you in the night; my spirit within me earnestly seeks you. For when your judgments are in the earth, the inhabitants of the world learn righteousness. (Is.26:9)

11:19

¹⁹ And when evening came they went out of the city.

4 Jesus left when the leaders rejected the truth.

When the religious leaders rejected Jesus and the truth for which He had stood, He left Jerusalem. His life was being threatened; it was dangerous to stay overnight in the city. He could not foolishly expose Himself, for it was not yet God's appointed time for Him to die. He still had some things to do for God. His hour had not yet arrived, so He returned to the Mount of Olives which was safer during the night hours (see note 2 and DEEPER STUDY # 1—Lu.21:37).

THOUGHT 1. In doing things for God and in carrying out His will, we are not to foolishly expose ourselves to danger and threats.

> Behold, I am sending you out as sheep in the midst of wolves, so be wise as serpents and innocent as doves. (Mt.10:16)

(Mt.21:21-22)

²⁰ As they passed by in the morning, they saw the fig tree withered away to its roots.
 	
²¹ And Peter remembered and said to him, "Rabbi, look! The fig tree that you cursed has withered."
 	
²² And Jesus answered them, "Have faith in God.
 	
²³ Truly, I say to you, whoever says to this mountain, 'Be taken up and thrown into the sea,' and does not doubt in his heart, but believes that what he says will come to pass, it will be done for him."
 	
²⁴ "Therefore I tell you, whatever you ask in prayer, believe that you have received it, and it will be yours."
 	
²⁵ "And whenever you stand praying, forgive, if you have anything against anyone, so that your Father also who is in heaven may forgive you your trespasses."
	1. The setting: The disciples noticed the withered fig tree, vv.12–14
	
	a. Jesus had cursed the tree
	b. Peter was surprised by the outcome of Jesus' prayer
	2. The 1st condition of prayer: Faith in God
	a. The object of faith: God
	b. The purpose of faith: To move mountains
	c. The way to gain faith: Prayer
	  1) Not doubting in your heart
	  2) Believing in God's authority
	d. The results of faith
	3. The 2nd condition of prayer: Asking and believing
	a. Involves emotions: Desiring
	b. Involves the will: Asking
	c. Involves the spirit: Believing
	4. The 3rd condition of prayer: Forgiving others—even while praying, forgive
	a. If we forgive, we will be forgiven
	b. If we do not forgive, we will not be forgiven

Division VII

The Son of God's Last Jerusalem Ministry:
Jesus' Warning and Conflict with Religionists, 11:1–12:44

D. The Conditions of Prayer, 11:20–26

(Mt.21:21-22)

11:20–26
Introduction

A startling sight sparked a mighty message from the Messiah about power in prayer. Jesus used the withered fig tree to teach us what the conditions of prayer are. When we pray as Jesus taught in this passage, we too will see the supernatural power of God released in our lives. This is, *The Conditions of Prayer*, 11:20-26.

1. The setting: The disciples noticed the withered fig tree, vv.12-14 (vv.20-21).
2. The first condition of prayer: Faith in God (vv.22-23).
3. The second condition of prayer: Asking and believing (v.24).
4. The third condition of prayer: Forgive others—even while praying, forgive (vv.25-26).

1 The setting: The disciples noticed the withered fig tree.

As the disciples returned to the temple on Tuesday morning of the week Christ would be crucified, they noticed the fig tree was completely dried up (v.20). Apparently, they had not noticed it the previous evening, perhaps because they either took a different route out of the city to Bethany or it was too dark to notice when they passed by.

11:20-21

²⁰ As they passed by in the morning, they saw the fig tree withered away to its roots.

²¹ And Peter remembered and said to him, "Rabbi, look! The fig tree that you cursed has withered."

a. Jesus had cursed the tree (v.21).

This was the same tree Jesus had cursed just the day before (vv.12-14). When Jesus cursed this tree, He was teaching a lesson about Israel (see *Introduction*—11:12-14 for discussion). The fig tree was full of leaves, appearing fruitful, but it had no fruit. Israel appeared to be full, to be religious, professing spiritual fruit; but the nation bore no fruit. Its religion was barren, legalistic, and fruitless. Thus, the tree was a sign of disappointment and of coming judgment.

On this occasion, however, this was not the lesson drawn by Jesus. Here, the application made by Jesus was clearly power, power that comes through faith and prayer (see outline and notes—Mt.21:17-22). Mark approaches the subject from a slightly different angle, an angle that can be titled "*The Conditions of Prayer.*"

b. Peter was surprised by the outcome of Jesus' prayer (v.21).

Peter was *surprised* at the answer to Jesus' prayer or pronouncement in cursing the fig tree. His surprise was both at the *effectiveness* and the *quickness of the answer.* Just twenty-four hours earlier, Jesus had cursed this very tree. Now it was completely dead and dried up, a process that would normally take many days.

THOUGHT 1. Those who meet the conditions of prayer will be more effective and be more likely to have quick answers to their prayers.

11:22-23

²² And Jesus answered them, "Have faith in God.

²³ Truly, I say to you, whoever says to this mountain, 'Be taken up and thrown into the sea,' and does not doubt in his heart, but believes that what he says will come to pass, it will be done for him."

2 The first condition of prayer: Faith in God.

Jesus' response to Peter's amazement was immediate and to the point. He revealed the secret to the almost instant demise and deterioration of the fig tree: faith in God (v.22). If we want to have spiritual power, power that brings the supernatural into the natural, we must, as Jesus teaches, "Have faith in God." Notice four lessons Jesus taught in this simple statement and the subsequent truth He expressed regarding it—God will move mountains for those who believe in Him wholeheartedly (v.23).

a. The object of faith: God (v.22).

The object of faith is God Himself. The critical words are "in God." Jesus did not say, "Have faith," but "Have faith *in God.*" Faith has to have an object. "In God" is where we are to have faith, where we are to place our faith. Faith has no value by itself; only the object (God) has value.

The Bible never says to have faith *in faith,* yet this is the experience of many. Too often, a great difficulty or problem arises, and we feel we have to *stir up* our faith. We think that if we can just *muster* enough faith, we will whip the problem. But in reality, we are demonstrating faith *in faith.* Our mind, our attention, and our heart have been focused on faith—not on God.

Faith itself has no power; it is the *object of faith* that has power. No matter how strongly we believe, our faith is not going to remove the mountain. *God* is going to remove the mountain. The strength of faith is not faith, but God. In the Bible, practically everyone who came to God had weak faith. Only a few had strong faith, yet God saved them and granted their requests (see Mt.14:22-33).

Faith requires knowing the object. The more we know the object of faith, the more we believe in the object (see He.11:6). For example, consider two men who want to go out on a frozen lake to fish. One man is told to go ahead and cross the lake. He is assured by his friend that the ice will hold him up. Yet, when he begins to step out on the ice, he cautiously and tremblingly takes step after step—usually until he can stand it no more and returns. But the other man walks out courageously and boldly, cuts a hole in the ice, sits down, and begins to fish.

➢ What supported the man sitting out on the ice? Not his faith, but the ice—the object of his faith.

➢ Who had the strongest faith? Of course, the man out on the ice. The one with the weak faith is the man who slowly inched his way back.

➢ What made the difference between the faith of the two? One thing: one man *knew* the ice, and the other man *did not know* the ice.

b. The purpose of faith: To move mountains (v.23a).

A second fact to note about faith is its purpose. The purpose of faith is to move mountains. Jesus' teaching says, "Have faith in God . . . [and then] say to this mountain, 'Be taken up [removed, lifted up].'" Mountains represent the immovable, the impossible. It is something almost too steep to climb, almost too high to cross, almost too overwhelming to see beyond.

This is the reason Jesus discussed prayer and communion along with faith. We learn to have faith in God as we pray and commune with God. And the more we pray and commune with God, the better we will know God. Then the better we know God, the better we can experience faith in God and experience the moving of mountains that hinder our progress through life (see note and DEEPER STUDY # 3—Mt.17:20 for more discussion).

c. The way to gain faith: Prayer (v.23b).

Jesus proceeded to teach the way to possess faith. The way is prayer. Jesus explicitly says that if we will not doubt, but unwaveringly believe that *what we say* will come to pass, *what we say* will be done. There are two crucial conditions in this promise.

First, we must not doubt at all. This means never having a thought whether a thing can be done or not. It means not hesitating, not wondering, not questioning, not considering, not being concerned at all. Realistically, only God Himself can know if a thing will happen or not—know so perfectly that no wondering thought would ever cross His mind. What Christ is after is that we grow in belief and trust. He wants us to believe that all things are possible through Christ who strengthens us, and He wants us to trust the unlimited ability of God (Ph.4:13; Ep.3:20; see outlines and notes—Mt.17:15-20; DEEPER STUDY # 3—Mk.9:18).

Second, we must believe in God's authority. Note the word "says" (see note and DEEPER STUDY # 3—Mt.17:20). The power of Christ came from the authority of God. All He had to do was *say*, that is, speak the word and it was done. That is the very point our Lord was making to us. If we believe, doubting not, then we stand in the authority of God. We may *say*, speak the word, and it will be done.

d. The results of faith (v.23c).

A fourth fact to note about faith is the result of faith. When we pray with faith, truly having faith *in God,* we will have what we say. The mountains which confront us will be moved, *effectively and quickly* (see note—vv.20-21).

And whatever you ask in prayer, you will receive, if you have faith. (Mt.21:22)

And Jesus said to him, " 'If you can'! All things are possible for one who believes." (Mk.9:23)

Truly, truly, I say to you, whoever believes in me will also do the works that I do; and greater works than these will he do, because I am going to the Father. Whatever you ask in my name, this I will do, that the Father may be glorified in the Son. If you ask me anything in my name, I will do it. (Jn.14:12-14)

When he calls to me, I will answer him; I will be with him in trouble; I will rescue him and honor him. (Ps.91:15)

When the poor and needy seek water, and there is none, and their tongue is parched with thirst, I the LORD will answer them; I the God of Israel will not forsake them. (Is.41:17)

11:24

²⁴ "Therefore I tell you, whatever you ask in prayer, believe that you have received it, and it will be yours."

3 The second condition of prayer: Asking and believing.

The second condition of prayer is expectancy. We must believe and expect that we will have what we ask. We have to be confident and assured, anticipating and looking for the answer (see note—Mt.21:22). The exact words of Jesus' promise are interesting (glance at the verse). Expectancy involves all of a person's being. The spirit of expectancy . . .

- involves a person's emotions: we *desire*
- involves a person's will (volition): we *ask*
- involves a person's spirit: we *believe*

But let him ask in faith, with no doubting, for the one who doubts is like a wave of the sea that is driven and tossed by the wind. (Js.1:6)

And this is the confidence that we have toward him, that if we ask anything according to his will he hears us. And if we know that he hears us in whatever we ask, we know that we have the requests that we have asked of him. (1 Jn.5:14–15)

Before they call I will answer; while they are yet speaking I will hear. (Is.65:24)

11:25–26

²⁵ "And whenever you stand praying, forgive, if you have anything against anyone, so that your Father also who is in heaven may forgive you your trespasses."

4 The third condition of prayer: Forgive others—even while praying.

a. If we forgive, we will be forgiven (v.25).

b. If we do not forgive, we will not be forgiven (v.26).[1]

The third condition to prayer is forgiveness. This is a critical condition in prayer, a condition that is stressed time and again by Jesus (Mt.5:23–24; 6:14–15; 18:32–33). Note, it is while a person is *actually praying*—"whenever you stand praying"—that we must forgive (v.25). It does no good to pray unless we forgive. When praying, there must always be forgiveness of those who have wronged us. Hard feelings or anger against a person is sin. It is evidence that we have not truly turned from our sins and are not really sincere in seeking forgiveness. Jesus emphasized this truth when teaching His disciples to pray (see outline and notes—Mt.6:14-15 for detailed discussion). Note the stress Jesus puts on the condition of receiving forgiveness in prayer. No request for forgiveness is granted unless we completely forgive all others.

Blessed are the merciful, for they shall receive mercy. (Mt.5:7)

And forgive us our debts, as we also have forgiven our debtors . . . For if you forgive others their trespasses, your heavenly Father will also forgive you, but if you do not forgive others their trespasses, neither will your Father forgive your trespasses. (Mt.6:12, 14–15)

Be merciful, even as your Father is merciful. Judge not, and you will not be judged; condemn not, and you will not be condemned; forgive, and you will be forgiven. (Lu.6:36–37)

---

1 Verse 26 does not appear in the manuscripts from which many newer Bible versions including the ESV are translated. Regardless of the variance between manuscripts, the truth expressed in the verse is firmly established by the fact that this is not the only occasion when Jesus stated it (see Mt. 6:14-15).

E. The Authority of Jesus Questioned: Two Choices Concerning Jesus, 11:27–33

(Mt.21:23–27; Lu.20:1–8)

²⁷ And they came again to Jerusalem. And as he was walking in the temple, the chief priests and the scribes and the elders came to him,

²⁸ and they said to him, "By what authority are you doing these things, or who gave you this authority to do them?"

²⁹ Jesus said to them, "I will ask you one question; answer me, and I will tell you by what authority I do these things.

³⁰ Was the baptism of John from heaven or from man? Answer me."

³¹ And they discussed it with one another, saying, "If we say, 'From heaven,' he will say, 'Why then did you not believe him?'

³² But shall we say, 'From man'?"— they were afraid of the people, for they all held that John really was a prophet.

³³ So they answered Jesus, "We do not know." And Jesus said to them, "Neither will I tell you by what authority I do these things."

1. **The setting: The temple in Jerusalem**
   a. Jesus was walking in the temple courts
   b. The religionists approached and questioned Jesus
2. **The question about Jesus' authority**
   a. The authority for His works
   b. The authority for His person, His claims
3. **The choices people have: Illustrated by John the Baptist**

   a. Choice one: He was from God
   b. Choice two: He was a mere man
   c. The religionists' dilemma

4. **The tragic answer: No decision due to hypocrisy**

Division VII

The Son of God's Last Jerusalem Ministry: Jesus' Warning and Conflict with Religionists, 11:1–12:44

E. The Authority of Jesus Questioned: Two Choices Concerning Jesus, 11:27–33

(Mt.21:23–27; Lu.20:1–8)

11:27–33
Introduction

This passage presents the first of a series of six combative situations for Jesus. Both religious and civil leaders confronted Jesus head-on, doing all they could to trap and discredit our Lord before the people so they could arrest Him and have Him killed. All the events of this section as well as the Olivet Discourse (Mt.24–25) seem to have taken place on Tuesday in the week Christ was crucified (see Mt.22:23; 25:1; 26:1–2). A quick reading of this section is an eye-opener into the great tragedy and problem with self-righteousness and unbelief. Jesus was very forceful in attacking these two arrogant attitudes that result in eternal condemnation. He delivered a *sustained attack*, leaving no doubt that a person, even a religious person, who continues in self-righteousness is unworthy of God's kingdom. Obstinate unbelief will doom any individual to eternal separation from God. This is, *The Authority of Jesus Questioned: Two Choices Concerning Jesus, 11:27-33.*

1. The setting: The temple in Jerusalem (v.27).
2. The question about Jesus' authority (v.28).
3. The choices people have: Illustrated by John the Baptist (vv.29-32).
4. The tragic answer: No decision due to hypocrisy (v.33).

11:27

²⁷ And they came again to Jerusalem. And as he was walking in the temple, the chief priests and the scribes and the elders came to him,

1 The setting: The temple in Jerusalem.

Jesus was in the temple, apparently walking through one of the arcades meditating and praying. He seems to have been alone. When we picture the background, we see the intense drama of the scene.

The temple actually had two arcades surrounding the Court of the Gentiles. They were just as films picture the arcades of the Greek and Roman eras: stately, magnificent, and awe-inspiring. There was an east arcade and a south arcade. The east arcade was known as Solomon's porch. Several biblical events took place in this magnificent passageway (Jn.10:23; Ac.3:11; 5:12). It was an area used for teaching, and rabbis often strolled among the colonnades while instructing their pupils. The arcades were also large enough to allow large crowds to gather for classroom-type instruction. Their magnificence can be imagined by picturing the stately columns which towered thirty-five feet above the ground. The arcades provided both shelter from rain and sun in an inspiring setting.

a. **Jesus was walking in the temple courts.**

b. **The religionists approached and questioned Jesus.**

Jesus was apparently walking along in one of the two arcades when the religionists approached Him. Again, they were an official delegation from the ruling body of the Jews, that is, from the Sanhedrin. Representatives from the three major groups were there: the chief priests, the Scribes, and the elders (see DEEPER STUDY # 1—Mt.16:21). They were all furious. All that had happened—the triumphal entry, Jesus' acceptance of the people's homage and the title of Messiah, the cleansing of the temple and the disruption of the priests' profits from those who sold and bought, the healing of the blind and lame, the worship of the children—naturally created a crisis for the ruling body. What Jesus was doing sent them into a rage. It provoked them to ask the question, "Who does this Jesus of Nazareth think He is?" (Mt.21:10-11).

This question was one of contempt, not of seeking. The question was an attempt to discredit Christ, not to learn the truth about Him. The question was stirred within them because their own position, esteem, and gain were disturbed; not because they really wanted to know if Jesus were the Messiah. Their minds were closed and shut to His claims. They had many claims and many proofs of His Messiahship, but they willfully ignored and denied His divine mission. They had plenty of opportunities to learn the truth (see note—Jn.3:1-2), yet they would allow nothing to change them. Their obstinate unbelief held a firm grip on them. (See DEEPER STUDY # 1—Mt.12:1-8; note and DEEPER STUDY # 1—12:10; note—15:1-20; DEEPER STUDY # 2—15:6-9. These notes will give some background to the opposition against Jesus.)

11:28

²⁸ and they said to him, "By what authority are you doing these things, or who gave you this authority to do them?"

2 The question about Jesus' authority.

Specifically, the Jewish religious leaders questioned Jesus' authority. This was the basic question that should have been asked, a question that probed into the very nature of Jesus: What was His authority? Who sent Him? Who empowered Him? Who gave Him the right to do as He was doing? Where had He come from?

The leaders wanted to know what right Jesus had to interfere with their lives and area of responsibility. *They* were the authorized guardians and rulers of the temple and of the people. He was interfering with their management, and, from their perspective, He had no right to do so. They asked Him two questions.

a. The authority for His works.

First, the religious leaders asked Jesus what was the authority for His works. He marched triumphantly into Jerusalem as a king, receiving the homage of the Messianic King from the people; He cast the market traders out of the temple; He healed the blind and lame (Mt.21:14), and He accepted the homage of small children's proclaiming Him to be the Messiah. What authority did He have to do these things?

The leaders were asking the basic question that needed to be asked. Perhaps they were unaware of it, but they were asking the question that would determine their eternal fate. Every person needs to ask, "What is the authority, the explanation, for the works of Christ?" There are the works of . . .

- ministry
- raising the dead
- healing
- ascending into heaven
- preaching

- teaching
- rising again
- foretelling the future
- calming the storms of nature
- dying and fulfilling Scripture

b. The authority for His person, His claims.

Second, the religionists indignantly asked Jesus what was the authority of His person. Who gave Him the authority to claim . . .

- to be the promised Messianic King by entering the city as He did?
- to be the Head, the God of the Temple; to call the temple, "My house?"
- to be the Light of the world to the blind and the Messianic Healer to the lame (Mt.21:14)?
- to be the Messianic fulfillment of Scripture by receiving the praise of the children?

The authorities knew exactly who Jesus was claiming to be. They simply rejected His claims and refused to believe. They chose the course of obstinate unbelief. They had proof upon proof, but they still refused to believe.

There are two possible answers Jesus could have given to the question about who He is. First, Jesus could have claimed to act by His own authority, could have said the power was His own. This would have made Him an egomaniac or a great imposter, the greatest in history. Of course, if He had claimed to act of His own authority, the authorities would have been able to discredit Him immediately and to arrest Him for causing so much havoc.

Second, Jesus could have claimed to act by the authority of God, to be of and from God. Now note: Jesus did make such a claim time and again. But if He had made it in the face of the authorities, they would have arrested Him immediately for blasphemy. They would have claimed that God would never have given orders to cause such turmoil in the temple.

Again, the leaders were asking the basic question that needs to be asked by every individual: *Who gave Jesus His authority?* Who is He: a mere man or truly the Son of God? Is He of man or of God? Is His authority of men or from within, of His very own nature as God?

3 The choices people have: Illustrated by John the Baptist.

Jesus answered the religionists' questions by asking them a question that would lead to the answer to their question (v.29). The question involved the ministry of John the Baptist, whom Jesus was using to illustrate the truth about Himself (v.30).

Jesus knew exactly what the authorities were plotting, and He responded to them both wisely and shrewdly. Jesus simply asked them, "Was John's baptism from heaven (from God) or from men?" Note the wisdom and shrewdness of our Lord.

First, He met them on their own ground. He said He would answer them, but they must first answer a question, then He would answer them.

29 Jesus said to them, "I will ask you one question; answer me, and I will tell you by what authority I do these things.

30 Was the baptism of John from heaven or from man? Answer me."

31 And they discussed it with one another, saying, "If we say, 'From heaven,' he will say, 'Why then did you not believe him?'

32 But shall we say, 'From man'?"—they were afraid of the people, for they all held that John really was a prophet.

Second, He formulated and asked a question that was astounding in its effect.

➤ It actually answered their question.

➤ It silenced them, for if they answered they would indict themselves.

➤ It ended the discussion and their questioning of Christ and immediate threat to Him.

➤ It revealed their obstinate unbelief and made them even more inexcusable before God (heaping wrath upon themselves).

a. Choice one: He was from God (v.31).

Jesus' question for the religionists had two possible answers. The first choice: Was John from God? If so, then Jesus was from God. Why? Because being from God, John would not lie, and John testified that Jesus was the Messiah, the Son of God sent from God.

> **The next day he saw Jesus coming toward him, and said, "Behold, the Lamb of God, who takes away the sin of the world! And I have seen and have borne witness that this is the Son of God." (Jn.1:29, 34)**

b. Choice two: He was a mere man (v.32).

The second choice: Was John's authority human; was he a mere man? If so, then Jesus could be a mere man acting in His own human authority. But how could this ever be? If John's and Jesus' ministry were really of men—not of God, of strictly human authority and power—then how could so many *changed lives* and *miraculous works* be accounted for? This one question alone shows the absurdity and sin of unbelief, not only of unbelievers in Jesus' day but of unbelievers in our day as well (see outline and notes—Mt.3:1-17).

c. The religionists' dilemma (vv.31–32).

Jesus' question presented quite a dilemma for the manipulative religious leaders. They discussed their answer to Jesus' question among themselves. Scripture is clear: they did not just reason within (which would be expressed by the use of the Greek word *en*) themselves, with each left to his own thoughts; but *with* or *among* (pros) themselves. This was a planned attack against Jesus, a deliberate rejection of Jesus and a group effort to destroy Him.

The Lord's questioners immediately knew their predicament. If they replied that John's ministry was of God, then Jesus would ask them why they did not believe John's testimony about the Messiah (v.31). If they replied that John's ministry was of men, they would incite the people against themselves, for the people believed strongly that John was a true prophet from God (v.32).

Note how the questioners reasoned among themselves. Their concern was not to discover the truth; but to save face and protect their position, esteem, and security. Consequently, they committed a threefold sin.

First, they deliberately denied Jesus. To confess that John was of God would force them to acknowledge Jesus. And they were not willing to confess Him. They feared the loss of all they possessed (position, power, wealth, esteem, image, security).

Second, they feared the people; they were deliberately cowardly. They feared the people's reactions (abuse, ridicule, persecution).

Third, they chose expediency—the easy way out, the way that was most beneficial to them personally—to deliberately be ignorant. They feared being shamed, embarrassed, ridiculed. To confess Jesus would mean confessing they had been wrong all along. It would mean denying self completely and doing so publicly. Like these spineless men, so many people . . .

• choose expediency rather than principle

• choose to play it safe rather than to stand for the truth

• choose to say "I don't know" rather than to speak the truth

THOUGHT 1. We have the same two choices as the authorities. Christ is either a mere man (egomaniac or imposter) or He is as John declared, "the Lamb of God . . . the Son of God" (Jn.1:29, 34).

(When all the people heard this, and the tax collectors too, they declared God just, having been baptized with the baptism of John.) (Lu.7:29)

Jesus answered them, "I told you, and you do not believe. The works that I do in my Father's name bear witness about me. . . . Do you say of him whom the Father consecrated and sent into the world, 'You are blaspheming,' because I said, 'I am the Son of God'? If I am not doing the works of my Father, then do not believe me; but if I do them, even though you do not believe me, believe the works, that you may know and understand that the Father is in me and I am in the Father." (Jn.10:25, 36-38)

And many came to him. And they said, "John did no sign, but everything that John said about this man was true." And many believed in him there. (Jn.10:41-42)

Do you not believe that I am in the Father and the Father is in me? The words that I say to you I do not speak on my own authority, but the Father who dwells in me does his works. (Jn.14:10)

4 The tragic answer: No decision due to hypocrisy.

After conferring among themselves, the authorities decided to answer, "We do not know." They lied. They knew perfectly well that John's baptism was of God. They just were not willing to run the risk of losing their position, prosperity, and security. They loved the world more than they loved God and the hope He extended toward them. Therefore, they acted cowardly and chose the route of expediency. They were hypocrites.

33 So they answered Jesus, "We do not know." And Jesus said to them, "Neither will I tell you by what authority I do these things."

The decision of these unbelievers to make no decision was tragic (see notes and DEEPER STUDY # 5—Mt.8:21-22). Indecision and agnosticism are always tragic. They simply would not be convinced of the truth. It was not that they *could not* be convinced, but that they *would not*. Such obstinate unbelief seldom, if ever, sees the truth of Christ. Even if Christ openly revealed the truth to them, they would reject Him. In their attempt to make no decision, they made their decision: they rejected the truth about Christ, condemning their souls eternally.

THOUGHT 1. Every person has to choose and make a decision. To avoid or circumvent the question—to not choose—is to choose. It is to reject Jesus and to choose instead to spend eternity separated from God in hell.

And sent his servants to call those who were invited to the wedding feast, but they would not come. (Mt.22:3)

He said to him, 'If they do not hear Moses and the Prophets, neither will they be convinced if someone should rise from the dead.' (Lu.16:31)

Whoever believes in him is not condemned, but whoever does not believe is condemned already, because he has not believed in the name of the only Son of God. (Jn.3:18)

Yet you refuse to come to me that you may have life. (Jn.5:40)

And now, because you have done all these things, declares the LORD, and when I spoke to you persistently you did not listen, and when I called you, you did not answer, . . . And I will cast you out of my sight, as I cast out all your kinsmen, all the offspring of Ephraim. (Je.7:13, 15)

I call heaven and earth to witness against you today, that I have set before you life and death, blessing and curse. Therefore choose life, that you and your offspring may live, loving the LORD your God, obeying his voice and holding fast to him, for he is your life and length of days, that you may dwell in the land that the LORD swore to your fathers, to Abraham, to Isaac, and to Jacob, to give them. (De.30:19-20)

CHAPTER 12

F. The Parable of the Wicked Tenants:
God and Israel, or God and Humanity, 12:1–12

(Mt.21:33–46; Lu.20:9–19; Is.5:1–7)

1. **God is generous: He gives mankind everything needed**
2. **God is trusting: He gives mankind the responsibility and freedom to govern life**

3. **God is responsible: He expects payment**
4. **God is patient: He sends messengers to receive payment**
   a. One suffers mild abuse

   b. Another suffers severe abuse

   c. Still another suffers death

5. **God is love: He sends His very own Son to the world**

   a. Man's plot: To kill the Son[DS1]
   b. Man's reason: To steal the inheritance

   c. Man's crime: They killed the Son

6. **God is just: He will come to destroy the evil tenants (Israel or mankind)**

7. **God is trustworthy: He fulfills His promises**
   a. The promise to send the Messiah: He is the stone
   b. The promise to exalt the Messiah: He is God's marvelous work
8. **Conclusion: The great tragedy**
   a. Reacting instead of repenting
   b. Being mistaken about Jesus' identity: Feared people more than the Messiah, God's Son
   c. Leaving the Messiah (Christ) and going their own way

And he began to speak to them in parables. "A man planted a vineyard and put a fence around it and dug a pit for the winepress and built a tower, and leased it to tenants and went into another country."

² "When the season came, he sent a servant to the tenants to get from them some of the fruit of the vineyard."

³ And they took him and beat him and sent him away empty-handed.

⁴ Again he sent to them another servant, and they struck him on the head and treated him shamefully.

⁵ And he sent another, and him they killed. And so with many others: some they beat, and some they killed."

⁶ "He had still one other, a beloved son. Finally he sent him to them, saying, 'They will respect my son.'

⁷ But those tenants said to one another, 'This is the heir. Come, let us kill him, and the inheritance will be ours.'

⁸ And they took him and killed him and threw him out of the vineyard."

⁹ "What will the owner of the vineyard do? He will come and destroy the tenants and give the vineyard to others."

¹⁰ "Have you not read this Scripture: 'The stone that the builders rejected has become the cornerstone;

¹¹ this was the Lord's doing, and it is marvelous in our eyes'?"

¹² And they were seeking to arrest him but feared the people, for they perceived that he had told the parable against them. So they left him and went away.

Division VII

The Son of God's Last Jerusalem Ministry:
Jesus' Warning and Conflict with Religionists, 11:1–12:44

F. The Parable of the Wicked Tenants: God and Israel or God and Humanity, 12:1–12

(Mt.21:33–46; Lu.20:9–19; Is.5:1–7)

12:1–12
Introduction

This parable continues Jesus' discussion with the Jewish religious leaders (11:27–33). *Them* (v.1) refers to the chief priests, scribes, and elders (11:27). It is one of the most interesting parables ever told by Jesus because it is both historical and prophetic. Jesus covered the history of Israel from God's perspective, just as God sees it (vv.1–5). He then predicted or revealed exactly what was going to happen to Israel: they were going to reject God's own Son (v.6), and because of their rejection and cruelty, God was going to reject them by giving the kingdom of God to another people (v.9).

What is said throughout this passage is applicable to all people as well as to Israel. Just as God once entrusted His vineyard to Israel, God has now entrusted the vineyard of the church and of the world to us (Mt.28:19–20), the new nation, the new creation of God (see notes—Ep.2:11–18; pt.4; 4:17–19). Every point covered in Israel's history should, therefore, be a dynamic message speaking to our hearts. This is, *The Parable of the Wicked Tenants: God and Israel or God and Humanity,* 12:1–12.

1. God is generous: He gives mankind everything needed (v.1).
2. God is trusting: He gives mankind the responsibility and freedom to govern life (v.1).
3. God is responsible: He expects payment (v.2).
4. God is patient: He sends messengers to receive payment (vv.2–5).
5. God is love: He sends His very own Son to the world (vv.6–8).
6. God is just: He will come to destroy the evil tenants (Israel or mankind) (v.9).
7. God is trustworthy: He fulfills His promises (vv.10–11).
8. Conclusion: The great tragedy (v.12).

1 God is generous: He gives mankind everything needed.

12:1a

Jesus began this parable by introducing His audience to a man who planted a vineyard and provided everything it needed to flourish. He provided every conceivable resource to take care of His vineyard and those assigned to manage and work it. Everything was provided to assure growth and fruitfulness. The cultivators of the vineyard had no excuse for not producing.

> And he began to speak to them in parables. "A man planted a vineyard and put a fence around it and dug a pit for the winepress and built a tower, and leased it to tenants and went into another country."

The man represents God, our Creator who generously provided everything Israel needed—and provides everything we now need—to accomplish His purposes. Note three marvelous, generous things that God did for His vineyard.

First, God put a fence (hedge, wall) around it. This was a wall built around the vineyard to keep the animals away from the grapes. The fence *assured* growth and fruitfulness.

Second, God dug a pit for the winepress. This was a trough or vat into which the wine was pressed. The trough was sometimes dug in rock, sometime built out of wood. The vat and the winepress stand for the resources which God provides to get His work done.

Third, God built a tower. It was a watchtower used to guard and protect the vineyard from thieves. The tower stands for the assurance and security of God's care that He gives to His servants (see Mt.6:25–34).

THOUGHT 1. God is generous to every person.

1) God has given us the world and our space in it to tend to (see note—Mk.12:1 for discussion and verses).

2) God has hedged His followers and the church round about. He protects us and assures our growth and fruitfulness (Jn.15:1–8).

> You did not choose me, but I chose you and appointed you that you should go and bear fruit and that your fruit should abide, so that whatever you ask the Father in my name, he may give it to you. (Jn.15:16)

> Filled with the fruit of righteousness that comes through Jesus Christ, to the glory and praise of God. (Ph.1:11)

> So as to walk in a manner worthy of the Lord, fully pleasing to him: bearing fruit in every good work and increasing in the knowledge of God; being strengthened with all power, according to his glorious might, for all endurance and patience with joy. (Col.1:10–11)

3) God gives His followers the gifts of the Spirit, the "equipment" we need to carry out our task on earth (1 Co.12:4–11).

> To one he gave five talents, to another two, to another one, to each according to his ability. Then he went away. (Mt.25:15)

> But you will receive power when the Holy Spirit has come upon you, and you will be my witnesses in Jerusalem and in all Judea and Samaria, and to the end of the earth. (Ac.1:8)

> Having gifts that differ according to the grace given to us, let us use them: if prophecy, in proportion to our faith. (Ro.12:6)

> Now there are varieties of gifts, but the same Spirit. (1 Co.12:4)

4) God gives His followers the assurance and security of His care (Mt.6:25–34).

> Therefore do not be anxious, saying, 'What shall we eat?' or 'What shall we drink?' or 'What shall we wear?' For the Gentiles seek after all these things, and your heavenly Father knows that you need them all. (Mt.6:31–32)

> Why, even the hairs of your head are all numbered. Fear not; you are of more value than many sparrows. (Lu.12:7)

> And my God will supply every need of yours according to his riches in glory in Christ Jesus. (Ph.4:19)

> Casting all your anxieties on him, because he cares for you. (1 Pe.5:7)

12:1b

And he began to speak to them in parables. "A man planted a vineyard and put a fence around it and dug a pit for the winepress and built a tower, and leased it to tenants and went into another country."

2 God is trusting: He gives mankind the responsibility and freedom to govern life.

After planting His vineyard and furnishing the cultivators with everything they needed to make it productive, the man went to a country far away. The message is this: God is trusting. He gives responsibility and freedom to govern life. God entrusted His vineyard to cultivators. The cultivators were the nation and people of Israel, in particular the leaders (both religious and civil). Everyone was to take care of the whole body of people. Everyone was responsible, thereby contributing to the welfare and provision of all. (See the whole body of the church and every member's responsibility to labor in the vineyard doing his or her part.)

Grasp the truths taught in this simple statement. God trusts us. Think what a glorious privilege it is to be trusted by God. Imagine how dear God's vineyard is to Him, and then think about how He entrusts its care to us and not to angels or some other higher form of being. What a wonderful and marvelous thing that God would trust us with His most precious vineyard!

In addition, God gives us freedom. God left the cultivators to care for His vineyard as they wished. They were to exercise their will, their choices, their drive to care for the vineyard. They had the glorious privilege of freedom, of not having someone looking over their shoulder, forcing them to work and micromanaging them.

THOUGHT 1. Two of the greatest gifts God has given us are *trust* and *freedom*. The very fact of being trusted by God is one of the most glorious privileges of life. And being given the freedom to care for God's immense creation is beyond comprehension. How marvelous are these two glorious gifts! Yet, note how humanity has neglected, abused, violated, and even worked to destroy these great gifts.

> For it will be like a man going on a journey, who called his servants and entrusted to them his property. (Mt.25:14)

> Calling ten of his servants, he gave them ten minas, and said to them, 'Engage in business until I come.' (Lu.19:13)

> Moreover, it is required of stewards that they be found faithful. (1 Co.4:2)

> So God created man in his own image, in the image of God he created him; male and female he created them. And God blessed them. And God said to them, "Be fruitful and multiply and fill the earth and subdue it, and have dominion over the fish of the sea and over the birds of the heavens and over every living thing that moves on the earth." (Ge.1:27–28)

> You have given him dominion over the works of your hands; you have put all things under his feet. (Ps.8:6)

3 God is responsible: He expects payment.

When the harvest time came, the owner of the vineyard sent one of his employees to collect what it had produced. God expects payment. He is businesslike; He holds people accountable. Note two truths taught in this verse:

> ² "When the season came, he sent a servant to the tenants to get from them some of the fruit of the vineyard."

- Fruit was expected. Every cultivator, that is, every person responsible for the vineyard, was expected to labor and produce.
- A day of accountability did come. Every person was expected to pay their dues, to make their contribution for the wonderful privilege of living in the beautiful vineyard and being blessed by it. (The kingdom of God, the world, the church—however one applies this passage—all are wonderful vineyards for which we are responsible to produce what fruit we can.)

> And he told this parable: "A man had a fig tree planted in his vineyard, and he came seeking fruit on it and found none." (Lu.13:6)

> Every branch in me that does not bear fruit he takes away, and every branch that does bear fruit he prunes, that it may bear more fruit. . . . I am the vine; you are the branches. Whoever abides in me and I in him, it is that bears much fruit, for apart from me you can do nothing. If anyone does not abide in me he is thrown away like a branch and withers; and the branches are gathered, thrown into the fire, and burned. (Jn.15:2, 5–6)

4 God is patient: He sends messengers to receive payment.

a. **One suffers mild abuse (vv.2–3).**

b. **Another suffers severe abuse (v.4).**

c. **Still another suffers death (v.5).**

The vineyard owner sent a series of messengers to collect the fruit of the harvest—what belonged to him. The sending of many messengers to make repeated attempts is a picture of God's patience. Time and again, He gave Israel a chance to be fruitful for Him. In relation to Israel, the messengers sent to gather the fruits of the vineyard

> ² "When the season came, he sent a servant to the tenants to get from them some of the fruit of the vineyard.
> ³ And they took him and beat him and sent him away empty-handed.
> ⁴ Again he sent to them another servant, and they struck him on the head and treated him shamefully.
> ⁵ And he sent another, and him they killed. And so with many others: some they beat, and some they killed."

385

represent the prophets and the good and godly leaders throughout Israel's history (judges, kings, and priests). All through Israel's history, God showed His lovingkindness by not reacting hastily and rejecting the nation. God treats us the same way; He gives us chance after chance. He sends messengers across our path time after time. He loves and aches for us to bear fruit by living for Him as we should.

Tragically, most cultivators continue as always: rebelling and claiming all rights to the vineyard and to their own lives. Therefore, they continue to resist God's messengers. This was true of Israel. They rebelled and refused to give the Master what belonged to Him. In fact, their rebellion led to the persecution and murder of God's servants.

The truth is, people do deliberately rebel against God. The workers want to rule the vineyard themselves. They want to be the kings of the kingdom, the rulers of the earth, and even the heads of the church. They want things to go their way and to rule and reign as they desire and will. They want no authority above themselves. They want to live and do things as they wish, and they want to claim the fruits for themselves. They want their own way so badly that they ridicule, slander, persecute, and even murder the true servants of God.

> Which of the prophets did your fathers not persecute? And they killed those who announced beforehand the coming of the Righteous One, whom you have now betrayed and murdered. (Ac.7:52; see also Mt.23:34-37; He.11:36-38)

God's messengers must understand that they are called to suffer (see DEEPER STUDY # 2—Mt.20:22-23). Note the detailed description of the world's treatment of God's messengers in these verses:

➢ They *beat and gave no fruit* to the first messenger (v.3).
➢ They struck and wounded the head of and shamefully handled the second messenger (v.4).
➢ They killed the third messenger (v.5).
➢ They beat "many others" (v.5).
➢ They killed "many others" (v.5).

> And he said to the vinedresser, 'Look, for three years now I have come seeking fruit on this fig tree, and I find none. Cut it down. Why should it use up the ground?' And he answered him, 'Sir, let it alone this year also, until I dig around it and put on manure. Then if it should bear fruit next year, well and good; but if not, you can cut it down.' (Lu.13:7-9)

> The Lord is not slow to fulfill his promise as some count slowness, but is patient toward you, not wishing that any should perish, but that all should reach repentance. (2 Pe.3:9)

> For my name's sake I defer my anger; for the sake of my praise I restrain it for you, that I may not cut you off. (Is.48:9)

THOUGHT 1. How many believers, laymen and ministers alike, are mistreated by the world! If we are going to serve Christ, we should expect to be persecuted.

> For it has been granted to you that for the sake of Christ you should not only believe in him but also suffer for his sake. (Ph.1:29)

> Indeed, all who desire to live a godly life in Christ Jesus will be persecuted. (2 Ti.3:12)

> Beloved, do not be surprised at the fiery trial when it comes upon you to test you, as though something strange were happening to you. But rejoice insofar as you share Christ's sufferings, that you may also rejoice and be glad when his glory is revealed. (1 Pe.4:12-13; see also 1 Pe.2:21; 4:5-6; Mt.19:29; Ro.8:16-17).

12:6-8

6 "He had still one other, a beloved son. Finally he sent him to them, saying, 'They will respect my son.'
7 But those tenants said to one another, 'This is the heir. Come, let us kill him, and the inheritance will be ours.'
8 And they took him and killed him and threw him out of the vineyard."

5 God is love: He sends His very own Son to the world.

The vineyard owner had but one remaining messenger to send: his son whom He dearly loved. He thought the cultivators would surely respect his son, but they killed his son as well.

The meaning of this part of the parable is obvious. God is love. Therefore, God sent His very own Son to the world to speak personally to people. He condescended and asked

His Son to leave the glory of eternity and to bring His Word to earth, speaking face to face with humanity.

a. Man's plot: To kill the Son (v.7a).

Jesus claimed to be God's Son. He was different from all the servants sent before. He was more than another human messenger; He was God's very own Son. There is no question that Jesus was clearly making this unique claim for Himself in this parable.

The cultivators—Israel, especially the religious leaders to whom Jesus was directly speaking—saw God's Son. An abundance of evidence clearly identified Him: Old Testament prophecies, the testimony of John the Baptist, Jesus' own claim and the miraculous works to prove His deity, the fulness or signs of the times (Ga.4:4). There was a feeling that He was the promised Messiah even among those who opposed Him (see note—Jn.3:1-2; see Jn.11:47-53). This is the tragic indictment against the Jewish leaders. Down deep within, they had a sense that Jesus really was the Messiah; but sin and greed for position, esteem, power, and security kept them from acknowledging Him. Their unbelief was deliberate and obstinate (see outline and notes—Mt.21:23-27). Consequently, they plotted His death (see Deeper Study # 1; Mt.12:14; Jn.11:53).

b. Man's reason: To steal the inheritance (v.7b).

The cultivators planned to seize the Son's inheritance. People wanted to possess the kingdom, the nation, the property, the power, the rule, the reign, the position, the esteem, the fame, the recognition, the wealth. Whatever the possession is, unbelieving people want the possession themselves. And they will deny, deceive, lie, cheat, steal, and even kill to get it (see notes—Mt.12:1-8; note and Deeper Study # 1—12:10; note—15:1-20; Deeper Study # 2—15:6-9).

c. Man's crime: They killed the Son (v.8).

The cultivators committed the worst crime of human history: they killed the Son of God Himself. Note two paramount truths in this part of the parable:
- Jesus Himself was prophesying His death at the hands of the Jewish leaders. He was looking them personally in the eye and confronting them with the crime they were plotting.
- Jesus' death was a willing act on His part. He knew death lay ahead, so He could have escaped. But He chose to die. It was in "the predetermined plan and foreknowledge of God" for Him to die (Ac.2:23, NASB).

For God so loved the world, that he gave his only Son, that whoever believes in him should not perish but have eternal life. (Jn.3:16)

Men of Israel, hear these words: Jesus of Nazareth, a man attested to you by God with mighty works and wonders and signs that God did through him in your midst, as you yourselves know—this Jesus, delivered up according to the definite plan and foreknowledge of God, you crucified and killed by the hands of lawless men. (Ac.2:22-23)

But God shows his love for us in that while we were still sinners, Christ died for us. (Ro.5:8)

But God, being rich in mercy, because of the great love with which he loved us, even when we were dead in our trespasses, made us alive together with Christ—by grace you have been saved. (Ep.2:4-5)

DEEPER STUDY # 1

(12:7) **Man, Error:** some unbelieving people feel God is too far away to do anything about their rejection of His Son. They feel God is too inactive and irrelevant. This is seen in the "far country" (v.1), the continuous rejection (vv.3-5), and the final denial of God's Son (vv.6-8).

6 God is just: He will come to destroy the evil tenants (Israel or mankind).

When the cultivators killed the owner's son, he came and destroyed them and committed his vineyard to others. The picture is clear in relation to Israel. When the Jews crucified Christ, God gave His vineyard to others—the Gentiles, the church. In relation to unbelieving humanity, God is just—He will come and destroy all who reject His Son. Three important details are presented here.

First, Jesus said the Lord of the vineyard is coming. He is coming to avenge the death of His only Son.

Second, God is coming to destroy the wicked. The destruction is to be miserable, terrible. Matthew's account reveals that Jesus' audience answered His question about what the vineyard owner would do (Mt.21:41). It was both the Jewish rulers and the people who said that justice would be executed. People, by their very nature, expect injustice to be punished.

12:9

[9] "What will the owner of the vineyard do? He will come and destroy the tenants and give the vineyard to others."

Third, God is going to trust His vineyard to others. Again, it was the crowd who said this. Everybody knows that a responsible vineyard owner will not allow his property to lie unkept. It will be cultivated by someone. God would raise up a new people to care for it—the church, the new creation of God (see DEEPER STUDY # 8—Mt.21:43; notes—Ro.9:25–33; Ep.2:11–18; pt.4—2:14–15; 4:17–19 for more discussion).

> Even now the axe is laid to the root of the trees. Every tree therefore that does not bear good fruit is cut down and thrown into the fire. (Mt.3:10)

> For the wrath of God is revealed from heaven against all ungodliness and unrighteousness of men, who by their unrighteousness suppress the truth. (Ro.1:18)

> In flaming fire, inflicting vengeance on those who do not know God and on those who do not obey the gospel of our Lord Jesus. They will suffer the punishment of eternal destruction, away from the presence of the Lord and from the glory of his might, when he comes on that day to be glorified in his saints, and to be marveled at among all who have believed, because our testimony to you was believed. (2 Th.1:8–10)

> But if it bears thorns and thistles, it is worthless and near to being cursed, and its end is to be burned. (He.6:8)

12:10–11

[10] "Have you not read this Scripture: 'The stone that the builders rejected has become the cornerstone;
[11] this was the Lord's doing, and it is marvelous in our eyes'?"

7 God is trustworthy: He fulfills His promises.

Jesus brought the parable to its conclusion. Quoting Psalm 118:22-23, He declared that He is the fulfillment of its prophecy (see note—Lu.2:34). God is trustworthy. He fulfills His promises, and He was fulfilling the promise of Psalm 118 *through Christ.*

a. The promise to send the Messiah: He is the stone (v.10).
Psalm 118:22-23 was recognized as a Messianic prophecy. The Messiah was to be the head cornerstone who was to begin building the kingdom of God and who was to support all other stones or leaders who came later. The religious leaders standing around Christ knew that He was referring to the Messiah (Is.28:16; Da.2:34; Zec.3:9). And they understood clearly what He was saying: He is the Messiah of whom the psalmist prophesied (see outline and notes—Ps.118:22-24 for discussion). He is the stone.

But note the promises. The stone was to be rejected at first. It was to be considered unsuitable and useless for the building. The builders would not allow the stone to be a part of the building; they would cast it aside and treat it as unusable.

However, the great Architect overruled the builders. He raised the stone from the graveyard of rejected stones and exalted it to the position of head cornerstone, the stone which supports all other stones and which holds the building of God's kingdom both up and together (see notes—Ep.2:20; see also Ph.2:9-11).

The symbolism of the head cornerstone says at least two significant things to us.

First, the cornerstone is the first stone laid. All other stones are placed after it. It is the preeminent stone in time. So it is with Christ. He is *the first* of God's new movement:

➤ Christ is the captain of our salvation. All others are crew members or soldiers who follow Him.

> **For it was fitting that he, for whom and by whom all things exist, in bringing many sons to glory, should make the founder of their salvation perfect through suffering. (He.2:10)**

➤ Christ is the author of eternal salvation and of our faith. All others are the characters of the story.

> **And being made perfect, he became the source of eternal salvation to all who obey him. (He.5:9)**

> **Looking to Jesus, the founder and perfecter of our faith, who for the joy that was set before him endured the cross, despising the shame, and is seated at the right hand of the throne of God. (He.12:2)**

➤ Christ is the beginning and the end. All others come after Him.

> **"I am the Alpha and the Omega," says the Lord God, "who is and who was and who is to come, the Almighty." (Re.1:8; see 21:6; 22:13)**

➤ Christ is the forerunner into the very presence of God. All others enter God's presence after Him.

> **We have this as a sure and steadfast anchor of the soul, a hope that enters into the inner place behind the curtain, where Jesus has gone as a forerunner on our behalf, having become a high priest forever after the order of Melchizedek. (He.6:19–20)**

Second, the cornerstone is the supportive stone. All other stones are placed upon it and held up by it. They all rest upon it. It is the preeminent stone in position and power. So it is with Christ. He is the support and power, the Foundation of God's new movement:

➤ Christ is *the head cornerstone,* the only true foundation upon which people can build. All crumble who are not laid upon Him.

> **For no one can lay a foundation other than that which is laid, which is Jesus Christ. (1 Co.3:11)**

➤ Christ is *the chief cornerstone* upon which all others are fitly joined together. All who wish to be formed together have to be laid upon Him.

> **Built on the foundation of the apostles and prophets, Christ Jesus himself being the cornerstone, in whom the whole structure, being joined together, grows into a holy temple in the Lord. In him you also are being built together into a dwelling place for God by the Spirit. (Ep.2:20–22)**

➤ Christ is *the living stone* upon which all others are built up a spiritual house. All others have to be built upon Him if they wish to live and have their spiritual sacrifice accepted by God.

> **As you come to him, a living stone rejected by men but in the sight of God chosen and precious, you yourselves like living stones are being built up as a spiritual house, to be a holy priesthood, to offer spiritual sacrifices acceptable to God through Jesus Christ. (1 Pe.2:4–5)**

b. The promise to exalt the Messiah: He is God's marvelous work (v.11).

This work, the work of exalting Christ as the Messiah, is all of God. It was entirely His doing. He was the One who raised up the Savior. And the One whom God raised up is the object of marvel and wonder. *He* is God's marvelous work.

8 Conclusion: The great tragedy.

Jesus' parable concluded with a great tragedy. Time and again, this tragedy has been repeated in so many people's lives down through the centuries.

a. Reacting instead of repenting.

There was the tragedy of reacting instead of repenting. The leaders saw that Jesus was speaking to them. But

¹² And they were seeking to arrest him but feared the people, for they perceived that he had told the parable against them. So they left him and went away.

their consciences had been numbed by obstinate unbelief (1 Ti.4:2). They were insensitive to His warnings (v.9). Therefore, they reacted instead of repenting. They should have heeded Christ's warnings and received Him as their Messiah, their Savior, but they did not. They were set against Him, seeking to destroy Him and thereby silencing His claim.

b. **Being mistaken about Jesus' identity: Feared people more than the Messiah, God's Son.**
There was the tragedy of holding the wrong view of the Messiah. This is seen in the people. The leaders were afraid to arrest Jesus because of the people. The people saw Jesus as some great prophet (a great teacher) and not as the Messiah, the Son of the Living God. This, too, was tragic; but God was able to use their respect to protect Christ until the appointed time for His death.

c. **Leaving the Messiah (Christ) and going their own way.**
There was the tragedy of leaving Jesus and going their own way. When they were directly confronted by Jesus and convicted of their sin and unbelief, they turned from Him—instead of to Him—and walked away. Even more tragic, countless millions of others through the centuries have followed their misguided example (see note, *Decision*—Mk.11:33 for Scripture application).

G. The Question Concerning Civil and Religious Power: The State and God, 12:13–17

(Mt.22:15–22; Lu.20:20–26)

¹³ And they sent to him some of the Pharisees and some of the Herodians, to trap him in his talk.

¹⁴ And they came and said to him, "Teacher, we know that you are true and do not care about anyone's opinion. For you are not swayed by appearances, but truly teach the way of God. Is it lawful to pay taxes to Caesar, or not? Should we pay them, or should we not?"

¹⁵ But, knowing their hypocrisy, he said to them, "Why put me to the test? Bring me a denarius and let me look at it."

¹⁶ And they brought one. And he said to them, "Whose likeness and inscription is this?" They said to him, "Caesar's."

¹⁷ Jesus said to them, "Render to Caesar the things that are Caesar's, and to God the things that are God's." And they marveled at him.

1. **The leaders' false concepts**
   a. Religion is supreme[DS1]
   b. The state is supreme (Herodians)[DS2]
2. **The sins common to false concepts about the state[DS3]**
   a. Selfish ambition: Leads to compromise
   b. Deception: Leads to insincere flattery and destruction
   c. Obstinate unbelief: Leads to denial of truth, condemnation
3. **Life within the state depends upon God, not money: Jesus does not even have a coin**
4. **The state is ordained by God: Some things belong to the state**
5. **The state is limited in its power: God is due the things that belong to God**

Division VII

The Son of God's Last Jerusalem Ministry: Jesus' Warning and Conflict with Religionists, 11:1–12:44

G. The Question Concerning Civil and Religious Power: The State and God, 12:13–17

(Mt.22:15–22; Lu.20:20–26)

12:13–17
Introduction

This passage reports the Jewish leaders' second challenge against Jesus. The Sanhedrin, the ruling body of the Jews, had met officially and plotted how they might manipulate Jesus into making a statement that would condemn Him (v.13). They devised a question dealing with taxes and a person's citizenship in the state, asking if it was a violation of Jewish law to pay taxes to Caesar (v.14). A *yes* answer would discredit Jesus with the people because they opposed paying taxes to a foreign conqueror (Rome). A *no* answer would cause Him to be arrested by the Roman authorities for opposing the law and threatening a revolt. Christ's arrogant, scheming opponents smugly thought they had finally devised a way to place Him in a no-win situation.

Jesus, being the all-wise Son of God Himself, saw through their plot. And Jesus used the occasion to teach the truth about citizenship, a truth which was both astounding and earth-shaking to the people of that day. It was earth-shaking because the Jews had always believed that the loyalty of a citizen belonged only to God, and the rest of the world believed that their loyalty belonged to the ruling monarch of their territory. Jesus astounded the world of His day by declaring that there is an earthly citizenship to which some things are to be given, and there is a spiritual, heavenly citizenship to which some things are to be given. The principle He taught continues to guide His followers today. This is, *The Question Concerning Civil and Religious Power: The State and God,* 12:13–17.

1. The leaders' false concepts (v.13).
2. The sins common to false concepts about the state (v.14).
3. Life within the state depends upon God, not money: Jesus does not even have a coin (v.15).
4. The state is ordained by God: Some things belong to the state (vv.16–17).
5. The state is limited in its power: God is due the things that belong to God (v.17).

12:13

¹³ And they sent to him some of the Pharisees and some of the Herodians, to trap him in his talk.

1 The leaders' false concepts.

In their plotting to trap Jesus, the Pharisees and the Herodians were led by the idea that God's people cannot be loyal to both their faith and the earthly government under which they live. Either their religion or the state must reign supreme in their conduct as citizens. As Jesus would reveal, their concepts were false. But it must be remembered that the world did not know the concepts were false until this experience.

a. Religion is supreme.

The Pharisees believed that religion is supreme (see DEEPER STUDY # 1). They believed strongly in the heavenly, spiritual world, so much so that they believed all obedience and loyalty were due God and God alone. In fact, all things on earth were due God. The state and all other power and authority were to be subject to religious rule. Therefore, they were strongly against paying taxes to a foreign king. From their perspective, paying taxes to a secular government was an infringement on God's right. They also argued that using Roman currency, which was stamped with the image of the emperor, violated the second commandment, which forbids the making of graven images.

b. The state is supreme.

The second false concept is that the state is supreme. This is seen in the view of the Herodians (see DEEPER STUDY # 2).

Picture the scene, how strange it was. The Pharisees held that religion was dominant over government. They despised Roman authority and taxation. The Herodians held that government was dominant over religion. They would agree that taxes must be paid to Caesar rather than to God. They and the Pharisees were bitter enemies. To find them together was strange indeed. But their hatred of Jesus had brought them together against One whom they considered a common enemy (see notes—Mk.3:6; DEEPER STUDY # 3—Ac.23:8).

DEEPER STUDY # 1

(12:13) **Pharisees:** see DEEPER STUDY # 3—Ac.23:8.

DEEPER STUDY # 2

(12:13) **Herodians:** the Herodians were not a religious party, but a political party of Herod, the king of Galilee. They were supportive of Rome, compromising wherever they could in order to preserve their own power and influence. They had compromised to such a point that they gave some degree of consent to pagan temples. Religiously, they were mainly Sadducees who gave their first loyalty to the state (see DEEPER STUDY # 3—Ac.23:8). Therefore, they opposed all Messianic claims because of the disturbance such claims caused among the people. They would agree that taxes must be paid to Caesar rather than to God.

2 The sins common to false concepts about the state.

These strange allies—the Pharisees and the Herodians—asked Jesus which of their concepts God's people should follow. On the surface, their question appears innocent. It was a question asked by some in every generation: "Should we be loyal to God or the government?" But answering this question was a dangerous proposition for Jesus. If He had said taxes were due Caesar, the people would have called Him a traitor and turned against Him as a Roman stooge. If He had said it was unlawful to pay taxes, the religionists would have reported Him to the Romans and accused Him of insurrection (see DEEPER STUDY # 3).

14 And they came and said to him, "Teacher, we know that you are true and do not care about anyone's opinion. For you are not swayed by appearances, but truly teach the way of God. Is it lawful to pay taxes to Caesar, or not? Should we pay them, or should we not?"

Lurking beneath the surface was something even more repulsive and horrible than their trickery. It was the camouflage of their trickery with flattery. Note how the flattery flowed on and on, distastefully so. They hoped the flattery would make Jesus think they were sincere and do away with any suspicions He had.

Holding a false concept of citizenship can lead people to commit abhorrent sins. Some of these sins are seen in the plot of the Pharisees and Herodians against Jesus.

a. Selfish ambition: Leads to compromise.

The first sin is *selfish ambition*, which often leads to compromise and intrigue. Nothing could be more surprising than to see Pharisees and Herodians working together. They stood diametrically opposed to one another. Pharisees thought Herodians were no better than the heathen doomed to hell. Yet they are seen working with Herodians against Jesus. What was it that brought them together? Selfish ambition. They feared the loss of their position, influence, power, wealth, and security. (See notes—Mt.12:1-8; note and DEEPER STUDY # 1—12:10; note—15:1-20; DEEPER STUDY # 2—15:6-9. These notes will help considerably in understanding why the rulers feared Jesus so much.)

The depth of sin in selfish ambition is seen in that the primary plotters were religious leaders. They were not only willing to plot evil; they were trying to put a man to death. Just *how* *evil* selfish ambition can be, in both government and religion, is clearly seen in this passage.

> How can you believe, when you receive glory from one another and do not seek the glory that comes from the only God? (Jn.5:44)

THOUGHT 1. People who live for this world will become a bedfellow with almost anyone to protect their security. The degree or strange appearance of the compromise will seldom matter.

> Do not be unequally yoked with unbelievers. For what partnership has righteousness with lawlessness? Or what fellowship has light with darkness? (2 Co.6:14)

> You adulterous people! Do you not know that friendship with the world is enmity with God? Therefore whoever wishes to be a friend of the world makes himself an enemy of God. (Js.4:4)

> Do not love the world or the things in the world. If anyone loves the world, the love of the Father is not in him. (1 Jn.2:15)

b. Deception: Leads to insincere flattery and destruction.

The second sin is *deception*, which usually leads to flattery and destruction. The Pharisees' deception is seen in that they themselves did not go to Jesus. They sent some of their disciples— "Pharisees in training," so to speak—to question Jesus (Mt.22:16). These trainees were learners, students who would actually be seeking the answer to such a question. Herodians accompanied them to give the appearance that these disciples had asked them first but were not satisfied with their answer. It would seem they wanted to know what He (One who claimed to be the Messiah) would answer. Thus, Jesus would think the question was the legitimate, earnest question of a student, never suspecting a plot to entrap Him.

Deception of the lowest kind is seen in the words of flattery which are used in approaching Jesus in this situation:

> "Teacher . . .
> "we know that You are true, truthful, a man of integrity . . .
> "and teach the way of God truthfully. . . ."
> "and do not care about anyone's opinion . . .
> "for you are not swayed by appearances, do not show partiality . . ."

Note that everything they said about Jesus was true. He *was* a teacher, a rabbi. He was even more: He was the Master and Lord of the universe. He *was* true and truthful: a teacher from God. (Contrast their hypocritical approach with the sincerity of Nicodemus, Jn.3:2.) He *did* teach the way of God: how people are to live and behave if they wish to please God. He *did not* care what people said about Him: it did not influence Him or His actions. He *did not* show partiality or favoritism.

The problem was that these schemers did not mean what they were professing, not in their hearts. What they were professing about Jesus was coming from an evil motive. They wanted to use Him to secure their own selfish purposes. Although they did not prevail in this encounter, in the end they were successful; they were able to do what they were plotting. They were able to have Christ destroyed.

THOUGHT 1. Deception always destroys that which is truthful and strong and lovely.

> Their throat is an open grave; they use their tongues to deceive. The venom of asps is under their lips. (Ro.3:13)

> For such persons do not serve our Lord Christ, but their own appetites, and by smooth talk and flattery they deceive the hearts of the naive. (Ro.16:18)

> Do not be unequally yoked with unbelievers. For what partnership has righteousness with lawlessness? Or what fellowship has light with darkness? (2 Co.6:14)

> For your iniquity teaches your mouth, and you choose the tongue of the crafty. (Jb.15:5)

> For there is no truth in their mouth; their inmost self is destruction; their throat is an open grave; they flatter with their tongue. (Ps.5:9)

> A man who flatters his neighbor spreads a net for his feet. (Pr.29:5)

c. **Obstinate unbelief: Leads to denial of truth, condemnation.**
The third sin is *obstinate unbelief*. This sin is the natural fruit of closed-mindedness, and it leads to denial of the truth and self-condemnation. Consider the simple question asked of Jesus: "Is it lawful to pay taxes to Caesar, or not?"
> The Pharisees, sincere Jewish religionists, would shout, "No!"
> The Herodians (and those securing position and wealth by Roman rule) would insist, "Yes!"

Standing there, the questioners thought they had entrapped Jesus. Whichever answer He gave would result in His rejection and condemnation.

DEEPER STUDY # 3

(12:14) **Tax—Tribute:** the tax Jesus was asked about was the poll tax. It was a tax that had to be paid by every person between the ages of twelve (for women) or fourteen (for men) and sixty-five.[1] The poll tax amounted to about one day's wage in that time (see DEEPER STUDY # 1—Ro.13:6).

---

1 Geoffrey W. Bromiley, ed., *The International Standard Bible Encyclopedia*, (Grand Rapids, MI: Wm. B. Eerdmans Publishing Co., 1986). Via Wordsearch digital edition.

3 Life within the state depends upon God, not money: Jesus does not even have a coin.

Apparently, Jesus did not have a penny to His name. He had to ask His questioners to give Him a coin to prove His point. He was living in the state of Israel and living under the rule of another state, the rule of Rome. He was, theoretically, a citizen of two states, yet He did not have a single coin. His sustenance and existence did not rest in the state nor in the things of the state. It rested in God's hands. His trust was in God, not in the state. He modeled an important principle: as citizens under an earthly government, we are to depend on God, not money, and not the government.

15 But, knowing their hypocrisy, he said to them, "Why put me to the test? Bring me a denarius and let me look at it."

THOUGHT 1. God has ordained civil government, and the state is necessary for order and justice in this world. But it is not necessary for life. The state can be and should be helpful to our lives, but it is not necessary. However, God is necessary, for we do not live by bread—earthly or material substances and possessions—alone. We cannot live an abundant life apart from God. With God we have purpose, fulfillment, and life—eternally. But without God we have none of these life-giving qualities, not permanently. The state can offer some liberties that allow some opportunities to pursue life; but God can make life free, completely free, instilling within the human heart a perfect assurance that we will live forever.

> But seek first the kingdom of God and his righteousness, and all these things will be added to you. (Mt.6:33)

> 'In him we live and move and have our being'; as even some of your own poets have said, 'For we are indeed his offspring.' (Ac.17:28)

> You shall serve the LORD your God, and he will bless your bread and your water, and I will take sickness away from among you. (Ex.23:25)

> You shall remember the LORD your God, for it is he who gives you power to get wealth, that he may confirm his covenant that he swore to your fathers, as it is this day. (De.8:18)

> And if you will indeed obey my commandments that I command you today, to love the LORD your God, and to serve him with all your heart and with all your soul, he will give the rain for your land in its season, the early rain and the later rain, that you may gather in your grain and your wine and your oil. And he will give grass in your fields for your livestock, and you shall eat and be full. (De.11:13–15)

> He who gives food to all flesh, for his steadfast love endures forever. (Ps.136:25)

4 The state is ordained by God: Some things belong to the state.

Jesus confirmed the truth that the state is ordained by God. He clearly demonstrated that, consequently, some things *belong* to the state. Therefore, we have some responsibilities and obligations that are *due* the state. What belongs to Caesar belongs to Caesar. Caesar—civil government—is responsible primarily for three functions: law and order, community services, and protection. No individual is an island within a state. Nobody exists in, of, and for themselves. Every person owes the state for the services and goods the state provides. Citizenship carries with it responsibility.

16 And they brought one. And he said to them, "Whose likeness and inscription is this?" They said to him, "Caesar's."
17 Jesus said to them, "Render to Caesar the things that are Caesar's, and to God the things that are God's." And they marveled at him.

Jesus was brilliant and brief as He dealt with the Pharisees and their false concept of citizenship. "Bring me a coin . . . whose image is on it?" He simply asked.

With this ingenious, simple question, Jesus forced the Pharisees (religion is supreme concept) to admit that some things belong to an earthly power. There is an *earthly citizenship*. The image was Caesar's; the superscription was Caesar's; and the coin had been made or coined by Caesar's government. Therefore, the coin was Caesar's if Caesar said it was due him. The point was clear.

Since the religionists *used what was owned and provided by Caesar*, they owed to Caesar what was due him. Jesus strikingly said, "Render to Caesar the things that are Caesar's."

In addition, Jesus revealed a very important truth for believers of every generation. We *have a dual citizenship*. We are citizens of heaven, yes, but we are also citizens of this world. Therefore, we have an obligation to the government under which we live. We receive the benefits of government just as the worldly-minded do (for example, roads, sewage, water, protection, and public transportation). Therefore, believers are to pay our due share. (See note—Ro.13:1-7. This note is a thorough discussion of citizenship.)

> However, not to give offense to them, go to the sea and cast a hook and take the first fish that comes up, and when you open its mouth you will find a shekel. Take that and give it to them for me and for yourself. (Mt.17:27)

> Let every person be subject to the governing authorities. For there is no authority except from God, and those that exist have been instituted by God. (Ro.13:1)

> Remind them to be submissive to rulers and authorities, to be obedient, to be ready for every good work. (Tit.3:1)

> Be subject for the Lord's sake to every human institution, whether it be to the emperor as supreme, or to governors as sent by him to punish those who do evil and to praise those who do good. For this is the will of God, that by doing good you should put to silence the ignorance of foolish people. (1 Pe.2:13–15)

> Honor everyone. Love the brotherhood. Fear God. Honor the emperor. (1 Pe.2:17)

> "Whoever will not obey the law of your God and the law of the king, let judgment be strictly executed on him, whether for death or for banishment or for confiscation of his goods or for imprisonment." (Ezr.7:26)

> I say: Keep the king's command, because of God's oath to him. (Ec.8:2)

12:17b

⁵ The state is limited in its power: God is due the things that belong to God.

¹⁷ Jesus said to them, "Render to Caesar the things that are Caesar's, and to God the things that are God's." And they marveled at him.

At the same time, we are to render to God the things that are God's. The state is limited in its power. God is due the things that are God's. God's people have a heavenly citizenship; we are beneficiaries of things that belong to God.

Jesus was equally brilliant in dealing with the Herodians and their false concept of citizenship. The Herodians not only subjected religion to the state, but they were worldly-minded and denied much of the supernatural, including life after death and the spiritual world or dimension of being. Jesus declared unequivocally to the Herodians that there *is* a spiritual world. God is; He does exist; therefore, there are some things which belong to God. Again, the point is clear. Since the Herodians (representing "the state is supreme" concept), as citizens of the world and of life itself, used what was owned and provided by God, they owed God what was due Him.

Jesus revealed a very important truth to all generations of people. We are beings of God as well as of this world, spiritual as well as physical beings. Therefore, we are responsible to live as citizens of God as well as citizens of this world. All people—believers and unbelievers alike—have received so much from God . . .

- life that was made to exist with God forever; therefore people owe God their life
- a spirit that can be *born again* and live a self-denying life of love and joy and peace for the sake of all people everywhere (Ga.5:22-23)
- a mind and body that have the power to enjoy the beauty of the earth and to learn, reason, and produce for the betterment and service of all mankind

THOUGHT 1. All people receive these benefits and many more from God. Therefore, we all are to pay our due share to God.

1) We are to love God supremely.

> Jesus answered, "The most important is, 'Hear, O Israel: The Lord our God, the Lord is one. And you shall love the Lord your God with all your heart and with all your soul and with all your mind and with all your strength.'" (Mk.12:29-30)

2) We are to seek the Lord.

> The God who made the world and everything in it, being Lord of heaven and earth, does not live in temples made by man, nor is he served by human hands, as though he needed anything, since he himself gives to all mankind life and breath and everything. And he made from one man every nation of mankind to live on all the face of the earth, having determined allotted periods and the boundaries of their dwelling place, that they should seek God, and perhaps feel their way toward him and find him. Yet he is actually not far from each one of us. (Ac.17:24–27)

3) We are to know that the Lord is God, and He alone is to be worshiped.

> Know that the LORD, he is God! It is he who made us, and we are his; we are his people, and the sheep of his pasture. Enter his gates with thanksgiving, and his courts with praise! Give thanks to him; bless his name! (Ps.100:3–4)

4) We are not to forget the Lord.

> And have forgotten the LORD, your Maker, who stretched out the heavens and laid the foundations of the earth, and you fear continually all the day because of the wrath of the oppressor, when he sets himself to destroy? And where is the wrath of the oppressor? (Is.51:13)

5) We are not to profane God's covenant.

> Have we not all one Father? Has not one God created us? Why then are we faithless to one another, profaning the covenant of our fathers? (Mal.2:10)

God will draw those who do these things—those who acknowledge and honor Him—to salvation through His Son, Jesus Christ. By recognizing what every person can recognize about God through His creation and through human conscience (Ro.1:18–21; 2:14–15)—general revelation—a person begins to believe through illumination God gives. Therefore, God will give that person additional illumination, the light of the gospel that is in Jesus Christ (2 Co.4:4–6).

> For the wrath of God is revealed from heaven against all ungodliness and unrighteousness of men, who by their unrighteousness suppress the truth. For what can be known about God is plain to them, because God has shown it to them. For his invisible attributes, namely, his eternal power and divine nature, have been clearly perceived, ever since the creation of the world, in the things that have been made. So they are without excuse. For although they knew God, they did not honor him as God or give thanks to him, but they became futile in their thinking, and their foolish hearts were darkened. (Ro.1:18–21)

> For when Gentiles, who do not have the law, by nature do what the law requires, they are a law to themselves, even though they do not have the law. They show that the work of the law is written on their hearts, while their conscience also bears witness, and their conflicting thoughts accuse or even excuse them. (Ro.2:14–15)

> In their case the god of this world has blinded the minds of the unbelievers, to keep them from seeing the light of the gospel of the glory of Christ, who is the image of God. For what we proclaim is not ourselves, but Jesus Christ as Lord, with ourselves as your servants for Jesus' sake. For God, who said, "Let light shine out of darkness," has shone in our hearts to give the light of the knowledge of the glory of God in the face of Jesus Christ. (2 Co.4:4–6)

(Mt.22:23–33; Lu.20:27–38)

1. The Sadducees attempted to discredit Jesus

2. The resurrection is challenged and scoffed at: The unbelieving Sadducees asked a sarcastic question about an unlikely situation

   a. The first of seven brothers married a wife and then died, leaving no children
   b. The remaining six brothers, in turn, married the same woman; each man died leaving no children
   c. The woman died last

   d. The question: Whose wife will she be in heaven?

3. The resurrection is declared in the Scriptures and based on the power of God

4. The resurrection is different from any earthly experience: It is of another world, another dimension
5. The resurrection brings about a living relationship that cannot be broken
   a. God is the living God of past saints who are now living with Him

   b. God is the God of the living
   c. Any other belief is a great error

18 And Sadducees came to him, who say that there is no resurrection. And they asked him a question, saying,
19 "Teacher, Moses wrote for us that if a man's brother dies and leaves a wife, but leaves no child, the man must take the widow and raise up offspring for his brother.
20 There were seven brothers; the first took a wife, and when he died left no offspring.
21 And the second took her, and died, leaving no offspring. And the third likewise.
22 And the seven left no offspring. Last of all the woman also died.
23 In the resurrection, when they rise again, whose wife will she be? For the seven had her as wife."
24 Jesus said to them, "Is this not the reason you are wrong, because you know neither the Scriptures nor the power of God?"
25 "For when they rise from the dead, they neither marry nor are given in marriage, but are like angels in heaven."
26 "And as for the dead being raised, have you not read in the book of Moses, in the passage about the bush, how God spoke to him, saying, 'I am the God of Abraham, and the God of Isaac, and the God of Jacob'?
27 He is not God of the dead, but of the living. You are quite wrong."

Division VII

The Son of God's Last Jerusalem Ministry: Jesus' Warning and Conflict with Religionists, 11:1–12:44

H. The Question About and Proof of the Resurrection, 12:18–27

(Mt.22:23–33; Lu.20:27–38)

12:18–27
Introduction

It was still Tuesday of the Lord's last week before His death. On this particular day, the chief priests and lay leaders (elders) had challenged His authority (see outline and notes—Mt.21:23–27). Jesus had met the challengers head-on and disarmed them. But in so doing, His mind had been focused on His death and Israel's rejection. The very thought that Israel, in whom God had put so much trust, was failing God by putting His Son to death was surely heart wrenching to Jesus (see outline and notes—Mt.21:33-46; 22:1-14).

The Pharisees and Herodians (Herod's political party) had attempted to discredit Jesus by pitting Him either against the government or the people (see outlines and notes—Mt.22:15-22). Again, Jesus had met and outsmarted His challengers. But the struggle had been tiring and pressuring, hard and heavy.

Now we see for a third time, a different group confronting and challenging the Lord. And again, the challenge came from a group who tried to out-argue and discredit Him. His challengers this time were the Sadducees, the religious and political liberals of the day. As Matthew points out, "[They] say that there is no resurrection" (Mt.22:23). Luke adds, "The Sadducees say there is no resurrection, nor angel, nor spirit" (Ac.23:8) (see DEEPER STUDY # 3—Mt.16:12; DEEPER STUDY # 2—Ac.23:8). Their liberal position caused them to stumble at the spiritual and supernatural. They ridiculed and scorned both. Therefore, in their minds, the teachings of Jesus were those of an unthinking and illogical man, teachings lacking philosophical analysis and natural proof.

Christ's teachings also caused the Sadducees to feel threatened and to oppose Jesus. Many people were flocking to Jesus and soaking up His teachings. This meant the Sadducees were losing their grip on the people. Their position and wealth were being jeopardized; therefore, they were compelled to attack and discredit Him before the people. But, like the Pharisees, they would walk away frustrated, infuriated, and humiliated. This is, *The Question About and Proof of the Resurrection*, 12:18-27.

1. The Sadducees attempted to discredit Jesus (v.18).
2. The resurrection is challenged and scoffed at: The unbelieving Sadducees asked a sarcastic question about an unlikely situation (vv.19-23).
3. The resurrection is declared in the Scriptures and based on the power of God (v.24).
4. The resurrection is different from any earthly experience: It is of another world, another dimension (v.25).
5. The resurrection brings about a living relationship that cannot be broken (vv.26-27).

1 The Sadducees attempted to discredit Jesus.

12:18

Thinking themselves smarter and more sophisticated than the Pharisees, the Sadducees arrogantly thought they would succeed where their religious rivals had failed (see DEEPER STUDY # 2—Ac.23:8 for discussion). They strategically decided to challenge Jesus in the area in which they specialized—their "pet" doctrine: their belief that there is no resurrection, that death marks the end of our existence, that there is no life after death.

[18] And Sadducees came to him, who say that there is no resurrection. And they asked him a question, saying,

2 The resurrection is challenged and scoffed at: The unbelieving Sadducees asked a sarcastic question about an unlikely situation.

12:19-23

Down through the centuries many people have scoffed at the resurrection. The Sadducees are among these (see 1 Co.15:12-58; 2 Pe.3:3-18). They asked Jesus a ridiculous, sarcastic question revolving around a hypothetical situation that would seldom, if ever occur. The subpoints of the outline adequately convey the unlikely circumstances they created:

[19] "Teacher, Moses wrote for us that if a man's brother dies and leaves a wife, but leaves no child, the man must take the widow and raise up offspring for his brother. [20] There were seven brothers; the first took a wife, and when he died left no offspring. [21] And the second took her, and died, leaving no offspring. And the third likewise. [22] And the seven left no offspring. Last of all the woman also died. [23] In the resurrection, when they rise again, whose wife will she be? For the seven had her as wife."

a. The first of seven brothers married a wife and then died, leaving no children (v.20).

b. The remaining six brothers, in turn, married the same woman; each man died leaving no children (vv.21–22a).

c. The woman died last (v.22b).

d. The question: Whose wife will she be in heaven (v.23)?

The Sadducees used Moses' law, the Levirate law, as the basis for their argument (De.25:5-6). When a husband died without a son, the Levirate law said that his brother was to marry his wife and bear a son. This law had been given to help preserve and to enlarge the nation of Israel (see Ru.4:5). By law, the son was considered the first-born son of the deceased brother. It assured two things: that the family name continued, and that the property holdings were kept in the family.

The hypothetical question was now asked, the question which in the Sadducees' mind showed the absurdity of the resurrection. Note three things by reading through verses 23-28 several times.

First, the Sadducees' spirit was mocking. The situation they proposed was logical, and, though highly unlikely, possible; but their spirit was cold and coarse, egotistical and unbelieving, regrettable and revolting. The unbeliever's spirit is often self-incriminating and self-condemning.

Second, the Sadducees thought their argument was irrefutable. They believed it pointed out just how foolish the idea of another world, of a spiritual world, was to the thinking person.

Third, the Sadducees were thinking that the spiritual world would be just like the physical world, that it would be nothing more than a continuation of this world, both in *its nature and in its relationships.*

THOUGHT 1. A picture of what the Scripture says about the natural person—the unregenerate person who has only the sin nature—is clearly seen in this event.

> The natural person does not accept the things of the Spirit of God, for they are folly to him, and he is not able to understand them because they are spiritually discerned. (1 Co.2:14)

THOUGHT 2. The resurrection and return of the Lord are often questioned.

> Now if Christ is proclaimed as raised from the dead, how can some of you say that there is no resurrection of the dead? (1 Co.15:12; see v.13–34 for a full discussion)

> But someone will ask, "How are the dead raised? With what kind of body do they come?" (1 Co.15:35; see v.36–58 for a full discussion)

> Knowing this first of all, that scoffers will come in the last days with scoffing, following their own sinful desires. They will say, "Where is the promise of his coming? For ever since the fathers fell asleep, all things are continuing as they were from the beginning of creation." (2 Pe.3:3–4; see vv.5–15 for a full discussion)

12:24

[24] Jesus said to them, "Is this not the reason you are wrong, because you know neither the Scriptures nor the power of God?"

3 The resurrection is declared in the Scriptures and based on the power of God.

Jesus said very pointedly to the Sadducees and to all who follow their position: "You are in error. Your reasons for denying the resurrection are unsound."

First, Jesus told these arrogant skeptics that they did not know the Scriptures. The Scriptures are plain and clear. They leave no doubt that there is a spiritual world and that a resurrection into the spiritual world and dimension of being will take place. The resurrection is not just a New Testament doctrine. The Old Testament is filled with the truth of the resurrection. But the Sadducees denied most of the Old Testament, accepting only the Pentateuch as Scripture. Note the following sampling of verses from the poetic and prophetic books—books rejected by the Sadducees—that declare the truth of the resurrection:

> For I know that my Redeemer lives, and at the last he will stand upon the earth. And after my skin has been thus destroyed, yet in my flesh I shall see God, whom I shall see for myself, and my eyes shall behold, and not another. My heart faints within me! (Jb.19:25–27)

> But God will ransom my soul from the power of Sheol, for he will receive me. Selah (Ps.49:15; see Ps.71:20; Ho.13:14)

> Your dead shall live; their bodies shall rise. You who dwell in the dust, awake and sing for joy! For your dew is a dew of light, and the earth will give birth to the dead. (Is.26:19)

> And many of those who sleep in the dust of the earth shall awake, some to everlasting life, and some to shame and everlasting contempt. (Da.12:2)

An abundance of New Testament verses support and expand the doctrine of the resurrection. The following verses are just a few of many:

> Truly, truly, I say to you, an hour is coming, and is now here, when the dead will hear the voice of the Son of God, and those who hear will live. . . . Do not marvel at this, for an hour is coming when all who are in the tombs will hear his voice and come out, those who have done good to the resurrection of life, and those who have done evil to the resurrection of judgment. (Jn.5:25, 28–29)

> For this is the will of my Father, that everyone who looks on the Son and believes in him should have eternal life, and I will raise him up on the last day. (Jn.6:40)

> Jesus said to her, "I am the resurrection and the life. Whoever believes in me, though he die, yet shall he live." (Jn.11:25)

> Having a hope in God, which these men themselves accept, that there will be a resurrection of both the just and the unjust. (Ac.24:15)

> If the Spirit of him who raised Jesus from the dead dwells in you, he who raised Christ Jesus from the dead will also give life to your mortal bodies through his Spirit who dwells in you. (Ro.8:11)

> For as in Adam all die, so also in Christ shall all be made alive. (1 Co.15:22)

> Knowing that he who raised the Lord Jesus will raise us also with Jesus and bring us with you into his presence. (2 Co.4:14)

> For the Lord himself will descend from heaven with a cry of command, with the voice of an archangel, and with the sound of the trumpet of God. And the dead in Christ will rise first. (1 Th.4:16)

THOUGHT 1. There are three reasons why people who have the Bible may not know the Scriptures.
1) They have not *really studied* the Scriptures.
2) They do not believe the Scriptures. They reject the Scripture as God's Word.
3) They do not take the Scriptures literally for what they say. They spiritualize and allegorize them.

Second, Jesus told the Sadducees that they did not know the power of God. They did not believe that God was mighty enough to raise the dead.

THOUGHT 2. There are three reasons why people do not know the power of God.
1) They are ignorant of God. They know nothing about God and seldom, if ever, give any thought to God and His power.
2) They do not believe in God nor in His power. They prefer to acknowledge God's eternal power and Godhead seen in creation and to go about *creating* (mentally and physically) gods of their own (Ro.1:20–32). They simply refuse to acknowledge the facts of nature:

> You foolish person! What you sow does not come to life unless it dies. And what you sow is not the body that is to be, but a bare kernel, perhaps of wheat or of some other grain. But God gives it a body as he has chosen, and to each kind of seed its own body. (1 Co.15:36–38)

3) They believe, but their belief in God and His power is weak. They cannot picture much happening beyond the physical world and the power of natural laws.

THOUGHT 3. The idea of a spiritual world is perplexing to the natural man—the sinful human nature, the lost person who is not indwelled by God's Spirit. Just imagine! While we are sitting here surrounded by all that we see . . .
- there is another world, an unseen spiritual dimension of being, that actually exists
- there is a spirit, the real life within our bodies, that is destined to exist forever
- there is to be a resurrection of all the dead bodies that have been lying and decaying in the graves for ages and ages, and the bodies of believers will be perfected and glorified to live and work again—forever and ever in the new heavens and earth.

Belief in the truth of the resurrection is impossible apart from God's Word and His power. Apart from God's Word, people *can never know the truth* about the spiritual world. They are bound by the physical and material world of which they are a part. They can only think and guess and hypothesize that a spiritual world exists and speculate on details such as a resurrection. People cannot, while living in this world, penetrate the spiritual world with their bodies to scientifically prove the existence of the spiritual world.

God alone could reveal the reality of the spiritual dimension and the fact of a resurrection yet to take place. And only the power of God can bring about a resurrection. No human being has the power to bring it about. If a resurrection is to take place, God's power will have to do it.

THOUGHT 4. Two things will keep a person from error.
1) Knowing the Scriptures
2) Trusting the power of God

12:25

²⁵ "For when they rise from the dead, they neither marry nor are given in marriage, but are like angels in heaven."

4 The resurrection is different from any earthly experience: It is of another world, another dimension.

The Sadducees did not know the Scriptures nor the power of God. Therefore, when they thought of the resurrection into another world, they saw life simply as continuing on as it does now. They pictured heaven as being a continuation of this world. Very simply, they could not conceive that God would change the qualities of life and give people a totally new environment in which to live. Jesus explained that life after the resurrection—life in heaven—is different from this life. It is of another dimension of being.

Jesus taught that future life and relationships will exceed earthly relationships, even the bond of marital relationships. That which bonds us together in eternity will be greater and stronger than that which bonds us together on earth. Future life and relationships will be like that experienced by the angels and God. What does this mean? (Note: Jesus had just affirmed the existence of angels, refuting the Sadducees' disbelief.)

First, heavenly life and relationships will be perfected. Our relationships as they are known on earth will cease to be in heaven. They will be changed in that they will be perfected; selfishness and sin will not affect our love and lives. Our love will be perfected; therefore, we will love everyone perfectly. People will not be loved as they were on this earth, imperfectly. They will be loved more, loved perfectly. Everyone will love everyone else perfectly. God will change all relationships into perfection, even as the relationships between angels and God are perfected.

Second, heavenly life and relationships will be eternal. There will be no ending of relationships. People who love each other will always have the other to love. One will not cease to be (die) before the other (as is the case now). They will never be separated again. Everyone will always have everyone else to love. God will change the brief time that we now have with each other into an eternal relationship. We will enjoy each other's presence eternally, even as the relationship between angels and God is enjoyed eternally.

THOUGHT 1. Two warnings must always be issued when thinking of heaven and eternal life.
1) A person can *materialize heaven* and *humanize eternal life*. That is, we can conceive heaven to be nothing more than a glorified world, and we can conceive eternal life to be nothing more than physical life, plus a little more. This was the mistake of the Sadducees, and it is often the concept pictured by liberal thinkers today when they hear about the resurrection.
2) A person can *idealize heaven* and *allegorize eternal life*. We can think of heaven as little more than an ideal land which we should seek and toward which we should direct our lives. And we can think of eternal life as little more than a dream, or we can think of it as floating around and being free of trouble and trials, or we can think of it as simply a place to which we go after our departure from this world.

We need to always keep the teaching of Scripture, of God's revelation, in mind when thinking of heaven and eternal life. Scripture teaches that the very nature of things will be changed.

Scripture says that heaven is a spiritual dimension, a real world of being. And Scripture declares that the heavens and earth that now are will one day be transformed into that spiritual dimension of being (2 Pe.3:3–13; Re.21:1, 5).

In addition, Scripture teaches that eternal life is life that will exist forever in the spiritual world and dimension of being. The Scripture says:

> So is it with the resurrection of the dead. What is sown is perishable; what is raised is imperishable. It is sown in dishonor; it is raised in glory. It is sown in weakness; it is raised in power. It is sown a natural body; it is raised a spiritual body. If there is a natural body, there is also a spiritual body. (1 Co.15:42–44; see 1 Th.5:13–18.)

> Just as we have borne the image of the man of dust, we shall also bear the image of the man of heaven. I tell you this, brothers: flesh and blood cannot inherit the kingdom of God, nor does the perishable inherit the imperishable. Behold! I tell you a mystery. We shall not all sleep, but we shall all be changed, in a moment, in the twinkling of an eye, at the last trumpet. For the trumpet will sound, and the dead will be raised imperishable, and we shall be changed. For this perishable body must put on the imperishable, and this mortal body must put on immortality. When the perishable puts on the imperishable, and the mortal puts on immortality, then shall come to pass the saying that is written: "Death is swallowed up in victory." (1 Co.15:49–54)

(See notes and DEEPER STUDY # 1—Mt.19:28; DEEPER STUDY # 1—Jn.17:2–3; DEEPER STUDY # 1—2 Ti.4:18. See DEEPER STUDY # 2—Jn.1:4 for discussion.)

5 The resurrection brings about a living relationship that cannot be broken.

12:26–27

The resurrection brings about a living relationship with God that cannot be broken. To prove this, Jesus referred back to the Pentateuch, which the Sadducees accepted as Scripture. Specifically, Jesus pointed the Sadducees back to Moses' encounter with God in the burning bush. There, God identifies Himself as "the God of Abraham, the God of Isaac, and the God of Jacob" (v.26; Ex.3:6). From this Scripture, Jesus makes two points.

26 "And as for the dead being raised, have you not read in the book of Moses, in the passage about the bush, how God spoke to him, saying, 'I am the God of Abraham, and the God of Isaac, and the God of Jacob'?

27 He is not God of the dead, but of the living. You are quite wrong."

a. God is the living God of past saints who are now living with Him (v.26).

God is the God of past saints, believers who have passed on. Jesus was saying that God's relationships are active relationships, not inactive. God says, "I *am* the God of. . . ." not, "I *was* the God of. . . ." His relationships with His people are continuous. They are maintained. God is eternal; therefore, He creates and maintains eternal, active relationships. God's people do enter into the spiritual realm of His presence and actively relate to Him. The Sadducees believed that death ends all; there is no life after death. But Jesus established that we do live on after we die (2 Co.5:7; 1 Th.4:14).

In addition, God's relationships are good and rewarding. The patriarchs of old were promised rewards, personal rewards (see He.11:13–16). There has to be a resurrection if our relationship with God is good and rewarding. To die and be left dead as a decaying corpse is not good or rewarding. Abraham, Isaac, and Jacob have a good and rewarding relationship with God. They are alive, more alive than they were while on earth, for they are perfected and eternal. They are with God Himself. And so shall we be. Again, we do live on after we die.

b. God is the God of the living (v.27a).

God is the God of the living, not of the dead. He is the God of Abraham, Isaac, and Jacob, not the God of decaying corpses. When Moses wrote these words, the three patriarchs had been dead for many years. If they were entirely dead—body, soul, and spirit—God was not their God. Since He was their God, they were alive, living in God's presence in relationship to Him, perfect and eternal. Their bodies may have been resting in their graves, but their spirits were alive in the presence of the Lord. Their spirits are still very much alive today! Humans are not just spirits; we are also bodies. And our bodies will be resurrected and reunited with our spirits when Jesus comes again (1 Co.15:12–58; 1 Th.4:13–18).

One simple fact clearly comes to the forefront in these points made by Christ: *since God is* ("I am"), God is not the God of the dead, but of the living.

> **Having a hope in God, which these men themselves accept, that there will be a resurrection of both the just and the unjust. (Ac.24:15)**

> **Why is it thought incredible by any of you that God raises the dead? (Ac.26:8)**

> **For none of us lives to himself, and none of us dies to himself. For if we live, we live to the Lord, and if we die, we die to the Lord. So then, whether we live or whether we die, we are the Lord's. For to this end Christ died and lived again, that he might be Lord both of the dead and of the living. (Ro.14:7–9)**

c. Any other belief is a great error (v.27b).

Jesus concluded by bluntly telling the Sadducees that their belief that there is no resurrection—no life after death—was a grievous, dangerous error. Jesus said that they were *quite wrong* or *greatly mistaken* (Gk. polu panasthe; pronounced *pa-nas'-they*). Jesus emphasized the severity of their error. To deny the resurrection—to say that death marks the end of a human's existence—is one of the most dangerous errors any person can make. (See note—Mt.22:31-32 for more detailed discussion and for Scriptures dealing with the resurrection.)

(Mt.22:34–40; Lu.10:25–37)

²⁸ And one of the scribes came up and heard them disputing with one another, and seeing that he answered them well, asked him, "Which commandment is the most important of all?"

²⁹ Jesus answered, "The most important is, 'Hear, O Israel: The Lord our God, the Lord is one.

³⁰ And you shall love the Lord your God with all your heart and with all your soul and with all your mind and with all your strength.'

³¹ The second is this: 'You shall love your neighbor as yourself.' There is no other commandment greater than these."

³² And the scribe said to him, "You are right, Teacher. You have truly said that he is one, and there is no other besides him.

³³ And to love him with all the heart and with all the understanding and with all the strength, and to love one's neighbor as oneself, is much more than all whole burnt offerings and sacrifices."

³⁴ And when Jesus saw that he answered wisely, he said to him, "You are not far from the kingdom of God." And after that no one dared to ask him any more questions.

1. **The setting: A teacher of the law approached Jesus**^{DS1}
   a. Observed Jesus' arguments
   b. Posed a test question: Which is the most important commandment?
2. **The greatest commandment**
   a. To first acknowledge the Lord our God as the one and only God^{DS2}
   b. To love the Lord our God wholeheartedly—with all our heart, soul, mind, and strength

   c. To love our neighbors as ourselves^{DS3,4}

3. **The scope of the greatest commandment**
   a. So great it causes honest and thinking people to agree
   b. So great it exceeds all offerings and sacrifices

   c. So great it almost assures salvation to those who truly understand it

Division VII

The Son of God's Last Jerusalem Ministry: Jesus' Warning and Conflict with Religionists, 11:1–12:44

I. The Question About the Greatest Commandment, 12:28–34

(Mt.22:34–40; Lu.10:25–37)

12:28–34
Introduction

Jesus had silenced His third group of challengers, the Sadducees. The Pharisees, the strict religionists of that day, heard about Jesus' conquering His challengers again. In their minds, His threat to their security remained. All three attempts to discredit Him had failed. They somehow felt they must discredit Christ before the people in order to break His hold on them. A very dangerous possibility existed: the people might follow through with their proclaiming Him to be the Messiah and rise up against the Roman authorities. The responsibility for such action, of course, would lie at their feet as Jewish leaders; and they would be replaced as the ruling body of the Sanhedrin, losing their position, authority, esteem, and wealth.

They met together to plan and plot against Jesus again (see Mt.22:34). This time they took a different approach. Earlier they had challenged Him as a body of questioners. Now they chose only one member from among their body to attack Jesus. He was their brightest and best hope of going face-to-face with Jesus, a Scribe who was most brilliant and versed in the law.

Jesus used the occasion to teach humanity the greatest *provision* and *duty* of human life: love. Love will provide for every need people have; therefore, to love is our greatest duty. This is, *The Question About the Greatest Commandment*, 12:28–34.

1. The setting: A teacher of the law approached Jesus (v.28).
2. The greatest commandment (vv.29–31).
3. The scope of the greatest commandment (vv.32–34).

12:28

²⁸ And one of the scribes came up and heard them disputing with one another, and seeing that he answered them well, asked him, "Which commandment is the most important of all?"

1 The setting: A teacher of the law approached Jesus.

The man who approached Jesus was a lawyer (Mt.22:35; see DEEPER STUDY # 1). Apparently, something about Jesus had struck a chord within this man. His heart had been touched and stirred rather deeply, for Jesus said that he was not far from the kingdom of God (v.34).

a. Observed Jesus' arguments.

Mark tells us that the man was present when Jesus had been debating the Sadducees (Mt.12:28). He was impressed with Jesus and acknowledged that Jesus had answered them well.

True, he was being put forward by the official body to challenge Jesus. But personally, there was something about Jesus when Jesus was answering the Sadducees—the spirit, the wisdom, the self-confidence, the authority—that had stirred the lawyer's heart to wonder and to want to learn more about Jesus.

b. Posed a test question: Which is the most important commandment?

Through the years, Jewish teachers had set up six hundred commandments. There were so many commandments that in day-to-day life no person could keep them all. So, the question was often discussed: Which commandments must be absolutely obeyed? Which ones are important and which ones are not? Can the failure to obey some be condoned or not? Which commandments are heavy, and which are light? If a person keeps the greatest of the precepts, can he be excused for his failure to keep the others (see Mt.19:16f)? This is the question the lawyer posed to Jesus.

Opinions as to the most important commandment differed. Various groups believed the greatest commandment to be different things such as circumcision, sacrifices, and the Sabbath. The Pharisees hoped that Jesus, by stating His opinion, would upset the people who held a position different from His and they would turn against Him. By saying that a particular commandment was the greatest, they hoped that people would feel He was lessening the weight of other very important commandments.

THOUGHT 1. The Jewish people were trying to find a way to excuse their inability to keep all of the law, instead of learning the lesson God intended from it. God wanted people to learn that they could not live up to His righteous demands. Therefore, they need a Savior (Ga.3:19–24). To break the law in one area is to be guilty of breaking it all (Js.2:10).

At the same time, Jesus taught that some laws were weightier or more important than others (Mt.23:23).

Woe to you, scribes and Pharisees, hypocrites! For you tithe mint and dill and cumin, and have neglected the weightier matters of the law: justice and mercy and faithfulness. These you ought to have done, without neglecting the others. (Mt.23:23)

Why then the law? It was added because of transgressions, until the offspring should come to whom the promise had been made, and it was put in place through angels by an intermediary. Now an intermediary implies more than one, but God is one. Is the law then contrary to the promises of God? Certainly not! For if a law had been given that could give life, then righteousness would indeed be by the law. But the Scripture imprisoned everything under sin, so that the promise by faith in Jesus Christ might be given to those who believe. Now before faith came, we were held captive under the law, imprisoned until the coming faith would be revealed. So then, the law was our guardian until Christ came, in order that we might be justified by faith. (Ga.3:19–24)

For whoever keeps the whole law but fails in one point has become guilty of all of it. (Js.2:10)

DEEPER STUDY # 1

(12:28) **Lawyer** (Gk. nomikos; see Mt.22:35): a profession of laymen who studied, taught, interpreted, and dealt with the practical questions of Jewish law. They were specialists within the profession, commonly called Scribes, who dealt with the study and interpretation of the law. They functioned both in the court and synagogues (see Lu.7:30; 10:25; 11:45, 46, 52; 14:3; Tit.3:13).

2 The greatest commandment.

12:29–31

What was the greatest commandment in the law? Jesus answered without hesitation or equivocation. He answered with all the authority of God Himself, and what He said was an eye-opener to people steeped in man-made religions.

a. To first acknowledge the Lord our God as the one and only God (v.29).

To answer the question, Jesus quoted from the Shema. *Shema* is the "transliteration of [the] Hebrew imperative meaning, 'Hear,' (De.6:4) and applied to 6:4–9 as the basic statement of the Jewish law. The Shema became for the

[29] Jesus answered, "The most important is, 'Hear, O Israel: The Lord our God, the Lord is one.

[30] And you shall love the Lord your God with all your heart and with all your soul and with all your mind and with all your strength.'

[31] The second is this: 'You shall love your neighbor as yourself.' There is no other commandment greater than these."

people of God a confession of faith by which they acknowledged the one true God and His commandments for them."[1]

The Shema begins with the statement, "The Lord our God, the Lord is one" (see note, *God, Nature*—Ro.3:29–30 for more discussion). Note the following analysis of this foundational statement of the truth about God:

- He is *the Lord*, Jehovah, Yahweh. There is no other. Monotheism (one God) is the true belief (see DEEPER STUDY # 2). Polytheism (many gods) is a false belief.
- He is *our God*. This is a personal relationship between a worshiper and God. It is a daily experience. We are related to Him; we are His people, the sheep of His pasture. Therefore, we should love, adore, and worship Him.
- He is *one Lord*. He is the focus and concentration of our life, attention, worship, love, and praise. He is the only Subject of our devotion. There is no reason, no excuse for distraction by any other subject. He is *the One Lord, the only Subject*.

Therefore, as to the eating of food offered to idols, we know that "an idol has no real existence," and that "there is no God but one." (1 Co.8:4)

One God and Father of all, who is over all and through all and in all. (Ep.4:6)

---

1 Trent C. Butler, ed., *Holman Bible Dictionary,* (Nashville: Holman Bible Publishers, 1991). Via Wordsearch digital edition.

> For there is one God, and there is one mediator between God and men, the man Christ Jesus. (1 Ti.2:5)
>
> Therefore you are great, O Lord God. For there is none like you, and there is no God besides you, according to all that we have heard with our ears. (2 S.7:22)
>
> For you are great and do wondrous things; you alone are God. (Ps.86:10)
>
> "You are my witnesses," declares the Lord, "and my servant whom I have chosen, that you may know and believe me and understand that I am he. Before me no god was formed, nor shall there be any after me. I, I am the Lord, and besides me there is no savior." (Is.43:10–11)
>
> For thus says the Lord, who created the heavens (he is God!), who formed the earth and made it (he established it; he did not create it empty, he formed it to be inhabited!): "I am the Lord, and there is no other." (Is.45:18)

b. **To love the lord our God wholeheartedly—with all our heart, soul, mind, and strength (v.30).** The Shema commands us to love the Lord our God. Love God as *your* very own God. This is a personal relationship, not a distant relationship. God is not impersonal, far out in space someplace, distant and removed. God is personal, ever so close, and we are to be personally involved with God on an intimate basis. The command is to *"love the Lord your God."* Loving God is alive and active, not dead and inactive. We are, therefore, to maintain a personal relationship with God that is alive and active.

Note that Jesus says to love God with all your being. Jesus breaks our being down into three parts: the heart, the soul, and the mind (see Deeper Studies 4, 5, 6—Mt.22:37 for discussion).

Note also that Jesus adds "with all your strength." Love is mankind's chief duty. Humans are responsible to maintain a loving relationship with God. Very practically, loving God involves the very same factors that loving a person involves (see outlines and notes—Ep.5:22-33).

First, a loving relationship involves commitment and loyalty. True love does not desire others. True love does not covet and does not care for a carnal definition that allows fleshly acts and sensual relationships with others.

To the contrary, true love is commitment and loyalty to one person. It is quite significant that the very first commandment God gives deals with commitment and loyalty: "You shall have no other gods" (Ex.20:3). God strikes at the very core of humanity's carnal behavior and tendency to define love in terms that allow people to satisfy their lust.

Second, a loving relationship involves trust and respect for the person loved. It is loving the person for who he or she is. We love God because of Himself, because He is who He is:
➢ He is the Creator and Sustainer of life; therefore we love Him.
➢ He is the Savior and Redeemer; therefore we love Him.
➢ He is the Lord and Owner of life; therefore we love Him.

Third, a loving relationship involves the *giving and surrendering* of oneself. The drive is to give oneself, to surrender oneself to the other, not to get from the other.

Fourth, a loving relationship involves *knowing and sharing*. The desire is to know and to share, to be learning, growing, working, and serving, ever so closely together.

THOUGHT 1. We are to love God supremely.

> May the Lord direct your hearts to the love of God and to the steadfastness of Christ. (2 Th.3:5)
>
> Keep yourselves in the love of God, waiting for the mercy of our Lord Jesus Christ that leads to eternal life. (Jude 21)
>
> And now, Israel, what does the Lord your God require of you, but to fear the Lord your God, to walk in all his ways, to love him, to serve the Lord your God with all your heart and with all your soul, (De.10:12)
>
> You shall therefore love the Lord your God and keep his charge, his statutes, his rules, and his commandments always. (De.11:1)
>
> Only be very careful to observe the commandment and the law that Moses the servant of the Lord commanded you, to love the Lord your God, and to walk in all his ways and to keep his commandments and to cling to him and to serve him with all your heart and with all your soul. (Jos.22:5)

Love the Lord, all you his saints! The Lord preserves the faithful but abundantly repays the one who acts in pride. (Ps.31:23)

12:28–34

c. **To love our neighbors as ourselves (v.31).**

The Lord our God commands that we love our neighbors as ourselves. Because of the length of this discussion, it is handled in a dedicated study (see DEEPER STUDIES 3, 4).

DEEPER STUDY # 2

(12:29) **God—Monotheism:** see De.6:4; (see note—Ro.3:29–30).

DEEPER STUDY # 3

(12:31) **Love—Brotherhood:** the Lord our God commands that we love our neighbors as ourselves. This is actually a second commandment. Jesus said so. The lawyer had not asked for it, but the first commandment is abstract; it cannot be seen or understood standing by itself. There has to be a *demonstration, an act, something done* for love to be seen and understood. A profession of love without demonstration is empty. It is only profession. Love is not known unless it is shown to others.

Several important things need to be said about love at this point.

1. Love is an active experience, not inactive and dormant. That is what Christ is pointing out in Mark 12. Love for God *acts.* Love acts by showing and demonstrating itself. It is inaccurate and foolish for a person to say, "I love God"; and then be inactive, dormant, doing nothing for God. If people truly love God, they will *do things* for God. Any person who loves does things for the one loved.

2. The primary thing God wants from us involves loving our neighbor, *not the doing of religious things.* Doing religious things is good; but it only deals with things such as rituals, observances, ordinances, or laws. Such things are lifeless, unfeeling, unresponsive. They are immaterial. They are not helped by our doing them. Only we are helped. Doing religious things makes us feel good and religious, which is beneficial to our growth, but religious things are not what demonstrate our love for God. Loving our neighbor is what proves our love for God. People may say they love God, but if they hate and act unkindly toward their neighbor, everyone knows their religion is only profession; it is not genuine.

> A new commandment I give to you, that you love one another: just as I have loved you, you also are to love one another. By this all people will know that you are my disciples, if you have love for one another. (Jn.13:34–35)

> If anyone says, "I love God," and hates his brother, he is a liar; for he who does not love his brother whom he has seen cannot love God whom he has not seen. And this commandment we have from him: whoever loves God must also love his brother. (1 Jn.4:20–21)

3. The great commandment to love God flows downward into another great commandment: to love our neighbor as ourselves. The fact is inescapable.

> But God shows his love for us in that while we were still sinners, Christ died for us. (Ro.5:8)

When people really see the love of God, they cannot help but love God and share the love of God with their neighbors. It is the love of Christ for us, His death and sacrifice, that compels us to go and love all people everywhere.

> For the love of Christ controls us, because we have concluded this: that one has died for all, therefore all have died; and he died for all, that those who live might no longer live for themselves but for him who for their sake died and was raised. (2 Co.5:14–15)

> We love because he first loved us. And this commandment we have from him: whoever loves God must also love his brother. (1 Jn.4:19, 21)

4. We are to love self.
   a. There is a corrupt love of self that feels the world should center around oneself. This self-love . . .
      • wants all attention centered around oneself
      • pushes self forward
      • insists on one's own way
      • demands and revels in recognition
      • shows conceit and ignores others
   b. However, there is a godly love for self that is natural and pleasing to God. It is a love that stirs a strong self-image, confidence and assurance, and even helps in preventing some physical ailments. The right love of self or the godly love of self comes from knowing three things:
      ➢ You are actually the creation of God: the highest creation possible.
      ➢ You are actually the object of God's love: the most supreme love possible.
      ➢ You are actually the steward of God's gifts: the greatest gifts possible.
   c. The godly love of self has three traits that are clearly seen.
      ➢ It esteems others better than itself. It does esteem self ever so highly as God's glorious creation, but it esteems others more highly.

      Do nothing from selfish ambition or conceit, but in humility count others more significant than yourselves. (Ph.2:3)

      ➢ It looks on the things of others. It does look on one's own things as a steward of God's gifts, but it also looks on the things of others.

      Let each of you look not only to his own interests, but also to the interests of others. (Ph.2:4)

      ➢ It walks humbly before others.

      The greatest among you shall be your servant. Whoever exalts himself will be humbled, and whoever humbles himself will be exalted. (Mt.23:11–12)

      Likewise, you who are younger, be subject to the elders. Clothe yourselves, all of you, with humility toward one another, for "God opposes the proud but gives grace to the humble." (1 Pe.5:5)

5. We are to love our neighbor as ourselves. Note three very specific things about this second great commandment.
   a. To love our neighbor is a command, not an option. If the commandment is not obeyed, God is displeased, and we stand guilty of having broken the law of God.
   b. To love our neighbor stirs the question: Who is our neighbor? Jesus answered the question Himself in the Parable of the Good Samaritan. A good neighbor is a person who shows mercy on any who need mercy, even if the needy person is socially despised (Lu.10:25-37, esp. 36-37). Everyone in the world needs mercy; therefore, our neighbor is everyone in the world, no matter regardless of status, condition, or circumstance. Every person is to be valued ever so highly and helped no matter who they are. No individual is to be injured or wronged. Every individual is always to be esteemed better than oneself (Ph.2:3).
   c. To love our neighbor is a very practical command. It involves some very practical acts that are spelled out in Scripture (see 1 Co.13:4-7).
      ➢ Love is patient (suffers long).
      ➢ Love is kind.
      ➢ Love does not envy (is not jealous).
      ➢ Love does not boast (parade itself).
      ➢ Love is not arrogant (puffed up).
      ➢ Love does not behave rudely.
      ➢ Love is not self-seeking, insisting on its own way.
      ➢ Love is not easily provoked, not irritable (not touchy, short-tempered).

➢ Love is not resentful, thinks no evil (harbors no evil or immoral thoughts, takes no account of a wrong done it).

➢ Love does not rejoice in wrongdoing or iniquity (not in wrong, sin, evil, injustice); but rejoices in the truth (what is right, just, righteous).

➢ Love bears all things.

➢ Love believes all things (exercises faith in everything; is ready to believe the best in everyone).

➢ Love hopes all things (keeps up hope in everything, under all circumstances).

➢ Love endures all things (keeps a person from weakening; gives the power to endure or persevere).

DEEPER STUDY # 4

(12:31) **Love—Brotherhood:** see Le.19:18.

3 The scope of the greatest commandment.

12:32–34

This commandment, the greatest of all according to Jesus, is unlimited in its scope. When people truly grasp it and accept it, it will have a powerful effect on them, potentially leading them to saving faith.

[32] And the scribe said to him, "You are right, Teacher. You have truly said that he is one, and there is no other besides him.

[33] And to love him with all the heart and with all the understanding and with all the strength, and to love one's neighbor as oneself, is much more than all whole burnt offerings and sacrifices."

[34] And when Jesus saw that he answered wisely, he said to him, "You are not far from the kingdom of God." And after that no one dared to ask him any more questions.

a. So great it caused honest and thinking people to agree (v.32).

Unlike the others who had tested Jesus, the lawyer agreed with Him. The commandment of love is so great that it causes thinking and honest people to agree. This lawyer was a thinking man, and he was open and honest. Imagine the bitter hatred of this man's peers against Jesus, yet he was open and honest enough to listen to Jesus and face the truth of what Jesus said. (How many are as open and honest today?)

b. So great it exceeds all offerings and sacrifices (v.33).

The man had been wrapped up in offerings and sacrifices all his life. His life as a Scribe was literally dedicated to and possessed by a religion that was steeped in offerings and sacrifices. But he willingly acknowledged the truth that the commandment of love is so great that it exceeds all offerings and sacrifices.

The lawyer's making this statement shows that he had come a long way in his understanding of truth. He was beginning to see that life and religion were not ritual and ceremony and rules and regulations. Life is love—loving God with all of your being and loving your neighbor as yourself.

c. So great it almost assures salvation to those who truly understand it (v.34).

Jesus made an encouraging statement to the man, telling him that he was not far from the kingdom of God—not far from being born again. The commandment of love is so great that it almost assures salvation to those who understand it. When a person acknowledges the truth about God and accepts His great commandment, that person is close to being saved. Upon believing this foundational truth about God and our responsibility to Him, God will give a person more light, more insight to His truth, leading that person ultimately to repentance and saving faith.

THOUGHT 1. How many people really think and are at the same time open and honest? Some do think through the deeper issues of life, but there are fewer who are open and honest.

THOUGHT 2. How many are not "far from the kingdom of God?" Some are not far away, but note: they are still away. They are not in the kingdom. It is not enough to just believe in God and His commandments. A person must repent—turn from sin and self to God—and believe on Jesus Christ, accepting His substitutionary death as payment for their sin.

> And they said, "Believe in the Lord Jesus, and you will be saved, you and your household." (Ac.16:31)

> But what does it say? "The word is near you, in your mouth and in your heart" (that is, the word of faith that we proclaim); because, if you confess with your mouth that Jesus is Lord and believe in your heart that God raised him from the dead, you will be saved. For with the heart one believes and is justified, and with the mouth one confesses and is saved. (Ro.10:8–10)

> For there is one God, and there is one mediator between God and men, the man Christ Jesus, who gave himself as a ransom for all, which is the testimony given at the proper time. (1 Ti.2:5–6)

> You believe that God is one; you do well. Even the demons believe—and shudder! (Js.2:19)

(Mt.22:41-46; Lu.20:39-44)

³⁵ And as Jesus taught in the temple, he said, "How can the scribes say that the Christ is the son of David?"

³⁶ "David himself, in the Holy Spirit, declared, 'The Lord said to my Lord, "Sit at my right hand, until I put your enemies under your feet."'

³⁷ David himself calls him Lord. So how is he his son?" And the great throng heard him gladly.

1. **Jesus questioned people about the Messiah**
2. **The mistaken concept about the Messiah: He is David's son—a mere man**
3. **The accurate concept about the Messiah: He is the Lord of David—God Himself** [DS1]
4. **The crowds listened to Jesus with amazement and delight**

Division VII

The Son of God's Last Jerusalem Ministry: Jesus' Warning and Conflict with Religionists, 11:1-12:44

J. The Puzzling Concept of the Messiah, 12:35-37

(Mt.22:41-46; Lu.20:39-44)

12:35-37
Introduction

It was still Tuesday of the Lord's last week on earth. He had just been challenged four different times by four different opponents. He had met each group, each questioner head-on by turning the questions around to teach much needed truths (see Mt.21:23f; 22:15f; 22:23f; 22:34f). In each case, Jesus had silenced those who opposed His claim to be the Messiah.

Now it was His turn to question His opponents. But note that Jesus did not stand against them as an opponent. He questioned them as men who were in error and needed to see the truth. He was giving them an opportunity to receive the truth of His Messiahship and accept Him as the Son of God. The spirit of His questioning is seen in the brief discussion He had with them. The question He asked of them is the all-important question which He asks of every individual: "What do you think about the Christ, the Messiah?" (Mt.22:42). This is, *The Puzzling Concept of the Messiah*, 12:35-37.

1. Jesus questioned people about the Messiah (v.35).
2. The mistaken concept about the Messiah: He is David's son—a mere man (v.35).
3. The accurate concept about the Messiah: He is the Lord of David—God Himself (vv.36-37).
4. The crowds listened to Jesus with amazement and delight (v.37).

1 Jesus questioned people about the Messiah.

12:35

When Jesus questions people, it is for important reasons. These reasons are clearly seen in His dealing with these men.

First, Jesus is long-suffering and tender. These men had challenged Jesus time and again, trying to discredit and embarrass Him before the crowd. Yet He never reacted once.

³⁵ And as Jesus taught in the temple, he said, "How can the scribes say that the Christ is the son of David?"

He answered their questions honestly, opening up new truths which they desperately needed to know. He questioned them because He was patient and long-suffering. He wanted to open up further truths to them. He longed for them to see and know and surrender to His Messiahship.

Second, Jesus continues to question in order to reach out to people over and over. In the case of these men, Jesus was making a last-ditch effort, a last appeal to them. They had rejected and rejected Him until there was little hope. But Jesus was still hoping, still reaching out to them. He questioned in order to lead them to see that He is the Messiah, the Lord, the Son of God Himself.

While considering the Lord's questioning, another fact—a critical one—needs to be considered: there is an end to His questioning, a time when there is no hope and no chance that a person will repent and believe. There is a time when He begins to pronounce judgment. Jesus offered one last question. Once it was answered, He began to pronounce judgment. Jesus discussed and questioned repeatedly, but after these men had rejected so many times, they became steeped in their unbelief. Therefore, Jesus ceased the discussion and pronounced judgment on them (see Mt.23:1-39).

12:35

35 And as Jesus taught in the temple, he said, "How can the scribes say that the Christ is the son of David?"

2 The mistaken concept about the Messiah: He is David's son—a mere man.

What puzzled people about the Messiah was that He was David's son. This fact led the people to mistakenly believe that He was *a mere man*. The most important question that can be asked of any person is, who do you believe Jesus is? Matthew says that Jesus had first asked the Scribes, "What do you think about the Christ [Messiah]? Whose Son is He?" (Mt.22:42). Their response was that the Messiah is the "Son of David," not the "Son of God." Note four important observations.

First, the Greek uses the definite article "*the* Christ" or Messiah (ho Christos). Jesus was trying to stir them to think about the Messiah. He did not ask these men what they thought of Him, but what they thought about *the Messiah*.

Second, Jesus asked a specific question about the Messiah: "Whose Son is He?" Think about the Messiah. What is His origin? Who gave birth to Him? In practical day-to-day living, Jesus was asking three things:

- Where does your deliverance come from? The Messiah is to deliver humanity from all the evil and enslavements of the world. Where will such a Person come from?
- Where does your Lord come from—the Person you are to follow? The Messiah is to be the Lord who is to rule and reign and govern all lives, executing perfect justice and care.
- Where does your concept of a perfect society come from—the Person who is to bring about the perfect world and all that is good and beneficial? Where does the Person come from who is to bring the kingdom of God to earth?

Third, the common title for the Messiah was "the Son of David." Old Testament passages definitely state the Messiah was to come from the line of David. It was from such passages as these that the Messiah was known as "the Son of David" (see note, *Jesus Christ, Son of David*—Lu.3:24-31; DEEPER STUDY # 3—Jn.1:45 for verses and fulfillment).

Once for all I have sworn by my holiness; I will not lie to David. His offspring shall endure forever, his throne as long as the sun before me. (Ps.89:35-36)

For to us a child is born, to us a son is given; and the government shall be upon his shoulder, and his name shall be called Wonderful Counselor, Mighty God, Everlasting Father, Prince of Peace. Of the increase of his government and of peace there will be no end, on the throne of David and over his kingdom, to establish it and to uphold it with justice and with righteousness from this time forth and forevermore. The zeal of the LORD of hosts will do this. (Is.9:6-7)

There shall come forth a shoot from the stump of Jesse, and a branch from his roots shall bear fruit. And the Spirit of the LORD shall rest upon him, the Spirit of wisdom and understanding, the Spirit of counsel and might, the Spirit of knowledge and the fear of the LORD. And his delight shall be in the fear of the LORD. He shall not judge by what his eyes see, or decide disputes by what his ears hear, but with righteousness he shall judge the poor, and decide with equity for the meek of the earth; and he shall strike the earth with the rod of his mouth, and with the breath of his lips he shall kill the wicked. Righteousness shall be the belt of his waist, and faithfulness the belt of his loins. (Is.11:1-5)

The Messiah was to do four specific things. (See notes—Mt.1:1; Deeper Study # 2—1:18; Deeper Study # 3—3:11; notes—11:1-6; 11:2-3; Deeper Study # 1—11:5; Deeper Study # 2—11:6; Deeper Study # 1—12:16; notes—Lu.7:21-23. These notes are important for the full concept of the Messiah.)

- He was to free Israel from all enslavement. Enslavement was to be abolished, and all people were to be set free under God's domain.
- He was to give victory over all enemies. Israel was to be established as the seat of His rule. This, of course, meant Israel was to be the leading nation of the world.
- He was to bring peace to earth. All were to serve God under the government established by the Messiah.
- He was to provide plenty for all. The Messiah was to see that all people had the benefits of God's rule and care.

Fourth, the common idea of the Messiah's origin was that He was to be human, born of a man. The idea that He might be of divine origin, of God Himself was simply unacceptable to the religious leaders.

3 The accurate concept about the Messiah: He is the Lord of David—God Himself.

12:36-37a

Quoting Psalm 110:1, Jesus pointed out the claim of Scripture: the Messiah is Lord, the Lord of David (v.36; see Deeper Study # 1). Scripture does not only say that the Messiah is the Son of David, it also says that He is the *Lord* of David. This verse is strong in its statement. Four facts are clear and definite.

First, David called the Messiah "Lord" *in* or *by the Holy Spirit*. That is, David's words were written under the inspiration of the Holy Spirit. God was supernaturally directing Him (see 1 Co.12:3; 2 Ti.3:16; and 2 Pe.1:21).

In addition, David said, "The Lord [Jehovah God] said to *my* Lord [the Messiah]." David unquestionably called the Messiah, "*My Lord.*"

A third fact is, David said that *my* Lord sits on God's "right hand." The Messiah is *Lord*, for He is *exalted* by God.

> That he worked in Christ when he raised him from the dead and seated him at his right hand in the heavenly places. (Ep.1:20)

> Therefore God has highly exalted him and bestowed on him the name that is above every name. (Ph.2:9)

> Now the point in what we are saying is this: we have such a high priest, one who is seated at the right hand of the throne of the Majesty in heaven. (He.8:1)

Then, David said that *my* Lord's enemies will be put under His feet. The Messiah is Lord, for all His enemies are to be subjected under Him.

> So that at the name of Jesus every knee should bow, in heaven and on earth and under the earth, and every tongue confess that Jesus Christ is Lord, to the glory of God the Father. (Ph.2:10-11)

After quoting Scripture, Jesus asked the key question, the question that should have moved His opponents to recognize that He was the Messiah: How can the Messiah be both David's Lord and Son (v.37)?

In this question, Jesus is saying that to think of the Messiah only in human terms was inadequate—totally inadequate. It is not enough to think in terms of earthly power, of national, political, military, and institutional leaders. There is no way a *mere man* can bring faultless deliverance, leadership, and a perfect society to this earth. The Messiah is not merely a man; He is the Lord from heaven.

In addition, Jesus is claiming to be the Son of God Himself. A person's concept of the Messiah—the Deliverer and King—has to go beyond the mere human and physical. A person's understanding has to stretch upward into God's very own heart. God loves this earth; therefore, God sent His Son to earth, sacrificing Him in order to save it.

36 "David himself, in the Holy Spirit, declared, 'The Lord said to my Lord, "Sit at my right hand, until I put your enemies under your feet."'
37 David himself calls him Lord. So how is he his son?" And the great throng heard him gladly.

Simon Peter replied, "You are the Christ, the Son of the living God." (Mt.16:16)

For God so loved the world, that he gave his only Son, that whoever believes in him should not perish but have eternal life. (Jn.3:16)

The woman said to him, "I know that Messiah is coming (he who is called Christ). When he comes, he will tell us all things." Jesus said to her, "I who speak to you am he." (Jn.4:25-26)

So Jesus said to the twelve, "Do you want to go away as well?" Simon Peter answered him, "Lord, to whom shall we go? You have the words of eternal life, and we have believed, and have come to know, that you are the Holy One of God." (Jn.6:67-69)

I told you that you would die in your sins, for unless you believe that I am he you will die in your sins. (Jn.8:24)

Jesus said to her, "I am the resurrection and the life. Whoever believes in me, though he die, yet shall he live, and everyone who lives and believes in me shall never die. Do you believe this?" She said to him, "Yes, Lord; I believe that you are the Christ, the Son of God, who is coming into the world." (Jn.11:25-27)

But Saul increased all the more in strength, and confounded the Jews who lived in Damascus by proving that Jesus was the Christ. (Ac.9:22)

And Paul went in, as was his custom, and on three Sabbath days he reasoned with them from the Scriptures, explaining and proving that it was necessary for the Christ to suffer and to rise from the dead, and saying, "This Jesus, whom I proclaim to you, is the Christ." (Ac.17:2-3)

Everyone who believes that Jesus is the Christ has been born of God, and everyone who loves the Father loves whoever has been born of him. (1 Jn.5:1)

THOUGHT 1. Note a tragedy: the religionists missed the truth of the Messiah because . . .
- they misread the Scripture, not letting the Scripture speak for itself
- they did not pay close enough attention to the exact words of the Scripture (note how Christ takes a simple statement and shows how its exact words predicted the Messiah)
- they studied their teachers and authorities more than the Scripture itself
- they were dogmatic about their own ideas and notions about the future and how events would actually take place; prophecies concerning the coming of the Messiah were made a matter of fellowship

---

DEEPER STUDY # 1

(12:36) **Prophecy, of Messiah:** see Ps.110:1. The Pharisees recognized these Scriptures as being Messianic.

12:37b

[37] "David himself calls him Lord. So how is he his son?" And the great throng heard him gladly.

4 The crowds listened to Jesus with amazement and delight.

The crowds, that is, the common people, listened to Jesus with delight. Just as before, they were amazed and stricken with awe at such profoundness of character and ability. Jesus was such an able teacher, and He was equally able in refuting those who were His avowed enemies.

THOUGHT 1. The people heard Jesus gladly. Why? Because of the debating? Argument and dissension attract interest in a worldly and fleshly sense. Many enjoy seeing a heated argument and fight, especially when an underdog is getting the upper hand. Yet, there is no mention of the people's trusting Christ and becoming His followers. Some may have, but there is no mention of the fact. Again, it is not just enough to believe the facts about Jesus, to believe that He was a great speaker and teacher, or to be impressed or even astonished by Him. In order to be saved, we must believe on Him as our personal Savior and Lord.

K. The Warning to the Crowds and Religionists: Some Things to Guard Against, 12:38-40

(Mt.23:5-6, 14; Lu.20:45-47)

³⁸ And in his teaching he said, "Beware of the scribes, who like to walk around in long robes and like greetings in the marketplaces"

³⁹ "and have the best seats in the synagogues and the places of honor at feasts,"

⁴⁰ "who devour widows' houses and for a pretense make long prayers. They will receive the greater condemnation."

1. **Dressing differently: To draw attention to self**
2. **Coveting special greetings and titles: To exalt self**
3. **Sitting in the front seats and high places: To be seen, admired, and honored**

4. **Devouring widows: To steal their estates for personal gain**
5. **Praying long prayers: To show piety**

Division VII

The Son of God's Last Jerusalem Ministry: Jesus' Warning and Conflict with Religionists, 11:1–12:44

K. The Warning to the Crowds and Religionists: Some Things to Guard Against, 12:38–40

(Mt.23:5-6, 14; Lu.20:45-47)

12:38–40
Introduction

People are not always what they present themselves to be. Sadly, this is true of some religious leaders. There have always been, and always will be, those who use their spiritual office for personal purposes. Paul warned of those who use the ministry for "dishonest [shameful] gain" (Tit.1:11).

In this passage, Jesus called out and condemned the Scribes for their pride and greed. He listed some specific practices through which they fed their egos and lined their pockets. Why did He do this? Because God's people need to be warned. Not all ministers and religious leaders can be trusted. Some are not what they present themselves to be. Some are not worthy of the office they hold and the trust that has been committed to them.

The five sinful practices Jesus mentions here all have to do with pride or flaunting oneself, either by elevating oneself above others or by exploiting others. We need to not only beware of religious leaders who follow in the Scribes' and Pharisees' footsteps, but we also need to guard against these sins in our own lives. This is, *The Warning to the Crowds and Religionists: Some Things to Guard Against*, 12:38-40.

1. Dressing differently: To draw attention to self (v.38).
2. Coveting special greetings and titles: To exalt self (v.38).
3. Sitting in the front seats and high places: To be seen, admired, and honored (v.39).
4. Devouring widows: To steal their estates for personal gain (v.40).
5. Praying long prayers: To show piety (v.40).

1 Dressing differently: To draw attention to self.

The Scribes' prideful, insincere hearts were seen in the way they dressed. They dressed in a way that drew attention to themselves. As Jesus warned the people about their hypocritical leaders, He also warned that we need to guard against dressing to draw attention. Consider three ways a person can dress to draw attention.

38 And in his teaching he said, "Beware of the scribes, who like to walk around in long robes and like greetings in the marketplaces"

First, a person can desire and love to wear the clothing of the extravagant and wasteful. Jesus condemned the Scribes for wearing long robes. This was the dress of the nobility, the rich, the well-known. It was a long robe reaching to the ground. A man was unable to work in it; therefore, it was the sign of *higher society* or of a man of leisure. Jesus was not speaking against fine clothing. What He said in a nutshell was, "Beware of those who *love* to walk around in fine clothing." He condemned the person whose mind is on attracting attention, on self, on impressing others through their appearance. Our minds are not to be focused on vain, prideful things, but on things of a much higher nature:

> Finally, brothers, whatever is true, whatever is honorable, whatever is just, whatever is pure, whatever is lovely, whatever is commendable, if there is any excellence, if there is anything worthy of praise, think about these things. (Ph.4:8)

> If then you have been raised with Christ, seek the things that are above, where Christ is, seated at the right hand of God. Set your minds on things that are above, not on things that are on earth. (Col.3:1-2)

Our lives are not defined by the things we have, but by the service we render to others (Mt.23:11; Lu.12:15). The world is desperate, swamped with enormous needs. God's will is for people to be focused on meeting the needs of the world and not on vainly impressing others. This is especially God's desire for the Christian. The Christian's concern is to be righteousness. We are to work for Christ and His kingdom, not vain pursuits such as expensive, extravagant clothing.

> Let the thief no longer steal, but rather let him labor, doing honest work with his own hands, so that he may have something to share with anyone in need. (Ep.4:28)

Second, people can change their dress, their clothing, and their appearance *in order to attract attention*. People often desire attention, so they seek to attract it by being different and making themselves stand out. This was a sin of the religionists in Christ's day. They wanted to draw attention to their "spirituality." They wanted to stand out from the common people. Therefore, they vainly flaunted their religious devotion by the way they dressed.

The Scribes and Pharisees wore little leather-type boxes which contained a piece of parchment with four passages of Scripture written on it. The Scriptures were Exodus 13:1-10; 13:11-16; Deuteronomy 6:4-9 and 11:13-21. These boxes were called phylacteries.

The use of the phylacteries apparently arose from an extremely literal translation of Exodus 13:9 and Proverbs 7:3. The true meaning of these two passages seems to be that we are to have the Word of God in our minds just as clearly as if we had it before our eyes. The great fault of the religionists was that they not only interpreted the passages literally and wore little leather boxes on their forehead, but they enlarged the little leather boxes to draw attention to themselves as being religious.

The Jewish religious leaders also enlarged the borders of their garments; that is, they wore outside tassels. God had instructed the Jews to make fringes or tassels on the borders of their outer robes. When people noticed them, they were to be reminded to keep God's commandments. Again, the error was that the religionist changed his appearance from others; he enlarged the tassels, drawing attention to his being more religious than others.

Third, a person can wear clothes that expose the body, that actually attract attention to certain parts of the body. A person can wear clothes that are too tight, too low cut, too high cut, too thin. A person can wear too little clothing, clothing that fails to cover enough of the body.

Jesus very simply was saying to beware of dressing to attract attention. The religionists did it to appear righteous. Others do it to appear worldly (appealing).

Do not present your members to sin as instruments for unrighteousness, but present yourselves to God as those who have been brought from death to life, and your members to God as instruments for righteousness. (Ro.6:13)

Likewise also that women should adorn themselves in respectable apparel, with modesty and self-control, not with braided hair and gold or pearls or costly attire, but with what is proper for women who profess godliness—with good works. (1 Ti.2:9-10)

Do not let your adorning be external—the braiding of hair and the putting on of gold jewelry, or the clothing you wear—but let your adorning be the hidden person of the heart with the imperishable beauty of a gentle and quiet spirit, which in God's sight is very precious. For this is how the holy women who hoped in God used to adorn themselves, by submitting to their own husbands. (1 Pe.3:3-5)

2 Coveting special greetings and titles: To exalt self.

The religionists loved to be greeted with *titles* that exalted them with honor. The title they loved most was "rabbi," meaning teacher or master (Mt.23:7). It was only a simple title, yet some loved and reveled in the recognition it gave them above others. It took a man who was supposed to be God's messenger and said, "Here I am; look at me." It honored the man and not the Lord.

[38] And in his teaching he said, "Beware of the scribes, who like to walk around in long robes and like greetings in the marketplaces"

The religious leaders especially loved to be called by these titles in the marketplaces. The marketplaces were wherever the people were, the public places where people were seen by others—the streets, the offices, the schools, the stores, the restaurants, and so on. We are not to attempt to vainly attract attention or elevate ourselves above others in public.

THOUGHT 1. People exalt themselves with titles: reverend, doctor, director, executive, chairman—all to elevate self above others. Think of those who demand to be called by a title, even going as far to correct others when they do not refer to them by it.

Some ministers covet the tile "doctor" so strongly that, instead of earning it, they scheme and manipulate to have an "honorary doctorate" bestowed on them. Knowing the vain nature of such ministers, unethical institutions and colleges use honorary doctorates as a means of gaining support.

While a title itself is not wrong, using it vainly and pridefully is. We need to guard against letting titles that we have earned or that have been bestowed on us become a source of pride.

Whoever exalts himself will be humbled, and whoever humbles himself will be exalted. (Mt.23:12)

For when he dies he will carry nothing away; his glory will not go down after him. (Ps.49:17)

Though you soar aloft like the eagle, though your nest is set among the stars, from there I will bring you down, declares the LORD. (Ob.4)

THOUGHT 2. What Christ is after is love—love among all men and women, boys and girls. And the only way love will ever rule on the earth is for all to begin serving and *lifting up others* instead of self. Dressing and using titles to draw attention to oneself do not lead one to love others. Such practices tend to elevate self and to destroy the moral fabric and stability of both family and community.

For "All flesh is like grass and all its glory like the flower of grass. The grass withers, and the flower falls." (1 Pe.1:24)

3 Sitting in the front seats and high places: To be seen, admired, and honored.

In the synagogue, the religious leaders and other distinguished people sat on a bench in front of the chest (where the Scripture was kept), and they sat facing the congregation. No leader could be missed.

12:39

³⁹ "and have the best seats in the synagogues and the places of honor at feasts,"

On social occasions the most honored sat at the right hand of the host, then the next most honored at his left hand, and so on, alternating from the right to the left down the table. Position and recognition were set. The Scribes and Pharisees loved, and often demanded, to be seated in these special places.

We need to guard against loving positions of honor, special seats, and places of recognition. Think of those today who love the restricted neighborhoods and clubs, the preferred lists. They love the preeminence (3 Jn.9). Note that Jesus does not condemn being in these positions and places, but the *loving* of them and the lengths to which people go to attain such status. Someone has to hold the upper positions and fill the major places. It is the *love* of such, the seeking of elevated status and the feeling of pride that goes with it that is wrong.

> **How can you believe, when you receive glory from one another and do not seek the glory that comes from the only God? (Jn.5:44)**
>
> **Man in his pomp will not remain; he is like the beasts that perish. (Ps.49:12)**

12:40

⁴⁰ "who devour widows' houses and for a pretense make long prayers. They will receive the greater condemnation."

4 Devouring widows: To steal their estates for personal gain.

Not only did Jesus condemn the Scribes for their prideful vanity, but He also condemned them for their greed. Specifically, He said that they "devour[ed] widows' houses." This is a "vivid figure of speech for exploiting the generosity of people of limited means, especially widows. They unethically appropriated people's property."¹

Of course, others were guilty of exploiting the weak and helpless as well, but the ones who stood before Jesus were lawyers. They used their legal position to manage the wills and other legal business for widows, and they cheated, devouring the widows by skimming too much out of their estates.

They were also religious leaders, professing to be men of God. Some used the guise of religion to fleece the people whom they served.

THOUGHT 1. Some today—lawyers, financial managers, preachers, and other Christian leaders, institutional and civic—court the attention and favor of people, especially widows, for the purpose of securing money. They seek large donations, endowments, trusts, investments, and gifts *to promote themselves* and line their own pockets. Many preachers twist Scripture to manipulate people to give. And the great tragedy is, many such false and hypocritical hearts use the guise of religion or charity to promote themselves and their false ideas. Their call to people is to institutional religion, not to the honor of God and the spirit of self-denial. Vain people, of course, are susceptible to such appeals, but widows in particular are exposed to those who seem to be so devoted to God or to a worthy cause.

Religious leaders who dishonestly exploit their followers are going to be judged severely by the Lord. Some sins are more horrible than others. Using religion for selfish ends is one of them. Something should be noted here. Widows hold a special place in God's heart. He has always instructed His people to care for them in a very special way.

---

1 John Walvoord and Roy B. Zuck, eds., *The Bible Knowledge Commentary New Testament: An Exposition of the Scriptures by Dallas Seminary Faculty,* (Wheaton, IL: Victor Books). Via Wordsearch digital edition.

If then you have been raised with Christ, seek the things that are above, where Christ is, seated at the right hand of God. Set your minds on things that are above, not on things that are on earth. (Col.3:1–2)

Religion that is pure and undefiled before God the Father is this: to visit orphans and widows in their affliction, and to keep oneself unstained from the world. (Js.1:27)

He executes justice for the fatherless and the widow, and loves the sojourner, giving him food and clothing. (De.10:18)

'Cursed be anyone who perverts the justice due to the sojourner, the fatherless, and the widow.' And all the people shall say, 'Amen.' (De.27:19)

Father of the fatherless and protector of widows is God in his holy habitation. (Ps.68:5)

Learn to do good; seek justice, correct oppression; bring justice to the fatherless, plead the widow's cause. (Is.1:17)

5 Praying long prayers: To show piety.

Finally, Jesus condemned the Scribes' and Pharisees' practice of praying long, pretentious prayers. They prayed publicly to impress others, not to worship and beseech God. Of all their vain and prideful sins, this was surely the most deplorable. Jesus seems to have saved the religious leaders' worst sins—exploiting others and exploiting prayer—for last.

40 "who devour widows' houses and for a pretense make long prayers. They will receive the greater condemnation."

We need to guard against the *danger of praying publicly for attention and to impress others.* The problem in Jesus' day dealt with *long public prayers*; however, in our day short public prayers are just as big a problem. People too often pray publicly . . .

- to sound good
- to demonstrate their speaking ability
- to show their devotion to God
- to simply impress people—make people think they are spiritual

Again, some use long prayers while others use short prayers to show their piety.

We need to also guard against *the danger of boasting of our private prayer life with others.* Some are prone to boast of spending a long time in prayer (all night or hours) or of their consistency in daily prayer. Sharing such personal prayer matters, even with one's closest friends, can cause a *surge* of spiritual pride, of *super-spirituality*, of being a little bit better than another Christian brother or sister. We must not make our prayer lives a cause for boasting, a source of pride.

And when you pray, do not heap up empty phrases as the Gentiles do, for they think that they will be heard for their many words. Do not be like them, for your Father knows what you need before you ask him. Pray then like this: "Our Father in heaven, hallowed be your name. Your kingdom come, your will be done, on earth as it is in heaven. Give us this day our daily bread, and forgive us our debts, as we also have forgiven our debtors. And lead us not into temptation, but deliver us from evil." (Mt.6:7–13)

After naming and condemning the Scribes' prideful and greedy practices, Jesus made a statement that should strike the heart of every minister: religious leaders—preachers, pastors, bishops, elders, missionaries, evangelists, and all others—are going to receive the greater condemnation. They will be judged more severely because of the trust that has been extended to them both from God and from the people they serve. And those who violate that trust, who exploit the ministry and serve for personal vanity and gain, will especially be judged harshly by God.

But the one who did not know, and did what deserved a beating, will receive a light beating. Everyone to whom much was given, of him much will be required, and from him to whom they entrusted much, they will demand the more. (Lu.12:48)

Keep a close watch on yourself and on the teaching. Persist in this, for by so doing you will save both yourself and your hearers. (1 Ti.4:16)

Obey your leaders and submit to them, for they are keeping watch over your souls, as those who will have to give an account. Let them do this with joy and not with groaning, for that would be of no advantage to you. (He.13:17)

Not many of you should become teachers, my brothers, for you know that we who teach will be judged with greater strictness. (Js.3:1)

L. The Widow's Offerings:
Real Giving, 12:41–44

(Lu.21:1–4)

1. **Real giving is demonstrated: Jesus observed various people giving at the temple**
   a. Saw the wealthy give much
   b. Saw a poor widow give little
2. **Real giving is sacrificial giving**
 	
3. **Real giving is measured by how much a person keeps back—not by how much a person gives**
 	
4. **Real giving is giving in spite of need**
5. **Real giving is giving all to the Lord**
	⁴¹ And he sat down opposite the treasury and watched the people putting money into the offering box. Many rich people put in large sums. ⁴² And a poor widow came and put in two small copper coins, which make a penny. ⁴³ And he called his disciples to him and said to them, "Truly, I say to you, this poor widow has put in more than all those who are contributing to the offering box." ⁴⁴ "For they all contributed out of their abundance, but she out of her poverty has put in everything she had, all she had to live on."

Division VII

The Son of God's Last Jerusalem Ministry:
Jesus' Warning and Conflict with Religionists, 11:1–12:44

L. The Widow's Offerings: Real Giving, 12:41–44

(Lu.21:1–4)

12:41–44
Introduction

This passage presents one of the most touching—and most ignored—stories in all of Scripture. It is a story that shows how God's heart reaches out in tenderness and compassion and love to those in need. It is a story that shows how much devotion and commitment and boldness mean to Him. In addition, it is a story that shows how deeply God is moved by those who give all they are and have to Him (contrast the Rich Young Ruler, Mk.10:17–22). But, perhaps most of all, it is a story that shows what real giving is. This is, *The Widow's Offerings: Real Giving*, 12:41-44.

1. Real giving is demonstrated: Jesus observed various people giving at the temple (vv.41–42).
2. Real giving is sacrificial giving (v.42).
3. Real giving is measured by how much a person keeps back—not by how much a person gives (v.43).
4. Real giving is giving in spite of need (v.44).
5. Real giving is giving all to the Lord (v.44).

1 Real giving is demonstrated: Jesus observed various people giving at the temple.

Following all the plotting and arguing in the Court of the Gentiles (Mk.11:27-12:40), Jesus walked into the Court of the Women, over by the treasury. The treasury was an area in which there were thirteen trumpet shaped collection boxes where the worshipers dropped their offerings. The Lord sat down, apparently all alone, to get some relief and rest from the tension of the past hours. While resting, He watched the people dropping their offerings into the collection boxes (v.41a). *Watched* or *saw* (Gk. etheorei; pronounced *eh-theh-oh-reh'-eye*) means He was deliberately observing, discerning the motives of the people as they made their offerings.

⁴¹ And he sat down opposite the treasury and watched the people putting money into the offering box. Many rich people put in large sums.
⁴² And a poor widow came and put in two small copper coins, which make a penny.

a. **Saw the wealthy give much (v.41b).**
   Jesus saw many walk by and drop in sizeable offerings. Some were apparently quite large contributions. He could see the handfuls of coins and hear them clang against the sides as they slid down the funnel shaped trumpets. But none attracted His admiration.

b. **Saw a poor widow give little (v.42a).**
   Finally, a poor widow came along and threw in two *lepta* or mites, which were the smallest of coins, coins of very little value. Touched by what He saw, Jesus used the widow and her humble gift to teach His disciples what true giving really is.

2 Real giving is sacrificial giving.

Jesus accurately described this most generous giver as a "poor widow." *Poor* (ptoche, pronounced *pto-kay*) means pauper. She was not just poor, she was destitute, in deep poverty. Her poor dress and plain appearance showed her desperate plight. The coins were all she had, yet she gave them despite her own desperate need.

⁴² And a poor widow came and put in two small copper coins, which make a penny.

Unquestionably, what this poor widow gave was a *sacrifice*. What most of the others gave was not a sacrifice. It did not cost them nor hurt them. They still had plenty left, for they gave only what they could spare. But not the widow. Her gift cost her. It hurt to give, for she gave what she could not spare. She gave a *sacrificial gift*. She went without a meal or gave up something else so that she could give.

> **THOUGHT 1.** There is a great difference between giving what one can spare and giving sacrificially, actually giving up something in order to give. Sacrificial giving costs something. Sacrificial giving is giving when it hurts, when a person has nothing left, nothing to spare. The difference needs to be stressed, for God notices and honors sacrificial giving. If the world and its desperate needs are ever to be reached for Christ, then every believer must give sacrificially.
>
> > On the first day of every week, each of you is to put something aside and store it up, as he may prosper, so that there will be no collecting when I come. (1 Co.16:2)
> >
> > We want you to know, brothers, about the grace of God that has been given among the churches of Macedonia, for in a severe test of affliction, their abundance of joy and their extreme poverty have overflowed in a wealth of generosity on their part. For they gave according to their means, as I can testify, and beyond their means, of their own accord, begging us earnestly for the favor of taking part in the relief of the saints. (2 Co.8:1-4)
> >
> > Each one must give as he has decided in his heart, not reluctantly or under compulsion, for God loves a cheerful giver. . . . For the ministry of this service is not only supplying the needs of the saints but is also overflowing in many thanksgivings to God. By their approval of this service, they will glorify God because of your submission that comes from your confession

of the gospel of Christ, and the generosity of your contribution for them and for all others, . . . Thanks be to God for his inexpressible gift! (2 Co.9:7, 12–13, 15)

Every man shall give as he is able, according to the blessing of the LORD your God that he has given you. (De.16:17)

12:43

⁴³ And he called his disciples to him and said to them, "Truly, I say to you, this poor widow has put in more than all those who are contributing to the offering box."

3 Real giving is measured by how much a person keeps back—not by how much a person gives.

Jesus called His disciples to Him and used the great sacrifice that the widow made to teach a much-needed lesson. Note several facts.

First, they all gave an offering to God: both the people who had much (v.41) and the poor widow who had very, very little (v.42).

Second, the ones who had plenty gave more money, much more than the widow. Their contributions were generous. Their incomes were far more than sufficient for their needs, so their offerings were large.

Third, in the Lord's eyes, the widow gave more. Why? Because God measures what is *kept*, not what is given.

➤ The widow had less remaining; the others still had much.
➤ The widow had given more of what she had; the others had given less of what they had.
➤ The widow had sacrificed more; the others had sacrificed less.

In proportion to what she had, the widow gave a larger percentage. The others gave a much smaller percentage. After they had given, they still had a significant percentage of their income left to spend on themselves.

Jesus was teaching a critical lesson: God counts what we have left, not what we give. He counts the size of the sacrifice, not the amount of money. The gift that matters most to the Lord is the gift that costs the giver most. To the Lord, it is not the size of the gift that impresses, but the sacrifice the giver had to make in order to give the gift. The greater the sacrifice, the more God honors the gift.

For where your treasure is, there your heart will be also. (Mt.6:21)

And Zacchaeus stood and said to the Lord, "Behold, Lord, the half of my goods I give to the poor. And if I have defrauded anyone of anything, I restore it fourfold." (Lu.19:8)

For you know the grace of our Lord Jesus Christ, that though he was rich, yet for your sake he became poor, so that you by his poverty might become rich. (2 Co.8:9)

12:44

⁴⁴ "For they all contributed out of their abundance, but she out of her poverty has put in everything she had, all she had to live on."

4 Real giving is giving in spite of need.

Jesus noted that this woman gave out of her poverty. She had a great need for food, clothing, and shelter. Yet she had so little. She was the kind of person who would have had to wander about seeking odd jobs just to survive. Looking at her, a person could tell she never knew where she would get her next meal. She had no one to care for her and no one to help her. The weight of the world seemed to lie upon her shoulders. From all appearances, she had nobody who cared or expressed care for her. But she knew something: people may not care, but God cares. And what she did is a crucial lesson for us to learn: she gave in spite of her need.

She knew the great principle that God will take care of those who give to Him. She knew that if she gave what little she had to God, if she put His kingdom first, He would provide all her necessities (Mt.6:33).

Two needs are present and being met:

• God's house had a need. The widow, though poor, gave to help carry on the ministry of God.

- The poor widow had a need. She gave, believing God would see to it that she had food, clothing, and shelter.

> Give, and it will be given to you. Good measure, pressed down, shaken together, running over, will be put into your lap. For with the measure you use it will be measured back to you. (Lu.6:38)

> The point is this: whoever sows sparingly will also reap sparingly, and whoever sows bountifully will also reap bountifully. (2 Co.9:6)

> Honor the Lord with your wealth and with the firstfruits of all your produce; then your barns will be filled with plenty, and your vats will be bursting with wine. (Pr.3:9-10)

> Whoever brings blessing will be enriched, and one who waters will himself be watered. (Pr.11:25)

> Bring the full tithe into the storehouse, that there may be food in my house. And thereby put me to the test, says the Lord of hosts, if I will not open the windows of heaven for you and pour down for you a blessing until there is no more need. (Mal.3:10)

5 Real giving is giving all to the Lord.

Jesus knew that this poverty-stricken woman had given everything she had to the Lord's house, all she had to live on. Just imagine! *She gave her living*—not just part—not just a sacrifice—but *all!* She could have easily said what so many often feel:

44 "For they all contributed out of their abundance, but she out of her poverty has put in everything she had, all she had to live on."

> ➤ "My gift doesn't matter. It's so little."
> ➤ "I have so little. God will understand. He doesn't expect me to give it when I can't even buy food."

This woman viewed everything she had as belonging to God. Therefore, it was not beyond her to give all of the money she had to live on at that time to God. Such a gift comes only from a believer who has consecrated everything to Him. She had dedicated herself wholly to the Lord; she had presented everything she was and possessed to Him (Ro.12:1). She was a faithful steward, one who recognized that God was the owner of all she had, and she was the manager of it. Like the generous believers of Macedonia, when God prompted her to give an unusual gift to Him, she was willing to obey, for she had given herself "first to the Lord" (2 Co.8:5).

This is real giving. When we give all we are and have to God—when we see Him as the owner of it all and ourselves as stewards or managers—we are willing to give whatever He stirs us to give, even if He should lead us at some point to give everything we possess.

THOUGHT 1. The lesson is twofold.
1) We lack devotion and dedication in our commitment to God, whether commitment of life, time, gifts, or money.
2) We lack boldness in giving and using what we have for God.

> Jesus said to him, "If you would be perfect, go, sell what you possess and give to the poor, and you will have treasure in heaven; and come, follow me. . . . And everyone who has left houses or brothers or sisters or father or mother or children or lands, for my name's sake, will receive a hundredfold and will inherit eternal life." (Mt.19:29)

> Just as I try to please everyone in everything I do, not seeking my own advantage, but that of many, that they may be saved. (1 Co.10:33)

CHAPTER 13

VIII. THE SON OF GOD'S OLIVET MINISTRY: JESUS' PROPHECY OF HIS RETURN AND THE END TIME,[DS1, 2, 3] 13:1–37

A. The Signs of the End Time, 13:1–13

(Mt.24:1–14; Lu.21:5–19)

1. **Events that led to the great prophecies**
   a. The disciples admired the temple buildings

   b. Jesus predicted the destruction of the buildings

   c. The disciples asked two questions

   1) When is the destruction to come?
   2) What is the sign of the destruction?
   d. Jesus warned: Watch out for deceivers

2. **Sign 1: Spiritual deception and false messiahs**

3. **Sign 2: Wars and rumors of war, international disturbances**

4. **Sign 3: Natural disasters**
   (Note: these signs are the beginning of sorrows)[DS4]

5. **Sign 4: Persecution by civil and religious authorities**

6. **Sign 5: Worldwide evangelization**

7. **Sign 6: Empowerment by a supernatural witness**

And as he came out of the temple, one of his disciples said to him, "Look, Teacher, what wonderful stones and what wonderful buildings!" ² And Jesus said to him, "Do you see these great buildings? There will not be left here one stone upon another that will not be thrown down." ³ And as he sat on the Mount of Olives opposite the temple, Peter and James and John and Andrew asked him privately, ⁴ "Tell us, when will these things be, and what will be the sign when all these things are about to be accomplished?" ⁵ And Jesus began to say to them, "See that no one leads you astray." ⁶ "Many will come in my name, saying, 'I am he!' and they will lead many astray." ⁷ "And when you hear of wars and rumors of wars, do not be alarmed. This must take place, but the end is not yet. ⁸ For nation will rise against nation, and kingdom against kingdom. There will be earthquakes in various places; there will be famines. These are but the beginning of the birth pains." ⁹ "But be on your guard. For they will deliver you over to councils, and you will be beaten in synagogues, and you will stand before governors and kings for my sake, to bear witness before them." ¹⁰ "And the gospel must first be proclaimed to all nations." ¹¹ "And when they bring you to trial and deliver you over, do not be anxious beforehand what you are to say, but say whatever is given you in that hour, for it is not you who speak, but the Holy Spirit."

¹² "And brother will deliver brother over to death, and the father his child, and children will rise against parents and have them put to death.

¹³ And you will be hated by all for my name's sake. But the one who endures to the end will be saved."

8. **Sign 7: Division within families**
   a. Betrayal

   b. Hatred and persecution
9. **Sign 8: Steadfast endurance that brings about salvation**

Division VIII

The Son of God's Olivet Ministry: Jesus' Prophecy of His Return and the End Time, 13:1–37

A. The Signs of the End Time, 13:1–13

(Mt.24:1–14; Lu.21:5–19)

13:1-37
DIVISION OVERVIEW

Noting the exact words of Jesus will help in understanding this chapter.

1. Jesus said "These are the beginning of birth pains or sorrows" (v.8). This statement indicates that Jesus was dealing with the beginning of a terrible period of trial for the believer ("you," v.9). He was not *just* referring to the normal trials that occur on earth or the regular persecutions that are launched against believers throughout the centuries (see DEEPER STUDY # 2—Mt.24:1-31). World trouble and persecutions against God's people have always existed, even from the beginning of time. The great sorrow He spoke about refers to some period of time which is to be exceedingly terrible. It is to be a period that is to be distinguished from all other trouble the world and believers will suffer throughout history.

2. Jesus said, "When you see the abomination of desolation . . . standing where he [or "it"] ought not . . . then let those who are in Judea flee" (v.14). Matthew words the warning this way: "Then . . . flee . . . for then there will be great tribulation or distress, "such as has not been since the beginning of the world" (Mt.24:15-16, 21). There is no question about this sign. It launches the worst period of tribulation the world has ever seen. This sign definitely points to a specific period of human history. As to what the period should be called, it is probably best to title it as Matthew does: "great tribulation" (Mt.24:21).

3. Now, note what Jesus has said in the verses referred to above:

> **For nation will rise against nation, and kingdom against kingdom. There will be earthquakes in various places; there will be famines. These are but the beginning of the birth pains. (v.8)**

> **But when you see the abomination of desolation standing where he ought not to be (let the reader understand), then let those who are in Judea flee to the mountains. (v.14)**

Or as Matthew says,

> **So when you see the abomination of desolation spoken of by the prophet Daniel, standing in the holy place (let the reader understand), then let those who are in Judea flee to the mountains. For then there will be great tribulation, such as has not been from the beginning of the world until now, no, and never will be. (Mt.24:15-16, 21)**

Jesus seems to be giving a list of signs, one of which is the abomination of desolation. In verses 6-13, He gives eight signs, the eighth saying, "The one who endures to the end will be saved" (v.13). But note in verse 14, how He seems to pick up identifying signs again, giving what looks to be the most visible and terrible sign for which to watch. Note His words, reading verses 13 and

14 together, "The one who endures to the end will be saved. But when you see the abomination of desolation standing where he (or "it") ought not . . . then let those . . . flee."

Jesus is saying there will be a difference between the signs that precede the abomination and the unparalleled trials that follow. When *the abomination of desolation* stands where he (or "it") ought not (in the holy place), the trials that follow will be much, much worse—unparalleled in human history.

The abomination of desolation will be the sign that launches the worst tribulation the world has ever known. Jesus did not say exactly when this abomination would appear, but his (or "its") appearance would be one of the nine signs Jesus gave; and his (its) appearance would signal the worst devastation the world has ever known.

A chart diagramming Jesus' own words will perhaps help in understanding what He said.

1. His words were: "These [signs] are but the beginning of the birth pains or sorrows" (v.8).

2. "But when ye *see* the abomination of desolation . . . then let those . . . flee" (v.14); or as Matthew says, "*then there will be great tribulation*" (Mt.24:15, 21).

3. "But in those days, *after that tribulation* . . . they will see the Son of Man coming" (vv.24–27).

THE END OF THE WORLD

Seeing the Sign of the *Abomination of Desolation* *In the Middle of the Time or Years* (v.14)		*Seeing the Son of* *Man Coming* (v.26)
3 1/2 years Signs which are "The beginnings of sorrow" (v.8).	3 1/2 years Unparalleled trials of "the great tribulation" (v.19; cp Mt.24:21)	"His angels . . . gather together His elect" (v.27)

DEEPER STUDY # 1

(13:1–37) **End Time—Daniel:** Jesus made another statement that helps in understanding this chapter. He said that the abomination of desolation was "spoken of by the prophet Daniel" (Mt.24:15). Three passages in Daniel refer to the abomination of desolation (see DEEPER STUDY # 1—Mk.13:14).

Note several facts in regard to Daniel's prophecy.

1. The prophecy has already seen fulfillment through Antiochus Epiphanes (see DEEPER STUDY # 1—Mk.13:14).

2. Jesus said the prophecy of Daniel also had a future fulfillment. Note the words, "When you see." The future fulfillment refers both to the fall of Jerusalem (vv.14–20) and to the end of the world, right before the Lord returns (vv.14, 24–27).

3. The words of Daniel give a division of time even as Jesus divided the signs into two periods. Daniel says, "for half of the week" or "in the middle of the week. . . ." Note two facts.

   a. The words "for half of the week" or "in the middle of the week" definitely point to a separation of the week into two periods of time.

   b. "The week" is the seventieth week, the last week of Daniel's vision of history. This indicates that the end of time is being dealt with.

      In discussing the end of time, Jesus was saying that He was discussing what Daniel prophesied. Now note what begins the second half of Daniel's week. It is the abomination of desolation or the prince's causing abomination of desolation in the holy place. Mark 13:14 actually uses the masculine participle which indicates that the abomination of desolation is a person, the prince himself. Note something else.

What Jesus called the "great [unparalleled] tribulation" begins with the abomination of desolation (Mt.24:15-16, 21).

The indication again is that the beginning of sorrows and the great tribulation are one period of time, but the period includes two parts (see Division Overview—Mk.13:1-37 for chart of the two periods).

4. The length of the last part or half is actually given by Scripture (see notes—Re.11:2; 12:6; 13:4-8).

> But do not measure the court outside the temple; leave that out, for it is given over to the nations, and they will trample the holy city for forty-two months. . . . And the beast was given a mouth uttering haughty and blasphemous words, and it was allowed to exercise authority for forty-two months. It opened its mouth to utter blasphemies against God, blaspheming his name and his dwelling, that is, those who dwell in heaven. (Re.11:2; 13:5-6)

> And the woman fled into the wilderness, where she has a place prepared by God, in which she is to be nourished for 1,260 days. (Re.12:6)

> He shall speak words against the Most High, and shall wear out the saints of the Most High, and shall think to change the times and the law; and they shall be given into his hand for a time, times, and half a time. . . . And I heard the man clothed in linen, who was above the waters of the stream; he raised his right hand and his left hand toward heaven and swore by him who lives forever that it would be for a time, times, and half a time, and that when the shattering of the power of the holy people comes to an end all these things would be finished. (Da.7:25; 12:7)

Based upon this timetable, the tribulation of which Jesus spoke can be said to be seven years, divided into two parts:
- "The beginning of sorrows or birth pains," or the first half of the tribulation.
- "The great tribulation," or the second half of the tribulation.

Again, seeing these two periods of time as discussed by Jesus (and referred to by Daniel) helps in understanding Jesus' answer to the disciples' two questions (Mk.13:4; Mt.24:3).

5. Jesus said that that He would return after the rise of the prince to whom Daniel referred: "after that tribulation . . . they will see the Son of Man coming in clouds with great power and glory. And then He will send out the angels, and gather His elect . . ." (Mk.13:24-27). In these words, our Lord answered the two questions: "When will these things be (the destruction of the temple)? And what will be the sign of Your coming and of the end of the age?" (Mk.13:4; Mt.24:3).

DEEPER STUDY # 2

(13:1-37) **End Time:** several other facts need to be kept in mind while studying this section of *Mark*.

1. Jesus was preparing His disciples for His death and departure from this world and preparing them to carry on after He was gone. His immediate disciples were to face some terrible times, ranging all the way from personal trials brought on by their witness for Jesus, to national trials involving the utter destruction of their nation. It would be generations stretching into centuries before He returned to earth. No one knew this at that time, but He did; so He needed to prepare His future disciples as well. They, too, were going to face all kinds of trials. There was always the danger that His disciples might tire waiting for His return. They were to see and experience so much trouble in the world that their faith might falter.

Jesus used this occasion to reveal some of the events that were to take place on the earth during "these last days," the days of the church (Ac.2:16-17; 1 Jn.2:18). By knowing some of the events, His disciples would be better prepared to endure and to keep their hope for His return alive.

2. Jesus was dealing with two questions throughout this passage. He was answering the questions: When will the temple be destroyed, and what will be the sign of His return and of the end of the world (Mk.13:4; Mt.24:3)?

Note something: Jesus was dealing with the end of the temple and with the end of the world, the destruction of the temple and the destruction of the world. He was covering the signs, the events that were to cause the judgment and to occur during the judgment of both the temple and the world. What is the point? Simply this: Scripture teaches that the same signs and events cause the judgment of anything. That is, the events (sins) that cause judgment upon one thing are the same events that will bring judgment upon everything else. Therefore, the signs that surrounded the destruction of Jerusalem are much the same as the signs that will surround the end of the world. Therefore, what Jesus was saying had a double meaning and application. (See DEEPER STUDY # 3—Mt.24:1-14; 24:15-28. Both notes will help to see the double application.)

The Lord's words applied both to the disciples of His day and to all disciples who were to follow in succeeding generations. As long as the earth stands, the disciples of *the last days* (or ages) will face many of the same signs faced by those who experienced the destruction of Jerusalem. But there is to be one difference: at the end of the age, the signs will increase and intensify. The day is coming that is so terrible that it can be called *the beginnings of sorrows* (v.8), and *the great tribulation* (v.21). (See DEEPER STUDIES 1, 2—Mt.24:1-31; note—24:15-28.)

3. A quick outline of the passage helps one understand what Jesus was doing.
   a. The eight signs of the last days (that is, the last days before both Jerusalem's destruction and the world's end) (Mk.13:1-13).
   b. The ninth and most terrible sign: the abomination of desolation and the great tribulation (Mk.13:14-23; see Mt.24:15, 21).
   c. The coming of the Son of Man (Mk.14:24-27).

The rest of what Jesus covered dealt with the actual time of the Lord's return (Mt.24:32-41) and the believer's duty to watch and be prepared (Mt.24:42-25:46 for discussion).

DEEPER STUDY # 3

(13:1-37) **End Time:** the great similarities between what Jesus said about the end time and what sections of *Revelation* say need to be noted (see DEEPER STUDIES 1, 2—Mt.24:1-31 for discussion).

13:1-13
Introduction

Just like Jesus' disciples, people today are curious about and seek to understand when Christ is coming and how the world will end (Mt.24:3). As we seek to understand what Jesus was saying about the end times, we have to be very careful not to add to or take away from what He said. Both mistakes were made by religionists concerning Jesus' first coming (Mt.2:4-6).

A major fact to keep in mind is, the disciples did think that all three events (Jerusalem's destruction, the Lord's return, and the world's end) would happen at about the same time. They did think in terms of the Messianic Kingdom of God (Ac.1:6 compared with the Jewish concept of the Messiah show this). (See notes—Mt.1:1; DEEPER STUDY # 2—1:18; DEEPER STUDY # 3—3:11; notes—11:1-6; 11:2-3; DEEPER STUDY # 1—11:5; DEEPER STUDY # 2—11:6; DEEPER STUDY # 1—12:16; notes—22:42; Lu.7:21-23.) When Jesus said that the temple would be destroyed (Mt.24:2), the disciples assumed it would happen at the same time that He returned and ended the world, thereby restoring the kingdom to Israel.

Jesus, however, gave no timetable. He did not say when the three events would occur. What He did was give signs that would occur before the events, signs that pointed toward His return and toward the end of Jerusalem and the end of the world.

It is important to keep in mind that most of the signs Jesus mentions occur regularly throughout history, but there is this difference: the signs increase and intensify right before the end of Jerusalem and the end of the world. There will be a period known as *"the beginning of birth pains or sorrows"* (v.8), and a period launched by the abomination of desolation known as *the great tribulation, such as has not been since the beginning of the world"* (Mt.24:21). This is, *The Signs of the End Time,* 13:1-13.

1. Events that led to the great prophecies (vv.1-5).
2. Sign 1: Spiritual deception and false messiahs (v.6).
3. Sign 2: Wars and rumors of war, international disturbances (vv.7-8).
4. Sign 3: Natural disasters (v.8).
5. Sign 4: Persecution by civil and religious authorities (v.9).
6. Sign 5: Worldwide evangelization (v.10).
7. Sign 6: Empowerment by a supernatural witness (v.11).
8. Sign 7: Division within families (vv.12-13).
9. Sign 8: Steadfast endurance that brings about salvation (v.13).

1 Events that led to the great prophecies.

13:1-5

The first five verses set the stage for the great prophecies given by Jesus in this chapter. His intriguing, yet clear, teaching was His answer to His disciples' questions about the future.

a. The disciples admired the temple buildings (v.1).

As Jesus was leaving the temple, the disciples admired the impressive structure's magnificence and drew Jesus' attention to its beauty. The temple was awe-striking. It sat upon the towering summit of Mount Zion, and it was built of white marble plated with gold. The temple had several porches that were supported by huge, towering pillars, each one so large that it took three to four men extended arm to arm to reach around it. The disciples apparently stood someplace where the view of the temple's magnificent beauty had struck them with awe, and they wanted Jesus to see the beautiful sight.

And as he came out of the temple, one of his disciples said to him, "Look, Teacher, what wonderful stones and what wonderful buildings!"

² And Jesus said to him, "Do you see these great buildings? There will not be left here one stone upon another that will not be thrown down."

³ And as he sat on the Mount of Olives opposite the temple, Peter and James and John and Andrew asked him privately,

⁴ "Tell us, when will these things be, and what will be the sign when all these things are about to be accomplished?"

⁵ And Jesus began to say to them, "See that no one leads you astray."

b. Jesus predicted the destruction of the buildings (v.2).

Jesus replied to the disciples' admiration of the temple with a startling prediction: it would be utterly destroyed. This prophecy stirred the disciples' interest in coming events.

c. The disciples asked two questions (vv.3-4).

The disciples curiously asked two questions of the Lord: When will the temple be destroyed, and what will be the sign that the time of its destruction is near? By these questions, Mark clearly shows that the disciples were thinking about the signs of Jesus' return and of the end of the world (Mt.24:3; see note—Lu.21:5-8).

d. Jesus warned: Watch out for deceivers (v.5).

Jesus warned His disciples that they needed to guard against being deceived. This can mean one or two things. People can be easily deceived when dealing with end-time prophecies, or they can be easily deceived when facing the end-time events. They can be deceived into thinking that certain cataclysmic events are infallible signs that the end is at hand (v.7). Such too often results . . .

- in wild guesses about the end time
- in universal predictions
- in the deceiving of others
- in discouragement of a person's faith when the end does not come as expected

13:6

⁶ "Many will come in my name, saying, 'I am he!' and they will lead many astray."

2 Sign 1: Spiritual deception and false messiahs.

The first sign of the end time is spiritual deception by false messiahs. Jesus stated three facts.

First, *many* false messiahs will come. There will not be just a few, but many.

Second, they will claim to be the Christ, the Messiah; that is, each one will claim to be *the one* sent to lead people into a perfect society. They will claim that they can solve humanity's problems and see to it that people have plenty of everything. They will claim to be *the one* who can fulfill the people's dreams, delivering them from conflict and war into a state of peace and freedom, plenty and comfort, equality or supremacy. The false messiahs are sometimes politicians and sometimes religious leaders, but in either case, they wield power and proclaim themselves to be the hope of humanity.

THOUGHT 1. Think of the promises so often made by some politicians and leaders of religions, promises that point toward them as the *personal answer* to people's hopes, dreams, and problems.

Third, they will mislead many. They are *deceivers, imposters, seducers, pretenders*. They are not able to fulfill people's dreams and hopes nor to solve humanity's problems. They are not able to bring about a perfect society, for they do not have such power. They are mere men. They are not the true Messiah, not the Messiah of God. But despite this, many will follow them, believing their false promises and entrusting their lives and welfare into their keeping. Many will follow them as though they are the true deliverer of mankind.

> For such persons do not serve our Lord Christ, but their own appetites, and by smooth talk and flattery they deceive the hearts of the naive. (Ro.16:18)

> For such men are false apostles, deceitful workmen, disguising themselves as apostles of Christ. (2 Co.11:13)

> So that we may no longer be children, tossed to and fro by the waves and carried about by every wind of doctrine, by human cunning, by craftiness in deceitful schemes. (Ep.4:14)

> While evil people and impostors will go on from bad to worse, deceiving and being deceived. (2 Ti.3:13)

> For many deceivers have gone out into the world, those who do not confess the coming of Jesus Christ in the flesh. Such a one is the deceiver and the antichrist. (2 Jn.7)

13:7-8

⁷ "And when you hear of wars and rumors of wars, do not be alarmed. This must take place, but the end is not yet.
⁸ For nation will rise against nation, and kingdom against kingdom. There will be earthquakes in various places; there will be famines. These are but the beginning of the birth pains."

3 Sign 2: Wars and rumors of war, international disturbances.

The second sign of the end time is national and international disturbances, wars and rumors of wars. Believers will hear of upheavals, both within their own country and throughout the world. Some, as citizens of a warring nation, will even be caught up in the conflict. The news will be bad and bleak, always filled with *wars and rumors of wars—always plural, always referring to many*.

However, we should not be alarmed. *Alarmed, troubled, or frightened* (throeisthe; pronounced *thra-ace'-thee*) means to be terrified, disturbed, crying out within one's inner being.

Jesus said that world disturbances and upheavals must take place. They exist because of *selfishness* and *greed,* man's sinful and depraved nature. The dark side of humans is and always will be revealed and exposed by . . .

- assaults
- killing
- stealing
- storing up
- attacks
- maiming
- abuse
- lusting

- fighting
- cheating
- neglect
- unbelief (Ph.4:6–7)
- arguments
- lying
- hoarding
- negative thinking (Ph.4:8)

Jesus told us plainly that world disturbances do not mean the end has come. Note that Christ was specific about this fact: "The end is not yet." Remember, He had just warned us about being deceived. We must not be deceived by people who falsely claim that the end of the world is here.

THOUGHT 1. Three things can happen to the believer in looking at worldwide trouble.

1) We can become overly affected by the news of world affairs and turmoil. Such news can become so interesting and captivating that it can dominate our life. We begin to live and thrive on the news.

2) We can become overly apprehensive about the personal safety of ourselves and our families. We can begin to fear so much that we forget that our security is in God, not in this world. Fear over world affairs tends to emphasize the importance of the earth over the importance of God; it tends to emphasize the worldly over the spiritual. The world, of course, is important; but we need to focus on the spiritual. And it is our responsibility to emphasize the spiritual, the security and peace of heart that is found in Christ.

3) We can become so troubled over world affairs that we neglect our spiritual duties. We should naturally be concerned over the world, as all people should be. But we should not allow world affairs to interfere with our witnessing for Christ. We are to be at peace and to be secure with God, and we are to demonstrate the peace and security of God, going about our daily duties as much as possible within a turbulent world. The point is, we are to witness for Christ no matter the turmoil of the world.

> **But watch yourselves lest your hearts be weighed down with dissipation and drunkenness and cares of this life, and that day come upon you suddenly like a trap. (Lu.21:34)**

> **Do not be anxious about anything, but in everything by prayer and supplication with thanksgiving let your requests be made known to God. (Ph.4:6)**

> **Casting all your anxieties on him, because he cares for you. (1 Pe.5:7)**

> **They were broken in pieces. Nation was crushed by nation and city by city, for God troubled them with every sort of distress. But you, take courage! Do not let your hands be weak, for your work shall be rewarded. (2 Chr.15:6–7)**

> **Go out of the midst of her, my people! Let every one save his life from the fierce anger of the LORD! Let not your heart faint, and be not fearful at the report heard in the land, when a report comes in one year and afterward a report in another year, and violence is in the land, and ruler is against ruler. (Je.51:45–46)**

4 Sign 3: Natural disasters.

13:8

Natural disasters are the fourth sign of the end time. Jesus specifically mentioned *earthquakes* and *famines.* Jesus spoke of these signs as being *the beginning of birth pains* or *sorrows* (see DEEPER STUDY # 4).

Earthquakes can cause unbelievable destruction and death. The historian Josephus refers to a devastating storm and earthquake prior to the fall of Jerusalem in A.D. 70 that

8 "For nation will rise against nation, and kingdom against kingdom. There will be earthquakes in various places; there will be famines. These are but the beginning of the birth pains."

appears to have been a fulfillment of Jesus' prophecy as it related to the destruction of the temple. As Josephus reports, this disaster was considered a sign of coming destruction.

> "... there broke out a prodigious storm in the night, with the utmost violence, and very strong winds, with the largest showers of rain, and continual lightnings, terrible thunderings, and amazing concussions and bellowings of the earth, that was in an earthquake. These things were a manifest indication that some destruction was coming upon men, when the system of the world was put into this disorder; and any one would guess that these wonders foreshowed some grand calamities that were coming"[1]

While countless earthquakes have wreaked havoc on the earth throughout history, an unusual number will occur in many places during the last days of the earth (Re.6:12; 11:12-13, 19; 16:17-19).

Jesus also referred specifically to famines. Scripture speaks of a great worldwide famine that devastated the world in the days of Claudius Caesar (Ac.11:28-30). Josephus describes the famine as being so terrible that when flour "was brought into the temple ... not one of the priests was so hardy as to eat one crumb of it ... while so great a distress was upon the land."[2] He says in another place, "A famine did oppress them [Jerusalem] ... and many people died for want of what was necessary to procure food."[3]

In the very last days before Jerusalem's fall, Josephus speaks of yet another terrible famine:

> "It was now a miserable case, and a sight that would justly bring tears into our eyes, how men stood to their food, while the more powerful had more than enough, and the weaker were lamenting (for want of it)."[4]

> "Then did the famine widen its progress, and devoured the people by whole houses and families; the upper rooms were full of women and children that were dying by famine; and the lanes of the city were full of the dead bodies of the aged; the children also and the young men wandered about the marketplaces like shadows, all swelled with famine, and fell down dead wheresoever their misery seized them."[5]

From what Jesus said, there is evidently to be terrible famine in the last days. The black horse of the four horsemen of the Apocalypse indicates terrible famine (see note—Re.6:5-6). The unbearable pain and horrible evil that hunger can cause is graphically described by Scripture:

Happier were the victims of the sword than the victims of hunger, who wasted away, pierced by lack of the fruits of the field. The hands of compassionate women have boiled their own children; they became their food during the destruction of the daughter of my people. (Lam.4:9-10)

Matthew adds a third disaster of nature: pestilence. Earthquakes and famines, of course, cause disease and pestilence (see note—Mt.24:7).

Deeper Study # 4

(13:8) **Birth pains or Sorrows** (odinon): labor-pains; travailings; intolerable anguish; quick, sharp, violent ongoing pain.

---

1 Flavius Josephus. *Josephus Complete Works* (*Wars*. 4. 4:5.), translated by William Whiston. (Grand Rapids, MI: Kregel, 1960).

2 Josephus, *Josephus Complete Works* (*Antiquities*. 3. 15:3.), translated by William Whiston. (Grand Rapids, MI: Kregel, 1960).

3 Josephus, *Ant*. 20. 2:5.

4 Josephus, *Wars*. 5. 10:3.

5 Josephus, *Wars*. 5. 12

5 Sign 4: Persecution by civil and religious authorities.

The fourth sign of the end time is persecution by civil and religious authorities. Jesus warned His followers to be on their guard against persecution. In the Greek, the command is literally translated "But take heed you to yourselves." The emphasis is on the reflexive pronoun *heautous* (pronounced heh-au-tous') which means "to or for yourselves." This word stresses the need to guard oneself. Believers must guard *themselves*; they themselves must take heed. Believers living in the end time will face not only the deceptions and normal conflicts of a selfish world, not only the terrible disasters of nature, but they will face persecution by others.

9 "But be on your guard. For they will deliver you over to councils, and you will be beaten in synagogues, and you will stand before governors and kings for my sake, to bear witness before them."

Jesus warned that believers will be abused, neglected, ignored, arrested, and tried before the councils or courts of the world and of religions. Why? To bear witness to them; to be a testimony of the truth and power of Christ. Believers will stand before persecutors *for the purpose of demonstrating loyalty to Christ*. Standing fast through the persecution is *a way of witnessing*. Believers show that Christ and eternity are real when we suffer for Christ.

Then they will deliver you up to tribulation and put you to death, and you will be hated by all nations for my name's sake. (Mt.24:9; see Lu.21:12-13)

Remember the word that I said to you: 'A servant is not greater than his master.' If they persecuted me, they will also persecute you. If they kept my word, they will also keep yours. (Jn.15:20)

Indeed, all who desire to live a godly life in Christ Jesus will be persecuted. (2 Ti.3:12)

Do not fear what you are about to suffer. Behold, the devil is about to throw some of you into prison, that you may be tested, and for ten days you will have tribulation. Be faithful unto death, and I will give you the crown of life. (Re.2:10)

My times are in your hand; rescue me from the hand of my enemies and from my persecutors! (Ps.31:15)

All your commandments are sure; they persecute me with falsehood; help me! (Ps.119:86)

6 Sign 6: Worldwide evangelization.

The fifth sign of the end time is world evangelization. Note the exact words of Christ: "The gospel *must first* be proclaimed or preached to all nations" before the end can come. Note three observations in regard to this statement.

10 "And the gospel must first be proclaimed to all nations."

First, the word "must" assures the fact. The fact is set in God's plan for the world. It cannot be changed. The gospel will be preached to all nations before the end of the world.

Second, the promise was fulfilled in the first century. The gospel was carried to all the known world at that time (Ro.10:18; Col.1:23; see note—Mt.24:14 for detailed discussion).

Third, the promise of world evangelization is to be fulfilled in the end time. All nations of the world will hear the gospel before the end comes. Christ's promise was unrestricted. He said "to all nations." There is to be a proclamation of the gospel to the whole world before time ceases.

And this gospel of the kingdom will be proclaimed throughout the whole world as a testimony to all nations, and then the end will come. (Mt.24:14)

Go therefore and make disciples of all nations, baptizing them in the name of the Father and of the Son and of the Holy Spirit, teaching them to observe all that I have commanded you. And behold, I am with you always, to the end of the age. (Mt.28:19-20)

And that repentance for the forgiveness of sins should be proclaimed in his name to all nations, beginning from Jerusalem. (Lu.24:47)

Ask of me, and I will make the nations your heritage, and the ends of the earth your possession. (Ps.2:8)

All the ends of the earth shall remember and turn to the LORD, and all the families of the nations shall worship before you. (Ps.22:27)

For from the rising of the sun to its setting my name will be great among the nations, and in every place incense will be offered to my name, and a pure offering. For my name will be great among the nations, says the LORD of hosts. (Mal.1:11)

13:11

¹¹ "And when they bring you to trial and deliver you over, do not be anxious beforehand what you are to say, but say whatever is given you in that hour, for it is not you who speak, but the Holy Spirit."

7 Sign 6: Empowerment by a supernatural witness.

The sixth sign of the end time is a supernatural witness (see note—Mt.10:19–20). There is going to be a strong surge of Spirit-led witnessing in the end time. Multitudes of believers are going to be called on to give an answer for the hope that is within them.

Our Lord instructed His followers to not worry or be anxious about what we will say to our persecutors. We are not to be *overly* concerned about what we should say, either in defense of ourselves or as a testimony to those who are mistreating us because of our faith. Why? Because the Holy Spirit will speak through us. Believers will not be left alone in defending themselves in persecution. God will speak through them, standing right with them (see Ac.4:8f; 2 Ti.4:16–18).

At my first defense no one came to stand by me, but all deserted me. May it not be charged against them! But the Lord stood by me and strengthened me, so that through me the message might be fully proclaimed and all the Gentiles might hear it. So I was rescued from the lion's mouth. The Lord will rescue me from every evil deed and bring me safely into his heavenly kingdom. To him be the glory forever and ever. Amen. (2 Ti.4:16–18)

So we can confidently say, "The Lord is my helper; I will not fear; what can man do to me?" (He.13:6)

Fear not, for I am with you; be not dismayed, for I am your God; I will strengthen you, I will help you, I will uphold you with my righteous right hand. (Is.41:10)

Behold, the Lord GOD helps me; who will declare me guilty? Behold, all of them will wear out like a garment; the moth will eat them up. (Is.50:9)

13:12–13a

¹² "And brother will deliver brother over to death, and the father his child, and children will rise against parents and have them put to death. ¹³ And you will be hated by all for my name's sake. But the one who endures to the end will be saved."

8 Sign 7: Division within families.

The seventh sign of the end time is divided families (see note—Mt.10:21). It is hard to fathom a brother betraying a brother, parents betraying their children, and children betraying their parents. But it happens. Some staunch unbelievers or followers of false religions turn completely against their closest relatives because of their relatives' faith in Jesus Christ. It happens today, and it will be even more rampant in the end times.

a. **Betrayal (v.12).**

Jesus said that some believers will be betrayed by their closest relatives. Some of these betrayals will even lead to the believer's death (v.12). This atrocity will seep into the family and be widely practiced, so much so that Christ says it will be a common trait of the end time.

b. **Hatred and persecution (v.13a).**

Jesus went on to say that there will be intense hatred among all (the emphasis is, even within the family). Note why: because the believer stands for the name of Christ. Their own family, as well as the world, will hate, persecute, and betray them because of their testimony for the Lord.

Brother will deliver brother over to death, and the father his child, and children will rise against parents and have them put to death. (Mt.10:21)

9 Sign 8: Steadfast endurance that brings about salvation.

Jesus assured believers that they will be able to endure these fierce, unprecedented sufferings. *Endure* (hupomeinas, *hoop-om-ane'-os*) means to bear up under suffering, to be courageous in suffering, to persevere and withstand patiently—but actively, not passively. It is enduring pain, actively bearing intense suffering. The believer is now called on and will be called on to stand firm through all forms of persecution and abuse, even if it leads to inhuman torture and death.

13 "And you will be hated by all for my name's sake. But the one who endures to the end will be saved."

It is critical to note that Jesus was talking to His disciples. Therefore, His promise of *being saved* was bound to mean the *soul's salvation in the last days*. It could not mean the safety of human life. He had just said some (many) would be killed (v.12; see Mt.24:9).

In addition, Jesus is not saying that the persecuted *must* endure to the end *in order to* be saved. Jesus is assuring believers that their salvation—heaven and eternal life in the Lord's presence—awaits them at the end of their persecution. Jesus is also teaching that believers who stand firm to the end prove that they are true believers. "Those who have genuine faith in Christ will not give up their faith under such intense persecution."[6] And when they stand face-to-face with the Lord, He will gloriously reward them with the crown of life (Js.1:12; Re.2:10).

> To those who by patience in well-doing seek for glory and honor and immortality, he will give eternal life; but for those who are self-seeking and do not obey the truth, but obey unrighteousness, there will be wrath and fury. There will be tribulation and distress for every human being who does evil, the Jew first and also the Greek. (Ro.2:7–9)

> Blessed is the man who remains steadfast under trial, for when he has stood the test he will receive the crown of life, which God has promised to those who love him. (Js.1:12)

> Behold, we consider those blessed who remained steadfast. You have heard of the steadfastness of Job, and you have seen the purpose of the Lord, how the Lord is compassionate and merciful. (Js.5:11)

> But you are a chosen race, a royal priesthood, a holy nation, a people for his own possession, that you may proclaim the excellencies of him who called you out of darkness into his marvelous light. (1 Pe.2:9)

> Do not fear what you are about to suffer. Behold, the devil is about to throw some of you into prison, that you may be tested, and for ten days you will have tribulation. Be faithful unto death, and I will give you the crown of life. (Re.2:10)

---

6   Holman Bible editorial staff, *Holman New Testament Commentary*, (Nashville: Holman Reference, 2001). Via Wordsearch digital edition.

B. The Most Terrible Sign:
The Abomination That Causes Desolation, 13:14–23

(Mt.24:15–28; Lu.21:20–24)

1. **So terrible, it is named the abomination that causes desolation because it stands where it does not belong (that is, in the temple)**[DS1]
2. **So terrible, it is to be fled from immediately**
   a. To forget all comforts of home[DS2]

   b. To forget all personal possessions

   c. To grieve for those who cannot flee rapidly

   d. To pray for good conditions when fleeing
3. **So terrible, it causes horrifying, unparalleled affliction (the great distress or tribulation, Mt.24:21)**

4. **So terrible, God has to intervene and shorten the days of affliction**

5. **So terrible, it causes false messiahs (deliverers) to appear and deceive many**

6. **So terrible, it requires foretelling and forewarning**

¹⁴ "But when you see the abomination of desolation standing where he ought not to be (let the reader understand), then let those who are in Judea flee to the mountains.

¹⁵ Let the one who is on the housetop not go down, nor enter his house, to take anything out,
¹⁶ and let the one who is in the field not turn back to take his cloak.
¹⁷ And alas for women who are pregnant and for those who are nursing infants in those days!
¹⁸ Pray that it may not happen in winter."
¹⁹ "For in those days there will be such tribulation as has not been from the beginning of the creation that God created until now, and never will be."
²⁰ "And if the Lord had not cut short the days, no human being would be saved. But for the sake of the elect, whom he chose, he shortened the days."
²¹ "And then if anyone says to you, 'Look, here is the Christ!' or 'Look, there he is!' do not believe it.
²² For false christs and false prophets will arise and perform signs and wonders, to lead astray, if possible, the elect."
²³ "But be on guard; I have told you all things beforehand."

Division VIII

The Son of God's Olivet Ministry: Jesus' Prophecy of His Return and the End Time, 13:1–37

B. The Most Terrible Sign: The Abomination That Causes Desolation, 13:14–23

(Mt.24:15–28; Lu.21:20–24)

13:14–23
Introduction

When Jesus spoke of the Abomination of Desolation, He was referring to two future events. First, He was speaking of the fall of Jerusalem in A.D. 70, when the temple would be desecrated and destroyed. However, He was also speaking of the rise and blasphemous activities of the antichrist (see notes and Deeper Study # 1; note—2 Th.2:4-9; Deeper Study # 1—Re.11:7; notes—13:1-18; 17:7-14; see Da.9:20-27, esp. 27; 12:11). The antichrist himself will be a sign that the end time has come. Jesus pointed this out in His answer to the double question of the disciples (see note—Mt.24:15-28). He clearly said that He had told them *all things* in advance (v.23). This statement and the words that follow, "But in those days, after that tribulation" (v.24) clearly show that Jesus was continuing His discussion of the signs that pointed to the end time. (See note—Mt.24:15-28. This is an important note for the background to this passage.) This is, *The Most Terrible Sign: the Abomination That Causes Desolation,*13:14-23.

1. So terrible, it is named the abomination that causes desolation because it stands where it does not belong (that is, in the temple) (v.14).
2. So terrible, it is to be fled from immediately (vv.14-18).
3. So terrible, it causes horrifying, unparalleled affliction (the great distress or tribulation, see Mt.24:21) (v.19).
4. So terrible, God has to intervene and shorten the days of affliction (v.20).
5. So terrible, it causes false messiahs (deliverers) to appear & deceive many (vv.21-22).
6. So terrible, it requires foretelling & forewarning (v.23).

1 So terrible, it is named the abomination that causes desolation because it stands where it does not belong (that is, in the temple).

13:14a

14 "But when you see the abomination of desolation standing where he ought not to be (let the reader understand), then let those who are in Judea flee to the mountains."

This sign is so terrible it is called the abomination that causes the temple to be abandoned and left desolate (see note—Mt.24:15). The reason is because he ("it" in some translations)—the antichrist—stands "where he ought not," that is, in the temple of God. In fact, he stands in the holy place where the very presence of God is symbolized as filling the atmosphere. The words "where he ought not" mean that he *stands as God, as a replacement for God*. He assumes the position of God within the temple of God. The picture is exactly what Paul describes in speaking of this sign of the end time:

> **Let no one deceive you in any way. For that day will not come, unless the rebellion comes first, and the man of lawlessness is revealed, the son of destruction, who opposes and exalts himself against every so-called god or object of worship, so that he takes his seat in the temple of God, proclaiming himself to be God. (2 Th.2:3-4)**

There is no greater crime than a human being usurping the place of God. In reality, all who reject God usurp God's place. They replace God with someone or something else in their lives. But the picture here includes much more than personal unbelief, even more than the corporate unbelief of false messiahs and their limited followings. It is a universal, worldwide attempt to replace God Himself in His own temple, so that *all believers* living at that time will actually see the event (v.14).

The prophecies of the abomination of desolation have been literally fulfilled twice in the past when Antiochus Epiphanes and later Titus stood in the temple and desecrated it. Scripture seems to clearly indicate that the sign will be repeated in the end time and literally fulfilled within the temple (see Deeper Study # 1; see also Da.9:24-27; 12:11; 1 Th.2:3-4; Re.13:14-15). However, some believe the words "the temple" refer to all religion. They believe the abomination will be the desolating of all religion, in particular genuine Christianity.

Note: the act of corrupting the temple of God is so terrible that God has given it the name of abomination—*the abomination of desolation*. How repulsive unbelief and rejection are to Him!

DEEPER STUDY # 1

(13:14) **Abomination of Desolation—Antichrist** (to bdelugma tes eremoseos, *tah bdel-loog'-mah tase er-ay-mo'-seh-ose*): the abomination that makes desolate. Note Jesus' words, "the abomination of desolation, spoken of by *Daniel the prophet*" (Mt.24:15). There are three passages in Daniel that speak of the abomination of desolation.

> Seventy weeks are decreed about your people and your holy city, to finish the transgression, to put an end to sin, and to atone for iniquity, to bring in everlasting righteousness, to seal both vision and prophet, and to anoint a most holy place. Know therefore and understand that from the going out of the word to restore and build Jerusalem to the coming of an anointed one, a prince, there shall be seven weeks. Then for sixty-two weeks it shall be built again with squares and moat, but in a troubled time. And after the sixty-two weeks, an anointed one shall be cut off and shall have nothing. And the people of the prince who is to come shall destroy the city and the sanctuary. Its end shall come with a flood, and to the end there shall be war. Desolations are decreed. And he shall make a strong covenant with many for one week, and for half of the week he shall put an end to sacrifice and offering. And on the wing of abominations shall come one who makes desolate, until the decreed end is poured out on the desolator. (Da.9:24-27)

> Forces from him shall appear and profane the temple and fortress, and shall take away the regular burnt offering. And they shall set up the abomination that makes desolate. (Da.11:31)

> And from the time that the regular burnt offering is taken away and the abomination that makes desolate is set up, there shall be 1,290 days. (Da.12:11)

In Daniel 9:27, the Hebrew says, "upon the wing [or pinnacle] of abominations [shall come] the desolater" or "upon wings as a desolater [shall come] abomination."

In Daniel 11:31, the Hebrew says, "they shall put [place] the abomination that desolates."

In Daniel 12:11, the Hebrew says, "and from the time the daily [sacrifice] shall be taken away, and the abomination that makes desolate set up, [shall be]. . . ."

Several matters need to be discussed about the abomination of desolation spoken of by Jesus and Daniel.

1. The first matter that needs to be considered is *when Daniel's prophecy was fulfilled*.

   a. One clear fulfillment of this prophecy has already taken place, before the time of Jesus about 168 B.C. Antiochus Epiphanes, the King of Syria, conquered Jerusalem and tried to force Grecian culture upon the Jews. He wanted the Jews to become full-fledged Greeks both in custom and religion. He knew that to be successful he had to destroy the Jewish religion. Therefore, He did three of the most horrible things that could ever be done in the minds of the Jewish people. He desecrated the temple by (1) building an altar in the courtyard to the Grecian god Zeus, (2) sacrificing pig's flesh upon it, and (3) setting up a trade of prostitution in the temple chambers (see the Apocrypha—1 Maccabees 1:20-62; see also Josephus, *Ant.* 12.5:3-4; *Wars.* 1.1:2).

   b. Jesus said there is to be a future fulfillment: "When you *see* the abomination of desolation spoken of by the prophet Daniel. . . ." There are four primary views of the future fulfillment of Daniel's prophecy. (1) One view says there is no future fulfillment remaining, that all the signs were fulfilled in the destruction of Jerusalem in A.D. 70 by Titus. (2) Others see Jesus referring to the Church Age and the trials the church has to go through before Christ returns. (3) Still others view the prophecy as referring exclusively to the end time, having nothing to do with the destruction of Jerusalem in A.D. 70 by Titus. (4) Others believe Jesus was answering the very questions the disciples asked; the prophecy refers to both the destruction of Jerusalem and to the end of the world.

   In looking at what Jesus was saying, it is best to let Him speak for Himself without *adding to or taking away* from what He says. An attempt at this has been made in other notes (see DEEPER STUDIES 1, 2—Mk.13:1-37 Division Overview; DEEPER STUDIES 1, 2—Mt.24:1-31). The conclusion of the notes is that the prophecy is *fulfilled* in both Jerusalem's destruction and the end of the world. The Lord is answering the disciples' question.

Jesus is saying that the same thing that happened under Antiochus Epiphanes would happen again to the holy place; in fact, the temple would suffer such total destruction that not one stone would be left upon another. And it did happen only a few decades after Christ uttered this prophecy. What Jesus said took place in a most literal sense under Titus in A.D. 70. (See outline, notes, and DEEPER STUDY # 3—Mt.24:1-14, especially the notes that quote Josephus, the Jewish historian. Reading Josephus' record of Jerusalem's desolation reveals just how terribly the temple, the city, and the people were devastated.)

However, as discussed in the former notes, Jesus was not only answering the disciples' question about when the destruction of Jerusalem would take place; He was *also answering* their question about His return and the end of the world. Daniel's prophecy, and the Lord's elaboration on Daniel's prophecy, are to have multiple fulfillment. The signs that point toward one who had sinned so terribly (Jerusalem) are much the same as the signs that point toward another who is guilty of terrible sin (the world in the end time). There is one critical difference, however. The sin of Jerusalem was the most heinous sin that could be committed: the killing of God's own Son. However, the sin of the world at the end of time will be just as terrible by following the abomination of desolation. Therefore, the world will witness an increase and intensification of the signs at the end of time. As a result there will be great trials such as the world has never seen (v.19). (Again, see the outline and notes—Mt.24:1f for detailed discussion.)

2. A second matter that needs to be discussed about the abomination of desolation is *the division of time* that both Jesus and Daniel seem to give. Jesus did say that the abomination of desolation would launch the worst tribulation the world has ever known (Mk.13:14, 19; Mt.24:15, 21). In His own words, the signs that will occur up until the abomination of desolation are called "the beginning of birth pains or sorrows" (Mt.24:8); and the trials that will occur after the abomination of desolation takes place are called "great tribulation." The tribulation will be unparalleled in history (Mt.24:21). Daniel also gives a division of time just as Jesus did.

> And he shall make a strong covenant with many for one week, and for half of the week he shall put an end to sacrifice and offering. And on the wing of abominations shall come one who makes desolate, until the decreed end is poured out on the desolator. (Da.9:27)

"For half of the week" or "in the middle of the week" (Daniel's seventieth week) definitely points to a period of time (one week) that is divided into two parts. Now note these factors.

a. Daniel is dealing with the "seventieth week," the end of his prophecy. The fact that Jesus is dealing with the end of Jerusalem and the end of the world and the fact that Jesus said He was elaborating on Daniel's prophecy tells us that Daniel is prophesying the end time just as Jesus was.

b. Daniel says that what begins the second half of his seventieth week is "the abomination of desolation" or the prince who causes "abominable idols."[1]

The words of Jesus should be carefully noted: "When you see the abomination of desolation, spoken of by Daniel the prophet. . . ." (Mk.13:14, NKJV; Mt.24:15). Jesus is about to explain what Daniel prophesied in more detail. Jesus explains that the first half of Daniel's week would consist of signs which are "*the beginnings of birth pains or sorrows*" (Mk.13:8; see 13:5-13; Mt.24:8; 24:5-14), and the last half of Daniel's week would consist of unparalleled trials of "*great tribulation.*" The second half of the week would be launched by the abomination of desolation standing in the holy place (Mk.13:14, 19; Mt.24:15, 21).

3. A third matter that needs to be looked at is *the time frame of the end time* (the seventieth week) as predicted by Jesus and Daniel. Scripture refers to the length in the following words (see notes—Rev.11:2; 12:6):

---

1 H.C. Leupold, *Exposition of Daniel*, (Grand Rapids, MI: Baker Book House, 1969), p.434.

- "Time, times, and half a time" (Da.7:25; 12:7).
- "1260 days" (Re.12:6).
- "42 months" (Re.11:2; 13:5-6).

Based upon the days and months given in *Revelation*, if Daniel's time equals one year, then his words, "Time (1 year), times (2 years), and half a time (1/2 year)" are equal to 3 ½ years. Daniel stated that the abomination of desolation will be executed in the middle of the week, that is, after three and one-half years. It is assumed that Christ's words "the beginning of birth pains or sorrows" (that is, the first half of the week) are also three and one-half years. Therefore, in combining the two periods of time (3½ years each) the length of the last days or end time is said to be a literal seven years. Based on the words of *Revelation*, the prophecy of Christ can be diagrammed as seen in the chart in the Division Overview—Mk.13:1-37.

However, it should be noted that many biblical scholars say that the words "times" in Daniel and "days" and "months" in Revelation (in fact, throughout all Scripture) are often used to refer to blocks of time, that is, longer periods or indefinite periods of time.

4. A fourth matter that needs to be looked at is, *What or who is meant by "the abomination of desolation"?* As has already been discussed, many excellent commentators hold that the prophecy refers to the destruction of Jerusalem under both Antiochus Epiphanes (B.C. 168) and under Titus (A.D. 70). There is strong historical evidence and evidence through Jesus answering a specific question of the disciples to support a past fulfillment of this prophecy (Mk.13:4; Mt.24:3). But what about future fulfillment? What or who is meant by "the abomination of desolation" occurring at the end of the world? (See DEEPER STUDY # 1—Rev.11:7; see notes—2 Th.2:3-4; Rev.13:1; 13:3; 13:5-6. See General Subject Index.)

a. Some indication is perhaps given by the phrase itself. In the Old Testament the word *abomination* is connected with idolatry or sacrilege. *Of desolation* means the same as *causes desolation*. In this case it is *the abomination* that causes *desolation*. That is, the abomination acts upon the holy place and personally causes it to be abandoned. This, of course points toward a person's fulfilling the prophecy in a more distant future (in the end times) just as there were two literal persons who have already fulfilled the prophecy, Antiochus and Titus.

b. Mark 13:14 actually uses the *masculine* participle which indicates strongly that the abomination of desolation is a person.

c. Daniel 9:25-27 speaks of a prince who causes the desolation. Leupold, the great Lutheran theologian, translates the prince as "the destroyer."[2] (Because of extraordinary scholarship and simplicity of writing, Leupold should be referred to in studying Daniel.)

d. *2 Thessalonians* and *Revelation* identify an *antichrist* who is to arise in the last days and cause unparalleled havoc upon the world and upon God's people.

(See notes—Mk.13:14; 2 Th.2:4-9; Re.6:2-7; DEEPER STUDY # 1—11:7; notes—13:1-18; 17:7-14. See also Da.9:20-27; 11:31; 12:11.)

---

2 Leupold, *Exposition of Daniel*, p.433.

2 So terrible, it is to be fled from immediately.

This sign is so terrible it is to be fled from immediately. The idea Jesus conveyed is that the abomination (he who makes desolate) will swoop upon the earth suddenly, unexpectedly. His rise and the war He launches against God's temple will be so quick that he takes people by surprise. He poses an immediate danger for believers; therefore, Jesus instructed His followers in Judea to flee immediately (v.14). The imminent danger and urgency is stressed by Christ in four statements.

a. To forget all comforts of home (v.15).

A person is to forget all comforts of home: pictured by a man arising from his roof and immediately fleeing (see DEEPER STUDY # 2; note—Mt.24:17). Picture a person on top of a house escaping some calamity, perhaps a fire or flood. That person would be foolish to reenter the house to retrieve personal belongings regardless of their literal or sentimental value.

b. To forget all personal possessions (v.16).

A person is to forget all personal possessions: pictured by a person working in the field not taking time to go home to get clothes (or possessions).

c. To grieve for those who cannot flee rapidly (v.17).

A person is to grieve for those who cannot flee rapidly: picturing pregnant women and small children.

d. To pray for good conditions when fleeing (v.18).

A person is to pray for good conditions in fleeing: pictured by both winter and the Sabbath day (Mt.24:20). Travel would be more difficult in winter. The Sabbath day represents certain religious rules that would forbid fleeing (travel) for the religiously strong.

> **But when he saw many of the Pharisees and Sadducees coming to his baptism, he said to them, "You brood of vipers! Who warned you to flee from the wrath to come? Bear fruit in keeping with repentance." (Mt.3:7-8)**

DEEPER STUDY # 2

(13:15) **House—Rooftop:** see DEEPER STUDY # 2—Mt.24:17.

---

14 "But when you see the abomination of desolation standing where he ought not to be (let the reader understand), then let those who are in Judea flee to the mountains.
15 Let the one who is on the housetop not go down, nor enter his house, to take anything out,
16 and let the one who is in the field not turn back to take his cloak.
17 And alas for women who are pregnant and for those who are nursing infants in those days!
18 Pray that it may not happen in winter."

---

3 So terrible, it causes horrifying, unparalleled affliction (the great distress or tribulation).

This sign is so terrible it causes horrifying, unparalleled affliction. Matthew actually calls it "great tribulation" or "distress." He says:

> **For then there will be great tribulation, such as has not been from the beginning of the world until now, no, and never will be. (Mt.24:21)**

It is from this verse that the term "the great tribulation" has come. It should be noted that it is the term Christ Himself used to describe the unbelievable afflictions of the end time. No better term could be chosen. "The great tribulation" (or period of unparalleled affliction) is an accurate term, a term chosen by our Lord to strike the truth home to the human heart.

19 "For in those days there will be such tribulation as has not been from the beginning of the creation that God created until now, and never will be."

The great tribulation is to be a period of affliction unparalleled in history. In the years A.D. 66–70, Jerusalem experienced one of the most terrible sieges in all of history. In A.D. 66 the Jews revolted against Roman oppressors, and the Roman army was swift to attack. But the city was difficult to take, primarily for two reasons: it sat upon a hill, well protected by the terrain, and the leaders of the revolt were religious fanatics. Well over a million people had fled into the city behind its protective walls.

As the siege wore on, the predictions of destruction mentioned by Jesus were literally fulfilled. Outside the walls was the Roman army and all the maiming and killing of war. Inside the walls neighbor after neighbor faced famine, pestilence, false deliverers (messiahs), betrayal, murder, revolt, rebellion, hatred. And all took their toll. Josephus says over one million people died and ninety-seven thousand were taken captive. He described well the horrors of the siege:

> *"It appears to me that the misfortunes of all men, from the beginning of the world, if they be compared to these of the Jews, are not so considerable as they were."*[3]

(See notes—Mt.24:7; 24:10; 24:11; See also Josephus, *Wars*. 5.12:3; 6.3:4; 6.8:5.)

In the end time, the world will experience great tribulation—unparalleled in history. Note that Jesus did not describe the great afflictions beyond what He had already said (vv.5–12). A quick glance at the great tribulation period covered in Revelation will give some idea of the horrors that will be experienced (see outlines and notes for all of the following; see also Da.12:1–2).

- ➤ Thunder, lightning, and an earthquake (Re.8:5; see 8:1–5).
- ➤ Natural catastrophes (Re.8:6–12).
- ➤ Demonic-like locust or plagues (Re.8:13–9:11).
- ➤ Demonic-like army (Re.9:12–21).
- ➤ Nations angry, destroying the earth (Re.11:18; see 11:14–19).
- ➤ An evil political ruler (Re.13:1–10).
- ➤ A false religious ruler (Re.13:11–18).
- ➤ Terrible destruction and suffering both upon nature and humanity (Re.16:1–21).
- ➤ An evil, deceptive world power (Re.17:1–18:24).

13:20

[20] "And if the Lord had not cut short the days, no human being would be saved. But for the sake of the elect, whom he chose, he shortened the days."

4 So terrible, God has to intervene and shorten the days of affliction.

The great tribulation is so terrible God has to intervene and shorten the days of affliction. This was a promise to the believers of Jesus' day who would be alive when Jerusalem was overthrown, and it is a promise to the believers of the end time.

God in His providence used His power to shorten the days of the siege of Jerusalem (A.D. 70) for Israel's sake. In the midst of judgment, He was merciful. Israel was not totally annihilated. The siege was shorter than expected. Many have listed *the natural causes* that led to the shorter siege.

- ➤ Division and factions—the Jewish leaders were divided from the first. They never could form a cohesive policy.
- ➤ A disastrous fire destroyed many weapons and provisions.
- ➤ Rampaging gangs were another factor. These were set on self-preservation, stealing, assaulting, and killing. Such occurrences are well documented by Josephus.
- ➤ Treason and betrayal—some surrendered even their fortifications without a fight.
- ➤ The quick attack by Rome—Rome sent the armed force under Titus much quicker than expected.
- ➤ Weak fortifications—Herod Agrippa had intended to strengthen the walls, but he never did.

The believer, of course, sees God's hand in these natural causes. God *worked all things out for good in order to shorten the days and to fulfill His Word*. Despite the terrible tribulation, some lives

---

3 Josephus, *Wars*. Preface 4.

were saved—saved because God was compassionate (2 Pe.3:9). Similarly, the tribulations of the end time will also be shortened.

> And then the lawless one will be revealed, whom the Lord Jesus will kill with the breath of his mouth and bring to nothing by the appearance of his coming. (2 Th.2:8)

> Therefore, rejoice, O heavens and you who dwell in them! But woe to you, O earth and sea, for the devil has come down to you in great wrath, because he knows that his time is short! (Re.12:12)

> They are also seven kings, five of whom have fallen, one is, the other has not yet come, and when he does come he must remain only a little while. (Re.17:10)

Jesus said that God will shorten the days of tribulation for the elect's sake. This proved true when Jerusalem was destroyed. Many Christians fled Jerusalem before the attack, around A.D. 66, apparently because they remembered the Lord's warning. They fled to a smaller town called Pella in the district of Decapolis. These believers prayed for their neighbors and their beloved city, and God heard their intercessions. He shortened the days of terrible trial—shortened them because of the prayers of the elect. In the end times, God will do the same. He will hear the prayers of His people and shorten the days of their tribulation.

God's mercy toward the lost, even toward civilizations and cities, and His willingness to save these in answer to the believers' intercessory prayer is clearly illustrated in Scripture. Abraham's prayer for Sodom and Gomorrah is an example. If just ten righteous people could have been found, the cities would have been spared, despite terrible sin (Ge.18:23f). Lot's prayer for Zoar is another example (Ge.19:20-22).

> Therefore, confess your sins to one another and pray for one another, that you may be healed. The prayer of a righteous person has great power as it is working. (Js.5:16)

> Run to and fro through the streets of Jerusalem, look and take note! Search her squares to see if you can find a man, one who does justice and seeks truth, that I may pardon her. (Je.5:1)

5 So terrible, it causes false messiahs (deliverers) to appear and deceive many.

This sign is so terrible it causes a frantic search for false messiahs (deliverers). False messiahs and prophets will arise. When people are unmercifully oppressed, witnessing scene after scene of death by hunger, pestilence, murder, and war, they cry for deliverance. They are ever so open to a deliverer arising on the scene. And some are always ready to assume the power and leadership for which the oppressed cry. Such people (deliverers who promised salvation from both the Romans and the natural disasters) arose during the siege of Jerusalem. Apparently, the people believed constant rumors that the Messiah had come, that He was either out in the desert or in some secret room within the city, just awaiting the hour to strike. The scene in Jerusalem was somewhat like Jeremiah's day:

> 21 "And then if anyone says to you, 'Look, here is the Christ!' or 'Look, there he is!' do not believe it.
> 22 For false christs and false prophets will arise and perform signs and wonders, to lead astray, if possible, the elect."

> Then I said: "Ah, Lord GOD, behold, the prophets say to them, 'You shall not see the sword, nor shall you have famine, but I will give you assured peace in this place.' " And the LORD said to me: "The prophets are prophesying lies in my name. I did not send them, nor did I command them or speak to them. They are prophesying to you a lying vision, worthless divination, and the deceit of their own minds." (Je.14:13-14)

The same kind of scene will repeat itself in the last days. Many false christs and false prophets will arise. One of these—the great false deliverer of the earth, the antichrist and his false prophet—will deceive the whole earth (see outlines and notes—Re.13:1-18 and related passages). Jesus very simply said, "Do not believe it." Do not believe the rumors about false messiahs, and do not believe the false deliverer—the antichrist.

Jesus warned that these false deliverers will perform great signs and wonders. Deliverers, local and national, always feel and lay claim to being destined. They point to signs and wonders. The end time will witness an increase and an intensification of signs and wonders that will stretch across the whole world. Many seemingly miraculous acts, no doubt, will be performed through manipulating technology and human tricks. Think of what magicians and illusionists are able to do in today's world. Think of what modern technology is capable of. However, the antichrist, and possibly some of the others who will claim to be deliverers, will be fueled by the supernatural power of Satan himself.

> And then the lawless one will be revealed, whom the Lord Jesus will kill with the breath of his mouth and bring to nothing by the appearance of his coming. The coming of the lawless one is by the activity of Satan with all power and false signs and wonders, and with all wicked deception for those who are perishing, because they refused to love the truth and so be saved. (2 Th.2:8–10)

> It performs great signs, even making fire come down from heaven to earth in front of people, and by the signs that it is allowed to work in the presence of the beast it deceives those who dwell on earth, telling them to make an image for the beast that was wounded by the sword and yet lived. (Re.13:13–14)

False deliverers will be so convincing they will threaten even the elect. The elect, of course, are genuine believers. They endure for Jesus regardless of the circumstance or trial. An excellent passage that describes much of the same picture is seen in 2 Thessalonians 2:1–17. The way the elect are able to stand is clearly stated.

> So then, brothers, stand firm and hold to the traditions that you were taught by us, either by our spoken word or by our letter. Now may our Lord Jesus Christ himself, and God our Father, who loved us and gave us eternal comfort and good hope through grace, comfort your hearts and establish them in every good work and word. (2 Th.2:15–17)

13:23

[23] "But be on guard; I have told you all things beforehand."

6 So terrible, it requires foretelling and forewarning.

The great tribulation is so crushing and threatening that Jesus forewarned the world about it. He has not left people unprepared and in the dark. He wants the world to know that God is still on the throne; God will not be taken by surprise when the abomination of desolation arises. God's people can have confidence and be assured of eternal deliverance, no matter the terrible affliction coming upon the earth.

THOUGHT 1. Imagine the horror and suffering that would be caused by atomic warfare. The picture of such terrible affliction gives some idea of what Christ said about the great tribulation. Out of His great love and mercy, God gives humanity a more detailed warning in *Revelation*.

(Mt.24:29–31; Lu.21:25–28)

²⁴ "But in those days, after that tribulation, the sun will be darkened, and the moon will not give its light,"

²⁵ and the stars will be falling from heaven, and the powers in the heavens will be shaken."

²⁶ "And then they will see the Son of Man coming in clouds with great power and glory."

²⁷ "And then he will send out the angels and gather his elect from the four winds, from the ends of the earth to the ends of heaven."

1. **The setting: After the distress or tribulation**
2. **Event 1: Astronomical events will take place worldwide**

3. **Event 2: People will see the Son of Man return in the clouds**

4. **Event 3: God's angels will gather the elect from all over the world**

Division VIII

The Son of God's Olivet Ministry: Jesus' Prophecy of His Return and the End Time, 13:1–37

C. The Coming of the Son of Man, 13:24–27

(Mt.24:29–31; Lu.21:25–28)

13:24–27
Introduction

The greatest event to happen in the history of the world is yet to come. This event is the return of Jesus Christ. The disciples wanted to know, "When will these things be?" (Mk.13:4), and "What will be the sign of Your coming?" (Mt.24:3). Jesus answered the first question in the previous passages (Mk.13:1-23), and He begins to answer the second question about His return in this passage. This is, *The Coming of the Son of Man,* 13:24-37.

1. The setting: After the distress or tribulation (v.24).
2. Event 1: Astronomical events will take place worldwide (vv.24-25).
3. Event 2: People will see the Son of Man return in the clouds (v.26).
4. Event 3: God's angels will gather the elect from all over the world (v.27).

1 The setting: After the distress or tribulation.

13:24

The disciples asked the same question many still ask today: When will Jesus return? Jesus answered their question directly, revealing exactly when He was going to return. He will return "in those days, after that tribulation." The idea is, immediately after the great tribulation. In fact, Matthew

²⁴ "But in those days, after that tribulation, the sun will be darkened, and the moon will not give its light,"

uses the word *immediately* (Mt.24:29). Jesus even said that the days of the great tribulation have to be shortened in order to save mankind (v.20). Apparently, it will be shortened by Jesus' return.

Remember that Jesus was answering two questions. In addition to asking when Jesus would return, the disciples also asked when the temple would be destroyed (vv.1-4). Accordingly, the terrible afflictions predicted by our Lord referred both to Jerusalem's fall in A.D. 70 and to the great tribulation that "has not been from the beginning of the creation" (v.19; see Mt.24:21). Obviously, Jesus did not return after the destruction of Jerusalem and the temple (see note—Mt.24:29-31 for detailed discussion). This is clearly evident as we stand here centuries later. Therefore, what Jesus says in this passage is bound to refer to His coming again. This also indicates that the tribulation just discussed will be the great tribulation of the future, known as the end times. Jesus will return "in those days, after that tribulation." Both the great tribulation and the Lord's return will be tied together. The Lord's return will follow immediately upon the heels of the great tribulation.

Jesus tells us that the most terrible days of suffering and trouble the world has ever seen are yet to come. But He also tells us some glorious, assuring news.

First, He is definitely God. He is omniscient. He knows the future of the earth (evidenced by Jerusalem's destruction about forty years after His death, and the great trial yet to come upon the earth).

Second, He is in control. He will return to shorten the days of trial. There will be an end to all trials (v.20).

13:24-25

24 "But in those days, after that tribulation, the sun will be darkened, and the moon will not give its light,
25 and the stars will be falling from heaven, and the powers in the heavens will be shaken."

2 Event 1: Astronomical events will take place worldwide.

Jesus' return will immediately follow this list of specific astronomical happenings:

➤ "The sun will be darkened."
➤ "The moon will not give its light."
➤ "The stars will be falling from heaven."
➤ "The powers in the heavens will be shaken."

Very practically, such astronomical events occur now. The earth is sometimes darkened by dust from earthly catastrophes such as volcanic eruptions, wind storms, and smoke from huge fires. At other times, an eclipse darkens the sun and moon temporarily. The stars, that is, meteorites of various sizes, fall throughout space often. "The powers of the heavens" being shaken could refer to the heavenly bodies outside our solar system that are called by the Bible "the host of heaven" (De.4:19).

Some speculate that these prophecies foretell modern atomic warfare. Of course, an atomic bomb exploding on earth is powerful enough to darken the sun and moon from earth's view. Worldwide atomic warfare would cause so much dust and pollution it would be difficult for anybody to see anything in outer space. But as the atom is known today, it could not affect the axis or rotation (the falling or shaking) of the sun and moon and stars unless there is to be an intergalactic war of some sort way out in the future. Of course, there is always the possibility that there is a power much greater than what we know today. This is not to say that atomic warfare will never happen. There will be wars and rumors of war as long as the earth stands. But what the Bible teaches is that God is going to end all things, not man. When the world ends, it will be God's ending it by His own will and act and power.

An extreme literalism needs to be avoided when interpreting these verses, for there is just so much we do not know about the laws (powers) of nature and the forces God has put in motion throughout the universe. However, there is no reason for failing to understand the Lord's words as actual or literal events.

What the present passage seems to mean is that the whole universe is going to be affected by Jesus' coming to earth. The sun and moon and the stars and the "powers in the heavens"—the natural laws that regulate the universe—will be affected in the sense that they will *open up and receive Him*. They will serve notice that this is the Creator, the Son of Man, God's very own Son, who is now coming to earth in great power and glory. Imagine an unforeseen meteor shower, a mysterious eclipse, and other unexpected cosmic displays taking place simultaneously, and perhaps it will give us a little glimpse of what Christ is saying. A simple question is: Why would not everything, including the heavenly bodies, put on a display (that would be terrifying to man) when its Creator, the Son of God, returns?

Note in the verses below that the astronomical bodies are affected because of *the evil of mankind and the wrath of God* that is being shown. That is, the scene of falling stars (meteorites) is not for the purpose of human beings witnessing a spectacular event; it is to point to the Son of God, to His judgment's falling on the earth. Every person is going to know beyond any doubt that Jesus is coming in all the power and the glory of God Himself (Re.1:7).

The words "great power and glory" indicate that He is coming to subject all people to His rule and reign and to execute judgment on the earth. Scripture definitely reveals that astronomical happenings will precede and accompany the coming of the Lord.

> **And there will be signs in sun and moon and stars, and on the earth distress of nations in perplexity because of the roaring of the sea and the waves, people fainting with fear and with foreboding of what is coming on the world. For the powers of the heavens will be shaken. (Lu.21:25–26)**

> **And I will show wonders in the heavens above and signs on the earth below, blood, and fire, and vapor of smoke; the sun shall be turned to darkness and the moon to blood, before the day of the Lord comes, the great and magnificent day. (Ac.2:19–20)**

> **For the stars of the heavens and their constellations will not give their light; the sun will be dark at its rising, and the moon will not shed its light. I will punish the world for its evil, and the wicked for their iniquity; I will put an end to the pomp of the arrogant, and lay low the pompous pride of the ruthless. I will make people more rare than fine gold, and mankind than the gold of Ophir. Therefore I will make the heavens tremble, and the earth will be shaken out of its place, at the wrath of the LORD of hosts in the day of his fierce anger. (Is.13:10–13)**

> **Terror and the pit and the snare are upon you, O inhabitant of the earth! He who flees at the sound of the terror shall fall into the pit, and he who climbs out of the pit shall be caught in the snare. For the windows of heaven are opened, and the foundations of the earth tremble. The earth is utterly broken, the earth is split apart, the earth is violently shaken. The earth staggers like a drunken man; it sways like a hut; its transgression lies heavy upon it, and it falls, and will not rise again. On that day the LORD will punish the host of heaven, in heaven, and the kings of the earth, on the earth. They will be gathered together as prisoners in a pit; they will be shut up in a prison, and after many days they will be punished. (Is.24:17–22)**

> **And I will show wonders in the heavens and on the earth, blood and fire and columns of smoke. The sun shall be turned to darkness, and the moon to blood, before the great and awesome day of the LORD comes. (Joel 2:30–31)**

3 Event 2: People will see the Son of Man return in the clouds.

13:26

Jesus plainly foretold that all people living at that time will see Him—the Son of Man—"coming in clouds with great power and glory." Those who believe in Him will look up and be thrilled; those who do not will look up and be terrified. Note exactly what Jesus said.

26 "And then they will see the Son of Man coming in clouds with great power and glory."

First, it is the Son of Man who comes. Jesus claimed that He is the Son of Man, the Son of God incarnate in human flesh as the Perfect Man (see DEEPER STUDY # 3—Mt.8:20). In that day, there will be no doubt about who He is (see Mk.14:61–62). Right now, He is recognized only by believers, but then it will be unmistakable: He is the Son of Man.

Second, all people and every eye will see Him return. This is what is meant by "they." Matthew actually says, "All the tribes [peoples] of the earth will mourn, and they will see the Son of Man coming" (Mt.24:30). Christ's return will be visible to every person on earth (see Re.1:7).

Third, Jesus is coming "in clouds with great power and glory." Picture the scene: the backdrop of heaven is pitch dark, without any major light from the sun and moon. And then, suddenly, as quickly as the flash of lightning, the most brilliant focus of light ever known to mankind appears. The Shekinah glory of God shines in the person of Jesus Christ as He appears to the world. The Son of Man is there, in the clouds, returning in great power and glory just as He said He would.

> **And said, "Men of Galilee, why do you stand looking into heaven? This Jesus, who was taken up from you into heaven, will come in the same way as you saw him go into heaven." (Ac.1:11)**

And to grant relief to you who are afflicted as well as to us, when the Lord Jesus is revealed from heaven with his mighty angels in flaming fire, inflicting vengeance on those who do not know God and on those who do not obey the gospel of our Lord Jesus. They will suffer the punishment of eternal destruction, away from the presence of the Lord and from the glory of his might, when he comes on that day to be glorified in his saints, and to be marveled at among all who have believed, because our testimony to you was believed. (2 Th.1:7–10)

And then the lawless one will be revealed, whom the Lord Jesus will kill with the breath of his mouth and bring to nothing by the appearance of his coming. (2 Th.2:8)

Behold, he is coming with the clouds, and every eye will see him, even those who pierced him, and all tribes of the earth will wail on account of him. Even so. Amen. (Re.1:7)

Then I saw heaven opened, and behold, a white horse! The one sitting on it is called Faithful and True, and in righteousness he judges and makes war. His eyes are like a flame of fire, and on his head are many diadems, and he has a name written that no one knows but himself. He is clothed in a robe dipped in blood, and the name by which he is called is The Word of God. And the armies of heaven, arrayed in fine linen, white and pure, were following him on white horses. From his mouth comes a sharp sword with which to strike down the nations, and he will rule them with a rod of iron. He will tread the winepress of the fury of the wrath of God the Almighty. On his robe and on his thigh he has a name written, King of kings and Lord of lords. (Re.19:11–16)

13:27

²⁷ "And then he will send out the angels and gather his elect from the four winds, from the ends of the earth to the ends of heaven."

4 Event 3: God's angels will gather the elect from all over the world.

When Jesus returns, He will gather together "His elect." Who are the elect?

➤ They are the people who have been justified by God through faith in Jesus Christ (Ro.5:1, 9; 8:33).

➤ They are the people who have been crying (praying, conversing, sharing) day and night unto God (Lu.18:7–8).

Jesus said that He will gather together "His elect" from throughout the entire earth and heaven. Believers who are yet alive on earth will be joined by those who are in heaven (Re.19:14; 20:4).

When the Son of Man comes in his glory, and all the angels with him, then he will sit on his glorious throne. Before him will be gathered all the nations, and he will separate people one from another as a shepherd separates the sheep from the goats. (Mt.25:31–32)

(Mt.24:32-51; Lu.21:29-36)

28 "From the fig tree learn its lesson: as soon as its branch becomes tender and puts out its leaves, you know that summer is near.

29 So also, when you see these things taking place, you know that he is near, at the very gates."

30 "Truly, I say to you, this generation will not pass away until all these things take place."

31 "Heaven and earth will pass away, but my words will not pass away."

32 "But concerning that day or that hour, no one knows, not even the angels in heaven, nor the Son, but only the Father."

33 "Be on guard, keep awake. For you do not know when the time will come.

34 It is like a man going on a journey, when he leaves home and puts his servants in charge, each with his work, and commands the doorkeeper to stay awake.

35 Therefore stay awake—for you do not know when the master of the house will come, in the evening, or at midnight, or when the rooster crows, or in the morning—

36 lest he come suddenly and find you asleep."

37 "And what I say to you I say to all: Stay awake."

1. **The signs point to the end and are recognizable**
   a. Even as a fig tree blossoms
   b. Even as a cause has its effect
   c. Even to the point of being immediate—near, right at hand, v.32

2. **The events occur rapidly—within one generation**

3. **The events are a surety—unchangeable**

4. **The exact time is unknown—neither the day nor the hour is known**

5. **The need is to be on guard—stay alert**
   a. Because the time is unknown
   b. Because believers need to focus on the work God has assigned them

   c. Because Christ is returning suddenly and unexpectedly

   d. Because a believer can be caught sleeping
6. **The warning is to all—watch!**[DS1]

Division VIII

The Son of God's Olivet Ministry: Jesus' Prophecy of His Return and the End Time, 13:1–37

D. The End Time and Its Warning to Believers, 13:28–37

(Mt.24:32–51; Lu.21:29–36)

**13:28-37
Introduction**

Christ had just covered the signs of the end time and of His return. The truth is glorious, for it stirs hope and gives a picture of the future glory that can be ours. But one thing is needful: we must turn our lives over to God or else we will be banished from the presence and glory of Christ forever. As our Savior continued to teach about His return, He gave six critical warnings. This is, *The End Time and Its Warning to Believers,* 13:28–37.

1. The signs point to the end and are recognizable (vv.28–29).
2. The events occur rapidly—within one generation (v.30).
3. The events are a surety—unchangeable (v.31).
4. The exact time is unknown—neither the day nor the hour is known (v.32).
5. The need is to be on guard—stay alert (vv.33–36).
6. The warning is to all—watch! (v.37).

13:28–29

²⁸ "From the fig tree learn its lesson: as soon as its branch becomes tender and puts out its leaves, you know that summer is near.
²⁹ So also, when you see these things taking place, you know that he is near, at the very gates."

1 The signs point to the end and are recognizable.

The end and the return of Christ will be discernable. The signs Jesus had just revealed will point to the fact that the end of the age and His return are near. Believers should be aware of these signs and recognize them when they appear.

a. Even as a fig tree blossoms (v.28a).

The fig tree illustrates what Christ means regarding His return. When the fig tree begins to put forth leaves, we know that summer is near. So when we see "these things" (v.29), the signs He had been sharing, we should *know* that our Lord's return is near. We are to *know*; He does not leave us an option. It is a command: we are to stay alert, looking for the signs of the time so that we *can know* when His return is near. This is the whole point of this passage. We are to be looking for His return *lest* it catch us unexpectedly.

b. Even as a cause has its effect (v.28b).

Christ was speaking of cause and effect: every cause has its effect. The signs covered by Christ are causes (vv.6–27). Christ was saying when the signs (causes) are seen, expect the result (effect): the coming again of the Son of Man. When believers see . . .

- an unusual number of wars and natural disasters, they can know "the beginning of sorrows" has started
- "many" false messiahs and prophets arise, they can know an enormous number of the lost and carnal will be tragically deceived
- bitter persecution, they can know that God will tolerate only so much against His people
- lawlessness abounding and love's growing cold, they can know that God will judge and stop such apostasy
- the earth about to be destroyed, they can know that God will not wait much longer

c. Even to the point of being immediate—near, right at hand (v.29).

Christ says when the signs appear, His return is immediate—near—at the gate or door. The signs point to the *immediacy* of His return. Even though nobody knows the day nor the hour when Christ will return (v.32), believers should discern that the time is at hand by recognizing the signs.

13:30

³⁰ "Truly, I say to you, this generation will not pass away until all these things take place."

2 The events occur rapidly—within one generation.

Christ warned that these events will occur rapidly. They happen in one generation. Just what is meant by "generation" is often disputed. However, it must always be kept in mind that the disciples had asked two questions, one about Jerusalem's destruction and the other about the end of the world. In answering their questions, Christ did not draw a definite line between the two questions. The signs and events that precede one shall precede the other. Therefore, just as the signs and destruction of Jerusalem took place

3 The events are a surety—unchangeable.

Christ warned that what He foretold will definitely come to pass. The events He prophesied are a surety; they are unchangeable and irrevocable. His words will outlast the existence of the present heaven and earth—a figure of speech for the universe.

> 31 "Heaven and earth will pass away, but my words will not pass away."

This present universe is going to pass away. Christ is saying that it is actually going to be done away with and cease to exist in its present condition (2 Pe.3:10-11; Re.21:1).

All that Christ has said—all about the great tribulation and His return—*will* happen. The great tribulation and His return are surer than heaven and earth.

In the eyes of many people, it has been a long, long time since Christ spoke these words; and an innumerable list of events have happened. Therefore, they assume the whole idea of the second coming is a fable, the figment of hopeful imagination. God knew this would happen.

> **Knowing this first of all, that scoffers will come in the last days with scoffing, following their own sinful desires. They will say, "Where is the promise of his coming? For ever since the fathers fell asleep, all things are continuing as they were from the beginning of creation." . . . But do not overlook this one fact, beloved, that with the Lord one day is as a thousand years, and a thousand years as one day. The Lord is not slow to fulfill his promise as some count slowness, but is patient toward you, not wishing that any should perish, but that all should reach repentance. But the day of the Lord will come like a thief, and then the heavens will pass away with a roar, and the heavenly bodies will be burned up and dissolved, and the earth and the works that are done on it will be exposed. Since all these things are thus to be dissolved, what sort of people ought you to be in lives of holiness and godliness, waiting for and hastening the coming of the day of God, because of which the heavens will be set on fire and dissolved, and the heavenly bodies will melt as they burn! But according to his promise we are waiting for new heavens and a new earth in which righteousness dwells. (2 Pe.3:3-4, 8-13)**

Three things are certain in human history: "the beginning of birth pains or sorrows" (v.8); the "great tribulation, such has not been from the beginning of the world" (v.24; Mt.24:21); and "the Son of Man coming in clouds with great power and glory" (v.26; Mt.24:30). The universe will pass away, but not the words Christ has spoken, not what He said would happen. What He said would happen will happen. The three events are certain.

4 The exact time is unknown—neither the day nor the hour is known.

The day and hour of Christ's return—the exact time—are not known to anyone. God alone knows when Christ is to return. The general time will be recognized by expectant believers, but the exact day and hour are known only by God.

> 32 "But concerning that day or that hour, no one knows, not even the angels in heaven, nor the Son, but only the Father."

The second coming is an actual event that is yet to happen. There is "that [fixed] day and hour" when Christ will return. However, the time of the second coming is secret. Throughout history some have thought they knew when Christ was going to return (see 2 Th.2:1-2). But Christ is explicit: only the Father knows.

Some things are to be left entirely in God's hands. The exact day and hour of the Lord's return is one of those things. The *watchful* believer will be sensitive to the season (fig tree, vv.28-29) and know the generation (v.30), but the exact hour and day are hid from human beings, even from the wisest and most spiritual people. *Only* God Himself knows the day. If a person claims to know the hour and day, he or she is a person from whom we should flee. That person's word is not of the Lord.

What did Christ mean when He said that even He did not know when He was to return to earth? If He is the Son of God, possessing the divine (omniscient) nature of God, how could He not know? When Christ came to earth, He "emptied Himself" (Ph.2:7). This means at least the following:

- He took on the nature of man; He became flesh and blood (Ph.2:7; Heb.2:14).
- He voluntarily surrendered and limited Himself to the nature of man *in some respects*. For example, people do not know the future. Christ limited Himself in knowing the future except when and where a demonstration of His divine omniscience was needed.
- While man, Christ willed not to know some things and not to be able to do some things (for example, to be present everywhere, His omnipresence, see Jn.16:7). This enabled Him to identify with the human race more effectively in his limitations and needs.

While man, Christ subjected Himself completely to the Father. This means, of course, that He had to *live in* the Father and *be taught* by the Father (just as we are to live in and be taught by God, except Christ did so perfectly). This is a phenomenal truth. It means that God took His Son and pioneered the Ideal, Perfect life, teaching Him exactly how to live and what to say. Christ had "emptied Himself" in order to cast Himself *perfectly* upon God, trusting God to teach Him how to live and what to say day by day. He was Man, but there was one difference. He was living a perfect life, trusting and depending upon God completely. Therefore, God the Father was able to fill His Son completely and teach Him perfectly. Very simply stated, God was able to take Christ day-by-day and teach Him how to live and what to say and to do it *perfectly*. This is what Scripture proclaims and what Christ emphasized time and again.

> "I have much to say about you and much to judge, but he who sent me is true, and I declare to the world what I have heard from him." . . . So Jesus said to them, "When you have lifted up the Son of Man, then you will know that I am he, and that I do nothing on my own authority, but speak just as the Father taught me." And he who sent me is with me. He has not left me alone, for I always do the things that are pleasing to him. (Jn.8:26, 28–29)

> For I have not spoken on my own authority, but the Father who sent me has himself given me a commandment—what to say and what to speak. And I know that his commandment is eternal life. What I say, therefore, I say as the Father has told me. (Jn.12:49–50)

> Do you not believe that I am in the Father and the Father is in me? The words that I say to you I do not speak on my own authority, but the Father who dwells in me does his works. (Jn.14:10)

> Whoever does not love me does not keep my words. And the word that you hear is not mine but the Father's who sent me. (Jn.14:24)

> For I have given them the words that you gave me, and they have received them and have come to know in truth that I came from you; and they have believed that you sent me. (Jn.17:8)

> Although he was a son, he learned obedience through what he suffered. (He.5:8)

Christ was God-Man, perfectly God, perfectly human in one Person. There is no question about the teaching of Scripture on the Lord's two natures. How did the two natures interwork? There is no way to know. We can never understand the two natures of Christ *beyond what Scripture says*. And this is the point: we are to live by faith, live by the revelation of Scripture. We either accept the record (message, testimony, news) about Christ's becoming Man, or we reject it. That is exactly what God is after: belief in Him and in His Word—that He "so loved the world, that He *gave* His only Son, that whoever believes in Him should not perish but have eternal life" (Jn.3:16).

13:33–36

³³ "Be on guard, keep awake. For you do not know when the time will come.

³⁴ It is like a man going on a journey, when he leaves home and puts his servants in charge, each with his work, and commands the door-keeper to stay awake.

³⁵ Therefore stay awake—for you do not know when the master of the house will come, in the evening, or at midnight, or when the rooster crows, or in the morning—

³⁶ lest he come suddenly and find you asleep."

5 The need is to be on guard—stay alert.

Christ warned that believers need to be on guard for His return. We need to keep awake, stay alert, watch and pray (see outline and notes—Mt.24:42–51; note and DEEPER STUDIES 1, 2—25:1–13; 25:14–30). There are four reasons why the believer must be on guard.

a. Because the time is unknown (v.33).

Believers must be on guard because the time of the Lord's return is unknown (v.32). Again, nobody knows the exact time when Jesus will come; only the Father knows.

b. Because believers need to focus on the work God has assigned them (v.34).

Believers must watch because we have been given a specific task to do, and we must complete the job before Christ returns. The greatest of tragedies would be for a believer not to have finished the job Christ gave him or her to do (see outline and notes—Mt.24:42-51; note and Deeper Studies 1, 2—25:1-13).

c. Because Christ is returning suddenly and unexpectedly (v.35).

Believers must watch because Christ is returning unexpectedly, suddenly. It may be any day, any hour.

d. Because a believer can be caught sleeping (v.36).

Believers must watch because we can be caught napping and sleeping. We need to be careful to not let the return of Christ slip from our awareness. We should not go through one single day of our lives without being alert to the fact that Jesus is coming. Believers who are living when the signs of which Jesus spoke come to pass must be even more alert to the reality of Christ's return.

THOUGHT 1. Four tragic things can happen to believers while we are waiting for the Lord to return.

1) Believers may fail to wait *long enough*. As the days, weeks, and years wear on and on, we can grow more and more drowsy, nodding more and more, becoming less and less alert to the reality of Christ's return—until we live as if Jesus is not going to return.
2) As believers, we may delay, postpone, or slack up in our work for the Lord. We may figure that we have time to do it later; therefore, we may feel that we can set it aside for a while. We may feel that getting a little sidetracked here and there will not hurt that much.
3) We as believers may think that we can go ahead and do what we wish and cover it with the Lord later. We may think that we will have time to correct the matter before the Lord returns.
4) We as believers may begin *to think* like the world. However, God knows how the world thinks, and He has described it clearly for the sake of His dear followers (see 2 Pe.3:3-4, 8-15).

> And I will say to my soul, "Soul, you have ample goods laid up for many years; relax, eat, drink, be merry." But God said to him, 'Fool! This night your soul is required of you, and the things you have prepared, whose will they be?' (Lu.12:19-20)

> Come now, you who say, "Today or tomorrow we will go into such and such a town and spend a year there and trade and make a profit"—yet you do not know what tomorrow will bring. What is your life? For you are a mist that appears for a little time and then vanishes. (Js.4:13-14)

> "Come," they say, "let me get wine; let us fill ourselves with strong drink; and tomorrow will be like this day, great beyond measure." (Is.56:12)

6 The warning is to all—watch! 13:37

Christ concluded this teaching by strongly reinforcing His command to watch (see Deeper Study # 1). Stay awake! Be alert to Christ's coming! No one is exempt: no believer, no unbeliever. Note that Christ expressed this warning repeatedly in five successive verses (vv.33-37).

37 "And what I say to you I say to all: Stay awake."

DEEPER STUDY # 1

(13:37) **Stay Awake, Watch, Be Alert** (gregoreite; pronounced *gray-gor-ay'-teh*): to keep awake, to stay alert, to be watchful and sleepless, to be vigilant. It also includes the idea of being motivated, that is, of desiring, of holding and keeping one's attention (mind) upon a thing. Watching also has the idea of being alert at the right time. It is at night that one really needs to stay awake and watch for the thief (see 1 Th.5:4-9).

Be watchful, stand firm in the faith, act like men, be strong. (1 Co.16:13)

So then let us not sleep, as others do, but let us keep awake and be sober. (1 Th.5:6)

As for you, always be sober-minded, endure suffering, do the work of an evangelist, fulfill your ministry. (2 Ti.4:5)

The end of all things is at hand; therefore be self-controlled and sober-minded for the sake of your prayers. (1 Pe.4:7)

IX. THE SON OF GOD'S PASSION MINISTRY: JESUS' SUPREME SACRIFICE—REJECTED AND CRUCIFIED, 14:1–15:47

A. Jesus' Death Plotted: A Picture of the Passover and Jesus' Death, 14:1–2

(Mt.26:1-5; Lu.22:1-2)

It was now two days before the Passover and the Feast of Unleavened Bread. And the chief priests and the scribes were seeking how to arrest him by stealth and kill him,

² for they said, "Not during the feast, lest there be an uproar from the people."

1. **Picture 1: The Passover, Ex.12:1–51**
2. **Picture 2: The religionists plotted Jesus' death**[DS1]
   a. Plotted by all the leaders
   b. Plotted to use deception and lies to arrest Jesus on false charges: After the pilgrims had left the feast

Division IX

The Son of God's Passion Ministry: Jesus' Supreme Sacrifice—Rejected and Crucified, 14:1–15:47

A. Jesus' Death Plotted: A Picture of the Passover and Jesus' Death, 14:1–2

(Mt.26:1–5; Lu.22:1–2)

14:1–2
Introduction

This passage presents the final stage of Jesus' life before He was crucified. Here, Mark dramatically sets the stage for what is coming. In two short verses, he mentions the Passover, and then he mentions the religionists' plotting Jesus' death—two scenes as opposite from one another as can be imagined. The Passover was a feast, a joyous and festive occasion. It was a celebration of God's glorious deliverance of Israel from the bondage of Egypt. Yet against the backdrop of this joyous celebration, Jesus' murder was being plotted. And tragically, religious leaders were the ones plotting, the very people who should have been taking the lead in Passover ceremonies. On the one hand, there was the celebration of deliverance, the saving of life; on the other hand, there was the plotting of death, the taking of life. This passage deliberately sets the stage for what is to come. This is, *Jesus' Death Plotted: A Picture of the Passover and Jesus' Death,* 14:1-2.

1. Picture 1: The Passover, Ex.12:1–51 (v.1).
2. Picture 2: The religionists plotted Jesus' death (vv.1-2).

1 Picture 1: The Passover, Ex.12:1–51.

The first picture is that of the Passover. For months Jesus had been drilling into His disciples that He was to die. Mark points to two brief facts:

• The Passover was going to be celebrated in just two days.

14:1a

It was now two days before the Passover and the Feast of Unleavened Bread. And the chief priests and the scribes were seeking how to arrest him by stealth and kill him,

- While preparations were being made for the Passover, preparations were also being made to kill Jesus.

In these two simple statements, Mark ties the death of Jesus to the Passover (see outline and notes—Mt.26:17-19). Throughout history, the Passover had pictured Jesus' death. Jesus would now fulfill the Passover by shedding His own blood on the cross.

Historically, the Passover refers back to the time when God delivered Israel from Egyptian bondage (Ex.11:1f). God had pronounced judgment (the taking of the firstborn) on the people of Egypt for their injustices. As He prepared to execute the final judgment, those who believed God were instructed to slay a pure lamb and sprinkle its blood over the door posts of their homes. The blood of the innocent lamb would then serve as a sign that the coming judgment had already been carried out. When seeing the blood, God would *pass over* that house.

Symbolically, the Passover pictures the coming of Jesus Christ as the Savior. The *lamb without blemish* pictures His sinless life, and the *blood sprinkled on the door posts* pictures His blood shed for sinners (Ex.12:5; see Jn.1:29). It was a sign that the life and blood of the innocent lamb had been substituted for the firstborn (believers). The *eating of the lamb* pictures the need for spiritual nourishment gained by feeding on Christ, the Bread of Life. The *unleavened bread* (bread without yeast) pictures the need for putting evil out of one's life and household (see Deeper Study # 1—Mt.26:17).

14:1b–2

It was now two days before the Passover and the Feast of Unleavened Bread. And the chief priests and the scribes were seeking how to arrest him by stealth and kill him,

2 for they said, "Not during the feast, lest there be an uproar from the people."

2 Picture 2: The religionists plotted Jesus' death.

Mark briefly relates a dramatic, yet tragic scene. While the people were in the streets openly preparing to praise God for His delivering power and the saving of life, the religionists were behind closed doors preparing to arrest and murder Jesus. Just imagine! The religious leaders themselves were plotting to take the life of God's very own Son (see Deeper Study # 1).

a. **Plotted by all the leaders (v.1b).**
Both bodies of Jewish religious leaders—the chief priests and the Scribes—were plotting Jesus' death. Matthew adds that the elders or lay leaders were also in on the plot. Matthew also shows the secretiveness of the plot by stating that the leaders met in the home (palace) of the High Priest instead of meeting in the official court (see note—Mt.26:3-5).

b. **Plotted to use deception and lies to arrest Jesus on false charges: After the pilgrims had left the feast (v.1c–2).**
The religious leaders had no legitimate grounds to arrest Jesus, so they had to resort to *deception and lies* (v.1c). They were seeking a way to arrest Him on false charges that would result in His execution (see outline, notes, and Deeper Study # 2—Lu.22:2; also Mt.26:60-66).

The chief priests and Scribes shrewdly decided to arrest Jesus quietly, after all the pilgrims had left the feast to return home (v.2). The *feast* refers to all eight days of the feast. The danger of an uprising would not have passed until all the pilgrims had left the city. Of course, the threat of an uprising was removed by Judas' willingness to betray Jesus. In the crowded mass of about two million people within the city, Judas was able to show them where Jesus was and to quietly identify Him. He was also able to show them how Jesus could be secretly taken in the dark of night (see Mt.26:47-50).

THOUGHT 1. When people are set on doing something wrong, they plot and maneuver to do it. And, too often, they are willing to pay any price to sneak around to do it. This was the case with the religionists plotting Jesus' death. They were willing to pay any price to get rid of Him, even the price of becoming murderers.

THOUGHT 2. Just think! These men were religious leaders, men who professed to know God. Think how deceived they were—how much they had to deceive themselves in order to carry out their evil plan.

> Their throat is an open grave; they use their tongues to deceive. The venom of asps is under their lips. (Ro.3:13)

> Let no one deceive you with empty words, for because of these things the wrath of God comes upon the sons of disobedience. (Ep.5:6)

> Little children, let no one deceive you. Whoever practices righteousness is righteous, as he is righteous. Whoever makes a practice of sinning is of the devil, for the devil has been sinning from the beginning. The reason the Son of God appeared was to destroy the works of the devil. (1 Jn.3:7-8)

> There are those who are clean in their own eyes but are not washed of their filth. (Pr.30:12)

> Everyone deceives his neighbor, and no one speaks the truth; they have taught their tongue to speak lies; they weary themselves committing iniquity. (Je.9:5)

> The heart is deceitful above all things, and desperately sick; who can understand it? (Je.17:9)

DEEPER STUDY # 1

(14:1-2) **Religionists, Plot to Kill Jesus:** the religionists' conflict with Jesus is often misunderstood. This is because so much of the conflict had to do with *rules and regulations* that seem petty and meaningless to *modern* minds (see Mk.2:23-28; 3:1-6, 22-30; notes—Mt.12:1-8; note and DEEPER STUDY # 1—12:10; note—15:1-20; DEEPER STUDY # 2—15:6-9). Four facts will help in understanding why the conflicts happened and were life-threatening, ending in the murder of Jesus Christ.

1. The Jewish nation had been held together through their religious beliefs. Through the centuries, the Jewish people had been conquered by army after army, and millions had been deported and scattered all over the world. Even in Jesus' time, they were subservient to Rome. Their religion was the *binding force* that kept Jews together—in particular their religious rules governing the Sabbath and the temple, and their religious belief that God had called them to be a distinctive people. It was they who worshiped the only true and living God. These rules and this belief protected them from alien beliefs and from being swallowed up by other nations through intermarriage. Their religion was what maintained their distinctiveness as a people and as a nation.

Jewish leaders knew this. They knew that their religion was the *binding force* that held their nation together. Therefore, they opposed anyone or anything that threatened to break the laws of their religion.

2. The religionists were men of deep conviction. They were strong in their beliefs; therefore, they became steeped in religious belief and practice, law and custom, tradition and ritual, ceremony and liturgy, rules and regulations. To break any law or rule governing any practice was a serious offense, for it taught *loose behavior*. And *loose behavior*, once it had spread enough, would weaken their religion, the binding force that held their people together. Therefore, they felt Jesus was committing a great offense by breaking their law. He was weakening the binding force of their nation, their religion.

3. The religionists were men who had profession, position, recognition, esteem, livelihood, and security. Anyone who went contrary to what they believed and taught was a threat to all they had. Some religionists undoubtedly felt that Jesus was a threat to them. Every time Jesus broke their law, He was undermining their very position in society and their security.

4. The religionists were exposed by Jesus. In order for people to know the truth, Jesus had to point out where they were wrong and what they needed to do to get right with God. Both the sin of people and the truth of God had to be proclaimed. The religionists just could not take it. They refused to accept the fact that they were unacceptable to God. They were,

after all, the religious leaders of the day, the very ones who professed God. In their minds, they had no sin, at least not enough sin to bar them from God. Anyone who accused them of being so wrong and so depraved could not conceivably be of God. He or she must be of Beelzebub (see outline and note—Mk.3:22-30).

The religionists presented at least four different responses to Jesus.

1. Some were sincere men of deep conviction. They actually thought Jesus was an imposter, a deceiver, a false messiah. Saul of Tarsus, who was later to become Paul the apostle, would be an example of this position.

2. Some were open-minded enough to seek the truth about Jesus. They observed and reasoned, being honest enough to consider what He was saying, and they sought Him out to discover the truth. Nicodemus would be an example of this response.

3. Some did believe and trust Jesus (see Lu.13:31; Ac.6:7; 15:5; 18:8, 17).

4. Some were *professional* priests and ministers who looked upon Christ as a threat. They held their positions because of the prestige, comfort, livelihood, and security they received from them. Therefore, they opposed Christ rather vehemently. Caiaphas and Annas would be examples of this response.

The error of the religionists was fourfold.

1. They misinterpreted and corrupted God's Word (see notes—Mt.12:1-3; DEEPER STUDY # 1—Jn.4:22; see DEEPER STUDY # 6—Ro.9:4).

2. They committed serious sin after serious sin in God's eyes (see notes—1 Th.2:15-16; see note and DEEPER STUDY # 1—Ro.2:17-29).

3. They rejected God's way of righteousness—God's Messiah, which is Jesus Christ (see notes—Ro.10:4; 1 Co.1:30; Ph.3:9).

4. They allowed religion in its tradition and ritual, ceremony and rules to become more important than meeting the basic needs of human life: religion was more important than a person's need for God and for spiritual, mental, and physical health. Jesus, being the true Messiah, was bound to expose such error. Therefore the battle lines were drawn. The Messiah had to liberate people from this enslaving behavior. He had to liberate them so they could be saved and worship God in freedom of spirit.

The religionists had to oppose anyone who broke their law. They had to oppose Jesus because He was a threat to their nation and to their own personal position and security.

B. Jesus' Anointing at Bethany:
A Study of Love,[DS1] 14:3–9

(Mt.26:6–13; Jn.12:1–8)

³ And while he was at Bethany in the house of Simon the leper, as he was reclining at table, a woman came with an alabaster flask of ointment of pure nard, very costly, and she broke the flask and poured it over his head.

⁴ There were some who said to themselves indignantly, "Why was the ointment wasted like that?

⁵ For this ointment could have been sold for more than three hundred denarii and given to the poor." And they scolded her.

⁶ But Jesus said, "Leave her alone. Why do you trouble her? She has done a beautiful thing to me."

⁷ "For you always have the poor with you, and whenever you want, you can do good for them. But you will not always have me."

⁸ "She has done what she could; she has anointed my body beforehand for burial."

⁹ "And truly, I say to you, wherever the gospel is proclaimed in the whole world, what she has done will be told in memory of her."

1. The woman's act of love was selfless and costly[DS2, 3]

2. The woman's act of love was questioned and she was rebuked harshly

3. The woman's act of love was a good and lovely thing

4. The woman's act of love grasped the opportune time

5. The woman's act of love was all she could do

6. The woman's act of love was rewarded

Division IX

The Son of God's Passion Ministry: Jesus' Supreme Sacrifice—Rejected and Crucified, 14:1–15:47

B. Jesus' Anointing at Bethany: A Study of Love, 14:3–9

(Mt.26:6–13; Jn.12:1–8)

14:3–9
Introduction

One of the tenderest and most touching acts of love to ever be performed is recorded in this passage. John tells us that the woman who performed this act was Mary, the sister of Lazarus (Jn.12:1f; see DEEPER STUDY # 1). Her act of love was simple and sincere; yet at the same time, it required a tremendous sacrifice. The title of this passage could easily be, *A Study of Sacrifice*. In it, we see a strong lesson on sacrifice or sacrificial giving. The message is clear: love and sacrificing for the one loved go hand-in-hand. This is, *Jesus' Anointing at Bethany: A Study of Love*, 14:3–9.

1. The woman's act of love was selfless and costly (v.3).
2. The woman's act of love was questioned, and she was rebuked harshly (vv.4-5).
3. The woman's act of love was a good and lovely thing (v.6).
4. The woman's act of love grasped the opportune time (v.7).
5. The woman's act of love was all she could do (v.8).
6. The woman's act of love was rewarded (v.9).

DEEPER STUDY # 1

(14:3-9) **Mary, Sister of Martha and Lazarus:** multitudes were flowing into the city and the excitement of the Passover was filling the air. There was a sense that something significant was about to happen. Of course, Mary had no idea of the events that were to take place in the last week of Jesus' life, events which were to begin the very next morning with the triumphal entry. But Mary, along with everyone else, sensed that the time for the kingdom to be established was at hand. As Mary once again sat at Jesus' feet, she sensed two things. She sensed the need to repent of her recent criticism of Jesus (see note—Jn.12:3), and she sensed a foreboding of trouble surrounding Him. She may have seen within His eyes a weight so heavy that she was *drawn* to express the most profound faith and appreciation in Him possible. She took the most precious thing she had, a valuable bottle of perfume, and anointed Him as the Messiah, and as her Lord.

Mary's act was one of the most loving and precious acts ever shown to Jesus. It was an act of supreme love and adoration. What He had to say about it reflects this (vv.6-9). Just how loving an act it was can be seen by picturing all that was going on throughout the city at this time and all that was yet to happen: the plotting, the intrigue, the hostility, the attacks, the planned murder, the crowds' streaming into the city by the teeming thousands—crowds who created a worldly, carnival atmosphere. Even Simon the leper's own household had an enormous crowd in it with all the disciples present. Just imagine the noise from the conversation alone. Yet, there sat Mary at Jesus' feet, once again soaking up all He said, loving and adoring Him. He had done so much for her family. Simon the leper may have been her brother-in-law (husband to Martha). He had probably been healed by her Lord. Her brother, Lazarus, had been raised from the dead. They had all been saved by Him. How she loved Him! How she wished to express her love and faith in Him! She wanted to encourage Jesus, to show Him that she cared for Him and loved Him. So, she arose and went to get the most precious thing she had to give Him, and she gave it in the most precious way she knew. She anointed her Lord, even as David and all the kings of Israel had been anointed in the past. She anointed Him not from any official position, but from her heart. It is for this reason that her memory lives on in Scripture. In behalf of all, she anointed the Lord to be the One to experience death for all. In behalf of everyone, she anointed Him as the Lord and Savior, the true Messiah of all hearts and lives who worship and serve Him as the anointed One of God.

14:3

³ And while he was at Bethany in the house of Simon the leper, as he was reclining at table, a woman came with an alabaster flask of ointment of pure nard, very costly, and she broke the flask and poured it over his head.

1 The woman's act of love was selfless and costly.

Because of the hot and dry climate, it was the custom of the day to anoint heads with oil, especially the heads of guests. But this was not Mary's purpose. Mary anointed Jesus *herself* (see DEEPER STUDY # 2). A servant would ordinarily do the anointing, and Simon, owning a home large enough to entertain so many guests, would certainly have had servants (see DEEPER STUDY # 3). Mary was not a servant; she was one of the heads of the household. Mary was not just anointing to fulfill a custom of the day. Her purpose was much greater than that.

Mary took the most precious thing she had and *gave* it to Jesus in the most significant way, in an act of anointing. The oil normally used for anointing the head cost only a mite, the smallest coin in circulation. But the oil Mary used was far more valuable. She took an extremely expensive oil which cost about 300 denarii per flask or bottle. It was the oil used by kings, and they used it only drop by drop. A denarius was the average pay for a day's work. Therefore, the bottle was worth about a whole year's wages.

Note how Mary gave the gift to Jesus. She did not just hand it to Him, nor did she sprinkle a few drops on His head. She broke the neck of the flask and poured the whole bottle on Jesus' head and feet (see Jn.12:3). Why? What was Mary doing?

Mary's anointing of Jesus was a selfless act, a costly act, an act of love for and faith in the Lord Jesus. Very simply put, Mary anointed Jesus to show Him how deeply she loved Him and believed Him to be the true Messiah, *the anointed One of God* (see DEEPER STUDY # 1—Mk.14:3-9; see DEEPER STUDY # 2—Mt.1:18). He was her Savior, Lord, and King. He had done so much for her and her family. She wanted Him to know how much she appreciated, loved, and believed Him.

Something else needs to be noted. Mary may have sensed something within Jesus: a foreboding, a preoccupation of mind, a heaviness of heart, a weight of tremendous pressure. Her heart reached out to Him and wanted to encourage and help Him. Being a young woman in the presence of so many men, she was not allowed to vocally express herself openly. Such privilege was not allowed women of that day, so she did all that she could: she acted. She arose and went for the most precious gift she could think of—a most costly bottle of perfume. And she gave it to Jesus in such a way that He would know that at least one person truly loved Him and believed Him to be the Messiah. She may have hoped that such worship, faith, and love would boost His spirits.

THOUGHT 1. True love is selfless and costly. True love forgets self and pays whatever price is necessary to demonstrate one's love. True love gives its most precious possession. True love is ...

- being all that one should be, changing (repenting) to become that person
- giving one's most prized possession, surrendering all that one is and has
- going wherever one can best share it
- serving wherever one will be most effective

> Grace be with all who love our Lord Jesus Christ with love incorruptible. (Ep.6:24)

> Though you have not seen him, you love him. Though you do not now see him, you believe in him and rejoice with joy that is inexpressible and filled with glory. (1 Pe.1:8)

> Keep yourselves in the love of God, waiting for the mercy of our Lord Jesus Christ that leads to eternal life. (Jude 21)

> Love the LORD, all you his saints! The LORD preserves the faithful but abundantly repays the one who acts in pride. (Ps.31:23)

DEEPER STUDY # 2

(14:3) **Anoint:** see DEEPER STUDY # 1—Ac.10:38.

DEEPER STUDY # 3

(14:3) **Simon the Leper:** see DEEPER STUDY # 1—Mt.26:6.

2 The woman's act of love was questioned, and she was rebuked harshly.

Some who witnessed Mary's act of love were indignant and rebuked her harshly. *Indignant* (Gk. aganaktountes) means to ache within, to be vexed and disturbed. *Scolded* or *criticized* (enebrimonto) means growled, expressed anger, or rebuked. It indicates strong emotions. But note: only some of the disciples felt this way; all did not.

14:4-5

⁴ There were some who said to themselves indignantly, "Why was the ointment wasted like that?

⁵ For this ointment could have been sold for more than three hundred denarii and given to the poor." And they scolded her.

What disturbed these disciples was *not* the fact that Mary anointed Jesus. Anointing Him was easy enough to understand since it was a common custom of the day. What disturbed them was the gift she gave. The gift . . .
- seemed too valuable and expensive
- seemed unnecessary and thoughtless
- seemed misplaced and wasted
- seemed too costly and sacrificial
- seemed to be a foolish and senseless act

Very simply, some of the disciples questioned the act, and even criticized it. They became quite emotional about the matter. They felt cheaper oil should have been used for the anointing, and the expensive oil should have been sold and the money given to the poor.

THOUGHT 1. There are always those who question the believer's love and sacrifices for the Lord. Some even criticize believers who make significant sacrifices. They do not understand the believer's love and commitment (sacrifice) for their Lord. They question the sacrifice of . . .
- money, possessions, comfort
- pleasure, partying, popularity
- position, recognition, prestige
- profession, promotion, security

THOUGHT 2. There are always those who feel the believer's love and sacrifice go too far. They feel . . .
- commitment of life is not necessary, not to the extent of total sacrifice (see Lu.9:23)
- commitment of money is not necessary, not to the extent of tithing (see 1 Co.16:2; Mal.3:10)
- commitment of behavior is not necessary, not to the extent of *separation from the world* (see 2 Co.6:17–18)
- commitment of the tongue is not necessary, not to the extent of cleaning up one's speech completely and witnessing courageously (see Ex.20:7; Mt.12:36–37)

14:6

⁶ But Jesus said, "Leave her alone. Why do you trouble her? She has done a beautiful thing to me."

3 The woman's act of love was a good and lovely thing.

Jesus knew that some of the disciples were questioning and criticizing Mary. He reacted strongly, ordering them to leave her alone and referring to her loving deed as a "beautiful thing" or "good work." The word Christ used for beautiful or good is not *agathos* which speaks of moral goodness. He chose to use the word *kalos,* which means both good and lovely. It means something so good that it is striking, appealing, attractive, and pleasant.

Mary was driven to express her faith and love for Jesus in the most meaningful way she could. She did this by anointing Him as her Lord with the most expensive perfume she possessed.

The most significant person in Mary's life was the Lord Jesus. He was the Messiah, the Savior and Lord of her life and family. She wished to show Him that He was deserving of all she was and had. Therefore, Mary's love and sacrifice was a *good work,* a *lovely work,* a *beautiful thing,* and it struck the attention of the Lord. There was no way such love and sacrifice could ever escape His sight.

THOUGHT 1. The love and sacrifice that leads a person to do *good works* and *lovely works* for Christ attract His attention. His eyes do not miss the good and lovely works of those devoted to Him. He is *struck* by their sacrifice of life, money, time, and whatever else they present to Him.

> **In the same way, let your light shine before others, so that they may see your good works and give glory to your Father who is in heaven. (Mt.5:16)**

> **Show yourself in all respects to be a model of good works, and in your teaching show integrity, dignity. (Tit.2:7)**

> **And let us consider how to stir up one another to love and good works. (He.10:24)**

> **I know your works, your love and faith and service and patient endurance, and that your latter works exceed the first. (Re.2:19; see Mt.25:34–40 for a descriptive picture of Jesus' knowledge about us.)**

4 The woman's act of love grasped the opportune time.

Mary grasped the opportunity to do something special for Jesus. Jesus made a significant point many people often miss. Opportunities come and go—and once they are gone, they are gone for good. Mary demonstrated the difference. The poor would always be present for believers to help, but the privilege of ministering to Jesus would not always be available. If the disciples were to minister to Him, they had to grasp the opportunity while Jesus was with them.

> [7] "For you always have the poor with you, and whenever you want, you can do good for them. But you will not always have me."

THOUGHT 1. What a lesson for mankind! The presence of Jesus, that is, a sense of His presence and of His Word, is not always pounding away at our minds and hearts. We need to grasp the opportunity to show our love and sacrifice for Christ when it presents itself. The opportunity will pass. In fact, the opportunity and privilege of life itself will soon pass. The servant of the Lord must love and act while it is still day. The night is coming when we will no longer be able to serve our Lord.

> **We must work the works of him who sent me while it is day; night is coming, when no one can work. (Jn.9:4)**

> **Making the best use of the time, because the days are evil. (Ep.5:16)**

5 The woman's act of love was all she could do.

Jesus said that Mary had "done what she could." She took all she had, symbolized in her most precious and valuable possession, and sacrificed it for Jesus. She could do no more. Her heart reached out toward Jesus, and she acted sacrificially with the deepest devotion.

> [8] "She has done what she could; she has anointed my body beforehand for burial."

> **But lay up for yourselves treasures in heaven, where neither moth nor rust destroys and where thieves do not break in and steal. (Mt.6:20)**

> **For whoever would save his life will lose it, but whoever loses his life for my sake and the gospel's will save it. For what does it profit a man to gain the whole world and forfeit his soul? (Mk.8:35–36)**

> **Indeed, I count everything as loss because of the surpassing worth of knowing Christ Jesus my Lord. For his sake I have suffered the loss of all things and count them as rubbish, in order that I may gain Christ. (Ph.3:8)**

Jesus remarked that Mary's anointing pointed toward His burial, His death. Some commentators think Mary knew what she was doing, having grasped what Jesus had been saying—that He was soon to die. They feel Mary grasped the fact when others did not. But this is unlikely. The atmosphere surrounding everyone was that the kingdom was about to be set up. However, whether she knew what she was doing or not, Jesus took her act and applied it to His death. He said that her love and faith, the anointing of His body, pointed toward His death. In simple terms,

Mary's love and faith, gift and anointing *were a witness of anticipation*. She was witnessing to the Lord's death by looking ahead to it.

Today, the believer's love and faith, gift and anointing *are a witness of fact*. The believer is to witness to the Lord's death by looking back to it. It is a fact: He did die for the sins of the world.

> But God shows his love for us in that while we were still sinners, Christ died for us. (Ro.5:8)

> He himself bore our sins in his body on the tree, that we might die to sin and live to righteousness. By his wounds you have been healed. (1 Pe.2:24)

14:9

⁹ "And truly, I say to you, wherever the gospel is proclaimed in the whole world, what she has done will be told in memory of her."

6 The woman's act of love was rewarded.

The Savior rewarded Mary for her sincere, sacrificial act of love. He honored her in a special way because she had so greatly honored Him. Today, centuries later, Mary is still receiving the reward Jesus promised her. Her beautiful act is forever preserved in God's inspired Word, and believers throughout the world are touched by it.

Several things about Mary stand as an ideal for all: her deep love and faith in Jesus, her sacrificial gift, her courage in proclaiming her strong love and faith by anointing Jesus before a room full of men. Such devotion and love could not be allowed to fade from history. Jesus memorialized it, and He will memorialize the faith and love of any believer who sacrifices for Him.

> As for the rich in this present age, charge them not to be haughty, nor to set their hopes on the uncertainty of riches, but on God, who richly provides us with everything to enjoy. They are to do good, to be rich in good works, to be generous and ready to share, thus storing up treasure for themselves as a good foundation for the future, so that they may take hold of that which is truly life. (1 Ti.6:17–19)

(Mt.26:14-16; Lu.22:3-6)

¹⁰ Then Judas Iscariot, who was one of the twelve, went to the chief priests in order to betray him to them.

¹¹ And when they heard it, they were glad and promised to give him money. And he sought an opportunity to betray him.

1. **Judas was personally irresponsible**
   a. Was full of jealousy
   b. Was full of ambition
   c. Was full of greed
   d. Was devil-possessed, Jn.13:27
2. **Judas forsook Christ: Deceived and betrayed Him**

Division IX

The Son of God's Passion Ministry: Jesus' Supreme Sacrifice—Rejected and Crucified, 14:1–15:47

C. Jesus' Betrayal by Judas: Why a Disciple Failed, 14:10–11

(Mt.26:14–16; Lu.22:3–6)

14:10–11
Introduction

Perhaps the most tragic aspect of Judas Iscariot's betrayal of Jesus is that Judas had known the Lord personally. He had walked with Jesus during the Lord's earthly ministry, professing to be one of His closest followers. The fact that he could know Jesus so well and still end up failing and being doomed eternally is a warning to all of us. All of us need to understand why Judas failed so miserably. This is, *Jesus' Betrayal by Judas: Why a Disciple Failed,* 14:10-11.

1. Judas was personally irresponsible (vv.10-11).
2. Judas forsook Christ: Deceived and betrayed Him (v.11).

1 Judas was personally irresponsible.

14:10–11

Judas was personally irresponsible. He forsook Jesus, denied and betrayed Him, and Judas alone is to be blamed. No one made him do it; he personally took the initiative. But why would Judas deny and betray Jesus? This passage suggests several reasons.

¹⁰ Then Judas Iscariot, who was one of the twelve, went to the chief priests in order to betray him to them.

¹¹ And when they heard it, they were glad and promised to give him money. And he sought an opportunity to betray him.

a. Was full of jealousy (v.10).

Judas seems to have been jealous of the other apostles. The exact words, "Judas Iscariot, who was one of the twelve" are significant. The Greek actually reads, "Judas Iscariot, *the one* of the twelve." The definite article "the" is a part of the text. There seems to be some kind of priority and importance suggested by this wording. At first, Jesus had noticed some great potential, some unusual qualities about Judas. Judas was not only called by Jesus, he was elevated and given a position of authority among the disciples. He had been appointed the treasurer of the group, an extremely important function. He was in charge of the Lord's funds and the purchasing of whatever was needed (Jn.12:6; 13:29; see Lu.8:2-3). Such a high position and responsibility indicates the high esteem with which he was held by Jesus and the others. But something happened. Judas was never a part of Christ's inner circle of three (Peter, James, and John).

Apparently, Judas' mood and attitude began to turn sour at some point. Jesus, of course, knew what was happening to his heart and character; therefore, Judas probably saw himself excluded more and more from intimacy with Jesus. He saw himself, who had been one of the first, becoming one of the last.

Most likely, jealousy and envy began to fill his heart, and he refused to deal with it. The result was inevitable: he became even more unreachable and felt less and less important. Judas could not take it. He began to be consumed with jealousy and envy and the urge to retaliate. He who *had been one* of the twelve denied Jesus and reacted against Him.

> **Let us not become conceited, provoking one another, envying one another. (Ga.5:26)**

> **A tranquil heart gives life to the flesh, but envy makes the bones rot. (Pr.14:30)**

b. Was full of ambition (v.10).

Judas was definitely ambitious. He approached the chief priests thinking they were the *winning* side. Right along with the other disciples, Judas was seen seeking after the higher positions in the government they thought Jesus would set up (see outline and notes—Mk.9:33-37; Mt.18:1-4; Lu.9:46-48).

There was one difference, however, between Judas and the other disciples. They never lost faith in Jesus' *Person*, that He was the true Messiah, but Judas did. They all thought that wealth, power, and position would be theirs when Jesus set up His kingdom. They simply misunderstood the Messiah's *method* for saving the world, not His *Person*; but Judas mistook both Jesus' method and Person. As the days passed, the fact that Jesus was not going to set up His kingdom at that time became more and more apparent. The authorities were mobilizing against Jesus to kill Him, and it seemed as though they were going to be successful. Jesus had even been teaching that they were to be successful; He had predicted that He was to be killed by their hands.

Judas became convinced that he had been mistaken about Jesus. Jesus was not the real Messiah. He was just another mistaken self-proclaimed messiah. He was doomed and there was no way out. Judas' dreams of wealth and power and position with Jesus were shattered. In going to the chief priests, he was trying to get whatever he could out of the situation. He wanted to be in good standing with the winning side and to get what he could.

> **It shall not be so among you. But whoever would be great among you must be your servant, and whoever would be first among you must be your slave, even as the Son of Man came not to be served but to serve, and to give his life as a ransom for many. (Mt.20:26-28)**

> **Whoever exalts himself will be humbled, and whoever humbles himself will be exalted. (Mt.23:12)**

> **How can you believe, when you receive glory from one another and do not seek the glory that comes from the only God? (Jn.5:44)**

c. Was full of greed (v.11).

Judas was a thief, consumed with greed and the love of money (Jn.12:6). In fact, this is the sin of Judas that is stressed above all the others by Scripture. Matthew records that Judas asked the chief priests *how much* they would give him to betray Jesus (Mt.26:15).

THOUGHT 1. Note four significant facts about greed.

1) Greed is a growing sin. It has to be fed to grow. We lust for more and more. Desiring is normal and natural. It is when we feed our desires that they become sinful and grow and grow. (See notes—Js.4:1-3; 4:2. These notes will stir additional thoughts for application in dealing with desires and lust.)

2) Greed or covetousness, the desire for more and more, will eat at us just like a cancer. Judas had what he needed: food, clothing, and housing. He did not go without. What was he after? The sin of lusting for more and more ate away at him, causing him to put his hand into the treasury.

3) Greed is sin. But note: it is not money that is sinful; it is the love of money (1 Ti.6:10). Money is a *thing*; it is *inanimate*, *lifeless*. It has no feelings, no desires, no will to act. People are the culprits. People are the ones who crave more and more; therefore, it is people who sin, not the piece of paper or metal.

4) Greed is very, very dangerous. It is one of the most dangerous sins.

> And he said to them, "Take care, and be on your guard against all covetousness, for one's life does not consist in the abundance of his possessions." (Lu.12:15)

> Put to death therefore what is earthly in you: sexual immorality, impurity, passion, evil desire, and covetousness, which is idolatry. (Col.3:5)

> For the love of money is a root of all kinds of evils. It is through this craving that some have wandered away from the faith and pierced themselves with many pangs. (1 Ti.6:10)

> Your gold and silver have corroded, and their corrosion will be evidence against you and will eat your flesh like fire. You have laid up treasure in the last days. (Js.5:3)

> Whoever is greedy for unjust gain troubles his own household, but he who hates bribes will live. (Pr.15:27)

> He who loves money will not be satisfied with money, nor he who loves wealth with his income; this also is vanity. (Ec.5:10)

THOUGHT 2. Judas allowed his strength to become his weakness. This is often true with us.

➢ Gifts of administration can lead to being overbearing.
➢ Gifts of loveliness can lead to being sensual.
➢ Gifts of humility can lead to no service.
➢ Gifts of leadership can lead to being self-seeking.
➢ Gifts of speaking can lead to being prideful or super-spiritual.

d. Was devil-possessed, Jn.13:27 (v.11).

Judas actively denied Jesus and sought how to betray Him. Only a person controlled by the devil denies and betrays Jesus. The devil did enter into Judas (Jn.13:27). Apparently, Judas had filled his heart with the lust for more and more instead of filling it with Jesus. He went too long without repenting and letting Jesus into his life, and the devil was able to fill his being. The devil blinded and took control of his thinking. Hence, Judas was able to justify his betrayal in his own mind. He was, after all, helping the religious body and saving himself from being arrested as one of the followers of Jesus. Therefore, he betrayed Jesus of Nazareth, who apparently in Judas' mind was just another mistaken self-proclaimed messiah who was doomed to be arrested and condemned as an insurrectionist.

In looking at the bargain to which Judas agreed in betraying Jesus, thirty pieces of silver seems a small price for betraying someone of the Lord's stature. It amounted to only about four or five months' wages. However, two things need to be kept in mind.

First, Judas probably expected to get much more, but he did not dictate the terms—the chief priests did. They were going to arrest Jesus in just a few days anyway, just as soon as the pilgrims left the city (Mt.26:5). All Judas did was move their schedule up a few days.

Second, Judas felt that Jesus was doomed, without any hope of escape. He had become convinced that Jesus was not the true Messiah, but just another mistaken self-proclaimed messiah. It is possible that Judas betrayed Jesus because he was angry for having been deceived and disillusioned. He was willing to get what he could, no matter how small the amount.

Once Judas had approached the leaders, he was forced to betray Jesus regardless of how much or how little they were willing to pay him. If he attempted to back out of the deal, he felt they would arrest him right along with Jesus and His disciples.

2 Judas forsook Christ: Deceived and betrayed Him.

11 And when they heard it, they were glad and promised to give him money. And he sought an opportunity to betray him.

Judas intentionally deceived and betrayed Jesus. It did not happen spontaneously in some sudden surge of emotion; Judas looked for the opportunity to betray Jesus. The picture is that of being on the prowl, searching and seeking, looking here and there for the right moment. Judas' heart was set, full of intrigue, plotting evil and planning its strategy. He did *not* believe in Jesus, but even more, He *willed* to do evil against Jesus, to hurt Him, to destroy Him; and he sought the opportunity to do so. Just how deceitful Judas was is clearly seen: immediately after bargaining with the authorities, he sat down to eat with Jesus. He sat at the very table where the Lord's Supper was being instituted.

THOUGHT 1. Note that Judas not only rejected Jesus, but he also sought to destroy Him. Many reject Jesus, but they do not seek to harm and destroy Him.

➤ Some curse Him, consciously or unconsciously dishonoring His name.
➤ Some talk and teach against His divine nature, against the fact that He is the Son of God.
➤ Some talk and teach against the written revelation of Himself and the truth, that is, the Word of God, the Holy Bible.
➤ Some talk and teach against His active presence in the life of the genuine believer.

> Beware of false prophets, who come to you in sheep's clothing but inwardly are ravenous wolves. (Mt.7:15)

> Now the Spirit expressly says that in later times some will depart from the faith by devoting themselves to deceitful spirits and teachings of demons, through the insincerity of liars whose consciences are seared. (1 Ti.4:1–2)

> But understand this, that in the last days there will come times of difficulty. For people will be lovers of self, lovers of money, proud, arrogant, abusive, disobedient to their parents, ungrateful, unholy, heartless, unappeasable, slanderous, without self-control, brutal, not loving good, treacherous, reckless, swollen with conceit, lovers of pleasure rather than lovers of God, having the appearance of godliness, but denying its power. Avoid such people. (2 Ti.3:1–5)

D. Jesus' Last Chance Given to Judas:
The Appeal to a Sinner, 14:12–21

(Mt.26:17–25; Lu.22:21–23; Jn.13:21–31)

¹² And on the first day of Unleavened Bread, when they sacrificed the Passover lamb, his disciples said to him, "Where will you have us go and prepare for you to eat the Passover?"

¹³ And he sent two of his disciples and said to them, "Go into the city, and a man carrying a jar of water will meet you. Follow him,

¹⁴ and wherever he enters, say to the master of the house, 'The Teacher says, Where is my guest room, where I may eat the Passover with my disciples?'

¹⁵ And he will show you a large upper room furnished and ready; there prepare for us."

¹⁶ And the disciples set out and went to the city and found it just as he had told them, and they prepared the Passover.

¹⁷ And when it was evening, he came with the twelve.

¹⁸ And as they were reclining at table and eating, Jesus said, "Truly, I say to you, one of you will betray me, one who is eating with me."

¹⁹ They began to be sorrowful and to say to him one after another, "Is it I?"

²⁰ He said to them, "It is one of the twelve, one who is dipping bread into the dish with me."

²¹ "For the Son of Man goes as it is written of him, but woe to that man by whom the Son of Man is betrayed! It would have been better for that man if he had not been born."

1. **The Setting: The Passover was approaching**
   a. The disciples asked where they were to observe the Passover
   b. It was Jesus' habit to worship and observe the Passover
2. **Jesus knew about Judas' denial and betrayal**
   a. He kept His plans and movement secret
   b. He shared only with His trusted disciples
      1) He had preplanned the arrangements
      2) He sent trusted disciples to carry out the arrangements
   c. He kept His plans despite the impending betrayal
3. **Jesus gave Judas every chance to repent**
   a. The first chance: He tried to stir conviction
      1) Stirred sorrow in the faithful
      2) Stirred self-examination in the faithful
   b. The second chance: He revealed monstrous deception
4. **Jesus gave Judas a last warning**

Division IX

*The Son of God's Passion Ministry: Jesus' Supreme
Sacrifice—Rejected and Crucified, 14:1–15:47*

D. Jesus' Last Chance Given to Judas: The Appeal to a Sinner, 14:12–21

(Mt.26:17–25; Lu.22:21–23; Jn.13:21–31)

14:12–21
Introduction

It was time to observe the Passover, and Judas had just plotted with the authorities to betray Jesus. They wanted to arrest Him in a quiet spot where the people would not be present and rise to His defense. Judas was just waiting for the right place and time (vv.10-11).

Jesus was fully aware of Judas' activities and plans. Yet, He gave him one last chance to repent. In spite of what Judas was in the process of doing—betraying Jesus and handing Him over to His executioners—Jesus still loved Judas and wanted him to be saved. This passage is a demonstration of the truth that the Lord does not want anybody to perish, but that He wants all to repent (2 Pe.3:9; 1 Ti.2:4). This is, *Jesus' Last Chance Given to Judas: The Appeal to a Sinner,* 14:12-21.

1. The Setting: The Passover was approaching (v.12).
2. Jesus knew about Judas' denial and betrayal (vv.13–17).
3. Jesus gave Judas every chance to repent (vv.18-20).
4. Jesus gave Judas a last warning (v.21).

14:12

¹² And on the first day of Unleavened Bread, when they sacrificed the Passover lamb, his disciples said to him, "Where will you have us go and prepare for you to eat the Passover?"

1 The Setting: The Passover was approaching.

Jerusalem was stirring with excitement, for the Passover was approaching. Josephus, the notable Jewish historian of that day, estimated that between two and three million people flooded into the city to observe the Passover. Pilgrims by the teeming thousands came from all over the world. The mass of people and the necessary housing, food, and other arrangements that had to be made—along with the commercial carnival atmosphere—can hardly be imagined.

a. The disciples asked where they were to observe the Passover.
The disciples had to ask Jesus where they were to celebrate the Passover. He had not told them, not even given them a hint. The day of unleavened bread was at hand, and so far as they knew, no arrangement had been made to secure a place for them to observe the Passover. Considering the housing shortage with the mass of pilgrims, such apparent oversight was most unusual. The disciples must have wondered and questioned why the Lord had not shared His plans earlier.

b. It was Jesus' habit to worship and observe the Passover.
The disciples did not ask Jesus *if* He was going to observe the Passover; they asked Him *where* He would do so. Jesus faithfully worshiped and kept the feasts of the Jews. He did not neglect the requirements of the law. The disciples knew this.

2 Jesus knew about Judas' denial and betrayal.

Judas had just plotted with the chief priests against Jesus (vv.10–11), and Jesus knew that Judas was looking for the ideal opportunity to betray Him. This seems to be the very point of what happened in these verses.

a. He kept His plans and movement secret (v.13a).

Jesus could not let Judas know where He was going to observe the Passover, lest Judas lead the authorities to arrest Him in the upper room before He had completed His mission with the disciples. For this reason, the Lord had kept His plans and movements secret. The disciples did not know where He wished to celebrate the Passover. He could not reveal the plans to a sinful, fallen disciple who was denying and betraying Him. That disciple (Judas) would only interrupt what Jesus was trying to do with the faithful disciples in the upper room location. He would only create havoc, cause disturbance, hindering and hampering the work of Jesus.

> ¹³ And he sent two of his disciples and said to them, "Go into the city, and a man carrying a jar of water will meet you. Follow him,
> ¹⁴ and wherever he enters, say to the master of the house, 'The Teacher says, Where is my guest room, where I may eat the Passover with my disciples?'
> ¹⁵ And he will show you a large upper room furnished and ready; there prepare for us."
> ¹⁶ And the disciples set out and went to the city and found it just as he had told them, and they prepared the Passover.
> ¹⁷ And when it was evening, he came with the twelve.

b. He shared only with His trusted disciples (vv.13b–16).

Jesus shared His plan with only two of His faithful and trusted disciples. Note that Jesus did have a plan, and He followed that plan to the most minute detail. He had apparently pre-planned the arrangements, and He sent two trusted disciples to carry out the arrangements. They followed His instructions exactly. But note how secretive the instructions were. Secret arrangements were necessary because Judas and the authorities were seeking to catch Jesus in a quiet place away from the people. This upper room would have been an ideal place to arrest Him.

Jesus directed the two disciples to look for a pre-planned sign: a man carrying a pitcher of water (v.13b). This was a most unusual sight. Women were usually the ones who carried pitchers, often on their heads. It was apparently a sign for the disciples to quietly follow.

Jesus did not name the homeowner or tell where the house was. He simply said to follow the man with the pitcher on his head and to tell the homeowner that "The Teacher" requests the room (v.14). The man would then lead the two disciples to the upper room of his home. The disciples did exactly as Jesus had instructed (v.16).

c. He kept His plans despite the impending betrayal (v.17).

Jesus kept His plans despite the betrayer and those who wanted to stop Him. Note the courage and power of Jesus to control the circumstances and events.

THOUGHT 1. Note several striking and convicting points.

1) Jesus knows about the denial and betrayal of any person, just as He knew about Judas.
2) Jesus does not reveal His plans or movements to the individual who is denying and betraying Him. Those who deny Jesus know this. They have no sense, no consciousness, no awareness of Jesus' presence. The Lord's plans are not known to them, and the movements of God's Spirit are neither felt nor experienced.
3) Jesus shares His plans and movement only with faithful and trusted followers.
4) Jesus' plans are sure; they are fixed. Just as they could not be stopped by Judas, so they cannot be stopped now, no matter the denial and betrayal. Jesus keeps His plans, working out whatever is necessary to fulfill them.

> So Jesus said to them, "The light is among you for a little while longer. Walk while you have the light, lest darkness overtake you. The one who walks in the darkness does not know where he is going." (Jn.12:35)

> And we know that for those who love God all things work together for good, for those who are called according to his purpose. (Ro.8:28)

> The natural person does not accept the things of the Spirit of God, for they are folly to him, and he is not able to understand them because they are spiritually discerned. (1 Co.2:14)

3 Jesus gave Judas every chance to repent.

14:18–20

As Jesus and His disciples were observing the Passover, the Lord stunned the disciples with a blood-chilling announcement: one of them would betray Him (v.18). He made this shocking announcement for a specific purpose: He was giving Judas every chance to repent.

¹⁸ And as they were reclining at table and eating, Jesus said, "Truly, I say to you, one of you will betray me, one who is eating with me."
¹⁹ They began to be sorrowful and to say to him one after another, "Is it I?"
²⁰ He said to them, "It is one of the twelve, one who is dipping bread into the dish with me."

a. The first chance: He tried to stir conviction (vv.18–19).

The first chance was an attempt to stir conviction within Judas. When Jesus said that one of the twelve would betray Him, Judas was seated there. He heard the words of Jesus. What were his thoughts? He had tried to hide his sin, and he had done a pretty good job of it. In his mind no one knew about his sin (plot), not even the disciples who were his closest associates. But he was surely wondering, "Does Jesus know; or is Jesus stabbing in the dark, guessing, suspicious, aware that something is brewing, but not quite sure what?" Scripture is silent about the betrayer's thoughts, but one thing is known: Judas was not convicted of his sin, not enough to repent. However, note what happened to the faithful and trusted disciples.

First, they were stirred with deep sorrow in their hearts (v.19a). The words *Be sorrowful* (Gk. lupeisthai; pronounced *loop-ace'-thigh*) mean to grieve, to sorrow with heaviness of heart. Their hearts were gripped with a real burden, a heavy weight of grieving.

Second, they were stirred to examine their own hearts (vv.19b–20). They asked, "Is it I?" Note how they had matured. They knew the weakness of the flesh, that it could so easily fail. Each one feared lest a great fall lay ahead of them. Note also how they did not look for the fault or weakness in others, but they looked at themselves. What a lesson for us all!

THOUGHT 1. The man who should have been . . .

- convicted, was not
- grieving, was not
- examining his own heart, was not
- sorrowing, was not
- repenting, was not

THOUGHT 2. Two things are critical, even for the most faithful and trusted.
1) To know the weakness of the human flesh, the great danger of falling.
2) To always be examining oneself and not others.

> How can you say to your brother, 'Brother, let me take out the speck that is in your eye,' when you yourself do not see the log that is in your own eye? You hypocrite, first take the log out of your own eye, and then you will see clearly to take out the speck that is in your brother's eye. (Lu.6:42)

> For I know that nothing good dwells in me, that is, in my flesh. For I have the desire to do what is right, but not the ability to carry it out. (Ro.7:18)

> Therefore let anyone who thinks that he stands take heed lest he fall. (1 Co.10:12)

> Let a person examine himself, then, and so eat of the bread and drink of the cup. (1 Co.11:28)

> Examine yourselves, to see whether you are in the faith. Test yourselves. Or do you not realize this about yourselves, that Jesus Christ is in you?—unless indeed you fail to meet the test! (2 Co.13:5)

b. The second chance: He revealed monstrous deception (v.20).

The second chance given to Judas left him without excuse if he refused to heed it. Jesus revealed that He knew about the *monstrous deception*. Jesus said directly that it was one of the twelve men who were eating with Him at that very moment who would betray Him. What deception! The sinner sat with Jesus, partaking of His Last Supper and being guilty of the most terrible sin.

Note that Judas was told that his sin was known. Yet, even after he was told, he still felt he could get away with it. He refused to repent. He continued on in his deception, rejecting chance after chance.

> No, I tell you; but unless you repent, you will all likewise perish. . . . No, I tell you; but unless you repent, you will all likewise perish. (Lu.13:3, 5)

> Repent therefore, and turn back, that your sins may be blotted out. (Ac.3:19)

> Repent, therefore, of this wickedness of yours, and pray to the Lord that, if possible, the intent of your heart may be forgiven you. (Ac.8:22)

4 Jesus gave Judas a last warning.

Jesus gave Judas one last warning, a warning that should have shaken the evil man to his core. He warned Judas of the terrible judgment that was to come on him. Jesus knew the destiny of the sinner, the terrible fate that awaited him. It would be better never to have been born than to deny and betray Christ.

> [21] "For the Son of Man goes as it is written of him, but woe to that man by whom the Son of Man is betrayed! It would have been better for that man if he had not been born."

THOUGHT 1. Note the grace of God in warning sinners of judgment.

1) Sinners are told in *advance*, before judgment ever comes or is ever pronounced. Judas was told. Sinners can still repent when they *first* hear about judgment. They can still be saved as long as they are living. It is God's grace that warns them of the consequences of their sin, of coming judgment.

2) Sinners are never compelled to repent of their denial or betrayal of Christ. Judas was not forced to turn from his evil; neither is any other sinner. It is God's grace that respects our will and desires. God loves and cares, warns and speaks frankly, but He never forces obedience.

> Woe to the world for temptations to sin! For it is necessary that temptations come, but woe to the one by whom the temptation comes! And if your hand or your foot causes you to sin, cut it off and throw it away. It is better for you to enter life crippled or lame than with two hands or two feet to be thrown into the eternal fire. And if your eye causes you to sin, tear it out and throw it away. It is better for you to enter life with one eye than with two eyes to be thrown into the hell of fire. (Mt.18:7–9)

> For the wages of sin is death, but the free gift of God is eternal life in Christ Jesus our Lord. (Ro.6:23)

> How shall we escape if we neglect such a great salvation? It was declared at first by the Lord, and it was attested to us by those who heard. (He.2:3)

> And just as it is appointed for man to die once, and after that comes judgment. (He.9:27)

> The soul who sins shall die. The son shall not suffer for the iniquity of the father, nor the father suffer for the iniquity of the son. The righteousness of the righteous shall be upon himself, and the wickedness of the wicked shall be upon himself. (Eze.18:20)

(Mt.26:26–30; Lu.22:7–20; Jn.13:1–30)

1. **The first act: Jesus took the bread**
   a. He gave thanks for it
   b. He broke it and passed it on, identifying it as His body
2. **The second act: Jesus took the cup**
   a. He gave thanks for it
   b. He offered it and they drank from it
   c. He identified the cup as His blood, which was to be poured out (offered) for many
3. **The third act: Jesus revealed the hope of a glorious kingdom, the kingdom of God**

4. **The fourth act: Jesus and His disciples sang a hymn**

²² And as they were eating, he took bread, and after blessing it broke it and gave it to them, and said, "Take; this is my body."

²³ And he took a cup, and when he had given thanks he gave it to them, and they all drank of it.

²⁴ And he said to them, "This is my blood of the covenant, which is poured out for many."

²⁵ "Truly, I say to you, I will not drink again of the fruit of the vine until that day when I drink it new in the kingdom of God."

²⁶ And when they had sung a hymn, they went out to the Mount of Olives.

Division IX

The Son of God's Passion Ministry: Jesus' Supreme Sacrifice—Rejected and Crucified, 14:1–15:47

E. Jesus' Institution of the Lord's Supper, 14:22–26

(Mt.26:26–30; Lu.22:7–20; Jn.13:1–30)

14:22–26
Introduction

So much happened in the upper room. John is the only Gospel writer to cover the upper room in great detail. He devotes five entire chapters to the event. In contrast, Mark covers only two events of the upper room, and both of these are given in only brief detail. Mark concentrates on Judas' betrayal and the Lord's Supper. In five fully-packed verses, he shares what Jesus did to establish this memorial meal for His followers. This is, *Jesus' Institution of the Lord's Supper,* 14:22–26.

1. The first act: Jesus took the bread (v.22).
2. The second act: Jesus took the cup (vv.23–24).
3. The third act: Jesus revealed the hope of a glorious kingdom, the kingdom of God (v.25).
4. The fourth act: Jesus and His disciples sang a hymn (v.26).

14:22

²² And as they were eating, he took bread, and after blessing it broke it and gave it to them, and said, "Take; this is my body."

1 The first act: Jesus took the bread.

As Jesus and His disciples observed the Passover meal, Jesus took bread into His hands. This symbolized that His death was a voluntary act. His destiny was in His hands. He was not forced to die, but He willingly died.

Just as the Father knows me and I know the Father; and I lay down my life for the sheep.... For this reason the Father loves me, because I lay down my life that I may take it up again. No one takes it from me, but I lay it down of my own accord. I have authority to lay it down, and I have authority to take it up again. This charge I have received from my Father. (Jn.10:15, 17–18)

a. He gave thanks for it.

Jesus gave thanks for the bread He and His disciples were about to share. But His giving of thanks for the bread had a deeper significance: He was not just thanking God for the physical sustenance provided, but for what the bread represented, the *deliverance and the provision and assurance of eternal life* through His sacrificial death.

b. He broke it and passed it on, identifying it as His body.

Jesus broke the bread, symbolizing that His body was to be broken; that is, sacrificed for humanity's deliverance (Is.53:5). This act was so significant that the early church sometimes called the Lord's Supper simply *the breaking of bread* (Ac.2:42; 1 Co.10:16). Under the Old Testament, the broken bread pictured the sufferings of the Israelites. Now, under the New Testament, the bread was to picture the broken body of Christ (1 Co.11:24).

> **But he was pierced for our transgressions; he was crushed for our iniquities; upon him was the chastisement that brought us peace, and with his wounds we are healed. (Is.53:5)**

The Lord gave the bread to the disciples to eat. Jesus' instruction to *take* it means that we are to take and receive Christ into our lives. The moment we take and receive Christ is the moment of redemption. It is that moment of redemption that is to be remembered in this ordinance (see DEEPER STUDY # 2—Mt.26:26; note—Jn.6:52–58).

> **This is the bread that comes down from heaven, so that one may eat of it and not die. I am the living bread that came down from heaven. If anyone eats of this bread, he will live forever. And the bread that I will give for the life of the world is my flesh. (Jn.6:50–51)**

2 The second act: Jesus took the cup.

Just as Jesus had done with the bread, He took the cup into His hands. Again, Jesus was teaching that His death was voluntary. He held His own life in His hands. His life was not being taken from Him; He was laying it down (see Jn.10:11, 17–18).

> ²³ And he took a cup, and when he had given thanks he gave it to them, and they all drank of it.
> ²⁴ And he said to them, "This is my blood of the covenant, which is poured out for many."

a. He gave thanks for it (v.23a).

Jesus gave thanks also for the cup. He thanked God for the deliverance that would come through His sacrifice, through the shedding of His blood.

b. He offered it and they drank from it (v.23b).

Jesus gave the cup to His disciples, and they all drank of it. Jesus was again saying that He must become a part of our very being if we wish to be delivered from sin. *Gave* (edoken) is in the Greek aorist tense. This means Christ gave the cup *once-for-all*. He died once and only once (Ro.6:10), and we partake of His death once and only once (Ro.6:6).

> **We know that our old self was crucified with him in order that the body of sin might be brought to nothing, so that we would no longer be enslaved to sin. (Ro.6:6)**

> **For the death he died he died to sin, once for all, but the life he lives he lives to God. (Ro.6:10)**

c. He identified the cup as His blood, which was to be poured out (offered) for many (v.24).

Jesus identified the cup as His blood of the New Covenant. He simply meant that His blood established a new covenant with God. His blood allowed a new relationship between God and people. Note the Lord's exact words.
- "This is my blood"—Christ's blood, which was shed from His body, was to become the sign, the symbol of the New Covenant. His blood was to take the place of the sacrifice of animals.
- "The covenant" or "the new covenant"—Christ's blood, the sacrifice of His life, established a new covenant between God and humanity (see He.9:11–15). We are now to approach God through faith in His blood, His sacrifice. Before, under the Old Covenant, people who wanted a right relationship with God approached God through the sacrifice of an animal's blood. Old Testament believers believed that God accepted them because of the sacrifice

of the animal. Now, under the New Covenant, we believe that God accepts us because of the sacrifice of Christ. This is what Jesus said: the blood of the New Covenant was *His* blood, and it was poured out or shed for many people (see Deeper Study # 4—Mt.26:28; note—He.9:18–22). Our sins are forgiven and we become acceptable to God by believing that Christ's blood was shed for us.

> In him we have redemption through his blood, the forgiveness of our trespasses, according to the riches of his grace. (Ep.1:7)

> But if we walk in the light, as he is in the light, we have fellowship with one another, and the blood of Jesus his Son cleanses us from all sin. (1 Jn.1:7)

> My little children, I am writing these things to you so that you may not sin. But if anyone does sin, we have an advocate with the Father, Jesus Christ the righteous. He is the propitiation for our sins, and not for ours only but also for the sins of the whole world. (1 Jn.2:1–2)

The point is, we must personally receive what Christ has done for us. We must drink, partake, absorb, assimilate Christ's blood into our life. That is, we must believe and trust the death of Christ to secure forgiveness of our sins. We must allow Christ's death to become the very nourishment, the innermost part and energy, the very flow of our life (see Deeper Study # 3—Mt.26:27–28).

> Whoever feeds on my flesh and drinks my blood has eternal life, and I will raise him up on the last day. For my flesh is true food, and my blood is true drink. Whoever feeds on my flesh and drinks my blood abides in me, and I in him. As the living Father sent me, and I live because of the Father, so whoever feeds on me, he also will live because of me. This is the bread that came down from heaven, not like the bread the fathers ate, and died. Whoever feeds on this bread will live forever. (Jn.6:54–58)

14:25

²⁵ "Truly, I say to you, I will not drink again of the fruit of the vine until that day when I drink it new in the kingdom of God."

3 The third act: Jesus revealed the hope of a glorious kingdom, the Kingdom of God.

Jesus' third act in instituting the Lord's Supper was the giving of two great promises:

➢ The promise of a glorious kingdom (see Deeper Study # 3—Mt.19:23–24).
➢ The promise of a glorious celebration (see outline and notes—Mt.22:1–14 for discussion).

Both promises are possible because of the body and blood of Christ, and both promises were given to the person who partakes of the body and blood of Christ. Partaking of the body and blood of Christ does not mean taking communion; it means taking Christ as Savior through faith in Him and acceptance of His sacrifice for one's sins. The act of taking communion (the Lord's Supper) does not save. The reality of what the Lord's Supper represents is what saves: His broken body and shed blood—His sacrificial, substitutionary death.

Jesus promised a day when all genuine believers will sit down with Him in the Kingdom of God. This is the promise of perfection, of living forever in the new heavens and earth, of sitting with Christ in the glorious kingdom of God which is to be established in the future.

> The Spirit himself bears witness with our spirit that we are children of God, and if children, then heirs—heirs of God and fellow heirs with Christ, provided we suffer with him in order that we may also be glorified with him. (Ro.8:16–17)

> For this light momentary affliction is preparing for us an eternal weight of glory beyond all comparison. (2 Co.4:17)

> When Christ who is your life appears, then you also will appear with him in glory. (Col.3:4)

> For in this way there will be richly provided for you an entrance into the eternal kingdom of our Lord and Savior Jesus Christ. (2 Pe.1:11)

4 The fourth act: Jesus and His disciples sang a hymn.

Despite the sorrow, perplexity, and uncertainty of what lay ahead—Calvary and the cross—Jesus and His disciples sang a hymn. They sang the hymn in praise to the Father for the salvation He was providing through the sacrifice of His Son. They sang the hymn in celebration of the great *hope* which God gives of *deliverance and salvation*. They sang the hymn out of thankful hearts in anticipation of being together again in the kingdom of God.

14:26

> 26 And when they had sung a hymn, they went out to the Mount of Olives.

> **These things I have spoken to you, that my joy may be in you, and that your joy may be full. (Jn.15:11)**

> **As sorrowful, yet always rejoicing; as poor, yet making many rich; as having nothing, yet possessing everything. (2 Co.6:10)**

> **Rejoice in the Lord always; again I will say, rejoice. (Ph.4:4)**

F. Jesus' Prediction of Peter's Denial:
How Jesus Treats Failure, 14:27–31

(Mt.26:31–35; Lu.22:31–34; Jn.13:36–38)

1. **Jesus showed tenderness in the face of weakness and failure**

2. **Jesus encouraged returning to Him after failure**
3. **Jesus tried to get the disciples to face their failures**
   a. Peter's verbal loyalty
   b. Jesus' appeal for conviction
4. **Jesus further pressed the disciples to recognize their weakness: Peter's flaming self-confidence**

27 And Jesus said to them, "You will all fall away, for it is written, 'I will strike the shepherd, and the sheep will be scattered.'"

28 "But after I am raised up, I will go before you to Galilee."

29 Peter said to him, "Even though they all fall away, I will not."

30 And Jesus said to him, "Truly, I tell you, this very night, before the rooster crows twice, you will deny me three times."

31 But he said emphatically, "If I must die with you, I will not deny you." And they all said the same.

Division IX

The Son of God's Passion Ministry: Jesus' Supreme Sacrifice—Rejected and Crucified, 14:1–15:47

F. Jesus' Prediction of Peter's Denial: How Jesus Treats Failure, 14:27–31

(Mt.26:31–35; Lu.22:31–34; Jn.13:36–38)

14:27–31
Introduction

We human beings are weak and sure to fail. Scripture attributes our failures to one basic reason: we are not perfect. By nature, that is, by thought, act and being, we fall short in so many ways.

➢ Our thoughts fall short: our thoughts are imperfect, incomplete, never absolute nor all-embracing.
➢ Our actions fall short: they are imperfect, incomplete, never all that they can be, not in an absolute sense.
➢ Our beings fall short: our beings are imperfect, incomplete, corruptible, and dying.

We are weak; we do fail. We are short of perfection by nature. Scripture expresses the same thought another way. Humans are flesh, beings with a nature that is basically driven by self-interest and selfish urges. People desire to please and pamper their flesh and will, body and mind. We seek to please and pamper our flesh through comfort and ease, pleasure and excitement, stimulation and feelings, recognition and fame. And we seek to please and pamper our will through power and conquest, achievement and position, knowledge and development.

It is not our urges and goals that are wrong; it is people who are wrong. The urges within us are good and healthy when we put them in their proper place, that is, when we use them to the glory of God and for the benefit of others as Scripture dictates. When we act for the glory of God and the welfare of others, there is nothing wrong with comfort and ease, with pleasure and excitement, with stimulation and feelings, with recognition and fame.

For example, God expects His people to possess power and to conquer spiritually, mentally, and physically. He expects us to achieve and secure better positions, to gain more knowledge and more development, to be ever increasing and growing. The problem arises when we are not able to control our flesh and will, body and mind. Too often people focus on themselves, misusing and depriving other people to fulfill their own urges. Their misdeeds can range all the way from minor deception to destroying life.

Christ's realistic assessment of selfish human tendencies are the heart of Mark 14:27-31. Humans have a weak and fallen nature that causes us to be imperfect and incomplete, corruptible and dying. Our flesh is weak and failing; therefore, we must receive a new nature from God, a supernatural nature. We cannot trust in the arm of the flesh; we must trust in the arm of God. We must receive a *God-given resurrected power* (nature) if we are to live a conquering and fulfilled life, a life that pleases God.

Peter and the disciples needed to learn this. They trusted their own flesh and their own strength. Therefore, they were destined to fail despite a determination that was as strong as it could be. Jesus needed to prepare them. They were to fail and fall away at His death because of the weakness of their flesh. But Jesus would arise from the dead. They would need to know they were not rejected because they had fallen away. And they would need to receive the power of the resurrection through the presence of the Holy Spirit so that they could conquer and not fail in the future. This is, *Jesus' Prediction of Peter's Denial: How Jesus Treats Failure,* 14:27-31.

1. Jesus showed tenderness in the face of weakness and failure (v.27).
2. Jesus encouraged returning to Him after failure (v.28).
3. Jesus tried to get the disciples to face their failures (vv.29-30).
4. Jesus further pressed the disciples to recognize their weakness: Peter's flaming self-confidence (v.31).

1 Jesus showed tenderness in the face of weakness and failure.

14:27

Jesus knew that His disciples—the ones who had followed Him most closely for the last three years and had just received the Lord's Supper—would stumble and fall away from Him that very night. He referred to the prophecy that foretold that, when He would be smitten, His followers would be scattered (Zec.13:7).

[27] And Jesus said to them, "You will all fall away, for it is written, 'I will strike the shepherd, and the sheep will be scattered.'"

In referring to this specific prophecy, Jesus also made the point that God was behind His death. The Scripture says, "I [God] will smite the shepherd" (Zec.13:7). There was a Godly purpose for Jesus' dying, an eternal purpose.

> **This Jesus, delivered up according to the definite plan and foreknowledge of God, you crucified and killed by the hands of lawless men. God raised him up, loosing the pangs of death, because it was not possible for him to be held by it. (Ac.2:23-24)**

Jesus said that, when He was killed, the disciples would tragically forsake Him. Not a single one would stand up for Him. The threat of the world and the weakness of their flesh would be too much to overcome. They would fail.

Note that Jesus *predicted* their failure. In so doing, He helped them in several ways:
- He taught them the weakness and failure of human flesh.
- He laid the groundwork of the resurrection, the basis for receiving the new power (nature) of God, the presence of the Holy Spirit.
- Their remembering His words would stir them to remember His tenderness and care, and it would draw them back to Him more quickly and easily.
- Their remembering His words would stir faith in Him as the Son of God who is omniscient, knowing all things.
- Their faith would be strengthened by understanding how the Old Testament prophecy was fulfilled in Jesus and them: "I will strike the Shepherd, and the sheep will be scattered."

2 Jesus encouraged returning to Him after failure.

Jesus encouraged the disciples to return to Him after their failure. Jesus had been blunt: they would fall. But now He was just as clear. He would go before them into Galilee. Their failure, even in so crucial an hour, would not cause Him to reject them. Despite their failure, they could return to Him, and there would be a glorious reunion.

14:28

²⁸ "But after I am raised up, I will go before you to Galilee."

Note: Jesus again predicted His resurrection. It was His resurrection that made both *repentance* and the glorious *reunion* possible.

THOUGHT 1. No matter how terrible the failure, we can repent and return to Christ and rest assured of being a part of the glorious reunion in the great day of His return.

> **Repent, therefore, of this wickedness of yours, and pray to the Lord that, if possible, the intent of your heart may be forgiven you. (Ac.8:22)**

> **If we confess our sins, he is faithful and just to forgive us our sins and to cleanse us from all unrighteousness. (1 Jn.1:9)**

> **Whoever conceals his transgressions will not prosper, but he who confesses and forsakes them will obtain mercy. (Pr.28:13)**

14:29–30

²⁹ Peter said to him, "Even though they all fall away, I will not."
³⁰ And Jesus said to him, "Truly, I tell you, this very night, before the rooster crows twice, you will deny me three times."

3 Jesus tried to get the disciples to face their failures.

Jesus wanted His disciples to face their weaknesses and failures. People will not work to help us with our weaknesses and failures until we first face them ourselves.

a. **Peter's verbal loyalty (v.29).**

b. **Jesus' appeal for conviction (v.30).**

Peter strongly declared his loyalty to Christ. In response, Jesus pressed the point, spelling out in detail that Peter would not only fall one time, but he would fall three times, all in the same night. Jesus' pressing of the point was an appeal for Peter to become convicted of the weakness of his flesh. Note what Peter reveals about himself in his prideful statement to the Lord.

First, Peter was sincere and full of genuine fervor for the Lord. He was thoroughly convinced he would not fall and fail his Lord.

Second, Peter did not know the weakness of the flesh, not in times of great trial.

Third, Peter looked at the weaknesses and failures of others, not at his own. He could see how others could perhaps fall, but not himself. He felt that he loved and cared for the Lord too much to fail Him.

Fourth, Peter's confidence was in himself, in his own natural strength. *As with all people*, his natural strength failed. The need for the Lord's strength, for the presence of the Holy Spirit to conquer self was the great lesson Peter had to learn. Very simply, he and the others had to learn to trust the strength of Jesus and not their own flesh, not if they wished to please God and be acceptable to Him.

THOUGHT 1. The cock's crowing was probably mentioned to trigger the warning about the weakness of the flesh in the mind of Peter and the other disciples. For any who have the opportunity to hear a rooster crow, it is a good trigger to remind them of the weakness of their own flesh and the great need to walk in the power of the Spirit of God.

> **Therefore let anyone who thinks that he stands take heed lest he fall. (1 Co.10:12)**

> **Whoever trusts in his own mind is a fool, but he who walks in wisdom will be delivered. (Pr.28:26)**

4 Jesus further pressed the disciples to recognize their weakness: Peter's flaming self-confidence.

Jesus' prediction of Peter's failure led him and the others to pledge their loyalty to Christ even more strongly. Peter went as far as to say that he would die with Christ rather than deny him, and the others affirmed that they would as well.

Notice exactly what Jesus had done: He had prompted these men to exaggerate their failure. The message about the weakness of human flesh provoked Peter to boast of his loyalty to Jesus, a loyalty rooted in confidence in his flesh. Jesus had to get the point across, so He stressed the fact that Peter would deny Him (v.30). But Peter refused to accept the truth. In a bold display of self-confidence, he declared that he would not deny Jesus, even if he had to die for Him. What caused Peter to be so confident, so sure, that he would be true to Christ, whatever the cost?

³⁰ And Jesus said to him, "Truly, I tell you, this very night, before the rooster crows twice, you will deny me three times."

³¹ But he said emphatically, "If I must die with you, I will not deny you." And they all said the same.

First, Peter's over-confidence was caused by being blind to the cross (Mt.26:34). Peter simply did not see the cross. It was the image of Jesus' hanging on the cross that was going to cause Peter to deny Him. Jesus had told Peter all about the cross, but he had refused to believe it (see notes—Mt.17:22; 18:1-2). The fact that human flesh was so sinful, so depraved that God would have to crucify His Son to set people free from the flesh was just too much to grasp (see outline, notes, and DEEPER STUDY # 1—Lu.9:23; notes—Ro.6:6-13; Ga.2:20; 5:24; 6:14; see also Ro.6:2; Col.3:3).

Second, Peter's over-confidence was caused by not knowing himself, his own personal weaknesses, the weaknesses of his human flesh. Peter's self-image was strong. He saw himself above *serious* sin and failure. He asserted with all the confidence in the world that he would die for Jesus before denying Him.

Third, Peter's over-confidence was caused by contradicting Jesus instead of listening to Him—caused by not listening to the Word of Jesus, to what Jesus was saying. Jesus was warning the disciples about the deceitfulness and weakness of the human heart. Peter and the rest just refused to accept the fact. They denied personal weaknesses; they rejected the Word of Jesus.

THOUGHT 1. We need to firmly understand Peter's tendencies in order to recognize them in ourselves.

1) Peter was a strong believer, one of the strongest.
2) Peter really failed to understand himself, his flesh. The one sin that a believer should not commit is to deny Jesus. To die for Jesus rather than to deny Him is the one thing a genuine believer would be expected to do.
3) Peter believed strongly that he, his flesh, was above serious sin (see Ro.3:9f; 7:8, 14-18; Ga.5:19f).
4) Peter failed not once, but three times, and all three times were in the same night with Christ right off to his side (Lu.22:61).

THOUGHT 2. Note that all the disciples declared their loyalty, boasting confidence in their flesh. Peter was only the spokesman for the group.

It is the Spirit who gives life; the flesh is no help at all. The words that I have spoken to you are spirit and life. (Jn.6:63)

For by works of the law no human being will be justified in his sight, since through the law comes knowledge of sin. (Ro.3:20)

For I know that nothing good dwells in me, that is, in my flesh. For I have the desire to do what is right, but not the ability to carry it out. (Ro.7:18)

Those who are in the flesh cannot please God. (Ro.8:8)

Thus says the LORD: "Cursed is the man who trusts in man and makes flesh his strength, whose heart turns away from the LORD." (Je.17:5)

THOUGHT 3. We need to listen and keep the Words of Jesus, and do just what He said. It is when we fail to listen to the Words of Jesus, to the Holy Scriptures, that we fall.

➢ Keeping the Words of Jesus assures us that we have eternal life.

It is the Spirit who gives life; the flesh is no help at all. The words that I have spoken to you are spirit and life. (Jn.6:63)

Simon Peter answered him, "Lord, to whom shall we go? You have the words of eternal life." (Jn.6:68)

Truly, truly, I say to you, if anyone keeps my word, he will never see death. (Jn.8:51)

➢ Keeping the Words of Jesus assures us of the presence of the Holy Spirit.

If you love me, you will keep my commandments. And I will ask the Father, and he will give you another Helper, to be with you forever. (Jn.14:15–16)

➢ Keeping the Words of Jesus assures us of fellowship with God and Christ.

Jesus answered him, "If anyone loves me, he will keep my word, and my Father will love him, and we will come to him and make our home with him." (Jn.14:23)

➢ Keeping the Words of Jesus assures us that we know Him.

And by this we know that we have come to know him, if we keep his commandments. (1 Jn.2:3)

➢ Failing to keep the Words of Jesus dooms us to judgment.

The one who rejects me and does not receive my words has a judge; the word that I have spoken will judge him on the last day. (Jn.12:48)

G. Jesus in the Garden of Gethsemane:
Bearing the Weight of Unspeakable Suffering, 14:32–42

(Mt.26:36–46; Lu.22:39–46; Jn.18:1; He.5:7–8; 12:3–4)

32 And they went to a place called Gethsemane. And he said to his disciples, "Sit here while I pray."

33 And he took with him Peter and James and John, and began to be greatly distressed and troubled.

34 And he said to them, "My soul is very sorrowful, even to death. Remain here and watch."

35 And going a little farther, he fell on the ground and prayed that, if it were possible, the hour might pass from him.

36 And he said, "Abba, Father, all things are possible for you. Remove this cup from me. Yet not what I will, but what you will."

37 And he came and found them sleeping, and he said to Peter, "Simon, are you asleep? Could you not watch one hour?"

38 "Watch and pray that you may not enter into temptation. The spirit indeed is willing, but the flesh is weak."

39 And again he went away and prayed, saying the same words.

40 And again he came and found them sleeping, for their eyes were very heavy, and they did not know what to answer him.

41 And he came the third time and said to them, "Are you still sleeping and taking your rest? It is enough; the hour has come. The Son of Man is betrayed into the hands of sinners."

42 "Rise, let us be going; see, my betrayer is at hand."

1. **Picture 1: Jesus' great need for prayer and for friends to be at His side**

2. **Picture 2: Jesus' heavy agony and pressure**

3. **Picture 3: Jesus' desperate search for relief**
   a. He got all alone: Prostrated Himself
   b. He prayed for the cup of the hour, the cross, to pass from Him
      1) For the cup to be taken away[DS1]
      2) For God's will to be done

4. **Picture 4: Jesus' disappointment in His friends**

5. **Picture 5: Jesus' continuing ministry—even under trial**

6. **Picture 6: Jesus' perseverance in prayer—despite no answer from God**

7. **Picture 7: Jesus' continued disappointment in friends**

8. **Picture 8: Jesus' relief of soul and spiritual strength**

9. **Picture 9: Jesus' acceptance of God's chosen path**

Division IX

The Son of God's Passion Ministry: Jesus' Supreme Sacrifice—Rejected and Crucified, 14:1–15:47

G. Jesus in the Garden of Gethsemane: Bearing the Weight of Unspeakable Suffering, 14:32–42

(Mt.26:36–46; Lu.22:39–46; Jn.18:1; He.5:7–8; 12:3–4)

14:32–42
Introduction

No person could ever understand the depth of sorrow and agony experienced by Jesus in the Garden of Gethsemane. His experience is the picture of a terrifying struggle—a struggle against sin and the awful judgment which is to fall upon sin. It is a picture which should cause every human being to bow in humble adoration and worship of the Lord Jesus, for Jesus bore the sorrow and agony of sin for every person. He bore the punishment of sin for all. This is, *Jesus in the Garden of Gethsemane: Bearing the Weight of Unspeakable Suffering,* 14:32–42.

1. Picture 1: Jesus' great need for prayer and for friends to be at His side (v.32).
2. Picture 2: Jesus' heavy agony and pressure (vv.33–34).
3. Picture 3: Jesus' desperate search for relief (vv.35–36).
4. Picture 4: Jesus' disappointment in His friends (v.37).
5. Picture 5: Jesus' continuing ministry—even under trial (v.38).
6. Picture 6: Jesus' perseverance in prayer—despite no answer from God (v.39).
7. Picture 7: Jesus' continued disappointment in friends (v.40).
8. Picture 8: Jesus' relief of soul and spiritual strength (v.41).
9. Picture 9: Jesus' acceptance of God's chosen path (v.42).

14:32–33

32 And they went to a place called Gethsemane. And he said to his disciples, "Sit here while I pray."
33 And he took with him Peter and James and John, and began to be greatly distressed and troubled.

1 Picture 1: Jesus' great need for prayer and for friends to be at His side.

Gethsemane was most likely a beautiful garden just outside the city of Jerusalem (see DEEPER STUDY # 1—Mt.26:36). Gardens were not allowed within the city walls because of the lack of space. Therefore, the wealthy secured beautiful spots right outside the walls and built their gardens. It was apparently Jesus' habit to pray in Gethsemane, as Judas knew exactly where to go to find Him (v.43; Jn.18:2). However, Jesus' need this time was much greater than before. He was facing the cross, unbelievable human suffering, and separation from God (see notes—Mt.20:19). He needed to pray, to be in the very presence of God and to be strengthened by Him. But He also needed the presence and prayers of His closest companions. Note what our Savior did.

First, Jesus said to His disciples, "Sit here while I pray" (v.32). His words implied that they too should begin to pray, for great trials were coming, and the billows of temptation would roll in upon them ever so heavily.

Second, taking Peter, James, and John, Jesus walked farther into the garden to be alone with these three (v.33). They were the closest to Him. In His darkest hour, He especially needed their presence and prayer support. But note: Jesus' need was not to talk the problem over with them. He just needed their presence and prayer support *while* He talked and shared with God. He knew who had the true answer to His need (see vv.34, 37–38, 40–41).

THOUGHT 1. Every believer should have a place where they get alone with God in prayer, and it should be their habit to visit it, daily approaching the throne of God.

THOUGHT 2. What a lesson! Too many talk their problems over with friends instead of with God. God is the One who holds the true answer to our problems. The proper order between friends and God is to seek God for the answer and friends for their prayer support.

> Ask, and it will be given to you; seek, and you will find; knock, and it will be opened to you. (Mt.7:7)

> And he told them a parable to the effect that they ought always to pray and not lose heart. (Lu.18:1)

> Is anyone among you suffering? Let him pray. Is anyone cheerful? Let him sing praise. (Js.5:13)

> Seek the Lord and his strength; seek his presence continually! (1 Chr.16:11)

2 Picture 2: Jesus' heavy agony and pressure.

As Jesus walked deeper into the garden with Peter, James, and John, He began to experience extreme agony and pressure beyond imagination (v.33). *Greatly distressed* (Gk. ekthambeisthai; pronounced *ek-thom-base'-thigh*) is a very strong term in the Greek. It speaks of utter and extreme fright, horror, terror, bewilderment. Jesus was staggering under "dreadful and great darkness," something like what fell upon Abraham, except Jesus' horror was much, much worse (Ge.15:12).

> 33 And he took with him Peter and James and John, and began to be greatly distressed and troubled.
> 34 And he said to them, "My soul is very sorrowful, even to death. Remain here and watch."

The word *troubled* (ademonein, *ad-ay-mon-ane'*) is expressive, perhaps as expressive as words can be. It means to be extremely heavy, excessively troubled, distressed beyond what one is able to bear. However, when looking at the root of the word (ademos), it means much more. It means *being not at home, homeless, out of one's usual surroundings*. The meaning is probably twofold.

First, Jesus suffered beyond all imagination. Imagine this: whatever suffering and whatever pain were involved in the *Perfect and Ideal Man's* bearing all the sins of the world and the judgment for those sins—all of it fell upon Jesus. No one could bear any of the suffering with Jesus. He had to bear it all alone. Upon the cross He had to *"be made sin for us"* (2 Co.5:21, emphasis added). In Gethsemane, He was facing the loneliness of bearing all sin for us. He was alone, and He experienced all the terrible emotions and distress of the solitary, the lonely, the *homeless*.

Second, Jesus had to be separated from God for the first time in His eternal existence. His *home*, His place, His very being was with God throughout all eternity. In Gethsemane, Jesus was anticipating the separation from God which He was shortly to experience upon the cross. He was to be *cut off from God*, left all alone to bear the sins and judgment of the human race. He again felt the terrible emotions and distress of being left all alone, cut off from God, of being left *homeless*.

Note in these verses how severely our Savior suffered because of the weight of all our sin. The terror and heaviness were so painful they almost killed Jesus *before* He went to the cross. He shared this fact with the disciples, saying that He was grieved to the point of death (v.34). The sorrow and weight of stress were life-threatening. The pressure was swelling up in Him to such a degree it was about to explode. He began to sweat large drops of blood (Lu.22:44). He was under such great distress—physically, mentally, emotionally, and spiritually—that God sent an angel to strengthen Him (see Deeper Study # 2—Mt.26:37–38).

Jesus told the three disciples to "watch," that is, to be praying. They knew a critical hour was at hand. They felt the pressure in the very atmosphere, and the Lord had just shared His own great need. He needed and wanted their presence and prayer support.

> And being in agony he prayed more earnestly; and his sweat became like great drops of blood falling down to the ground. (Lu.22:44)

> Greater love has no one than this, that someone lay down his life for his friends. (Jn.15:13)

> Reproaches have broken my heart, so that I am in despair. I looked for pity, but there was none, and for comforters, but I found none. (Ps.69:20)

3 Picture 3: Jesus' desperate search for relief.

Our suffering Savior searched desperately for relief from His indescribable sorrow. In confronting the cross (death), Jesus did the only thing He could: He turned to God.

14:35–36

³⁵ And going a little farther, he fell on the ground and prayed that, if it were possible, the hour might pass from him.

³⁶ And he said, "Abba, Father, all things are possible for you. Remove this cup from me. Yet not what I will, but what you will."

a. He got all alone: Prostrated Himself (v.35a).

Jesus went even further into the garden, away from Peter, James, and John. Luke says He withdrew "about a stone's throw" from the three (Lu.22:41). The pressure and weight of what He was about to face were unbearable. He was desperate and needed to be alone with God. He fell on the ground, prostrating Himself before His Father.

b. He prayed for the cup of the hour, the cross, to pass from Him (vv.35b–36).

Jesus prayed that the "hour" of the cross "might pass from Him" (v.35b). The term "the hour" or "My hour" is a constant symbol of His death (see note—Jn.12:23–24; see Mt.26:18, 45; Jn.7:6, 8, 30; 8:20; 12:27, 33; 13:1; 17:1). Jesus was definitely praying for God to choose another way to secure the redemption of the world.

Jesus prayed "Abba, Father" (v.36a). This was what small children called their father from day to day. It was the address of a child's love and dependency. Children knew that their father would hear and turn to them when they called, "Abba." Just like a child, our Savior cried out to *His Father* in childlike brokenness and dependency, knowing that His Father would hear and turn to help Him.

Jesus prayed, "All things are possible for you [God]" (v.36b). Why then did God not choose another way? As simply stated as possible, God does only what He has willed to do; and He wills only what His love and righteousness guide Him to will. God's love and righteousness led Him to demonstrate these attributes by giving His Son to die for the sins of the human race. The cross demonstrated in the very best way possible that "God so loved the world that He gave His only begotten Son" to bear the judgment of sin for every person (Jn.3:16). Therefore, God's will was subject to His love and righteousness.

In Gethsemane, Jesus knew this, but He struggled in His flesh, in His humanity, for God to choose another way. The pressure of it all, of being cut off from His Father, was just too heavy. He cried out in desperation for God to deliver Him from the terrible load. He knew that God would not, yet He cried for God to do it; He cried *expressing* His great dependence and love for God. He loved His Father so much that He did not want to be separated from Him. He wanted His Father to know that, so He pleaded for deliverance from the cross, *expressing* His love and dependence, knowing that God had determined the path of the cross. He was willing to bear it, to subject Himself to God's eternal will and love and righteousness.

Jesus continued praying, asking God to remove the cup from Him (v.36c; see DEEPER STUDY # 1; DEEPER STUDY # 4—Mt.26:39; DEEPER STUDY # 1—Mt.27:26-44; see Mt.20:19). Jesus' *human* nature and will are clearly seen in this request. He was as much man as any human is. Therefore, He begged God to choose another way other than the cup, if possible. The thought of being separated from God upon the cross was almost too much for Jesus to bear.

Christs' *divine* nature and will are also clearly seen in this request. Note the rest of the Lord's statement: He prayed for the Father's will to be done (v.36d). The first act, the first impulse and struggle and movement of His will had come from His human nature: to escape the cup of separation from God. But immediately, the second act, the second impulse and struggle and movement of His will, came from His divine nature: to do not as He willed, but as God willed.

THOUGHT 1. Christ's surrender to do God's perfect will in the Garden of Gethsemane was critical.

➤ It was through His surrender that He was made perfect and stood before God as the Ideal, Perfect Man.

➤ It was through His surrender to be the Ideal, Perfect Man that His righteousness was able to stand for every human being.

➤ It was through His surrender to be the Ideal, Perfect Man that He was able to bear the cup of God's wrath against sin *for every human being*.

➤ It was through His surrender to be the Ideal, Perfect Man that His sacrifice and sufferings were able to stand for every human being.

For our sake he made him to be sin who knew no sin, so that in him we might become the righteousness of God. (2 Co.5:21)

But we see him who for a little while was made lower than the angels, namely Jesus, crowned with glory and honor because of the suffering of death, so that by the grace of God he might taste death for everyone. For it was fitting that he, for whom and by whom all things exist, in bringing many sons to glory, should make the founder of their salvation perfect through suffering. (He.2:9-10)

Although he was a son, he learned obedience through what he suffered. And being made perfect, he became the source of eternal salvation to all who obey him. (He.5:8-9)

DEEPER STUDY # 1

(14:36) **Cup:** Jesus Christ was neither fearing nor shrinking from death itself. This is clearly seen in Jn.10:17-18. Death for a cause is not such a great price to pay. Many people have so died—fearlessly and willingly, some perhaps more cruelly than Jesus Himself. Shrinking from betrayal, beatings, humiliation, and death, due to foreknowledge is not what was happening to Jesus. As stated, some have faced horrible deaths courageously, even inviting martyrdom for a cause. The Lord knew He was to die from the very beginning, and He had been preparing His disciples for His death (see outlines and notes—Mk.8:31-33; 9:30-32; Mt.16:21-28; 17:22; 20:17-19). It was not human and physical suffering from which Jesus was shrinking. Such an explanation is totally inadequate in explaining Gethsemane. The great cup or trial Jesus was facing was separation from God (see note, pt.1 and DEEPER STUDY # 2—Mt.26:37-38). He was to be the sacrificial Lamb of God who takes away the sins of the world (Jn.1:29). He was to bear the judgment of God for the sins of the world (see note—Mt.27:46-49; see Is.53:19). Jesus Himself had already spoken of the "cup" when referring to His sacrificial death (see DEEPER STUDY # 2—Mt.20:22-23; DEEPER STUDY # 2—Jn.18:11).

Scripture speaks of the cup in several ways.

1. The cup is called "the cup of the Lord's wrath" or "fury" (Is.51:17).

2. The cup is associated with suffering and God's wrath (see Ps.11:6; Is.51:17; Lu.22:42).

3. The cup is also associated with salvation. Because Jesus drank the cup of suffering and wrath for us, we can "lift [take] up the cup of salvation and call on the name of the Lord" (Ps.116:13).

4 Picture 4: Jesus' disappointment in His friends.

14:37

The Lord returned to the three disciples and found them asleep. His words reveal His disappointment in His friends. He had turned to these three in His darkest hour, and they had failed Him.

37 And he came and found them sleeping, and he said to Peter, "Simon, are you asleep? Could you not watch one hour?"

Jesus spoke to all three, but He addressed Peter in particular. Peter was the one who had spoken up just an hour or two earlier declaring that he would stand with Jesus through anything. Yet he could not even stand with Jesus during a short season of prayer. Jesus spoke to him very bluntly about this. He did not address Peter by his new name, Peter, but by his old name, Simon. The flesh had gotten the best of Peter, and Jesus let Peter know it.

Note that Jesus had not asked Peter and the disciples to watch and pray *all night*. He had asked them to pray with Him for only one hour. This is significant in seeing their failure and weakness.

For I know that nothing good dwells in me, that is, in my flesh. For I have the desire to do what is right, but not the ability to carry it out. (Ro.7:18)

Those who are in the flesh cannot please God. (Ro.8:8)

For the desires of the flesh are against the Spirit, and the desires of the Spirit are against the flesh, for these are opposed to each other, to keep you from doing the things you want to do. (Ga.5:17)

14:38

[38] "Watch and pray that you may not enter into temptation. The spirit indeed is willing, but the flesh is weak."

5 Picture 5: Jesus' continuing ministry—even under trial.

Jesus was so heavily pressured, He was at the point of collapsing. Yet He was concerned over the needs of the disciples. They were going to face great temptation, and He knew it. He wanted them to know it. They must watch and pray, be prepared. Despite His own need in this hour—His own trials—Jesus ministered all He could to them, helping them and trying to awaken them to watch and pray as never before.

THOUGHT 1. We are to continue to minister even while we are in need or are going through extreme trials. Our life is to be a life of ministry.

Therefore be alert, remembering that for three years I did not cease night or day to admonish every one with tears. (Ac.20:31)

14:39

[39] And again he went away and prayed, saying the same words.

6 Picture 6: Jesus' perseverance in prayer—despite no answer from God.

Jesus had not yet found relief from God, yet He was not discouraged. He did not turn away from God. To the contrary, He went back, got alone, and sought God again. He even prayed the same words as before.

Jesus zeroed in on the same request: that the cup might pass from Him. He sought, wrestled, and agonized with God. He persevered, giving every indication that He was not going to quit praying until God heard and met His need.

Ask, and it will be given to you; seek, and you will find; knock, and it will be opened to you. (Mt.7:7)

Continue steadfastly in prayer, being watchful in it with thanksgiving. (Col.4:2)

Submit yourselves therefore to God. Resist the devil, and he will flee from you. Draw near to God, and he will draw near to you. Cleanse your hands, you sinners, and purify your hearts, you double-minded. (Js.4:7–8)

14:40

[40] And again he came and found them sleeping, for their eyes were very heavy, and they did not know what to answer him.

7 Picture 7: Jesus' continued disappointment in friends.

When Jesus returned from praying the second time, Peter, James, and John were asleep again. Some commentators excuse the disciples, saying their bodies and eyes were so heavy with the pressure of the hour, they just could not stay awake. But their failure to watch and pray was a continued disappointment to the Lord. Even after a rebuke (v.37), they would not struggle to stand with the Lord. They were guilty; "they did not know what to answer Him."

Blessed are those servants whom the master finds awake when he comes. Truly, I say to you, he will dress himself for service and have them recline at table, and he will come and serve them. (Lu.12:37)

For you are all children of light, children of the day. We are not of the night or of the darkness. So then let us not sleep, as others do, but let us keep awake and be sober. (1 Th.5:5–6)

Be sober-minded; be watchful. Your adversary the devil prowls around like a roaring lion, seeking someone to devour. (1 Pe.5:8)

I know, O LORD, that the way of man is not in himself, that it is not in man who walks to direct his steps. (Je.10:23)

8 Picture 8: Jesus' relief of soul and spiritual strength.

When Jesus returned to the three the third time only to find them yet asleep, He told them that it was enough; the hour of His betrayal had come. His words were evidence of a great release. Jesus' agony, His desperate need for friends to *watch* with Him, was now gone (vv.34, 38). God had given Him great relief of soul. The very tone of His words to His disciples revealed a calmness of spirit, a peace of mind, a relief of the physical and emotional strain that was about to kill Him. Through prayer and supplication, He had made His request known to God, and the peace of God had swept over His aching heart and troubled mind (Ph.4:6-7). God had met His need in a most wonderful way, giving Him the spiritual strength He needed to face the cross.

14:41

> 41 And he came the third time and said to them, "Are you still sleeping and taking your rest? It is enough; the hour has come. The Son of Man is betrayed into the hands of sinners."

And there appeared to him an angel from heaven, strengthening him. (Lu.22:43)

In the days of his flesh, Jesus offered up prayers and supplications, with loud cries and tears, to him who was able to save him from death, and he was heard because of his reverence. (He.5:7; see He.5:7–9)

9 Picture 9: Jesus' acceptance of God's chosen path.

14:42

Jesus had accepted God's will for Him, the cross. He told the three sleeping disciples to get up, that it was time to go and submit to His betrayal. There was no shrinking now, no agony, no desperation. Jesus was relieved and strengthened, ready to face the sufferings necessary to secure our salvation.

> 42 "Rise, let us be going; see, my betrayer is at hand."

Jesus said He was being "betrayed into the hands of sinners" (v.41). All those taking part in His death were sinners. His death was the most heinous crime of history, for He, the Son of Man, the Ideal and Perfect Man, was killed by men. But there is more here: He died for the sins of the world. It was every human's sins that caused Him to be crucified. Every sin is an act of rebellion, of simply saying "No" to God (Ro.3:23). Therefore every person is guilty of putting Christ to death. There is a sense in which every sin, every act of rebellion crucifies the Son of God again, subjecting Him to fresh contempt and shame (He.6:6).

Jesus' relief of soul and infusion of strength did not come from resigning Himself to death. Rather, He relinquished His will in favor of the Father's will. He deliberately gave up His own will and actively pursued the Father's will. This was the victory He fought to gain in Gethsemane. It should also be said that His submission was voluntary—not forced. He had a choice even up until His death on the cross (see note—Mt.26:39). Even when He died, it was because He submitted to death, voluntarily releasing His Spirit from His body (Lu.23:46).

I can do nothing on my own. As I hear, I judge, and my judgment is just, because I seek not my own will but the will of him who sent me. (Jn.5:30)

Who gave himself for our sins to deliver us from the present evil age, according to the will of our God and Father. (Ga.1:4)

And walk in love, as Christ loved us and gave himself up for us, a fragrant offering and sacrifice to God. (Ep.5:2)

Then I said, 'Behold, I have come to do your will, O God, as it is written of me in the scroll of the book.' When he said above, "You have neither desired nor taken pleasure in sacrifices and offerings and burnt offerings and sin offerings" (these are offered according to the law), then he added, "Behold, I have come to do your will." He does away with the first in order to establish the second. And by that will we have been sanctified through the offering of the body of Jesus Christ once for all. . . . But when Christ had offered for all time a single sacrifice for sins, he sat down at the right hand of God. (He.10:7–10, 12)

I delight to do your will, O my God; your law is within my heart. (Ps.40:8)

H. Jesus' Arrest:
A Study of Human Character, 14:43–52

(Mt.26:47–56; Lu.22:47–53; Jn.18:3–11)

1. The fallen disciple who betrayed Jesus
  a. His tragedy
    1) He was one of the disciples
    2) He led a crowd against Jesus

  b. His prearranged sign

  c. His hypocritical deception

2. The men who apprehended Jesus: Arrested Him
3. The disciple who acted courageously but wrongly
4. The Lord who showed a striking serenity in the midst of mass confusion
  a. His piercing question

  b. His obedience to Scripture, to God's will

5. The disciples who allowed their faith to fail
6. The young man who became terror-stricken when confronted

43 And immediately, while he was still speaking, Judas came, one of the twelve, and with him a crowd with swords and clubs, from the chief priests and the scribes and the elders. 44 Now the betrayer had given them a sign, saying, "The one I will kiss is the man. Seize him and lead him away under guard." 45 And when he came, he went up to him at once and said, "Rabbi!" And he kissed him. 46 And they laid hands on him and seized him. 47 But one of those who stood by drew his sword and struck the servant of the high priest and cut off his ear.

48 And Jesus said to them, "Have you come out as against a robber, with swords and clubs to capture me? 49 Day after day I was with you in the temple teaching, and you did not seize me. But let the Scriptures be fulfilled." 50 And they all left him and fled.

51 And a young man followed him, with nothing but a linen cloth about his body. And they seized him, 52 but he left the linen cloth and ran away naked.

Division IX

The Son of God's Passion Ministry: Jesus' Supreme Sacrifice—Rejected and Crucified, 14:1–15:47

H. Jesus' Arrest: A Study of Human Character, 14:43–52

(Mt.26:47–56; Lu.22:47–53; Jn.18:3–11)

14:43–52
Introduction

The scene is one of the most tragic and unjust in history. Jesus was betrayed, arrested, and deserted within just a few minutes. Mark's account of the chaotic event seems to focus on the people involved. It is a dramatic study of human character. Indeed, it is a mirror of mankind. As we look into this probing passage of God's Word, we should also look for ourselves in the people it highlights. This is, *Jesus' Arrest: A Study of Human Character*, 14:43-52.

1. The fallen disciple who betrayed Jesus (vv.43-45).
2. The men who apprehended Jesus: Arrested Him (v.46).
3. The disciple who acted courageously but wrongly (v.47).
4. The Lord who showed a striking serenity in the midst of mass confusion (vv.48-49).
5. The disciples who allowed their faith to fail (v.50).
6. The young man who became terror-stricken when confronted (vv.51-52).

1 The fallen disciple who betrayed Jesus.

Mark's account of Jesus' arrest begins with the focus on Judas, the fallen disciple who betrayed the Lord. As Judas led the soldiers to the Savior, his greedy, deceptive heart is displayed for all to see.

[43] And immediately, while he was still speaking, Judas came, one of the twelve, and with him a crowd with swords and clubs, from the chief priests and the scribes and the elders.

[44] Now the betrayer had given them a sign, saying, "The one I will kiss is the man. Seize him and lead him away under guard."

[45] And when he came, he went up to him at once and said, "Rabbi!" And he kissed him.

a. His tragedy (v.43).

What a tragedy that a professed follower of Jesus would betray Him! Judas was actually a disciple, one of the twelve, yet he is seen taking the lead against Jesus. Remember, he had begun his downward fall by stealing just a little at a time; but as with all thieves, he became bolder and began to take more and more. Scripture calls him a thief and a robber (Jn.10:1). He fell so deeply that he was a betrayer, a leader against Jesus.

THOUGHT 1. How many professing disciples have forsaken Jesus? How many now stand against Him? How many began with *little sins* but became involved in greater sins? Jesus warned that many who profess Him as Lord have never genuinely believed unto salvation (Mt.7:21-23).

Just as Paul exhorted the Corinthians, we need to examine ourselves to be sure we are truly "in the faith" (2 Co.13:5).

"Not everyone who says to me, 'Lord, Lord,' will enter the kingdom of heaven, but the one who does the will of my Father who is in heaven. On that day many will say to me, 'Lord, Lord, did we not prophesy in your name, and cast out demons in your name, and do many mighty works in your name?' And then will I declare to them, 'I never knew you; depart from me, you workers of lawlessness.' " (Mt.7:21-23)

Examine yourselves, to see whether you are in the faith. Test yourselves. Or do you not realize this about yourselves, that Jesus Christ is in you?—unless indeed you fail to meet the test! (2 Co.13:5)

b. His prearranged sign (v.44).

It was night and already dark, and some of the arresting party would not know Jesus, not well enough to arrest Him in the cover of darkness. So Judas arranged to identify Jesus with a kiss. It was the custom of the day for a disciple to greet his teacher with a slight kiss on the cheek.

c. His hypocritical deception (v.45).

Judas' hypocrisy is sickening. As he approached Jesus, he not only attempted to deceive Jesus, he pretended to deeply respect and love Him. The devil-influenced deceiver called Jesus "Rabbi" and kissed Him. The word "kiss" here is different from the word "kiss" in verse 44. In verse 44, the word is translated from the Greek *phileso*, which is the respectful kiss of greeting. But in verse 45 when Judas kissed Jesus, the word is translated from *kataphilesen*, which is a kiss of intense feelings. Judas was not only portraying hypocritical deception, he was drenching Jesus with false affection and soaking himself in hypocrisy. He was standing face to face with Jesus fervently declaring his discipleship, yet at that very moment, he was leading others in their sin against Jesus.

493

THOUGHT 1. How many approach Christ in church and feign devotion to Christ? They profess discipleship, yet at the same time, they live in sin and shame. How many feel they are actually getting away with it, actually able to keep the truth from Christ? How foolishly we deceive ourselves and attempt to deceive others!

> Take care, brothers, lest there be in any of you an evil, unbelieving heart, leading you to fall away from the living God. (He.3:12)

> Suffering wrong as the wage for their wrongdoing. They count it pleasure to revel in the daytime. They are blots and blemishes, reveling in their deceptions, while they feast with you. They have eyes full of adultery, insatiable for sin. They entice unsteady souls. They have hearts trained in greed. Accursed children! (2 Pe.2:13–14)

> The heart is deceitful above all things, and desperately sick; who can understand it? "I the LORD search the heart and test the mind, to give every man according to his ways, according to the fruit of his deeds." Like the partridge that gathers a brood that she did not hatch, so is he who gets riches but not by justice; in the midst of his days they will leave him, and at his end he will be a fool. (Je.17:9–11)

14:46

⁴⁶ And they laid hands on him and seized him.

2 The men who apprehended Jesus: Arrested Him.

Mark's brief statement about the men who arrested Jesus sparks a number of insights for our own lives and our modern world. The words "laid their hands on Him" are thought-provoking. Like so many today, they mistreated the Son of God. Note three simple observations.

First, the hands laid on Jesus were the hands of the rude, the abusive, the unconcerned, the neglectful, the violent. When they should have been concerned over Jesus and their own souls, they were rejecting and reacting against Him. Even though the Roman soldiers and the servants of the Jewish leaders were just doing what they had been ordered to do, they were still responsible for their actions. Their superiors who ordered them to seize Jesus by force were even more responsible.

Second, Jesus desires people to lay hold of Him in humility and belief, not in some sinful, negative reaction.

Third, the hands of people can take hold of Jesus in reaction. They can arrest His messenger and message, and they can sense triumph, but only temporarily. God will always raise up His messengers to carry on the glorious news of salvation, even if the messengers have to be new ones. The triumph will always be the Lord's, and in that glorious day of redemption, He will ultimately prevail. It was this that Judas and his cohorts failed to grasp. It was their rejection of God's Son that led them to forcefully lay hands on Jesus.

> He was in the world, and the world was made through him, yet the world did not know him. He came to his own, and his own people did not receive him. (Jn.1:10–11)

> "Father, glorify your name." Then a voice came from heaven: "I have glorified it, and I will glorify it again." (Jn.12:28)

> For those who live in Jerusalem and their rulers, because they did not recognize him nor understand the utterances of the prophets, which are read every Sabbath, fulfilled them by condemning him. (Ac.13:27)

14:47

⁴⁷ But one of those who stood by drew his sword and struck the servant of the high priest and cut off his ear.

3 The disciple who acted courageously but wrongly.

One of Jesus' disciples attempted to defend Jesus, drawing his sword and slicing off the ear of the high priest's servant. John records that this disciple was Peter (Jn.18:10). As soon as Jesus was accosted, Peter jumped to the Lord's defense. He was ready and prepared to stand with his Lord. However, the way he went about defending Jesus was wrong. His courage was commendable, but his method was wrong. He tried to attack and to defeat (kill) the enemy of Jesus with physical force. Physical force was not the way of Jesus. Jesus would have His attackers know His faith and trust, His gentleness and love, His submission and willingness to do the will of God. This is always the way into the presence of God.

In addition, Peter's bold attempt to defend Jesus was contrary to God's overall will. It was God's plan for His Son to die for the sins of the human race (see outline and notes—vv.41-42). Christ's arrest was necessary for God's plan to be carried out.

> **THOUGHT 1.** Courage is needed—but spiritual courage, not physical courage. Believers need to be courageous and zealous in their spirit, standing with Christ proclaiming the way of faith and trust, gentleness and love, submission and a willingness to do God's will.
>
>> But in your hearts honor Christ the Lord as holy, always being prepared to make a defense to anyone who asks you for a reason for the hope that is in you; yet do it with gentleness and respect. (1 Pe.3:15)
>>
>> Then he said to me, "This is the word of the LORD to Zerubbabel: Not by might, nor by power, but by my Spirit, says the LORD of hosts." (Zec.4:6)

> **THOUGHT 2.** Many are involved in attacking instead of proclaiming. Some Christians often treat opponents of Christ as though they are unreachable and untouchable by Christ. The wise disciple must treat everyone *in the truth*: sinners need to be loved and shown the way of Christ. Their sin is to be despised, but not the sinners themselves.

4 The Lord who showed a striking serenity in the midst of mass confusion.

14:48–49

Standing in stark contrast to the chaos was Jesus. The Lord showed a striking serenity in the midst of mass confusion. Jesus was calm throughout the whole affair. His serenity is a dynamic example as we face the trials of this life. He was able to be peaceful through it all because He lived moment by moment in obedience to the Scripture, that is, to the will of God.

[48] And Jesus said to them, "Have you come out as against a robber, with swords and clubs to capture me?
[49] Day after day I was with you in the temple teaching, and you did not seize me. But let the Scriptures be fulfilled."

a. His piercing question (v.48).

Jesus asked His arresters why they were treating Him like a robber—a criminal, why they felt they had to seize Him by force with weapons drawn. Consider how the worldly religious leaders treated Jesus as a thief. They acted as though He had stolen from them, for He had not preached a message that allowed them to live as they wished. He had not praised them, nor boosted their egos; He had not complimented their service and gifts. Rather, He had proclaimed that they were short of God's glory and were dying and doomed if they did not repent and begin to live as God commanded (see note—Mt.26:55-56).

Note a critical point too often overlooked: Jesus had to tell the truth in order for people to be saved. God is love, but His love is not the indulgence of a weak parent or soft-hearted grandparent who accepts wrongdoing. His love is the ache and acceptance of a true parent who receives a repentant and obedient Child. *Only through repentance and obedience can a person ever personally know the love of God* (see Jn.14:21, 23-24; 15:10, 14). God does not accept a person who does wrong and lives unrighteously. Therefore, Jesus had to tell people the truth. If people wanted to be acceptable to God and live in His love, then they had to turn away from sin and come to God, believing that God exists and diligently seeking Him (He.11:6).

b. His obedience to Scripture, to God's will (v.49).

Jesus pointed out the injustice of His arrest, noting that His opponents had ample opportunity to arrest Him publicly on any number of occasions. It was not necessary for them to track Jesus down and arrest Him at night, for He was neither hiding from them nor resisting them. To the contrary, He was submitting to His arrest in order to fulfill the Scriptures. He had to die; Scripture said so. God's will was fixed and set in Scripture. Consequently, Jesus was dying willingly. He laid down His life voluntarily just as Scripture said.

> For this reason the Father loves me, because I lay down my life that I may take it up again. No one takes it from me, but I lay it down of my own accord. I have authority to lay it down, and I have authority to take it up again. This charge I have received from my Father. (Jn.10:17–18)

> This Jesus, delivered up according to the definite plan and foreknowledge of God, you crucified and killed by the hands of lawless men. (Ac.2:23)

> But he was pierced for our transgressions; he was crushed for our iniquities; upon him was the chastisement that brought us peace, and with his wounds we are healed. All we like sheep have gone astray; we have turned—every one—to his own way; and the LORD has laid on him the iniquity of us all. He was oppressed, and he was afflicted, yet he opened not his mouth; like a lamb that is led to the slaughter, and like a sheep that before its shearers is silent, so he opened not his mouth. (Is.53:5–7)

THOUGHT 1. It was Jesus' obedience to God's will that brought the serenity and peace to His heart in the midst of mass confusion. Likewise, we secure peace and serenity through living for God and obeying Him.

> If you abide in me, and my words abide in you, ask whatever you wish, and it will be done for you. (Jn.15:7)

> Do not be anxious about anything, but in everything by prayer and supplication with thanksgiving let your requests be made known to God. And the peace of God, which surpasses all understanding, will guard your hearts and your minds in Christ Jesus. (Ph.4:6–7)

> Great peace have those who love your law; nothing can make them stumble. (Ps.119:165)

14:50

⁵⁰ And they all left him and fled.

5 The disciples who allowed their faith to fail.

Perhaps the saddest detail of that destined night is Jesus' disciples forsaking Him and running away. The disciples were not cowards (see v.47). Their problem was not lack of courage but weak faith and lack of spiritual understanding (carnality). When Jesus was arrested, their courage rose to the occasion. They were willing to stand up and fight although they were far outnumbered and had inferior weapons. But when they saw Jesus standing there submitting to His capture (Mt.26:52), they could not understand. They were disillusioned, wondering: "Why does Jesus not destroy His enemies? The Messiah could. He is supposed to have such power, and Jesus is the Messiah. Isn't He?" Their faith failed, and it is critical to understand *why* it failed.

First, they were close-minded. They had closed their minds to *part of the truth*, to Christ's full mission and purpose. They had *refused* to accept His word about dying and rising again literally. They had failed to grasp the spiritual and eternal nature of His kingdom. They spiritualized what He was saying rather than taking it literally. Now that it was happening, they were not prepared for it; their faith was too weak.

Second, they were worldly and materialistic minded. They had hung on to their earthly concept of the Messiah, that is, a Messiah who was coming to bring a perfect society to this material and physical world. They were, therefore, not prepared to deal with their earthly Messiah's being bound and taken prisoner. Their faith lacked the strength to bear such a trial.

> Jesus said to him, "No one who puts his hand to the plow and looks back is fit for the kingdom of God." (Lu.9:62)

> He is a double-minded man, unstable in all his ways. (Js.1:8)

> Blessed is the man who remains steadfast under trial, for when he has stood the test he will receive the crown of life, which God has promised to those who love him. (Js.1:12)

> Draw near to God, and he will draw near to you. Cleanse your hands, you sinners, and purify your hearts, you double-minded. (Js.4:8)

> You therefore, beloved, knowing this beforehand, take care that you are not carried away with the error of lawless people and lose your own stability. But grow in the grace and knowledge of our Lord and Savior Jesus Christ. To him be the glory both now and to the day of eternity. Amen. (2 Pe.3:17–18)

6 The young man who became terror-stricken when confronted.

Of the four Gospel authors, only Mark mentions a young man at the scene who became terror-stricken when confronted and attacked. Most commentators seem to think this young man was Mark himself. If so, he does not name himself out of modesty. Several facts lead to this conclusion:

- Why is the event recorded if it were not Mark? There seems to be little, if any, point to the event's being mentioned if the young man were not Mark. Apparently, Mark is saying, "I was there; I was an eyewitness to the happenings." (Not mentioning oneself by name is the practice of the Gospel writers. For example, John refers to many instances where he was an eyewitness, but he never gives his name.)
- Mary, Mark's mother, lived in Jerusalem (Ac.12:12).
- The level of detail in Mark's account points to his having been an eyewitness.
- The trait of fleeing Jesus when the going got rough is characteristic of Mark in *Acts* (Ac.13:13; 15:37–38).

⁵¹ And a young man followed him, with nothing but a linen cloth about his body. And they seized him,
⁵² but he left the linen cloth and ran away naked.

Mark's mother, Mary, had a house large enough to hold a fairly large prayer meeting. Some commentators think the upper room was even in her home. If so, they speculate that Judas may have returned to the upper room with the arresting party. Mark was probably lying in his bed, heard the commotion, and then left hastily in his nightclothes or clad in a sheet to warn Jesus. When Jesus was seized, one of the officers reached for the young man, but the young man was able to break loose and escape, leaving his garment in the officer's hands. Another possibility is that Mark followed Jesus and His disciples to Gethsemane.

The point again is weak faith (if it were Mark or some other believer) or lack of faith (if it were an unbelieving spectator). The young man failed to stand with Jesus. He had little if any faith in the Lord. His whole being surged with fear and terror. He sought to save himself at the expense of standing with the Messiah and witnessing for Him.

THOUGHT 1. Many seek to escape embarrassment, ridicule, threats, and persecution instead of standing with Christ and being a testimony for Him. Why? Weak faith. Their faith is not strong enough to cast out fear.

> **Disheartened by the saying, he went away sorrowful, for he had great possessions. (Mk.10:22)**

> **Therefore do not be ashamed of the testimony about our Lord, nor of me his prisoner, but share in suffering for the gospel by the power of God. (2 Ti.1:8)**

> **You then, my child, be strengthened by the grace that is in Christ Jesus. (2 Ti.2:1)**

> **Therefore, preparing your minds for action, and being sober-minded, set your hope fully on the grace that will be brought to you at the revelation of Jesus Christ. (1 Pe.1:13)**

> **I am coming soon. Hold fast what you have, so that no one may seize your crown. (Re.3:11)**

I. Jesus' Trial Before the High Priest:
A Look at Weak and Strong Character, 14:53–65

(Mt.26:57–68; Lu.22:54, 63–71; Jn.18:12–14, 19–24)

1. **The setting: Jesus was led before the High Priest and the Sanhedrin (the Jewish high court)**
2. **The confused, yet courageous Peter: He alone followed Jesus**

3. **The disturbed religionists: They sought testimony against Jesus**

   a. The witnesses were false and did not agree
   b. The final charge was formulated

   c. The final witnesses did not even agree
4. **The calm Lord: He stood silent before men but assured before God**

5. **The strong Lord: He claimed to be the Messiah, the Son of God**

6. **The frenzied mob of religionists: They got their satisfaction—the condemnation of their perceived enemy**
   a. The true character of the High Priest
   b. The true character of men[DS1]

⁵³ And they led Jesus to the high priest. And all the chief priests and the elders and the scribes came together. ⁵⁴ And Peter had followed him at a distance, right into the courtyard of the high priest. And he was sitting with the guards and warming himself at the fire. ⁵⁵ Now the chief priests and the whole council were seeking testimony against Jesus to put him to death, but they found none. ⁵⁶ For many bore false witness against him, but their testimony did not agree. ⁵⁷ And some stood up and bore false witness against him, saying, ⁵⁸ "We heard him say, 'I will destroy this temple that is made with hands, and in three days I will build another, not made with hands.'" ⁵⁹ Yet even about this their testimony did not agree. ⁶⁰ And the high priest stood up in the midst and asked Jesus, "Have you no answer to make? What is it that these men testify against you?" ⁶¹ But he remained silent and made no answer. Again the high priest asked him, "Are you the Christ, the Son of the Blessed?" ⁶² And Jesus said, "I am, and you will see the Son of Man seated at the right hand of Power, and coming with the clouds of heaven." ⁶³ And the high priest tore his garments and said, "What further witnesses do we need?

⁶⁴ You have heard his blasphemy. What is your decision?" And they all condemned him as deserving death. ⁶⁵ And some began to spit on him and to cover his face and to strike him, saying to him, "Prophesy!" And the guards received him with blows.

Division IX

The Son of God's Passion Ministry: Jesus' Supreme Sacrifice—Rejected and Crucified, 14:1–15:47

I. Jesus' Trial Before the High Priest: A Look at Weak and Strong Character, 14:53–65

(Mt.26:57-68; Lu.22:54, 63-71; Jn.18:12-14, 19-24)

14:53–65
Introduction

As Mark reports on Jesus' appearance before the High Priest, the study of human character continues. People with both weak and strong character emerge, presenting some traits we should follow and others we should avoid. This is, *Jesus' Trial Before the High Priest: A Look at Weak and Strong Character,* 14:53-65.

1. The setting: Jesus was led before the High Priest and the Sanhedrin (the Jewish high court) (v.53).
2. The confused, yet courageous Peter: He alone followed Jesus (v.54).
3. The disturbed religionists: They sought testimony against Jesus (vv.55-59).
4. The calm Lord: He stood silent before men but assured before God (vv.60-61).
5. The strong Lord: He claimed to be the Messiah, the Son of God (v.62).
6. The frenzied mob of religionists: They got their satisfaction—the condemnation of their perceived enemy (vv.63-65).

1 The setting: Jesus was led before the High Priest and the Sanhedrin (the Jewish high court).

14:53

The soldiers led Jesus to appear before the High Priest and the Sanhedrin. He stood before them on trial for His life. The Sanhedrin was the official Jewish ruling body, the high court of the Jews. Led by the High Priest, it consisted of the chief

[53] And they led Jesus to the high priest. And all the chief priests and the elders and the scribes came together.

priests, the elders, and the scribes, Pharisees and Sadducees alike. All the Jewish religious leaders gathered together to judge God's Son. The Greek word for *came together* or *assembled* (sunerchontai; pronounced *soon-air'-kon-tie*) means just that—to gather, to come together, to flock together. There is also the idea of herding together as a group. The picture is that of the Jewish leaders' surrounding or herding together around Jesus, of being called to accompany one another to their respective seats, ready to pounce on Jesus. There was no question about the evil of their hearts. They were ready to pounce on and execute Him. Several facts reveal the evil of their hearts.

- They had hastily assembled the court *at night*, which was illegal. All criminals were supposed to be tried during the day.
- They were meeting in Caiaphas' palace (home), not in the official court. This, too, was illegal. All cases were to be tried in court.
- They were trying Jesus during the Passover week, when no cases were to be tried.
- They had not met to try Jesus but to secretly devise charges and to condemn Him to death.

THOUGHT 1. People often *flock together* to do evil. People also *flock together* to oppose Christ, even in the church. It is easier to do evil or to oppose Christ in a group than when alone.

> Therefore go out from their midst, and be separate from them, says the Lord, and touch no unclean thing; then I will welcome you, and I will be a father to you, and you shall be sons and daughters to me, says the Lord Almighty. (2 Co.6:17–18)

THOUGHT 2. A heart that wishes to do evil will twist the rules. If people have a sinful desire to do something, they will usually figure out a way, rationalizing and justifying the matter in their mind.

> So whoever knows the right thing to do and fails to do it, for him it is sin. (Js.4:17)

> Beloved, do not imitate evil but imitate good. Whoever does good is from God; whoever does evil has not seen God. (3 Jn.11)

14:54

⁵⁴ And Peter had followed him at a distance, right into the courtyard of the high priest. And he was sitting with the guards and warming himself at the fire.

2 The confused, yet courageous Peter: He alone followed Jesus.

Peter had attempted to defend Jesus, but Jesus stopped him and even forbade him to come to His aid (Mk.14:47; Jn.18:10). In addition, Jesus was giving in to the injustices and indecencies of the mob instead of blasting them away and setting up His kingdom. Peter could not understand this surrender. In the Garden of Gethsemane, when Jesus stopped him from fighting the arresting party, Peter had to flee for his life. But Peter loved His Lord too much to flee too far away. His love for Jesus stopped him, turned him around, and led him back to Jesus. He followed the mob from a safe distance. The trail ended up in the courtyard of Caiaphas' palace. It took enormous courage for Peter to enter the courtyard, for Peter was risking his life by being there. But Peter was confused about what exactly was going on. He had to see what happened to his Lord. He hoped against hope that Jesus was just waiting to act and take over. He had to see.

THOUGHT 1. How much we need a deep love for Christ, a love so great that we would risk our lives to follow Him. Quite often, our love is so weak we will not even risk ridicule or embarrassment to witness for Him, much less risk our lives.

> There is no fear in love, but perfect love casts out fear. For fear has to do with punishment, and whoever fears has not been perfected in love. (1 Jn.4:18)

THOUGHT 2. Peter's love caused him to be courageous. Courage always needs to be rooted in love, and love must always rule over courage.

> For this reason I remind you to fan into flame the gift of God, which is in you through the laying on of my hands, for God gave us a spirit not of fear but of power and love and self-control. (2 Ti.1:6–7)

14:55–59

⁵⁵ Now the chief priests and the whole council were seeking testimony against Jesus to put him to death, but they found none. ⁵⁶ For many bore false witness against him, but their testimony did not agree. ⁵⁷ And some stood up and bore false witness against him, saying, ⁵⁸ "We heard him say, 'I will destroy this temple that is made with hands, and in three days I will build another, not made with hands.'" ⁵⁹ Yet even about this their testimony did not agree.

3 The disturbed religionists: They sought testimony against Jesus.

Imagine! It was the religious leaders who were actually seeking testimony against Jesus. They were so disturbed with Jesus, so determined to execute Him, that the evidence they gathered was meaningless. Their minds were closed; they rejected Him and opposed Him from the start. He was a threat to their way of life, their security and position, and their nation. Therefore, they were set on finding Him guilty. The truth did not matter. He was to be denied and done away with. They ignored all rules of justice to formulate a charge against Jesus (see notes—Mt.12:1-8; note and Deeper Study # 1—12:10; note—15:1-20; Deeper Study # 2—15:6-9; Deeper Study # 3—16:12 for a discussion of the reasons for their opposition).

a. The witnesses were false and did not agree (v.56).
The witnesses the Sanhedrin called to testify against Jesus were false witnesses who presented conflicting testimony. "Many" came charging Jesus, but they were all false, and their

testimonies would not stand up in court under the scrutiny of honest and objective minds. Therefore, the leaders faced a problem, for they had to formulate a charge that would convince Pilate and the Roman authorities that Jesus should die.

The witnesses could not agree. By law two witnesses had to agree for a formal charge to be made and a conviction secured. But two witnesses who agreed could not be found, despite the fact that "many" came forward.

b. The final charge was formulated (vv.57–58).

Finally, two witnesses did come forward with a charge that seemed strong enough to stand up in court and convince the Roman authorities. However, the charge against Jesus was still said to be false (v.57).

The two witnesses distorted Jesus' words (v.58). Jesus had said, "Destroy this temple, and in three days I will raise it up" (Jn.2:19). Jesus had actually said the Jews were to be the destroyers; but the false witnesses testified, "We heard him say, 'I will destroy this temple.'" They twisted what Jesus had actually said, making Him the destroyer.

These false witnesses also misunderstood Jesus' words. Jesus was referring to His body—to the temple of His body and to the resurrection of His body. The Jews apparently thought He meant He would destroy and rebuild the Jerusalem temple in three days. It was this charge—the charge of being a revolutionary—that the religionists believed they could use to convince the Romans to execute Jesus (see note—Mt.26:60-61 for additional discussion).

c. The final witnesses did not even agree (v.59).

Mark reemphasizes that this charge against Jesus was false. Even in this matter, the matter the Sanhedrin decided to use against Jesus, the lying witnesses contradicted each other.

THOUGHT 1. Many today have closed minds; they reject Christ. Some even oppose Him and actively struggle to gather evidence against Him. Why? Primarily for the same reason the religious leaders of Christ's day rejected Him. They desire . . .

- to live as they wish
- to build their image and preserve their current lives and lifestyles
- to gain personal recognition, position, security, and wealth as they want

> But his citizens hated him and sent a delegation after him, saying, 'We do not want this man to reign over us.' (Lu.19:14)

> The world cannot hate you, but it hates me because I testify about it that its works are evil. (Jn.7:7)

> If the world hates you, know that it has hated me before it hated you. . . . But the word that is written in their Law must be fulfilled: 'They hated me without a cause.' (Jn.15:18, 25)

THOUGHT 2. The religionists twisted and distorted the word of Christ. Similarly, we can abuse and misuse God's Word for our own purposes.

> Do your best to present yourself to God as one approved, a worker who has no need to be ashamed, rightly handling the word of truth. (2 Ti.2:15)

> And count the patience of our Lord as salvation, just as our beloved brother Paul also wrote to you according to the wisdom given him, as he does in all his letters when he speaks in them of these matters. There are some things in them that are hard to understand, which the ignorant and unstable twist to their own destruction, as they do the other Scriptures. (2 Pe.3:15–16)

> Woe to those who call evil good and good evil, who put darkness for light and light for darkness, who put bitter for sweet and sweet for bitter! (Is.5:10)

501

4 The calm Lord: He stood silent before men but assured before God.

In spite of the lies of the false witnesses and the injustice of His entire trial, the Lord was calm. He remained silent; He said nothing in defending Himself against the false charges.

14:60-61

⁶⁰ And the high priest stood up in the midst and asked Jesus, "Have you no answer to make? What is it that these men testify against you?"
⁶¹ But he remained silent and made no answer. Again the high priest asked him, "Are you the Christ, the Son of the Blessed?"

The High Priest and court became disturbed and perhaps confused by Jesus' silence. They needed Him to speak up, hoping He would add evidence to the charge and thereby incriminate Himself. The High Priest brow-beat Jesus, attempting to pressure Him into saying *something*, into giving *some* answer to the liars' accusations (v.60).

When Jesus refused to say anything, the High Priest asked Him directly if He was the Messiah, "the Son of the Blessed" (v.61). *Blessed* (Gk. eulogetou) is a reference to God. The Jews, when mentioning God's name, would usually say, "God, blessed for ever." The word "blessed" came to be a title for God. Jesus' answer to this question would definitely provide His unjust judges the evidence they sought to execute Him.

THOUGHT 1. Jesus set a powerful example for us to follow when under attack.
1) He set an example of *patience*. He had to stand there patiently while *false* charge after *false* charge was leveled against Him.
2) He had to *endure* it all.
3) He had to *control* Himself, his emotions and tongue, and not retaliate.

How difficult it is to remain silent and to control the tongue, especially when the accusations are false! When we are attacked or accused unjustly, we need to pray for strength to follow our Lord's example. Even though we might need to speak up and defend ourselves (Jesus did not defend Himself in accordance with God's purpose—His sacrificial death), we still need the sense of calm, the strength to endure, and the self-control our Lord exhibited.

> For "Whoever desires to love life and see good days, let him keep his tongue from evil and his lips from speaking deceit." (1 Pe.3:10)

> Whoever guards his mouth preserves his life; he who opens wide his lips comes to ruin. (Pr.13:3)

> Whoever keeps his mouth and his tongue keeps himself out of trouble. (Pr.21:23)

14:62

⁶² And Jesus said, "I am, and you will see the Son of Man seated at the right hand of Power, and coming with the clouds of heaven."

5 The strong Lord: He claimed to be the Messiah, the Son of God.

Jesus did not hesitate to state the truth. He answered that He was the Messiah, the actual Son of the Blessed (God). Jesus' answer was a strong claim. He pulled no punches, left no room for doubt. He used the striking words of deity: *I am* (ego eimi; see notes—Jn.6:20-21; DEEPER STUDY # 2—Mt.1:18 for discussion).

Calling Himself "the Son of Man" (see DEEPER STUDY # 3—Mt.8:20 for discussion), Jesus pointed to two proofs of His claim: His resurrection and His exaltation at His second coming. Both would prove His person and authority. Though not clearly stated, the fact of Christ's resurrected was implied. The Jews were going to kill Him, and He would obviously have to rise from the dead in order to come back to earth again. Note that the resurrection and exaltation at the second coming of Christ are a source of hope for believers, but the emphasis of Jesus to these unbelievers was judgment.

➢ His resurrection declared Him to be the Son of God with power.

> And was declared to be the Son of God in power according to the Spirit of holiness by his resurrection from the dead, Jesus Christ our Lord. (Ro.1:4)

➢ His exaltation declares His position and authority to rule and reign over all people (Ph.2:9-11).

> This Jesus God raised up, and of that we all are witnesses. Being therefore exalted at the right hand of God, and having received from the Father the promise of the Holy Spirit, he has poured out this that you yourselves are seeing and hearing. For David did not ascend into the heavens, but he himself says, "The Lord said to my Lord, 'Sit at my right hand, until I make your enemies your footstool.' Let all the house of Israel therefore know for certain that God has made him both Lord and Christ, this Jesus whom you crucified." (Ac.2:32–36)

> Therefore God has highly exalted him and bestowed on him the name that is above every name, so that at the name of Jesus every knee should bow, in heaven and on earth and under the earth, and every tongue confess that Jesus Christ is Lord, to the glory of God the Father. (Ph.2:9–11)

➤ His return will declare His execution of justice and judgment (Mt.24:30; Jn.5:28).

> Then will appear in heaven the sign of the Son of Man, and then all the tribes of the earth will mourn, and they will see the Son of Man coming on the clouds of heaven with power and great glory. (Mt.24:30)

> Do not marvel at this, for an hour is coming when all who are in the tombs will hear his voice and come out, those who have done good to the resurrection of life, and those who have done evil to the resurrection of judgment. "I can do nothing on my own. As I hear, I judge, and my judgment is just, because I seek not my own will but the will of him who sent me." (Jn.5:28–30)

6 The frenzied mob of religionists: They got their satisfaction—the condemnation of their perceived enemy.

The Jewish religious leaders got their satisfaction, what they needed to execute Jesus. They no longer had to rely on the flimsy testimony of false witnesses; Jesus had incriminated Himself by telling the truth about who He was, and is. They could charge God Son's with blasphemy, a charge that would bring about the death of their disturber.

⁶³ And the high priest tore his garments and said, "What further witnesses do we need?
⁶⁴ You have heard his blasphemy. What is your decision?" And they all condemned him as deserving death.
⁶⁵ And some began to spit on him and to cover his face and to strike him, saying to him, "Prophesy!" And the guards received him with blows.

a. The true character of the High Priest (vv.63–64a).

The bitter hatred Caiaphas felt toward Jesus reached its peak when Jesus made the strong claim to be the Son of God. The High Priest ripped his clothes, which was a custom when God's name was disgraced (2 K.18:37; 19:1; see Is.36:22; 37:1; Ac.14:14), and he shouted out for the verdict. The whole scene was a travesty, a terrible abuse of justice. Caiaphas pictures the character of every individual who chooses this world and its institutional religion over Jesus.

THOUGHT 1. Two things got the best of Caiaphas:
➤ He wished to have this world with its rewards of position and wealth, recognition and pleasure.
➤ He wished to have a religion of self-image instead of God's image.

Too often, the same two things get the best of us.

b. The true character of people (vv.64b–65).

The Sanhedrin lunged at the opportunity to sentence Jesus to death (v.64b). The mob of religious phonies went into a frenzy, openly displaying their bitter hatred of God's Son, the One sent to be their Savior. First, they spat in His face; and then they blindfolded the Lamb of God and beat Him (v.65). Spitting in the face was a sign of monstrous disrespect and rejection (see DEEPER STUDY # 1). Beating Jesus with fists and palms was an outburst of the inner bitterness within the religionists' hearts against Him. Coupled with the physical abuse was the ridicule of Jesus' claim and the heaping of sarcasm upon Him. As they struck God's Son, they mockingly commanded Him to "prophesy." Matthew adds that they called Him, "You Christ" and demanded that He tell them who it was that hit Him in spite of His being blindfolded (Mt.26:68).

I gave my back to those who strike, and my cheeks to those who pull out the beard; I hid not my face from disgrace and spitting. (Is.50:6; see Is.52:14)

Now muster your troops, O daughter of troops; siege is laid against us; with a rod they strike the judge of Israel on the cheek. (Mi.5:1)

DEEPER STUDY # 1

(14:65) **Jesus Christ—Spit Upon:** a sign of utter contempt (see Nu.12:14; De.25:9; Is.50:6).

J. Peter's Denial:
A Picture of Failure, 14:66–72

(Mt.26:69–72; Lu.22:54, 62; Jn.18:15–18, 25–27)

66 And as Peter was below in the courtyard, one of the servant girls of the high priest came,

67 and seeing Peter warming himself, she looked at him and said, "You also were with the Nazarene, Jesus."

68 But he denied it, saying, "I neither know nor understand what you mean." And he went out into the gateway and the rooster crowed.

69 And the servant girl saw him and began again to say to the bystanders, "This man is one of them."

70 But again he denied it. And after a little while the bystanders again said to Peter, "Certainly you are one of them, for you are a Galilean."

71 But he began to invoke a curse on himself and to swear, "I do not know this man of whom you speak."

72 And immediately the rooster crowed a second time. And Peter remembered how Jesus had said to him, "Before the rooster crows twice, you will deny me three times." And he broke down and wept.

1. **The cause of failure: Peter was below in the courtyard, among the worldly and unbelievers**
2. **Failure 1: Fearing an individual—caused a cowardly denial**
   a. A servant girl charged Peter with being a disciple
   b. Peter claimed ignorance and denied association with Christ
   c. The rooster crowed, 72
3. **Failure 2: Fearing a crowd—caused an emphatic denial**
   a. The servant girl charged Peter before a crowd
   b. Peter made an outright denial
4. **Failure 3: Fearing a crowd—caused a fiery denial**
   a. The crowd charged Peter
   b. Peter denied Christ by cursing and swearing
   c. The rooster crowed a second time
5. **The answer to failure: Repentance**
   a. Peter remembered
   b. Peter wept in repentance

Division IX

The Son of God's Passion Ministry: Jesus' Supreme Sacrifice—Rejected and Crucified, 14:1–15:47

J. Peter's Denial: A Picture of Failure, 14:66–72

(Mt.26:69–72; Lu.22:54, 62; Jn.18:15–18, 25–27)

14:66–72
Introduction

Failing the Lord is very, very serious. Peter failed Jesus in several areas, and his failure reached its climax in an actual denial of the Lord. We need to be reminded that if a man who walked so closely to Jesus—one of His inner circle—can so grievously fail the Lord, we can as well. For this reason, it is critical that we learn from Peter's failure. The Holy Spirit inspired all four Gospel authors to include it for our benefit. This is, *Peter's Denial: A Picture of Failure, 14:66–72.*

1. The cause of failure: Peter was below in the courtyard, among the worldly and unbelievers (v.66).
2. Failure 1: Fearing an individual—caused a cowardly denial (vv.67-68).
3. Failure 2: Fearing a crowd—caused an emphatic denial (vv.69-70).
4. Failure 3: Fearing a crowd—caused a fiery denial (vv.70-72).
5. The answer to failure: Repentance (v.72).

14:66a

⁶⁶ And as Peter was below in the courtyard, one of the servant girls of the high priest came,

1 The cause of failure: Peter was below in the courtyard, among the worldly and unbelievers.

The cause of Peter's failure is simply stated: "Peter was below in the courtyard." He was where he should not have been.

He was with the crowd of Christ rejecters, sitting with them and warming himself by their fire. As the case would be in any similar situation, the crowd was discussing the trial and mocking, joking, and cursing Jesus because of His claims. Peter should have been off alone or else with the other disciples in prayer, seeking an answer to their confusion. Besides being in the wrong place with the wrong people, what other factors contributed to Peter's failure?

First, Peter's failure was due to his misunderstanding of God's Word. In particular, he misunderstood the teaching concerning the Kingdom of God. He thought of the Kingdom of God in physical and material terms only. He failed to see the spiritual Kingdom of God, that is . . .

- the death and resurrection of Christ
- the Lord's indwelling power, His rule and reign within the human heart
- the remaking of a new heavens and earth, which he was later to understand in the clearest of terms (2 Pe.3:10)

Second, Peter's failure was due to confusion. Peter had drawn his sword and attacked. He had been ready to act in the flesh, to fight to establish the Lord's kingdom, but Jesus had rebuked him and stopped him (v.47; Jn.18:10-11). In addition, Jesus had not blasted His enemies nor made His move; but rather, He had allowed them to take Him, voluntarily surrendering to their abuse. Peter could not understand this surrender. He was confused. His mind was reeling and searching for answers.

Third, Peter failed because of his fear. Peter had created a bad situation for himself. He had attacked the arresting party. He had failed to wait on the Lord's direction, acting in the arm of the flesh and doing what he thought best. Therefore, to some degree he was now a hunted man. In the scuffle, he had forsaken the Lord and fled for his life. But, as mentioned before, Peter's great love for Jesus and his great hope that Jesus might yet make His move had stopped Peter and turned him around. He followed Jesus, although from a safe distance (see note—v.54). Throughout the whole incident, his heart had probably been palpitating with fear—fear of being recognized, arrested, and killed.

Fourth, Peter failed because of his weak faith. Peter had failed to trust Jesus in the midst of confusing and threatening *circumstances*. Jesus was being tried and condemned to die before Peter's eyes, yet Jesus had said He would arise. Peter had chosen to interpret Jesus' words symbolically, probably thinking Jesus was referring to raising up the kingdom after a struggle with the Romans (symbolically viewed as death, the death of enemies or fallen governments). The point is, Peter never interpreted the Lord's words literally; therefore, his faith was built on error. This led to weak faith and being unprepared for the events facing him.

THOUGHT 1. Being with a crowd of people who reject Christ, associating with and moving among the worldly, will always lead to the temptation to fail the Lord Jesus.

> **Therefore go out from their midst, and be separate from them, says the Lord, and touch no unclean thing; then I will welcome you, and I will be a father to you, and you shall be sons and daughters to me, says the Lord Almighty. (2 Co.6:17-18)**

> Now we command you, brothers, in the name of our Lord Jesus Christ, that you keep away from any brother who is walking in idleness and not in accord with the tradition that you received from us. (2 Th.3:6)

THOUGHT 2. The same four factors that caused Peter to fail Christ will cause us to fail Him as well . . .

> ➤ misunderstanding God's Word
> ➤ being confused
> ➤ fear
> ➤ weak faith (due to misinterpreting or not believing the Lord's words)

2 Failure 1: Fearing an individual—caused a cowardly denial.

Peter's first failure was that of fearing an individual, which caused cowardice. Note what happened.

a. A servant girl charged Peter with being a disciple (vv.66b–67).

One of the High Priest's maids simply walked up to Peter and remarked that he had also been with Jesus of Nazareth. She seems to have intended no threat or danger in this statement to Peter. At worst, it seems that it would have led only to some bantering and ridicule. The rejecters standing around were naturally jesting back and forth about Jesus and His claims. In their minds and talk, He was but a fool. Peter had an opportunity, perhaps, to be a witness for Jesus. He could have humbly shared about Jesus' love and enormous care for people. Perhaps he could have helped to turn some who were standing there to Jesus or at least stopped some of the mob from ridiculing Him. We must always remember that John was somewhere in the palace as well, and as far as we know, he was maintaining his composure and testimony for Jesus.

66 And as Peter was below in the courtyard, one of the servant girls of the high priest came,
67 and seeing Peter warming himself, she looked at him and said, "You also were with the Nazarene, Jesus."
68 But he denied it, saying, "I neither know nor understand what you mean." And he went out into the gateway and the rooster crowed.

b. Peter claimed ignorance and denied association with Christ (v.68b).

Peter crumbled under his fear. He denied Jesus, pretending he knew nothing about Him nor had anything to do with Him. He simply claimed ignorance of the whole matter.

c. The rooster crowed (v.68b).

At that precise point, immediately after Peter denied Jesus, the rooster crowed. Certainly, the crowing of a rooster is a common occurrence that does not normally draw much attention. However, considering the fact that Peter had *just* denied Christ, and considering the Lord's specific prediction of his denial and the rooster crowing, it would seem that Peter would have surely been stunned. Apparently, however, he was unfazed by the sound.

THOUGHT 1. The fear of ridicule and embarrassment often causes a person to deny Jesus. Sometimes the denial is . . .

- by voice
- by act (going along with the person or crowd)
- by silence

THOUGHT 2. When out in the world, too many pretend not to know Jesus. They profess Jesus on Sundays and among believers yet never say a word about Him during the week. Or, they live no differently from the world. No one ever knows they are professing believers. Such cowardice is denial.

> For whoever is ashamed of me and of my words in this adulterous and sinful generation, of him will the Son of Man also be ashamed when he comes in the glory of his Father with the holy angels. (Mk.8:38)

But in your hearts honor Christ the Lord as holy, always being prepared to make a defense to anyone who asks you for a reason for the hope that is in you; yet do it with gentleness and respect. (1 Pe.3:15)

The fear of man lays a snare, but whoever trusts in the LORD is safe. (Prov.29:25)

14:69-70a

⁶⁹ And the servant girl saw him and began again to say to the bystanders, "This man is one of them."

⁷⁰ But again he denied it. And after a little while the bystanders again said to Peter, "Certainly you are one of them, for you are a Galilean."

3 Failure 2: Fearing a crowd—caused an emphatic denial.

Peter's second failure was that of fearing a crowd. Just as it did with Peter, fearing a crowd sometimes causes outright denial.

a. The servant girl charged Peter before a crowd (v.69).

This time, the maid who had recognized Peter told the crowd standing around that he was one of Jesus' followers. The pressure on Peter was tremendous, and the hateful eyes of all those around him suddenly focused on him.

b. Peter made an outright denial (v.70a).

Just as the pressure on Peter was stronger because of the presence of a crowd, Peter's denial of Christ was stronger. Matthew says, "He denied [Christ] with an oath" (Mt.26:72). Peter actually denied Jesus before the crowd, and he denied Him using an oath. Instead of denying Jesus, he should have been upstairs in the courtroom standing by the Lord's side and testifying for Him. Instead, Peter was falling (progressing) deeper and deeper into sin.

➤ He was denying Jesus because he was not by His side; instead he was standing among the Lord's rejecters.

➤ He was standing among the Lord's rejecters because he had fled the Lord.

➤ He had fled the Lord because he had acted in the flesh.

➤ He had acted in the flesh because he had not accepted the Lord's words. The Lord had told Peter and the others exactly what was to happen, yet Peter had refused to open his mind to the truth. Therefore, he was utterly confused and caught off guard.

Peter's denial was rooted in fear. He feared persecution. This was the first time he was standing face to face with life-threatening persecution. And he was failing to stand for Christ. He was failing despite the fact that Jesus had told him time and again that he must suffer for God. Peter had followed Jesus ever so readily when Jesus was popular and had a huge following. But he could not stand the heat when Jesus was being opposed and rejected by most.

But whoever denies me before men, I also will deny before my Father who is in heaven. (Mt.10:33)

Therefore do not be ashamed of the testimony about our Lord, nor of me his prisoner, but share in suffering for the gospel by the power of God. (2 Ti.1:8)

Be strong and courageous. Do not fear or be in dread of them, for it is the LORD your God who goes with you. He will not leave you or forsake you. (De.31:6)

14:70b-72

⁷⁰ But again he denied it. And after a little while the bystanders again said to Peter, "Certainly you are one of them, for you are a Galilean."

⁷¹ But he began to invoke a curse on himself and to swear, "I do not know this man of whom you speak."

⁷² And immediately the rooster crowed a second time. And Peter remembered how Jesus had said to him, "Before the rooster crows twice, you will deny me three times." And he broke down and wept.

4 Failure 3: Fearing a crowd—caused a fiery denial.

Peter's third failure is also that of fearing the crowd. Fearing a crowd can sometimes cause a person to panic and say or do things they would not normally say or do, just as it did Peter (see notes—Mt.26:73-74; 5:33-37).

a. The crowd charged Peter (v.70b).

The angry crowd approached and confronted Peter. The pressure on this terrified disciple was growing by the second. His Galilean speech (accent) had given him away, and the crowd knew that Jesus and His disciples were from Galilee (Mt.26:73). Jesus had been arrested secretly, and few knew about it. They just assumed that no Galilean would be out this time of night unless he was a follower of Jesus.

b. **Peter denied Christ by cursing and swearing (v.71).**
Peter's chest was surely pounding with emotion and fear. His thoughts were flying, trying to figure out how to escape. Terror-stricken, his emotions burst forth in a forceful cursing and swearing denial: "I do not know this man." Note Peter called his Lord "this man," which was all He was to those standing around. (To all rejecters Jesus is no more than "this man.")

c. **The rooster crowed a second time (v.72a).**
Immediately upon Peter's vehement denial of Christ, the rooster crowed, and Peter heard it. The fear that consumed the disloyal disciple's heart and mind was suddenly shoved out by an emotion even more powerful—regret.

THOUGHT 1. A worldly crowd can and will put undue pressure upon a believer. A believer does not belong in the midst of a worldly crowd, hanging around worldly places.

> And with many other words he bore witness and continued to exhort them, saying, "Save yourselves from this crooked generation." (Ac.2:40)

> Take no part in the unfruitful works of darkness, but instead expose them. (Ep.5:11)

> And not frightened in anything by your opponents. This is a clear sign to them of their destruction, but of your salvation, and that from God. (Ph.1:28)

5 The answer to failure: Repentance.

14:72

In spite of his utter failure, Peter's heart was not hardened toward the Lord. When the rooster crowed, he was overcome with conviction, and he repented of his horrible sin.

> [72] And immediately the rooster crowed a second time. And Peter remembered how Jesus had said to him, "Before the rooster crows twice, you will deny me three times." And he broke down and wept.

a. **Peter remembered.**
As soon as Peter heard the rooster crow the second time, the Spirit of God brought the haunting words of the Lord to His mind. Jesus had said that he would deny Jesus three times before the second crow of the rooster—in a very short span of time.

b. **Peter wept in repentance.**
Quickly, emotion and sorrow arose in Peter's chest, and he felt the tears come. He was overcome by the conviction of failing his Lord and failing Him so miserably. Peter loved the Lord, and somehow he knew that he was not where he belonged. He might not understand what was happening to the Lord and the course the Lord had taken, but he should have been by His side all the time testifying for Him. As fast as he could, without attracting attention, he made his way out of the courtyard, and as soon as he reached the outside, he broke down in tears (Mt.26:75; Lu.22:62). The Greek word for *wept* (eklaien; pronounced *ek-lie'-en*) expresses that Peter sobbed and wailed loudly, illustrating his repentance through godly sorrow and weeping. The idea is that Peter was utterly heartbroken and added weeping upon weeping. He was a broken man, broken by his sin against the Lord he loved (see DEEPER STUDY # 1—2 Co.7:10; note and DEEPER STUDY # 1—Ac.17:29–30 for application).

➢ He wept, and the more he thought about the situation, the more he wept.
➢ He fell to the ground and wept, being heartbroken.
➢ He wept, being grieved with hurt and pain that was unbearable.
➢ He wept and wept and continued to weep.

> Repent, therefore, of this wickedness of yours, and pray to the Lord that, if possible, the intent of your heart may be forgiven you. (Ac.8:22)

If we confess our sins, he is faithful and just to forgive us our sins and to cleanse us from all unrighteousness. (1 Jn.1:9)

Whoever conceals his transgressions will not prosper, but he who confesses and forsakes them will obtain mercy. (Pr.28:13)

Only acknowledge your guilt, that you rebelled against the LORD your God and scattered your favors among foreigners under every green tree, and that you have not obeyed my voice, declares the LORD. (Je.3:13)

CHAPTER 15

K. Jesus' Trial Before Pilate:
The Picture of a Morally Weak Judge,[DS1] 15:1–15

(Mt.27:1-2, 11-25; Lu.23:1-25; Jn.18:28-40)

And as soon as it was morning, the chief priests held a consultation with the elders and scribes and the whole council. And they bound Jesus and led him away and delivered him over to Pilate.

2 And Pilate asked him, "Are you the King of the Jews?" And he answered him, "You have said so."

3 And the chief priests accused him of many things.

4 And Pilate again asked him, "Have you no answer to make? See how many charges they bring against you."

5 But Jesus made no further answer, so that Pilate was amazed.

6 Now at the feast he used to release for them one prisoner for whom they asked.

7 And among the rebels in prison, who had committed murder in the insurrection, there was a man called Barabbas.

8 And the crowd came up and began to ask Pilate to do as he usually did for them.

9 And he answered them, saying, "Do you want me to release for you the King of the Jews?"

10 For he perceived that it was out of envy that the chief priests had delivered him up.

11 But the chief priests stirred up the crowd to have him release for them Barabbas instead.

12 And Pilate again said to them, "Then what shall I do with the man you call the King of the Jews?"

13 And they cried out again, "Crucify him."

14 And Pilate said to them, "Why? What evil has he done?" But they shouted all the more, "Crucify him."

15 So Pilate, wishing to satisfy the crowd, released for them Barabbas, and having scourged Jesus, he delivered him to be crucified.

1. **Pilate was forced to make a decision concerning Jesus Christ**
   a. The religionists met to finalize their charge against Jesus
   b. They bound and took Jesus to Pilate
2. **Pilate was indecisive and rejected strong evidence**
   a. Jesus' strong claim: He is King
   b. Jesus' strong, enduring purpose: Under repeated questioning

   c. Jesus' strong control: Silence
   d. Jesus' impact: Pilate marveled
3. **Pilate attempted to compromise**
   a. The custom of Rome to pacify the Jews by releasing a prisoner
   b. The prisoner chosen: A murderer and an insurrectionist

   c. The frenzied mob

   d. The wish of Pilate: To release Jesus

   e. The reason: Pilate knew Jesus was innocent

4. **Pilate ignored the evil leaders' influence over the people**

5. **Pilate was too weak to act justly and responsibly**
   a. His first attempt at justice: Presented Jesus as king of the Jews

   b. His second attempt at justice: Declared Jesus to be innocent

6. **Pilate gave in to worldly pressure**

Division IX

*The Son of God's Passion Ministry: Jesus' Supreme
Sacrifice—Rejected and Crucified, 14:1–15:47*

K. Jesus' Trial Before Pilate: The Picture of a Morally Weak Judge, 15:1–15

(Mt.27:1–2, 11–25; Lu.23:1–25; Jn.18:28–40)

15:1–15
Introduction

Sometimes we call them spineless, and sometimes we call them gutless. Sometimes we say they are yellow-bellied, and sometimes we say they have a yellow-streak down their back. These and other terms of derision are used of people who are cowardly and morally weak. Pontius Pilate has gone down in history as a prime example of such a person.

After charging Jesus with blasphemy and sentencing Him to death, the Sanhedrin sent Jesus to Pilate, the Roman official responsible for their region (see DEEPER STUDY # 1). Pilate was morally weak both as a man and as a judge. His treatment of Jesus clearly demonstrated some of the shortcomings of a morally weak person—failures that every individual needs to reflect on. This is, *Jesus' Trial Before Pilate: The Picture of a Morally Weak Judge,* 15:1–15.

1. Pilate was forced to make a decision concerning Jesus Christ (v.1).
2. Pilate was indecisive and rejected strong evidence (vv.2–5).
3. Pilate attempted to compromise (vv.6–10).
4. Pilate ignored the evil leaders' influence over the people (v.11).
5. Pilate was too weak to act justly and responsibly (vv.12–14).
6. Pilate gave in to worldly pressure (v.15).

DEEPER STUDY # 1

(15:1–15) **Pilate:** Pilate was the procurator of Judea. He was directly responsible to the Roman Emperor for the administrative and financial management of the country. A man had to work himself up through the political and military ranks to become a procurator. Pilate was, therefore, an able man, experienced in the affairs of politics and government as well as the military. He had held this office for ten years, which shows that he was deeply trusted by the Roman government. However, the Jews despised Pilate, and Pilate despised them, in particular their intense practice of religion. When Pilate became procurator of Judea, he did two things that incited the people's bitter hatred against him forever. First, on his state visits to Jerusalem, he rode into the city with the Roman standard, an eagle sitting atop a pole. All previous governors had removed the standard out of respect toward Jewish opposition to idols. Second, Pilate launched the construction of a new water supply for Jerusalem. To finance the project, he took the money out of the temple treasury. The Jews never forgot nor forgave this act. They bitterly opposed Pilate all through his reign, and he treated them with equal contempt. On several occasions Jewish leaders threatened to exercise their right to report Pilate to the emperor. This disturbed Pilate tremendously, causing him to become even more bitter toward the Jews.

1 Pilot was forced to make a decision concerning Jesus Christ.

a. The religionists met to finalize their charge against Jesus.

b. They bound and took Jesus to Pilate.

The ruling body of the Jews (the Sanhedrin) dragged Jesus to Pilate for civil judgment. Jesus' fate was now in this Roman governor's hands. Pilate would have to make a decision as to what to do with God's Son.

The chain of events was most likely as follows: The Sanhedrin met to finalize its charges against Jesus. The charges had to be strong enough to convince the Romans to execute Him. The false witnesses had been secured the evening before (see Mk.14:53–65). The Sanhedrin probably met until the wee hours of the morning and then took a break for a little rest and breakfast. They were now returning to formulate in writing the charges against Jesus. They no doubt stated the charges in as grievous terms as possible so that the Romans would be forced to condemn Christ as a revolutionary. As soon as the charges were finalized, they bound Christ and led Him to Pilate.

THOUGHT 1. Note the picture of sacrifice in this verse. In the Old Testament, sacrifices were to be bound with cords (Ps.118:27). Christ was "bound" and "led away" and "delivered" as the great Sacrifice for us (He.10:5–14).

15:1

And as soon as it was morning, the chief priests held a consultation with the elders and scribes and the whole council. And they bound Jesus and led him away and delivered him over to Pilate.

2 Pilate was indecisive and rejected strong evidence.

The morally weak man was indecisive and rejected Jesus despite strong evidence to acquit Him of the charges against Him. The major charge against Jesus was that He claimed to be the king of the Jews. Pilate asked Jesus about the charge.

a. Jesus' strong claim: He is King (v.2).

The Greek text of Pilate's question points to Jesus' meekness and humility. The question was emphatic: "You! Are You the King of the Jews?" . . . the One who stands here . . .

- with no revolutionary fire in your eyes or voice
- with such a humble and meek attitude and appearance
- with no friends or followers supporting you
- with such poor clothing, the garb of a peasant

15:2–5

² And Pilate asked him, "Are you the King of the Jews?" And he answered him, "You have said so."

³ And the chief priests accused him of many things.

⁴ And Pilate again asked him, "Have you no answer to make? See how many charges they bring against you."

⁵ But Jesus made no further answer, so that Pilate was amazed.

Pilate was gazing at the meek Man standing before Him and saying, "How could *you* be a king?"

Jesus answered Pilate strongly and without hesitation, affirming that what Pilate had said was true. Jesus strongly claimed to be King. But it must always be noted: Jesus went on to explain that He was not a threat to Caesar nor to any other civil government. He was the King of people's spirits and of heaven, not of this earth (Jn.18:36–37). He wished to reign in people's hearts and lives, in the realm of the spiritual and eternal, not in the realm of the physical and temporal.

b. Jesus' strong, enduring purpose: Under repeated questioning (vv.3–4.).

At this point, the chief priests stepped up and read a list of charges against Jesus (v.3). The list was long and padded with every possible offense the religious leaders could drum up. Pilate urged Jesus to speak up and defend Himself (v.4). Standing before His determined accusers and the Roman official who held His life in his hands, the Lord said nothing, enduring their awful indignities. He submitted to their false, unjust attack because He was purposed to die for the sins of the human race.

c. Jesus' strong control: Silence (v.5a).

As human beings, we have the natural tendency to defend ourselves when attacked or accused falsely. However, even after Pilate implored Jesus to defend Himself, He remained stone silent before His accusers. Why would Jesus not defend Himself, not try to escape death? Why did He let the false charges levied against Him go unchallenged? Again, it was because of His purpose. His purpose was to surrender to the *sinful behavior* of mankind. The *sinful behavior* to which He submitted was . . .

- the very depth of sin itself
- the ultimate demonstration of sin
- the greatest sin that could be committed

The rejection and killing of the Son of God was the horrific sin to which Jesus ultimately subjected Himself.

d. Jesus' impact: Pilate marveled (v.5b).

As Pilate observed Jesus' silence—His steadfast refusal to defend Himself against outrageous charges—the Roman governor was amazed. *Was amazed* or *marveled* (Gk. thaumazein; pronounced *thaw-mah'-zane*) means more than to simply be astonished. It means "to esteem, to admire, to honour."[1] Pilate looked on Jesus with a sense of wonder and admiration because of the Lord's self-control, how He was able to endure such obviously manufactured charges without losing His composure. Nevertheless, the cowardly, indecisive governor would not acquit Jesus of the charges against Him. He rejected the strong evidence of Christ's innocence and let the bloodthirsty crowd decide the fate of God's Son.

THOUGHT 1. Indecision is one of the gross mistakes of weak people, a mistake that dooms many. There is no excuse for indecision when it comes to Jesus; the evidence that Jesus is the Savior of the world is clearly seen to an open and honest heart.

> No one can serve two masters, for either he will hate the one and love the other, or he will be devoted to the one and despise the other. You cannot serve God and money. (Mt.6:24)

> You cannot drink the cup of the Lord and the cup of demons. You cannot partake of the table of the Lord and the table of demons. (1 Co.10:21)

> He is a double-minded man, unstable in all his ways. (Js.1:8)

> And Elijah came near to all the people and said, "How long will you go limping between two different opinions? If the Lord is God, follow him; but if Baal, then follow him." And the people did not answer him a word. (1 K.18:21)

15:6–10

⁶ Now at the feast he used to release for them one prisoner for whom they asked.

⁷ And among the rebels in prison, who had committed murder in the insurrection, there was a man called Barabbas.

⁸ And the crowd came up and began to ask Pilate to do as he usually did for them.

⁹ And he answered them, saying, "Do you want me to release for you the King of the Jews?"

¹⁰ For he perceived that it was out of envy that the chief priests had delivered him up.

3 Pilate attempted to compromise.

The scene was set. The Jewish court (Sanhedrin) had accused Jesus, condemned Him to die, and had delivered Him to the Roman authority, Pilate. It was Pilate who had to pass the final sentence and actually carry out the execution. However, Pilate knew that Jesus was innocent and wished to release Him. But how? He must pacify and maintain fairly good relations with the Jewish authorities. It was the only way he could maintain peace and keep them from reporting him to Rome, threatening his own position (see DEEPER STUDY # 1—Mk.15:1–15). Therefore, the morally weak man attempted to compromise.

1 Gerhard Kittel and Gerhard Friedrich, *Theological Dictionary of the New Testament*, (Grand Rapids, MI: Wm. B. Eerdmans Publishing Co., 1987). Via Wordsearch digital edition.

a. **The custom of Rome to pacify the Jews by releasing a prisoner (v.6).**

Pilate thought of a way to escape his predicament. It was his custom to release a prisoner of the Jews' choosing at every Passover. This was one method he used to gain good will with the Jews.

b. **The prisoner chosen: A murderer and an insurrectionist (v.7).**

Pilate had a notorious criminal in prison at that very moment. Barabbas had committed serious offenses. He was a robber, an insurrectionist, and a murderer (Jn.18:40). Pilate felt sure that by pitting Barabbas against Jesus, the people would choose Jesus, the One who had ministered and helped so many of them. To release Barabbas instead of Jesus would be a gross miscarriage of justice of which Pilate did not think the religious nation would dare be guilty.

c. **The frenzied mob (v.8).**

The Jewish people had come to eagerly anticipate the annual release of a prisoner of their choosing. They relished the opportunity to exert this small measure of power over a government they bitterly despised. A frenzied mob had gathered outside Pilate's hall and began to demand that Pilate honor the custom.

d. **The wish of Pilate: To release Jesus (v.9).**

Pilate suggested to the Jews that they release Jesus. This was the decision he hoped for, the outcome that would solve his dilemma.

e. **The reason: Pilate knew Jesus was innocent (v.10).**

In addition, Pilate knew that releasing Jesus was the *right* thing to do. He knew Jesus was innocent. He knew the Jews sought to kill Jesus solely because they envied Him. However, Pilate was a morally weak man. Jesus should have been released immediately, but Pilate attempted a compromise instead of standing up for the truth. How wrong the man of compromise was! The Jews thirsted for the blood of Jesus; the world will always cry out against Jesus to get rid of Him.

THOUGHT 1. Note a crucial point: when the truth is known, it should be proclaimed and not compromised. Compromise results in three tragedies.

1) Compromise weakens character and testimony.
2) Compromise means that the truth is not being done or lived. A person is agreeing to do something less than what he or she should be doing.
3) Compromise weakens principle, position, and life.

> I will ponder the way that is blameless. Oh when will you come to me? I will walk with integrity of heart within my house. (Ps.101:2)

> I have chosen the way of faithfulness; I set your rules before me. (Ps.119:30)

> And your ears shall hear a word behind you, saying, "This is the way, walk in it," when you turn to the right or when you turn to the left. (Is.30:21)

THOUGHT 2. God accepts no compromise concerning His Son, Jesus Christ. A person either stands for Him or against Him. There is no neutral ground. Jesus is the innocent, sinless Son of God in whom all people are to place their trust and lives.

> Whoever is not with me is against me, and whoever does not gather with me scatters. (Lu.11:23)

> That all may honor the Son, just as they honor the Father. Whoever does not honor the Son does not honor the Father who sent him. Truly, truly, I say to you, whoever hears my word and believes him who sent me has eternal life. He does not come into judgment, but has passed from death to life. (Jn.5:23–24)

> Submit yourselves therefore to God. Resist the devil, and he will flee from you. Draw near to God, and he will draw near to you. Cleanse your hands, you sinners, and purify your hearts, you double-minded. Be wretched and mourn and weep. Let your laughter be turned

to mourning and your joy to gloom. Humble yourselves before the Lord, and he will exalt you. (Js.4:7-10)

And this is the testimony, that God gave us eternal life, and this life is in his Son. Whoever has the Son has life; whoever does not have the Son of God does not have life. (1 Jn.5:11-12)

15:11

¹¹ But the chief priests stirred up the crowd to have him release for them Barabbas instead.

4 Pilate ignored the evil leaders' influence over the people.

The morally weak man overlooked just how much influence the Jewish religious leaders carried with the people. What happened now was tragic. The religionists moved out among the crowd, inciting them to protest for Barabbas' release. Note that Pilate did nothing. He just sat still and said nothing, ignoring the reality of evil influence.

THOUGHT 1. People who are set on evil will try to influence others in order to get their way. The influence of the wicked upon other people cannot be ignored. Evil people do influence others. To ignore the fact is to allow the infiltration and growth of more and more evil.

> For, as it is written, "The name of God is blasphemed among the Gentiles because of you." (Ro.2:24)

> Do not be overcome by evil, but overcome evil with good. (Ro.12:21)

> While evil people and impostors will go on from bad to worse, deceiving and being deceived. (2 Ti.3:13)

15:12-14

¹² And Pilate again said to them, "Then what shall I do with the man you call the King of the Jews?"
¹³ And they cried out again, "Crucify him."
¹⁴ And Pilate said to them, "Why? What evil has he done?" But they shouted all the more, "Crucify him."

5 Pilate was too weak to act justly and responsibly.

The morally weak man had neither the integrity nor the fortitude to act justly and responsibly. He chose to attempt to reason with the Jewish people rather than to stand boldly for the truth.

a. **His first attempt at justice: Presented Jesus as king of the Jews (vv.12-13).**
Pilate presented Jesus to the people as their king, the One whom they called the King of the Jews. He was *appealing* to the hope they had for a deliverer. Many had, after all, called Jesus their king, the One for whom they had been looking. He had ministered to and cared for so many. He had declared His kingdom to be concerned only with the spiritual (Jn.18:36-37). He was no threat to Caesar. Why should the people condemn One who had shown so much care and interest in their needs? But the people cried out for Jesus' death.

b. **His second attempt at justice: Declared Jesus to be innocent (v.14).**
Pilate plainly declared Jesus to be innocent. He had done no evil, and Pilate knew it. The spineless Roman governor tried to persuade the crowd to think about the fact. He cried out loudly, "Why, what evil has He done?" But it was all to no avail. His voice was drowned out by the savage cries of the bloodthirsty mob. Inflamed even more, the crowd screamed, "Crucify Him!"
Indeed Pilate was a morally weak man.
➢ He was not strong enough to do what he knew was right.
➢ He lacked the moral strength to stand up for an innocent Man.
➢ He was too weak to declare the truth.

> I call heaven and earth to witness against you today, that I have set before you life and death, blessing and curse. Therefore choose life, that you and your offspring may live. (De.30:19)

And Elijah came near to all the people and said, "How long will you go limping between two different opinions? If the LORD is God, follow him; but if Baal, then follow him." And the people did not answer him a word. (1 K.18:21)

6 Pilate gave in to worldly pressure.

Pilate cared more about satisfying and pleasing the people than doing what was right. Fear, of course, lay behind Pilate's action—the fear . . .

- of losing the people's favor
- of causing problems for himself
- of losing his position and security

> [15] So Pilate, wishing to satisfy the crowd, released for them Barabbas, and having scourged Jesus, he delivered him to be crucified.

Therefore, Pilate moved forward with punishing Jesus. First, Pilate released the criminal Barabbas. Then, he ordered that Jesus be scourged (see note—Mt.27:26–38). Finally, he delivered Jesus over to the soldiers to be crucified.

Pilate had the authority and the duty to do what was right. But he failed. The morally weak man gave in to worldly pressure. He was too weak to stand for the truth, too weak to do the right thing, too weak to free himself from the evil influence of the world.

> Do not be conformed to this world, but be transformed by the renewal of your mind, that by testing you may discern what is the will of God, what is good and acceptable and perfect. (Ro.12:2)

> By faith Moses, when he was grown up, refused to be called the son of Pharaoh's daughter, choosing rather to be mistreated with the people of God than to enjoy the fleeting pleasures of sin. (He.11:24–25)

> Do not love the world or the things in the world. If anyone loves the world, the love of the Father is not in him. For all that is in the world—the desires of the flesh and the desires of the eyes and pride of life—is not from the Father but is from the world. (1 Jn.2:15–16)

L. Jesus' Cross:
An Outline of Its Mockery and Events, 15:16–41

(Mt.27:26–56; Lu.23:26–49; Jn.19:16–37)

1. **The abuse by Pilate's soldiers: A misunderstanding of Jesus' claim**
   a. They called others to join in abusing Him
   b. They mocked and tortured Him
      1) Put a purple robe on Him (v.17)
      2) Thrust a crown of thorns on His head (v.17)
      3) Mocked His claim to be a king (v.18)
      4) Repeatedly struck Him on the head with a staff (v.19)
      5) Again mocked His claim (v.19)
2. **The switching of Jesus' clothes: His life was valued less than the royal clothing**

3. **The man who carried Jesus' cross: A picture of conversion by picking up the cross**

4. **The place of the crucifixion: A symbol of death—Jesus died just like all human beings**
5. **The refusal of drugs: A resolve to taste death at its bitterest**
6. **The gambling for Jesus' clothes: An indifferent and insensitive spirit**

7. **The crucifixion: The depth of sin and the summit of love**
8. **The inscription on the cross: A misunderstood charge**
9. **The two thieves crucified with Jesus: A picture of Jesus' life—to the end He was numbered with sinners, Is.53:12**
10. **The mocking by the people: Misunderstanding Jesus' salvation**
    a. The mockery by those passing by: Misunderstanding Jesus' resurrection

    b. The mockery by religionists: Misunderstanding God's Messiahship

16 And the soldiers led him away inside the palace (that is, the governor's headquarters), and they called together the whole battalion.

17 And they clothed him in a purple cloak, and twisting together a crown of thorns, they put it on him.

18 And they began to salute him, "Hail, King of the Jews!"

19 And they were striking his head with a reed and spitting on him and kneeling down in homage to him.

20 And when they had mocked him, they stripped him of the purple cloak and put his own clothes on him. And they led him out to crucify him.

21 And they compelled a passerby, Simon of Cyrene, who was coming in from the country, the father of Alexander and Rufus, to carry his cross.

22 And they brought him to the place called Golgotha (which means Place of a Skull).

23 And they offered him wine mixed with myrrh, but he did not take it.

24 And they crucified him and divided his garments among them, casting lots for them, to decide what each should take.

25 And it was the third hour when they crucified him.

26 And the inscription of the charge against him read, "The King of the Jews."

27 And with him they crucified two robbers, one on his right and one on his left.

29 And those who passed by derided him, wagging their heads and saying, "Aha! You who would destroy the temple and rebuild it in three days,

30 save yourself, and come down from the cross!"

31 So also the chief priests with the scribes mocked him to one another, saying, "He saved others; he cannot save himself.

³² Let the Christ, the King of Israel, come down now from the cross that we may see and believe." Those who were crucified with him also reviled him.

³³ And when the sixth hour had come, there was darkness over the whole land until the ninth hour.

³⁴ And at the ninth hour Jesus cried with a loud voice, "Eloi, Eloi, lema sabachthani?" which means, "My God, my God, why have you forsaken me?"

³⁵ And some of the bystanders hearing it said, "Behold, he is calling Elijah."

³⁶ And someone ran and filled a sponge with sour wine, put it on a reed and gave it to him to drink, saying, "Wait, let us see whether Elijah will come to take him down."

³⁷ And Jesus uttered a loud cry and breathed his last.

³⁸ And the curtain of the temple was torn in two, from top to bottom.

³⁹ And when the centurion, who stood facing him, saw that in this way he breathed his last, he said, "Truly this man was the Son of God!"

⁴⁰ There were also women looking on from a distance, among whom were Mary Magdalene, and Mary the mother of James the younger and of Joses, and Salome.

⁴¹ When he was in Galilee, they followed him and ministered to him, and there were also many other women who came up with him to Jerusalem.

c. The mockery by two thieves: Misunderstanding Jesus' claim

11. **The frightening darkness: A symbol of separation and loneliness**

12. **The terrible cry of separation: A horrifying judgment**

13. **The confused mob: A picture of the world's people**
    a. A man of pity: Offered Jesus a drink
    b. Men of hardness: Ridiculed Jesus

14. **The loud cry of death: A picture of glorious triumph**

15. **The torn veil of the temple: A symbol of open access into God's very presence**

16. **The centurion's confession: A picture of the great confession to be made by many**

17. **The women at the cross: A proof that Jesus lived and served well**

Division IX

The Son of God's Passion Ministry: Jesus' Supreme Sacrifice—Rejected and Crucified, 14:1–15:47

L. Jesus' Cross: An Outline of Its Mockery and Events, 15:16–41

(Mt.27:26–56; Lu.23:26–49; Jn.19:16–37)

15:16–41
Introduction

The death of Jesus on the cross is the most important event in history; in fact, it is the crucial focal point of history. Eternal salvation was secured for the human race through the death of Jesus on the cross. Because Jesus died, we can live forever in a perfect state of being. Therefore, the events of the cross are all-important. They hold lesson after lesson for the person who seeks the truth of God's Son. This is, *Jesus' Cross: An Outline of Its Mockery and Events,* 15:16-41.

1. The abuse by Pilate's soldiers: A misunderstanding of Jesus' claim (vv.16-19).
2. The switching of Jesus' clothes: His life was valued less than the royal clothing (v.20).
3. The man who carried Jesus' cross: A picture of conversion by picking up the cross (v.21).
4. The place of the crucifixion: A symbol of death—Jesus died just like all human beings (v.22).
5. The refusal of drugs: A resolve to taste death at its bitterest (v.23).
6. The gambling for Jesus' clothes: An indifferent and insensitive spirit (v.24).
7. The crucifixion: The depth of sin and the summit of love (v.25).
8. The inscription on the cross: A misunderstood charge (v.26).
9. The two thieves crucified with Jesus: A picture of Jesus' life—to the end He was numbered with sinners, Is.53:12 (vv.27-28).
10. The mocking by the people: Misunderstanding Jesus' salvation (vv.29-32).
11. The frightening darkness: A symbol of separation and loneliness (v.33).
12. The terrible cry of separation: A horrifying judgment (v.34).
13. The confused mob: A picture of the world's people (vv.35-36).
14. The loud cry of death: A picture of glorious triumph (v.37).
15. The torn veil of the temple: A symbol of open access into God's very presence (v.38).
16. The centurion's confession: A picture of the great confession to be made by many (v.39).
17. The women at the cross: A proof that Jesus lived and served well (vv.40-41).

15:16-19

[16] And the soldiers led him away inside the palace (that is, the governor's headquarters), and they called together the whole battalion.
[17] And they clothed him in a purple cloak, and twisting together a crown of thorns, they put it on him.
[18] And they began to salute him, "Hail, King of the Jews!"
[19] And they were striking his head with a reed and spitting on him and kneeling down in homage to him.

1 The abuse by Pilate's soldiers: A misunderstanding of Jesus' claim.

Mark's account of the crucifixion begins with Jesus being abused by Pilate's soldiers. Jesus had explained to Pilate that His kingdom was a spiritual kingdom, but Pilate had not understood what He meant (Jn.18:36-37). The soldiers, of course, knew little if anything about the conversation between Jesus and Pilate. But they had heard about the man Jesus, a carpenter from Nazareth who claimed to be the Messiah, the Son of God. Jesus of Nazareth now stood before them, declared guilty of insurrection and of claiming to be the King of the Jews. This, of course, was a threat to their own rule and power. In their eyes, seeing Jesus standing there as a captive, beaten and bloody, showed Him to be anything but a king. He was a man condemned as a threat to their power as soldiers and to their government which they had sworn to uphold. To them, He was worthy of death. The soldiers tortured Jesus so severely because of . . .

- His claim to be the Messiah and the Son of God
- His being condemned as an insurrectionist

a. They called others to join in abusing Him (v.16).
The soldiers who took possession of Jesus called all the other soldiers to join in on the "fun" of torturing Jesus. They were in the Praetorium, which was the main quarters of the soldiers. It was a large court within the palace itself. The whole company—between two and six hundred soldiers—taunted and tortured God's Son (see note, pt.2—Mt.27:26-38).

b. They mocked and tortured Him (vv.17-19).
The band of cruel soldiers stripped Jesus and threw a worn-out purple soldier's cloak on His mangled, bleeding body. The cloak was a mocking symbol of the royal cloak worn by kings. Then, several soldiers went outside and wove a crown from a thorn bush. Returning, they tortured Jesus by slamming the crown of thorns into His head and brow (v.17). As the blood from the fresh wounds streamed down our Lord's face, they mocked His claim to be the King of the Jews (v.18).

The soldiers continued abusing Jesus both physically and mentally. They grabbed the reed which they had given to Him as a mock scepter (Mt.27:29) and beat Him in the head. When the vulgar stick would make contact with the barbed crown, it would drive the large thorns deeper into Christ's scalp. They also spat on Him and continued to mock His claim, bowing before Him and pretending to worship Him (v.19).

THOUGHT 1. What the soldiers did in mocking Jesus demonstrates perfectly the *nature* of the Lord's Kingship. Earthly royalty is symbolized by a royal robe, gold crown, scepter, and bowing of the knee—all standing for the pomp and power of earthly royalty. Christ could not accept such, not at His first coming.

The worn, faded robe, the crown of thorns, the reed scepter, the mocking—all show that the nature of Christ's Kingship is love, *sacrificial love.*

> Who, though he was in the form of God, did not count equality with God a thing to be grasped, but emptied himself, by taking the form of a servant, being born in the likeness of men. And being found in human form, he humbled himself by becoming obedient to the point of death, even death on a cross. (Ph.2:6–8)

2 The switching of Jesus' clothes: His life was valued less than the royal clothing.

15:20

After the soldiers had their fill of mocking and beating Jesus, they stripped the purple cloak—now matted into Jesus' bloody, exposed flesh—off Him and put His own clothes back on Him. The life of God's Son was valued less than worn-out royal clothing. This verse is both interesting and revealing. It shows the depth of human depravity. The soldiers would save an old, faded robe, yet they thought nothing of taking the life of an innocent person (even more, the very Son of God). The cloak was no good; it was a throw-away. They never would have put a *good* cloak on such a mangled, bloody mass of flesh. The blood and the ongoing torture would have ruined a good cloak.

20 And when they had mocked him, they stripped him of the purple cloak and put his own clothes on him. And they led him out to crucify him.

The soldiers, of course, did not want a criminal wearing a soldier's cloak through the streets, even if it were a throw-away. So they stripped the cloak from Jesus. The dried blood had naturally caused the robe to stick to the Lord's back; therefore, His wounds were reopened and bled again.

THOUGHT 1. Note two applications.

1) The cloak and what it stood for were valued and honored more than the life of Jesus, more than the very One who had come to reveal God's love and salvation to mankind. So many people value things more highly than Jesus instead of valuing Jesus more highly than all else combined.

> Do not love the world or the things in the world. If anyone loves the world, the love of the Father is not in him. For all that is in the world—the desires of the flesh and the desires of the eyes and pride of life—is not from the Father but is from the world. (1 Jn.2:15–16)

> I counsel you to buy from me gold refined by fire, so that you may be rich, and white garments so that you may clothe yourself and the shame of your nakedness may not be seen, and salve to anoint your eyes, so that you may see. (Re.3:18; see also Ep.4:23–24)

> I said to him, "Sir, you know." And he said to me, "These are the ones coming out of the great tribulation. They have washed their robes and made them white in the blood of the Lamb." (Re.7:14)

2) The soldier's robe had been only a mockery of kingly authority, but it symbolized the world's attitude toward giving homage to God's Son. Nobody determines the authority of God's Son. He possesses authority because He is God's Son, not because people give Him authority. God has given Him all authority and rule because He bore the sufferings and death of the cross for the human race. We should worship Him sincerely and submit to His authority over our lives.

> And Jesus came and said to them, "All authority in heaven and on earth has been given to me." (Mt.28:18)

For the Father judges no one, but has given all judgment to the Son, that all may honor the Son, just as they honor the Father. Whoever does not honor the Son does not honor the Father who sent him. (Jn.5:22–23)

15:21

²¹ And they compelled a passerby, Simon of Cyrene, who was coming in from the country, the father of Alexander and Rufus, to carry his cross.

3 The man who carried Jesus' cross: A picture of conversion by picking up the cross.

Evidently, Jesus was so weak from the severe beatings that He could not carry His own cross. Therefore, the soldiers forced a bystander, Simon of Cyrene, to carry Jesus' cross. Note three observations.

First, see the plan and providence of God. Nothing happens by chance, not to the Christian believer. God oversees the life of His people. Thus, Simon's being pressed into carrying the cross for Jesus was in the plan of God. God led Simon to be at that place at that time, granting him the holy privilege of helping the Savior bear His indescribable burden.

Second, Simon was standing along the roadway watching the armed procession make its way through the streets. Apparently, there was some expression of concern and sympathy for Jesus, something within his heart that was touched and moved him to reach out to Jesus. God knew this and directed the soldiers to enlist his help in carrying the Lord's cross.

Third, Simon was "the father of Alexander and Rufus." This comment by Mark is interesting. Evidently, they were known believers at the time of Mark's writing (see Ac.13:1; Ro.16:13). The indication from Mark's reference is that Simon and his two sons had later been converted.

THOUGHT 1. The symbol and application are clear. Simon represents the person who has been genuinely converted, who takes up the cross and dies to self and becomes a true follower of Christ.

And he said to all, "If anyone would come after me, let him deny himself and take up his cross daily and follow me." (Lu.9:23)

15:22

²² And they brought him to the place called Golgotha (which means Place of a Skull).

4 The place of the crucifixion: A symbol of death—Jesus died just like all human beings.

Jesus died just like all other people, a truth symbolized by the place of the crucifixion. Golgotha was a hill outside Jerusalem. It was known as a place of death, a place where executions took place. The word "Golgotha" means the place of a skull. The very place where Jesus was crucified symbolized death itself; it's very form and face of the hill to this day resembles a human skull, stirring thoughts of death and corruption. Here upon Golgotha, Jesus died to deliver humanity from the bondage of death.

Since therefore the children share in flesh and blood, he himself likewise partook of the same things, that through death he might destroy the one who has the power of death, that is, the devil, and deliver all those who through fear of death were subject to lifelong slavery. (He.2:14–15)

15:23

²³ And they offered him wine mixed with myrrh, but he did not take it.

5 The refusal of drugs: A resolve to taste death at its bitterest.

Christ's executioners offered Him a mixture of wine and myrrh to numb His suffering. The drink was strong and intoxicating, deadening the senses to some degree. It was given to crucifixion victims to dull the pain somewhat.

Jesus' purpose was to die for mankind. God's will was not to be done in a drunken stupor, in a drugged, insensitive, and unthoughtful state. He was to taste death for every person, being fully conscious of doing God's will, being as mentally alert as possible.

Jesus died as our substitute. He took upon Himself the punishment for our sin. By refusing to take the drugs offered to Him, Jesus pointed to the horrifying truth that there is no relief from the penalty of sin. There is no drug, no painkiller, nothing whatsoever to ease the suffering of those eternally separated from God in hell. Our Savior suffered the full force of that punishment for us, fully awake and fully aware of every pain. From the slightest twinge to the most excruciating jolt, Jesus felt it all.

> But we see him who for a little while was made lower than the angels, namely Jesus, crowned with glory and honor because of the suffering of death, so that by the grace of God he might taste death for everyone. (He.2:9)

> In burnt offerings and sin offerings you have taken no pleasure. Then I said, 'Behold, I have come to do your will, O God, as it is written of me in the scroll of the book.' . . . For it was fitting that he, for whom and by whom all things exist, in bringing many sons to glory, should make the founder of their salvation perfect through suffering. (He.10:6-7, 10)

6 The gambling for Jesus' clothes: An indifferent and insensitive spirit.

15:24

The hardened soldiers rudely gambled for Jesus' clothes, displaying an indifferent and insensitive spirit to Jesus' suffering as well to the suffering of those who cared for Him. Mary, Jesus' mother, was standing by the cross; yet the soldiers showed no compassion whatsoever in sharing His belongings with her (see Ps.22:18).

24 And they crucified him and divided his garments among them, casting lots for them, to decide what each should take.

The stripping of Jesus' clothing pictures a spiritual truth of His crucifixion. He allowed all of His mortality to be stripped so that He might abolish death and bring life and immortality to light.

> And which now has been manifested through the appearing of our Savior Christ Jesus, who abolished death and brought life and immortality to light through the gospel. (2 Ti.1:10)

7 The crucifixion: The depth of sin and the summit of love.

15:25

"They crucified Him." Oh, that we might be able to absorb the full impact of these three words that, so briefly yet so powerfully, express the sacrificial death of God's Son—the summit of sin and love.

25 And it was the third hour when they crucified him.

Jesus was crucified at "the third hour," 9 a.m., and darkness swept the land from noon until 3 p.m. (the sixth to the ninth hour, vv.33-34; see Deeper Study # 1—Mk.6:48; see also Mt.27:45-46; Lu.23:44).

Mankind demonstrated the height of depravity by putting God's Son to death. God demonstrated the height of love by not sparing His Son, but by allowing Him to die for humanity's sins.

> For God so loved the world, that he gave his only Son, that whoever believes in him should not perish but have eternal life. (Jn.3:16)

> But God shows his love for us in that while we were still sinners, Christ died for us. (Ro.5:8)

8 The inscription on the cross: A misunderstood charge.

15:26

The inscription on Christ's cross indicates the misunderstood charge against Him. Pilate had placed a sign saying, "The King of the Jews," above Jesus' head to mock the Jewish authorities and to reproach Jesus' claim. However, God overruled and used the title to proclaim the truth of Jesus' Lordship to the whole world (Lu.23:38). The very charges against Jesus proclaimed His deity and honor.

26 And the inscription of the charge against him read, "The King of the Jews."

523

And being found in human form, he humbled himself by becoming obedient to the point of death, even death on a cross. Therefore God has highly exalted him and bestowed on him the name that is above every name, so that at the name of Jesus every knee should bow, in heaven and on earth and under the earth, and every tongue confess that Jesus Christ is Lord, to the glory of God the Father. (Ph.2:8-11)

To keep the commandment unstained and free from reproach until the appearing of our Lord Jesus Christ, which he will display at the proper time—he who is the blessed and only Sovereign, the King of kings and Lord of lords, who alone has immortality, who dwells in unapproachable light, whom no one has ever seen or can see. To him be honor and eternal dominion. Amen. (1 Ti.6:14-16)

15:27-28[2]

²⁷ And with him they crucified two robbers, one on his right and one on his left.

9 The two thieves crucified with Jesus: A picture of Jesus' life—to the end He was numbered with sinners.

The fact that Jesus was crucified between two thieves is an appropriate picture of His life. He who was known as the "Friend of sinners" (Mt.11:19) died between two sinners; to the end He was numbered with sinners, fulfilling Isaiah's prophecy:

Therefore I will divide him a portion with the many, and he shall divide the spoil with the strong, because he poured out his soul to death and was numbered with the transgressors; yet he bore the sin of many, and makes intercession for the transgressors. (Is.53:12)

The saying is trustworthy and deserving of full acceptance, that Christ Jesus came into the world to save sinners, of whom I am the foremost. (1 Ti.1:15)

For Christ also suffered once for sins, the righteous for the unrighteous, that he might bring us to God, being put to death in the flesh but made alive in the spirit. (1 Pe.3:18)

15:29-32

²⁹ And those who passed by derided him, wagging their heads and saying, "Aha! You who would destroy the temple and rebuild it in three days,
³⁰ save yourself, and come down from the cross!"
³¹ So also the chief priests with the scribes mocked him to one another, saying, "He saved others; he cannot save himself.
³² Let the Christ, the King of Israel, come down now from the cross that we may see and believe." Those who were crucified with him also reviled him.

10 The mocking by the people.

As Jesus endured excruciating suffering on the cross, those at the scene mocked Him openly. Passersby, the Jewish religious leaders, and even the thieves who hanged beside Him failed to understand what was taking place before their very eyes: God's Son was dying for their—and our—sins.

a. The mockery of those passing by: Misunderstanding Jesus' resurrection (vv.29-30).

As people traveled in and out of the city, they slowed down, and some stopped to see what was going on. When they stopped, they saw the charge above the cross that Jesus claimed to be "The King of the Jews." They were aware of His claim of enormous power—power to destroy and rebuild the temple in three days. Such notions were ridiculous in their minds. Therefore, they joined in the mocking and verbal abuse. Of course, they did not understand that Christ was speaking of His resurrection. However, if they had, they would have no doubt mocked Him for claiming that He would rise from the dead.

He was oppressed, and he was afflicted, yet he opened not his mouth; like a lamb that is led to the slaughter, and like a sheep that before its shearers is silent, so he opened not his mouth. (Is.53:7)

b. The mockery by religionists: Misunderstanding God's Messiahship (vv.31-32a).

The Jewish religious leaders gloated as Jesus suffered for their sins. Even as He bled and died before them, their proud, stony hearts refused to believe that He was God's Messiah.

---

2 Verse 28 does not appear in the manuscripts from which many modern versions, including the ESV, are translated. Accordingly, it is not included in those versions.

> The saying is trustworthy and deserving of full acceptance, that Christ Jesus came into the world to save sinners, of whom I am the foremost. (1 Ti.1:15)
>
> For there is one God, and there is one mediator between God and men, the man Christ Jesus, who gave himself as a ransom for all, which is the testimony given at the proper time. (1 Ti.2:5-6)

c. **The mockery by two thieves: Misunderstanding Jesus' claim (v.32b).**

The two thieves also misunderstood Jesus' claim. The thieves heard the mob's mockery about Jesus' claiming to be the Messiah. A man's making such a claim while dying seemed to be insane and to merit abuse. Thus, they joined the mockers.

> When he was reviled, he did not revile in return; when he suffered, he did not threaten, but continued entrusting himself to him who judges justly. He himself bore our sins in his body on the tree, that we might die to sin and live to righteousness. By his wounds you have been healed. (1 Pe.2:23-24)

11 The frightening darkness: A symbol of separation and loneliness. 15:33

The darkness that swept the land for three hours that dreadful day is a symbol of separation and loneliness. The darkness proclaimed a message about mankind's sinful condition, the cause of Christ's death (see note—Mt.27:45 for detailed discussion):

³³ And when the sixth hour had come, there was darkness over the whole land until the ninth hour.

- Humanity was separated from the light.

> And this is the judgment: the light has come into the world, and people loved the darkness rather than the light because their works were evil. For everyone who does wicked things hates the light and does not come to the light, lest his works should be exposed. (Jn.3:19-20)

- The human race stands all alone. People cannot see in the dark, not well. They are, so to speak, standing in the world all alone, responsible for their own behavior. And because of what they have done, they must face God someday all alone to give an account for their behavior.

> And just as it is appointed for man to die once, and after that comes judgment. (He.9:27)

12 The terrible cry of separation: A horrifying judgment. 15:34

At the ninth hour, God's Son released a terrible cry of separation—a statement indicating horrifying judgment upon Him. What did Jesus mean when He cried out that God had forsaken Him?

³⁴ And at the ninth hour Jesus cried with a loud voice, "Eloi, Eloi, lema sabachthani?" which means, "My God, my God, why have you forsaken me?"

Jesus was not referring to the suffering and ill treatment of the cross, the suffering at the hands of men which He was going through. All through His ministry He knew suffering and foretold of suffering for His followers, even martyrdom.

Scripture tells us what Jesus meant (see note—Mt.27:46-49 for detailed discussion):

- He was being made sin for us.

> For our sake he made him to be sin who knew no sin, so that in him we might become the righteousness of God. (2 Co.5:21)

- He was bearing our sins as the sacrificial Lamb of God.

> For if the blood of goats and bulls, and the sprinkling of defiled persons with the ashes of a heifer, sanctify for the purification of the flesh, how much more will the blood of Christ, who through the eternal Spirit offered himself without blemish to God, purify our conscience from dead works to serve the living God. . . . so Christ, having been offered once to bear the sins of many, will appear a second time, not to deal with sin but to save those who are eagerly waiting for him. (He.9:13-14, 28)

- He was suffering for sins, the just for the unjust.

> For Christ also suffered once for sins, the righteous for the unrighteous, that he might bring us to God, being put to death in the flesh but made alive in the spirit. (1 Pe.3:18)

- He was bearing the curse of the law.

> Christ redeemed us from the curse of the law by becoming a curse for us—for it is written, "Cursed is everyone who is hanged on a tree." (Ga.3:13)

Note a critical point: the only thing that could have caused God to separate Himself from Christ was sin (Is.59:2; Ro.5:12; see Deeper Study # 1—He.9:27). Sin is the only thing that causes God to withdraw from anyone. Since Christ was perfect and sinless, it was not His own sin that caused God to forsake Him—it was our sin (2 Co.5:21; He.4:15; 7:26; 1 Pe.1:10; 2:22). While on the cross, He was separated from God so that we do not have to be—if we believe in Him.

15:35-36

[35] And some of the bystanders hearing it said, "Behold, he is calling Elijah."
[36] And someone ran and filled a sponge with sour wine, put it on a reed and gave it to him to drink, saying, "Wait, let us see whether Elijah will come to take him down."

13 The confused mob: A picture of the world's people.

When Jesus cried out to God, some of the onlookers thought He was calling out to Elijah, most likely because of the similarity of the words *eloi*, which Jesus spoke, and *Elian*, the Greek form of "Elijah" (v.35). The confused mob pictures the people of the world who never understand who Jesus truly is.

a. **A man of pity: offered Jesus a drink (v.36a).**
Jesus had said, "I thirst" (Jn.19:28-29). One man felt compassion for the Lord. He filled a sponge with sour wine (vinegar), put it on a stick, and raised it up to wet Jesus' parched mouth. This act was another fulfillment of prophecy (Ps.69:21).

b. **Men of hardness: Ridiculed Jesus (v.36).**
The other men standing around—those with hard hearts—stopped the man who pitied Jesus and attempted to refresh Him (see Mt.27:49). Thinking that Jesus was calling on a prophet of old to save Him, they mockingly wanted to see what would happen.

What a telling scene! Jesus was seen hanging and suffering on the cross, expressing the utmost pity for sinful humanity. Yet, when one man tried to show compassion for Christ, the man was stopped.

> But God shows his love for us in that while we were still sinners, Christ died for us. (Ro.5:8)

> And this is his commandment, that we believe in the name of his Son Jesus Christ and love one another, just as he has commanded us. (1 Jn.3:23)

15:37

[37] And Jesus uttered a loud cry and breathed his last.

14 The loud cry of death: A picture of glorious triumph.

Jesus' death cry was one of glorious triumph. It was one word in the Greek, *tetelestai*, "It is finished" (Jn.19:30). It is a cry of purpose, a shout of triumph. God's Son was dying for a specific purpose, and that purpose was now fulfilled (see note—Mt.27:50 for detailed discussion). The price for the sin of the human race had been paid in full.

> I am the door. If anyone enters by me, he will be saved and will go in and out and find pasture. . . . I am the good shepherd. The good shepherd lays down his life for the sheep. . . . just as the Father knows me and I know the Father; and I lay down my life for the sheep. . . . For this reason the Father loves me, because I lay down my life that I may take it up again. No one takes it from me, but I lay it down of my own accord. I have authority to lay it down, and I have authority to take it up again. This charge I have received from my Father. (Jn.10:9, 11, 15, 17-18)

15 The torn veil of the temple: A symbol of open access into God's very presence.

When Jesus took His last breath, the veil of the temple was split in two. This supernatural occurrence was a symbol of open access into God's very presence.

[38] And the curtain of the temple was torn in two, from top to bottom.

The veil (curtain) that was torn was the inner *veil* or *curtain* (Gk. katapetasma) which separated the Holy of Holies from the Holy Place. There was another veil, an *outer curtain* (kalumma), which separated the Holy Place from the outer court of the temple.

The Holy of Holies was the most sacred part of the temple, the place where the very presence of God was symbolized as dwelling in a very special way. It was closed *forever* to everyone except the High Priest. But even he could enter the Holy of Holies only once a year, on the Day of Atonement (Ex.26:33).

At the very hour that Jesus died, the priests would have been conducting the evening sacrifice. Most likely, the High Priest was rolling back the outer curtain in order to expose the Holy Place to the people, to those who had gathered to worship in the surrounding court. As he did so, both he and the worshipers stood in amazement. They saw the inner veil split from the top to the bottom. There they stood, seeing and experiencing for the very first time the Holy of Holies, the very special presence of God Himself.

The veil was torn from top to bottom. This indicates that it was torn by an act of God Himself. It symbolized God's giving direct access into His presence (He.6:19; 9:3-12, 24; 10:19-23). The torn veil symbolized that all people could now enter the presence of God by the sacrifice of Christ, His blood and His body.

> But now in Christ Jesus you who once were far off have been brought near by the blood of Christ. For he himself is our peace, who has made us both one and has broken down in his flesh the dividing wall of hostility (Ep.2:13-14)

> And by that will we have been sanctified through the offering of the body of Jesus Christ once for all. (He.10:10)

16 The centurion's confession: A picture of the great confession to be made by many.

[39] And when the centurion, who stood facing him, saw that in this way he breathed his last, he said, "Truly this man was the Son of God!"

The centurion's actions show him to be a thoughtful and honest man. He was in charge of the crucifixion. He was responsible for overseeing all that took place. As the events unfolded upon the cross, he was stricken more and more with the claim of Jesus and the way in which the events were happening. When Jesus shouted out that His purpose was finished, that His death was the climax of His purpose on earth, the centurion was convinced that Jesus was who He claimed to be. The very fact that Jesus' death was purposeful sealed his conviction. God convinced the soldier's heart of the glorious truth, and this man confessed that Jesus was the Son of God.

The centurion was a Gentile. He symbolizes the people of all nations who would confess Jesus in coming generations.

> Because, if you confess with your mouth that Jesus is Lord and believe in your heart that God raised him from the dead, you will be saved. For with the heart one believes and is justified, and with the mouth one confesses and is saved. (Ro.10:9-10)

527

17 The women at the cross: A proof that Jesus lived and served well.

Mark mentions the women who were at the cross despite the danger. Although they stood some distance away, they were there nonetheless. They still loved and cared about Jesus, no matter what. Their presence testified that Christ's life was not in vain, that He had lived and served well.

15:40–41

For whoever would save his life will lose it, but whoever loses his life for my sake and the gospel's will save it. (Mk.8:35)

⁴⁰ There were also women looking on from a distance, among whom were Mary Magdalene, and Mary the mother of James the younger and of Joses, and Salome.

⁴¹ When he was in Galilee, they followed him and ministered to him, and there were also many other women who came up with him to Jerusalem.

M. Jesus' Burial:
A Discussion of Courage, 15:42-47

(Mt.27:57-66; Lu.23:50-56; Jn.19:38-42)

⁴² And when evening had come, since it was the day of Preparation, that is, the day before the Sabbath,

1. The need for haste because the Sabbath was approaching

⁴³ Joseph of Arimathea, a respected member of the council, who was also himself looking for the kingdom of God, took courage and went to Pilate and asked for the body of Jesus.

2. The courage to request and to look after the body of Jesus

⁴⁴ Pilate was surprised to hear that he should have already died. And summoning the centurion, he asked him whether he was already dead.

⁴⁵ And when he learned from the centurion that he was dead, he granted the corpse to Joseph.

3. The courage to experience a broken heart and to die for God's cause: Seen in Christ's early death

⁴⁶ And Joseph bought a linen shroud, and taking him down, wrapped him in the linen shroud and laid him in a tomb that had been cut out of the rock. And he rolled a stone against the entrance of the tomb.

4. The courage to make an unashamed commitment to Jesus
   a. Took Jesus down from the cross
   b. Cared for and buried the body of Jesus

⁴⁷ Mary Magdalene and Mary the mother of Joses saw where he was laid.

5. The courage to take a public stand by the cross

Division IX

The Son of God's Passion Ministry:
Jesus' Supreme Sacrifice—Rejected and Crucified, 14:1–15:47

M. Jesus' Burial: A Discussion of Courage, 15:42–47

(Mt.27:57–66; Lu.23:50–56; Jn.19:38–42)

15:42–47
Introduction

If we truly love Jesus, genuinely love Him with all our hearts, we will serve Him and stand for Him whatever the cost. Staying loyal to Christ sometimes requires tremendous courage and involves great risk. Some will put their jobs, families, homes, and even their lives on the line by staying true to the Savior. But those who genuinely love the Lord will summon the courage necessary to serve Him and stand for Him.

Mark's account of Jesus' burial highlights such a man. Joseph of Arimathea was a secret disciple, a man afraid to stand for Jesus. But when He saw Jesus die, he was suddenly infused with boldness. His burial of Jesus presents a strong picture of courage, the kind of courage that sets a dynamic example for all to follow. This brand of courage is found when we gaze at our Savior dying on the cross for our sins. This is, *Jesus' Burial: A Discussion of Courage,* 15:42–47.

1. The need for haste because the Sabbath was approaching (v.42).
2. The courage to request and to look after the body of Jesus (v.43).
3. The courage to experience a broken heart and to die for God's cause: Seen in Christ's early death (vv.44-45).
4. The courage to make an unashamed commitment to Jesus (v.46).
5. The courage to take a public stand by the cross (v.47).

15:42

⁴² And when evening had come, since it was the day of Preparation, that is, the day before the Sabbath,

1 The need for haste because the Sabbath was approaching.

The Sabbath was the day of worship for Jews. The day began at 6 p.m. (Jewish days began at 6 p.m. and ran until 6 p.m. the next night, that is from sundown to sundown.) Strict Jewish law said that once the Sabbath began, no work could be done. This included burying the dead.

Jesus died at 3 p.m. on Friday, the day of preparation for the Sabbath (see vv.33-34, 37). If anything was to be done with Jesus' body, it had to be done immediately and quickly. Only three hours remained for work.

The Romans either dumped the bodies of crucified criminals in the trash heaps or left them hanging on the cross for the vultures and animals to consume. The latter served as an example to the public of the punishment criminals would face. If Jesus' body was not removed quickly within these three hours, the fate of His body was set. The Romans would not care what happened to Him, and no Jew could remove Him until the Sabbath was over. Therefore, the need for haste in burying the body of the Lord was urgent.

15:43

⁴³ Joseph of Arimathea, a respected member of the council, who was also himself looking for the kingdom of God, took courage and went to Pilate and asked for the body of Jesus.

2 The courage to request and to look after the body of Jesus.

A man, Joseph of Arimathea, was stirred to step forth for Jesus. The Gospel writers share the following information about him:

➢ He was from Arimathea.
➢ He was now a permanent citizen of Jerusalem. He had bought a tomb in Jerusalem for his burial.

➢ He was "a respected member of the council," that is, a member of the Sanhedrin (Mk.15:43).
➢ He was a good and just man (Lu.23:50).
➢ He waited for the kingdom of God (Mk.15:43).
➢ He was rich (Mt.27:57).
➢ He did not vote for Jesus' execution in the Sanhedrin decision (Lu.23:51).
➢ He was a disciple, but a secret one, fearing his fellow Jews (Jn.19:38).

It was this last fact that revealed a marked change in Joseph. Up until the death of Jesus, he had been a secret disciple. He had probably had several meetings with Jesus when the Lord had visited Jerusalem; but now, after the Lord's death, he was no longer a secret disciple. He became bold in standing for Jesus.

Joseph actually marched in boldly to Pilate and requested permission to look after the body of Jesus. This was a tremendous act of courage, for Pilate was extremely upset and wearied with the whole situation. He had been forced to give in to the Jewish authorities who were always causing problems for him. He despised them. He could react severely and cause some serious problems for Joseph, especially since Joseph was one of the leaders of the nation.

The thing that turned Joseph from being a secret disciple to a bold Christ-follower seems to be the phenomenal events surrounding the cross (for example, the behavior and final words of Jesus, the darkness, the earthquake, etc.). When Joseph witnessed all this, his mind likely connected the claims of Jesus with the Old Testament prophecies of the Messiah, and Joseph saw the prophecies fulfilled in Jesus. He stepped forward, braved all risks, and took his stand for Christ. His act is most effectively expressed by the New American Standard Bible (NASB) translation of the Greek word *tolmesas*: "he gathered up courage." A remarkable courage! A courage stirred by the death of Jesus.

THOUGHT 1. The primary thing that stirs courage in the believer is the cross. Seeing the cross and what the cross really means will empower a secret disciple to courageously step forward for Christ.

THOUGHT 2. Joseph courageously asked to take care of the body of Jesus. Today the body of Jesus is the church (Ep.1:22). We are to boldly step forward and take care of the church, in particular when there are special times of need. But note: we often need a strong dose of courage to step forward and show care. In those times, we need to take a fresh look at the cross. God can use the cross to stir us.

> For if I cause you pain, who is there to make me glad but the one whom I have pained? (2 Co.2:2)

> Knowing that he who raised the Lord Jesus will raise us also with Jesus and bring us with you into his presence. For it is all for your sake, so that as grace extends to more and more people it may increase thanksgiving, to the glory of God. (2 Co.4:14–15)

> And he died for all, that those who live might no longer live for themselves but for him who for their sake died and was raised. (2 Co.5:15)

3 The courage to experience a broken heart and to die for God's cause: Seen in Christ's early death.

Joseph must have rushed to Pilate immediately after Jesus died, for Scripture seems to indicate that the governor who had cowardly permitted Jesus' execution heard the news about Christ's death from Joseph. Mark reports that Pilate *marveled* or *was surprised to hear* that Jesus was already dead. Victims usually lingered for days before dying from exposure to the sun and from thirst and loss of blood due to the scourging and nail wounds. In fact, the victims' legs were often broken to hasten their death (Jn.19:31).

[44] Pilate was surprised to hear that he should have already died. And summoning the centurion, he asked him whether he was already dead.

[45] And when he learned from the centurion that he was dead, he granted the corpse to Joseph.

All indications point to Jesus dying from a broken heart (see notes—Jn.19:31-37). The weight of sin and its inevitable separation and judgment from God were just too much to bear (see notes—v.34; Mt.27:46-49). The weight that Jesus felt in the Garden of Gethsemane continued up to the point of His death on the cross (see note—Mk.14:33-34; see notes and DEEPER STUDY # 2—Mt.26:37-38 for detailed discussion).

This detail points to the courage of Jesus. Our Savior was willing to bear terrible sorrow and pain, so much suffering that it would actually burst His heart and speed up His inevitable death (see note, pt.2—Jn.19:31-37). Just imagine! He did it for us.

> He himself bore our sins in his body on the tree, that we might die to sin and live to righteousness. By his wounds you have been healed. (1 Pe.2:24)

> For Christ also suffered once for sins, the righteous for the unrighteous, that he might bring us to God, being put to death in the flesh but made alive in the spirit. (1 Pe.3:18)

THOUGHT 1. The heart of Jesus was broken over sin and the sinner. He loved sinners (all of us). He was always seeking for, praying for, and weeping over sinners. He ached so much for sinners to personally know God, *ached* so much that He never knew what it was to be free from *suffering in heart* for sinners. His hurt was so deep for sinners that it was the pain of sin and the needs of sinners that eventually crushed His heart.

Note the great lesson. It took enormous, unswerving courage to bear a broken heart for sinners. What a lesson for us in courage—the courage to experience brokenness for sinners, brokenness in prayer, weeping and seeking.

For I could wish that I myself were accursed and cut off from Christ for the sake of my brothers, my kinsmen according to the flesh. (Ro.9:3)

Brothers, my heart's desire and prayer to God for them is that they may be saved. (Ro.10:1)

So, being affectionately desirous of you, we were ready to share with you not only the gospel of God but also our own selves, because you had become very dear to us. (1 Th.2:8)

Those who sow in tears shall reap with shouts of joy! He who goes out weeping, bearing the seed for sowing, shall come home with shouts of joy, bringing his sheaves with him. (Ps.126:5-6)

15:46

⁴⁶ And Joseph bought a linen shroud, and taking him down, wrapped him in the linen shroud and laid him in a tomb that had been cut out of the rock. And he rolled a stone against the entrance of the tomb.

4 The courage to make an unashamed commitment to Jesus.

Joseph summoned the courage to demonstrate His commitment to the Lord publicly and unashamedly. Remember, the disciples had fled and forsaken Jesus. But Joseph, witnessing the events of the cross, became thoroughly convinced of Jesus' Messiahship and made a firm, visible commitment to Him.

a. **Took Jesus down from the cross.**

Joseph personally took care of Jesus. A man of Joseph's wealth could have hired servants to tend to Jesus' body, but he personally took his Lord down from the cross, wrapped the linen cloth around Him, and laid Jesus in his own tomb. It was doubtful that Joseph understood all that was surrounding the cross and all that was about to take place in the resurrection. No one did. But he apparently believed in Jesus and courageously acted on that belief.

By tending to Jesus' body, Joseph risked—and most likely experienced—the disfavor and discipline of the Sanhedrin. They were the ruling body who had instigated and condemned Jesus, and Joseph was a member of the council. Most likely he faced some harsh reaction from some of his fellow Sanhedrin members and from some of his closest friends.

b. **Cared for and buried the body of Jesus.**

Joseph demonstrated a care, even an affection, for Jesus. He demonstrated this affection by giving his own tomb to Jesus. This act alone would leave no question about his stand for Christ.

Joseph also eliminated himself from taking part in the great Passover Feast—and this was never done, even for the most serious reasons. Joseph, by handling Jesus' body, was considered defiled for seven days for having come in contact with a corpse. Once defiled, Jewish law forbade a person from taking part in Jewish ceremonies.

Simply stated, Joseph, who had been a secret disciple, now stepped forward to make an unashamed commitment to Jesus. Everyone would know that he was the one who tended to Jesus' body. They would know that he had even given his own tomb for Jesus' burial. Joseph was risking his position, esteem, wealth, and even his life by making such a pronounced commitment to the Savior.

THOUGHT 1. The courage Joseph demonstrated is desperately needed by all.
1) The courage to make an unashamed commitment to Christ.
2) The courage to risk all for Christ, even if it does cost our position, esteem, wealth, and life.
3) The courage to unashamedly care for the body of Christ, His church and its affairs.
4) The courage to be an unashamed witness for Christ, no matter the cost.

Then they left the presence of the council, rejoicing that they were counted worthy to suffer dishonor for the name. (Ac.5:41)

Indeed, I count everything as loss because of the surpassing worth of knowing Christ Jesus my Lord. For his sake I have suffered the loss of all things and count them as rubbish, in order that I may gain Christ. (Ph.3:8)

Therefore do not be ashamed of the testimony about our Lord, nor of me his prisoner, but share in suffering for the gospel by the power of God. (2 Ti.1:8)

Be strong and courageous. Do not fear or be in dread of them, for it is the Lord your God who goes with you. He will not leave you or forsake you. (De.31:6)

The Lord is on my side; I will not fear. What can man do to me? (Ps.118:6)

5 The courage to take a public stand by the cross.

The women who stood by the cross also loved Jesus enough to demonstrate their affection and loyalty for Him (vv.40-41). They did not understand, but they did *love and believe.* The men who walked side by side with Jesus may forsake Him, but not these women. They stood by the cross from beginning to end—despite the danger and possible threat of being arrested for being followers of Jesus. Apparently, they loved Christ and believed in Him so strongly that nothing could have driven them away.

47 Mary Magdalene and Mary the mother of Joses saw where he was laid.

A number of women who followed Jesus were present at the cross (v.41). After Jesus died, all but two women either returned to their own homes or else escorted Mary, the mother of Jesus, to her residence. The two women who remained behind saw Joseph come to bury Jesus. They watched, probably even accompanied him, so they would know where their Lord was buried.

These women had courage, the kind of courage that takes a stand by the cross. The women . . .

- were not ashamed to stand by the cross
- did not allow the fear of others to run them away from the cross
- did not allow discouragement to defeat them despite not understanding what was going on

For whoever is ashamed of me and of my words in this adulterous and sinful generation, of him will the Son of Man also be ashamed when he comes in the glory of his Father with the holy angels. (Mk.8:38)

For I am not ashamed of the gospel, for it is the power of God for salvation to everyone who believes, to the Jew first and also to the Greek. (Ro.1:16)

For the Scripture says, "Everyone who believes in him will not be put to shame." (Ro.10:11)

As it is my eager expectation and hope that I will not be at all ashamed, but that with full courage now as always Christ will be honored in my body, whether by life or by death. (Ph.1:20)

CHAPTER 16

X. THE SON OF GOD'S SUPREME MINISTRY:
JESUS' VICTORY OVER DEATH AND HIS GREAT COMMISSION, 16:1–20

A. The Proofs of the Resurrection,[DS1] 16:1–13

(Mt.28:1-15; Lu.24:1-49; Jn.20:1-23)

1. The sad and despairing women
 a. They witnessed His death and burial
 b. They bought spices to anoint His body
 c. They were strict believers who obeyed the law

 d. They were practical, sensible, thinking women—not hysterical, deceived women
2. The rolled-away stone

3. The young man in a white robe
 a. He sat on the right side
 b. He alarmed the women

 c. He commanded authority
4. The missing body of Jesus

5. The compassionate, encouraging word to Peter
6. The fulfillment of the Lord's promise

7. The fright and silence of the women

8. The appearance of Jesus to Mary Magdalene[DS2]

9. The immediate unbelief of the disciples

When the Sabbath was past, Mary Magdalene, Mary the mother of James, and Salome bought spices, so that they might go and anoint him. ² And very early on the first day of the week, when the sun had risen, they went to the tomb. ³ And they were saying to one another, "Who will roll away the stone for us from the entrance of the tomb?" ⁴ And looking up, they saw that the stone had been rolled back—it was very large. ⁵ And entering the tomb, they saw a young man sitting on the right side, dressed in a white robe, and they were alarmed. ⁶ And he said to them, "Do not be alarmed. You seek Jesus of Nazareth, who was crucified. He has risen; he is not here. See the place where they laid him." ⁷ "But go, tell his disciples and Peter that he is going before you to Galilee. There you will see him, just as he told you." ⁸ And they went out and fled from the tomb, for trembling and astonishment had seized them, and they said nothing to anyone, for they were afraid. ⁹ [[Now when he rose early on the first day of the week, he appeared first to Mary Magdalene, from whom he had cast out seven demons. ¹⁰ She went and told those who had been with him, as they mourned and wept. ¹¹ But when they heard that he was alive and had been seen by her, they would not believe it.

¹² After these things he appeared in another form to two of them, as they were walking into the country.

¹³ And they went back and told the rest, but they did not believe them.

10. The appearance of Jesus to two disciples

11. The continued unbelief of other disciples

Division X

The Son of God's Supreme Ministry:
Jesus' Victory over Death and His Great Commission, 16:1-20

A. The Proofs of the Resurrection, 16:1-13

(Mt.28:1–15; Lu.24:1–49; Jn.20:1–23)

16:1–13
Introduction

We believe that Jesus rose from the dead largely because we have faith in God and in His Word. However, is the resurrection a matter that can only be supported by faith? Is there any evidence that Christ rose from the dead? How can we convince those who do not have faith that Jesus really did rise from the dead?

Mark's account of the resurrection is one of the Bible passages that provide solid, historical evidence of Christ's resurrection. The events he highlights in these verses offer eleven proofs of the resurrection—proofs that should stir faith in the Lord Jesus Christ. This is, *The Proofs of the Resurrection,* 16:1-13 (see DEEPER STUDY # 1).

1. The sad and despairing women (vv.1-3).
2. The rolled-away stone (v.4).
3. The young man in a white robe (vv.5-6).
4. The missing body of Jesus (v.6).
5. The compassionate, encouraging word to Peter (v.7).
6. The fulfillment of the Lord's promise (v.7).
7. The fright and silence of the women (v.8).
8. The appearance of Jesus to Mary Magdalene (vv.9-10).
9. The immediate unbelief of the disciples (v.11).
10. The appearance of Jesus to two disciples (v.12).
11. The continued unbelief of other disciples (v.13).

DEEPER STUDY # 1

(16:1-13) **Jesus Christ—Resurrection:** the order of the resurrection events seems to be as follows: (1) Mary discovers the empty tomb (Jn.20:1-2), and (2) runs to inform Peter and John; (3) they in turn run to see and verify for themselves (Jn.20:3-10).

After this, some additional resurrection appearances take place. It should be noted that just how long Jesus stayed with the apostles when He visited them is not given. Some of the visits may have been for days. In fact, He may have even appeared to some of whom we have no record. The exact order of the appearances mentioned by Scripture is hazy, but some order is possible (see 1 Co.15:5-11): (1) to Mary Magdalene (Mk.16:9-11; Jn.20:11-18); (2) to the women running to tell the disciples about the empty tomb (Mt.28:8-10); (3) then apparently to Peter, probably to assure him of restoration (Lu.24:34; 1 Co.15:5); (4) to the two Emmaus disciples sometime in the early evening (Mk.16:12; Lu.24:13-42); (5) to the disciples, with Thomas absent (Mk.16:14; Lu.24:36-43; Jn.20:19-25). (6) The next recorded appearance seems to be one week later, on Sunday evening, when Jesus appears to the disciples who had gone fishing (Jn.21:1-25). There were also other appearances although the order is unknown: (7) to 500 believers (1 Co.15:6); (8) to the apostles (Mt.28:16-20; Mk.16:15-18); (9) to James, the Lord's half-brother (1 Co.15:7); (10) then there was the appearance to the believers at His ascension (Mk.16:19-20; Lu.24:44-53; Ac.1:3-12).

16:1-3

When the Sabbath was past, Mary Magdalene, Mary the mother of James, and Salome bought spices, so that they might go and anoint him.

² And very early on the first day of the week, when the sun had risen, they went to the tomb.

³ And they were saying to one another, "Who will roll away the stone for us from the entrance of the tomb?"

1 The sad and despairing women.

The women who came to anoint Christ's body are the first proof of His resurrection. They are not fictional characters; they are real, specifically-named individuals. And, as Mark's record shows, they were credible, trustworthy witnesses to the Lord's resurrection. They approached the tomb filled with sadness and despair, for they fully expected to find the dead body of their Lord.

a. They witnessed His death and burial (v.1a).

These ladies were actual witnesses of Christ's death and burial. They knew He was dead, and they knew where He had been laid to rest because they had been part of the procession to the tomb (Mk.15:40-41, 47; see Mt.27:55-56, 61; Lu.23:55-56). There was no question in their minds whatsoever about His being dead and buried.

b. They bought spices to anoint His body (v.1b).

The grieving women bought spices to anoint the Lord's body. Apparently, they had purchased the spices Saturday evening when the Sabbath ended, for they came "very early" on Sunday morning to embalm Him (v.2). Again, they knew Jesus was dead; but they cared about Him deeply, so they wanted to take care of His body just as loved ones would do.

c. They were strict believers who obeyed the law (v.2).

These women strictly obeyed the law; they observed the Sabbath faithfully. Imagine, their loved One was dead, yet they would not break the Sabbath law even to take care of Him (see Lu.23:56). The women were obedient to the commandments of God. They were moral, truthful women who would never even consider lying about the death and resurrection of Jesus.

d. They were practical, sensible, thinking women—not hysterical, deceived women (v.3).

Note what was on these women's minds: how they were going to remove the stone from the entrance of the tomb. Their senses were present; they were thinking about solving the practical problems facing them. Note also that they had stayed with Joseph of Arimathea until he had closed the tomb. They knew that a large stone had sealed the entrance. Luke even says they actually saw the tomb and how Christ's body was laid in it (Lu.23:55). Apparently, they went in, looked over the tomb, and perhaps helped Joseph and Nicodemus all they could. They probably stayed with them until the *great* stone was rolled across the entrance.

The point is, these women, despite their sadness and bereavement, were sensible. They knew Jesus was dead. They were not mistaken or deceived. Every step they took was evidence that what they experienced was true: Jesus did arise from the dead.

2 The rolled-away stone.

The second proof of the resurrection is the rolled-away stone (see DEEPER STUDY # 1—Mt.27:65-66 for a detailed description of the stone). The stone was not rolled back for the benefit of Jesus but for the witnesses to the resurrection. When Jesus arose, He was in His resurrection body, the body of the spiritual dimension of being which has no physical bounds. He did not need any barriers removed to free Himself from the tomb. However, the witnesses needed to enter the tomb to see the truth. The stone was rolled back for their benefit (see outline and notes—Jn.20:1-10).

⁴ And looking up, they saw that the stone had been rolled back—it was very large.

Note also that soldiers were guarding the tomb (Mt.27:62-66; 28:2-4, 11-15.) The fact that the stone was rolled back is a proof of the resurrection.

3 The young man in a white robe.

a. **He sat on the right side (v.5a).**

b. **He alarmed the women (v.5b).**

c. **He commanded authority (v.6).**

A young man clothed in a white robe was sitting in the tomb. He was an angel sent by God as proof of the resurrection. God sent him for four reasons:

⁵ And entering the tomb, they saw a young man sitting on the right side, dressed in a white robe, and they were alarmed.
⁶ And he said to them, "Do not be alarmed. You seek Jesus of Nazareth, who was crucified. He has risen; he is not here. See the place where they laid him."

- To roll the stone back for the witnesses (Mt.28:2).
- To deal with the soldiers guarding the tomb (Mt.28:4).
- To reassure the women (vv.5-6). They were already grieving over Jesus' death. If they found the tomb empty without any explanation, they would have been devastated even more. The angel was a ministering spirit of God, one who ministered by reassuring God's people (see DEEPER STUDIES 1, 2—He.1:4-14).
- To validate and proclaim the resurrection and to give instructions (vv.6-7).

It is important to note the clear, specific details Mark's account provides. He says that the young man was sitting on the *right side* of the tomb dressed in a white robe (v.5a). When the women saw him, they were alarmed (v.5b). He spoke to them authoritatively, comforting them, revealing what had taken place, and inviting them to see the place where Jesus had been laid (v.6). Such specific details could only have come from an eyewitness to the scene.

4 The missing body of Jesus.

The fourth proof of the resurrection is the missing body of Jesus. The angel clearly stated that Jesus' body was no longer in the tomb, for He had risen from the dead. The angel went as far as to encourage the women to see for themselves that he was telling them the truth. He even told them where Jesus was, where they would find Him (v.7).

⁶ And he said to them, "Do not be alarmed. You seek Jesus of Nazareth, who was crucified. He has risen; he is not here. See the place where they laid him."

5 The compassionate, encouraging word to Peter.

The compassion and wisdom of God are clearly seen in this personal word sent to Peter. It serves as a fifth proof of the resurrection. God knew that Peter was crushed, despite his repentance, and that it would be extremely difficult for him to face the other disciples. He had proclaimed his loyalty too loudly and failed too greatly, even to the point of denying his Lord (see Mk.14:26-31, 66-72). Peter was devastated, more than most believers could ever imagine. This is evident from the fact

⁷ "But go, tell his disciples and Peter that he is going before you to Galilee. There you will see him, just as he told you."

that he needed both this personal word of encouragement from an angel and a personal visit from the resurrected Lord. Apparently, the Lord would visit him first, all alone, before He appeared to the rest of the disciples (Lu.24:34; 1 Co.15:5).

This personal word to Peter points to God's being behind the whole event. It demonstrates God's compassion and perfect wisdom. It is evidence of the resurrection.

> When I saw him, I fell at his feet as though dead. But he laid his right hand on me, saying, "Fear not, I am the first and the last, and the living one. I died, and behold I am alive forevermore, and I have the keys of Death and Hades." (Re.1:17–18)

> Fear not, for I am with you; be not dismayed, for I am your God; I will strengthen you, I will help you, I will uphold you with my righteous right hand. (Is.41:10)

> But now thus says the LORD, he who created you, O Jacob, he who formed you, O Israel: "Fear not, for I have redeemed you; I have called you by name, you are mine. When you pass through the waters, I will be with you; and through the rivers, they shall not overwhelm you; when you walk through fire you shall not be burned, and the flame shall not consume you." (Is.43:1–2)

16:7

6 The fulfillment of the Lord's promise.

⁷ "But go, tell his disciples and Peter that he is going before you to Galilee. There you will see him, just as he told you."

Jesus had told the disciples that He would go into Galilee after He had risen (Mk.14:28). Fulfilling His promise was proof that Jesus had risen.

Being told to meet Jesus in Galilee would ignite some degree of wonder and hope in the disciples' hearts. It would give them hope that their relationship with the Lord could be restored. They would know that everything would be explained to them in Galilee.

It would also prompt them to remember the Lord's promise and give evidence that Jesus had actually risen from the dead. The very fact that He met them in Galilee, fulfilling His promise, is evidence of His resurrection. The promise could not be fulfilled if He had not risen, and since He arose, the promise was to be fulfilled.

> Fully convinced that God was able to do what he had promised. (Ro.4:21)

> For all the promises of God find their Yes in him. That is why it is through him that we utter our Amen to God for his glory. (2 Co.1:20)

> If we are faithless, he remains faithful—for he cannot deny himself. (2 Ti.2:13)

> By which he has granted to us his precious and very great promises, so that through them you may become partakers of the divine nature, having escaped from the corruption that is in the world because of sinful desire. (2 Pe.1:4)

16:8

7 The fright and silence of the women.

⁸ And they went out and fled from the tomb, for trembling and astonishment had seized them, and they said nothing to anyone, for they were afraid.

The women who discovered the empty tomb reacted as anyone would: they were trembling, amazed, silent, and afraid. Their fright and silence is a proof of the resurrection. The women ran to tell Peter and the disciples why were they silent and afraid, saying nothing to anyone?

First, the angel had instructed them to tell only "His disciples and Peter" (v.7). They were to tell no one else.

Second, they feared others might think them *crazy*, so grieved that they were imagining things.

Third, they feared the Jewish and Roman authorities, that they might be accused of stealing the body.

Every emotion of the women and their very reaction (fear, amazement, and visible trembling) are proof of the resurrection. They reacted in a normal way, just as any people would react, and their normal reaction is evidence of the resurrection. (Note: despite the effect on their emotions, their thought processes were still very active. They did exactly as the angel instructed. They reasoned and knew to keep the matter quiet.)

8 The appearance of Jesus to Mary Magdalene.

The eighth proof of the resurrection is Jesus' appearance to Mary Magdalene (see outline and notes—Jn.20:11-18). The very fact that Jesus visited Mary first, before He visited anyone else, is evidence of the resurrection. It is true to the character of Jesus. He *responds* to love and deep devotion. And Mary, above all others, seems to have loved Jesus more and held Him closer to her heart with more devotion than anyone else. Her need for Him seems to have been greater and more visibly displayed than anyone else's.

9 [[Now when he rose early on the first day of the week, he appeared first to Mary Magdalene, from whom he had cast out seven demons.
10 She went and told those who had been with him, as they mourned and wept.

> ➤ She had been forgiven and healed of so much. (Note that even in this reference to her, mention is made that Jesus cast seven devils out of her.)
> ➤ She was at the cross through the whole ordeal, and her name is one of the names always given, even above Jesus' own mother, Mary (Mk.15:40-41).
> ➤ She was present when Jesus was taken down from the cross and until the very last moment at His burial (Mk.15:47; Lu.23:55).
> ➤ She was foremost in making preparations for embalming the body over the weekend (Mk.15:56).
> ➤ She visited the tomb after the Sabbath at the earliest possible moment, arising very early in the morning when it was still dark (vv.1-2; Jn.20:1).
> ➤ She refused to leave the tomb after Peter and John verified that the body was missing (Jn.20:11f).

Mary was a most unusual follower of the Lord, a woman of deep devotion and love, humility and grace; a precious saint who felt the loss of her Lord perhaps more deeply than anyone else. Therefore, Jesus responded to her, meeting her need first of all. This definitely lends proof to the fact that the Lord was risen.

THOUGHT 1. Every genuine believer can attest to the same glorious truth that Mary's experience proclaims: Jesus is risen, for He is ever present with us, responding to our love and devotion and meeting our every need. How precious and strong is the presence of our wonderful Lord!

> If you love me, you will keep my commandments. And I will ask the Father, and he will give you another Helper, to be with you forever. (Jn.14:15–16)
>
> Greater love has no one than this, that someone lay down his life for his friends. (Jn.15:13)
>
> For the Father himself loves you, because you have loved me and have believed that I came from God. (Jn.16:27)
>
> Who shall separate us from the love of Christ? Shall tribulation, or distress, or persecution, or famine, or nakedness, or danger, or sword? (Ro.8:35)

DEEPER STUDY # 2

(16:9-10) **Scripture:** these verses are not in the two oldest manuscripts, the Sinaiticus and Vaticanus. Only portions are found in other manuscripts and then in various forms. However, they are found in the Latin Vulgate and Syriac Versions.

9 The immediate unbelief of the disciples.

The disciples did not believe Mary's report that Jesus was alive. Their immediate unbelief is another proof of the resurrection. Again, the disciples are painted in a bad light, a picture that most likely would not be shown if the resurrection had not really happened. The disciples would be seen as

11 But when they heard that he was alive and had been seen by her, they would not believe it.

stalwarts of great belief and heroic examples if the resurrection were being fabricated. The very fact that they are seen failing again and again, and that they are actually the ones to fail the most tragically and are to be blamed the most, is a clear evidence of the resurrection.

> **Afterward he appeared to the eleven themselves as they were reclining at table, and he rebuked them for their unbelief and hardness of heart, because they had not believed those who saw him after he had risen. (Mk.16:14)**
>
> **Whoever believes in him is not condemned, but whoever does not believe is condemned already, because he has not believed in the name of the only Son of God. (Jn.3:18)**
>
> **Take care, brothers, lest there be in any of you an evil, unbelieving heart, leading you to fall away from the living God. (He.3:12)**
>
> **Let us therefore strive to enter that rest, so that no one may fall by the same sort of disobedience. (He.4:11)**

16:12

10 The appearance of Jesus to two disciples.

[12] After these things he appeared in another form to two of them, as they were walking into the country.

The tenth proof of the resurrection is Jesus' appearance to two disciples. Most likely, Mark is referring to the appearance to the two on the road to Emmaus (Lu.24:13-35). Just who they were is not known. They were simply two disciples of the Lord who were to go to the apostles and prepare them even more for the Lord's appearance to them. Again, the very way in which the Lord appeared and went about preparing His disciples for confrontation with Him is evidence of His having truly risen. His perfect wisdom, tenderness, and care—which is so evident in the way everything is handled—are clear evidence.

16:13

11 The continued unbelief of other disciples.

[13] And they went back and told the rest, but they did not believe them.

The eleventh proof Mark offers of the resurrection is the continued unbelief of the disciples. Again, no fabricated story would paint its main characters in such a bad light, not time after time. In fact, the disciples are not presented as heroes but as tragic failures throughout the whole gospel story. This is seldom remembered and mentioned by preachers and teachers, yet these men are seen in the Gospels as tragic failures, unbelievably weak time and again. They were a far cry from the type of men we would choose as heroes. Why does Scripture paint them in such a bad light? Because what they said *did* happen. Their testimony is the truth. Jesus arose and appeared to Mary and the two disciples, and when they shared their experiences with the other disciples, they simply refused to believe. (They were without excuse. For many months Jesus had drilled the fact of His death and resurrection into them. See notes—Mt.16:21-28; 17:1-13, 22, 24-27.) The weakness of the disciples and their continued unbelief are evidence that what happened was true. It is proof of the resurrection. The truth—exactly what happened—was being told simply and clearly by honest and moral eyewitnesses.

> **He said to them, "Why are you so afraid? Have you still no faith?" (Mk.4:40)**
>
> **And he said to them, "O foolish ones, and slow of heart to believe all that the prophets have spoken!" (Lu.24:25)**
>
> **Whoever believes in the Son has eternal life; whoever does not obey the Son shall not see life, but the wrath of God remains on him. (Jn.3:36)**
>
> **I told you that you would die in your sins, for unless you believe that I am he you will die in your sins. (Jn.8:24)**

(Mt.28:16–20; Lu.24:46–49; Jn.20:21. See Jn.17:18; Ac.1:8)

14 Afterward he appeared to the eleven themselves as they were reclining at table, and he rebuked them for their unbelief and hardness of heart, because they had not believed those who saw him after he had risen.

15 And he said to them, "Go into all the world and proclaim the gospel to the whole creation."

16 "Whoever believes and is baptized will be saved, but whoever does not believe will be condemned."

17 "And these signs will accompany those who believe: in my name they will cast out demons; they will speak in new tongues;

18 they will pick up serpents with their hands; and if they drink any deadly poison, it will not hurt them; they will lay their hands on the sick, and they will recover."

19 So then the Lord Jesus, after he had spoken to them, was taken up into heaven and sat down at the right hand of God.

20 And they went out and preached everywhere, while the Lord worked with them and confirmed the message by accompanying signs.]]

1. **The two hindrances to the Great Commission**
   a. Lack of faith
   b. A stubborn refusal to believe and to go forth to bear witness

2. **The Great Commission: Go—preach**
   a. What: The gospel
   b. Where: All the world

3. **The reason for the Great Commission**
   a. If believe: Saved[DS1]
   b. If disbelieve: Condemned

4. **The promise to the believer who carries out the Great Commission: Power**

5. **The confirmation of the Great Commission**
   a. The Lord's ascension to the position of power
   b. The Lord's working through the disciples' ministry

Division X

The Son of God's Supreme Ministry:
Jesus' Victory over Death and His Great Commission, 16:1–20

B. The Lord's Great Commission, 16:14–20

(Mt.28:16–20; Lu.24:46–49; Jn.20:21. See Jn.17:18; Ac.1:8)

16:14–20
Introduction

This closing passage of Mark's Gospel records the first appearance of Jesus to all the disciples. It is important to keep in mind that it was Sunday evening, the same day that Jesus had risen from the dead. The day had been an extremely busy one for the Lord. He had spent it encouraging those who had needed special attention and sending word of His resurrection to the disciples, who were hovered behind closed doors in fear of the Jews. Jesus needed to send word of His resurrection to them bit by bit so they would be prepared to see Him risen and in His resurrected body. The day included the following appearances:

- The appearance to Mary Magdalene (vv.9-11).
- The appearance to the women as they were going to tell the disciples (Mt.28:9).
- The appearance to Peter, which probably was a long conference lasting for hours (Lu.24:34).
- The appearance to two disciples on the road to Emmaus (vv.12-13).
- The appearance to the disciples mentioned in this passage (v.14; this appearance is discussed more fully in Lu.24:36f; Jn.20:19f).

Note that in this closing section of His Gospel, Mark's focus is clear. He stresses the Great Commission, and it is the whole focus of his attention. This is, *The Lord's Great Commission*, 16:14-20.

1. The two hindrances to the Great Commission (v.14).
2. The Great Commission: Go—preach (v.15).
3. The reason for the Great Commission (v.16).
4. The promise to the believer who carries out the Great Commission: Power (vv.17-18).
5. The confirmation of the Great Commission (vv.19-20).

16:14

1 The two hindrances to the Great Commission.

¹⁴ Afterward he appeared to the eleven themselves as they were reclining at table, and he rebuked them for their unbelief and hardness of heart, because they had not believed those who saw him after he had risen.

a. **Lack of faith.**

b. **A stubborn refusal to believe & to go forth to bear witness.**

Luke and John present a number of details about the risen Lord's first appearance to His disciples (Lk.24:36f; Jn.20:19f). Mark, however, focuses on only one: Jesus rebuked the disciples for their lack of faith and their hardness of heart—their stubborn refusal to believe the witnesses of Christ's resurrection and to bear witness of it themselves. *Rebuked* or *reproached* (Gk. oneidisen; pronounced *oh-nay-dih'-sen*) means to rebuke strongly or scold harshly. This is the only place in the New Testament this particular Greek verb is used of Jesus. Why was Jesus so harsh with His disciples, harsher than He had ever been before? Our Lord rebuked the eleven so strongly because these two sins—unbelief and hardness of heart—would hinder the apostles from fulfilling His Great Commission. Note three observations.

First, the skeptical disciples deserved the rebuking and scolding. Their unbelief and stubbornness were inexcusable. They had witnessed Jesus' power, that is, God's power, throughout His ministry. They had seen His power over both nature and disease. They had even witnessed His power over death when He raised up Jairus' daughter, a young man, Lazarus, and perhaps others of which there is no record.

In addition, the disciples had witnessed Jesus' life, His purity and holiness. And they had been taught that sin caused death; that is, that a person dies because of sin (Jn.3:19; see 3:16-21; 5:24-29; 8:34-35; see Ro.5:12; 6:23). Jesus was without sin; therefore, death could never hold Him and enforce its power over Him. They should have been able to reason and see this glorious fact, especially in light of the Scriptures.

> Concerning his Son, who was descended from David according to the flesh and was declared to be the Son of God in power according to the Spirit of holiness by his resurrection from the dead, Jesus Christ our Lord. (Ro.1:3-4)

> For you will not abandon my soul to Sheol, or let your holy one see corruption. . . . For you will not abandon my soul to Hades, or let your Holy One see corruption. . . . Therefore he says also in another psalm, " 'You will not let your Holy One see corruption.' " (Ps.16:10; Ac.2:27; 13:35)

For months, Jesus had taught His disciples that He was to die and be raised again. When He did rise, just as He had promised, the Lord had sent them word by Mary Magdalene and the other two disciples (Mk.16:9-13). Yet, they had rejected this testimony of His resurrection.

The disciples' unbelief and hardness of heart was very, very serious. Jesus' rebuke (and Mark's emphasizing) of their unbelief and hardness show this (16:11, 13, 14). The unbelief had to be dealt with if the Great Commission were to be carried out.

The *root cause* of the disciples' unbelief and hardness of heart was very simply the misinterpretation of Scripture and of Jesus' words. Jesus had told them time and time again that He would die and rise from the dead. But the disciples refused to believe the word of Christ; they ...

- refused to see the Messiah as a suffering Savior, choosing instead to think in terms of a conquering king (Lu.24:44-45; see notes—Lu.3:24-31; 7:21-23)
- refused to see the kingdom of God as a spiritual kingdom, choosing instead to think in terms of a physical kingdom, a kingdom on earth
- refused to see the death and resurrection of Jesus as a literal fact, choosing instead to think of it in symbolic terms (see note, pt.5—Mt.20:20-21)

THOUGHT 1. Unbelief and hardness of heart are inexcusable within a believer. Jesus dealt with these sins with the eleven, and He deals with such sins in us as well. When we begin to believe that souls are lost and doomed unless they hear and receive Jesus, then we will take the Great Commission seriously and preach the gospel to the whole world. It has now been two thousand years, and a place as relatively small as our world has not even been completely reached. Unimaginable, when we have had the means of transportation and communication as well as the resources at our disposal to do the job.

> And he said to them, "O foolish ones, and slow of heart to believe all that the prophets have spoken!" (Lu.24:25)
>
> But exhort one another every day, as long as it is called "today," that none of you may be hardened by the deceitfulness of sin. (He.3:13)
>
> Those whom I love, I reprove and discipline, so be zealous and repent. (Re.3:19)
>
> Blessed is the one who fears the LORD always, but whoever hardens his heart will fall into calamity. (Pr.28:14)
>
> He who is often reproved, yet stiffens his neck, will suddenly be broken beyond healing. (Pr.29:1)

2 The Great Commission: Go—preach.

16:15

After rebuking the disciples' faithlessness and stubbornness, Jesus gave them—and us—the Great Commission. The Great Commission is a straightforward command. It is brief, yet forceful and uncompromising: *go—preach*. Jesus makes two critical points.

15 And he said to them, "Go into all the world and proclaim the gospel to the whole creation."

a. What: The gospel.

We are to preach the gospel—not our own thoughts and ideas, humanistic and man-centered beliefs, world religions and philosophies. The gospel of Jesus Christ—salvation through His death, burial, and resurrection—is the news which the world desperately needs to hear.

> Paul, a servant of Christ Jesus, called to be an apostle, set apart for the gospel of God, which he promised beforehand through his prophets in the holy Scriptures, concerning his Son, who was descended from David according to the flesh and was declared to be the Son of God in power according to the Spirit of holiness by his resurrection from the dead, Jesus Christ our Lord. (Ro.1:1-4)
>
> I am under obligation both to Greeks and to barbarians, both to the wise and to the foolish. So I am eager to preach the gospel to you also who are in Rome. (Ro.1:14-16)
>
> Now I would remind you, brothers, of the gospel I preached to you, which you received, in which you stand, and by which you are being saved, if you hold fast to the word I preached to you—unless you believed in vain. For I delivered to you as of first importance what I also received: that Christ died for our sins in accordance with the Scriptures, that he was buried, that he was raised on the third day in accordance with the Scriptures. (1 Co.15:1-4)

b. Where: All the world.

Christ commanded that the gospel be carried "into all the world" and preached to every person. The fulfillment of Christ's command hinges on two simple facts.

First, the Great Commission was given to the whole church, to every believer. It is a permanent commission given to the church of every generation, not only to the first disciples. After a person believes and is baptized, Jesus says that person is to go forth with power and proclaim the gospel (vv.16-17). Every believer who is genuinely saved is to proclaim the gospel (v.16; see Mt.28:19-20; Jn.20:21; Ac.1:8; 2 Ti.2:2; 1 Pe.3:15).

Second, the Great Commission does not consider difficulties, dangers, or barriers to be reasons for not going. Jesus did not discuss excuses for not sharing the gospel. His command was *uncompromising*. The issue of eternal life vs. eternal damnation is too critical an issue to allow anything to stop the gospel from going forth (v.16). The gospel has to be carried to the world. No land is to be neglected; no people are to be ignored. The believer is to be undaunted and unswerving in devotion to the Great Commission. The believer is commanded: "Go into all the world" (v.15).

16:16

[16] "Whoever believes and is baptized will be saved, but whoever does not believe will be condemned."

3 The reason for the Great Commission.

Jesus was clear: people are either saved or condemned. There is no other status or standing before God. There is no "in between." If the gospel is shared with others and they believe and are baptized (see DEEPER STUDY # 1), they will be saved; but if they do not believe, they will be condemned.

The reason for the Great Commission is the great love and salvation of God. The Lord wants all people to be saved. He does not want any to be condemned:

> **Paul, a servant of Christ Jesus, called to be an apostle, set apart for the gospel of God, which he promised beforehand through his prophets in the holy Scriptures, concerning his Son, who was descended from David according to the flesh and was declared to be the Son of God in power according to the Spirit of holiness by his resurrection from the dead, Jesus Christ our Lord. (Ro.1:1-4)**

> **This is good, and it is pleasing in the sight of God our Savior, who desires all people to be saved and to come to the knowledge of the truth. (1 Ti.2:3-4)**

> **The Lord is not slow to fulfill his promise as some count slowness, but is patient toward you, not wishing that any should perish, but that all should reach repentance. (2 Pe.3:9)**

a. If believe: Saved.

People can be saved. They no longer need to wander through life seeking and searching for fulfillment and completeness, questioning if there is really any purpose to life. They can be saved and live eternally. Every human being can be delivered . . .

- from sin and its power (Ro.6:6-7)
- from death and its fear and corruption (Jn.5:24; He.2:14-15)
- from hell and its torture and separation from God (see DEEPER STUDY # 2—Mt.5:22; DEEPER STUDY # 1—He.9:27)

We must carry this message—the message that life is available—to the whole world.

b. If disbelieve: Condemned.

People are lost and condemned if they do not believe the gospel. *Does not believe* (apistesas) means to disbelieve or to be unbelieving. It is the opposite of having faith; it is to be faithless. All who reject Jesus Christ, who refuse to believe and follow Him, will be condemned. Condemned to what?

➢ To the power and enslavement of sin (Jn.3:19; Ro.3:12, 23).
➢ To the fear and corruption of death (Ro.5:12; 6:23).
➢ To the torture and separation of hell (see DEEPER STUDY # 2—Mt.5:22; DEEPER STUDY # 1—He.9:27).

Therefore, the great motive for reaching the world is the desperate need of every human being to be saved: saved from sin, death, and hell—saved to the uttermost—saved to live forever in the presence of God Himself (Jn.3:16; 5:24-29).

DEEPER STUDY # 1

(16:16) **Baptism—Belief—Salvation—Obedience:** two things are said here to be essential for salvation—belief and baptism. There are two basic positions on baptism: first, one must be baptized to be saved, and, second, baptism is a symbol or sign that one believes and has been saved. Note four insights that help in understanding what Jesus said about baptism.

1. Perhaps what is often overlooked by both positions is this: *belief* is an *act of obedience* to God's command if a person wishes to be saved, and *baptism* is an *act of obedience* to God's command if a person believes.

Baptism is an act of obedience to God's command, just as belief is an act of obedience to God's command. Very simply, if a person wishes to be saved, God commands that he or she *believe*; and if a person believes, God commands him or her to *be baptized*.

A legitimate and straightforward question needs to be asked: "How can a person honestly be saved if they immediately rebel against being baptized? How can a person really believe, be genuine in their confession, if they rebel at obeying their Lord about baptism?"

Facing the reality of the situation, Scripture is strong: a person who truly believes in the Lord will not refuse to follow their Lord *in baptism*. To believe and to obey are the same thing. The two, belief and obedience, are one and the same.

> And being made perfect, he became the source of eternal salvation to all who obey him. (He.5:9. See DEEPER STUDY # 1—He.5:9 as well.)

Another way to say the same thing is, there is no such thing as faith alone, not without works or fruit. Faith without obedience is not what the Scripture means by faith. In the Scripture, faith is the movement of the heart which embraces the Lord, the Lord who is the fulfillment of the law (Mt.5:17-18; see note—Mt.5:17-18 as well). Faith is coming to God believing that He is, and *diligently seeking* Him (He.11:6). Faith, Biblical faith, diligently seeks to obey the Lord. Therefore, the person who truly believes will follow the Lord in baptism and in everything else.

This does not mean the person will be perfect and never fail. Far from it. Genuine believers will fail, but they will *not continue in sin* (1Jn.3:9). They will get up out of their sin, ask God to forgive them, and begin to follow the Lord even more diligently. Their faith works and bears fruit, for they know that God exists and that He is a rewarder of them that diligently seek Him.

> What good is it, my brothers, if someone says he has faith but does not have works? Can that faith save him? (Js.2:14)

> So also faith by itself, if it does not have works, is dead. But someone will say, "You have faith and I have works." Show me your faith apart from your works, and I will show you my faith by my works. (Js.2:17-18)

> Do you want to be shown, you foolish person, that faith apart from works is useless? Was not Abraham our father justified by works when he offered up his son Isaac on the altar? You see that faith was active along with his works, and faith was completed by his works; and the Scripture was fulfilled that says, "Abraham believed God, and it was counted to him as righteousness"—and he was called a friend of God. You see that a person is justified by works and not by faith alone. (Js.2:20-24)

THOUGHT 1. There is no such thing as cheap salvation, not the kind that is too often preached and stressed. Following Jesus or being saved costs. It costs all that a person *is and has*. A person who is not willing to follow Jesus has not been saved (Lu.9:23, 25), and following Jesus begins with being baptized and continues with diligently seeking Him (living righteously).

2. The person who is condemned is said to be the person who does not believe, not the person who is not baptized. This is a matter for close attention. Jesus *did not say,* "Whoever does not believe *and is not baptized* will be condemned." Not being baptized is not mentioned as a reason for being condemned. This does establish that *not believing* is the reason for condemnation, and conversely, *believing* is the reason for salvation. However, as discussed above, it is very difficult to explain how a person can be genuinely saved and not be baptized if he or she is physically able to be baptized. Believing involves commitment, doing what God says, and commitment involves believing (see DEEPER STUDY # 1—Jn.2:24). Therefore, a person who genuinely believes does what God says: believes, is baptized, lives righteously. A person who refuses to do what God says proves that he or she does not truly believe, that is, he or she has not been genuinely saved. A person who is truly saved will be committed to Jesus Christ, committed to being baptized and to living righteously.

3. The nature of belief and baptism should also be considered. Belief and baptism are two different substances, of two different natures, of two different dimensions. In dealing with belief, the same things can be said about belief that is said about salvation. Both are of the spirit, not of the body or of the physical world. Belief is a spiritual thing or substance. Its nature is spiritual; it is of the spiritual dimension of being; it is an act of the spirit of a person.

However, baptism is of a different nature. It is a person's physical body being placed into water (a material thing or substance). Baptism is of the physical or material dimension of being; it is an act of the body.

4. Very practically, in a world of billions of people, some are born mentally alert and responsible; yet they are tragically deformed, or injured, or diseased. Some are so deformed and physically affected they could never be immersed in the waters of baptism. Many of these do come to believe in Christ and do live righteously, obeying God in so far as their heart and body allows them. Would God condemn these people because they physically cannot be baptized? If one *must* be baptized to be saved, then how can they be saved?

In conclusion, the thrust of Scripture seems to be that a person who genuinely believes *will be* baptized and will not fail to be baptized unless it is physically impossible, nor will they fail to live righteously. Yet the moment of salvation is neither at baptism nor at any other act or work of doing righteousness. It is at the moment of believing in the Lord Jesus Christ. When a person really believes and really *entrusts* their life into the hands of Christ, *God knows that moment,* the very second of trust. Therefore, at that very moment God gives life to the person's spirit, causing him or her to be *born again,* and making him/her alive spiritually (not physically; it is not a physical thing or substance). Then, the person arises from their confession of faith, is baptized, and begins to follow the Lord in righteousness.

16:17–18

4 The promise to the believer who carries out the Great Commission: Power.

[17] "And these signs will accompany those who believe: in my name they will cast out demons; they will speak in new tongues;

[18] they will pick up serpents with their hands; and if they drink any deadly poison, it will not hurt them; they will lay their hands on the sick, and they will recover."

Christ promises power to believers as they carry out the Great Commission. The signs Jesus mentioned in these verses are evidence of His supernatural power on those who believe. The same power of God that produced them is for every believer.

This promise is critical; believers must have *supernatural power* as we go forth throughout the world. The world is a dangerous place. The believer will sometimes be called upon to face treacherous land, violent storms within nature, savage and venomous animals, hostile unbelievers, spiritual evil of unbelievable force. The evil of humanity, of nature, and of demonic spirits can be so threatening to the believer that the believer's witness would be stopped if God did not provide His strength and power. God did, does, and will exercise His supernatural power to protect His messengers to accomplish His purposes. He did, does, and will do the supernatural when He chooses to do so.

This is the point of this passage. God *does* give power to the believer—all the power necessary to carry the gospel "into all the world" and "to the whole creation."

This, of course, does not mean that *every* believer will be delivered from every threat and from ever being martyred. Some believers are persecuted, and some even martyred. As God wills, He teaches and touches lives and moves history and society itself through the persecution and martyrdom of believers. Things do not always go smoothly for believers. But God does give power to believers—the power to walk through difficulties in His confidence and peace, even through the fire of martyrdom if faced. It is often the witness of the God-given power, confidence, and peace that reaches others for Christ and that causes an enormous movement toward God.

Nor does this mean that believers should voluntarily perform foolish acts, such as handling venomous snakes or drinking poisonous substances, or walking across hot coals or broken glass, or any other dangerous act, as an exhibition of their faith. The power of God preserved His servants when they were involuntarily subjected to these kinds of things, not when they did them voluntarily and foolishly (Ac.28:3-5).

To repeat, this is the point of these two verses: as the believer carries out the Great Commission, God promises power, the power needed to get the task done. Note the power or signs mentioned by Mark. Such power will be present in the lives of believers (when needed) as they proclaim the gospel around the world.

> **But you will receive power when the Holy Spirit has come upon you, and you will be my witnesses in Jerusalem and in all Judea and Samaria, and to the end of the earth. (Ac.1:8)**

> **And my speech and my message were not in plausible words of wisdom, but in demonstration of the Spirit and of power. (1 Co.2:4)**

> **That according to the riches of his glory he may grant you to be strengthened with power through his Spirit in your inner being. (Ep.3:16)**

> **Because our gospel came to you not only in word, but also in power and in the Holy Spirit and with full conviction. You know what kind of men we proved to be among you for your sake. (1 Th.1:5)**

> **For God gave us a spirit not of fear but of power and love and self-control. Therefore do not be ashamed of the testimony about our Lord, nor of me his prisoner, but share in suffering for the gospel by the power of God. (2 Ti.1:7-8)**

> **But as for me, I am filled with power, with the Spirit of the LORD, and with justice and might, to declare to Jacob his transgression and to Israel his sin. (Mi.3:8)**

> **Then he said to me, "This is the word of the LORD to Zerubbabel: Not by might, nor by power, but by my Spirit, says the LORD of hosts." (Zec.4:6)**

5 The confirmation of the Great Commission.

16:19-20

Mark closes His Gospel by mentioning two acts that took place sometime after Jesus' giving of the Great Commission to His disciples. These two acts are confirmation of the Great Commission.

¹⁹ So then the Lord Jesus, after he had spoken to them, was taken up into heaven and sat down at the right hand of God.

²⁰ And they went out and preached everywhere, while the Lord worked with them and confirmed the message by accompanying signs.]]

a. The Lord's ascension to the position of power (v.19).

The first act is the Lord's ascension to the right hand of God, that is, the position of power (see Lu.24:50-51; Ac.1:9-11). Christ's ascension assures (proves, confirms) that seven things are absolutely certain (see note, *Ascension*—Jn.6:62 for more discussion).

First, the ascension assures us that God exists and that He is alive. Christ could be raised from the dead and taken up into heaven *only* by the power of God. The fact that Christ was raised up from the dead and "carried up into heaven" (Lu.24:51) proves that God exists. Only God could do such a thing (1 Co.6:14; 2 Co.4:14; see also Jn.3:16; Ac.2:24, 32; 3:15, 26; 4:14; 5:30; 10:40; 13:30, 33-34; 17:31).

Second, the ascension assures us that Christ is God's Son. The very fact that God raised up Christ and received Him into heaven proves that Christ is God's Son (Ro.1:3-4; Ph.2:5-11).

547

Third, the ascension assures us that heaven is real (Ph.3:20-21). Jesus ascended to an actual place, a place called heaven.

Fourth, the ascension assures us that the gospel is true. When God raised up Christ and received Him into heaven, God showed that the message of Christ is true. What Christ proclaimed and revealed is true. The problem with humanity is sin and death, a future of condemnation and separation from God. But people can be saved, saved by the cross of Christ (v.16; 1 Pe.2:24).

Fifth, the ascension assures us that the Great Commission is the call and mission of believers. Two facts show this:

➢ Christ has ascended into heaven. He is gone, no longer on earth. If the gospel is to be carried to the ends of the earth, believers have to do it. We are the ones left on earth to do it.

➢ It is the risen and ascended Lord who gave the Great Commission. As the ascended Lord, He demands that His commission be fulfilled (Mk.16:15; see Mt.28:19-20).

Sixth, the ascension assures us that power is available to carry out the Great Commission (Mt.28:18; see v.20).

Seventh, the ascension assures us that we have a very special Helper in heaven, One who really loves and cares for us. He is One who "sympathize[s] with our weaknesses," One who was tempted in every way that we are, "yet without sin" (He.4:15). Therefore, He is ever ready to forgive us and to look after us and to carry us through all of life.

b. The Lord's working through the disciples' ministry (v.20).
The Great Commission is confirmed by the Lord's working through the disciples' ministry. The early disciples "went out" and "preached everywhere." As they went, the Lord Himself "worked with them" and confirmed their message with powerful signs. A record of some of their ministries is given in *Acts*.

> And with great power the apostles were giving their testimony to the resurrection of the Lord Jesus, and great grace was upon them all. (Ac.4:33)

THOUGHT 1. The believers of every generation are to go forth immediately and preach the gospel everywhere. The Great Commission was, and still can be, carried out. We must embrace our Lord's command to proclaim the gospel to every person throughout the earth. We must spread the gospel personally wherever God places or leads us, and we must help send those whom He calls to carry the good news to the peoples of all corners of the earth (Ac.1:8).

> And Jesus came and said to them, "All authority in heaven and on earth has been given to me. Go therefore and make disciples of all nations, baptizing them in the name of the Father and of the Son and of the Holy Spirit, teaching them to observe all that I have commanded you. And behold, I am with you always, to the end of the age." (Mt.28:18-20)

> But you will receive power when the Holy Spirit has come upon you, and you will be my witnesses in Jerusalem and in all Judea and Samaria, and to the end of the earth. (Ac.1:8)

THOUGHT 2. As we proclaim the gospel, we can go out with the assurance that we are not working alone. The Lord will work with us, just as He worked with the apostles, and He will infuse us with the same power with which He infused them.

> For we are God's fellow workers. You are God's field, God's building. (1 Co.3:9)

> Working together with him, then, we appeal to you not to receive the grace of God in vain. (2 Co.6:1)

OUTLINE AND SUBJECT INDEX

REMEMBER: When you look up a subject and turn to the Scripture reference, you have not only the Scripture, you have an outline and a discussion (commentary) of the Scripture and subject.

This is one of the GREAT VALUES of the **every**WORD˙ series. Once you have all the volumes, you will have not only what all other Bible indexes give you, that is, a list of all the subjects and their Scripture references, BUT you will also have . . .

- An outline of every Scripture and subject in the Bible.
- A discussion (commentary) on every Scripture and subject.
- Every subject supported by other Scriptures or cross references.

DISCOVER THE GREAT VALUE for yourself. Quickly glance below to the very first subject of the Index of Mark. It is:

ABOMINATION OF DESOLATION (See **ANTICHRIST**)
Discussed. Mk.13:14-23

Turn to the reference. Glance at the Scripture and outline of the Scripture, then read the commentary. You will immediately see the GREAT VALUE of the INDEX of the **every**WORD˙ series.

ABOMINATION OF DESOLATION (See **ANTICHRIST**)
Discussed. 13:14-23
Predicted. By Daniel the prophet. 13:14

ACCEPTANCE—ACCEPTABLE
Condition. Discussed. 9:38-41

ACCESS
Available. Into Jesus' presence. Any hour or day. 1:33

ACCOUNTABLE—ACCOUNTABILITY
Who is **a**. A property owner. 12:1-12
Why men are **a**. Rejecting God's message. 12:1-12

ADULTERY
Committed. By marrying a divorced person. 10:1-12
Described. As remarriage. 10:10-12
Meaning. 7:21

ALEXANDER
A son of the man who carried Jesus' cross. 15:21

AMBITION
Discussed. 9:33-37; 10:35-45
Evil **a**. Causes arguing, conflict. 9:33-34; 10:41
Motives of. True vs. false. 10:36-37
Price of. Sacrifice & pain. 10:38-39
Problem with. Discussed. 9:33-37; 10:35-45
World's view vs. Lord's view. 10:42-44

ANDREW, THE APOSTLE
Discussed. 3:18
Call of. 1:16-18

ANGER
Of Jesus. Over hard hearts. 3:5

ANOINTING
Kinds. Day-to-day courtesy. 6:13; 14:3
Of Christ. By a thankful person—Mary. 14:3-9

ANTICHRIST
Appearance of. 13:14-23
Deception by. 13:21-23
Described. Abomination of Desolation 13:14-23
Discussed. 13:14
Persecution by. 13:21-23
Prophesied.
    By Daniel. 13:1-27; 13:14
    Past & future fulfillment. 13:14

ANXIETY—ANXIOUS
Caused by. Worrying over witnessing. 13:9-11

APOSTASY (See **DENY—DENIAL**)
Example. Judas. 14:10-11

APOSTLE—APOSTLES (See **DISCIPLES**)
Ambition of. Seeking, arguing over positions. 9:33-37
Call of.
    Andrew & Peter. 1:16-18
    Cost Matthew more than most. 2:14
    James & John. 1:19-20
    Matthew. 2:14
    Twelve. Called, appointed, changed. 3:13-19
Discussed. Each of twelve. 3:16-19
Former life. Successful businessmen. 1:20
Inner circle of. Peter, James, & John. 9:2
Mission of. To preach the gospel. 16:15
Prepared for Christ's death. 9:2-13; 9:30-32
Training of.
    Intensive **t**. for six months. 7:31
    New stage launched. Prepared for Jesus' death. 8:31; 9:30-32
Weakness—Failure of.
    Deserted Christ. Foretold. 14:27
    Forsook Christ. (See **DESERTION**)
    Spiritualized Jesus' death & resurrection. 9:32; 16:11; 16:13

APPEARANCE, OUTWARD
Warning. Against dressing to attract attention. 12:38

APPROACH—APPROACHABLE
Jesus is **a**. any hour, any day. 1:32

ASS—COLT—DONKEY
Discussed. 11:1-7

ASSURANCE
Needed. In launching a new ministry. 1:11

ATTITUDE
Kinds of. Discussed. 5:22-24; 5:25-34; 5:35-43

AUTHORITY
Dangers of. Seeking with evil motive. 10:35-45
Of Christ. **A**. of His teaching. 1:22

BACKSLIDING (See **DENY—DENIAL**)
Caused by. Why a believer **b**. 14:10-11
Described as.
    Being offended by Christ. 14:27-31
    Denying Christ. 14:27-31
Examples. Disciples. Stumbling, falling away. 14:50-52

BAPTISM
Meaning. 1:9-11
Of Jesus Christ.
    A decision for God. 1:9-11
    Discussed. 1:9-11
    Ministry of **b**. 1:7-8
Of John the Baptist. **B**. only in water, not in the Spirit. 1:7-8
Of suffering. Meaning 10:38-39
Views of. Discussed. 16:16

BARABBAS
Criminal chosen over Christ. 15:6-10

BARTHOLOMEW—NATHANAEL, THE APOSTLE
Discussed. 3:18

BARTIMAEUS, BLIND
Steps to getting help from God.
10:46-52

BEELZEBUB
Discussed. Prince of the devils. 3:22

BELIEVE—BELIEVING—BELIEF (See
FAITH)
By demons. Christ rejected. Reasons.
1:25-26
Essential—Importance of. Reasons. 1:15

BELIEVER (See **APOSTLES; DISCIPLES;**
LABORERS; MINISTERS)
Duty—Work.
To bear fruit. 4:20
To be responsible. World's fate
depends upon. 6:30
To beware of some things. 12:38-40
To deny self. 8:34
To love life for the sake of the gospel.
8:35
To rise & stand up. 3:3
Growth of. Parable of Growing Seed.
4:26-29
Names—Titles. Sheep. 6:34
Nature. Made children, sons &
daughters of God. 3:34-35
Traits of. Cp. sheep. 6:34
Warning.
About the end time. 13:28-37
Beware of some things. 12:38-40

BEWARE
Meaning. 8:15

BLASPHEMY
Against the Holy Spirit. Unforgivable.
3:29-30
Charged against. Christ. 2:6-7
Is forgiven. 3:28
Meaning. 7:22

BLESSED OF THE LORD
Meaning. 11:10

BLIND—BLINDNESS (See **SPIRITUAL**
BLINDNESS)

BOAST—BOASTING
Warning against. **B**. in conversion.
1:44

BODY
Sins against. Defilement of. Things that
defile. 7:14-23

BREAD
Of Lord's supper. Discussed. 14:22

BROTHERHOOD
Duty—Essential.
To follow Christ. 1:19
To love neighbor as self. 11:31
Meaning of. True **b**. 3:31-35
Nature of. Spiritual, not blood
relationship. 3:33
Source of. The Spirit. 3:31-35
Verses. List of. 3:34-35

CAESAR
And God. Asked Jesus about the state &
God. 12:13-17

CAESAREA PHILIPPI
Discussed. 8:27

CALL—CALLED
Of disciples. (See **APOSTLE**)
Of whom.
Choice men. 3:13-19
Kind of person **c**. 1:16-20
The industrious, visionary,
successful. 1:16-20

CAMEL
Cp. to a rich man. Going through the
eye of a needle. 10:25

CANAANITES
Vs. Jews. Bitter enemies. 7:25-26

CANDLE
Parable of. Truth & man's duty 4:21-25

CARE—CARING
Duty to **c**.
For life 4:35-41
For one's needs. 8:1-9
For the home & the individual.
1:29-31
For the rejected. 7:24-30
For the whole world. 1:32-34
Necessity. 8:22-26
Steps to **c**. Threefold. 7:24-30

CARNAL—CARNALITY
Deliverance from **c**. How to conquer.
Praying and fasting. 9:28-29
Described as.
Faithlessness. 9:19-22
Immaturity. 9:14-29
Prayerlessness. 9:28-29
Result. Grieving the Lord. 9:19-22
Verses. List of. 8:32-33

CEMETERIES
Discussed. 5:3

CEREMONY—CEREMONIAL LAW (See
SCRIBAL LAW; RELIGION; RITUAL)
Broken—Violated.
By disciples of Christ. 2:23-24
By Jesus. 3:4
Emptiness of. Discussed. 7:1-13
Facts about. Less important than man
& his needs. 2:23-24
Laws of.
Eating with unwashed hands. 7:1-13
Governing Sabbath. Against work.
2:23-24
Over six hundred **l**. 12:28

CHARACTER (See **BELIEVER**; and
Related Subjects)
Weakness of. Discussed. 6:14-29

CHILDREN—CHILDLIKENESS
Discussed. 10:13-16
Duty toward. To be warned about the
end time. 13:1-37
Needs of. Discussed. 9:36-37
Problems—Weaknesses of.
Immaturity. Example. Salome's
dependency upon evil mother.
6:24-25
Truth about. 10:13-16
Symbolize—Illustrate.
Coming to Christ. 10:13-16
Disciples. 10:24
Greatness. 9:36-37
Requirements to enter heaven.
10:15-16

Traits of. Discussed. 10:14
Treatment—Reactions toward.
Jesus' protection of. 10:14
Prevented from coming to Christ.
10:13
Treated as a nuisance. 10:13-16
What it takes to receive **c**. 9:36-37

CHRISTIAN (See **BELIEVER**)

CHRISTIANITY (See **CHURCH;**
KINGDOM OF GOD)
Defined as. A family relationship.
3:31-35
Growth of. How it grows. 4:26-29;
4:30-32

CHURCH
Abuse of. Warning against. 11:15-19
Discipline. (See **CHURCH**
DISCIPLINE)
Growth of. Essentials. 4:30-32
How it grows. Discussed. 4:26-29;
4:30-32
Nature. Mixture of good & bad. 4:32
Problems. Failing to meet needs. Dead,
formal, lifeless. 1:23-24
Worship. (See WORSHIP)

CHURCH DISCIPLINE
Who is **d**. Five persons are cast out by
Christ. 11:15-17

CITIZENSHIP (See **GOVERNMENT;**
STATE)
Discussed. 12:13-17
Basis of. True **c**. 12:15
Vs. God. 12:13-17
Duty toward government. To pay taxes.
12:13-17
False concept of. Twofold. 12:13
Of believers
Has two **c**. 12:13-17
Often misunderstood. 12:13-17

CLEAVE—CLEAVING
In marriage. Meaning. 10:7-8

CLOTHING (See **DRESS**)
Illustrated. New **c**. sewn on old **c**. 2:21
Warning.
Against dressing to attract attention.
12:38
Against extravagant styles. 12:38

CLOUD
Symbolic of. Shekinah glory. Discussed.
9:7

COLT—ASS
Discussed. 11:1-7

COMMANDMENT (See **LAW**)
Greatest **c**. Discussed. 12:28-34
Ten **c**. Real meaning of. 5:21-43

COMMISSION
Described.
As preaching. 16:15
As sharing one's testimony. 5:18-20
Discussed. Sent forth. Equipped &
going forth. 6:7-13
Duty. To go to own home & friends
first. 2:15
Given to. A new convert. 5:18-20
Great **c**. 16:14-20

Hindrances; reason; promise; confirmation. 16:14-20

Purpose.
Discussed. 6:7-13
Fourfold. 3:14-15
To be with Jesus. 3:14-15
Verses. List of. 1:17-18; 3:14-15

COMMITMENT
Needed desperately for reaching the world. 4:30-32

COMPASSION (See **JESUS CHRIST**, Compassion of)
Essentials. Involves six things. 8:1-9
Of Jesus.
For the helpless. 9:22
For the needy. 1:32-34
To cleanse the most unclean. 1:41

COMPROMISE
Illustrated. By Pilate. 15:1-15

CONFESS—CONFESSION
Essential.
A willingness to stand up. 3:3
C. vs. being ashamed. 8:38
Must c. Jesus or be doomed. 3:11-12
Must make the c. that Christ wants. 1:25-26
Of Christ. Peter's great c. Who Jesus is. 8:27-30

CONFORM—CONFORMITY
To the world. Herod illustrates. 6:14-29

CONSCIENCE
Function—Purpose—Work. To disturb, stir quietly. 6:16-23
Guilty. What causes a guilty c. 6:16-23

CONSERVATIVE
Vs. liberal schools in Christ's day. 10:2-4

CONTRITE—CONTRITION
Essential. For confession. 3:11-12

CONVERSION—CONVERTED (See **SALVATION**; and Related Subjects)
Essential. Must be willing to be changed. 3:16-19
Illust. Centurion's confession at the cross. 15:39
Nature of. A convulsive experience. 1:25-26

COOPERATION—COOPERATIVE
Essential. To follow Christ. 1:10

CORBAN
Discussed. 7:11

COURAGE
Example.
A new convert. 3:3
Joseph of Arimathaea. 15:46; 15:47

COVENANT
New c. Established by blood of Christ. 14:23

COVETOUSNESS
Meaning. 7:22

CRITICISM—CRITICIZING
Object of c. A person who differs. Conditions of tolerance. 9:38-41

CROSS—SELF-DENIAL (See **SELF-DENIAL**)
Duty. To bear the c. 8:34-38
Meaning. 8:34
Pictures conversion. 15:21

CROWD
Excitement of. Not always wise. 6:45
Followed Jesus. Came from all over. Discussed. 3:7-8

CUP
Meaning. Symbol of three things. 14:36
Of Lord's Supper. Meaning. 14:23
Of suffering. Meaning. 14:36

CURIOUS—CURIOSITY
Need.
To come to Christ. 1:33
To seek Christ out of c. 2:1-2

DALMANUTHA
City of. Discussed. 8:10

DANCING
Example of. Suggestive d. 6:21-22

DANIEL
Predicted. Antichrist. 13:1-37
Seventieth week. 13:1-37; 13:14

DAVID
Example of. Man more important than rules & regulations. 2:25-27
Kingdom of. Given to Christ. 11:10
Predictions of. Messiah to be Lord. 12:35-37

DEATH—DYING
Form of capital punishment. By drowning. 9:42
Dead raised. By Jesus. Jairus' daughter. Approach that lays hold of Jesus. 5:21-24, 35-43
Preparation for. Tasting d. vs. seeing God's kingdom. 9:1
To self. (See **CROSS; SELF-DENIAL**)

DECEIVE—DECEPTION
Described. As self-deception. 14:1-2
Meaning. 7:22

DECISION
Duty—Essential.
One decision required. "He does all things well." 7:31-37
To follow Christ.
Attacked by Satan. 1:12
Cost of. 1:9
Rejection of Christ. By Israel. 12:12
Responses to Christ. Two choices men make. 11:27-33
Results of. Discussed. 1:12
Steps involved in. Discussed. 10:46-52
Tragic d. 11:33

DEDICATED—DEDICATION (See **COMMITMENT; LOYALTY**)
Duty. To labor to point of exhaustion. 4:35-36
Marks—Acts of. Sacrificing & doing all one can. 14:8
Meaning. Sacrificial giving. 10:17-22
Of Jesus Christ. D. to do God's will at any cost. 14:33-34; 14:41-42
Why one should be d. Degrees of. 4:20

DEFILE—DEFILEMENT (See **SIN**)
Causes of d. The heart. 7:14-23
Things that d. Discussed. 7:14-23

DELIVERANCE (See **SALVATION**)
Source. By whom. God's presence. 10:32
Verses. List of. 6:50-51
Who is delivered.
Most enslaved, helpless. 1:23-28
Most wild & mean. 5:1-20

DEMONS (See **EVIL SPIRITS**)

DENARII
Money. One d. was the average pay for a day's work. 14:3

DENIAL OF SELF
Meaning. 8:34

DENY—DENIAL (See **APOSTASY; BACKSLIDING**)
By whom.
Disciples.
Foretold. 14:27
Reasons. 14:50
When Jesus was arrested. 14:48-49
Judas
Double-dealing; deception; hypocrisy. 14:43-45
Why a disciple failed & ended up doomed. 14:10-11
Peter. Lesson in failure. 14:66-72
Causes. Discussed. 14:10-11; 14:66-72
Repentance of. Example of Peter. 14:72

DESERTION (See **APOSTASY; DENY—DENIAL**)

DESPERATE—DESPERATION
Answer to. Jesus. Steps. 5:21-43

DEVOTION
Of Jesus. Prepared Himself spiritually. 11:11

DIDYMUS
The Apostle. Discussed. 3:18

DISCIPLES (See **APOSTLES; BELIEVERS; LABORERS; MINISTERS**)
Ambition of. Seek positions. 9:33-37
Call of.
Called, appointed, changed. 3:13-19
Kind of person called. 1:16-20
Who Christ called. 1:16-20
Character—Traits.
Kind of men called to be d. 1:16-20
Desert Christ. (See **APOSTASY; DENIAL**)
Duty.
To be responsible. World's fate determined by. 6:30
To go forth. Equipping; six instructions. 6:7-13
Impact of Jesus upon. Young d. & theologians. 2:18-22
Message. (See **GOSPEL; MINISTERS**)
Preeminence of Christ. 1:7-8
Repentance. 6:12
Mission—Commission. (See **COMMISSION; MISSION**)

DISCIPLES (*Continued*)
Sent forth. (See **COMMISSION; MISSION**)

DISCIPLESHIP
Cost of **d.**
Discussed. 8:34-38
Everything. 2:14
Method of. Used by Christ. 6:7

DISCRIMINATION (See **DIVISION; PREJUDICE**)
Jews vs. Gentiles. One race vs. another. 7:24-30

DISEASE
Vs. demon possession. 3:15

DIVISION—DISSENSION
Cause. Opposing one who differs. 9:38
Examples. Jews vs. Gentiles. 7:24-30
Results. Destroys. 3:24-26

DIVORCE
Caused by. Hardness of heart. 10:2-5
Old vs. New Testament law. 10:2-4
Problem of. Positions of. 10:1-12
Schools of thought. Conservative vs. liberal. 10:1-12

DOG
Discussed. 7:27

DRESS (See **CLOTHING**)
Warning against.
D. in extravagant styles. 12:38
D. to draw attention. 12:38
Exposure of body. Drinking & dancing parties. 6:24-25

DRINKING—DRUNKENNESS
Example of. Partying spirit. 6:21-22

DROWNING
Form of capital punishment. 9:42

ELIJAH
Appeared at Jesus' transfiguration. Discussed Jesus' death. 9:2-4

EMOTIONS
Stirring of. Not always wise. 6:45

ENCOURAGE—ENCOURAGEMENT
Duty. To **e.** spiritual growth. 4:28

END TIME (See **JESUS CHRIST**, Return)
Believer's duty. To watch. 13:9; 13:23; 13:33-37
Chart of. 13:1-37
Christ's return and the world's end. Gathering of the elect. 13:26-27
Seventieth week of Daniel. 13:1-27
Signs of—Events.
Abomination of desolation. 13:14-23
Antichrist. 13:14-23
Astronomical events. 13:24-25
Discussed. 13:1-37
Great tribulation. 13:14-23; 13:24-27
Occur in one generation. 13:30
Return of Christ. 13:24-27
The book of destiny. 13:1-37
Warning to believers. 13:28-37

ENDURANCE
Result. Salvation. 13:13

ENSLAVED
Power to deliver. 1:23-28

EPILEPSY
Caused shame. 9:14-18

ETERNAL LIFE
How to secure. Giving everything. Feared, neglected by men. 10:21-22
Misconception.
Humanize or allegorize. 12:25
Secured by good works. 10:17; 10:18
Nature of. Discussed. 12:25
Problem of. Discussed. 10:17-22
Results of rejecting. Losing one's life. 8:35
Seeking. How to **s.** 10:17; 10:18
Source. How to receive. 10:17-22

EVANGELISM (See **COMMISSION**)
Hindrances to. Unbelief & hardness. 16:14
Power to **e.** Supernatural power. 16:17-18
Predicted. Whole world **e.** 13:10

EVIL
Concept of. Threefold. 7:23
Problem of.
Discussed. 7:14-23
From within, not without. 7:14-23
Man makes three mistakes in dealing with **e.** 7:23
Source. Heart. 7:23

EVIL EYE
Meaning. 7:22

EVIL SPIRITS
Acknowledged Jesus' deity. Rejected by Jesus. 1:23-26; 3:11-12
Delivered from.
Boy with dumb spirit. 9:14-29
Most enslaved. 1:23-28
Most wild & mean. 5:1-20
Discussed. 5:1-20
Nature of. Discussed. 5:6-7
Power over.
By Jesus.
Acknowledged by religionists. 3:22-23
Impact upon. Discussed. 3:11-12
Many in mass meeting. 1:34
Many when confronting Jesus. 3:7-12
Given to disciples. 6:7
Relation to God & Christ. Four facts about. 5:6-7
Vs. sickness. 3:15
Work of.
Effects of work. Described. Sixfold. 5:2-5
To enslave, control, possess. 1:23-24; 5:1-20
To heighten & aggravate existing conditions. 9:17-18
To possess people. 1:23-28; 3:11-12; 5:1-20; 9:14-29

EVIL THOUGHTS
Meaning. 7:21

EXCITEMENT
Of crowds. Not always wise. 6:45

Problem with. Stirred by worldly desires. 6:45

EXHAUSTION
Need for rest. Dangers of too much rest. 6:30-34

EXORCISM (See **EVIL SPIRITS; JESUS CHRIST**, Power of)
By Jesus. Discussed. 3:22-23

EYE
Evil. Meaning. 7:22
Sins. Seriousness of. 9:47-48

FAILURE
Causes. Four things. 14:66
How Jesus treats. Discussed. 14:27-31

FAITH (See **BELIEVE—BELIEF**)
Attitude. Wrong vs. right **a.** 5:35-43
Discussed. 11:22-23
Essential.
Discussed. 1:15
For answered prayer. 2:3-4
For forgiveness. 2:3-4
Must be accompanied with repentance. 1:15
To remove mountains, problems. 11:22-23
Example. Of friends. Saves another. 8:22-26
Lack of. (See **UNBELIEF**)
Meaning. Obedience. 16:16
Object of. Discussed. 11:22-23
Purpose. To remove mountains, problems. 11:22-23
Results. 11:22-23
Answered prayer. 11:22-23
Lays hold of Jesus' power. 5:21-43
Stages—Kinds.
Intercession. Saves a friend. 8:22-26
Persevering. 2:3-5
Prevailing **f.** 5:21-43
Vs. fear. **F.** eliminates fear. 5:36
Vs. works. Discussed. 16:16
What a person must believe. 1:15

FAITHFUL—FAITHFULNESS
Duty. To labor to point of exhaustion. 4:35-41
Essential. For power. 1:39

FALSE PROFESSION (See **HYPOCRISY; PROFESSION, FALSE**)

FAMILY
Dissension—Divisiveness. 13:12-13
Duty. To care for all members, even elderly parents. 7:11
Problems of. Persecution of believing members. 13:12-13

FAMILY OF GOD
Basis of.
Spiritual, not blood or social relationship. 3:33-35
True kinship. 3:33-35

FASTING
Of Jesus. Questioned. 2:18
When to **f.**
Two times. 2:20

FAVORITE—FAVORITISM
Feeling as though one is a **f.** of God. 10:36-37

FEAR, HUMAN
Deliverance from. By God's presence.
10:32
Duty. To cry for help. 6:47-49
Results.
Deserting Jesus. 14:50; 14:51-52
Failure. Denying Christ. 14:66
Pretension, denial, cursing.
14:66-72
Vs. faith. 5:36

FELLOWSHIP (See **BROTHERHOOD;
UNITY**)
Of believers. True **f.** 3:33-35

FERVENCY (See **ZEAL**)
Duty. To arise and stand forth. 3:5

FIG TREE
Cursed by Christ. Fruitless life.
11:12-14
Symbolized.
Israel. 11:20-21
Judgment in all of life. 11:12-14

FLESH (See **CARNAL**)
Duty. To put off old garment of **f.** 2:22
Verses. List of. 8:32-33
Works—Shortcomings of. Men seek to
please & pamper. 14:27-31

FOLLOW
Meaning. 8:34

FOOLISHNESS
Meaning. 7:22

FORGIVENESS, HUMAN
Condition. For answered prayer.
11:25-26
Results. Assures prayers being
answered. 11:25-26

FORGIVENESS, SPIRITUAL
Essential—Necessity. Most important
thing in life. 2:5
How one receives.
By coming & believing. 2:3-4
By forgiving others. 11:25-26
Power to forgive. 2:1-12
Most unclean. 1:41-42
Sin. Discussed. 2:1-12
Source. Jesus Christ. 2:8-11; 3:28
Who is **f.** Anyone—no matter how great
the sin. 3:28

FORNICATION
Meaning. 7:21

FREEDOM
Gift of God. To use **f.** to care for the
world. 12:1

FRUIT BEARING (See **BELIEVER;
DEDICATION**)
Purpose for Jesus' coming. Seeks
fruitful men. 11:12
Results. Are assured of some **f.** if sow
seed. 4:1-20; 4:3-9; 4:30-32
Steps to. Threefold. 4:20

FULNESS OF TIME
Meaning of. 1:15

GALILEE
Population: 200 cities over fifteen
thousand. 3:7-10

GALILEE, SEA OF
Discussed. 1:16

GENESARET, LAKE OF
Discussed. 1:16

GENTILES
Described. As "dogs." 7:27
Salvation of **G.** To be evangelized.
Foreshadowed by Christ. 7:24

GETHSEMANE
Jesus & **G.** Confronting death & terrible
trial. 14:32-42

GIVE—GIVING (See **STEWARDSHIP**)
Attitudes toward. Human need & **g.**
6:35-44
Described. Widow's mite. 12:41-44
Facts—Principles.
G. determines how much one gets in
life. 4:24-25
Measured by how much one has left.
12:43
More one **g.** more he receives.
4:24-25
Purpose. To seek to have a need met.
12:44
Verses. List of. 10:21-22

GLORY
Of Christ. Described. 9:2-4

GOD
And Israel. Discussed. 12:1-12
Concepts of. Stress love. Indulgent
"grandfather" type. 8:32-33
Duty. To love supremely. 12:29-31
Family of. True kinship. 3:33-35
Nature.
Good & severe. 11:12-14
Is one God. 12:29-31
View of. By men. Seems far away.
12:7

GOLGOTHA
Meaning. 15:22

GOSPEL
Beginning of. Discussed. 1:1-8; 1:1-2
Duty.
To lose life for sake of **g.** 8:35
To plant the **g.** in a world that is
barren & lost. 4:30-32
To preach to all nations. 13:10;
16:15
Message.
For whole world. Foreshadowed by
Christ. 7:24
Is Jesus Christ. 1:1-2
Preached by Jesus Christ. 1:14-15

GOVERNMENT (See **STATE;
CITIZENSHIP**)
And God. Question of civil & religious
authority. 12:13-17
Concepts of. Two false **c.** 12:13
Leaders. Sins of. 12:14

GRAVEYARDS
Discussed. 5:3

GREAT COMMISSION (See
COMMISSION, GREAT)

GREATNESS
Discussed. 9:33-37; 10:35-45

GREED
Discussed. Four significant facts.
14:10-11
Example of. A people choose
possessions over Christ. 5:14-17
Verses. List of. 14:11

GREETINGS
Warning. Against using titles for
attention. 12:38

GRIEVE—GRIEVED
Meaning. 3:5; 8:12

GROWTH (See **SPIRITUAL GROWTH;
MATURITY**)

GUILT
Example of. Herod's sinful life. 6:14-29

HANDICAP
Duty. Must care for **h.** 8:22-26

HANDS
How **h.** lay hold of Jesus. 14:46
Sins of. How. Seriousness of. 9:43-44

HARD—HARDNESS OF HEART
Cause. Forgetting. Attached to earth.
6:52
Examples of.
Disciples. 6:52; 8:17
Religionists. 3:5
Men easily forget. 6:52
Result. Blinds to truth. 6:52
Warning against. Discussed. 8:16-20

HEAL—HEALING
And forgiveness. **H.** is less important
than forgiveness. 2:1-12
By Jesus Christ. Examples of.
Blind Bartimaeus. Steps for getting
help. 10:46-52
Blind man. Necessity for caring.
8:22-26
Deaf & dumb. Doing all things well.
7:31-37
Demon possessed.
Boy with dumb spirit. 9:14-29
Caring for the rejected. 7:24-30
Delivering the most enslaved.
1:23-28
Hope for the most wild & mean.
5:1-20
Seeking & fearing Christ. 3:7-12
Evil spirits. Delivering the most
enslaved. 1:23-28; 1:34; 3:11-12;
5:1-20
Hemorrhaging woman. How to
approach Christ. 5:25-34
Leper. The most unclean. 1:23-28;
1:40-45
Man with a withered hand. 3:1-2;
3:1-6
Many among crowds. Seeking &
fearing Christ. 3:7-12
Palsy. Forgiveness of sins. 2:1-12
People in the streets. Caring for the
whole world. 1:32-34
Peter's mother-in-law. Caring for the
house. 1:29-31
Raised the dead. Jairus' daughter.
5:21-24, 35-43
Method. Anointing with oil. 6:8-13
Steps to. Discussed. 6:53-56

HEART

Condition of. Hard; shallow; thorny; soft. 4:1-20

Defilement of. Things that defile. 7:14-23

Duty. To receive the Word of God. Four ways. 4:1-20

Essential. Must be broken for salvation. 3:11-12

Hard—Hardened. (See HARD—HARDNESS OF HEART)

Kinds of.
Corrupt h. 7:14-23
Four kinds. 4:13-20
Hard h. 3:5; 6:52; 8:17

Meaning. 7:21

Source. Of evil. 7:23

What the h. does. Defiles a man. 7:14-23

HEAVEN

Characteristics—Nature. Love perfected. 12:25

Glory of. Glimpse of g. 9:2-13

Misconceptions—Errors. Idealize, materialize, humanize h. 12:25

Relationships in. Love perfected. 12:25

HEED, TAKE

Meaning. 8:15

HELL

Described.
Fire. 9:43-44
Worm that dies not. 9:43-44

HELP—HELPING

Steps for getting help. Discussed. 10:46-52

HEROD ANTIPAS (B.C. 4—A.D. 39)

Murdered John the Baptist. The immoral vs. the righteous. 6:14-29

Reaction to Jesus. Guilty conscience. 6:16-23

HERODIANS

Discussed. 12:13

Joined forces with the Pharisees. 3:6

Plotted Jesus' death. 3:6

HERODIAS

Wife of Herod. Plotted John's death. Vengeful. 6:24-25

HIGHEST, IN THE

Meaning. 11:10

HILLEL

Liberal school of thought. Scripture. Divorce. 10:1-12

HISTORY

Pivotal point of. Death of Jesus Christ. 15:16-41

HOLY SPIRIT

Promised. Verses. List of. 1:7-8

Sins against. Blasphemy. Unpardonable sin. 3:29-30

HOME

Duty.
To care for the h. & the individual. 1:29-31
To invite the presence of Jesus into the h. 1:29-31

Essential. Jesus' presence. 1:29-31

Hope of. Jesus Christ. 1:30; 1:31

HONOR

Seeking (See AMBITION)

Warning. Against seeking. 12:39

HOPELESSNESS

Answer to. Discussed. 5:25-34

HOSANNA

Meaning. 11:9

HOUSES

Of Jesus' day. Discussed. 2:4

HUMILITY

Essential. For true confession. 3:11-12

HYPOCRISY—HYPOCRITE (See PROFESSION, FALSE)

Appearing fruitful, but bearing no f. 11:12-14

Traits of. False profession. 7:6

Warning against. Discussed. 11:12-14

IMMATURITY (See SPIRITUAL IMMATURITY)

IMMORALITY

Example of. Party of Herod. Suggestive dancing. 6:21-22

INDECISION

Example of. Pilate. 15:2-5

Verses. List of. 15:2-5; 15:6-10

INDIGNATION

Meaning. 10:14

INITIATIVE

Essential. To seize opportunity. 1:21

INTERCESSION

Result. Brings healing to a friend. 8:22-26

INVITATION

Verses. List of. 1:33

ISRAEL (See JEWS)

And God. Discussed. Parable of the Wicked Tenants. 12:1-12

History. Blessed by God. Two b. 12:1

Prophecy. Future of. Told by Christ. 12:1-12

Sin of. Rejected. God's servants. 12:3

JAIRUS

Daughter raised from the dead. How to approach Jesus. 5:21-24, 35-43

JAMES, THE APOSTLE, THE SON OF ALPHAEUS

Discussed. 3:18

Had a believing mother. 3:18

JAMES, THE APOSTLE, THE SON OF ZEBEDEE

Brother of John. Discussed. 3:17

Called Boanerges, son of thunder (anger). 3:17

Called to be a disciple. 1:19-20

Discussed. 3:17

Fate of. Martyred. 10:39

Self-seeking. Sought chief position. 10:35-45

Wealthy. Father owned fishing business. 10:36-37

JERICHO

Discussed. 10:46

JERUSALEM

Jesus' ministry in. John covers; other Gospels say little. 11:1-13:37

JESUS CHRIST (See SEEKING, Jesus Christ)

Access to. (See ACCESS)

Accused—Accusation against.
A megalomaniac. 11:28
A traitor, a Roman stooge. 12:14
By religionists. Fourfold charge. 3:22
Listed. 3:22
Of Beelzebub. 3:22-30
Of being demon possessed. 3:22-30
Of being insane. By friends. 3:20-21
Of blasphemy. 2:6-7
Of breaking the ceremonial law. 2:23-28
Of not fasting or keeping the rituals of religion. 2:18-22
Of using ungodly authority. 11:27-28

Anger.
Against hardness of hearts. 3:5; 10:14
Over abuse of God's temple. 11:15-19

Anointed. At Bethany. A study of love. 14:3-9

Approached. How to a. 5:21-43

Arrested. Study of human character. 14:43-52

Ascension.
Assures seven things. 16:19-20
Sits in the position of power. 16:19

Authority (See JESUS CHRIST, Power)
Approaches that lay hold of. 5:21-43
Astonished man. 1:22
Over nature. 4:35-41
Questioned. Two choices. 11:27-33
Rejected. Why r. 6:1-6
Vs. a. of men. 1:22

Baptism—Baptized.
A decision for God. 1:9-11
Why Jesus was b. 1:9-11

Betrayed.
By Judas. Study of deception, hypocrisy, double-dealing. 14:43-45
Why a disciple failed & ended up doomed. 14:10-11
Why b. for thirty pieces of silver. 14:10

Burial. Discussion of courage. 15:42-47

Challenged about. (See JESUS CHRIST, Accused—Accusation)
Authority. 11:27-33
Greatest law. 12:28-34
Resurrection. 12:18-27
State and religion. 12:13-17

Claims.
I AM. 14:62
King of the Jews. 15:2-5
Lord of David. 12:36-37
Messiah. 14:62
Verses. List of. 1:23-24
Son of God. 3:21
To be of God. 11:27-33
To have the rights & dignity of a King. 11:1-11

555

LAW (See **CEREMONIAL LAW; COMMANDMENT**)
Breaking. Satisfaction, payment must be made. 1:15
Ceremonial l. (See **CEREMONIAL LAW**)
Defined. Greatest l. Is l. of love. 12:28-34
Man-made. Less important than man & his needs. (See **CEREMONIAL LAW**)

LAWYER
Discussed. 12:28
Questioned Christ. About great law. Heart touched. 12:28-34

LAZY
Fact. Useless to Christ. 1:16

LEAVEN
Of Herod. 8:15
Of Pharisees (religionists). 8:15

LEPER—LEPROSY
Discussed. 1:40-45
Sin. 1:40-45
Symbolized. The most unclean. 1:40-45

LEVI
Matthew. Call of. 2:14

LIBERAL—LIBERALS
Errors of. Twofold. 12:24
Vs. conservative. Two schools in Christ's day. 10:2-4

LIFE (See **SALVATION**)
Christ and l. Kinds of l. Christ brings. 2:18-22
Concepts of. Threefold. 8:32-33
Essential—Duty. Losing vs. gaining life. 8:35
Kinds of. Fruitless l. 11:12-14
Nature. Kind of l. Christ brings. Fourfold. 2:18-22
Source.
  Christ. 2:18-22
  Christ came to bring l. 11:12-14
Storms of. Calmed by Christ. Rest & peace. 4:35-41

LIGHT
Described. As nature & witness of believer. 4:21
Essential—Duty. To share the l. 4:21
Parable of. Truth & man's duty. 4:21-25

LISTEN—LISTENING
Need to l. Only way to hear man's need. 7:32

LORD'S SUPPER
Bread of. Meaning. 14:22
Cup. Meaning. 14:23
Instituted. Discussed. 14:22-26

LOST, THE
Sought. By Jesus. 2:13-17

LOVE (See **BROTHERHOOD**)
Acts. Listed. 12:31
Concepts of. Threefold. 8:32-33
Described.
  As greatest commandment. 12:29-31
  Not inactive, but active. 12:31
Discussed. 12:28-34

Essential—Duty.
  Chief duty of man. 12:29-31
  To l. God. 12:29-31
  To l. neighbor. 12:31
  To l. self. 12:31
Example of. Peter at civil trials of Jesus. 14:54
Nature. What l. involves. 12:29-31
Study of. Jesus' anointing at Bethany. 14:3-9
Vs. doing religious things. 12:31

MAN
Attitude. To world & soul. 8:36-37
Blessed. (See **BLESSED—BLESSINGS**)
Deliverance. (See **DELIVERANCE; SALVATION**) 5:1-20
Depravity.
  Progress of sin within. 7:21
  Short of perfection. Incomplete. 14:27-31
  Sinful from within. 7:18-23
  Under the influence of evil. 1:23-24
Described.
  As sheep without a shepherd. 6:34
Duty—Behavior.
  Things of men & things of God. 8:34-9:1
  To beware of some things. 12:38-40
  To love God supremely. 12:29-30
  To love neighbor. 12:31
  To love self. 12:31
  To oversee the world for God. 12:1
  Truth & man's duty. 4:21-25
Errors of.
  Feels God is far away. 12:7
  Insensitive. Inconsiderate. 15:24
  Misconception of Christ. Discussed. 8:32-33
  Misses truth of Christ. Reasons. 12:36-37
  Self-confidence. 14:31
Nature.
  Can be enslaved. By evil spirits. 1:23-24
  Misconceptions of life. 8:32-33
  Short of perfection. Self-centered. 14:27-31
  Spiritually blind. 8:10-13
  To be light, truth. 4:21
Needs of. (See **NEEDS**)
Response to Christ. (See **JESUS CHRIST**, Responses To)
  His ministry. Questioning who He is. 1:27-28
  Rebels against God. 12:2
State of.
  Future. Exists forever. In heaven or hell. 8:36-37
  Given dominion over the world. 12:1
  Present. Rejects God. 12:2-5
  Spiritual blindness. 8:10-13
Value—Worth. More important than rules & regulations. 2:23-24
Weaknesses of. Discussed. 14:27-31

MARK, JOHN
Deserted Christ at His arrest. 14:51-52

MARKETPLACE
Warning. Against displaying self in the **m**. 12:38

MARRIAGE—MARRIED (See **DIVORCE**)
Discussed. 10:1-12
In heaven. Love will be perfected. 12:25
Nature of. Creative, logical, spiritual union. 10:6; 10:7; 10:8; 10:9
Ordained. By God. 10:6
Problems. Are serious. 10:10-12
Union of. Cleaving. 10:6; 10:7; 10:8; 10:9

MARRIAGE SUPPER OF THE LAMB, THE
Promised. To believers. Meaning. 14:25

MARY MAGDALENE
First to whom Jesus appeared after His resurrection. 16:9-10

MARY, MOTHER OF JESUS
Embarrassed over J. Reasons. 3:31-32
Special, but still only human. 3:31-32

MARY, SISTER OF MARTHA
Anointed Jesus. A study of love. 14:3-9

MATERIALISM (See **MONEY; WEALTH**)
Desire for.
  By a people who choose **m**. over Jesus. 5:14-17
  By Matthew. 2:14
Problem with. Dangers of. 10:23-27

MATTHEW—LEVI, THE APOSTLE
Call of. Reaching the outcast & sinner. 2:14
Discussed. 3:18

MATURITY (See **SPIRITUAL GROWTH**)
Assured. No need for discouragement. 4:28

MERCY
Need for. Crying for. 10:47

MESSENGER (See **MINISTER**)
Gospel & the **m** of God. 1:1-8
Message of. 1:7-8

MESSIAH—MESSIAHSHIP
Claimed. By Jesus. (See **JESUS CHRIST**, Claims; Deity)
  Confronting death. 14:62
  In Jerusalem. His major thrust in J. Reason. 11:1-12:44
  Is Lord. 12:36-37
Confession.
  By the disciples. Who Jesus is. 8:27-30
  Vs. being ashamed. 8:38
Demonstrated.
  Fulfilled prophecy as a warning. 11:1-7
  In Jerusalem. Time & again. Reasons. 11:1-12:44
  Triumphal entry. Warning, He is **M**. 11:1-11
False concept—Misunderstood.
  Entangled idea of. 12:35-37
  False **m**. In last days. 13:21-22
  False vs. true. 8:27-30; 8:31-33; 10:35-45; 11:1-11
  Jewish **c**. Messiah was to do four things. 12:35
  Man's concept vs. God's concept. 8:27-9:50; 8:31-33
Ignorance of. A problem of ambition. 9:33-37

MESSIAH—MESSIAHSHIP (Continued)
Names—Titles.
    Son of David (Man) & Lord of David
      (God). 12:36-37
Origin.
    Called Lord by David. 12:35-37
    Of man vs. of God. 12:35-37
Predicted. By Scripture. 12:35; 12:36;
    22:43-45
Proclaimed. By John. 1:1-8
Proof. Power of Christ. 1:25-26
Way of God's **M.** vs. man's **m.** 8:31-33

MILLSTONE
Discussed. 9:42

MIND
Evil thoughts. Meaning. 7:21
Meaning. 12:29-31

MIND, SPIRITUAL
Result. Melts a hard heart. 6:52

MINISTERS (See **BELIEVERS;**
    DISCIPLES)
Call—Called.
    Discussed. 3:13-19
    Kind of person called. 1:16-20
    Saved to **m.** 1:31
    To preach. First calling. 2:1-2
Commission—Mission. (See
    COMMISSION; MISSION)
    Equipped & sent forth. 6:7-13
    Threefold. 1:3
    To "be with"; send; preach; receive
      power. 3:14-15
    To minister, to serve. 10:42-45
Discussed. Called; appointed; changed.
    3:13-19
Duty—Work.
    Five specific instructions. 6:8-13
    Five wise lessons. 6:45-52
    To be responsible. World's fate at
      stake. 6:30
    To be tolerant, accepting. 9:38-41
    To lose life for the sake of the gospel.
      8:34
    To minister at all hours. 1:32
    To pray after preaching. 6:46
    To preach. First calling. 2:1-2
    To sow the seed. How men receive.
      4:1-20
Equipped—Resources.
    To heal, anointing with oil. 6:8-13
    With power. Over evil spirits. 6:7
Example. John the Baptist. 1:1-8
Gospel & the **m.** of God. 1:1-8
Message. 1:7-8
    Threefold. 1:14-15
    To focus upon Christ. 1:7-8
Personal matters. Need for rest & its
    dangers. 6:30-34
Purpose. (See **MINISTERS,**
    Commission; Duty)
Reward. Greatness assured. 10:42-44
Treatment.
    Authority questioned. 6:3
    Conditions for receiving **m.**
      9:38-41
    Ignored. By people. Reasons. 3:20
    Rejected. Reasons. 6:1-6
Verdict upon. Doing all things well.
    7:31-37

MINISTRY—MINISTERING
Call. Hard work, vision, cooperation,
    sacrifice. 1:16-20
Cost of. Total sacrifice of everything. 1:9
Duty.
    Five wise lessons for **m.** 6:45-52
    Of elderly. Elderly expected to **m.** 1:31
    To **m.** to individuals & homes.
      1:29-31
    To restore people to wholeness. 3:4;
      3:5
    To save life, not to be religious. 3:4,
      cp. 1-5
    To seek a verdict of faithfulness.
      7:31-37
Preparation. Launching a new **m.**
    Discussed. 1:21-22
Result. Verdict upon. Doing all things
    well. 7:31-37

MISSION—MISSIONS (See **BELIEVERS;**
    COMMISSION; DISCIPLES;
    MINISTERS)
Duty. To preach. First calling. 2:1-2
Hindrances. Discussed. 16:14
Of Christ. Sense of. 1:36-38
Predicted. World to be evangelized.
    13:10
Source. Power of the Word. 16:17-18
Verses. List of. 1:17-18; 3:14-15

MOTIVES
Wrong **m.**
    For rejection of Christ. 8:11
    Of ambition. 10:36-37

MOUNTAINS
Meaning. 11:22-23

MULTITUDES
Feeding of.
    Attitudes toward human need &
      resources. 6:35-44
    Spiritual food, compassion,
      evangelism. 8:1-9

MUSTARD SEED
Discussed. 4:31
Parable of. Growth of God's Kingdom.
    4:30-32

MURDER
Meaning. 7:21

NATURAL MAN (See **MAN**)
Depraved. By nature. 14:27-31
Errors of.
    Discussed. 8:32-33
    Misunderstands spiritual dimension,
      spiritual world. 12:24

NATURE
Power over. Christ **p.** over. (See **JESUS**
    CHRIST, Power)

NAZARETH
Hometown of Christ. Rejected Him.
    6:1-6

NEEDLE
Camel passing through. Meaning. 10:25
Cp. a rich man. 10:25

NEEDS—NECESSITIES
Attitude toward. **N.** & resources.
    6:35-44
Duty. To cry for help. 6:47-49

Met—Provided. Steps for getting help &
    meeting needs. 10:46-52
Personal responsibility vs. social
    responsibility. 6:35-37
Provision of. By God. 12:15

NEEDY, THE
Care for. By Jesus. For people in streets.
    1:32-34
Seeking Jesus. (See **SEEK—SEEKING**)

NEIGHBOR (See **LOVE**)

NEW CREATION
Nature. A new & an adventuresome
    life. 2:21-22
Necessary—Essential. Reasons.
    14:27-31
Source. Christ. 2:21

NEW MAN
Necessary—Essential. Reasons.
    14:27-31

OBEY—OBEDIENCE
Basis. Of being accepted into the family
    of God. 3:34-35
Duty. To **o.** will of God. 3:34-35
Of Jesus Christ. To God. 11:11

OFFEND—OFFENDING
How. Six ways. 9:42
Meaning. 14:27
Verses. List of. 9:42

OIL
Anointing with. To heal. 6:13

OPPORTUNITY
Duty.
    To grasp **o.** Verses. List of. 1:21
    To seize while can. 14:7
Grasping. While there is time. 14:7
Missing. Four causes. 1:21

ORDAINED
Meaning. 3:14

OUTCAST
Attitude toward.
    By church. 2:15
    By society. 2:16-17
Power to reach. Discussed. 2:13-17

PALM SUNDAY
Meaning. 11:1-11

PARABLE
Meaning. 4:2
List of.
    Bridegroom. A new life & a new age.
      2:19-20
    Candle. Under a bushel basket. Truth
      & man's duty. 4:21-25
    Divided kingdom. Strife destroys
      nations. 3:24-25
    Growing Seed. Growth of believers.
      4:26-29
    House divided against itself destroys
      homes. 3:25
    Mustard Seed. Growth of God's
      kingdom. 4:30-32
    New and old cloth. New vs. old life.
      2:21
    New wine and old bottles. New vs.
      old life. 2:22
    Salt. Serving God. 9:50

Sower. How one receives the gospel. 4:1-20

Wicked Tenants. God & Israel. 12:1-12

Use of. Why Jesus used illustrations. 4:33-34

PARENTS (See **FAMILY**)

Care of. Not forsaking & abandoning. 1:20

Duty. To bring children to Christ. Prevented. 10:13

Evil. Influence of. Worldliness. 6:24-25

Verses. List of. 10:14

PARTYING

Results.

Drinking & dancing **p**. 6:21-22

Passion & immoral decisions. 6:21-22

Example of. Herod. Suggestive, lustful, drinking. 6:21-22

PASSOVER

Atmosphere. Commercial, carnival **a**. 14:12

Attendance. Multitudes of pilgrims. Two to three million. 14:12

Discussed. 14:1

Preparation of. Jesus makes secret **p**. Reasons. 14:13-17

Symbolized. Pictured. Death of Jesus. 14:1

PEACE

Source.

Christ. Came to bring **p**. 11:1-7

Presence & power of Christ. 4:35-41

PEOPLE (See **WORLD**)

PERSECUTION—PERSECUTORS

By whom.

Families. 13:12-13

Leaders. 13:9

Described. As a reward. 10:30

Discussed. 13:9

How to overcome.

Endurance. 13:13

Supernatural protection & strength. 13:11

Predicted. In end time. 13:9

Results. Fills up & completes the sufferings of Christ. 10:30

Verses. List of. 10:30

Warning of. Discussed. 13:9

Who is to be **p**. God's messengers. 12:2; 12:3-5

PERSEVERANCE—PERSISTENCE (See **STEADFASTNESS**)

Duty. To **p**. in seeking forgiveness. 2:3-4

Essential. To get help. 10:48

Example.

Blind man. Steps for getting help. 10:46-52

Rejected woman. Caring for the rejected. 7:24-30

Results.

Demonstrates faith. 2:4

Fivefold. 10:48

PETER, SIMON THE APOSTLE

Conversion—Call.

Called to be a disciple. 1:16-18

Discussed. 3:16

Courage. Followed Christ through trials. 14:54

Denial of Christ.

Foretold. How Jesus treats failure. 14:27-31

Lesson in failure. 14:66-72

Repented. 14:72

Discussed. 3:16

Great confession of. Jesus is Messiah. 8:27-30

Home of. Jesus visited. 1:29

Mother-in-law healed. 1:30

Weaknesses & strengths. Discussed. 3:16

PHARISEES (See **RELIGIONISTS**)

Belief—Teaching. Tradition. 7:1-13

Error—Fault of.

Hypocritical religionists, false teachers. 7:1-13; 8:14-21

Separated selves from sinners. 2:15-17

Spiritual blindness. 8:11

Joined by John's disciples. 2:18-22

Opposed Jesus. Joined forces with Herodians. 3:6

Vs. Jesus. Plotted Jesus' death. 3:6

PHILIP THE APOSTLE

Discussed. 3:18

PILATE

Discussed. 15:1-15

Picture of a morally weak man. 15:1-15

POSITION (See **AMBITION**)

Seeking.

Discussed. 10:35-45

Problem of ambition. 9:33-37

POSSESSIONS (See **MATERIALISM; WEALTH; WORLDLINESS**)

POWER

Duty. To seek. Problem of ambition. 9:33-37; 10:35-45

Lack of. Reasons & results. 9:18

Purpose. To control evil spirits. 6:7

Source of. Discussed. 1:35-39

Verses. List of. 3:14-15

POWERLESSNESS

Cause. Spiritual immaturity & **p**. 9:14-29

Results. Discussed. 9:18

PRAY—PRAYER—PRAYING

Answers to. Conditional. 11:20-26

Conditions for. Discussed. 11:20-26

Essentials. Discussed. 11:25-26

Hindrances.

Failing to pray. 14:34

Long prayers. 12:40

Prayer life of Christ. (See **JESUS CHRIST**, Prayer Life)

When to **p**.

After ministry. 6:46

At meals. 6:41

PREACHER (See **MINISTER**)

PREACHING

Call to. First call. 2:1-2

Conditions. For receiving messengers. 9:38-41

Described. As sowing seed. How men receive. 4:1-20

Meaning. 3:14

Message of.

Good news of gospel. 1:14-15

Preached by Jesus. 1:14-15

Mission.

Of believers. 1:36-38; 1:39

Of Christ. 1:36-38; 1:39; 2:1-2

Results. Crowd's excitement. Not always wise. 6:45

PREJUDICE

Broken down—Abolished. Steps to. 7:24-30

Kinds.

Gentiles called "dogs." 7:27

Racial **p**. 7:25-26

PRIDE

Caused by. Wealth. 10:24

Described. As saying "But for grace of God, there go I." 1:44

Meaning. 7:22

PROFESSION

Essential **p**. Jesus is Messiah. 8:27-30

Steps required. Discussed. 10:46-52

PROFESSION, FALSE—PROFESSION ONLY

Error—Mistakes of.

Lacks conviction against error & evil. 3:5

Refuses to accept Jesus as Messiah. 7:6

Identified. Resting under the church's umbrella. 4:30-32

Judgment of. Seen, examined, condemned. 11:12-14

Results.

Deception. 11:13

One's life being condemned. 11:12-14

Vs. true. Discussed. 8:27-30

Warning against. Discussed. 11:12-14

PROMISES

Essential.

To believer. 16:7

Verses. List of. 16:7

PROPHECY

About John the Baptist. Forerunner. 1:2

RAISING THE DEAD (See **DEAD**, Raised)

RANSOM

Meaning. 10:45

Verses. List of. 10:45

REDEEM—REDEMPTION

Source. The death of Jesus. 9:31

Verses. List of. 9:31; 10:45

REGENERATION

Described. A new life and religion. 2:21; 2:22

REJECTION

Described. 7:24-30

Of Christ. (See **JESUS CHRIST**, Response to; **UNBELIEF**)

RELIGION (See **RITUAL**)
Christ used established **r**. 1:39
Described as.
Ritual, tradition. 7:1-13
Rules and regulations. 2:23-28;
3:1-6
Position—Hold to.
Ritual, tradition. 7:1-13
Rules and regulations. 2:23-28;
3:1-6
Problem with—Errors.
Emptiness of. 7:1-13
Evils of. 8:14-21
Man-made. 7:1-13
Spiritually blind. 8:10-13
Purpose. To serve, not master, man.
2:25-27
True religion.
Is not ritual & ceremony, rules &
regulations. 2:23-24
What true **r**. really is. Five things.
3:1-6
Vs. love. 12:31
Vs. the state, government. 12:13-17

RELIGIONISTS
Leaven of. Evil & dangers of. 8:14-21
Opposed Christ.
Called Jesus demon-possessed.
3:22-30
For associating with outcasts &
sinners. 2:13-17
For breaking ceremonial law. 3:4
For breaking tradition. Scribal law.
2:23-24; 3:1-6; 7:1-13
For casting out demons. 3:22-30
For disciples working on the
Sabbath. 3:1-6
For forgiving sins. 3:5-6
For healing on the Sabbath. 3:1-6
For not fasting, not keeping the
ritual of **f**. 2:18-22
Four reasons why **o**. 14:1-2
Questioned Christ. (See **JESUS
CHRIST**, Challenged)
Plotted Jesus' death. Reasons. 3:6;
11:18; 14:1-2
Put Jesus on trial. (See **JESUS
CHRIST**, Trials)
Reasons. Several events of last week.
3:22; 11:27
Rejected Christ. Reasons. 11:32
Tried to discredit. 10:1-4;
11:27-33
Position—Holds to. Rules & regulations.
Ceremonial law. 2:23-28; 3:1-6
Problem with—Errors.
Attitude toward sinner & outcast.
2:16-17
Fear sinner & outcast. Two reasons.
2:16-17
Fourfold **e**. 14:1-2
Inadequate religion. Example of.
Herod. 6:20
Misses the truth of Christ. Reasons.
12:36-37
Seek signs of proof. 8:10-13
Warned—Fate of. Beware of some
things. 12:38-40

REMARRIAGE
Discussed. 10:1-12; 10:10-12

REPENT—REPENTANCE (See
SALVATION; and Related Subjects)
Duty. To preach. 1:15
Essential.
Must accompany faith. 1:15
Reasons. 1:15
Example of. Peter. 14:72
Verses. List of. 1:3-5; 1:15

REPRODUCTION
Law of. Discussed. 4:32

RESOURCES
Attitude toward. Fivefold. 6:37-44

RESPECTABILITY
Inadequate for salvation. 10:19-20

REST—RELAXATION, PHYSICAL
Duty. To allow interruptions
sometimes. 7:25-26
Need for.
Dangers of. 6:30-34
Sought by Jesus for preparation.
7:24
Source. Jesus. Power to bring **r**. & peace.
4:35-41

REST, SPIRITUAL
Source. The presence & power of
Christ. 4:35-41

RESURRECTION
Denied. Reasons. 12:19-23; 12:24
Discussed. 12:18-27
Nature of. Discussed. 12:25
Proof of. Discussed. 12:18-27
Questioned. Discussed. 12:18-27
Verses. List of. 12:24

REVENGE
Reasons for. Threefold. 6:24-25

REWARDS
Degrees. The great vs. the first. 10:40
How to secure—Basis of.
Leaving all & following Christ.
10:28
Ministering in Christ's name. 9:41
Seeking. By Christ & by Moses.
10:28-31
Misconception of. Thought to be
mercenary. 10:28-31
Promised. In both this life & in the
next life. Four **r**. 10:29

RICH—RICHES (See **MATERIALISM;
MONEY; WEALTH**)
Desire for. Matthew. 2:14
How a rich man can be saved.
Discussed. 10:21-22; 10:27
Meaning. 10:23
Problem—Danger of. Choosing over
Jesus. 10:23-27

RICH YOUNG RULER
Problem of eternal life. 10:17-22

RITUAL (See **RELIGION**)
Purpose. To serve, not master, man.
2:25-27

ROADS
Of ancient day. Discussed. 1:3

RUFUS
Son of Simon of Cyrene who bore Jesus'
cross. 15:21

RULES—REGULATIONS (See
CEREMONIAL LAW; RELIGION)
Facts about.
Are not to be put before man's
welfare. 3:1-6
Are to be subject to Christ. 2:23-28
Problem with. Emptiness of. 7:1-13

SABBATH—SUNDAY
Discussed. Understanding the **S**.
2:23-28
Laws governing. Broken by disciples.
2:23-24
Purpose. To serve man. 2:25-27
Meaning. True **m**. of. 2:23-28

SACRIFICE
Of Christ. Cost of. 1:9
Vs. common sense. 14:4-5

SADDUCEES
Liberal position caused two things.
12:24

SALT
Symbol—Type. Of judgment. Salted
with fire. 9:49

SALVATION—SAVED
Conditions—How one is **s**.
Approaches that lay hold of Jesus.
5:21-43
By God recreating a person. through
new birth. 4:27
By endurance. 13:13
Confession needed. Great **C**. Who
Jesus is. 8:27-30
Costs. Everything. Matthew
illustrated. 2:14
Giving all one is & has. 10:21-22;
10:27
Not by love of Jesus. Not enough.
10:21
Not respectability. 10:19-20
Repentance & belief. 1:15
Requirements for. 10:17-22
Steps to. Discussed. 6:53-56; 10:46-52
Deliverance. A conversion experience.
1:25-26
Duty. To carry the message of **s**. to all.
1:36-39
Results. Sets free from three things.
1:12
Who is **s**.
Anyone—no matter how great a
sinner. 3:28
Most enslaved & helpless. 1:23-28
Most rejected. 7:24-30
Most unclean. 1:40-45
Most wild & mean. 5:1-20
Outcast & sinner. 2:13-17
The sick. 1:29-31; 1:32-34

SANHEDRIN
And Jesus.
Sent an investigative delegation to **i**.
Jesus. 2:6-7
Tried Jesus.
For treason. Weak & strong
character. 14:53-65
Met to formulate charges. 15:1

SATAN
Defeated—Destroyed. By Christ. House
spoiled by **C**. 3:27

Existence—Nature of.
Does not act against his **n**. 3:22-26
Opposed to Christ. 5:6-7
Relationship to God & Christ. Four facts. 5:6-7
Work—Strategy of. To attack new converts. 1:12

SCRIPTURES (See **WORD OF GOD**)

SCRIBES (See **PHARISEES; RELIGIONISTS**)
Problem with.
Hypocritical religionists, false teachers. 7:1-13
Vs. Jesus.
Accused Jesus of devil possession. 3:22-30
Plotted Jesus' death. 14:1-2

SEA OF GALILEE
Discussed. 1:16

SECOND CHANCE
Given to Judas. 14:18-20

SEED
Parable of. Growing **S**. Growth of believers. 4:26-29
S. & Sower. How Word is received. 4:1-20

SEEK—SEEKING (See **PERSEVERANCE**)
Christ **s**. men.
Sought, questioned by **C**. Reasons. 12:35
Duty. To seek Christ with fervor. 3:7-8
Men **s**. Christ.
By helpless. 2:1-5
By most unclean. 1:40
Crying for help. 10:47
His special presence. 2:20
How to **s**. 5:21-43; 6:55
Is approachable any day or hour. 1:32
Reasons do not. 3:20
When. Two special times. 2:19
Verses. List of. 2:20
Men **s**. life. How to secure. 2:20

SELF-CENTERED
Cause. Depraved nature. 14:27-31

SELF-CONFIDENCE
Cause. Forgetting human weakness, carnality. 14:27-31
Not knowing one's true self. 14:29-30

SELF-DENIAL (See **CROSS**)
Cost of discipleship. Discussed. 1:9
Example. John the Baptist. 1:6
Verses. List of. 1:23-24

SELF-LOVE
Vs. Godly love. 12:31

SELF-RIGHTEOUS
Attitude of. Toward the outcast. 2:15
Essential. To acknowledge, confess need. 2:15

SELF-SEEKING (See **AMBITION**)
Motives of. Wrong **m**. Fivefold. 10:36-37
Problem with. Ruins ambition. 9:33-37; 10:35-45
Of attention, honor, position. 12:38-40
Results. Conflict. 10:41

SENSATIONALISM—SPECTACULAR (See **SIGNS**)

SERVE—SERVICE (See **BELIEVERS; MINISTERS—MINISTERING**)
Duty. To do all things well. 7:31-37
How to **s**. Five wise lessons. 6:45-52

SHAMMAI
Conservative school of thought. 10:1-12

SHEEP
Describes. Lost world. 6:34
Traits of. Discussed. 6:34

SHEPHERD
Duty. What happens to sheep if no **s**. 6:34

SICKNESS
Vs. demon-possession. Distinction made. 3:15

SIGNS
Desire for.
Reasons no **s**. given. Seven **r**. 8:12
Seeking **s**. 8:10-13
Purpose. To prove Jesus is the Messiah, the Son of God. 8:11

SIMON OF CYRENE
Discussed. 15:21

SIMON PETER (See **PETER, SIMON**)

SIMON, THE CANAANITE—SIMON THE ZEALOT, THE APOSTLE
Discussed. 3:18

SIN (See **TEMPTATION**; and Related Subjects)
Acts of—Behavior of.
Cheat, devour widows. 12:40
Common to government leaders. 12:14
Displaying self in marketplace, streets. 12:38
Dressing to attract attention. 12:38
Eye sins. 9:47-48
Foot sins. 9:45-46
Hands sin. 9:43-44
Holding back. 10:21-22
Long deceptive public prayers. 12:40
Misleading others to sin. Six ways. 9:42
Not caring. 7:24-30
Offending, leading others astray. 9:42
Rejecting others. 7:24-30
Seeking chief seats, honor, recognition. 12:39
Self-seeking. (See **SELF-SEEKING**)
Stealing from widows. 12:40
Terribleness of sin. 9:42-50
Things that defile. 7:14-23
Using titles & greetings to exalt man. 12:38
Caused by. Heart. 7:14-23
Deliverance from.
Cleansing the most unclean. 1:40-45
Forgiveness of. Power to forgive. 2:1-12
Described. As defilement. Things that defile. 7:14-23

Growth of. Progress. Within man. 7:23
Results—Penalty.
Condemnation. Greater **c**. of seven sins. 12:38-40
Held personally responsible. 9:42-50
Symbol—Type of. Leprosy. 1:40-45
Unpardonable **s**. Blasphemy against the Holy Spirit. 3:29-30
Warning against. Worst thing to fall upon. 1:43

SINNER
And Christ. **C**. associated with. 2:15
Attitude toward.
By church. 2:15
By society. 2:16-17
Duty. To seek cleansing. 1:40; 1:43
Hope. For most wild & mean. 5:1-20
Power to reach. Discussed. 2:13-17

SOCIETY
Attitude. Toward sinner. 2:16-17

SODOM
Illustrates—Symbolizes. Judgment. 6:11

SOUL
Attitude toward. Discussed. 8:36-37
Duty. To save the **s**. Vs. gaining the world. 8:36-37
Meaning. 8:36-37

SOWER, PARABLE OF
How men receive the Word of God. 4:1-20

SPIRITUAL BLESSINGS (See **BLESSINGS**)
Secured. Three ways. 9:23-27

SPIRITUAL BLINDNESS (See **UNBELIEF**)
Faults of. Discussed. 8:10-13
Inexcusable. Motive for. 8:11; 8:12
Results. Fail to see the truth. 6:52

SPIRITUAL GROWTH—MATURITY
Assured. No need for discouragement. 4:28
Of believers. Parable of Seed. Four facts. 4:26-29

SPIRITUAL HUNGER (See **HUNGER & THIRST**)

SPIRITUAL IMMATURITY
Conquered. Two ways. 9:28-29
Problem. Spiritual **i**. & powerlessness. 9:14-29

SPIRITUAL WORLD—DIMENSION
Denied. Reasons. Minimize, ignore. 8:11
Misconception. Misunderstood by natural man. 12:24
Nature of. Discussed. 12:25
Relationships in. Discussed. 12:25
Revealed. By God alone. 12:24

SPIT—SPITTING
Sign of utter contempt. 14:65

STATE (See **CITIZENSHIP; GOVERNMENT**)
And God. Question of civil & religious power. 12:13-17
Concepts of. Two false **c**. 12:13
Nature. Ordained by God. 12:16-17

Keeps one out of God's kingdom. 10:17-22; 10:23-27; 10:28
Judgment of. How **w.** is to be judged. 10:27
View of. Jewish 10:26
Meaning. 10:23
Misunderstanding—Misconception. Popular view of. 10:26
Sign of God's blessings, spirituality. 10:26

WICKED HUSBANDMAN
Parable of. God & Israel. 12:1-12

WICKEDNESS
Meaning. 7:22

WIDOWS
Sins against. Deceived & cheated by some. 12:40

WIDOW'S MITE
Real giving. 12:41-44

WILL
Of Christ. Subjection of. Absolute submission. 14:41-42
Of God.
Meaning. 3:34-35
Obedience to. Essential. 3:34-35

WILLS—INHERITANCE
Dedicated to God. 7:11
Meaning. 8:34

WINE SKINS
Parable. New wine put in old **w.s.** Old vs. new life. 2:22

WITNESS—WITNESSING
Called to. Must be saved to **w.** 1:25
Duty.
To go to sinners. 2:16-17
To go to the rejected. 2:16-17
To share, to be the very nature of the believer. 4:21
To sow the seed, the Word of God. 4:1-20; 4:26
To **w.** to most unclean. 1:44
Example.

By new convert. People prepared for message. 8:1-2
Of Matthew. Right after conversion. 2:15
How to go—Method.
Beginning where a person is. 8:23
Sharing one's testimony. 5:18-20
Two by two. Reasons. 6:7
Power to **w.** Discussed. 16:17-18
Predicted. Whole world evangelized. 13:10
Results. Are assured. 4:1-20; 4:3-9
Verses. List of. 1:17-18; 3:14-15

WOMEN
Position in ancient world. 10:5

WORD OF GOD
Described. How it is used in Scripture. Seventeen ways. 4:33
Duty.
To desire. 6:35-44; 8:1-2
To place before tradition. 7:8; 7:9-12; 7:13
Meaning. 4:33
Response to. How men receive the **W.** 4:1-20

WORKS
Essential. To follow Christ. 1:16
Vs. love. 12:31
Weakness of. Emptiness of. 7:1-13

WORLD
Attitudes of. Toward the outcast. 2:13-17
Created by—Creation. Blessed by God. Given everything needed. 12:1
Deliverance from.
By Word of God. Strong witness. 4:30-32
Gaining **w.** vs. saving soul. 8:36-37
Hope of Christ. 1:32-34
Described. As sheep without a shepherd. Traits. 6:34
Judgment of. End of. Predicted. 13:1-37
Leaders of. Evil & dangers of. 8:14-21
Nature.

Fades away. 8:36-37
Fruitless, sterile, empty, barren. 4:30-32
Under influence of evil. 1:23-24
State of.
Described. 1:32-34
Discussed. 6:7
View of success & ambition. 10:42-43
Vs. Christ.
Christ warns the **w.** 11:1-11
Cries to be left alone. 1:23-24
Guilty of Christ's death. 10:33
Ignores Christ. Reasons. 3:20
Rebel. 12:6-8
Rejects. Reasons. Refuse to give all. 8:38
Vs. soul. Attitude toward. 8:36-37
Warning about. Discussed. 11:1-11

WORLD, END OF (See **END TIMES**)

WORLD HISTORY (See **HISTORY**)

WORLDLY—WORLDLINESS
Example of.
Herod's lavish party. 6:14-29
Pilate. 15:15
Problem of. Dangers. 10:23-27
Results—Effects of.
Chokes the Word, spiritual growth. 4:18-19
Discussed. 6:14-29
Sin of. Attached to, preoccupied with **w.** 8:16-21

WORSHIP
Duty. To be faithful. 1:21
Failure—Weakness of.
Can be empty, worthless, useless. 7:7
Sitting in church, but failing to **w.** 1:23-24
Results. Brings Christ into home. 1:29
Warning to those who abuse. 11:15-19

ZEBEDEE, FATHER OF JAMES & JOHN, THE APOSTLES
A successful businessman. 1:20

LEADERSHIP MINISTRIES WORLDWIDE

Leadership Ministries Worldwide (LMW) exists to equip ministers, teachers, and lay workers in their understanding, preaching, and teaching of God's Word by publishing and distributing worldwide *The Preacher's Outline & Sermon Bible*® and related Outline Bible Resources; to reach & disciple men, women, boys, and girls for Jesus Christ.

OUTLINE BIBLE RESOURCES

The **Outline Bible Resources** have been given to LMW for printing and distribution worldwide at/below cost, by those who remain anonymous. Our daily prayer is that each volume will lead thousands, millions, yes even billions, into a better understanding of the Holy Scriptures and a fuller knowledge of Jesus Christ the Incarnate Word, of whom the Scriptures so faithfully testify.

This material, like similar works, has come from imperfect man and is thus susceptible to human error. We are nevertheless grateful to God for both calling us and empowering us through His Holy Spirit to undertake this task. Because of His goodness and grace, *The Preacher's Outline & Sermon Bible*® New Testament and the Old Testament volumes are complete and are now being revised and expanded in the **everyWORD**® commentary series.

In addition, *The Minister's Personal Handbook, The Believer's Personal Handbook, The Business Leader's Personal Handbook* and other helpful **Outline Bible Resources** are available in printed form as well as on various digital platforms.

Our Mission is to make the Bible so understandable—its truth so clear and plain—that men and women everywhere, whether teacher or student, preacher or hearer, can grasp its message, receive Jesus Christ as Savior, and become fully-equipped disciples of Jesus Christ. It is our goal that every leader around the world, both clergy and lay, will be able to understand God's Holy Word and present God's message with more clarity, authority, and understanding—all beyond his or her own power.

God has given the strength and stamina to bring us this far. Our confidence is that as we keep our eyes on Him and remain grounded in the undeniable truths of the Word, we will continue to produce other helpful **Outline Bible Resources** for God's dear servants to use in their Bible study and discipleship.

We offer this material first to Him in whose name we labor and serve and for whose glory it has been produced and, second, to everyone everywhere who studies, preaches and teaches the Word.

LMW (Leadership Ministries Worldwide) publishes the world's leading outline commentary Bible series, *The Preacher's Outline & Sermon Bible*®. Our mission is to provide pastors in the global church with this and other gospel-centered resources:

The Preacher's Outline & Sermon Bible® - a Bible outline commentary series (44 volumes in KJV, 40 in NIV).

The LMW app - our Bible outline commentary digital app

everyWORD® - our Bible outline commentary series in ESV (call for availability)

Handbook Series
What the Bible Says to the Believer – The Believer's Personal Handbook
What the Bible Says to the Minister – The Minister's Personal Handbook
What the Bible Says to the Business Leader – The Business Leader's Personal Handbook
What the Bible Says about the Tabernacle
What the Bible Says about the Ten Commandments

The Teacher's Outline & Study Bible™ - various New Testament books

Practical Illustrations
Practical Word Studies in the New Testament
Old Testament Prophets Supplement

Study Booklets:
Faith
Prayer
The Passion of Jesus
Wisdom

All books are available at **lmw.org**, on **amazon.com**, and at your local bookstore. *The Preacher's Outline & Sermon Bible*® is also available for sale digitally from Wordsearch, Logos, Olive Tree, Accordance and others.

Proceeds from sales, along with donations from donor partners, go to underwrite our translation and distribution projects. These projects equip pastors and leaders in the global church who have limited access to the books, resources, and training they need to prepare them to preach the Word of God clearly, plainly, and confidently.

Visit LMW's website at **lmw.org** to learn more about our mission and how you can partner with us:

PRAY: Please pray for the spread of the gospel and our role in it. Go to **lmw.org/stories** to join our prayer network.

CONNECT: LMW partners with other like-minded ministries around the world. Do you know someone who might like to connect with us? Let us know at: **info@lmw.org**

GIVE: The work of LMW is sustained by faithful giving. Impact the world with God's Word at **lmw.org/give.**

LMW is a 501(c)(3) ministry founded in 1992 to share God's Word, clearly explained, with pastors, bible students and Christian leaders worldwide.

lmw.org   1928 Central Ave.   1-(800) 987-8790
info@lmw.org   Chattanooga, TN 37408   (423) 855-2181